Praise for

GORDON S. WOOD'S

The Radicalism of
THE AMERICAN REVOLUTION

"Wood proclaims the culturally and politically transforming character of the American Revolution in this deeply intelligent and beautifully written masterwork." —*Patricia U. Bonomi, New York University*

"In his splendid new book Gordon Wood rescues the American Revolution from those who would see it as a conservative or backward-looking event...In a rapidly changing world, Wood provides a timely reminder of the radical energy that drives popular democracy."
—*T. H. Breen, Northwestern University*

"A landmark study, a superb achievement...The clarity of Wood's prose, the richness of his insights, and his choice of quotations and anecdotes make this powerful book a delight to read."
—*Richard D. Brown, University of Connecticut*

"Startlingly original...An authoritative account of one of the most significant and hitherto elusive transformations in our nation's past."
—*Richard Buel, Jr., Wesleyan University*

"Indisputably the work of a remarkably creative and gifted historian."
—*Ronald Hoffman, University of Maryland*

"A work that vividly re-creates the new American society with almost Tocquevillean power and a bri[...]lexities of his subject." [...]*niversity*

D0951450

GORDON S. WOOD

The Radicalism of
THE AMERICAN REVOLUTION

Gordon S. Wood received his A.B. from Tufts University and his Ph.D. from Harvard University. He has taught at the College of William and Mary, Harvard University, and the University of Michigan, and was Pitt Professor at Cambridge University in 1982–83. Since 1969 he has been at Brown University, where he is presently University Professor and Professor of History. In 1970 his book *The Creation of the American Republic, 1776–1787* was nominated for the National Book Award and received the Bancroft and the John H. Dunning prizes.

ALSO BY GORDON S. WOOD

The Creation of the American Republic,
1776–1787

GORDON S. WOOD

The Radicalism of
THE AMERICAN
REVOLUTION

VINTAGE BOOKS
A DIVISION OF RANDOM HOUSE, INC.
NEW YORK

FIRST VINTAGE BOOKS EDITION, MARCH 1993

Copyright © 1991 by Gordon S. Wood

All rights reserved under International and Pan-American Copyright Conventions.
Published in the United States by Vintage Books, a division of Random House, Inc., New
York, and simultaneously in Canada by Random House of Canada Limited, Toronto.
Originally published in hardcover by Alfred A. Knopf, Inc., New York, in 1992.

Library of Congress Cataloging-in-Publication Data
Wood, Gordon S.
Radicalism of the American Revolution / Gordon S. Wood.
p.   cm.
Originally published: New York: A.A. Knopf, 1992.
Includes bibliographical references and index.
ISBN 0-679-73688-3 (pbk.)
1. United States—History—Revolution, 1775–1783—Social aspects.
2. United States—Politics and government—1775–1783.
3. Radicalism—United States—History—18th century.   4. Political
culture—United States—History—18th century.   I. Title.
[E209.W65   1993]
973.3′1—dc20   92-56347
CIP

Manufactured in the United States of America

3579C8642

To Louise

Contents

Preface

This book is part of a continuing inquiry into the democratization of early America that I have been engaged in during the past several decades. Few subjects are more important to Americans, and perhaps to the rest of the world as well. Americans were not born free and democratic in any modern sense; they became so—and largely as a consequence of the American Revolution. After eighteenth-century Americans threw off their monarchical allegiance in 1776, they struggled to find new attachments befitting a republican people. Living in a society that was already diverse and pluralistic, Americans realized that these attachments could not be the traditional ethnic, religious, and tribal loyalties of the Old World. Instead, they sought new enlightened connections to hold their new popular societies together. But when these proved too idealistic and visionary, they eventually found new democratic adhesives in the actual behavior of plain ordinary people—in the everyday desire for the freedom to make money and pursue happiness in the here and now. To base a society on the commonplace behavior of ordinary people may be obvious and understandable to us today, but it was momentously radical in the long sweep of world history up to that time. This book attempts to explain this momentous radicalism of the American Revolution.

An early version of the book was presented in February 1986 as the Anson G. Phelps Lectures at New York University. I am very grateful to New York University and its History Department for the honor of inviting me to give the Phelps Lectures, which are the most prestigious in the field of early American history. I especially want to thank Carl Prince and Patricia U. Bonomi for their kindness and hospitality during my visit to New York University.

A fellowship at the Center for the Advanced Study of the Behavioral Sciences provided the opportunity to enlarge the lectures and write the bulk of the book. I am very grateful to the Center and its staff for their help. I particularly wish to thank Margaret Amara, Leslie Lindzey, Kathleen Much, and Rosanne Torre, who met every request with care and good cheer. My thanks also to Jonathan Clark of All Souls College for his knowledgeable reading of the first part of the manuscript. I am especially indebted to my friends and colleagues in early American history, Patricia U. Bonomi, Richard Buel, Jr., and Jack Rakove, who read the entire manuscript and offered perceptive and helpful criticism.

As always, I owe the most of all to my wife, Louise, not only for her editorial expertise but for everything else. To her this book is lovingly dedicated.

GORDON S. WOOD

THE RADICALISM OF

THE AMERICAN REVOLUTION

Introduction

We Americans like to think of our revolution as not being radical; indeed, most of the time we consider it downright conservative. It certainly does not appear to resemble the revolutions of other nations in which people were killed, property was destroyed, and everything was turned upside down. The American revolutionary leaders do not fit our conventional image of revolutionaries—angry, passionate, reckless, maybe even bloodthirsty for the sake of a cause. We can think of Robespierre, Lenin, and Mao Zedong as revolutionaries, but not George Washington, Thomas Jefferson, and John Adams. They seem too stuffy, too solemn, too cautious, too much the gentlemen. We cannot quite conceive of revolutionaries in powdered hair and knee breeches. The American revolutionaries seem to belong in drawing rooms or legislative halls, not in cellars or in the streets. They made speeches, not bombs; they wrote learned pamphlets, not manifestos. They were not abstract theorists and they were not social levelers. They did not kill one another; they did not devour themselves. There was no reign of terror in the American Revolution and no resultant dictator—no Cromwell, no Bonaparte. The American Revolution does not seem to have the same kinds of causes—the social wrongs, the class conflict, the impoverishment, the grossly inequitable distributions of wealth—that presumably lie behind other revolutions. There were no peasant uprisings, no jacqueries, no burning of châteaux, no storming of prisons.

Of course, there have been many historians—Progressive or neo-Progressive historians, as they have been called—who have sought, as Hannah Arendt put it, "to interpret the American Revolution in the light of the French Revolution," and to look for the same kinds of internal violence, class conflict, and social deprivation that presumably lay behind the French Revolution and other modern revolutions.' Since the beginning of the twentieth century these Progressive historians have formulated various social interpretations of the American Revolution essentially designed to show that the Revolution, in Carl Becker's famous words, was not only about "home rule" but also about "who was to rule at home.''² They have tried to describe the Revolution essentially as a social struggle by deprived and underprivileged groups against entrenched elites. But, it has been correctly pointed out, despite an extraordinary amount of research and writing during a good part of this century, the purposes of these Progressive and neo-Progressive historians—"to portray the origins and goals of the Revolution as in some significant measure expressions of a peculiar economic malaise or of the social protests and aspirations of an impoverished or threatened mass population—have not been fulfilled.''³ They have not been fulfilled because the social conditions that generically are supposed to lie behind all revolutions—poverty and economic deprivation—were not present in colonial America. There should no longer be any doubt about it: the white American colonists were not an oppressed people; they had no crushing imperial chains to throw off.⁴ In fact, the colonists knew they were freer, more equal, more prosperous, and less burdened with cumbersome feudal and monarchical restraints than any other part of mankind in the eighteenth century. Such a situation, however, does not mean that colonial society was not susceptible to revolution.

Precisely because the impulses to revolution in eighteenth-century America bear little or no resemblance to the impulses that presumably account for modern social protests and revolutions, we have tended to think of the American Revolution as having no social character, as having virtually nothing to do with the society, as having no social causes and no social consequences. It has therefore often been considered to be essentially an intellectual event, a constitutional defense of American rights against British encroachments ("no taxation without representation"), undertaken not to change the existing structure of society but to preserve it. For some historians the Revolution seems to be little more than a colonial rebellion or a war for independence. Even when we have recognized the radicalism of the Revolution, we admit only a political, not a social radicalism. The revolutionary leaders, it is said, were peculiar "eighteenth-century radicals concerned, like the eighteenth-century British radicals, not with the need to recast the social order nor with the problems of the economic inequality and the injustices of stratified societies but with the need to purify a corrupt constitution and fight off the apparent growth of prerogative power.''⁵ Consequently, we have generally described the Revolution as an unusually conservative affair, concerned almost exclusively with politics and constitutional rights, and, in comparison with the social radicalism of the other great revolutions of history, hardly a revolution at all.

If we measure the radicalism of revolutions by the degree of social misery or economic deprivation suffered, or by the number of people killed or manor houses burned, then this conventional emphasis on the conservatism of the American Revolution becomes true enough. But if we measure the radicalism by the amount of social change that actually took place—by transformations in the relationships that bound people to each other—then the American Revolution was not conservative at all; on the contrary: it was as radical and as revolutionary as any in history. Of course, the American Revolution was very different from other revolutions. But it was no less radical and no less social for being different. In fact, it was one of the greatest revolutions the world has known, a momentous upheaval that not only fundamentally altered the character of American society but decisively affected the course of subsequent history.

It was as radical and social as any revolution in history, but it was radical and social in a very special eighteenth-century sense. No doubt many of the concerns and much of the language of that premodern, pre-Marxian eighteenth century were almost entirely political. That was because most people in that very different distant world could not as yet conceive of society apart from government. The social distinctions and economic deprivations that we today think of as the consequence of class divisions, business exploitation, or various isms—capitalism, racism, etc.—were in the eighteenth century usually thought to be caused by the abuses of government. Social honors, social distinctions, perquisites of office, business contracts, privileges and monopolies, even excessive property and wealth of various sorts—all social evils and social deprivations—in fact seemed to flow from connections to government, in the end from connections to monarchical authority. So that when Anglo-American radicals talked in what seems to be only political terms—purifying a corrupt constitution, eliminating courtiers, fighting off crown power, and, most important, becoming republicans—they nevertheless had a decidedly social message. In our eyes the American revolutionaries appear to be absorbed in changing only their governments, not their society. But in destroying monarchy and establishing republics they were changing their society as well as their governments, and they knew it. Only they did not know—they could scarcely have imagined—how much of their society they would change. J. Franklin Jameson, who more than two generations ago described the Revolution as a social movement only to be roundly criticized by a succeeding generation of historians, was at least right about one thing: "the stream of revolution, once started, could not be confined within narrow banks, but spread abroad upon the land.''[6]

By the time the Revolution had run its course in the early nineteenth century, American society had been radically and thoroughly transformed. One class did not overthrow another; the poor did not supplant the rich.[7] But social relationships—the way people were connected one to another—were changed, and decisively so. By the early years of the nineteenth century the Revolution had created a society fundamentally different from the colonial society of the eighteenth century. It was in fact a new society unlike any that had ever existed anywhere in the world.

Of course, there were complexities and variations in early American society and culture—local, regional, sectional, ethnic, and class differences that historians are uncovering every day—that make difficult any generalizations about Americans as a whole. This study is written in spite of these complexities and variations, not in ignorance of them. There is a time for understanding the particular, and there is a time for understanding the whole. Not only is it important that we periodically attempt to bring the many monographic studies of eighteenth-century America together to see the patterns they compose, but it is essential that we do so—if we are to extend our still meager understanding of an event as significant as the American Revolution.

That revolution did more than legally create the United States; it transformed American society. Because the story of America has turned out the way it has, because the United States in the twentieth century has become the great power that it is, it is difficult, if not impossible, to appreciate and recover fully the insignificant and puny origins of the country. In 1760 America was only a collection of disparate colonies huddled along a narrow strip of the Atlantic coast—economically underdeveloped outposts existing on the very edges of the civilized world. The less than two million monarchical subjects who lived in these colonies still took for granted that society was and ought to be a hierarchy of ranks and degrees of dependency and that most people were bound together by personal ties of one sort or another. Yet scarcely fifty years later these insignificant borderland provinces had become a giant, almost continent-wide republic of nearly ten million egalitarian-minded bustling citizens who not only had thrust themselves into the vanguard of history but had fundamentally altered their society and their social relationships. Far from remaining monarchical, hierarchy-ridden subjects on the margin of civilization, Americans had become, almost overnight, the most liberal, the most democratic, the most commercially minded, and the most modern people in the world.

And this astonishing transformation took place without industrialization, without urbanization, without railroads, without the aid of any of the great forces we usually invoke to explain "modernization." It was the Revolution that was crucial to this transformation. It was the Revolution, more than any other single event, that made America into the most liberal, democratic, and modern nation in the world.

Of course, some nations of Western Europe likewise experienced great social transformations and "democratic revolutions" in these same years. The American Revolution was not unique; it was only different. Because of this shared Western-wide experience in democratization, it has been argued by more than one historian that the broader social transformation that carried Americans from one century and one kind of society to another was "inevitable" and "would have been completed with or without the American Revolution." Therefore, this broader social revolution should not be confused with the American Revolution. America, it is said, would have emerged into the modern world as a liberal, democratic, and capitalistic society even without the Revolution.[8] One could, of course, say the same thing about the relationship between the French Revolution and the emergence of France in the nineteenth century as a liberal, democratic, and capitalistic society; and indeed, much of the current revisionist historical writing on the French Revolution is based on just such a distinction. But in America, no more than in France, that was not the way it happened: the American Revolution and the social transformation of America between 1760 and the early years of the nineteenth century were inextricably bound together. Perhaps the social transformation would have happened "in any case," but we will never know. It was in fact linked to the Revolution; they occurred together. The American Revolution was integral to the changes occurring in American society, politics, and culture at the end of the eighteenth century.

These changes were radical, and they were extensive. To focus, as we are today apt to do, on what the Revolution did not accomplish— highlighting and lamenting its failure to abolish slavery and change fundamentally the lot of women—is to miss the great significance of what it did accomplish; indeed, the Revolution made possible the anti-slavery and women's rights movements of the nineteenth century and in fact all our current egalitarian thinking. The Revolution not only radically changed the personal and social relationships of people, including the position of women, but also destroyed aristocracy as it had been understood in the Western world for at least two millennia. The Revolution brought respectability and even dominance to ordinary people long held in contempt and gave dignity to their menial labor in a manner unprecedented in history and to a degree not equaled elsewhere in the world. The Revolution did not just eliminate monarchy and create republics; it actually reconstituted what Americans meant by public or state power and brought about an entirely new kind of popular politics and a new kind of democratic officeholder. The Revolution not only changed the culture of Americans—making over their art, architecture, and iconography—but even altered their understanding of history, knowledge, and truth. Most important, it made the interests and prosperity of ordinary people—their pursuits of happiness—the goal of society and government. The Revolution did not merely create a political and legal environment conducive to economic expansion; it also released powerful popular entrepreneurial and commercial energies that few realized existed and transformed the economic landscape of the country. In short, the Revolution was the most radical and most far-reaching event in American history.

i MONARCHY

1. *Hierarchy*

To appreciate the extent of change that took place in the Revolution, we have to re-create something of the old colonial society that was subsequently transformed. Despite all the momentous transformations that had taken place since the seventeenth-century settlements, mid-eighteenth-century colonial society was in many ways still traditional—traditional in its basic social relationships and in its cultural consciousness. All aspects of life were intertwined. The household, the society, and the state—private and public spheres—scarcely seemed separable. Authority and liberty flowed not as today from the political organization of the society but from the structure of its personal relationships. In important respects this premodern or early modern society still bore traces of the medieval world of personal fealties and loyalties out of which it arose.

To be sure, already by the middle of the century a thousand different aberrations and peculiarities, a thousand different anomalies and inconsistencies, cried out for resolution and explanation. Powerful social and economic developments were stretching, fraying, and forcing apart older personal bonds holding people together, and people everywhere were hard pressed to explain what was happening. New ideas, new values, were emerging in the English-speaking world, but the past was tenacious. Like all Englishmen, the colonists continued to embrace deeply rooted assumptions about the order and stability needed in a monarchical society.

Living in a monarchical society meant, first of all, being subjects of the king. This was no simple political status, but had all sorts of social, cultural, and even psychological implications. As clarified by Sir Edward Coke and other jurists in the seventeenth century, the allegiance the English subject owed his monarch was a personal and individual matter. Diverse persons related to each other only through their common tie to the king, much as children became brothers and sisters only through their common parentage. Since the king, said William Blackstone, was the "*pater familias* of the nation," to be a subject was to be a kind of child, to be personally subordinated to a paternal dominion. In its starkest theoretical form, therefore, monarchy, as Americans later came to describe it, implied a society of dependent beings, weak and inferior, without autonomy or independence, easily cowed by the pageantry and trappings of a patriarchal king. The whole community, said Benjamin Franklin in 1763, is regulated by the example of the king.[1]

Because monarchy had these implications of humiliation and dependency, the Anglo-American colonists could never be good monarchical subjects. But of course neither could their fellow Englishmen "at home" three thousand miles across the Atlantic. All Englishmen in the eighteenth century were known throughout the Western world for their insubordination, their insolence, their stubborn unwillingness to be governed. Any reputation the North American colonists had for their unruliness and contempt for authority came principally from their Englishness.

In our enthusiasm to contrast the "traditional" society of the mother country with the "modernity" of the colonies, we have often overlooked how dominantly British and traditional the colonists' culture still was; indeed, in some respects colonial society was more traditional than that of the mother country. Most colonial leaders in the mid-eighteenth century thought of themselves not as Americans but as Britons. They read much the same literature, the same law books, the same history, as their brethren at home read, and they drew most of their conceptions of society and their values from their reading. Whatever sense of unity the disparate colonies of North America had came from their common tie to the British crown and from their membership in the British empire. Most colonists knew more about events in London than they did about occurrences in neighboring colonies. They were provincials living on the edges of a pan-British world, and all the more British for that. Their little colonial capitals resembled, as one touring British officer remarked of Williamsburg, nothing so much as "a good Country Town in England." Philadelphia seemed only a smaller version of Bristol. Most English visitors in fact tended to describe the colonists simply as country cousins—more boorish, more populist, more egalitarian perhaps, with too much Presbyterianism and religious nonconformity—but still Englishmen, not essentially different from the inhabitants of Yorkshire or Norwich or the rest of rural and small-town provincial England. Observer after observer thought that "the manners, morals and amusements" of America in the mid-eighteenth century were "in a humbler degree . . . much the same . . . as in the mother country."[2]

In fact, it is very difficult to find contemporary descriptions of the colonists that were not applicable as well to the English at home. True, the colonists were thought to be a particularly unruly lot, crude if not barbarous, and especially defiant of social and political authority. But this reputation did not make them any less subjects of the English king; it only made them more English. Had not Montesquieu written that the English were too busy with their interests to have politeness and refinement?[3] Englishmen everywhere simply made poor subjects for monarchy, and they were proud of it. The king had his birthright to the crown, but the people had theirs too: they were "free-born Englishmen," and they had rights and liberties that no other people in the world enjoyed. They had in fact more rights and liberties than any traditional hereditary monarchy could accommodate; and consequently the British monarchy was very different not only from any other but also from what it had been in the days of James I.

Since the early seventeenth century the English had radically transformed their monarchy: they had executed one king and deposed another, written charters and bills of rights, regularized the meetings of their parliaments, and even created a new line of hereditary succession. In the years following the Glorious Revolution of 1688 they had become increasingly aware of the marvelous peculiarity of their limited monarchy. "The constitution of our English government (the best in the World)," they told themselves, "is no arbitrary tyranny, like the Turkish Grand Seignior's, or the French King's, whose wills (or rather lusts) dispose of the lives and fortunes of their unhappy subjects."[4] Representation in the House of Commons even allowed for the participation of His Majesty's subjects in the affairs of government. It was a constitution specially dedicated to liberty.

Liberty: Englishmen everywhere of every social rank and of every political persuasion could not celebrate it enough. Every cause, even repression itself, was wrapped in the language of English liberty. No people in the history of the world had ever made so much of it. Unlike the poor enslaved French, the English had no standing army, no lettres de cachet; they had their habeas corpus, their trials by jury, their freedom of speech and conscience, and their right to trade and travel; they were free from arbitrary arrest and punishment; their homes were their castles. Although few Englishmen and no Englishwomen could vote for representatives, they always had the sense of participating in political affairs, even if this meant only parading and huzzahing during the periodic elections of the House of Commons. It would be impossible to overemphasize the degree to which eighteenth-century Englishmen reveled in their worldwide reputation for freedom. Even the young Prince of Wales, soon to be George III, shared in this unmonarchical celebration of liberty. "The pride, the glory of Britain, and the direct end of its constitution," he said, "is political liberty."[5] No unruly American provincial could have put it better.

Many of the characteristics for which the eighteenth-century colonists were noted were in truth English characteristics or exaggerations of English characteristics. Continental critics accused the English of being crude and unpolished. But like the colonists, the English turned this lack of cultivation into an advantage: Frenchmen, they said over and over, were overrefined, foppish, and effeminate, sunk in luxury and misery, and overawed by superstitious priests in wooden shoes—no match for their own sturdy, brawling, beef-eating John Bull character. Just as the English commented on the uniformity of speech among the different social ranks of the colonists, so too did Europeans comment on the same characteristic among the English themselves. Americans may have had a multiplicity of religious groups and a consequent reputation for religious toleration. But so too did the mother country. "If there were only one religion in England," wrote Voltaire in his *Philosophical Letters,* "we should have to fear despotism; if there were two, they would cut each other's throats; but there are thirty, and they live in peace and happiness."[6]

Englishmen on both sides of the Atlantic bragged of their independence. To be sure, most colonial farmers owned their own land and were thus different from the mass of tenant farmers who characterized English agricultural life. Yet too much can be made of this contrast, for dependent as English tenant farmers may have been, they were not seen to be dependent either by themselves or by foreigners. Although the farmers of New York held their lands "in Fee simple," said Lieutenant Governor Cadwallader Colden in 1765, "they are as to condition of life in no manner superior to the common Farmers in England." English tenant-farmers were in fact celebrated for their independence, particularly in comparison with the cringing peasants of France, where, as Dr. Johnson's friend Mrs. Thrale observed, "everyone seems to belong to some other man and no man to himself." Independence and dependence were relative and not absolute statuses, and most colonists, like most Englishmen at home, were never as free as they made themselves out to be.[7]

America had a reputation for egalitarianism, but so too did England.

Unlike the Continent, England had no legal or customary barriers to set off its landed aristocracy from the rest of society, and the consequent uninterrupted circulation among the various ranks impressed European observers. When even a Manchester cobbler in 1756 could dream and celebrate the mobility of English society—"leaving the Coast open for new adventurers"—it is not surprising that foreigners thought the English were mad for equality. European visitors from across the Channel thought that ordinary Englishmen had no respect for authority; common people hooted at their social superiors in the streets and jeered at social pretensions everywhere. Foreigners were stunned to discover common workingpeople of England, even apprentices and streetwalkers, mingling with and emulating their betters on Sunday strolls in Greenwich Park. In France the peasants dressed like peasants, noted the Swedish visitor Peter Kalm, but in England laboring men and women wore knee breeches and perukes, bonnets and panniered dresses. In the eyes of Europeans everywhere, Englishmen appeared much too liberty-loving and egalitarian and indeed seemed infected with a "republican spirit."[8]

To be the subject of an English king who celebrated liberty as proudly as the humblest plebeian was to be a member of a very unusual state indeed. By continental standards the English monarchy was scarcely a real monarchy. Yet, however superficial and hollow, it was still a monarchical society the colonists lived in, and it was still a king to whom they paid allegiance. In fact, because the growth of royal authority and influence in America was such a recent and novel development, the colonists in the mid-eighteenth century could at times be more enthusiastic monarchists than the English themselves. South Carolinians, said Dr. David Ramsay, "were fond of British manners even to excess," and similar comments were made of other colonists up and down the seaboard. No metropolitan Englishman could have matched the awe felt by the Pennsylvanian Benjamin Rush when in 1768 he first saw the king's throne in London. It was as if he were "on sacred ground," and he "gazed for some time at the throne with emotions that I cannot describe." Rush importuned his reluctant guide to let him sit upon it "for a considerable time," even though the guide said that visitors rarely did so. The experience was unsettling, to say the least: "I was seized with a kind of horror," said Rush, and "a crowd of ideas poured in upon my mind." This was all a man could want in this world; "his passions conceive, his hopes aspire after nothing beyond this throne." No wonder Rush eventually came to rue the degree to which people's "affections" had been "absorbed by kings and nobles": too many colonists, including himself, had once spoken "only of George the 3rd" and ignored their fellow countrymen.[9]

Perhaps, as David Hume slyly noted, the colonists revered the king so much more than metropolitan Englishmen precisely because they were so far away and thus never knew what a king was really like. Certainly the colonists' excitement over the accession of George III in 1760 equaled that of Englishmen at home. William Henry Drayton of South Carolina thought that no people were ever "more wrapped up in a king" than were Americans in 1763.[10]

Of course, most colonists knew little about monarchy firsthand. Unlike Rush, they never saw the throne, never witnessed royal progresses, and never saw much royal pomp and ceremony. But colonial newspapers reported royal occasions in detail, and colonial authorities did what they could to maintain respect for the crown. They displayed royal arms and emblems in public buildings and celebrated royal occasions like the king's birthday by firing cannons, setting off fireworks, and dispensing drinks. The royal governors were increasingly anxious to establish styles of living that would befit their rank as the crown's viceregents and do honor to the king—by building distinguished government houses, by dressing lavishly, by entertaining generously.[11] They had the power to pardon condemned criminals, and sometimes they used it, like a new king succeeding to the throne, when they took up their gubernatorial offices. The governors' ability to set aside the law in this way was designed to induce awe among the people and to enhance royal authority: the condemned persons usually pleaded for their lives on their knees in open court. Royal authority being as thin as it was in the colonies, the governors resorted to this pardoning power quite freely, in some colonies sparing as many as one-quarter to one-half of those condemned to death.[12]

In the mid-eighteenth century Englishmen on both sides of the Atlantic made new efforts to embellish royal authority. Since the colonial courts were hardly awesome by English standards, every little effort was made to dignify the king's dispensing of justice, even if this only involved raising the justices' bench in a Virginia courtroom a foot or so above the floor. In 1764 the New York Supreme Court, in emulation of the mother country and several other colonies, ordered the judges and the counsel appearing before them to don robes or gowns and bands in order to advance the "Dignity Authority Solemnity and Decorum of the Court," and to promote "many useful consequences." John Adams recalled that in the early 1760s the Massachusetts authorities had likewise introduced a new "scenery" in the supreme court—"of scarlet and sable robes, of broad bands, and enormous tie wigs"—in order to create a more "theatrical" and "ecclesiastical" setting for the doing of justice. Full-length, gold-framed portraits of Charles II and James II, said Adams, were "hung up on the most conspicuous sides" of the courtroom "for the admiration and imitation of all men." "The colors of the royal ermines and long flowing robes were the most glowing, the figures the most noble and graceful, the features the most distinct and characteristic"—these portraits of these particular Stuart kings were designed to overawe. All this, thought Adams, made the council chamber in Boston's old town hall "as respectable an apartment as the House of Commons or the House of Lords in Great Britain, in proportion."[3]

However recently contrived or artificially imposed, royal authority in the colonies was more deep-rooted and more effective by mid-century than ever before. Despite widespread smuggling of goods, especially in New England, most American trade was being carried on within the confines of the British navigation laws: British or colonial ships carried the goods, colonial staples such as sugar, tobacco, and rice were sent to Britain, the colonists imported increasing amounts of British manufactures, and most European imports came to America through England. Although the colonists grumbled about and evaded some of these imperial regulations, their compliance was remarkably high; legal commerce soared and all participants prospered as never before. With the resumption of Anglo-French warfare in the 1750s, British funds poured into the colonies, and the colonists responded to the empire's war needs in unprecedented fashion; by the end of the decade many of the colonies had mobilized huge proportions of their manpower and resources to fight on behalf of the British crown. At the same time there were more successful strong royal governors in the colonies than ever before—from William Gooch and Francis Fauquier in Virginia to William Shirley and Thomas Pownall in Massachusetts.[4]

Religion tended to bolster monarchical authority and order, especially among ordinary people for whom Christian revelation (and magic) remained the major means for understanding and manipulating the world. The European tradition of centralized state-supported churches that had been only fitfully applied in the colonies during the seventeenth century was dramatically expanded in the first third of the eighteenth century. Although religious groups in most of the colonies lacked the kind of legally established dominance that the Church of England achieved in the mother country, all of their churches, including the dissenting ones, extended their institutional and disciplinary hold over colonial society. Everywhere in the decades following 1690 governments helped the churches assert coercive Christian authority over increasing numbers of people who had hitherto been neglected or ignored. In all the colonies clerical power was reinvigorated, new parishes were laid out, larger and more elegant churches were built, new and more elaborate ceremonies were established, and more and more unchurched were brought under the control of formal religion; in these different ways monarchical authority and obedience were subtly fortified. Even the Puritan churches of New England reversed their original exclusivity and localism by attempting to strengthen the central authority of the clergy and by reaching out to embrace larger and larger proportions of the society. By offering religious rituals and services to everyone, however, the revived Anglican church during the first half of the century did the most to extend the crown's Christian authority into the remotest areas and the lowliest ranks of American society. Although the leaders of all religious groups tended to support hierarchical authority to one degree or another—for example, by preaching from Romans 13 that all were "subject unto the higher powers . . . for conscience sake" and by exalting personal and emotional loyalties over calculating and conditional ones—none of them supported and spread the ethic of monarchy more forcefully than did the Anglicans. By the time of the Revolution there were some four hundred Anglican congregations in the North American colonies. Even moderate Anglican preachers continually stressed the sacredness of authority and the need for subjects to honor and revere those set over them and thereby lent a more monarchical tone to the culture than it otherwise would have had. Although the Anglican church often appealed to the poorest and the most powerless of the colonists, as the king's church it was also especially attractive to the top of the social scale—to royal officials and other elites. Indeed, by mid-century Anglicans held public office in numbers out of proportion to their numbers in the society, which further contributed to a strengthening of monarchy in the colonies.[15]

Royal authority never seemed more impressive and acceptable to the colonists than at mid-century, not simply because wars naturally favored a growth in the influence of the crown and the Anglican church was growing in strength, but also because the theoretical underpinnings of their social thought still remained largely monarchical. They may not have known much of real kings and courts, but they knew very well the social hierarchy that the subjection and subordination of monarchy necessarily implied. Monarchy presumed what Hume called "a long train of dependence," a gradation of degrees of freedom and servility that linked everyone from the king at the top down to the bonded laborers and black slaves at the bottom. The inequalities of such a hierarchy were acceptable to people because they were offset by the great emotional satisfactions of living in a society in which everyone, even the lowliest servant, counted for something. In this traditional world "every Person has his proper Sphere and is of Importance to the *whole*."[16] Ideally, in such a hierarchy no one was really independent, no one was ever alone and unattached. Hence followed the fascination of the eighteenth century with the fate of isolated individuals, like Robinson Crusoe, strangers without relatives or connections cast alone in the world.[17]

In the eighteenth century, as in the time of John Winthrop, it was nearly impossible to imagine a civilized society being anything but a hierarchy of some kind, in which, in the words of the famous Calvinist preacher Jonathan Edwards, all have "their appointed office, place and station, according to their several capacities and talents, and everyone keeps his place, and continues in his proper business." In such a society it was inconceivable, unnatural, for inequality not to exist.

> Order is Heav'n's first law; and this confest,
> Some are, and must be, greater than the rest,
> More rich, more wise . . .

The hierarchy of a monarchical society was part of the natural order of things, part of that great chain of existence that ordered the entire universe, part of what John Adams called that "regular and uniform Subordination of one Tribe to another down to the apparently insignificant animalcules in pepper Water."[18]

A proper society was like the plenitude of nature: nothing was ever lost, nothing was ever wasted. This traditional society contained a limited number of places and goods, with the implication that no one could really advance and prosper except at someone else's expense. Movement from one rank to another was not only possible, of course, but necessary if people were to find their allotted positions; but such mobile persons had to possess and demonstrate the qualifications of the rank or position into which they moved. It was unnatural to pretend to be something that one was not equipped to be. "A man of low stature may add something to his height, but nothing to his comeliness by strutting upon stilts." Ideally, people were expected to find and attend to "the proper

Business" of their particular place within the social order and to "consider their mutual Relations and Dependencies, and duly perform the Duties of their respective Stations" and thus promote the moral consensus and harmony essential for a healthy society. "God hath in great wisdom," said the Reverend Thomas Cradock of Maryland at midcentury, "given variety of abilities to men, suitable to the several stations in life, for which he hath design'd them, that everyone keeping his station, and employing his respective abilities in doing his own work, all might receive advantage."[19]

Both the New England towns with their ancient "warning out" regulations and the southern colonies with their vagabond legislation expected everyone to belong somewhere, and they used the force of law to maintain their inherited sense of community. Under the warning-out laws, for example, towns could legally eject "strangers" and have constables convey them from town to town until they were returned to the town where they legally belonged.[20] Society had to be an organic whole. The colonists repeatedly invoked those powerful lines from Corinthians—"that there should be no Schism in the Body but the Members should have the Same Care for one another"—and widely condemned all selfish persons and parties, indeed "anything that dissolved in a moment the solidest friendship."[21]

The colonies were simple, underdeveloped provincial societies, and they lacked the great inequalities and the intricate calibrations of the more complicated society of the mother country. Yet they had their own degrees and subordinations. Although eighteenth-century Americans were "without nobility, or orders of gentry," recalled Arthur Browne, an Anglican clergyman who lived in several New England cities, there was evidence everywhere in the colonies of "how necessarily some differences of rank, some inequality must and ought to grow up in every society."[22]

The colonists' sense of hierarchy was reinforced in a multitude of ways. The military seemed to reproduce the society, and thus it was natural for land grants to veterans of the French and Indian wars to be made according to rank, with field-grade officers receiving 5,000 acres each, captains 3,000 acres, and so on, down to privates, who received 50 acres each. College students learned, sometimes through harsh punishments, the importance of hierarchy. They were required, in the words of Yale president Thomas Clap, to "show due Respect and Distance to those who are in Senior and Superior Classes" and were taught through a variety of means the intricacies of rank and precedence within the college. Students, for example, had to remove their hats at varying distances from the person they approached, depending on the status of that person: ten rods for the president, eight rods for a professor, and five rods for a tutor. All had some sense of where they stood and how they ought to behave toward others in this social hierarchy. And if they did not, there were guidebooks, like that copied by a young George Washington, telling them when to pull off their hats "to Persons of Distinction," how to bow "according to the Custom of the Better Bred and Quality of the Person"—what to do, in short, in order to "give to every Person his due title According to his Degree."²³

Social ranks carried designations, and such designations, whether "Mr.," "Esq.," "Yeoman," or whatever, were virtually part of a person's name. Pleadings in courts of law often depended on plaintiffs or defendants getting their social rank correct. "If it is of any Consequence to society that Ranks and subordination should be established in it," argued the young attorney John Adams in 1761, "it is of Consequence that the Titles denoting those Ranks should not be confounded." Every title from the local militia was carried over into private life; there was hardly a justice of the peace who was not a colonel. When William Brattle went on a mission to New Hampshire on behalf of the Massachusetts governor, he took care to let all "the Country People" know that "he was General Brattle, that he might make them Stare," and that his words "might have more weight." New England farmers prized the subtle shade of difference between husbandman and yeoman. Church pews were assigned on the basis of family heads' age and social position; and entering students at Harvard and Yale were ranked according to the social respectability of their families. On the eve of the Revolution the colonists squabbled over the proper seating order at the governors' tables to the point where Joseph Edmundson, the Mowbray herald extraordinary of the English College of Arms, had to be called in to prepare "Rules of Precedency" to lay down the precise social position of the various colonial officials.²⁴

These differences of title and quality did not resemble our modern conception of "class." Although the colonists talked of "gentlemen of the first rank," people of "middling circumstances," and the "meaner sort," they did not as yet think clearly in terms of those large-scale horizontal solidarities of occupation and wealth with which we are familiar today. Distinctions in colonial society were measured by far more subtle, far more emotionally powerful criteria. Money and property were of course critically important, but by themselves they could not create and sustain the inequalities of this social hierarchy. Indeed, the distribution of wealth in eighteenth-century colonial society was far more equal than it would become in the nineteenth century.[25] But a more equitable distribution of wealth did not make this traditional society more equal than the one that would emerge in the decades following the Revolution. It was just differently organized.

There were, of course, a number of occupational categories. Men were in fact considered to be *bred* to their occupations and were usually labeled by occupation as coopers, tradesmen, laborers, and so on.[26] Usually occupational designations were for common people only—for all those who were defined by what they did rather than by who they were. The learned professions—medicine, law, and divinity—were not yet regarded as occupations in any modern sense of the term. Indeed, "profession" still bore traces of its ancient meaning as something publicly and voluntarily professed, like a religious avowal; and therefore members of the learned professions were generally not defined by how they occupied themselves but by who they were—by their "quality" or gentlemanly status. Although designations of quality were becoming harder to make in the increasingly complex eighteenth-century pan-British society, nonetheless efforts were continually made.[27] Some positions—government officeholders and the liberal professions—usually carried with them a presumption of high social status and the title of "Mr." or "Esq." It was thought, for example, that clergymen were "often by birth, and always by education and profession gentlemen."[28]

Most people in the society were planters or farmers; a few of them possessed a high degree of quality, most did not. Calling oneself a planter or farmer could be confusing, however, for gentlemen who applied such titles to themselves never meant to say that they were cultivators by trade. Those involved in overseas commerce, and hence creating wealth for the country, were designated as merchants—a very respectable but not genteel title. There were, moreover, many different sorts of merchants. In large port cities there were great ones, like Able James of Philadelphia, deeply involved in the lucrative and prestigious dry-goods trade with Great Britain. But for every such great merchant in Philadelphia, New York, or Boston, there were scores of smaller traders and shopkeepers, not only in the large ports but in lesser places such as Hartford or Norfolk, sometimes dealing in coastwise or West Indian routes but often just scrambling every which way in an endless search for goods and places with which to trade. Various sorts of artisans and mechanics existed everywhere—on southern plantations, in small towns, and in the port cities. Indeed, one-third to one-half of the male population of the large cities was composed of artisans or mechanics, and they ran the gamut from very rich to very poor. Some were beginning teenaged apprentices, others were journeymen working for wages, and many were masters, ranging from those who hired themselves out to those few who ran huge manufacturing establishments employing dozens of workers. No matter how wealthy an artisan became, however, his social status or quality remained at best only middling—along with most other laboring people in this society. Below these were the "meaner sort," distinguished from everyone above them by their lack of property—their lack, that is, of either land, goods for trading, or a skill of some sort.[29]

Out of these occupational categories and differing levels of wealth a class consciousness of a sort would begin to rise by the early nineteenth century.[30] But in the mid-eighteenth century most Americans still conceived of their society in a traditional manner, composed not of broad and politically hostile layers or classes but of "various individuals, connected together and related and subservient to each other."[31] They thought of themselves as connected vertically rather than horizontally, and were more apt to be conscious of those immediately above and below them than they were of those alongside them. Probably nothing captures more succinctly the peculiar vertical nature of this social hierarchy than a passage from Henry Fielding's great comic novel *Joseph Andrews* (1742). Fielding saw the degrees of dependence in the society as "a kind of ladder":

> as, for instance: early in the morning arises the postilion, or some other boy, which great families, no more than great ships, are without, and falls to brushing the clothes and cleaning the shoes of John the footman; who, being drest himself, applies his hands to the same labours for Mr. Second-hand, the squire's gentleman; the gentleman in the like manner, a little later in the day, attends the squire; the squire is no sooner equipped than he attends the levee of my lord; which is no sooner over than my lord himself is seen at the levee of the favourite, who, after the hour of homage is at an end, appears himself to pay homage to the levee of his sovereign. Nor is there, perhaps, in this whole ladder of dependence, any one step at a greater distance from the other than the first from the second; so that to a philosopher the question might only seem, whether you would choose to be a great man at six in the morning, or at two in the afternoon. And yet there are scarce two of these who do not think the least familiarity with the

persons below them a condescension, and, if they were to go one step
farther, a degradation.[32]

Although individuals in this graded society might on occasion erupt
in passion against the rich and the moneyed, few groups or occupations
could as yet sustain any strong corporate or class consciousness, any
sense of existing as a particular social stratum with long-term common
interests that were antagonistic to the interests of another stratum. In
fact, most people could locate themselves only in superiority or in subordination to someone else. Their behavior and courtesies were always
relative, for it was "absurd to act the same with a Clown and a Prince."
Thus the colonists' literature on how to behave in society always had to
advise for both directions at once, above and below: "with Superiors,
courteous and fair-spoken; not over familiar nor surly, with inferiors."
Individuals were simultaneously free and subservient, independent and
dependent, superior and inferior—depending on the person with whom
they were dealing. Thus they did not have class positions or occupations
as much as they had relationships; and the degrees of these relationships
could sometimes be calculated with startling precision. When a new
tutor to a household of children was even advised to "let the same
distance be observed in every article of behaviour between you and the
eldest Son, as there ought to be, by the latest and most approved pre-
cepts of Moral-Philosophy, between the eldest Son, and his next youngest Brother," then we know we are dealing with a society that took its
degrees of subordination seriously.[33]

2. Patricians and Plebeians

Despite the fact that most of colonial society was vertically organized,
there was one great horizontal division that cut through it with a significance we can today scarcely comprehend—that between extraordinary and ordinary people, gentlemen and commoners. Although the
eighteenth century was becoming increasingly confused over who precisely ought to make up each of these basic groups, there was little
question that in all societies some were patricians and most were plebeians, that some were officers and most were common soldiers, that
some were polished and literate and most were rude and unlettered, that
some were gentlemen and most were not. There were the few who
were sometimes called "the reverend" or "right reverend," "the hon-

ourable," or "excellent," or "noble," or "puissant," or "royal," and there were the many who were often called "the Mob," "the Vulgar," or "the Herd." This social cleavage, this "most ancient and universal of all Divisions of People," overwhelmed all others in the culture, even the one between free and enslaved that we find so horribly conspicuous. The awareness of the "difference between *gentle* and *simple,*" recalled the Anglican minister Devereaux Jarrett of his humble youth in colonial Virginia, was "universal among all of my rank and age." Since this distinction has lost almost all of its older meaning (Jarrett himself lived to see "a vast alteration, in this respect"), it takes an act of imagination to recapture its immense importance in the eighteenth century. Southern squires entered their churches as a body and took their pews only after their families and the ordinary people had been seated. Massachusetts courts debated endlessly over whether or not particular plaintiffs and defendants were properly identified as gentlemen. More than any other distinction, this difference between aristocrats and commoners, between gentlemen and ordinary people, made manifest the unequal and hierarchical nature of the society.[1]

In the English-speaking world the aristocracy composed a small but immensely powerful proportion of the society, constituting perhaps only 4 or 5 percent of the population, though in the northern colonies of North America that proportion approached 10 percent. Originally the term "aristocracy" referred to a form of government, government by the most distinguished in birth and fortune; but by the eighteenth century "aristocracy" had been popularly extended to embrace the entire patrician order to which such a governing body belonged. Although this aristocracy was a group distinct from the main body of the social hierarchy, it was itself marked by severe degrees of rank. At its top was the king. Below him were the peers of the realm, rarely numbering more than two hundred at any one moment in the eighteenth century. These dukes, marquesses, earls, viscounts, and barons had huge estates and hereditary titles and, in the case of the English peers at least, automatically sat in the House of Lords (Scottish peers elected a proportion of their number to the House of Lords). Baronetcies, too, were inheritable but gave the holder no right to a seat in the House of Lords. Below these were several titled ranks of knights and esquires. The entire aristocracy was bottomed on the large body of gentry, the lowest social rank entitled to bear a coat of arms.[2]

"Gentleman" originally meant noble by birth and applied to all of the aristocracy, including even the king. But from the sixteenth century on, with the enlargement of the aristocracy from below by the entry of numerous lesser gentry, the hereditary peerage sought to confine the term "gentleman" to all those who stood as "a middle rank betwixt the nobles and common people." But although this distinction between the nobility and the gentry developed to the point where Dr. Johnson defined a gentleman as "not noble," most eighteenth-century Englishmen still considered gentlemen to be part of the aristocracy.[3]

When the gentry are included in the eighteenth-century English aristocracy, the numbers were in proportion to the population not all that different from the numbers of the eighteenth-century French nobility. Indeed, the English aristocracy and the French nobility may have been much more alike than we used to think. Certainly entry into the upper ranks of the English aristocracy and the French nobility was equally difficult. During most of the eighteenth century the English peerage was scarcely accessible to anyone who was not already well established and well connected. In fact, the English kings gave many of the new titles only to those who already had one. What did distinguish the aristocracies of the two countries was the extent to which the status of nobility was hereditary. In France, the aristocracy was defined legally, and all children of a French nobleman inherited noble status (though it could be forfeited by marriage outside the nobility or by the pursuit of ignoble employment). In England, only the topmost ranks of the aristocracy were hereditary, and even then the titles descended only in the eldest male line. The rest of the children of the titled nobility were thrown off into the lower gentry ranks of the aristocracy. By the eighteenth century the gentry was defined largely in social, not legal, terms. It was the legally uncontrolled access to this category of gentleman at the bottom that gave the English aristocracy its reputation for openness.

By modern standards, perhaps even by eighteenth-century French standards, that reputation was greatly exaggerated. However amorphous and accessible the bottommost level of the eighteenth-century English aristocracy may have been, gentlemen in the English-speaking world constituted a distinct group separated from ordinary people to a degree that can only astonish late-twentieth-century Americans. "The title of a gentleman," wrote one early-eighteenth-century observer, "is commonly given in England to all that distinguish themselves from the common sort of people, by a good garb, genteel air, or good education, wealth or learning." Yet becoming a gentleman was no easy matter. "A finished Gentleman," concluded Richard Steele, "is perhaps the most uncommon of all the great Characters in Life."[4]

So distinctive and so separated was the aristocracy from ordinary folk that many still thought the two groups represented two orders of being. Indeed, we will never appreciate the radicalism of the eighteenth-century revolutionary idea that all men were created equal unless we see it within this age-old tradition of difference. Gentlemen and commoners had different psyches, different emotional makeups, different natures. Ordinary people were made only "to be born and eat and sleep and die, and be forgotten." Like Mozart's Papageno, they knew "little of the motives which stimulate the higher ranks to action, pride, honour, and ambition. In general it is only hunger which can spur and goad them on to labour." Ordinary people were thought to be different physically, and because of varying diets and living conditions, no doubt in many cases they were different. People often assumed that a handsome child, though apparently a commoner, had to be some gentleman's bastard offspring. At times the aristocracy thought that common people resembled Jonathan Swift's Yahoos, having only appetites and being little more than "cattle." George Washington called ordinary farmers "the grazing multitude." Colonel Landon Carter, a leader of one of Virginia's most distinguished families, saw little to respect among ordinary people and thought that some of them were "but Idiots." Even John Adams early in his career referred to them as the "common Herd of Mankind." "Common Persons," he said, "have no Idea [of] Learning, Eloquence, and Genius," and their "vulgar, rustic Imaginations" were easily excited. To Nathanael Greene "the great body of the People" were always "contracted, selfish, and illiberal," and not to be confused with the "noble" natures of gentlemen. As the ambitious son of a Rhode Island ironmonger desperate for distinction and feeling surrounded by a "mist [of] ignorance," Greene was bound to exaggerate the inferiority of the vulgar. But often other, more established gentry also regarded the common people as narrow-minded and bigoted with little awareness of the world. Despite the best efforts of enlightened elites to spread orthodox Christianity and reason, many ordinary people still believed in an occult world of spirits and demons and still relied on a wide variety of magical practices. They were presumably unimaginative and unreflective and rarely saw beyond their own backyards and their own bellies. They had, said Gouverneur Morris, "no morals but their interests."[5]

No wonder some aristocrats believed that such ignorant, superstitious, small-souled ordinary folk were made for monarchy. The "unthinking mob," the "ignorant vulgar," were easily taken in by their senses, especially by their sight, and were often overawed by elaborate displays of color and ermine. Even at the end of his long life and a decade's experience with republican government, Benjamin Franklin could still conclude that "there is a natural inclination in mankind to Kingly Government."[6]

Compared with what young Alexander Hamilton called "the unthinking populace," the members of the aristocracy were very different. They were those "whose Minds seem to be of a greater Make than the Minds of others and who are replenished with Heroic Virtues and a Majesty of Soul above the ordinary Part of our Species." These great-souled men were driven by passions that ordinary people could never comprehend, by ambition, by pride, by honor, and by "a Prospect of an Immortality in the Memories of all the Worthy, to the End of Time." In war, the arts, or government, they were the source of achievement and works of genius. The aristocracy were those from whom rulers were drawn; it was from their ranks that the Caesars and Catos, the Cromwells and Marlboroughs, emerged, which is why such men were to be feared as much as admired. Men of soaring ambition were those in the society who made things happen; they were the men of "extraordinary Character" who were destined to distinguish their "Path thro' the World by any Great Effects." A fifteenth-century nobleman had thought that in a description of political events it was "sufficient to speak of the high-ranking people, for it is through them that God's power and justice are made known." And so it had always been through the ages and was still for many in the eighteenth century: only the ambitions and actions of the great, of the high-ranking, of kings and generals, of aristocrats and gentlemen, counted in the direction and movement of events. John Locke thought that in educating a society the "most to be taken Care of is the Gentlemen's Calling. For if those of that rank are by their Education once set right, they will quickly bring the rest into Order." Most gentlemen in that age, like some people even in our own time, believed that the intentions and concerns of ordinary men and women did not matter much in history. Even Thomas Jefferson thought that the ordinary people most often seen by travelers—"tavern keepers, Valets de place, and postilions"—were "the hackneyed rascals of every country" who "must never be considered when we calculate the national character."[7]

Before the mid-eighteenth century few patricians paid much attention to what Thomas Gray, in his "Elegy Written in a Country Churchyard," called the "homely joys and destiny obscure" of ordinary lowly people. In their "noiseless tenor," "the short and simple annals of the poor" were scarcely worth recording (which was what gave Gray's great poem its ironic significance). Certainly no writer or artist thought the vulgar capable of noble and glorious actions. Yet writers of course could use common people for satiric or comic effect, largely by playing upon the natural repulsion eighteenth-century audiences would feel in seeing plebeian characters doing what they were not meant to do. Both English and provincial playwrights, from Oliver Goldsmith to Robert Munford, sought to make their audiences laugh by setting forth the ingenious ways inferiors might pretend to be something they were not. Nothing more amused eighteenth-century theatergoers than to watch servants and other lowly sorts attempting to strike the heroic poses of their betters.[8]

Although the formal status of most members of the English aristocracy was not defined legally, the law did recognize their distinctiveness from commoners. Only gentlemen could display coats of arms and presumably be officers in the army or navy. Their treatment in law was different. Common soldiers captured in war were imprisoned; captured officers, however, could be released "on parole," after giving their word to their fellow gentlemen officers that they would not flee the area or return to their troops. Although English law was presumably equal for all, the criminal punishments were not: gentlemen, unlike commoners, did not have their ears cropped or their bodies flogged.

In just such ways were common people made to recognize and feel their inferiority and subordination to gentlemen. People in lowly stations, Jarrett remembered, were apt to be filled with consternation and awe when confronted with "what were called *gentle folks* . . . beings of a superior order." They often stood red-faced and fumbling, caps in hand, when talking with gentlemen. No wonder many of the most humble developed what was called a "down look." Old George Hewes of Massachusetts, seventy years after the event, still had seared into his mind the memory of being scared "almost to death" during a visit he made as a twenty-year-old apprentice cobbler to the home of Squire John Hancock. Common people, noted the Maryland physician Alexander Hamilton, knew "how to fawn and cringe" before "a person of more than ordinary rank." They stared "like sheep" at a gentleman's "laced hat and sword." The sight of a periwig was apt to send them running. They often shook their heads in bewilderment at an elaborately printed page or gaped in awe at a gentleman's spouting of Latin or Greek. But since their ignorance, inferiority, and subordination seemed part of the natural order of things, many common folk felt little shame in their differentness. They dutifully made their bows and doffed their caps before ladies and gentlemen; they knew their place and willingly walked while gentlefolk rode; and as yet they seldom expressed any burning desire to change places with their betters.[9]

"My parents," Jarrett recalled, "neither sought nor expected any titles, honors, or great things, either for themselves or children. . . . They wished us all to be brought up in some honest calling, that we might earn our bread, by the sweat of our brow, as they did." The naturalist John Bartram felt the same way about his son William. "I don't want him to be what is commonly called a gentleman," he said in 1755. "I want to put him to some business by which he may, with care and industry, get a temperate reasonable living."[10] We will never comprehend the distinctiveness of that premodern world until we appreciate the extent to which many ordinary people still accepted their own lowliness. Only then can we begin to understand the radical changes in this consciousness of humility, among other things, that the American Revolution brought about.

Of course, in the outlying colonies of the greater British world the aristocracy was bound to be different from what it was in the metropolitan homeland. In the colonies there were few peers or titled gentry, a deficiency that bothered a good many imperial officials. Since the colonists only occasionally saw someone with a title—a visiting landlord, a royal governor, a British general—their sense of aristocracy was largely confined to the category of gentry. But this limitation did not make their aristocracy any less distinctive in their minds. In Virginia, for example, the distinction was there practically from birth: "Before a boy knows his right hand from his left, can discern black from white, good from evil, or knows who made him, or how he exists, he is a Gentleman." And as a gentleman, "it would derogate greatly from his character, to learn a trade; or to put his hand to any servile employment." Because of the lack of a titled aristocracy in the colonies, being a gentleman became all that more important."

In the southern colonies perhaps as few as one in twenty-five adult white males was readily acknowledged as a gentleman, while in the northern colonies maybe one in ten was accorded that status; but all the North American colonies recognized this distinction between the great and the humble, gentlemen and commoners. Even among the New Jersey farmers, who were remarkably "Level" in wealth and estate, there were some "Gentlemen in the first rank of Dignity and Quality" with "high-born, long-recorded Families." Limited as these New Jersey gentry may have been in their property, they were still quite distinguishable from "the laborious part of Men, who are commonly ranked in the middling or lower Class." In the Chesapeake region these differences were of course far greater. In Virginia in 1771 the top 7.9 percent of the planters controlled one-third of the land in the colony. Some of these aristocratic planters had truly grand pretensions, as Philip Fithian, the College of New Jersey (later Princeton) graduate who became tutor to the family of the great Virginia planter Robert Carter, was at pains to point out. The great planters' "amazing property" in land and slaves, no matter how burdened with debts, had created in all the owners' minds, said Fithian, a belief "that they are exalted as much above other Men in worth and precedency, as blind stupid fortune has made a difference in their property." The South Carolina aristocracy, with its "state and magnificence, the natural attendants on great riches," was even more overwhelming, especially to someone like Josiah Quincy, who knew only plain Puritan Boston. Charleston with its "grandeur and splendor . . . ," Quincy wrote in 1773, "far surpasses all I ever saw, or ever expect to see, in America." All the colonial cities, in fact, were breeding grounds for aristocrats. There in the urban centers select individuals, "by more information, better polish and greater intercourse with strangers, insensibly acquired an ascendency over the farmer of the country; the richer merchants of these towns, together with the clergy, lawyers, physicians and officers of the English navy who had occasionally settled there, were considered as gentry." It was in the great towns, all travelers agreed, where one found the "more civilized" inhabitants, those who were distinguished from the common herd by their refinement and learning.[12]

Although the precise nature of the "men of quality," the "better sort," was more in doubt in the eighteenth century than ever before in Western history, the colonists still had some lingering inherited ideas of who a gentleman was. John Adams in 1761 at least thought he knew when someone was not a gentleman, "neither by Birth, Education, Office, Reputation, or Employment," nor by "Thought, Word, or Deed." A person who springs "from ordinary Parents," who "can scarcely write his Name," whose "Business is Boating," who "never had any Commissions"—to call such a person a gentleman was "an arrant Prostitution of the Title." The colonists had a number of ways of distinguishing this genteel status.[13]

The most important measure was still "Birth and Parentage," as befitting a monarchical society with an inherited crown. All men were created unequal. God, it was said, had been "pleas'd to constitute a Difference in Families." Although most children were of "low Degree or of Common Derivation, Some are Sons and Daughters of the Mighty: they are more honorably descended, and have greater Relations than others." The word "gentry" was, after all, associated with birth, derived from "gens" or stock. English and colonial writers like Henry Fielding and Robert Munford, even when poking fun at the false pretensions of the aristocracy, had to have—for the harmony of their stories—their apparently plebeian heroes or heroines turn out to be secretly the offspring of a gentleman. A monarchical society necessarily had a deep cultural prejudice against what the Maryland physician Alexander Hamilton called people of "low extraction."[4]

Wealth, too, was important in distinguishing a gentleman, for "in vulgar reckoning a mean condition bespeaks a mean man." One sardonic observer of the gentry of King William County, Virginia, in the 1760s said that any male who had "Money, Negroes and Land enough" was automatically considered a "compleat gentleman"; even a man "looked upon . . . as unworthy of a Gentleman's notice because he had no Land and Negroes" could, if he, "by some means or other, acquired both," become "a Gentleman all of a sudden." But for many, property and riches alone were never enough to make someone a gentleman. Not only did some impoverished persons claim gentry status, but some common laboring people had more property than some gentlemen. Increasingly in this early modern society, wealth and even birth—the traditional sources of aristocratic or gentry status—were surrounded and squeezed by other measures of distinction, by cultivated, man-made criteria having to do with manners, taste, and character. "No man," it was more and more said, "deserves the appellation a Gentleman until he has done something to merit it."[5]

Gentlemen walked and talked in certain ways and held in contempt those who did not. They ate with silver knives and forks while many common people still ate with their hands. They took up dancing and fencing, for both "contribute greatly to a graceful Carriage." They were urged by their parents to study poetry and to learn to play musical instruments and to "become perfectly easy and natural" in their manners, particularly in "real humility, condescension, courteousness, affability." "A Gentleman," they were told, "should know how to appear in an Assembly [in] Public to Advantage, and to defend himself if attacked." Philip Fithian said that any young gentleman traveling through

Virginia was presumed to be acquainted with dancing, boxing, card- and fiddle-playing, and the use of a small sword. Gentlemen prided themselves on their classical learning, and in both their privately cir- culated verse and their public polemics they took great pains to display their knowledge. Unlike common people, gentlemen wore wigs or pow- dered their hair, believing that "nothing [was] a finer ornament to a young gentleman than a good head of hair well order'd and set forth," especially when appearing "before persons of rank and distinction." They dressed distinctively and fashionably. In contrast to the plain shirts, leather aprons, and buckskin breeches of ordinary men, they wore lace ruffles, silk stockings, and other finery. They sought to build elaborate houses and to have their portraits painted. Little gratified their hearts more than to have a "coach and six," or at least a "chariot and four," to have servants decked out in "fine liveries," to have a reputation for entertaining liberally, to be noticed. Some colonial gentry or would-be gentry, like Jonathan Trumbull, an obscure trader from Lebanon, Con- necticut, even refined the spelling of their names and acquired coats of arms from the Herald's office in London.[16]

Ultimately, beneath all these strenuous efforts to define gentility lay the fundamental classical characteristic of being free and independent. The liberality for which gentlemen were known connoted freedom— freedom from material want, freedom from the caprice of others, free- dom from ignorance, and freedom from having to work with one's hands. The gentry's distinctiveness came from being independent in a world of dependencies, learned in a world only partially literate. and leisured in a world of laborers.

We today have so many diverse forms of work and recreation and so much of our society shares in them that we can scarcely appreciate the significance of the earlier stark separation between a leisured few and a laboring many. In the eighteenth century, labor, as it had been for ages, was still associated with toil and trouble, with pain, and man- ual productivity did not yet have the superior moral value that it would soon acquire. To be sure, industriousness and hard work were every- where extolled, and the Puritan ethic was widely preached—but only for ordinary people, not for gentlemen, and not for the sake of increas- ing the society's productivity. Hard, steady work was good for the char- acter of common people: it kept them out of trouble; it lifted them out of idleness and barbarism; and it instilled in them the proper moral values; but it was not thought to expand the prosperity of the society. Although Locke had argued that labor was the source of property, most conventional thinking did not yet regard labor as a source of wealth. People labored out of necessity, out of poverty, and that necessity and poverty bred the contempt in which laboring people had been held for centuries. Freedom was always valued because it was freedom from this necessity to labor. Most people, it was widely assumed, would not work if they did not have to. "Everyone but an idiot," said the English agricultural writer Arthur Young in a startling summary of this traditional view, "knows that the lower class must be kept poor or they will never be industrious." It was "poverty," wrote Lieutenant Governor Thomas Hutchinson of Massachusetts in 1761, that "will produce industry and frugality." To many ordinary people in this premodern age (as indeed to many even today in the Third World) leisure seemed more attractive than work, for as yet they could see no reason why they should work harder. Which is why gentlemen spent so much time and energy urging the common people to be industrious.[7]

In time the consumption by ordinary people of goods beyond necessities—everything from china dishes to lace curtains—would provide a sufficient incentive for working harder, but this possibility was only beginning to be noticed in the middle of the eighteenth century. Traditionally consumption was regarded as both the privilege of the gentry and as an obligation of their rank. Gentlemen responded to unemployment among the laboring ranks by ordering another pair of boots or a new hat. In the seventeenth century Thomas Mun had argued that "the purse of the rich" maintained the poor. In the eighteenth century Montesquieu still agreed: "If the rich do not spend so lavishly," he wrote, "the poor would die." When unemployed silk workers rioted in London in 1765, the king's natural reaction was to ensure that the ladies of his court ordered expensive silk gowns for the next ball. "To be born for no other Purpose than to consume the Fruits of the Earth," wrote Henry Fielding in 1751, "is the Privilege (if it may be really called a Privilege) of a very few. The greater Part of Mankind must sweat hard to produce them, or Society will no longer answer the Purposes for which it was ordained." Sir Joseph Banks, the famous botanist, agreed: he even worried that farmers were growing rich enough to send their sons to college to become "Lawyers, Parsons, Doctors, etc.," and thus turning them "into Gentleman Consumers and not Providers of Food."[18]

"An Aged Farmer" of New Jersey in 1770 urged his fellow farmers to stop complaining about the gentry's fox-hunting on their land. "Begrudging the young Men of [Philadelphia] the Use of this Diversion in our Woods" was shortsighted, he said. These gentlemen more than made up for "all the little injuries that they may do by Accident, in Pursuit of those *noxious Animals,*" by consuming our produce. Who else, he asked, would purchase our watermelons if not these gentry? Fox-hunting may have been a "Luxury" as charged, but so were water-melons. "They are of no Kind of Use as Food," and yet the gentry "pay us *some Thousand Pounds a Year*" for them. The Jersey farmers were indebted to the gentry's luxuries. Being able to dispose of his *"Truck"* in "the Philadelphia Market . . . for Cash, without paying . . . *Toll* for having the Liberty of selling it," was for this old Jersey farmer an "Indulgence" that had brought him "much good living in my Time," for which he acknowledged his gratitude, "as should also my Country-men, who are mostly under the same Obligations."[19] Consumption was a gentry prerogative that could be used quite purposefully. The psy-chology of the Americans' resistance movement in the 1760s and 1770s— its resort to various nonimportation agreements and boycotts of British goods—rested on this traditional assumption about the nature of genteel consumption: that it was a kind of indulgence or favor done for those producers dependent on it and the refusal to consume was a form of coercive punishment. In the Association of October 1774 members of the Continental Congress further revealed their genteel biases by agreeing to "discountenance and discourage every species of extravagance and dissipation," including the fashionable resort to elaborate mourning dress and the giving of gloves and scarves at funerals.[20]

The debate over luxury that emerged in the pan-British world in the eighteenth century was directly related to the increased consumption of genteel goods by ordinary people. Luxury, which Benjamin Franklin's friend Richard Jackson defined as "a greater expense of subsistence than in prudence a man ought to consume," was relative to social rank: much of what a gentleman needed a commoner did not, and thus many of the necessities of a gentleman were a common man's luxuries. Lux-ury therefore was a serious social vice, a symptom of social disarray. Although all social ranks were presumably capable of luxurious living— of consuming beyond their needs—the spending habits of ordinary people were what most concerned and alarmed their betters. The aris-tocracy needed to display its status by spending, but the responsibility of common people was to produce, not to consume. Thus followed the many traditional attempts to impose sumptuary laws on ordinary people and the continual calls for more frugality among the commonality. The evil of luxury was the evil of ordinary people violating the social hier-archy and living beyond their allotted social rank. Luxurious spending by the aristocracy provided useful work for common people; it was, as Gibbon said, a voluntary tax paid by the rich for the sake of the poor. But if this luxurious spending extended throughout all social ranks, then, according to the received wisdom, common people would reduce their exertions, become idle, begin to act like aristocrats, and thus confound all social distinctions.[21]

Idleness, leisure, or what was best described as *not* exerting oneself for profit, was supposed to be a prerogative of gentlemen only. Gentlemen, James Harrington had written, were those who "live upon their own revenue in plenty, without engagement either to the tilling of their lands or other work for their livelihood." In the early eighteenth century Daniel Defoe defined "the gentry" as "such who live on estates, and without the mechanism of employment, including the men of letters, such as clergy, lawyers and physicians." A half century later Richard Jackson similarly characterized the gentry as those who "live on their fortunes." Aristocrats lived upon what we today might call "unearned income"; they did not work for a living. Although some northern colonists might suggest that gentlemen farmers ought to set "a laborious example to their Domesticks," perhaps by taking an occasional turn in the fields, a gentleman's activity was supposed to be with the mind. Managing their landed estates meant exercising authority—the only activity befitting a truly free man. Of course, like the ancient Roman landed aristocrats whom many eighteenth-century gentlemen sought to emulate, landed gentry such as Thomas Nelson of Virginia were deeply involved in all sorts of commercial and entrepreneurial activities— breeding their cattle, upgrading their soil, improving their fruit trees, speculating in land, or even trafficking and trading.[22] But they engaged in these commercial activities in something other than a pure money-making spirit, and that presumably made all the difference.

If they had sufficient aristocratic status, they could scorn commercial profiteering as greedy and ungenteel and yet at the same time exploit every possible means to increase their wealth without any sense of contradiction. But ideally, of course, they were not to work for a living; their income was supposed to come to them indirectly from their wealth—from rents and from interest on bonds or money out on loan— and much of it often did. Immense cultural pressure often made them pretend that their economic affairs were for pleasure or for the good of the community, and not for their subsistence.[23] They saw themselves and, more important, were seen by others as gentlemen who happened to engage in some commercial enterprises. Unlike ordinary people, gentlemen traditionally were not defined or identified by what they did, but by who they were. They had avocations, not vocations. The great French naturalist the Comte de Buffon did not like to think of himself as anyone other than "a gentleman amusing myself with natural history." He did not want to be called a "naturalist," or even a "great naturalist." "Naturalists, linkboys, dentists, etc."—these, said Buffon, were "people who live by their work; a thing ill suited to a gentleman." Clergymen, doctors, lawyers, were not yet modern professionals, working long hours for a living like a common artisan. Their gentry status depended less on their professional skills than on other sources—on family, wealth, or a college education in the liberal arts; and doctors, lawyers, and clergymen who had none of these were therefore something less than gentlemen—pettifoggers, charlatans, or quacks.[24]

One thing seemed clear: as John Locke had said, "Trade is wholly inconsistent with a gentleman's calling." Prominent merchants dealing in international trade brought wealth into the society and were thus valuable members of the community, but their status as independent gentlemen was always tainted by their concern to "serve their own private separate interest." Retail trading was even worse. The Charleston merchant-planter Henry Laurens was keenly aware of the bad image buying and selling had among southern planters. In 1764 he advised two impoverished but aspiring gentry immigrants heading for the backcountry to establish themselves as planters before attempting to open a store. For them to enter immediately into "any retail trade in those parts," he warned, "would be mean, would lessen them in the esteem of people whose respect they must endeavour to attract." Only after they were "set down in a creditable manner as planters" might they "carry on the sale of many specie of European and West Indian goods to some advantage and with a good grace." Even that might not work, as former staymaker and wealthy merchant Charles Wallace of Annapolis discovered after he purchased a plantation and sought to become a Maryland aristocrat. Although Wallace eventually did get appointed to the governor's council and did associate with the prominent gentry of Maryland, he was never really accepted; as his nephew pointed out, "he was not quite a patrician."[25]

From the beginning of the eighteenth century a number of thinkers—Daniel Defoe, Bernard Mandeville, Richard Steele, and Joseph Addison among them—had attempted to reconcile the astonishing growth of English commerce with traditional notions of gentility. Some even went so far as to extol the exertion for profit as superior to aristocratic leisure, but the classical aversion to moneymaking remained strong. Although Addison in *The Spectator* tried to make his merchant character Sir Andrew Freeport respectable, in the end he had to have Sir Andrew retire from business and buy a landed estate in order to become a full-fledged gentleman. Thus it was natural for many Englishmen on both sides of the Atlantic to conclude that having a landed estate worked by others was "the only Gentlemanlike Way of growing rich . . . ; all other Professions have something in them of the *mean* and *subservient;* this alone is free and noble."[26]

Labor or working in order to live was thus traditionally considered to be servile, associated with dependency and a lowly status. Even Benjamin Franklin, for all his praise of the work ethic, never valued toil for its own sake, and certainly not for a gentleman. "Who is there," he once wrote, "that can be handsomely Supported in Affluence, Ease and Pleasure by another, that will chuse rather to earn his Bread by the Sweat of his own Brows?" Men worked from necessity, he said, not from choice. As soon as Franklin acquired enough wealth not to have to work, he retired from business at the age of forty-two, and became a gentleman of leisure. Nobody who continued to work for a living, especially with his hands—no plowman, no printer, no artisan—no matter how wealthy he became, no matter how many employees he managed, could ever legitimately claim the status of gentleman. Only when the small-time Charleston trader John Marley and the prosperous printer Benjamin Franklin actually gave up their businesses and freed themselves from mandatory labor could they enter the ranks of gentlemen. Anyone who worked with his hands, even a great painter with noble aspirations like John Singleton Copley, was socially stigmatized. Copley painted the portraits of dozens of distinguished colonial gentlemen, and he knew what his patrons thought of his art. For them, Copley said bitterly in 1767, painting was "no more than any other useful trade, as they sometimes term it, like that of a Carpenter tailor or shoemaker."[27]

But it was not enough for a man to avoid trade or manual labor and to think himself a gentleman. Ultimately the rank of the "better sort," especially in colonial America, which lacked any legal titles for its aristocracy, had to rest on reputation, on opinion, on having one's claim to gentility accepted by the world. Once this reputation was gained, it was worth a great deal, both materially and psychologically. Gentry status brought respectability and credit, and for that very personal eighteenth-century world that lacked most of our impersonal modern devices for money transactions, respectability and credit were very nearly everything. Among the Virginia planters, noted Fithian, just the fact of a Princeton education meant that "you would be rated, without any more questions asked, either about your family, your Estate, your business, or your intention, at 10,000£ and you might come, & go, & converse, & keep company, according to this value; & you would be dispised & slighted if you rated yourself a farthing cheaper." It is thus understandable why, when given the choice, New York traders preferred to list themselves as "gentleman" rather than as "merchant." One tutor refused to continue teaching in a Chesapeake household unless the family began treating him as the "gentleman" he felt himself to be. If only he could be regarded as a gentleman, then the poverty that was being thrown up to him would soon be remedied.[28]

No wonder, then, that eighteenth-century gentlemen so jealously guarded their reputations. "Scarcely anything is so important to an individual as a good Name" was a maxim every gentleman valued. The poet John Trumbull thought that, in Connecticut at least, "three or four well invented lies, properly circulated and coming from the right Persons, will ruin any but the most Respectable Character." This is why the polemics of the period could be so personally vicious and vituperative. No accusation was too coarse or outrageous to be made by one gentleman against another—from drunkenness and gambling to impotence and adultery—for the purpose of such accusations was to destroy the gentlemanly reputation of one's opponents and thereby bring into question both their social authority and the legitimacy of their arguments.[29]

This reputation was another name for honor—a traditional quality still much invoked by the eighteenth century. Honor was the value genteel society placed on a gentleman and the value that a gentleman placed on himself. Honor suggested a public drama in which men played roles for which they were praised or blamed. It subsumed self-esteem, pride, and dignity, and was akin to glory and fame. Gentlemen acted or avoided acting for the sake of their honor. Honor was, in fact, as one American said, "as strong an incentive to Action as self-Preservation and perhaps more so." Honor was a stimulus for ambition, which was thought to be an exclusively aristocratic passion. Everyone had appetites and interests, but only the restless-minded, the great-souled, the extraordinary few, had ambition—that overflowing desire to excel, to have precedence, and to achieve fame. It was the kind of passion that in 1769

led Alexander Hamilton, a fourteen-year-old merchant's clerk on the
obscure island of St. Croix, to wish for a war so he could risk his life
and gain honor.[30]

War was so exciting and inspiring to eighteenth-century gentlemen
precisely because it offered so many more opportunities for achieving
honor and fame than did other endeavors. "The more danger the greater
glory," declared a young and ambitious John Adams. Yet Adams always knew instinctively, and to his great frustration, that he was not
cut out "to make a Figure in Arms," which is why he never could quite
forgive George Washington his eventual success.[31]

There was, of course, something old-fashioned, even feudal, about
this gentlemanly concern with reputation and honor—as the new democratic world of the nineteenth century would increasingly discover.
Since it was "the nature of honor to aspire to preferments and titles,"
honor, Montesquieu had written, was ideally suited to a monarchical
society. In fact, he said, honor was the very life and soul of monarchy.
It set all parts of a monarchical society in motion and by its very action
connected them together. Honor was the means by which kings gained
the allegiance and support of the ambitious heroes and gentlemen of the
society. Honor made sense only in an unequal society, observed the
English philosopher David Hartley. "Men that are much commended,
presently think themselves above the Level of the rest of the World. . . .
It is evident from the very Nature of Praise, which supposes something
extraordinary in the Thing praised, that it cannot be the Lot of many."
Honor was exclusive, heroic, and elitist, and it presumed a world very
different from the world that was emerging and from our own, a hierarchical world in which a few could unabashedly claim a moral superiority over the rest.[32]

This gentlemanly superiority was so great and so distinctive that it
had its own rules of respectability. This superiority or honor was generally recognized by demonstrations of respect for the head, either by
the gentry's wearing of wigs or by the doffing of caps by ordinary folks
in the presence of gentlefolk. Any affront to the head, ranging from a
slap in the face to scalping, was an act of dishonor. Such a concept of
honor lay behind the practice of dueling. Dueling was the means by
which gentlemen protected their reputations or their honor among other
gentlemen. Indeed, for some, dueling was the ultimate recognition of
the distinctiveness of being a gentleman. The law's remedy for insults
may have been good enough for ordinary people, but "there are those

of a *different* character who know how to resent and to *punish* men for ill usage, without troubling a magistrate or a court of justice."[33] Gentlemen were answerable for their honor to their equals alone. They could be insulted only by other gentlemen. A superior could ignore the affront of an inferior, since his honor or his reputation among other gentlemen was not thereby challenged.

Gentlemanly honor was bound up with the moral commitment to tell the truth or to keep one's word. Young William Paterson of New Jersey let his enthusiasm over becoming a gentleman carry him to the point of saying that legal devices such as "Contracts and evidence, and seals and Oaths were devised to tie fools, and knaves, and cowards: Honor and Conscience are the more firm and sacred ties of gentlemen." Few went that far, but most gentlemen thought that a gentleman's word was due only to those who socially deserved it—that is, to other gentlemen. This is why captured military officers (that is, gentlemen, not common soldiers) could be released "on parole." To call into question a gentleman's word or to give him the lie publicly was thus the most serious kind of affront, demanding satisfaction. The entire elaborate code worked out over centuries presumed a distinctive category of gentlemen that transcended ordinary social and even national lines. Even in wartime, gentlemen officers in opposing armies recognized that they often had more in common with one another than they did with the common soldiers in their own armies.[34]

The very clarity of gentlemen's social superiority over the rest of society could at times permit what later generations would regard as an unbecoming familiarity between different social ranks. Gentlemen mingled affably with their inferiors at sporting events and other popular entertainments and rubbed shoulders in taverns and streets more easily than would be the case a half century later. Only a hierarchical society that knew its distinctions well could have placed so much value on a gentleman's capacity for condescension—that voluntary humiliation, that willing descent from superiority to equal terms with inferiors. Rufus Putnam, a young Massachusetts enlisted man serving with the provincial forces attached to the British army in northern New York during the Seven Years' War, thought that Brigadier General George Augustus, Viscount Howe, possessed such a perfect ability to condescend that "every soldier in the army had a personal attachment to him." Howe, who was second-in-command in the 1758 expedition against Fort Ticonderoga, frequently came among the men, said Putnam, "and his man-

ner was so easy and fermiller, that you loost all that constraint or diffi-
dence we feele when addressed by our Superiours, whose manners are
forbiding.''[35]

Gentlemen drank with their inferiors, joked with them, and sometimes teased them, as with children. Southern gentry planters called
their neighboring freeholders by their first names, but expected to be
called "Mr." or "Your Honor" in return. Gentlemen often took the
vulgarities of their inferiors for granted and felt little threatened by them.
Sometimes they scarcely thought about those far beneath them. What
is extraordinary about the Itinerarium of Dr. Alexander Hamilton—
that remarkably detailed report of a four-month trip northward in 1744
by a learned and observant Maryland physician—was Hamilton's ignoring of the presence or activities of his Negro servant, who accompanied him throughout. The more confident gentlemen were of their
superiority, the more familiar they might be. Thus William Byrd could
blithely eat the corn pone served to slaves while a boatwright looked on
in disgust.[36]

By the early nineteenth century men looked back puzzled by the
"unsophisticated" and "illiberal" "semi-barbarism" of their
eighteenth-century childhood. It was a more boisterous, more violent,
and more freewheeling world then, Samuel Breck recalled, and people
behaved in strange ways. Wild revels and bloody street fights were condoned by people of quality. Pope's Day, the anniversary of Guy
Fawkes's attempt to blow up the Houses of Parliament on November 5,
1605, was celebrated in eighteenth-century Boston by parades, with effigies of the pope, the devil, and the "guy" carried about the streets
and later hanged and burned. During the day the north and south ends
of Boston had rival parades and stoned and fought each other viciously.
In the evening, companies of the vulgar, remembered Breck, actually
used to enter the homes of the gentry, put on mummeries, and then
insolently demand money. What was most astonishing to Breck in rec-
ollecting these memories of his youth was that the colonial gentry of his
parents' generation put up with such behavior and paid the money
demanded; the new enlightened and refined nineteenth-century society,
he declared, "would not brook such usage a moment." He could not
comprehend that his genteel nineteenth-century world might have lost
much more than it had gained.[37]

3. Patriarchal Dependence

The gentlemanly elites of the eighteenth century could condescend and be affable with their subordinates and inferiors because they often thought of themselves as parents dealing with children. Since most relationships in this hierarchical society were still very personal, they were also necessarily paternalistic. It was only natural for the family—that oldest and most intimate of institutions—to be the model for describing most political and social relationships, not only those between king and subjects but also those between all superiors and subordinates. Some traditionalists still believed, as Montesquieu complained, "that nature having established paternal authority, the most natural government was that of a single person." Even a good whig like Daniel Defoe could argue that there was "a sort of Patriarchal Affection, as well as obligation, between a King on the Throne and the People he Governs." "The Obedience of Children to Parents is the Basis of all Government," wrote Addison in *The Spectator*. In fact, the family was "the measure of that Obedience which we owe to those whom Providence hath placed over us." The language of paternalism and filial obligation still provided the common metaphors eighteenth-century Englishmen on both sides of the Atlantic used to describe their hierarchical experiences.[1]

"Approach the Almighty with Reverence, thy Prince with Submission, thy Parents with Obedience, and thy Master with Respect" was the conventional advice given to all. The king, said Governor James Glen of South Carolina, had "Paternal care of his People," even in these "the most distant parts of his Dominions." If the people were good subjects, Lieutenant Governor Robert Dinwiddie told the Virginia House of Burgesses in 1752, they "will deserve the paternal Affection of his Majesty." Could there ever be a more powerful image of authority? Even "Almighty God . . . ," said Dinwiddie, "has not disdained to be called the Father of us all." All superiors, all magistrates, all masters, were "fathers" or "tender parents." Thus the kind of paternalistic ordering of social relations expressed in the early eighteenth century in the prescriptions of the Puritan divine Samuel Willard retained much of its vitality at mid-century: "The Fifth Commandment hath a proper respect to the Order which God hath placed among Mankind; and the Relative Duties which do flow from the Nature of that Order."[2]

Paternalism was meaningful to the colonists because much of their society was organized in families or in those stark dependencies that resembled the relationship between parents and children. For the colonists, the family, or what modern scholars call the household, was still the basic institution in the society and the center of all rights and obligations. A "little commonwealth," the original Puritan settlers had called it, and it remained for eighteenth-century Americans the fundamental source of community and continuity. Almost everyone spent some time in his or her life living in an extended household. And everyone in the household was dependent on the will of the father or master (the terms were indistinguishable). The family was, in fact, not simply those living under one roof but all those dependent on the single head. And this head, the patriarch, was the only one who dealt with the larger world. Thus it was easy to conclude, as one New England clergyman did in 1754, that

> as the *Civil State*, as well as the *Churches of Christ*, is furnish'd with Members from private Families: if the Governors of these little Communities, were faithful to the great Trust reposed in them, and Family-Religion & Discipline were thoroughly, prudently & strictly, maintained & exercised . . . , the Civil State, would prosper and flourish from Generation to Generation.[3]

The household and hence patriarchy may even have been stronger in America than in England precisely because of the weakness in the colonies of other institutions, such as guilds. The family household was still the place where most of the work in the society was done and where most of the education and training took place. In the absence of all the elaborate institutions of modern society—from hospitals and nursing homes to prisons and asylums—the family remained the primary institution for teaching the young, disciplining the wayward, and caring for the poor and insane. No wonder that the colonists believed that society was little more than a collection of family households, to which all isolated and helpless individuals necessarily had to be attached. Everywhere families reached out and blended almost imperceptibly into the larger community.

Sometimes colonial communities seemed to be only enlarged families. Inbreeding and intermarrying, particularly through the remarriages of widowed spouses, often created incredibly tangled webs of kinship. Some of these kinship networks grew in time to permeate or encompass entire villages, counties, or even colonies. One-third of the

135 taxpayers in the early-eighteenth-century town of East Guilford, Connecticut, came from only five families; indeed, nearly 40 percent of all the families of the village were related to one another. Joseph Emerson of Pepperell, Massachusetts, said he "sometimes regretted that he did not marry a Shattuck, for he should then have been related to the whole town." All the landed gentry of western Massachusetts were bound together by blood or marriage. The members of six families of Hampshire County held two-thirds of all county offices—creating what has been called "a county-wide family magistracy." The half dozen families that dominated the eighteenth-century South Carolina council were linked in a similar way. Governor William Bull, for example, had three daughters and two nieces, who married two Draytons, two Middletons, and an Izard. In Virginia seats on the grand juries as well as on the vestries and the county courts fell to the same families year after year. At the funeral of Abraham De Peyster of New York in 1767, more than a hundred relatives attended, bearing twenty-five different family names. Every colony had its few dominant aristocratic families, and some of these, like the Shippens of Pennsylvania and the Lees of Virginia, were linked through marriage across colonial boundaries.[4]

Gentry families in many of the colonies, in emulation of the English nobility, created the legal devices of primogeniture and entail, built "seats" for themselves in the country, and strenuously sought to amass estates they could pass on to their heirs. Parents at all social levels almost always named children after themselves and their relatives and created numerous 2nds, 3rds, and 4ths, and in the case of the intermarrying first families of Virginia a veritable polyphony of names: Nelson Page, Page Nelson, Carter Page, Page Carter, Mann Page, William Byrd Page, Carter Harrison, Harrison Carter, Shirley Harrison, Byrd Harrison, Shirley Carter, Carter Braxton, and so on and on.

During the second third of the eighteenth century 43 percent of all marriages among the planters of one Maryland county were between blood kin or persons previously related by marriage. New England was no different. The Minutemen of the towns were held together less by chains of command than by familial loyalties. The 3,047 Massachusetts soldiers who served in the Seven Years' War had only 1,443 family names. Over one-quarter of the Lexington militiamen mustered by Captain John Parker on April 19, 1775, were related to him by blood or marriage.[5]

Family relationships determined the nature of most people's lives. Land was the basis of life in most American communities, and most rights in land depended on ties of kinship. Before mid-century there was apparently much more continuity and stability in many colonial rural areas, at least in New England, than historians long imagined. In fact, the colonists were far more likely to have kin alive and to live close to them than were the English in the mother country.[6] Many farmers were enmeshed in narrowly circumscribed worlds whose roots reached back to the seventeenth century. Sometimes as many as half of the younger sons without land might leave their communities, but most people did not: they lived out their entire lives in the locality in which they were born. Most New England farmers, and perhaps most others too, thought mainly of providing for their families and rarely justified their acquisitiveness in any other terms than the needs of their families. What they principally wanted out of life was sons to whom they could pass on their land and who would continue the family name. For Virginians as well as New Englanders, "a man's patrimony . . . is a sacred depositum." Probably few ordinary farmers ever owned much more than what was handed down to them by their families. When they did accumulate wealth, they generally used it to buy more land in order to provide for their heirs.[7]

The land belonged to the male line. English laws of inheritance provided for primogeniture (all lands passing to the eldest son) when there was no will, and for entail (allowing a testator to keep the landed estate intact through the stem line of the family). Entail was used in nearly all the colonies, but most commonly in Virginia. Primogeniture was often used too, but not in the New England colonies, which in cases of intestacy provided for partible inheritance among all children of the decedent, usually reserving a double portion for the eldest son. But the New Englanders' practice, even when they wrote wills, of dividing up their estates among all the children, or at least the males, instead of leaving them entirely to the eldest sons, does not mean they were modern in their outlook. Far from it: New England families scarcely conceived of themselves simply as conjugal units with the children sharing and sharing alike in the estates. They were traditional in their outlook, and not all that different from contemporary Europeans. Most premodern European families likewise preferred to partition their land among all their sons and to burden the land with various provisions for their daughters, if their tenure rights were secure and there was no danger of the land fragmenting into pieces too small to support a family. It was not unusual, therefore, for premodern parents to seek to secure the independence of as many of their children as possible without morseling the estate and impairing the social standing of the family.[8]

In most of the colonies, at least before mid-century, land was sufficiently plentiful for fathers to be able to take care of more than the eldest son in passing on their estates. Indeed, given the abundance of land in America compared with England, what is remarkable is not that the colonists resorted to partible inheritance but that they tried to institute primogeniture and entail at all. The sole existing study we have of primogeniture and entail in Virginia is more ambiguous than we have been led to believe. Virginians held much land in fee simple and docked many of their entailed estates; yet even as they were struggling to free some of their entailed land for disposal, they were entailing other portions in their continuing efforts to establish their family estates. Even in New England, especially after 1750 when land became less available, most farmers favored one of the sons over the others in the distribution of the land. Nearly half of the inheritances in the little town of Chebacco, Massachusetts, left one or more surviving sons landless. Where there were no male heirs, the fathers often gave the estate to a married daughter and her husband to hold in trust for one of their sons; or sometimes they created male heirs by selecting a brother's son, particularly if the nephew bore the testator's own Christian name. At age eight John Hancock became a full member of the childless household of his uncle Thomas Hancock and thereby became the heir to one of the largest fortunes in New England.[9]

In their inheritance practices New Englanders followed what has been called the premodern European tradition of "favored heir plus burdens." And these burdens could be heavy. Although New England farmers apparently never sought to entail estates, their heirs usually found themselves enmeshed in networks of obligations to their mothers and less favored siblings, including caring for aged kin, granting use-rights to the estate, and paying legacies out of future revenues. The task of defining these rights and obligations could be an intricate business, and it was often done in a very pecuniary and unsentimental manner. Calculating the price of past services of a son to his deceased father, or detailing the different heirs' proportional rights to the use of haylofts, barnyards, and wells, or specifying the cords of wood to be delivered to a widow, resembled nothing so much as contractual business arrangements between masters and apprentices or between neighbors. They were one more indication that the colonial family was still largely indistinguishable from the surrounding community; it was not yet a modern private institution bound together only by ties of affection.[10]

In all the colonies, business and politics usually began with the family. As a matter of course brothers took in each other's sons in order to teach them trades or simply to apply discipline. Merchants often formed partnerships with their relatives and counted on members of their extended families to act as the trusted agents they needed in distant ports. Most craftsmen organized their trade around their families, either in their own home or in an attached shop. An ironmaster, John Lesher, called the employees in his forges his "family," even though the group consisted of nearly thirty persons, not counting the colliers, woodcutters, and other day laborers.[11]

Families everywhere built up local networks of kin and used them in politics. The dominant force in the North Carolina provincial assembly in the early eighteenth century was a group of Cape Fear promoters, led by Maurice Moore, Roger Moore, and Edward Moselly, who were so closely tied together by kinship that their enemies called them the "Family." By 1731 at least half of the twenty-eight patentees of the rich Cape Fear area were related to the Moores, who themselves held 83,000 out of the 105,000 acres patented. In many of the colonies people used family names—the De Lanceys in New York, the Ogdens in New Jersey, the Wentworths in New Hampshire—to designate political groups. In Cambridge, Massachusetts, between 1700 and 1780 three successive Andrew Boardmans not only served almost continuously as town clerk and town treasurer but also were elected for ninety-three terms as selectman, representative, and moderator. During the half century before the Revolution, more than 70 percent of the representatives elected to the New Jersey assembly were related to previously elected legislators. The situation in South Carolina was similar. Dominant families everywhere monopolized political offices and passed them among themselves even through successive generations. Whether it was the town clerkship in Norwich, Connecticut, or the clerk of the court in Lancaster County, Virginia, in each case a single family held the office for forty or so years before the Revolution. John Adams knew of what he was speaking when he later stressed the importance of family dynasties in New England politics. "Go into every village in New England," he said, "and you will find that the office of justice of the peace, and even the place of representative, which has ever depended only on the freest election of the people, have generally descended from generation to generation, in three or four families at most."[12]

Living within a family meant a state of dependence for everyone but the patriarch. Women rarely had an independent existence, at least in law. In public records women were usually referred to simply as the "wife of," or the "daughter of," or the "sister of" some male. Before marriage they legally belonged to their fathers and after marriage to their husbands. Most husbands in their wills refused to give their wives outright ownership of their landed estates; at best the wife got a life-use of the estate, which the widow usually lost upon her remarriage. With their husbands alive women were considered legally to be like children: they could not sue or be sued, draft wills, make contracts, or deal in property. Even the bodices and ankle-length petticoats commonly worn by women, girls, and young boys in portraits suggest the similarity of their subordinate and dependent status. Women were in fact often treated as children by their husbands. Husbands might address their wives as "dear child" or by their Christian names but be addressed in return as "Mr." "I never know when to leave off," said one woman of her rambling letters to her husband, "but I depend on your sense to make allowances for the imperfections of a poor foolish Girl, whose Study & greatest pleasure always has & shall be to please you." "Sir," declared Elizabeth Byrd to her husband, William Byrd III, "your Orders must be obeyed whatever reluctance I find thereby." No wonder women who did not like to act the part of submissive children declared their "dependence" to be "a wrached state."[3]

The traditional patriarchal view held that children and other family members were absolutely dependent on the head of the household. In the seventeenth century Sir Robert Filmer had declared that "the Father of a family governs by no other law than by his own will," and some of that attitude lingered on. The head of the household remained a kind of miniature king, a governor or protector to whom respect and subjection were due. In the eighteenth century English law in the colonies still distinguished ordinary murder from the murder of masters by servants or husbands by wives by providing for harsher punishments for these petit treasons, similar to those for high treason. Parents were told that they "should carefully subdue the wills of their children and accustom them to obedience and submission."[4]

Nearly all of the traditional child-rearing manuals advocated the physical punishment of children. Heads of household expected their authority to be instantly acknowledged, and they beat their children and other dependents with a readiness and fierceness that today leaves us wincing. Such discipline and punishment could emotionally distance children from their fathers, and children often lived in fear and awe of their fathers. Nothing is more revealing than the note written by the twenty-seven-year-old Robert Bladen Carter to his father, Robert Carter, describing his attempt that morning to wait "on you in your Library with an intention of asking you for some employment." Nothing came of the effort: "It has and ever will be the case I am afraid, when before you," said young Carter; "in my serious reflections, I have observed a stoppage in my throat and intellect vastly confused: what it proceeds from God only knows."[5]

Children sometimes felt this dependence on their parents well into adulthood. One of the most widely read advice manuals in the colonies stressed that "children are so much the goods, the possessions of their Parents, that they cannot without a kind of theft, give away themselves without the allowance of those that have the right in them." William Byrd forbade his daughter "never more to greet, speak, or write" to a suitor he disapproved of, simply on the grounds of "the sacred duty you owe a parent, & upon the blessing you ought to expect upon the performance of it"; more to the point: if she disobeyed, she was "not to look for one brass farthing."[6]

In the face of a growing scarcity of land in older communities, many young men were waiting for their inheritance well into middle age. At mid-century close to half of the sons in Chebacco, Massachusetts, were over forty when they inherited their land. In many northern communities at least half the adult males were without land. Young men were growing up, marrying, and yet remaining dependent on their fathers, even to the extent of continuing to live in their fathers' households. In some towns in New England one-third or more of married couples shared a house with parents. Temporary as this filial dependence might be, many sons felt its burden, knew what it meant. One Rhode Island son experienced it in his father's angry will that left him only a pittance "by reason he has disobeid my comands and left me in a strait of time before he was of full age." Often fathers used the threat of disinheritance to control their children; even John Locke in his educational writings had recognized the use of such a threat when all other methods failed. William Shippen urged his daughter, whose marriage was broken, to allow her child to be brought up by her mother-in-law because, as Shippen warned her, the child's "fortune depends on the old Lady's pleasure."[7]

These paternalistic dependencies involved not only those linked by blood or marriage. Paternal authority reached beyond the household to bind large numbers of Americans in various degrees of legal dependency. Indeed, at any one moment as much as one-half of colonial society was legally unfree.[18]

Most conspicuously unfree, of course, were the half million Afro-Americans reduced to the utterly debased position of lifetime hereditary servitude. Henry Laurens, the South Carolina merchant and planter, had several hundred black slaves on the eve of the Revolution. Like many other large slaveholders, Laurens regarded his slaves as "poor Creatures who look up to their Master as their Father, their Guardian, and Protector, and to whom there is a reciprocal obligation upon the Master." Most black slaves were held in the South, but slavery was not inconsequential in the northern colonies. By the second quarter of the eighteenth century, one out of every five families in Boston owned at least one slave. At mid-century black slaves made up nearly 12 percent of the population of Rhode Island. By 1746 more than a quarter of New York City's working-age males were black slaves; perhaps one-half the households in the city held at least one slave.[19]

It is evident that many Northerners as well as Southerners experienced the master-slave relationship and exercised or witnessed this most severe sort of patriarchal authority at some point in their lives. The consequences were damaging for both masters and slaves: the prevalence of slavery in the South, as Thomas Jefferson pointed out, meant that children, both black and white, enslaved and free, were "nursed, educated, and daily exercised in . . . the most boisterous passions, the most unremitting despotism on the one part, and degrading submission on the other." Slavery etched deeply into people's consciousness what outright dependence could mean.[20]

Legal unfreedom, however, was not confined to blacks. Tens of thousands of whites, usually young men and women, were indentured as servants or apprentices and bound to masters for periods ranging from a few years to decades. As late as 1759 Benjamin Franklin thought that most of the labor of the middle colonies was being performed by indentured servants brought from Britain, Ireland, and Germany. It has been estimated that one-half to two-thirds of all immigrants to the colonies came as indentured servants. Among these immigrants there were an estimated 50,000 British and Irish convicts and vagabonds shipped to America between 1718 and 1775 and bound over as servants for periods of seven or fourteen years, or even in some cases for life. Yet being bound out in service or apprenticeship for a number of years was not always an unrespectable status, and it was by no means confined to the lowest ranks of the society. Many of the mid-eighteenth-century immigrants—redemptioners who redeemed the cost of their passage across the Atlantic by contracting their labor—were skilled craftsmen; even schoolmasters offered to sell themselves, usually with few buyers.[21]

Indentured apprenticeship was different from servitude; it existed at all social levels and still provided the primary means by which young men, even from well-to-do families, learned a skill and entered the world. Parents were often eager to place their adolescent children in another household; such placement, as one father put it, was better for discipline, "submission to a stranger [being] more eligible and easy." Jeremiah Wadsworth, who eventually became one of the leading merchants of the Connecticut Valley and commissary general during the Revolution, got his start at age fourteen by being bound out to the New York mercantile firm of Philip Livingston. In Charleston, Henry Laurens said in 1768, most of the merchant houses were overloaded with "engagements to take the sons, nephews, or relatives of some of their Principal Customers." Yet Laurens found room to take on the son of the royal governor of Georgia.[22]

Apprenticeship among the upper ranks or among urban artisans in the colonies resembled that in England. In both societies formal apprenticeship bound master and apprentice by written contract for a term of years. Although it is true that English masters more often had to be paid to take an apprentice than masters did in America, the practice of apprenticeship was similar. But the practice of servitude was not.[23]

Servitude was common on both sides of the Atlantic; indeed, nothing sets off that distant eighteenth-century world from our own more than the ubiquitous presence of servants. It has been estimated that servants in England made up over 13 percent of the population, and that 60 percent of young people between fifteen and twenty-four were servants. British colonial America was no different, at least in the North. Even middling households often contained one or two servants, and any family of the highest rank was apt to have a half dozen or more, ranging from butler to scullery maid. But servitude in this premodern society was not confined to the domestic or house servants that we are familiar with today. Indeed, most servants in the eighteenth-century pan-British world were engaged in agriculture. In England, however, the status of rural servants was very different from that of rural servants in the colonies.[24]

By colonial standards rural servitude was remarkably mild and loose in England. Although English servants were still members of their masters' households, these households were usually in localities close to their homes, and the servants saw themselves essentially as hired labor. Their contracts with their masters were usually oral and bound them for only a year at a time. Servants moved easily and often from master to master, and many of them received wages and acquired property. This was not the servitude that most colonists either experienced or witnessed.[25]

In the colonies servitude was a much harsher, more brutal, and more humiliating status than it was in England, and this difference had important implications for the colonists' consciousness of dependency. Colonial bonded servants in fact shared some of the chattel nature of black slaves. Although they were members of their master's household and enjoyed some legal rights, they were a kind of property as well, valuable property. Colonial servants were not simply young people drawn from the lowest social ranks but, more commonly, indentured immigrants who had sold their labor in order to get to the New World. Precisely because these imported servants were expensive, their indentures or contracts were written and their terms of service were longer than those of English servants—five to seven years rather than the year-long agreements usual in England.[26]

Because labor was so valuable in America, the colonists enacted numerous laws designed to control the movement of servants and to prevent runaways. There was nothing in England resembling the passes required in all the colonies for traveling servants. And as expensive property, most colonial servants could be bought and sold, rented out, seized for the debts of their masters, and conveyed in wills to heirs. Colonial servants often belonged to their masters in ways that English servants did not. They could not marry, buy or sell property, or leave their households without their master's permission.[27]

No wonder newly arriving Britons were astonished to see how ruthlessly Americans treated their white servants. "Generally speaking," said William Eddis upon his introduction to Maryland society in 1769, "they groan beneath a worse than Egyptian bondage." Eddis even thought that black slaves were better treated. As late as the 1750s immigrant redemptioners, as one observer noted, were being bought in parcels at Philadelphia and driven in tens and twenties "like cattle to a Smithfield market and exposed to sale in public fairs as so many brute beasts." Like black slaves, white servants, too, could be advertised for sale as "choice" and "well-disposed." Young Matthew Lyon, who came to the colonies in 1764 at the age of fifteen, was later sold by his master for a "yoke of bulls" valued at £12. Actually, all colonial servants, even those American-born, were treated harshly. "As is too commonly the case," one such Connecticut servant complained after having been bound out at the age of four by his father, "I was rather considered as a slave than a member of the family, and . . . was treated by my master as his property and not as his fellow mortal." It is not surprising, then, that a colonial father might discipline his errant child by threatening, "I'll bind you out."[28]

The subjugation of colonial servitude was thus much more cruel and conspicuous than it was in England, where the degrees of dependence were more calibrated and more gradual. Consequently, the colonists were much more acutely conscious of legal dependence—and perhaps of the value of independence—than Englishmen across the Atlantic. Under such circumstances it was often difficult for the colonists to perceive the distinctive peculiarity of black slavery. Slavery often seemed to be just another degree of servitude, another degree of labor, more severe and more abject, to be sure, but not in the eyes of most colonists all that different from white servitude and white labor. Both kinds of servants shared the necessity of laboring and the contempt in which manual labor was traditionally held, and both were plainly dependent in a world that valued only independence. Slaves, like servants, were often described simply as another kind of dependent in the patriarchal family. "Next to our children and brethren by blood," said the Reverend Thomas Bacon of Maryland in 1743, "our servants, and especially our slaves, are certainly in the nearest relation to us. They are an immediate and necessary part of our household." As late as 1720 some southern planters still lumped black slaves and white servants together as dependents. William Byrd in his *Secret Diary* mentioned about fifty servants by name, but he rarely differentiated between black and white servants; when he did so, it was only to distinguish between two servants bearing the same name.[29]

By the middle of the eighteenth century black slavery had existed in the colonies for several generations or more without substantial questioning or criticism. The few conscience-stricken Quakers who issued isolated outcries against the institution hardly represented general colonial opinion. Southern planters showed no feelings of guilt or defensiveness over slavery, and even the most liberal of masters coolly and callously recorded in their diaries the savage punishments they inflicted on their slaves—"I tumbled him into the Sellar and there had him tied Neck and heels all night and this morning had him stripped and tied up to a limb." White servants could be ferociously punished too. One drunken and abusive servant being transported by ship to Virginia in the 1770s was horsewhipped, put in irons and thumbscrewed, and then handcuffed and gagged for a night; he remained handcuffed for at least nine days.[30]

By modern standards it was a cruel and brutal age, and the life of the lowly seemed cheap. Slavery could be regarded, therefore, as merely the most base and degraded status in a society of several degrees of unfreedom, and most colonists felt little need as yet either to attack or to defend slavery any more than other forms of dependency and debasement.

In addition to these stark forms of unfreedom, many people in this monarchical society experienced other kinds of inferiority and dependency. Closest to the legally unfree in dependence were those who did not own their own land. Although most colonial farmers, unlike most English tenant farmers, were freeholders, in some areas of America in the middle of the eighteenth century tenantry was rapidly growing. Sometimes it was used as a device by speculators to develop otherwise uncultivated land, but increasingly it was becoming a much more settled and broadly based form of dependence. Not only were the great proprietors like the Baltimore and Penn families reviving, reordering, and exploiting old feudal landlord claims, but many lesser landowners were increasingly relying on rents as the major source of their income. By the 1760s Lord Baltimore had twenty-three tenanted manors encompassing 190,000 acres of Maryland. In New York six to seven thousand tenants were living on about fourteen baronial estates. Some of these manors—Philipsborough, Livingston, and Rensselaerswyck—were returning annual incomes for their landlords equal to those enjoyed by middling gentry in England. By the time of the Revolution the bulk of the income of the great Virginia planter Robert Carter came from the rents of tenants. George Washington had tenants working portions of his lands in four different counties of Virginia. On the eve of the Revolution as many as one-third to one-half of the households of some established Chesapeake counties were tenants. Nor was tenantry confined to the countryside. In a fast-growing town like Lancaster, Pennsylvania, more than a quarter of its heads of families were classified as "tenants."[31]

Although the loose and scattered nature of many of the leaseholds tended to reduce the landlord-tenant relationship to a predominantly monetary one, this was not always so. Tenants often appealed to the landlords' sense of moral responsibility, and aristocratic paternalism sometimes made the landlords remarkably indulgent and lenient. The great New York landlord Frederick Philipse lent money to half his tenants and then was very slow to collect any interest or to call in the debts. Henry Beekman and other New York landlords were remarkably casual and lax in collecting rents from their tenants. Beekman was never sure what was owed him and tended to take his tenants' word as to what they had paid. Some of the tenants of Robert Carter of Virginia were as much as ten years behind in their rent. Nor did tenants believe they owed their landlords only rents in money or produce; the dependent relationship often demanded more than that. During the mid-century disturbances in New York, manor lords were easily able to raise companies of forty to fifty loyal tenants to put down some New England-inspired insurrections in their neighborhoods. Although, as we shall later see, most of these American tenants leased their land or houses under more favorable conditions than did English tenants, they were nonetheless tenants, and thus technically at least still dependents of their landlords.[32]

Many colonists, therefore, not only black slaves but white servants and young men and a variety of tenants and of course all women, knew firsthand what dependence meant. Dependence, said James Wilson in 1774, was "very little else, but an obligation to conform to the will . . . of that superior person . . . upon which the inferior depends." People who were dependent could not be free; in fact, "freedom and dependency" were "opposite and irreconcilable terms." Dependents were all those who had no wills of their own; thus like children they could have no political personalities and could rightfully be excluded from participation in public life. It was this reasoning that underlay the denial of the vote to women, servants, apprentices, short-term tenants, minors, and sons over twenty-one still living at home with their parents.[33]

As common and as manifest as these legal forms of dependency were, however, they were not experienced by large portions of white male society, or if they were, not for full lives. Most farmers were not short-term tenants, and white servitude and apprenticeship were usually temporary statuses, largely confined to the young. But all dependency in this still very traditional and hierarchical society was not so limited and so obvious. These conspicuous examples of legal and contractual dependence did not begin, in fact, to comprehend the thousand and one other, less palpable ways in which paternalism and dependence made themselves felt. This monarchical society had many other, more elusive devices for extracting obedience and deference.

4. Patronage

Many colonists who were quick to scorn all forms of legal or contractual dependence, many who owned their own land and prided themselves on their independence, were nevertheless enmeshed in the diffuse and sometimes delicate webs of paternalistic obligation inherent in a hierarchical society. There was no doubt, wrote British polemicists John Trenchard and Thomas Gordon, that between men there should be "no such Relation as Lord and Slave, lawless Will and blind Submission." But these most radical whigs, with whom the colonists shared many ideas, did not expect equality between men; indeed for Trenchard and Gordon the only proper relationship was still "that of Father and Children, Patron and Client, Protection and Allegiance, Benefaction and Gratitude, mutual Affection and mutual Assistance." The ties that bound people together in this society were still explained and given meaning by terms that looked to the past more than the future, to the personal world of the family as much as the impersonal world of commerce. It was taken for granted that "Dependence and social Obligation take place at the first Dawn of Life, and as its Thread lengthens," they would "continually multiply and invigorate." The world still seemed small and intimate enough that the mutual relationships that began with the family could be extended outward into the society to describe nearly all other relationships as well.[1]

Despite the traditional English celebration of independence and liberty, no one in this hierarchical society could be truly independent, truly free. No relationship could be exclusive or absolute; each was relative, reciprocal, and complementary. "Every service or help which one man affords another, requires its corresponding return." These "returns . . . due from one person to another, according to the several circumstances or relations in which they stand, with respect to each other," were in fact "the bands of society, by which families, neighborhoods, and nations are knit together."[2] Society was held together by intricate networks of personal loyalties, obligations, and quasi-dependencies. These personal loyalties were not the same as the legal bondage of the unfree; they were not like the explicit subjection of the landless; and they were not even precise reproductions of the many subserviencies of patronage-ridden England. Still, these personal relationships were forms of paternalism, dependence, and subordination—vague and subtle as they often may have been.

Some referred openly to these social relationships as "paternalistic"; others called them "connections" or "interests." Yet by the middle of the eighteenth century so repugnant was the idea of dependency among free men in the English-speaking world, and so elusive and presumably mutual were these innumerable personal attachments, that only the term "friendship" seemed universal and affective enough to describe them.[3]

Indeed, every variety of personal attachment and connection, no matter how unequal, could be described as friendship. "Friendship, I take it," said John Adams, "is one of the distinguishing Glorys of man. And the Creature that is insensible of its Charms, tho he may wear the shape of Man, is unworthy of the Character." Kin relations could be "friends"; so too could patrons or customers. Charles Willson Peale advertised the opening of his upholstery and harness shop in 1761 by expressing his "hopes to have the Employ of his friends, who may depend upon being well and faithfully served." The chief justice of South Carolina promised the itinerant Anglican minister Charles Woodmason, as Woodmason put it, "to be my Friend and to take me under his protection." "Friendships" were what a person's age and rank would lead him to form—they were euphemisms for all sorts of dependencies. Sons were the friends of their fathers, wives were the friends of their husbands, and sons and daughters called their mother their "best friend." Even a common soldier might talk about "the Friendship of my officers" or a servant refer to his master as his "principal friend."[4]

The American colonies, even more than the mother country, necessarily had to be organized in these personal terms. In the strung-out colonies there were no institutions, no arenas, in which impersonal relationships might dominate. Of course, in America there was nothing remotely resembling the teeming metropolis of London—at three-quarters of a million the largest city in the Western world. But in America there were not even any cities that could rival the secondary urban areas of Great Britain. By 1760 England had a half dozen cities with populations over 30,000; America had none of that size. By 1760 England had over twenty cities with populations over 10,000; America had three. Indeed, the colonies had only a half dozen or so urban centers larger than 5,000 people, and even its largest—Philadelphia with a population of about 20,000 in 1760—could seem to be little more than an overgrown village.[5] Looking back from the urban sprawl of the early nineteenth century, one Philadelphian believed that in the colonial period he had known "every person, white and black, men, women, and children in the city of Philadelphia by name."[6] Nothing comparable in scale or importance to England's economic growth and industrialization was occurring in America: there were no burgeoning manufacturing centers, no Leeds, no Manchester, no Birmingham; indeed, by contemporary English standards there was in America not much manufacturing at all. In England less than half the labor force was employed in agriculture, whereas nineteen out of twenty colonists still were farmers; and the bulk of them lived in tiny rural communities in which most people knew one another. In comparison with much of England the colonies were still a very primitive and undeveloped society.

In such a small-scale society, privacy as we know it did not exist, and our sharp modern distinction between private and public was as yet scarcely visible. Living quarters were crowded, and people who were not formally related—servants, hired laborers, nurses, and other lodgers—were often jammed together with family members in the same room or even in the same bed. Members of New England communities thought nothing of spying on and interfering with their neighbors' most intimate affairs, in order, as one Massachusetts man put it in 1760, "not to Suffer Sin in My Fellow Creature or Neighbour." People took the injunction to be their brother's keeper very seriously and turned one another in for adultery, wife-beating, or any other violation of community norms.[7]

Since people in this society noticed everything, personal reputations counted a great deal: a man could go a long way just on what others thought of him. Benjamin Franklin, as he tells us in his *Autobiography*, was able "to secure my Credit and Character as a Tradesman" in Philadelphia not only by being "in *Reality* Industrious and frugal" but, more important in such a face-to-face society, by avoiding "all *Appearances* of the Contrary." He dressed plainly and never let people see him idle, and "to show that I was not above my Business I sometimes brought home the Paper I purchas'd at the Stores thro' the Streets on a Wheelbarrow." That these circumscribed worlds resembled theaters attended by everyone was no trivial metaphor in this culture.[8]

John Adams, too, knew what sort of society he was living in. He repeatedly advised his young protégé William Tudor "to mix yourself with the World and through yourself in their sight." He told Tudor a homily about Cicero, who had admirably administered an office in Sicily, but who to his mortification had received no commendation from the Romans; apparently Cicero was so far from their eyes that he was out of their thoughts as well. From then on, said Adams, "it was his Policy to keep himself always in their Sight; nor to be so solicitous how to make them hear of him, as to make them see him." Adams advised Tudor even to change his church in Boston, so "you will be seen by more People, and those of more Weight and Consequence."[9]

In these little worlds one's good name seemed as precious as life itself, and whenever it was defamed, people were quick to seek legal redress. The court records are thus full of actions for slander and defamation. To call someone "a Devillish Lyar," to accuse a minister of being "as drunk as the Devil last night," to say of a boat manufacturer that he made boats "only fit to drown people"—all these offenses were open to either criminal or civil prosecution. We today may be astonished by the "triviality" of these defamation cases, but slander was anything but a frivolous matter for the people of that very different society.[10]

People were expected to know those with whom they were dealing—which was why letters of introduction were so common and so essential. People were immediately conscious of strangers and unattached persons and subjected them either to intense questioning or to openmouthed staring. Runaway servants, as one British visitor noted, could not hope to lose themselves in such small-scale societies, so detailed were the descriptions of the runaways in the newspapers and so vigilant were the communities "in detecting persons under suspicious circumstances." For a newspaper to describe an escaped shipwright wearing "a great Coat of an ordinary dark brown Ratteen, with the Cuff of the right sleeve off, a green Grogram Vest, patch'd under one Arm, and bound down the Buttonholes with green Bays, with two rows of buttonholes, black Mohair Buttons and no lining, a new ozenbrigs Shirt, red Plush Breeches, the Breeches good but the Plush ordinary, a new silk handkerchief, an old Beaver hat, light grey yarn stockings, new shoes"—to set forth a description in this extraordinary detail was to presume a society in which all strangers were closely scrutinized.[11]

In this face-to-face society, particular individuals—specific gentlemen or great men—loomed large, and people naturally explained human events as caused by the motives and wills of those who seemed to be in charge, headed the chains of interest, and made decisions. No one as yet could conceive of the massive and impersonal social processes—industrialization, urbanization, modernization—that we invoke so blithely to describe large-scale social developments. Such complicated processes were simply not part of people's consciousness.

In this culture the question asked of events was not "how did they happen?'' but "who did them?" Specific identifiable individuals did things and were personally accountable for what happened. If the price of bread rose suddenly, then a particular baker or merchant could be blamed. If a merchant's cargo was seized for violating the navigation acts, then a particular and well-known official could be singled out. The political and social world still seemed small and intimate enough to hold particular men morally responsible for all that occurred within it. Which is why the colonists especially were quick to explain a concatenation of events as caused by a conspiracy.[12]

The provincial governments were lilliputian by modern standards. They were not impersonal bureaucracies, but particular familiar persons whose numbers could usually be counted on one's hands. Prominent colonists knew personally the governors, justices, customs collectors, naval officers, and other leading magistrates with whom they dealt. They drank and dined with them, played cards or the violin with them, and sometimes went to church with them. Even the provincial assemblies were minuscule. New Hampshire's assembly had thirty-five members; New York's, twenty-eight; New Jersey's, twenty; Maryland's, sixty. Massachusetts's house of representatives was extraordinarily large at 117. The combined membership of the New York colonial assembly and council was even smaller than a committee in today's House of Representatives. Gentlemen in such tiny political worlds were necessarily familiar with one another. The vitriolic burlesques of public officials, like the satiric closet dramas of Mercy Otis Warren, derived much of their force from the intimate knowledge the audience or readers had of the persons being ridiculed or satirized. Without such familiarity and inside knowledge, much of the fun of the pieces—the disguised characterizations, obscure references, private jokes, and numerous innuendos—would have been lost.[13]

Government authority in the colonies was intimate, and none of its activities was too insignificant to be dealt with by a leading official. A royal governor might respond personally to the public grievance of an obscure shipmaster and call him to his home to work out a solution. When William Eddis arrived in Maryland in 1769, he was astonished to discover that the meanest person in the colony seemed to have "an easy and immediate access to the person" of the governor. It has been said that the speaker of the South Carolina house was not exaggerating when he declared that he was "well acquainted with the circumstances of most of our Inhabitants," so small was the society. In 1756 Governor Robert Morris of Pennsylvania took to roaming the waterfront of Philadelphia at night in search of smugglers, even using his bare hands to force his way into warehouses suspected of being storage places for contraband. Local government could be even more personal and familiar. In 1763 the town council of Bristol, Rhode Island, lent Joseph Maxfield the money to buy a cord of wood, which, the council declared, he was to pay back "when he gets his money from Mr. Bosworth."[14]

Just as colonial public buildings were no more than elaborate private residences, so too was much public business only an extension into government of private social relationships. Consequently, private feelings often blended imperceptibly into public ones. James Otis's attack on Lieutenant Governor Thomas Hutchinson of Massachusetts in the early 1760s so intermingled personal and political motives that no one was (or has been since) able to separate them. Not only was Otis angry at Hutchinson for taking the chief-justiceship that Otis thought had been promised his father, but he bitterly resented the social superiority he felt Hutchinson and his clan pretended to. Otis's fury ran deep, and following a private confrontation it exploded in 1761–62 in a series of blisteringly sarcastic public denunciations of Hutchinson that left the lieutenant governor bewildered. There Otis was, he wrote of his confrontation with Hutchinson in the Boston *Gazette*, "entering the Lists with a Gentleman so much one's Superior"; it was, he said, like some insignificant army subaltern dueling with a general. "His Honour" was "very condescending" to debate such an inferior as Otis. Was not Hutchinson risking a loss of his reputation by stooping so low? But then again, said Otis, "from those who have, and desire but little, but little can possibly be taken away." Otis had reputedly sworn "revenge" against Hutchinson for his father's loss of the office, and he searched for a public issue that might embarrass the lieutenant governor. First he tried the money standard, and when that proved too complicated to arouse the public, he turned to the more inflammatory issue of plural officeholding. To be sure, there was political significance in all this maneuvering, but no one could be certain where that began and Otis's private animosity left off.[15]

Henry Laurens of Charleston, South Carolina, was another who had trouble separating his private emotions from his political attitudes in this small intimate society. In 1765 Laurens was no patriot. No one more vigorously denounced the Stamp Act riots than he. But by the late 1760s he had become much more radical, largely as the result of a series of personal confrontations, first with Daniel Moore, customs collector of Charleston, and later with Egerton Leigh, judge of the vice-admiralty court and Laurens's friend and kinsman. When Moore tried to use his position to create dependents among the Charleston merchants and in particular sought to exploit his initial "intimacy" with Laurens for "mean" purposes, Laurens became angry: Moore's behavior, he said, "made me sit loose & speak my mind plainly to him." One thing led to another, and Laurens became the "object" of the collector's "resentment." Following Moore's arbitrary seizure of several of Laurens's ships, Laurens confronted Moore in public and wrung his nose. This resulted in a challenge to a duel that was never fought. When Leigh, in the vice-admiralty court, tried in the meantime to mediate between the two men, he only managed to embroil himself in a heated quarrel with Laurens. Laurens and Leigh then attacked each other viciously in the press, and this resulted in another aborted challenge to a duel. The whole affair ended with Leigh's colonial career in ruins. Laurens naturally and defensively denied that his new stand on behalf of American rights was the consequence of these private quarrels; but there is no doubt that his dislike of Moore and his anger with Leigh did more to make him a patriot by the late 1760s than all the whig pamphlets he might have read. Obnoxious officials like Moore and Leigh, Laurens said in 1767, were "the most likely instruments to effect a disunion between the Mother Country & her American offspring." They are "the Men who shake the affections of the Americans & drive them to a greater distance from the powers in the Mother Country."[16]

And so it was everywhere in this small face-to-face society: personal and official affairs could scarcely be separated. Merchants used public money for private purposes, and vice versa. Soldiers sued their captains for their back pay. Magistrates lived off the fees and fines they levied. And governors sometimes drew on their personal accounts to raise money to supply troops. That the North Carolina governor even offered in 1765 to pay that portion of the stamp tax pertaining to official documents out of his own pocket tells us just how lost to us that eighteenth-century world really is.[17]

Personal relationships of dependence, usually taking the form of those between patrons and clients, constituted the ligaments that held this society together and made it work. The popular "deference" that historians have made so much of was not a mere habit of mind; it had real economic and social force behind it. Artisans in America, like their counterparts in Britain, still had patrons more than they had customers. Tradesmen and shopkeepers were told that "the Seller is Servant to the Buyer." At the end of the Seven Years' War wealthy Maryland planters flocked to Annapolis and began building town houses and consuming luxuries at unprecedented rates. By the early 1770s all the hundreds of newly arrived craftsmen and shopkeepers in the town had become dependent on the spending habits of the rich. Elsewhere it was the same. Although a few artisans in some places were already running large manufacturing establishments and turning out goods for distant markets, most colonial craftsmen still made wigs or boots or built homes or ships on demand for familiar gentlemen ("bespoke work") and felt obliged to them. And that sense of obligation and dependency could have emotional and economic satisfactions that often more than compensated for any loss of freedom and independence, as Philadelphia carpenter William Falk discovered. In the 1750s Falk decided to cut loose from his paternalistic relationship with the wealthy merchant Isaac Norris in order to try selling his labor by the day to the highest bidder. But the experience of too many days without work soon drove him back to the security of Norris's patronage.[18]

Everywhere, it seemed to John Adams, "all the rich men have many of the poor, in the various trades, manufacturing and other occupations in life, dependent upon them for their daily bread; many of smaller fortunes will be in their debt, and in many ways under obligations to them." Such relationships between patrons and clients were pervasive, and men could be both at the same time. John Goodrich was a prosperous and influential Virginia merchant who owned and operated a dozen vessels and a large number of warehouses and stores in Portsmouth. Although his business gave Goodrich many clients of his own, he was himself dependent on the patronage of the great planter Robert Carter, a patronage that could be quickly withdrawn. When the merchant failed to perform satisfactorily, Carter ordered his agent in the port "not in the future to employ any of Capt. Goodrich's Craft to do service for me." In just such ways was influence exerted.[19]

Much of the economy was organized into webs of private relationships. Indeed, the economy in this premodern world was still often thought of in traditional terms as the management of a household. Economy was defined as the art of providing for all the wants of the family, or in the case of the royal household of the king, the nation, which was his extended family. In such an antique conception the distribution of persons and goods in accordance with the organic social hierarchy—everything in its proper and needed place—became the key to proper political management. Although in England modern commercial developments were fast eroding such medieval and mercantilist notions—viewing the economy as an enlarged household administered by patriarchal authorities from the top down—they still lingered on in people's minds, especially in the colonies, which were commercially backward compared with the mother country.[20]

The financial and commercial revolutions that were transforming English society were slow to take hold in America. Before 1750 the colonies still had undeveloped economies engaged essentially in small-scale farming or in producing provisions and agricultural staples for the greater Atlantic world. The colonies had no Bank of England, no stock exchange, no large trading companies, no great centers of capital, and no readily available circulating medium of exchange. Although by 1750 most of the colonies had experimented with several forms of paper currency, there was little in America resembling the complicated array of monetary notes of England or the dozens upon dozens of private and country banks that had sprung up all over Great Britain in the decades after 1690 to facilitate inland trade. By 1774 there were fifty-two private banks in London alone.[21]

To this extent the colonies were not yet commercial societies like Britain, where the importance of inland or internal trade matched that of overseas or external trade. Instead, the colonies were what were called trading societies, dominated by their external commerce. This emphasis on overseas trade confirmed the traditional mercantilist assumption which held that each colony could increase its aggregate wealth only by selling more beyond its borders than it bought. The economic goal of a colony therefore was to have more exports than imports—that is, a favorable balance of trade, which would result in gold and silver specie (the only real money most people recognized) remaining within the colony. But since the colonists tended to import far more than they exported, they always had an acute shortage of gold and silver specie; sometimes farmers had to pay even their taxes in bits and pieces of produce.

In the absence of other forms of currency, this shortage of specie limited the colonists' ability to make exchanges with one another within their borders; it limited, that is, what was commonly called their "inland trade." Before mid-century the colonists' inland trade remained remarkably primitive, especially by English standards. But it was not only primitive, it was unappreciated as well. The colonists believed that their internal trade—say, between Lancaster and Philadelphia—had no real value unless goods were further shipped outside of the colony. Inland trade by itself could never increase a colony's aggregate wealth; it could only redistribute it, move it about. The "meer *handling of Goods one to another,* no more increases any wealth in the Province, than Persons *at a Fire,* increase the *Water in a Pail,* by passing it thro' Twenty or Forty hands.'' Such passing of wealth around the community from hand to hand, said William Smith of New York in 1750, ''tho it may enrich an Individual,'' meant that ''others must be poorer, in an exact proportion to his Gains; but the Collective Body of the People not at all.'' With such zero-sum mercantilist assumptions domestic trade was not much valued, and internal traders and retail shopkeepers did not have much respectability. They certainly did not yet have the status, or the right to claim the title, of ''merchants,'' those who by exporting and importing goods from abroad brought real wealth into the society.[22]

To carry on what internal trade they desired the colonists experimented with several crude forms of paper currency—land-bank certificates and government bills of credit. The certificates of land banks, which by 1750 were in use in every colony but Virginia, were loans to individual colonists, often only middling farmers, at 5 percent interest and repayable over a long period of time. These circulating certificates were secured by mortgages on land, but the bills of credit, issued mainly during wartime by desperate colonial governments that were spending far more than they were receiving in taxes, were backed by nothing more than the governments' promises to accept them as taxes at some future date.

By the middle of the eighteenth century England's century-long experience with its highly developed inland trade had made Englishmen at home familiar with a variety of sophisticated paper notes and checks. But not the colonists; before 1750 many of them regarded paper money as only a wartime expedient, as peculiar and special, and not as something essential to their economies. Since many colonists did not yet believe that their inland trade was very important, they did not believe that paper money (which made such inland trade possible) was very important. And because the paper currency the colonists issued usually could be exchanged at the rate of 133 to 100 pounds sterling (but sometimes through overprinting of the paper the rate could skyrocket to 160 or 180 to 100 pounds sterling), established merchants who imported from abroad and had to pay their bills in sterling were generally anxious to limit the amounts of paper currency in circulation. Since paper money was therefore not readily available, colonists who needed money for their businesses usually had to rely on loans from local moneyed men, thus increasing their sense of personal clientage and dependency.

Thus colonial economic life remained remarkably simple and personal, and few colonists other than overseas merchants knew anything of the large impersonal institutions and public worlds that were transforming the consciousness of Englishmen at home. This backwardness, this primitiveness, of colonial society put a premium on patronage and individual relationships and to this extent at least riddled colonial society with more personal monarchical-like dependencies than England itself had.

Without banks, without many impersonal sources of credit, without even in some cases a circulating medium, most economic exchanges in the colonies had to be personal, between people who knew one another. Economic relations in this society could never be strictly pecuniary; people rarely dealt directly in "ready pay" or cash—in a paid-and-be-done-with-it manner. Although a cash nexus was emerging here and there, most economic exchanges were by credit and were still clothed in moral and social terms. "Trade ought to be managed with truth, justice and charity: for without these," it was said, "it is only a more cleanly art of cheating or oppression." A businessman had to act morally even if it meant "the diminution of his trade." Merchants, shopkeepers, and craftsmen all tended to regard their businesses as a series of personal transactions with familiar persons. Their records exhibit these personal relationships—a single page of their ledgers for each person they dealt with. Often they treated their economic activities simply as extensions of their personal life: they mingled their domestic and business accounts to the point where they had little or no awareness at any one moment of the profitability of their enterprises.[23]

Many northern farmers—how many is a matter of controversy—were not as yet deeply involved in the larger market economy of the Atlantic world. Many, as the common appellation "husbandman" suggests, did not yet think of themselves as agricultural entrepreneurs out to maximize profits. They were acquisitive, to be sure, and few were truly self-sufficient; and thus they produced "surpluses" when they could and swapped goods and services with each other and with local shopkeepers and merchants. Some of the exchanges were simple and direct barters: a farmer might lend his oxen to a neighbor in return for help in harvesting his crop. A midwife might trade her services for wool or tobacco.[24]

But more often the exchanges took the form of credits and debits and were recorded in monetary terms. A farmer hired out his children or rented his boat to a neighbor for a fee of, say, 2s. 6d.; at the same time he used another neighbor's mill or bought a pair of shoes at the local store at a cost of, say, 3*s.* 4*d.* In the absence of much specie, these fees and costs were usually not paid in cash but were instead entered in each person's account book. Through these numerous exchanges farmers built up in their localities incredibly complicated webs of credits and debts, "book accounts" among neighbors that ran for years at a time.[25]

Although litigation could and did result from these obligations, such credits and debts more often worked to tie local people together and to define and stabilize communal relationships. Because such debts were individually small, were locally owed, and often lacked any explicitly stated promise to pay, they implied a measure of mutual trust between people. Such debts could even be regarded as social bonds linking people together.[26]

For the very wealthy, moneylending became a common and stable source of income and influence—more stable in America certainly than that resulting from land speculation or tenantry. Indeed, money lent out on interest was a principal means by which many colonial gentlemen maintained their superiority and their leisure. As a source of income for those whom George Washington called "the monied Gentry," it was akin to rent from tenants.[27] It was, in fact, just a form of what one historian, in reference to the eighteenth-century French aristocracy, has called "proprietary wealth"—meaning rents, bonds, and interest from loans.[28] Such proprietary wealth was generally static and stable and was based on noncapitalist forms of property. It produced income that came without work or without participation in trade and was thus genteel and free from the taint of self-interested profiteering. This proprietary wealth was what the English on both sides of the Atlantic meant when they talked about property as the source of that "independence" sought by all would-be ladies and gentlemen. So many hundreds of pounds a year from one's estate was the only kind of property someone like Jane Austen really thought about or valued. Independence, as Josiah Quincy pointed out in 1768, really meant independence from "the fickleness and inconstancy" of the marketplace.[29]

For gentry like Quincy, modern commercial venture capital was scarcely property at all: it could never be a source of independence, and there was too much risk and exertion involved in earning it. Such capital was not aristocratic property, certainly not the kind of proprietary wealth that sustained the English gentry. The dominant aristocratic position of the landed gentry, said Adam Smith, came from their unique source of "revenue." Their income from the rents of tenants on their landed estates "costs them neither labour nor care, but comes to them, as it were, of its own accord, and independent of any plan or project of their own." But in America, as John Witherspoon pointed out, such tenantry and rent-producing land could never be as secure a source of income as in England. In the New World, said Witherspoon, where land was more plentiful and cheaper than it was in the Old World, gentlemen seeking a steady income "would prefer lending money at interest to purchasing and holding real estate."[30]

The little evidence we have suggests that Witherspoon was correct. The probate records of wealthy colonists show large proportions of their estates out on loan. All sorts of persons lent money, said John Adams: merchants, professionals, widows, but especially "Men of fortune, who live upon their income." In 1776 Cadwallader Colden was the creditor of seventy-three different people. Even many of the great planters of the South earned more from such presumably ancillary activities as lending money than they did from selling their staple crops. Charles Carroll of Annapolis had £24,000 on loan to his neighbors. A large landowner in the Shenandoah Valley, James Patton, had 90 percent of his total estate in the form of bonds, bills, and promissory notes due him. When merchants and wealthy artisans wanted to establish their status unequivocally as leisured gentlemen, they withdrew from their businesses and, apart from investing in land, lent out their wealth at interest. Benjamin Franklin did it; so did Roger Sherman, John Hancock, and Henry Laurens. As soon as the trader Josiah Dwight of Springfield, Massachusetts, had any profits, he began removing them from his business and lending them out at interest. By the time of his death more than 60 percent of his assets were out on loan. This was how men became gentlemen and exerted influence in their communities. In fact, it was often through loans to friends and neighbors that great men were able to build up networks of clients and dependents. The Virginia planters, who were debtors to British investors abroad but creditors within their own communities, knew only too well that "every debtor does in some measure feel the imperiousness of his creditor."[31]

In the absence of banks and other impersonal institutions, such personal credit was usually the only source of capital for local communities, and gentry creditors could rightly regard their patrimonial property as indispensable to the trade and prosperity of the society. Although other, more dynamic and more volatile kinds of property were already emerging, often in the hands of those protocapitalist debtor developers who were demanding paper money, the gentry creditors could scarcely conceive of any property other than their established proprietary wealth, and considered those who wanted inflationary paper money to be "generally of low condition among the plebeians and of small estate, and many of them perhaps insolvent." They "consisted," wrote Thomas Hutchinson, one of the most established of the established gentry of Massachusetts, "of persons in difficult or involved circumstances in trade, or such as was possessed of real estates, but had little or no ready money at command, or men of no substance at all."[32]

If we take this language literally, as many historians have, we will be hopelessly confused, for many of the debtors and paper-money advocates were not poor uncommercial people but in fact prosperous farmers and substantial entrepreneurs and artisans who were eager to advance their wealth at the expense of those proprietary gentry standing in their way; they were poor or without substance only to the extent that their wealth was not as stable or as patrimonial as the wealth of those that opposed them. Unable to appreciate the growing entrepreneurial need for more money, or unwilling to share their dominance with newcomers, the established gentry considered attacks on their patrimonial wealth by debtors promoting paper money and other forms of debt relief to be dishonest and unjust public evils that threatened not merely their personal well-being but the bonds that held the traditional society together. Since their credit was often liberally extended and sometimes only slowly paid back, such patrimonial gentry saw themselves not as profiteers but as social benefactors fulfilling their paternalist obligations to the community. Of course, lending money in this liberal manner reinforced their political dominance. Although powerful creditor families like the Stoddards, Williamses, and Worthingtons of western Massachusetts took seriously their prescribed charitable responsibilities toward their debtors, they also expected gratitude and respect in return.[33]

Even the most impersonal and modern of marketing arrangements in colonial America—that involving the production and sale of southern staples—remained deeply grounded in personal and patronage connections. The southern economy was geared to the production of staple crops for distant markets, but well into the eighteenth century only the largest planters had direct access to the great merchant houses of Britain. Small and middling farmers of the Chesapeake, with their plantations of one or two hundred acres, lived in a world of dependency that was as much social as it was economic. The primary market for their tobacco was through the great planters.[34] Only these great planters—perhaps only one in fifty or more of all families—experienced firsthand the impersonalities of the larger Atlantic economy through the consignment system of tobacco marketing. They were in fact middlemen in the economy and the society of the Chesapeake. They collected together the small tobacco crops of their neighbors for consignment abroad and sold in their country stores goods imported from England or manufactured on their own plantations. They bought and sold land, extended credit, and resolved disputes among their numerous dependents and clients. They were land speculators, merchants, storekeepers, and bankers as well as farmers. In fact, most of the large fortunes these great planters amassed resulted from activities other than growing tobacco. And the patronage that came from such activities was what distinguished them from the mass of ordinary farmers in the Chesapeake.[35]

No wonder, then, that the great planters of Virginia and Maryland could speak so readily of mobilizing their "interest" among their neighboring freeholders. Their sense of paternalism—being addressed as "your honor" by friends and clients—had substance behind it. There was more truth in the maxim set forth in Robert Munford's play *The Candidates* than perhaps Munford intended:

> 'Tis said self-interest is the secret aim,
> Of those uniting under Friendship's name.

The great planters were the protectors, creditors, and counselors—"friends"—of the lesser farmers. They lent them money, found jobs or minor posts for their sons, stood as godfathers for their children, handed down clothing to their families, doctored them, and generally felt responsible for the welfare of "our neighbors who depended upon us." During a particularly bad "ague and fever Season" in 1771, "the whole neighbourhood," Landon Carter proudly noted in his diary, "are almost every day sending to me. I serve them all." They boasted of their paternalism, declaring, as the wealthy Charles Carroll of Annapolis did in 1759, "how commendable it is for a gentleman of independent means . . . to be able to advise his friends, relations, and neighbors of all sorts." These great Chesapeake planters had the wealth and, more important, the influence to make themselves the strongest aristocracy America has ever had.[36]

Perhaps no activity in colonial society revealed its paternalistic nature more than the way people governed their localities and handled their disputes. Much of the local administration and law enforcement for communities in both the northern and southern colonies rested with the local justice of the peace and the county courts. These courts were remarkably autonomous local bodies, composed of neighborhood gentry whose amateur knowledge of the law was more than offset by the social respect they commanded in the local community. That local social superiority, and not any professional legal expertise, was what gave the justices the extraordinary discretionary authority they exercised. Law at times seemed to be pretty much what they said it was. For their judgments they scarcely worried about English practices or collections of ancient cases; they instead relied on their collective memory and on their own untrained but ritualized sense of justice. Sometimes they even reinterpreted provincial statutes to fit their local needs.

The county courts were the places where the local communities reaffirmed their hierarchical relationships and reconciled their various obligations. The courts acted as clearinghouses for the many credits and debts crisscrossing though the local community. Since the justices were always more interested in people's relationships than in the letter of the law, they made great efforts to resolve disputes over debts informally or out of court. With all social relationships dependent on mutual trust, it is not surprising that the courts treated instances of cheating and deception far more severely than they did overt acts of violence. The courts tended to treat all culprits as fathers might treat wayward children: they lectured and reprimanded those brought before them and disciplined them in a highly discretionary and patriarchal manner. A person who offended the court by forgetting to take his hat off, "by readily acknowledging his fault & begging pardon for the same" might satisfy the magistrate's paternal sense of justice. Occasionally offenders even acted the part of children. In this familial world it was not startling for a man presented for profanity to send word to the justice that he "confessed himself to be guilty and was ashamed to appear before the Court, but would Willingly Submit to the Courts Judgment."[37]

Only a society that intuitively conceived of individuals as enmeshed in social relationships—bound tightly to the community in a variety of personal ways—could make sense of such public confessions and of the traditional public punishments still common in the eighteenth century. Subjecting criminals to public censure at the pillory or whipping and mutilating their bodies in front of neighbors and friends was designed both to involve the community in the punishment and to make the criminals feel shame for their actions. Men and women in eighteenth-century Boston were taken from the huge cage that had brought them from the prison, tied barebacked to a post on State Street, and lashed thirty or forty times "amid the screams of the culprits and the uproar of the mob." In New York, criminals with labels on their breasts were brought to the whipping post on a wooden horse set upon a "triumphal car." Everywhere criminals had their heads and hands pilloried and were exposed for hours on end to insults and pelting by onlookers. The stocks were even moved about, often to the particular neighborhood of the criminals so they could feel their mortification more keenly. Executions were likewise conducted in public (New York's gallows stood on the Common), and they drew thousands of spectators. In every punishment the authorities were determined to expose the offender to public scorn, and with the lowliest of criminals to do so permanently through mutilation. Persons with a brand on their forehead or a piece of ear missing were forever condemned to the contempt of the intimate worlds in which they lived.[38]

A society organized like this accentuated the difference between the few and the many, gentlefolk and commoners, and gave meaning to the age-old distinction between rulers and ruled. "In all Societies whatsoever," it was said, "there are, and must be, people that lead, and people that are led." Everywhere men of wealth and property, those with easier access to markets and political and legal influence, played crucial mediating roles as patrons for numerous clients and dependents. Someone like William Allen of Pennsylvania cultivated both those above and those below him on his chain of interest. He sent gifts of wine to Colonel Barré and Lord Shelburne and pine bud tea to William Pitt, and he married one of his daughters to the governor of Pennsylvania and another to the son of the governor of New York. At the same time he consolidated his interest among those beneath him by the selective use of his power and patronage. In 1764, for example, he secured positions as justices of the peace for some fellow Presbyterians, got the price of land on the frontier lowered, and reduced corruption in the land office. Even in his absence his friends and clients—his "interest"—rewarded him with election to the assembly from Cumberland County. His control of governmental patronage in the colony was awesome. When a young governor ignored Allen's recommendation for an office, Allen quickly got the proprietor, Thomas Penn, to set the governor straight and to instruct him "to advise with Mr. Allen upon every occasion." As a reward for Samuel Purviance having spent £300 in creating a network of Presbyterian committees to support Allen, Allen asked the proprietor to give Purviance "5 or 6,000 acres of land." Not surprisingly, such influence enabled the Allen family and its connections to dominate much of the executive activity in Pennsylvania on the eve of the Revolution.[39]

Paternalism, patronage, and friendship of one sort or another necessarily determined much of what went on in this society. Like the elder
James Otis of Barnstable, Massachusetts, dominant individuals at both
the local and provincial levels were repeatedly asked by supplicants to
"use your Interest" in their behalf, and when they did so, they created
"obligations" among those they helped. The provincial armies of the
eighteenth-century colonies were still little more than quasi-feudal bands
of patrons and clients. The system of recruitment for the Massachusetts
forces in the Seven Years' War of the 1750s depended largely on the
personal loyalties that local men had for the officers who enlisted them.
Governor William Shirley, commander in chief of the provincial forces,
expected ascending ranks of officers, who were appointed in accord with
their corresponding social influence, to be able to recruit increasing
numbers of men: each ensign, fifteen; each lieutenant, twenty-five; each
captain, fifty. Of course, this system of personal influence also worked
in reverse: gentlemen who could raise a company might be entitled by
that very demonstration of patronage to a captaincy.[40]

In the absence of the elaborate and impersonal selection procedures
and institutions that we today take for granted, personal influence had
to be the principal source of recruitment and mobility in all areas. To
get ahead in the law, young John Adams told a friend in 1756, one
needed not only knowledge, time, and a large collection of books, but
most important, "the Friendship and Patronage of the great Masters in
the Profession." George Washington got his start as a surveyor and
militia officer through the influence of Lord Fairfax and his family in
the Northern Neck of Virginia. The elder James Otis's rapid four-year
rise in Massachusetts politics was due mainly to the sponsorship of personal and kinship connections. Even someone like Jasper Yeates of Philadelphia, with a distinguished grandfather and a college degree,
ultimately came to depend "intirely" on his marriage into the great
Shippen family "for his promotion."[41]

This system of personal influence did not necessarily scorn merit or
discourage social mobility. It did require, however, that a talented person attract the attention of some patron in a position to help him. When
that happened, a person's rise from obscurity could be spectacular, as
the case of Benjamin Waller of Virginia suggests. One evening in 1720,
John Carter, the provincial secretary and "a man of immense wealth,"
was accidentally detained by a swollen river at the home of a "plain
planter," John Waller. Carter's eye caught the "quickness" and the
"uncommon parts" of Waller's ten-year-old son, Benjamin, and he

talked the father into allowing him to take the boy and make something of him. Carter virtually adopted young Waller as part of his family, sent him to the College of William and Mary, appointed him his secretary, and trained him in the law. Carter's "liberality" as a patron eventually made Waller at age twenty-five clerk of the General Court, which in turn led to the "friendship" of Governor William Gooch. Before Waller's career was over he had become a member of the House of Burgesses, holder of several crown offices, and a great man in his own right.[42]

Influential patrons everywhere were on the lookout to sponsor the mobility of young talent. Benjamin Robinson, clerk of Caroline County, Virginia, rescued fourteen-year-old Edmund Pendleton from poverty and set him on his way to becoming one of Virginia's distinguished leaders. So, too, was the penniless immigrant indentured servant Daniel Dulany, Sr., patronized by a wealthy Marylander. In a like way friends recognized the precocity of the teenaged Alexander Hamilton and plucked him from the "grov'ling" condition of a merchant's clerk in St. Croix "to which," as Hamilton lamented, "my Fortune, etc., condemns me." Wealthy apothecary Dr. Daniel Lathrop of Norwich, Connecticut, saw great promise in his young apprentice, Benedict Arnold, whose alcoholic father died just as he came of age and his apprenticeship ended. Lathrop's patronage was generous: he not only gave the twenty-one-year-old orphan the enormous sum of £500 but also deeded him the Arnold family home, whose £300 mortgage he had held, and wrote letters of introduction for him.[43]

Rescuing genius in this way was thought to redound to the credit of sponsors and patrons. Different groups of colonial gentlemen in Pennsylvania and Maryland organized subscriptions to send two struggling young painters, Benjamin West and Charles Willson Peale, to Europe to study art. That was what real aristocrats presumably did. Of course, some talented individuals of humble origins in this greater British world did make it on their own. John Paul Jones, son of a Scottish gardener, was apprenticed to sea at thirteen; through drive and luck he became at age twenty-one a master of a merchant vessel in the West Indies trade. But for most men seeking to move up through this personally organized hierarchy, ambition and ability were usually not enough. They also needed the patronage or "friendship" of someone who had power and influence—whether it was a governor awarding a printing contract, a merchant taking on an apprentice, or a minister helping a communicant's son get to Yale.

We are too apt to think of social mobility in eighteenth-century America in terms of the career of Benjamin Franklin, printer. But Franklin's career was extraordinary, to say the least; and in his lifetime in America he was rarely celebrated as the common man who had made good. In fact, at every crucial point in Franklin's meteoric rise it was not simply his hard work, brilliance, and character that moved him upward; most important was his ability to attract the attention of an influential patron. As a bright teenager who could read and write, Franklin immediately caught the eyes of two colonial governors. Governor William Keith of Pennsylvania, "surpris'd" that a seventeen-year-old boy could have written a letter he saw, concluded that Franklin "appear'd a young Man of promising Parts, and therefore should be encouraged." A year later Governor William Burnet of New York, told that a ship passenger "had a great many Books," and that being sufficiently rare, had young Franklin brought to his home, where the two "had a good deal of Conversation about Books and Authors." For "a poor Boy" like Franklin all this gubernatorial attention was "very pleasing" indeed. But it was just the beginning of decades of encouragement and sponsorship that Franklin received from "leading Men" such as James Logan, William Allen, and Andrew Hamilton. Hamilton especially, said Franklin, "interested himself for me strongly . . . continuing his Patronage till his death."[44]

Franklin understood better than most the kind of dependent society in which he lived. He learned early the pose of "the humble Enquirer," and constantly preached the virtues of calculation and civility.

> Wouldst thou extract the purest Sweet of Life,
> Be nor Ally nor Principal in Strife. . . .
> On *Hate* let *Kindness* her warm Embers throw
> And mould into a Friend the melting Foe.

Such caressing and cultivating of feelings was good not only for society but for oneself; for

> The weakest Foe boasts some revenging Pow'r;
> The weakest Friend some serviceable Hour.[45]

Franklin spent much of his long lifetime seeking patronage and place within English society and politics—not surprisingly, since, in 1749 at least, he believed that social mobility was actually easier in England than in the colonies ("Something seems wanting in America to incite and stimulate Youth to Study").⁴⁶ He became deputy postmaster general of North America in 1753, and by the 1760s he was angling for something bigger in the imperial hierarchy. But ultimately he was to find, as his old enemy Thomas Penn had predicted, that the topmost sphere of English politics remained closed to him. However brightly his scientific achievements may have shone in the eyes of British and European philosophes, they counted for very little in the eyes of the "great People" at the center of British imperial power. Thus, as Franklin told David Hume in 1762, he was perhaps better off carrying his talent away from this English land of plenty back to "where from its Scarcity it may probably come to a better Market." Yet it was not until the late 1760s, when all his hopes for English preferment seemed squashed, that Franklin began to think of himself as an American. The first part of his *Autobiography* was written at the moment in 1771 when his grandiose English political and social ambitions seemed most lost, and it became a kind of justification of his failure, a salve for his disillusionment, and ultimately to readers of the nineteenth century—who actually established Franklin's modern reputation as Poor Richard, the self-made man—a vindication of the American Revolution and the changes it had made in the old patronage society.⁴⁷

5. Political Authority

Patronage was most evident in politics, and there its use was instinctive. When Benjamin Franklin was made deputy postmaster general of North America in 1753, he wasted no time in appointing all his friends and relatives to positions under his control. His son became postmaster in Philadelphia. One brother was made postmaster in Boston; when the brother died, Franklin gave the office to his brother's stepson. He made his nephew postmaster in New Haven, appointed the son of a friend postmaster in Charleston, and made another friend in New York controller. A year or so later he promoted his son to be controller and moved the husband of his wife's niece into the vacated Philadelphia position. When this office again became open, he brought another brother down from Newport to fill it.¹

Such patronage politics was simply an extension into governmental affairs of the pervasive personal and kin influence that held the colonial social hierarchies together. The appointing to governmental offices, the awarding of military commissions or judgeships, the granting of land or contracts for provisions—all these were only the visible political expressions of the underlying system of personal obligations and reciprocity that ran through the whole society.[2] The key to Sir Lewis Namier's great success as a historian in illuminating the nature of eighteenth-century English politics was his perception of the special personal character of the vertical bonds that tied people together and his understanding of the peculiar behavior of the leading politicians in whom the chains of influence and patronage converged. Namier taught us what many in the eighteenth century, from the Duke of Newcastle to David Hume, already knew: that patronage was what made the English monarchy work.

In a monarchical society the king was "the Head & Fountain" of all offices and honors. Subjects were expected to look upward for favors and rewards, if not to the king himself, then at least to those who were dependent on him. The experience of living in a monarchy, said Hume, tended "to beget in everyone an inclination to please his superiors." Lines of influence radiated outward from the crown through the colonial governors into even the remotest localities of American society. Through such influence, wrote the English whig John Brown contemptuously, a "great Chain of political Self-Interest was at length formed; and extended from the lowest Cobler in a Borough, to the King's first Minister." "We may . . . give to this influence what name we please," said Hume; "we may call it by the invidious appellations of *corruption* and *dependence*; but some degree and some kind of it" were absolutely necessary for all royal government. Patronage was the lifeblood of monarchy.[3]

If this was so, how monarchical was government in the colonies? Historians have commonly stressed the weakness of royal influence in the colonies. Following the Revolution, observers ranging from loyalist supporters to radical whigs concluded that "the King and government of Great Britain had no patronage in the country, which could create attachment and influence sufficient to counteract that restless, arrogating spirit . . . in popular assemblies."[4] It is certainly true that royal influence in the colonies was meager compared with what it was in the mother country. There were no elaborate civil bureaucracies, no bishoprics, no deaneries, no prebends, few regular army or navy posts, and not much to speak of in the way of crown livings. During the first half of the eighteenth century much of the crown's appointing power had been progressively stripped away from below—by the provincial assemblies and by local authorities. And the political effectiveness of royal officials was continually weakened by divisions within the imperial hierarchy and by the governors' need to share influence with the British court and bureaucracy above them. Yet for many Americans the crown's manipulation of offices and patronage remained pervasive and powerful enough to arouse their continual exasperation and anxiety.

Weak in fact as royal authority may have been in America, the crown was responsible for the empire, and as such it ultimately bore the burden of nearly all personal political influence exercised in the colonies. Even when local notables encroached on the crown's authority and built up their own countervailing connections with which to combat royal officials, the notables still seemed somehow to be only links in that long chain of dependency whose end disappeared into the distant and murky corridors of Whitehall. The rich merchant William Pepperell had the most powerful "interest" in all of Maine, and naturally the governor of Massachusetts appointed him commander of the military expedition to take Louisburg in 1745 because he was "most likely to raise Soldiers soonest." Yet Pepperell's subsequent appointment to a regular command in the British army and the award of a baronetcy made it impossible for him to separate his "interest" from that of the crown, and thus inevitably, he was regarded as a royal dependent.[5]

Any Briton whose sources of political strength lay in the metropolitan center was bound to be associated with crown authority. Henry McCulloh was never a royal governor of North Carolina, but he exercised more political power than most royal governors ever did. For four decades this British merchant and land speculator, whose "political Connections" in England, as his son delicately put it, "are far from contemptible," almost single-handedly kept North Carolina's politics in turmoil. McCulloh never lost any opportunity to pursue his interest. He defied and replaced royal governors and acquired for himself hundreds of thousands of acres of Carolina land, which he also managed to exempt from the normal payment of quitrents. Although he spent only a half dozen years in America, he had friends and agents in North Carolina for whom he secured offices and privileges. The royal governors by themselves may have lacked sufficient patronage power to govern, but in the face of the activities of men like McCulloh, the colonists had a hard time perceiving the weakness of crown authority in America.[6]

Few royal governors could match the power of Lord Baltimore's secretary, Cecilius Calvert, who conceived of the Maryland proprietary as a "Political Warehouse" of positions and favors similar "in Miniature" to the patronage of the Duke of Newcastle in Great Britain. But they did what they could with what they had, and with the underdeveloped nature of American society less could often go a long way. Although "we have few places in the governor's gift," noted the Boston physician William Douglass, "a great many small farms well leased out may be equivalent to a few great farms." In fact, in all the royal colonies except Virginia, local officials—sheriffs, judges, justices of the peace, militia officers, clerks, and so on—remained more dependent on royal favor than their counterparts in the mother country. In New Jersey, for example, one-quarter of the gentry could be affected by such crown appointments to local offices. The situation was no different in Massachusetts, where in the course of the eighteenth century the proportion of members of the assembly who were simultaneously justices of the peace rose steadily, reaching a peak of 71 percent in 1763. All in all, concluded Douglass, this power to appoint local officials "gives the Governors vast Influence."[7]

The more equal the society, the more ferocious the scrambling "for any little distinction in title or name." Even Englishmen thought that the colonists solicited for offices "more eagerly than in any Country upon Earth," and "it matters not how menial those offices may seem." For those struggling up from near the bottom of this provincial hierarchy three thousand miles from the metropolis, it took little enough to create an "interest." The Commission of a Subaltern, in the Militia," noted John Adams, "will tempt these little Minds, as much as Crowns, and Stars and Garters will great ones." Sometimes the crown's influence took the form of a carpetbagging official's elevation to the chief-justiceship of a colony through the connections of some English lord's mistress; at other times it was simply a New England town deputy's "taking a favour from the Governor" and being made a justice of the peace. But however petty this royal patronage may have been, it exerted an influence in local colonial affairs that we have only begun to measure. Certainly it provided much of the colonists' antagonism to the imperial system; indeed, the power of appointment became the great political evil against which they struck out most vigorously in their new revolutionary state constitutions of 1776.[8]

It is almost impossible today to comprehend the ancient monarchy in its own terms or to understand the role that patronage played in sustaining its authority. We apply modern republican standards that were already emerging in the eighteenth century. "Corruption" is nearly all we see. Indeed, we find it very difficult to understand why members of that society put up to the extent they did with the flagrant efforts of political officials to exploit their positions for their personal gain. Charges of "covetousness" and "corruption" were repeatedly made, to be sure, but before mid-century these accusations were much less effective than they would be on the eve of the Revolution. In fact, before 1745 in Massachusetts opponents of royal authority remained preoccupied with technical constitutional issues—the right of the assembly to elect its own speaker, adjourn itself, and so on—and rarely attacked the government in the radical whig language of "corruption."[9] For that monarchical society there was something traditional and justifiable in the crown's patronage authority that ultimately allowed it to persist as long as it did in the face of the notorious abuse of it and the continual criticism of it.

Eighteenth-century monarchical government still rested largely on inherited medieval notions that are lost to us today. The modern distinctions between state and society, public and private, were just emerging and were as yet only dimly appreciated. The king's inherited rights to govern the realm—his prerogatives—were as much private as they were public, just as the people's ancient rights or liberties were as much public as they were private. Public institutions had private rights and private persons had public obligations. The king's prerogatives or his premier rights to govern the realm grew out of his private position as the wealthiest of the wealthy and the largest landowner in the society; his government had really begun as an extension of his royal household. But in a like manner all private households or families—"those small subdivisions of Government," one colonist called them—had public responsibilities to help the king govern.[10]

Governments in this premodern society were not supposed to have much to do beyond carrying out the king's duty to preserve the peace and to adjudicate disputes among his subjects. "The Business of Government," declared the radical whig "Cato," was to do justice—"to secure to every Man his own, and to prevent the Crafty, Strong, and Rapacious, from pressing upon or circumventing the Weak, Industrious, and Unwary." Royal governors did not have legislative policies, and assemblies did not enact legislative programs. Many of the colonial governments' activities were private, local, and adjudicatory. Even the assemblies spent a good deal of time hearing private petitions, which often were only the complaints of one individual or group against another.[11]

The modern distinctions between legislation and adjudication were far from clear. Many of the county courts not only settled disputes but exercised a general paternalistic authority over the localities and handled a wide variety of what we today would call "administrative" tasks, drawing on the community for help. The county courts were as much instruments of government as they were judicial bodies. They assessed taxes, granted licenses, oversaw poor relief, supervised road repair, set prices, upheld moral standards, and all in all monitored the localities over which they presided.[12]

These colonial governments carried out their responsibilities without the aid of elaborate bureaucracies. On the eve of the Revolution all the expenses of the government of South Carolina came to less than £8,000 a year. Colonial Massachusetts had a society of 300,000 people, yet it spent less than £25,000 a year on its government, which employed only six "full-time officials" and fewer than a thousand "part-time officials." Even this notion of "full-time" and "part-time" officials is anachronistic and misleading, for no one yet conceived of politics as a paid profession or of a permanent civil service in the local colonial governments. It is true that members of the Massachusetts assembly were paid for their services, but this practice was unusual, and it horrified many observers. "The Honour, and Pleasure of doing Good," it was said, should be "Recompence sufficient to a Patriot." Most officeholding was still regarded, with varying degrees of plausibility, as a public obligation that private persons *"serving gratis or generously"* owed to the community.[13]

Indeed, all government was regarded essentially as the enlisting and mobilizing of the power of private persons to carry out public ends. "Governments," it has been said, "did not act so much as they ensured and sanctioned the actions of others." If the eighteenth-century city of New York wanted its streets cleaned or paved, for example, it did not hire contractors or create a "public works" department; instead it issued ordinances obliging each person in the city to clean or repair the street abutting his house or shop. In the same way, if the colony of Connecticut wanted a college, it did not build and run the college itself, but instead gave legal rights to private persons to build and run it. Most public action—from the building of wharfs and ferries to the maintaining of roads and inns—depended upon private energy and private funds. For the most part governments had only legal authority at their disposal. They issued sanctions against private persons for failure to perform their public duties, and they enticed private persons into fulfilling public goals by offering charters, licenses, and various other legal immunities together with fee-collecting offices. Given the difficulty in that premodern world of raising tax revenues, it was understandable that governments insisted on shifting the costs of most public action to private sources.

This practice has been called "government by delegation, government committed to a policy of externalizing the costs of action." Even criminal defendants who were acquitted were required to pay the costs of their trials![14]

Only in the context of these traditional assumptions about the nature and limitations of premodern government can we appreciate the role of royal patronage and the apparent "private" exploitation of "public" offices in the colonies; in fact, it was to be the other way 'round: the "public" exploitation of "private" power. Since everyone in the society had an obligation to help govern the realm commensurate with his social rank—the king's being the greatest because he stood at the top of the social hierarchy—important offices were supposed to be held only by those who were already worthy and had already achieved economic and social superiority. Just as gentlemen were expected to staff the officer corps of the army, so were independent gentlemen of leisure and education expected to supply leadership for government. Since such well-to-do gentry were "exempted from the lower and less honourable employments," wrote the philosopher Francis Hutcheson, they were "rather more than others obliged to an active life in some service to mankind. The publick has this claim upon them." All the founding fathers felt the weight of this claim and often agonized and complained about it. At a moment of bitterness Jefferson actually debated with himself the question "whether the state may command the political services of all its members to an indefinite extent." He had little doubt, he said, that "public service and private misery [were] inseparately linked together."[15]

Governmental service, in other words, was generally thought to be a personal sacrifice required of certain gentlemen because of their talents, independence, and social preeminence. Officeholding was supposed to be a burden, "attended," said George Washington in 1758, "with a certain Expense and trouble without the least prospect of gain"; and plural officeholding was just that much more of a burden. Thomas Hutchinson never regarded his many offices as anything but public obligations placed upon him by virtue of his distinguished and wealthy position in Massachusetts society. "I never sought or solicited any posts," he said in 1765; and he insisted that he would willingly give up all claim to honors and emoluments if it would serve the peace of his country. Presumably Hutchinson never lost money from his officeholding—his confiscated estate as a loyalist was worth £98,000—but many local officeholders, from grand jurors to justices of the peace, did serve without salary; and in some places communities had trouble getting people to take on certain offices. Of course, many offices offered the holders incentives in the form of fees, rewards, or benefits, sometimes quite lucrative ones. But always it was assumed that granting such offices together with their perquisites was the best way for these premodern governments to get things done without incurring any direct public costs.[16]

Since the society and the state were assumed to be identical, social honors and titles were necessarily related to the offices of government. Justices of the peace were invariably "Esq."; assemblymen and many selectmen were "Mr." In fact, wrote the great English jurist William Blackstone, "honours and offices are in their nature convertible and synonymous." Social distinctions, including titles, were the prerequisite of high government office: "that the people may know and distinguish such as are set over them, in order to yield them their due respect and obedience." In this sense government office seemed to belong to men of property and high social rank in the same way that the throne belonged to the king. Officeholding at times even seemed patrimonial. Some men tended to regard their offices as a virtual species of private property that they could pass on to members of their families. Seats on Virginia grand juries were perpetuated within families almost as frequently as seats on the vestries and county courts. Everywhere in the colonies men resigned offices in favor of their sons and then exulted, as Joseph Read of Pennsylvania did to Edward Shippen III in 1774: "Is it not agreeable to find our Descendants thus honoured?" The practice of "a father resigning his place to his son" was common enough that even Thomas Hutchinson complained that it was "tending to make all offices hereditary."[17]

Because office was an extension into government of the private person, the greater the private person, the greater the office. Access to government therefore often came quickly and easily to those who had the necessary social credentials. Thus wealthy John Dickinson could be elected to the Delaware assembly in 1760 at the age of twenty-eight and promptly be made its speaker. When James Allen at the age of twenty-seven returned from his education at the Middle Temple in London, he immediately was elected alderman of the city of Philadelphia, a lifetime position that was as distinguished as nearly any in the colony; six years later he succeeded his father as a member of the Pennsylvania assembly from Cumberland County. So also in 1753 Daniel Dulany of Maryland, precisely because he inherited great wealth and social position, could at once take over those political offices that his father had spent decades in achieving. So, too, could Jonathan Trumbull, a poor, obscure country merchant, be catapulted into the speakership of the Connecticut assembly at twenty-eight and into the council at the age of twenty-nine simply by the fact that his marriage into the ancient and prestigious Robinson family had given him, as Samuel Peters put it, "the prospect of preferment in civil life."[18]

Since these colonial governments lacked most of the coercive powers of a modern state—a few constables and sheriffs scarcely constituted a police force—officeholders relied on their own social respectability and private influence to compel the obedience of ordinary people. Common people could become hog reeves or occupy other lowly offices, but they had no business exercising high political office, since, in addition to being caught up in their petty workaday interests, they had no power, no connections, no social capacity for commanding public allegiance and deference. Thus, when, in 1759, the governor of Massachusetts appointed as a justice of the peace in Hampshire County someone whose company the other local justices declared they were "never inclined to keep," eleven of the justices resigned in protest, saying that such an appointment would make the office contemptible in the eyes of the people and diminish their ability to enforce the law. For mechanics and other manual laborers, holding high office was virtually impossible while they remained in their inferior status and were involved in market interests.[19]

Although many artisans and petty traders who had wealth and political ambitions, such as Roger Sherman of Connecticut, found that retirement from business was a prerequisite for high public office, none was as scrupulous on this point as Benjamin Franklin—perhaps because his sights were higher and his enemies more numerous. Franklin shrewdly perceived that the secret to his rising in America was not to presume too much and get ahead of himself. As a printer and businessman, no matter how rich, Franklin knew he was not really a gentleman, and, unlike some of his fellow artisans in Pennsylvania, he made no effort to appear to be one. When, in 1747, the officers of the Philadelphia militia elected him colonel of their regiment, he "declin'd that Station, . . . conceiving myself unfit." Colonels were supposed to be gentlemen. A year later, however, at the age of forty-two, Franklin thought he had acquired "sufficient tho' moderate Fortune" to retire finally from business and become a gentleman. Only then did he believe he had "secur'd Leisure during the rest of my Life" to do what enlightened and virtuous gentlemen were supposed to do—engage in "Philosophical Studies and Amusements," serve in important political offices (for which "the Public now considering me as a Man of Leisure, laid hold of me for their Purposes"), and, finally assume the colonelcy of the Philadelphia regiment that he had earlier declined and for which he was now fit. At the time this coming into gentility was a significant, even a ceremonial, event for Franklin: he commissioned Robert Feke to paint a mannered and foppish portrait to honor the occasion. Later in his life, however, after he had become a wigless republican hero, he conveniently forgot about this monarchical portrait.[20]

The stability of the political system thus depended on the social authority of the political leaders being visible and incontestable. No wonder, then, that officials were so sensitive to public criticism of their private character. They knew only too well—"these are dry commonplace observations, known to everyone"—that their ability to govern rested on their personal reputations. In fact, as future loyalist Jonathan Sewell put it in 1766, "the *person* and the *office* are so connected in the minds of the greatest part of mankind, that a contempt of the *former*, and a *veneration* for the *latter* are totally incompatible."[21]

This patrimonial conception of officeholding, this identification between social and political authority, private and public leadership, ran deep in this traditional monarchical world. No presumption about politics was in fact more basic to this society and separated it more from the emerging democratic world of the nineteenth century. It lay behind much of the political squabbling of eighteenth-century America—from the continual resort to the law of seditious libel to the repeated complaints that the wrong sorts of persons were gaining office, either through arbitrary crown manipulations or through a demagogic courting of the populace. Rulers needed to be socially and morally respectable. "Whatever tends to create in the minds of the people, a contempt of the persons who hold the highest offices in the state," whatever convinced people that "subordination is not necessary, and is no essential part of government, tends directly to destroy it."[22]

Thus royal officials and other public magistrates tried to wrap themselves in the sacred mantle of God and religion and to establish their personal dignity in every way possible. They invoked the common law of seditious libel against scurrilous attacks on their personal character on the understandable grounds that such "speaking evil of dignities and reviling the rulers of the people" undermined their capacity to govern. Critics of government had to be careful to state that they were denouncing "measures, not men" and to avoid the full spelling out of the name of a public official in the press for fear of conveying contempt. But ensuring the people's respect for the personal dignity of public office-holders was difficult, if not impossible, if those holding office had no social respectability in the first place. And so both crown officials and colonial gentry complained constantly of the prevalence in government of men in "necessitous circumstances," or "plain illiterate husband-men," or "men without education, and of dissolute manners," or "ob-scure and inferior persons," or "those who have neither natural nor acquired parts to recommend them." Crown and colonists blamed each other for placing the wrong sorts of people—men without real wealth, esteem, and virtue—into offices of public trust. In an important sense the Revolution was fought over just this issue—over differing interpre-tations of who in America were the proper social leaders who ought naturally to accede to positions of public authority.[23]

The personal structure of eighteenth-century politics, the prevalence of numerous vertical lines of influence converging on particular people of wealth and power, was what made colonial politics essentially a con-test among prominent families for the control of state authority. This personal structure of politics, and not simply the age's abhorrence of division, explains the absence of organized political parties in the eigh-teenth century. Political factions existed, but these were little more than congeries of the leading gentry's personal and family "interests." And it was this personal structure of politics—not any elaborate legal restric-tions on the suffrage—that kept most common people from participating in politics. Although the contending gentry increasingly appealed to the "people" in electoral contests—so much so, as Governor William Shir-ley of Massachusetts observed in 1742, that the aroused people had "it in their power upon an extraordinary Emergency to double and almost treble their numbers" in elections—much of the time most ordinary folk were not deeply involved in provincial or imperial politics. Sometimes as many as one-third of the towns of Massachusetts failed to send rep-resentatives to the provincial legislature.[24]

Few if any of the common people regarded government as a means by which economic and social power might be redistributed or the prob-lems of their lives resolved. Usually they confined themselves to local issues and to wrangling over such questions as whether or not to allow their hogs to run free in their communities. And whenever they did discover the inclination to place demands on government, they lacked the power to challenge the personal influence of the dominant elites. In a 1758 election in Newport, Rhode Island, noted Ezra Stiles, two hundred out of six hundred eligible freemen did not vote; "one third lie still," he said, "silenced by Connexions." In 1773 in the Mohawk district of Tryon County, New York, at least four hundred men had the franchise. Yet in an election for five constables only fourteen electors turned out to vote; all fourteen were closely tied by interest or patronage to Sir William Johnson, the local grandee of the area, and all fourteen naturally voted for the same five candidates.[25]

Whatever acquiescence people gave to those who by virtue of their wealth, influence, and independence were considered best qualified to rule was based not simply on traditional habits of deference but on the dependency that patronage created. When in 1757 Jeremiah Gridley of Brookline, Massachusetts, thought his hopes of being elected to the House of Representatives were endangered, he asked the Earl of Loudoun, commander in chief of His Majesty's army in North America, to use his influence with Governor Thomas Pownall to secure his appointment as militia colonel for the regiment of his locality. Because the regimental commander had the power to impress men for provincial military service, Gridley told Loudoun, the colonelcy "will place my Townsmen in a Dependency upon me."[26]

Probably no one in late-eighteenth-century America used his property and patronage to create political dependencies more shamelessly than John Hancock. Hancock patronized everyone. He made work for people. He erected homes that he did not need. He built ships that he sold at a loss. He sponsored any and every young man who importuned him. He opened trade shops and staffed them. He purchased a concert hall for public use. He entertained lavishly and habitually treated the Boston populace to wine. John Adams recalled that "not less than a thousand families were, every day in the year, dependent on Mr. Hancock for their daily bread." He went through the mercantile fortune he had inherited from his uncle, but he formed one of the most elaborate networks of political dependency in eighteenth-century America and became the single most popular and powerful figure in Massachusetts politics during the last quarter of the century.[27]

Translating the personal, social, and economic power of the gentry into political authority was essentially what eighteenth-century politics was about. The process was self-intensifying: social power created political authority, which in turn created more social influence. Some members of the gentry, such as the Tidewater planters of Virginia or the wealthy landholders of the Connecticut River valley, had enough influence to overawe entire communities. Connecticut River valley gentry like Israel Williams and John Worthington, so imposing as to be called "river gods," used their power to become at one time or another selectmen of their towns, representatives to the Massachusetts General Court, members of the council, provincial court judges, justices of the peace, and colonels of their county regiments. It became impossible to tell where the circle of their authority began: the political authority to grant licenses for taverns or mills, to determine the location of roads and bridges, or to enlist men for military service was of a piece with their wealth and social influence.[28]

It was likewise substantial paternalistic and patronage power, and not merely the treating of the freeholders with toddy at election time, that enabled the great Virginia planters to mobilize their "interests" and to maintain law and order over their local communities without the aid of police forces. The leading Virginia gentry were the vestrymen of their parishes and the lay leaders of the Anglican church, so that the sacredness of religion and the patronage of poor relief further enhanced the hierarchy of authority. All this was the stuff of which aristocracies were made.[29]

Everywhere it was the same: those who had the property and power to exert influence in any way—whether by lending money, doing favors, or supplying employment—created obligations and dependencies that could be turned into political authority. When in 1743 Henry Beekman, a large New York landowner, interceded on behalf of several small freeholders of his county who were faced with an ejectment suit, he was exercising the power of patronage his position gave him. Although Beekman told the beneficiaries of his aid that he would "expect no other reward for this than your friendship," he clearly expected such "friendship" to manifest itself in political allegiance at election time.[30]

Even the recurrent mobbing and rioting of Anglo-American society, which seem to be challenges to the structure of authority, were in fact ultimately testimonies to the paternalism and personal organization of that society. The crowd riots were disorderly protests by common people, to be sure, and gentlemanly authorities were not at all happy with them. But the riots took place within the existing structure of authority and tended to reinforce that structure even as they defied it; often they grew out of folk festivals and traditional popular rites and had much in common with them. In fact, it was the awesomeness of personal and social authority in this premodern age that compelled common people to resort to mock ceremonies and rituals as a means of dealing with their humiliations and resentments. Such rituals momentarily allowed humble people to overcome their feelings of inferiority and subordination and to control the release of their pent-up anger and hostility. Consequently, role reversals, in which boys, apprentices, and servants became kings for a day, worked not to undermine but to reaffirm that existing hierarchy. Brief saturnalian transgressions of the society's rules by the populace tended to underscore the power of those rules. And the use of effigies and the heavily ritualized behavior of the mobs, such as those in Boston's Pope's Day celebrations of November 5, served to keep these challenges to authority at a distance.[31]

Often these popular mobs or riots were simply products of local frustration with the way the ordinary processes of society were operating; they indicated, said Samuel Adams, that the "wheels of government" were "somewhere clogged."[32] Whether destroying bawdy houses that magistrates had been unable to close, or protecting communities against the threat of smallpox, or preventing the king's ships from impressing local sailors, crowds of people periodically took to the streets to set things right in a direct and immediate fashion. Often the crowds acted to support traditional customs and moral relationships against changes brought on by new impersonal market conditions, maintaining by force, for example, customary prices and the traditional ways of distributing goods against the perceived forestalling and gouging practiced by unscrupulous shopkeepers and middlemen.

Such mobbing was a means by which ordinary people, usually those most dependent—women, servants, free blacks, sailors, and young men—made their power felt temporarily in a political system that was otherwise largely immune to their influence. Although the crowds usually acted outside the bounds of law and of existing institutions, they were not necessarily anti-authoritarian. The mobs' actions often enjoyed widespread support in the local community, and in fact were condoned or at least tolerated by many gentlemen who remained confident of their paternal hegemony and who often wanted to separate themselves from crass and greedy tradesmen and moneymakers. Sometimes members of the gentry even participated in the rioting and guided it. The mobs often showed remarkable restraint, pinpointing their objectives with extraordinary care, and limiting themselves to the intimidation of particular persons and to the selective destruction of property. These common crowd actions, at least before the imperial crisis deepened in the 1760s, were generally thought to pose no great threat to the hierarchy of the society. Popular uprisings were commonly viewed as momentary releases within the political system, temporary "Thunder Gusts" that "do more Good than Harm" in clearing the political atmosphere. Far from being symptoms of the breakdown of traditional authority, the behavior of the mobs indicated that the customary mechanisms of social control in the society were still working.[33]

Even the riots against royal officials and stamp agents in the 1760s were not always as deeply threatening to authority as they sometimes seemed. The mobs dared to whip, hang, and burn effigies but usually not real persons, and their mock ceremonies—the crowning of petty merchants and craftsmen as captains-general or kings, for example— were, like all parodies, backhanded tributes to what was being ridiculed. The severely ritualized nature of much of the crowds' behavior often kept the mobs from running amok. The destruction of Lieutenant Governor Thomas Hutchinson's home by a Boston mob on August 26, 1765, aroused so much more shock and fear in the community, even among whigs, than a riot against the Stamp Act twelve days earlier precisely because it ignored the prescribed rituals and effigy-parading that the previous riot had carefully followed. It seemed much more a private than a public mob.[34]

Perhaps nothing is more revealing of the paternal and face-to-face nature of this society than the way the prominent Charleston merchant-planter Henry Laurens dispersed a Stamp Act mob in 1765. Perceiving that the mob, disguised in blackened faces, sailors' clothes, and slouch hats, was about to force an entrance to his house in search of stamped paper, Laurens let the rioters in. Although held with a brace of cutlasses against his chest, Laurens called out the names of members of the mob— "to their great surprize"—and forced them by sheer familiarity to back down in their threats. The crowd eventually ended up praising Laurens: they said they "loved" him, gave him "three cheers," wished his "Lady" well and retired with "God bless your honour, Good night, Colonel."[35]

This sort of popular rioting was ultimately evidence that politics remained essentially a preserve of the dominant gentlemanly elite. The processes of government still depended on the face-to-face relations of gentlemen or on the widespread use of personal correspondence among gentlemen. Even much of the writing of pamphlets or newspaper essays was an extended form of personal correspondence among gentlemen who knew one another intimately. By filling their writings with personal references, Latin quotations, and esoteric allusions to the heritage of Western culture, gentlemen showed that they still thought of the audience for their political polemics as roughly commensurate with the social world comprised of other educated gentlemen.[36]

Such familiar elitist politics in a dependent hierarchical world necessarily involved a great deal of personal maneuvering and manipulation. Success of any sort in eighteenth-century Anglo-American society put a premium on certain traits of character—on circumspection, caution, and calculation; on the control and suppression of one's real feelings for the sake of cultivating the patronage of those superiors who could help or hurt one's rise. Throughout the pre-revolutionary crisis in Maryland the elder Charles Carroll, raised in this old society, continually exhorted his impetuous son of the same name, who was leading a newspaper assault on the government, to move carefully and to hide his bitter antagonism to the Maryland governor. For, as the father warned, "prudence directs you not to show that the governor's folly and want of spirit is mortifying to you. You may resolve to live in a desert if you will not generally associate with foolish, fickle, mean-spirited men." Such advice bred the civic-minded prudence and role-playing, the flattery and fawning, that made the eighteenth-century so distinctive and so repulsive to those who value sincerity and authenticity. Already by the time of the Revolution, however, a younger generation of American politicians, men like Carroll's son, were no longer willing to abide the insincere dissembling of that older monarchical courtier world.[37]

ii REPUBLICANISM

6. The Republicanization of Monarchy

In the end the disintegration of the traditional eighteenth-century monarchical society of paternal and dependent relationships prepared the way for the emergence of the liberal, democratic, capitalistic world of the early nineteenth century. This reordering of the society of the *ancien régime* was not confined to America, or even to the English-speaking world. It occurred throughout Western society, sometimes but not always accompanied by violence and revolution. Indeed, the late eighteenth century in the Atlantic world has been called "the age of the democratic revolution." It might better be called "the age of the republican revolution." For it was republicanism and republican principles that ultimately destroyed this monarchical society.[1]

But not at any one moment—neither in 1776 with the Declaration of Independence, nor in 1789 with the calling of the French Estates General, nor even in 1793 with the execution of Louis XVI. Republicanism did not replace monarchy all at once; it ate away at it, corroded it, slowly, gradually, steadily, for much of the eighteenth century. Republicanism seeped everywhere in the eighteenth-century Atlantic world, eroding monarchical society from within, wearing away all the traditional supports of kingship, ultimately desacralizing monarchy to the point where, as David Hume observed, "the mere name of king commands little respect; and to talk of a *king* as God's vice-regent on earth, or to give him any of these magnificent titles which formerly dazzled mankind, would but excite laughter in everyone."[2]

So confused and blended did monarchy and republicanism become in the eighteenth century that people, especially in the English-speaking world, had trouble precisely defining them. Republicanism, in particular, assumed a wide range of meanings and, as Alexander Hamilton said, was "used in various senses." By the early nineteenth century John Adams professed to believe that he had "never understood" what republicanism was and thought that "no other man ever did or ever will." He concluded in frustration that republicanism "may signify any thing, every thing, or nothing." And so it did, becoming at times virtually indistinguishable from monarchy. Certainly it stood for something other than a set of political institutions based on popular election. In fact, republicanism was not to be reduced to a mere form of government at all; instead it was what Franco Venturi has called "a form of life," ideals and values entirely compatible with monarchical institutions. Republicanism "was separated from the historical forms it had taken in the past, and became increasingly an ideal which could exist in a monarchy."[3]

Promoting republicanism as an actual form of government was of course forbidden in that monarchical world. No one in his right mind dared suggest deposing kings and replacing them with republican governments. That was dangerous, seditious, and treasonous.[4] Besides, few who believed in republicanism actually intended to foment revolution and overthrow monarchy. The self-proclaimed republics in Europe— the Swiss cantons, the Italian city-states, and the Dutch provinces—were scarcely fit models for the sprawling monarchies of the continent. And no one wanted to try the disastrous seventeenth-century English experiment in republican government again.

True, the intellectuals and critics who invoked republican principles and sentiments were opposed to the practices and values of the dominant monarchical world. But they sought to reform and revitalize their society; they wanted to enlighten and improve monarchy, not cut off the heads of kings. These critics and many others—including good loyal colonial subjects of His Britannic Majesty—used republicanism merely as a counterculture to monarchy. Though rarely cited specifically by name, republicanism represented all those beliefs and values that confronted and criticized the abuses of the eighteenth-century monarchical world.

But republicanism was no less revolutionary for all that. In fact, it was in every way a radical ideology—as radical for the eighteenth century as Marxism was to be for the nineteenth century. It challenged the primary assumptions and practices of monarchy—its hierarchy, its inequality, its devotion to kinship, its patriarchy, its patronage, and its dependency. It offered new conceptions of the individual, the family, the state, and the individual's relationship to the family, the state, and other individuals. Indeed, republicanism offered nothing less than new ways of organizing society. It defied and dissolved the older monarchical connections and presented people with alternative kinds of attachments, new sorts of social relationships. It transformed monarchical culture and prepared the way for the revolutionary upheavals at the end of the eighteenth century.

Many like Adam Smith believed that all governments in the world could be reduced to just two—monarchies and republics—and that these were rooted in two basic types of personalities: monarchists, who loved peace and order, and republicans, who loved liberty and independence. Late in his life Jefferson likewise thought that all people by nature could be divided into just two parties. They existed in all countries, he said, whether called tories and whigs, aristocrats and democrats, right and left, ultras and radicals, or serviles and liberals. Jefferson left no doubt where his own sympathies lay: "the sickly, weakly, timid man, fears the people, and is a Tory by nature. The healthy, strong and bold, cherishes them, is formed a Whig by nature."[5]

But most intellectuals in the mid-eighteenth century never tried to distinguish between monarchy and republicanism as sharply as Jefferson did. Instead, they usually discussed monarchy and republics as governments that mingled with and reinforced one another. David Hume thought that as perfect as the monarchical form may have appeared to some political leaders, "it owes all its perfection to the republican." It was not possible for a pure despotism established among a barbarous people to refine and polish itself. "It must borrow its laws and methods, and institutions, and consequently its stability and order, from free governments. These advantages," said Hume, "are the sole growth of republics." Such statements by a variety of intellectual figures helped to make republicanism a common and integral part of the dominant monarchical culture.

It was Montesquieu, however ("the most comprehensive and piercing genius of his age," the Reverend Thomas Robbins of Massachusetts called him), who most systematically and comparatively set forth the principles of monarchy and republicanism for that enlightened age. Although Montesquieu's ideal models of government were sometimes overly rigid and his moral and social prescriptions for each type of government often aphoristically concise ("as honor is the principle of a monarchical government, the laws ough to be in relation to this principle"; "the less luxury there is in a republic, the more it is perfect"), his influential treatise *The Spirit of the Laws* (1748) comprehensively weighed the advantages and disadvantages of monarchies and republics, described the cohesive forces of each, and suggested that most modern governments were mixtures of both to one degree or another.[6]

Most European readers of *The Spirit of the Laws,* even those who lived in the France of Louis XV and Louis XVI, could readily conclude that their societies shared in the spirit of both monarchy and republicanism. Had not Montesquieu himself previously written (in his *Persian Letters* of 1721) that there were no pure monarchies left in Europe? Surely monarchies like that of France could benefit from some further infusion of republican principles. Montesquieu and others even implied that France might borrow something from the balanced constitution of the English monarchy—that is, it might become more republican.

Among the monarchies of Europe, the English possessed by far the most republican constitution. England, Montesquieu said, "may be justly called a republic disguised under the form of monarchy." Already by the beginning of the century the English monarchy had lost much of its sacred aura. The man-made dynastic alterations of 1688 and 1714 and the rationalizing of religion inevitably weakened the sense of hereditary mystique, and the restrictions Parliament placed on the crown's prerogatives and finances diminished the king's ability to act independently. None of the Hanoverian monarchs before the American Revolution ever achieved more than a fleeting popularity. Neither George I nor George II seemed to care about the monarchy's public image, and both kings tended to avoid displaying the trappings of royalty. It was not easy for the English populace to get very excited about them, and more often than not London crowds accorded the monarchy in public less respect than they would pay to it in the nineteenth century. It was as if George I, by abolishing the royal touch, had begun a steady process of desacralizing the English crown. It reached the point where radical whigs like "Cato" could describe the king as being no different from the mayor of a town: "they are both civil officers."[7]

The English thought they lived in a republicanized monarchy, and they were right. Their famous "limited" or "mixed" monarchy was in fact a republicanized one. The English kings, it was said, were not typical kings. Far from being the traditional sort of power-hungry monarchs, the English kings were "the Scourges of Tyrants, and the Assertors of Liberty." They were "beloved by a nation of Freemen and Heroes," and they, like their people, aspired after "those brighter Trophies that are earn'd in the Paths of Virtue and heroic Deeds." The British king was the ultimate disinterested republican leader, the "sovereign umpire" of the realm.[8]

Nearly everyone agreed that the substantial element of republicanism in the English constitution was a crucial source of its strength. Some

Englishmen were even willing to admit openly that the English constitution was republican. Thomas Wentworth in 1710 said that the arrangement of "king, lords, and commons, each a check upon the other," was "calculated for the good of the whole," which meant "that it may more properly be called a commonwealth than a monarchy." The English constitution was judged by republican standards. Each part of the triad of king, lords, and commons was praised for its independence, and any loss of that independence was widely condemned as corruption, particularly when the crown gained power at the expense of the commons. Radical whigs were full of praise of republicanism. Trenchard and Gordon were certain "that our Government is a Thousand Degrees nearer akin to a Commonwealth (any sort of Commonwealth now subsisting or that ever did subsist in the World) than it is to absolute Monarchy." James Burgh went further in his celebration of republicanism and even suggested that the English people had a sovereign right to establish a republic if they wished. Many Britons agreed with Adam Smith's reputed view that for the English constitution "a commonwealth" was "the platform for the monarchy."[9]

Republicanism did not belong only to the margins, to the extreme right or left, of English political life. Monarchical and republican values existed side by side in the culture, and many good monarchists and many good English tories adopted republican ideals and principles without realizing the long-run political implications of what they were doing. Although they seldom mentioned the term, educated people of varying political persuasions celebrated republicanism for its spirit, its morality, its freedom, its sense of friendship and duty, and its vision of society. Republicanism as a set of values and a form of life was much too pervasive, comprehensive, and involved with being liberal and enlightened to be seen as subversive or as anti-monarchical.

Instead of constituting some thin eddy flowing only on the edges of British or even European culture, this republican tradition thus became an important current in its own right that blended and mingled with the monarchical mainstream and influenced its color, tone, and direction. Eighteenth-century republicanism did not so much displace monarchy as transform it. Republicanism was never a besieged underground ideology, confined to cellar meetings and marginal intellectuals. On the contrary: there were no more enthusiastic promoters of republicanism than many members of the English and French nobility, who were presumably closest to monarchy and who depended for their status upon it. All those French nobles who in 1785 flocked to the Paris salon to ooh and aah over Jacques-Louis David's severe classical painting *The Oath of the Horatii* had no idea they were contributing to the weakening of monarchy and their own demise. Nor did all those aristocrats who in 1786 applauded Mozart's *Marriage of Figaro*, with its celebration of humanistic and egalitarian values, believe that they were espousing republicanism and undermining monarchy. Likewise, all those aristocratic sponsors of the 1730 edition of James Thompson's whiggish poem *The Seasons*—including the queen, ten dukes, thirty-one earls and countesses, and a larger number of the lesser peerage and their sons and daughters—little sensed that they were contributing to the erosion of the values that made their dominance possible. When even hereditary aristocrats, "disclaiming as it were [their] birthright, and putting [themselves] upon the foot of a *Roman,*" could subscribe enthusiastically to the view voiced by Conyers Middleton in his *Life of Cicero* (1741) that "no man, how nobly soever born, could arrive at any dignity, who did not win it by his personal merit," then we know something of the power of these republican sentiments in the culture. "Radical chic" was not an invention of the twentieth century.[10]

In essence republicanism was the ideology of the Enlightenment. If the Enlightenment was, as Peter Gay has called it, "the rise of modern paganism," then classical republicanism was its creed.[11] In the eighteenth century to be enlightened was to be interested in antiquity, and to be interested in antiquity was to be interested in republicanism. Certainly classical antiquity could offer meaningful messages for monarchy too, but there is no doubt that the thrust of what the ancient world had to say to the eighteenth century was latently and at times manifestly republican.

All the ancient republics—Athens, Sparta, Thebes—were familiar to educated people in the eighteenth century (their names had "grown trite by repetition," said one American) but none was more familiar than Rome. People could not hear enough about it. "It is impossible," said Montesquieu, "to be weary of so agreeable a subject as ancient Rome." The eighteenth century was particularly fascinated by the writings of the golden age of Roman literature—"the First Enlightenment," as Peter Gay has called it—the two centuries from the breakdown of the republic in the middle of the first century B.C. to the reign of Marcus Aurelius in the middle of the second century A.D.[12]

These Roman writers—Cicero, Virgil, Sallust, Tacitus, among others—set forth republican ideals and political and social values that have had a powerful and lasting effect on Western culture. These classical ideals and values were revived and refurbished by the Italian Renaissance—becoming what has been variously called "civic humanism" or "classical republicanism"—and were carried into early modern Europe and made available to wider and deeper strata of the population. By the eighteenth century monarchical culture in Europe and particularly in Great Britain was thoroughly infused with these classical values and to that extent at least was republicanized.[13]

Of course, Englishmen subscribed to these classical republican values with varying degrees of intensity, and the term "republican" remained pejorative, something to hang on the head of an opponent in order to damage his credibility, if not his loyalty to the crown. Nevertheless, what is remarkable is the extent to which the thinking of eighteenth-century educated Englishmen on both sides of the Atlantic was republicanized in substance, if not in name. Many Englishmen were quick to respond as the editor of the *South Carolina Gazette,* Peter Timothy, did in 1749 when he was denounced as a republican for publishing *Cato's Letters*: he was not a "Republican . . . ," Timothy said, "unless Virtue and Truth be Republican."[14] Invoking these classical ideals became the major means by which dissatisfied Britons on both sides of the Atlantic voiced their objections to the luxury, selfishness, and corruption of the monarchical world in which they lived.

The literature of the first half of the eighteenth century in Great Britain—both belles lettres and political polemics—was a literature of social criticism, and this social criticism was steeped in classical republican values. Most English writers of the period—whether tory satirists like Pope and Swift or radical whig publicists like Trenchard and Gordon—expressed a deep and bitter hostility to the great social, economic, and political changes taking place in England during the decades following the Glorious Revolution of 1688. The rise of banks, trading companies, and stock markets, plus the emergence of the new moneyed men, the increasing public debt, and the corruption of politics all threatened traditional values and led opposition poets and polemicists alike to set classical models and morality against the spreading commercialization.[15]

Classical republican Rome, like some South Sea tribes for twentieth-century anthropologists, became the means by which enlightened eighteenth-century Englishmen could distance themselves from their own society and achieve the perspective from which to criticize it. Gibbon admired Juvenal for that Roman satirist's refusal to surrender his republican ideals in the face of monarchical realities. He had, said Gib-

bon, "the soul of a republican" and was "the sworn enemy of tyranny."
Thus Dr. Johnson found that the best way to condemn the corruption
of eighteenth-century London was to imitate Juvenal's third satire on
Nero's Rome.[16]

So pervasive, so dominant, was this literature of social criticism that
it is difficult to find anything substantial that stood against it. All the
great eighteenth-century British writers spoke in republican tones. The
long administration of Sir Robert Walpole (1721–42) eventually united in
intellectual opposition all of what William Pulteney called "the gay, the
polite and witty Part of the World"; and that opposition, whether the
tory John Gay in *The Beggar's Opera* or the whig James Thompson in his
poem *Liberty,* inevitably drew on classical republican values to voice its
love of freedom and its antagonism to corruption. Hume in 1742 thought
that more than half of what had been written during the previous twenty
years had been devoted to satirizing the machinations of Walpole, the
figure who seemed most responsible for what ailed Britain. One administration defender in 1731 concluded that, simply for the sake of getting
at Walpole, "the whole nation hath been abused, Corruption and Degeneracy universally charged." All the country-opposition citations to
Roman writers were moral strictures against a polluted court, and as
such they were often unwitting celebrations of republican values.

In fact, most of the eighteenth century's invocations of classical antiquity became covert and often unwitting championings of republicanism. Although some Englishmen in the late seventeenth century had
found in the age of Augustus a model of restored stability in which the
arts were allowed to flourish, after 1688 most Englishmen, even aristocrats close to the court, criticized Augustus and looked to the Roman
Republic for values and inspiration. Cicero and Cato, not Augustus,
were the Romans to be admired. To Voltaire, Augustus was *"ce poltron
qui osa exiler Ovide."* Augustus, Montesquieu said, had led the Romans
"gently into slavery," and most Englishmen agreed. "Augustus" became a code word for "tyrant," and as such he was attacked by nearly
everyone except royal absolutists. The tories, thinking of George I, called
Augustus a despot, but the court whigs and all defenders of the Hanoverian settlement, thinking of the Stuarts, did likewise. From 1688 on,
the need for the government to defend the whig settlement and attack
Stuart pretensions meant that a quasi-republican, anti-royalist bias was
necessarily built into the official center of English culture. During Walpole's era both court and country writers alike condemned Augustus as
an imperial dictator, the murderer of Cicero, and the destroyer of the

republic. From Addison to Dr. Johnson, English intellectuals expressed their admiration for Tacitus's anti-Augustan republican view of Roman history. Thomas Gordon originally dedicated his edition of Tacitus to Walpole, his patron, but the work so fully expressed a republican antagonism toward Augustus ("the best of his Government was but the sunshine of Tyranny") that it was celebrated by English commonwealthmen as well. David Hume thought that even the tories had been so long obliged to talk "in the republican stile" that they had at length "embraced the sentiments, as well as the language of their adversaries."[7]

These appeals to antiquity made anything other than a classical conception of leadership difficult to justify. It was almost always classical standards—Catonic and Ciceronian standards—that British opposition writers invoked to judge the ragged world of eighteenth-century politics. They placed the character of republicanism—integrity, virtue, and disinterestedness—at the center of public life. Whatever the partisan origins of a work like Richard Glover's *Leonidas* (1737), which contrasted the bravery and patriotism of the Spartan commander and his soldiers with the selfishness and corruption of Walpole and his followers, the repeated use of such antique models only led to the further spreading of classical ideals.[18]

Although set within a monarchical framework, these classical republican ideals established the foundations both for a liberal arts education and for political debate in the English-speaking world. The writings of classical antiquity provided more than window dressing for educated Englishmen on both sides of the Atlantic; they were, in fact, the principal source of their public morality and values. Political leaders were held to ancient republican standards:

> *You* then whose Judgment the right Course wou'd steer,
> Know well each ANCIENT's proper *Character*,
> His *Fable, Subject, Scope* in ev'ry Page,
> *Religion, Country, Genius*, of his Age.[19]

So Alexander Pope told his countrymen, and nearly every gentleman agreed. Public morality was classical morality; people could not read enough about Cato and Cicero. Although Hume attempted to explain the need for corruption in the working of the British constitution, it was virtually impossible, especially in the North American colonies, for anyone to justify holding office simply as a means of selfish aggrandizement. Classical republican values forbade it. Good monarchists inevitably accepted, at least rhetorically, the civic humanist ideals of disinterested public leadership. Even royal governors at times denied "all pretension to Eminence or Distinction" in favor of what was more valuable—the cultivation of "those Virtues of a social Nature."[20]

According to the classical republican tradition, man was by nature a political being, a citizen who achieved his greatest moral fulfillment by participating in a self-governing republic. Public or political liberty— or what we now call positive liberty—meant participation in government. And this political liberty in turn provided the means by which the personal liberty and private rights of the individual—what we today call negative liberty—were protected. In this classical republican tradition our modern distinction between positive and negative liberties was not yet clearly perceived, and the two forms of liberty were still often seen as one.[21] Liberty was realized when the citizens were virtuous— that is, willing to sacrifice their private interests for the sake of the community, including serving in public office without pecuniary rewards. This virtue could be found only in a republic of equal, active, and independent citizens. To be completely virtuous citizens, men— never women, because it was assumed they were never independent— had to be free from dependence and from the petty interests of the marketplace. Any loss of independence and virtue was corruption.

The virtue that classical republicanism encouraged was public virtue. Private virtues such as prudence, frugality, and industry were important but, said Hume, they only made men "serviceable to themselves, and enable them to promote their own interests"; they were not "such as make them perform their part in society." Public virtue was the sacrifice of private desires and interests for the public interest. It was devotion to the commonweal. All men of genius and leisure, all gentlemen, had an obligation to serve the state. "Let not your love of philosophical amusements have more than its due weight with you," Benjamin Franklin admonished New York royal official Cadwallader Colden in 1750. Public service was far more important than science. In fact, said Franklin, even "the finest" of Newton's "Discoveries" could not have excused his neglect of serving the commonwealth if the public had needed him.[22]

Republicanism thus put an enormous burden on individuals. They were expected to suppress their private wants and interests and develop disinterestedness—the term the eighteenth century most often used as a synonym for civic virtue: it better conveyed the increasing threats from interests that virtue now faced. Dr. Johnson defined disinterest as being "superior to regard of private advantage; not influenced by private profit." We today have lost most of this older meaning. Even some educated people now use "disinterested" as a synonym for "uninterested," meaning indifferent or unconcerned. Perhaps we cannot quite conceive of the characteristic that disinterestedness describes: we cannot quite imagine someone who is capable of rising above private profit and private advantage and being unselfish and unbiased where a personal interest might be present.[23]

Precisely because republics required civic virtue and disinterestedness among their citizens, they were very fragile polities, extremely liable to corruption. Republics demanded far more morally from their citizens than monarchies did of their subjects. In monarchies each man's desire to do what was right in his own eyes could be restrained by fear or force, by patronage or honor. In republics, however, each man must somehow be persuaded to sacrifice his personal desires, his luxuries, for the sake of the public good. Monarchies could tolerate great degrees of self-interestedness, private gratification, and corruption among their subjects. After all, they were based on dependence and subservience and had all sorts of adhesives and connections besides virtue to hold their societies together. Monarchies relied on blood, family, kinship, patronage, and ultimately fear, as one loyalist clergyman in western Massachusetts tried to make clear to several of his neighbors who were thinking of taking up arms against their king in 1775. Do not do it, the cleric warned. "The king can send a company of horse through the country and take off every head; and in less than six weeks you will be glad to labor a week for sheep's head and pluck."[24] But republics could never resort to such force. In their purest form they had no adhesives, no bonds holding themselves together, except their citizens' voluntary patriotism and willingness to obey public authority. Without virtue and self-sacrifice republics would fall apart.

One did not have to be a professed republican or a radical whig, however, to believe in virtue and the other classical values that accompanied it. Virtue, along with the concept of honor, lay at the heart of all prescriptions for political leadership in the eighteenth-century English-speaking world. Throughout the century Englishmen of all political persuasions—whigs and tories alike—struggled to find the ideal virtuous leader amid the rising and swirling currents of financial and commercial interests that threatened to engulf their society. Nothing more enhanced William Pitt's reputation as the great patriot than his pointed refusal in

1746 to profit from the perquisites of the traditionally lucrative office of paymaster of the forces. Pitt was living proof of the possibility of disinterestedness—that a man could be a governmental leader and yet remain free of corruption.[25]

If virtue was based on liberty and independence, then it followed that only autonomous individuals free from any ties of interest and paid by no master were qualified to be citizens. Jefferson and many other republican idealists hoped that all ordinary yeoman farmers who owned their own land and who depended for their subsistence only "on their own soil and industry" and not "on the casualties and caprice of customers" would be independent and free enough of pecuniary temptations and marketplace interests to be virtuous.[26]

Others, however, questioned the capacity of most ordinary people to rise above self-interest, particularly those who were dependent on "the casualties and caprice of customers." Common people and others involved in the marketplace were usually overwhelmed by their interests and were incapable of disinterestedness. Yet of course they were not to be the leaders of the society. Although republicanism compared to monarchy rested on a magnanimous view of common people, it retained a traditional patrician bias in regard to officeholding. Many good whigs and republicans believed that important public offices, even including membership of grand juries, ought to be filled only with "the better sort because they are less liable to temptations, less fearful of the frowns of power, may reasonably be supposed of more improved capacities than those of an inferior station." People who had occupations, who needed to engage in the market, who worked with their hands, who were without a liberal education—such ungenteel or ordinary people could scarcely possess the enlightenment and disinterestedness to resist the temptations of power and stand above the haggling of the marketplace and act as impartial umpires.[27]

For many this disinterested leadership could only be located among the landed gentry whose income from the rents of tenants came to them, as Adam Smith said, without their exertion or direct involvement in the interests of the marketplace. Merchants, unlike the landed gentry, gained their profits in the workaday world of interests and were considered to be necessarily motivated by avarice rather than by virtue. "It seems as difficult to restrain a Merchant from striking at Gain, as to prevent the keen spaniel from springing at Game, that he has been bred to pursue." Even Smith believed that the interest of merchants and all who thought more "about the interest of their own particular branch of business, than about that of the society" was "always in some respects different from, and even opposite to, that of the public."[28]

Perhaps only a classical education that made "ancient manners familiar," as Richard Jackson once told Benjamin Franklin, could "produce a reconciliation between disinterestedness and commerce; a thing we often see, but almost always in men of a liberal education." Yet no matter how educated merchants might become, while they remained actively engaged in commerce, they could never quite acquire the character of genteel disinterestedness essential for full acceptance as political leaders. Lord George Germain expressed conventional wisdom in declaring that he "would not have men in a mercantile cast every day collecting themselves together and debating on political matters." Consequently, in most places those merchants active in their businesses who wanted to participate in politics had great difficulty justifying their ambitions. If they did hold office, they usually had to have wealth and leisure sufficient to avoid any day-to-day involvement in their businesses. Otherwise, they were apt to be criticized, as Sir Henry Moore, governor of New York, said of some merchants nominated to the council, for possessing "no other merit than having dealt well by their correspondents in trade and [being] utterly unfit for the great ends of government."[29]

Mechanics and others who worked with their hands were thought servile and totally absorbed in their narrow occupations and thus unqualified for disinterested public office. Indeed, the very term "occupation," by which everyone except gentlemen was designated, meant being occupied and having no leisure for public service. Even members of the liberal professions, if they were too dependent on their work as a source of income, were regarded as ill equipped for virtuous leadership. On the eve of the Revolution, Virginians debated in the newspapers as to whether or not lawyers practiced "a grovelling, mercenary trade." Although one critic conceded that lawyers constituted one of the "three genteel Professions," he argued that they were surely guilty of more "petit Larceny" than doctors and clergymen. James Madison's college friend William Bradford was defensive about his decision to become a lawyer. He knew that the behavior of most lawyers was "reproachable," but he argued that they were at least different from merchants. The sole pursuit of merchants was gain, and thus they were "much more likely to contract an inordinate desire of wealth than the lawyers, whose pursuit is as much after fame as Wealth." Madison, reluctant himself to choose a profession, was not convinced by his friend; but he did concede that the profession of law would at least allow Bradford to use the knowledge both of them had acquired at Princeton. A liberal education, he said, "is a sort of General Lover that wooes all the Muses and Graces."[30]

Eighteenth-century Englishmen were preoccupied with the moral character of their leaders precisely because leaders were the source of despotism. The very abilities that made patricians and gentry likely leaders also made them potential tyrants. "Men of great talents by nature and polisht by Art" were no doubt necessary for all government. But, said Nathanael Greene in a common reckoning, such accomplished men, especially if they had "a general Acquaintance with mankind," were as well "the most dangerous persons to be connected with unless"—and this qualification identified the crux of the whole republican tradition—"unless they steadily persevere in the practice of Virtue." Such men knew "the secret avenues to the human Heart and, having the power to make the worse appear the better," they had the capacity for ensnaring ordinary people in chains. "Ninety-nine parts out of one hundred of mankind, are ever inclined to live at peace, and cultivate a good understanding with each other." Only members of "the remaining small part"—those whose "considerable abilities" were "joined to an intriguing disposition"—were "the real authors, advisers, and perpetuators of wars, treasons, and those other violences, which have, in all ages, more or less disgraced the annals of man."[31]

Controlling and channeling the overweening passions of these extraordinary men—the aristocratic passions of avarice and ambition: "the Love of Power and the Love of Money," as Benjamin Franklin called them—seemed to many to be the central political problem of the age. Some thought that "ambition and avarice are springs of action so utterly opposite, that they never did or ever will unite in the same person." Others, however, were convinced not only that these two great passions "may subsist together in the same breast," but that when "united in View of the same object, they have in many minds the most violent Effects. Place before the Eyes of such Men a Post of Honour, that at the same time be a Place of Profit, and they will move Heaven and Earth to obtain it."[32]

For all those who claimed to speak for the interests and the good of the people, the crown and all other rulers with soaring passions were dangerous, and the people were always justified in their suspicion and jealousy of power. Precisely because rulers in government were thought to be men of extraordinary and frightening capacities—"like elephants in war," said one colonial minister—they had to be watched constantly.

Radical whigs turned "political jealousy" into a "necessary and laudable Passion." The people had to be suspicious of their rulers, for, as Henry Laurens said in 1765, a "malicious Villain acting behind the Curtain . . . could be reached only by suspicion." Assuming as they did that patterns of events were always the intended consequence of particular human designs, the enlightened men of the age were ready to see plots and conspiracies everywhere.[33]

But suspicion and jealousy, essential as they might be in protecting liberty in a monarchy, were not noble or praiseworthy emotions in themselves. They were in fact necessary evils to offset the soaring passions of ambition and desires for power expressed by rulers or great men. And therefore to the degree that the rulers became virtuous and republicanized, the people could relax their jealousy and suspicion and become open and trustful. Barriers could be erected, bills of rights established, contracts negotiated, charters written, institutions arranged and balanced, and the people allowed a share of participation in government; but ultimately the most enlightened of that enlightened age believed that the secret of good government and the protection of popular liberty lay in ensuring that good men—men of character and disinterestedness—wielded power. In the end there was no substitute for classical republican virtue in the society's rulers; and everyone on the political spectrum paid at least lip service to the need for it. But no one paid more attention to this need for virtue than did members of that generation of North American colonial leaders who came of age in the middle decades of the eighteenth century.

7. A Truncated Society

Classical republican values existed everywhere among educated people in the English-speaking world, but nowhere did they have deeper resonance than in the North American colonies. Nowhere had the republicanizing of monarchy gone further. The Americans did not have to invent republicanism in 1776; they only had to bring it to the surface. It was there all along. The revolutionaries shed monarchy and took up republicanism, as Jefferson put it, "with as much ease as would have attended their throwing off an old and putting on a new suit of clothes.'"

Because English culture was so republicanized, it was often difficult for the colonists to appreciate how radical their thinking was. When the colonists in the 1760s and 1770s were accused of fomenting rebellion and promoting republican principles, they were surprised and indignant. The spirit of republicanism, they said, the spirit of Milton, Needham, and Sidney, was "so far from being uncompatible with the English constitution, that it is the greatest glory of it." In resisting tyranny the colonists saw themselves acting only as good Englishmen should. "We boast of our freedom," Samuel Adams told his fellow Englishmen across the Atlantic in 1767, "and we have your example for it. We talk the language we have always heard you speak." It was true. Americans read the same literature, the same law books, the same histories as those read by the English in the mother country. Even tories admitted that whig and republican principles of government were so ingrained in British culture, "so often transcribed by one from another," that there was no longer any need of having those principles "retailed in this enlightened age."[2]

Despite the colonists' sense that they were only thinking as any good Englishmen would, they did draw from that British culture its most republican and whiggish strains. For they were in fact the most republican of people in the English-speaking world. Every visitor to the New World sensed it. All the republican peculiarities for which Englishmen were noted were magnified in the colonies and carried to excess. If Englishmen were known to be liberty-loving and unruly, then the colonists seemed absolutely licentious. The colonists lived in a monarchy and were monarchical subjects, but, as General Guy Carleton noted in 1768, the conditions of their society gave them "a strong bias to Republican Principles."[3]

First, many colonists had little reason to feel part of His Majesty's realm or to respect royalty. Many white foreign immigrants had no natural allegiance to a British king, and they often settled far from established authority in the colonies. Even many of the eighteenth-century migrants from the British Isles—Scotch-Irish and Irish—came with bitter grievances against the English government. They had been pushed about and persecuted by the English government and Anglo-Irish landlords for so long that they could not feel much loyalty to the English crown.

But even those English colonists who were proud of being Englishmen were not very good monarchists. Many New Englanders ritualistically recalled their seventeenth-century Puritan heritage of defiance to king and church; and many of them remained a stern, sober people, not much given to the hierarchies and displays of monarchy. Massachusetts was accused in 1740 of being still "a kind of commonwealth where the king is hardly a stadtholder.'' Everywhere in America, even in the southern colonies where attempts to emulate English ways were strongest, most colonists had little sense of royal majesty: the crown was too far away to make its presence felt. The colonists were apt to think of King George, as one wealthy colonial merchant reputedly did, as simply a good honest fellow with whom they might like to smoke a pipe. The crown's viceregents in the colonies—the royal governors—did little to enhance royal dignity. They were often without titles, wealth, or the accouterments of power, and they complained constantly that their meager incomes allowed them to live no better than ''a private gentleman.'' In the 1750s the North Carolina governor did not even have a permanent residence: he was reduced, as he grumbled, to renting ''a small House'' in New Bern ''without either garden or field to keep either horse or cow.''[4]

Royal authority operated much of the time on the surface of American life, masking the confused reality of decentralized institutions and localized authorities that made up the central governance of the colonies. The harmonious compromise between central and local authorities that had developed in Britain since 1688 was not duplicated in America. The crown always seemed to the colonists to be an extraneous overlaid power antagonistic to their local institutions, especially the provincial assemblies. In England, Parliament provided an arena for reconciling crown and local interests, but in the colonies it had no such function. In this respect colonial society resembled more the hodgepodge of local privileges and liberties that confronted the French monarchy in the eighteenth century than it did the relatively agreeable and integrated relationship between the crown and local authorities worked out in Great Britain. Consequently, the colonists had little understanding of state authority, of a united autonomous political entity that was completely sovereign and reached deep into the localities. And thus they were not prepared to accept that authority when after 1763 it tried to intrude into their lives.

Not only did royal authority have trouble making itself felt in the colonies, but it lacked the religious backbone that an established church offered royalty at home. In England the Anglican church was firmly in the hands of the crown and operated essentially as a bureaucratic arm of the crown. But not in America. ''No Bishop, no King,'' James I had once warned—a ''stupid saying,'' declared radical English whigs, that had ''formerly filled our Prisons with Dissenters, and chased many of them to *America*.'' The colonies had many dissenters and no bishop—

and had never had one—and consequently the presence of the Church of England was fundamentally flawed; and royal officials saw a latent (and sometimes not so latent) rebellious presbyterianism everywhere.[5]

If England had thirty different religions, then America had hundreds, and none of them was traditionally organized. "There was no hierarchy or degrees of Eminence among the Clergy," complained William Knox, an imperial bureaucrat with a half dozen years of firsthand experience in the colonies, "no distinctions of Bishops, Priests or Deacons, no Rule or Order, no Deans Chapters or Archdeacons. All were Priests and nothing more." Control of religious life never flowed from the top down, and personal patronage within any of the numerous religious groups was never strong. Even where the Church of England was most solidly established—in Virginia—it was dominated by the local vestries. Regardless of the circumstances of their ordination, clergymen everywhere tended to be appointed by their congregations and thus dependent on them. The disorders and confusions of American religious life by themselves made difficult the maintenance of a traditional monarchical society in the colonies.[6]

But the meager royal authority and the disordered religious life only expressed a deeper social confusion—the weakness and incompleteness of America's social hierarchy. Despite increased social stratification during the eighteenth century, American society remained remarkably shallow and stunted by contemporary English standards. All the topmost tiers of English society were missing in America. There were no dukes, no marquesses, no court, and nothing like the fabulous wealth of the English nobility. The scale of everything was different in the colonies. While Charles Carroll of Maryland, one of the wealthiest planters in the South, was earning what the colonists regarded as the huge sum of £1,800 a year, the Earl of Derby's vast estates were bringing in an annual income of over £40,000. George Washington's estate was thought to be earning in the 1770s only "£300 per an. Virginia currency," which put Washington, according to a visiting Englishman, "in point of rank only equal to the better sort of yeoman in England." Major merchants in American cities were worth between £25,000 and £50,000; in contrast, their counterparts in England were worth between £200,000 and £800,000. Thomas Hancock of Boston, one of the richest merchants in America, left an estate of nearly £100,000; yet this enormous colonial fortune was scarcely a third of the sum bequeathed in 1753 by a London merchant, Henry Lascalles. Hancock's house in Boston and William Byrd's Virginia mansion of Westover may have been expensive and elaborate structures for the colonies, but they were dwarfed by the magnificent palaces the English nobility built for themselves. Hancock's two-storied house, like most gentry homes in America, had only eight rooms; the Sackville family's palace, Knole in Kent, had 365. Very few of the colonists' great houses even had secondary staircases for the servants. Byrd's Westover was sixty-five feet in length, but this was scarcely a tenth of the size of the Marquess of Rockingham's house, Wentworth Woodhouse, which was longer than two football fields.[7]

Everywhere even the wealthiest of colonial gentry strained to imitate the best of English taste. The practice of plastering and painting the wood, brick, and fieldstones of their homes in order to resemble classically precise-cut masonry was symptomatic of their plight. By English standards the colonial aristocracy was a minor thing—at best composed of middling and lesser gentry only. Charles Chauncy of Massachusetts was not exaggerating by much when he said in 1766 that "there is scarce a man in any of the colonies, certainly there is not in the New England ones, that would be deemed worthy of the name of a rich man in Great Britain."[8]

Although real and substantial distinctions existed in colonial America, the colonial aristocracy was never as well established, never as wealthy, never as dominant as it would have liked. As strong as the colonial gentry may have been in some places and at some times, they never were able to duplicate the mutual protection and allegiance between superiors and inferiors that made the eighteenth-century English squirearchy relatively so secure. As pervasive as personal and kinship influence was in the colonies, gentry use of this influence in the economy, in religion, or in politics was never as powerful as it was in England. Militia officers were often selected by their companies, ministers were hired by their parishioners, and a remarkably large proportion of political leaders were popularly elected, sometimes by an extremely broad electorate.

The American aristocracy, such as it was, was not only weaker than its English counterpart; it also had a great deal of trouble maintaining both the desired classical independence and its freedom from the marketplace. Few members of the American gentry were able to live idly off the rents of tenants as the English landed aristocracy did. Some landowners in New York and in the South leased out their lands to tenants, but their position was never quite comparable to the English landed gentry. Landlords were not able to preempt the produce of their tenants, and their rental income was often unreliable. Usually they acted more as land speculators than as landlords, offering tenants very advantageous terms simply to open up and clear land that otherwise would remain as useless wilderness. New royal governors, thinking of the English experience, tried to build up large rent rolls, but none of them realized his expectations.[9]

America could not sustain the stable pattern of tenantry that lay at the heart of a traditional landed society, and thus that dependency that lay at the heart of monarchical society was undermined. The tenants often lived on land far removed from their landlords and were very poorly supervised. Many landlords had trouble not only in collecting rents but in preventing their tenants from selling their leases and moving on without paying their debts. Since tenantry was often regarded as simply a first step toward an independent freehold, mobility was high. The New York manor leases, which were usually for life, turned over on the average every ninth year. In a society where land was so widely available, most men preferred to secure their own land. In fact, said Cadwallader Colden, "the hopes of having land of their own & becoming independent of Landlords is what chiefly induces people into America." In 1747 a North Carolinian advised a gentleman who was about to purchase from afar a plantation in the Cape Fear region to come and see it before he bought it; "for if you should not like to live their, you cannot Rent it," even at the low rate of 1 percent interest. "The poorest people here if they have been any time in the country, makes shift to get Land of their own either by taking up or Buying." The truth was, as the English bureaucrat Knox put it, that "the relation between Landlord and Tenant could have no existence where every Man held by the same tenure." Even though some gentlemen had vastly greater wealth and land than others, they could not be aristocrats in the English manner: "their riches brought them little influence for if they parcelled out their Lands it was upon the same tenure as they held it."[10]

Consequently, it is not surprising, particularly in the years after mid-century, that New York landlords expected less and less filial affection from their tenants and more and more monetary payments. Fewer of the landlords were able or willing to ignore or burn their tenants' overdue debts, as Colonel Frederick Philipse and Sir William Johnson continued to do. More and more landlords wanted their rents, and those like Beverly Robinson who raised them at every opportunity were willing to evict tenants who could not pay. Yet every act of exploitation, every suggestion that only profit mattered, eroded further the paternalistic bonds tying superiors and inferiors together.[11]

Most colonial aristocrats were never able to dominate their localities to the extent that English aristocrats did. In England local aristocrats were the primary patrons and consumers of local merchandise and skills. Their country houses were the centers of consumption and employment in their communities. They spent fortunes on building and maintaining their estates, and their patronage kept dozens and sometimes hundreds of artisans, shopkeepers, and laborers in work. Walpole employed twenty-nine men and fifty women just to lay out and plant his gardens at Houghton in 1721. Landowners with mines on their estates could employ entire communities. In the colonies a few aristocrats did spend huge amounts of money in their localities and developed dependencies among the local artisans and laborers. John Hancock went through a fortune in his aristocratic attempts to patronize local labor. But Hancock's example was conspicuously unusual in a way it would not have been in England; most American gentry had neither the funds nor the ability to do what he did. The southern planters built and maintained country houses, but they relied on their slaves to supply them with most of their needs, from making hogsheads to caring for their gardens. Thus not only did the great planters' reliance on the labor of their own slaves prevent the growth of large middling groups of white artisans in the South, but their patronage and hence dominance of the communities beyond their plantations was correspondingly reduced. Everywhere in America aristocrats tended to import from abroad many of their accouterments—from carriages to furniture; and to the extent that they did, they weakened their influence among artisans and workmen where they lived.[12]

Of course, the great planters of the South did enjoy a considerable amount of leisure based on the labor of their slaves; and consequently they came closest in America to fitting the classical ideal of the free and independent gentleman. By the middle of the eighteenth century the ruling southern planters in the Chesapeake and in South Carolina had thoroughly absorbed the classical republican ideology of leadership and saw themselves fulfilling it, and to a remarkable extent they did. In Virginia about forty or so interrelated wealthy families dominated the society and practiced a republican stewardship that rivaled that of the English squirearchy—laboring tirelessly in the county courts, the parish vestries, the House of Burgesses, and other offices out of a deep sense of public responsibility. In South Carolina planters and planter-merchants likewise saw themselves as independent English country gentlemen. They built country houses in the swamps, traced their genealogies, attempted to found families, and worked hard to make their General Assembly live up to the republican image of being a repository of virtue. Perhaps nowhere else on the continent did so many wealthy individual leaders take so much pride in their scorn of party and connections and their promotion of classical republican values.[13]

Yet despite the impressive ways these southern planters controlled and stabilized their societies and lived up to the classical republican image they had of themselves, they were not as free and independent as they would have liked. Some planters kept taverns on the side, and many others were intimately concerned in the day-to-day management of their estates. Even with overseers and agents and dozens of slaves, few of the great planters could treat their estates as self-perpetuating patrimonies. Their overseers were not comparable to the stewards and estate managers of the English gentry; thus the planters, despite their aristocratic poses, were often very busy, commercially involved men. Their livelihoods were tied directly to the vicissitudes of international trade, and they had always had an uneasy sense of being dependent on the market to an extent that the English landed aristocracy, despite its commitment to enterprising projects and improvements, never really felt. Even the wealthiest and most established of planters were incapable of being absentee owners; and those like William Byrd and the younger Charles Carroll, who might have liked to spend their days in Europe, had to return home or lose the source of their wealth. "Our affairs," Carroll told his father in 1764, "absolutely require my residence in Maryland."[14]

The legal devices of entail and primogeniture that in England worked to perpetuate family estates intact through a prescribed line of heirs had a contrary effect in America: by limiting a father's discretion in disposing of the estate, such devices tended to risk the family property on the particular talents—or shortcomings—of an eldest son. By the eve of the Revolution the great planters of the Chesapeake realized with growing concern that their painstakingly built fortunes could be suddenly wiped out by the mistakes of their heirs. Robert Carter gave his son Robert Bladen the management and profits of his Billingsgate plantation—1,200 acres and forty slaves—and then in dismay watched him squander it all away in only three years. The Nelsons were not the only great family in Virginia to disappear through the indebtedness and waywardness of a single generation. William Byrd III had no head for business: he mortgaged his silver plate and 159 slaves and went through a fortune before committing suicide on New Year's Day 1777. Some of the planters saw with mounting fear the accumulated gains of their lives being dissipated by the reckless gambling and drinking of their heirs, who, as Landon Carter moaned, "play away and play it all away." "In a commercial nation," noted the sober young Carroll, "the glory of illustrious progenitors will not screen their needy posterity from obscurity and want." The aristocrats of America had a much keener consciousness of mobility, both up and down, than their English counterparts. The huge debts of the Virginia planters, warned Thomas Nelson on the eve of the Revolution, were "but Preludes to Vast Changes of property among us, that must soon take place."[5]

In the years after mid-century the Virginia planters became more and more concerned about the state of their society. Pressure from their British creditors forced them to hound each other for repayment of debts. Circumstances were compelling them to cut through the appearance of independent country gentry they had sought to maintain and to expose the raw commercial character of their lives. They discovered, as James Mercer did, that they were not as free from the day-to-day business world as they made out. When Mercer gave up his law practice in 1765, he found that his plantation could not support him. Many of the planters were living on the edge of bankruptcy, seriously overextended and spending beyond their means in an almost frantic effort to live up to the aristocratic image they had created of themselves. Lieutenant Governor Francis Fauquier thought that the rising indebtedness of the planters was due to their unwillingness to "quit any one Article of Luxury." By the eve of the Revolution many planters were voicing a growing sense of impending ruin. Nonimportation of British luxuries was welcomed in the 1760s and 1770s precisely because, as Washington pointed out, it gave the planters a pretext to cut back on their ostentation and display without injuring either their aristocratic honor or their credit. By 1776 many Chesapeake planters were ready to believe that republicanism and republican values would save their society. Still, despite all their difficulties the great southern planters at least approached the classical image of disinterested gentlemanly leadership; they knew it and made the most of it throughout their history.[6]

Elsewhere, even in other parts of the South, elites never even came close to the English model. Perhaps no ruling group in the eighteenth-century colonies was weaker and more vulnerable to challenge than that of North Carolina. The majority of the colonial assembly in 1730 who were distinguished enough to leave any personal records were only middling planters even by Virginia standards—owning less than ten slaves and five hundred acres each. Even the council was composed of men whose claim to gentility was very doubtful. Of the twenty members of the council in 1730 only two are known to have been university-educated. One Virginian called them a "company of pirates, vagabonds and footmen." Put together, their estates, it was said, "won't amount to £1500." The royal governors continually complained that North Carolina lacked men of wealth and standing. The "characters" of the high officials, said Governor Gabriel Johnston, "alone were sufficient to bring all Magistracy and Government into contempt and ridicule." Of course, many of the governors were no better. Johnston himself was criticized for being "a Schoolmaster and of mean and low descent."[7]

No place was as confused as North Carolina; but in the northern colonies gentry elites also had trouble living up to the classical republican model of leadership, and challenges to their authority were common. Although eighteenth-century society was much tighter and less porous than American mythology would have it, the topmost ranks of the social hierarchy certainly remained more permeable and open to entry from below than in the mother country. Claiming the rank of gentleman in America was easier. Men who prescribed a few potions or displayed a knowledge of law might pretend to be doctors or lawyers and thus assert their membership in one of the gentlemanly liberal professions. Even in a settled area of Pennsylvania, noted the Maryland doctor Alexander Hamilton, a "very rough spun, forward clownish blade, much addicted to swearing," could attempt "to pass for a gentleman." In New England, to the chagrin of young John Adams, farmers called themselves both yeomen and gentlemen at the same time. More than half of the company officers of the Massachusetts militia mobilized for the Seven Years' War identified themselves with manual occupations.[18]

Because, as Benjamin Franklin said, "common Tradesmen and Farmers" in America were "as intelligent as most Gentlemen from other Countries," these common men often expected to pass as gentlemen more easily than elsewhere. David Harry, who had once been a fellow apprentice with Franklin, set himself up as a master printer in Philadelphia. But, said Franklin, "he was very proud, dress'd like a Gentleman, liv'd expensively, . . . ran in debt, and neglected his Business, upon which all Business left him"; eventually Harry fled the country. Franklin himself discovered early in his life how easy it was for a commoner with the right sponsorship to mingle comfortably with gentlemen. When he and James Ralph boarded the ship to sail to England in 1724, they "were forc'd to take up with a Berth in the Steerage," since, "none on board knowing us, [we] were considered as ordinary Persons." But when Colonel John French, justice of the Delaware Supreme Court, came on board, recognized the nineteen-year-old Franklin, and paid him "great Respect," he and Ralph were immediately invited "by the other Gentlemen to come into the Cabin." Franklin, however, did not let the incident go to his head; he realized, as we have seen, that it was wiser to keep to his allotted rank and wait until he had acquired sufficient wealth to retire permanently from business before formally becoming a gentleman.[19]

Other colonists were not so punctilious as Franklin. Everywhere wealthy commoners, even those who still worked with their hands, sought to buy their way into gentlemanly status. Building a second home in the country, for example, was very much a sign of being a gentleman. By the 1770s eighty-two Philadelphians owned places clearly defined as "country seats" in Philadelphia County alone. Yet these "seats" were by no means comparable to the great country seats of the English aristocracy. They were not even suburban villas: they had assessed values ranging from £4 to £200, and only ten of them were worth more than £50. And this distinction of having a "seat" was spread very widely: the list of eighty-two owners included thirteen esquires, nine gentlemen, five doctors, twenty-two merchants, four widows, three shopkeepers, two innkeepers, and twenty-six artisans of one sort or another.[20]

In the northern port cities there were only a few "merchant princes"—such as the Drinkers and Whartons of Philadelphia or the Amorys and Boylstons of Boston—whose wealth and standing were sufficient to allow them to imitate comfortably the lesser gentry of England. But even these few merchant princes, rich and genteel as they might be, knew that they were not real aristocrats exempt from the interests and worries of trade. Certainly they were not as patrician in manner or as free from failure as their counterparts in the mother country. Even the wealthiest American merchants realized that they could not ignore their businesses and take grand tours and live as nobly as rich English merchants did. Most ordinary colonial merchants—perhaps 85 percent or more of the two or three hundred merchants in Philadelphia—were ensnared in such "a hardharted Iron-Fisted & inhospitable world," unable "to lay up such a Stock, as would maintain me without dayly labour," and thus could not even pretend to gentility. Most were in fact very new to wholesale trade, often having begun their careers as artisans, shopkeepers, or smugglers. As Lieutenant Governor Colden of New

York pointed out, most of them "suddenly rose from the lowest rank of the People to considerable fortunes." Whereas in England it took £3,000 to become a merchant, in colonial Philadelphia it took only £400; which is why many young Englishmen who lacked the resources to become wholesalers at home migrated to the colonies. But business in America was always chancy, and being a colonial merchant was always precarious; and one could as readily slide into bankruptcy as rise into merchant status. Perhaps as many as one in three colonial merchants failed. Becoming a merchant in the colonies was far easier but also far riskier than it was in the more developed ports of Great Britain.[21]

The relative primitiveness of colonial economic conditions aggravated the uncertainty of many of the merchants and reduced their influence. Whatever authority they claimed in their home port, it rarely extended very far into the countryside. Rather than dictating to the farmers of the region, merchants often found themselves dependent on them. They needed supplies to trade, and farmers, many of whom were not regularly producing for the market, often lacked "surpluses" to sell. Not only were the merchants' sources of supply insecure; their markets were too. Consequently, even the most wealthy merchants usually ended up being only middlemen in extraordinarily complicated networks of exchanges. As such, they rarely could specialize; most merchants were forced to engage in a wide variety of tasks, being exporters, importers, wholesalers, retailers, manufacturers, insurance underwriters, shipbuilders, or privateersmen at one time or another. Such different roles blurred their special reputation as "merchants"—a term supposedly confined to those involved in overseas wholesale trade—and further weakened their status and thus their authority in their communities. Being merchants under such adverse circumstances no doubt bred peculiarly flexible and risk-taking personalities, but such aggressive and hustling arrivistes rarely possessed a patrician interest in public service. Many were apt to share Charles Pettit's view that politics was not worth the time and trouble it demanded, "unless it should eventually throw business in my hands by which I may obtain a profit." Consequently, most active merchants did not serve in government.[22]

Of course, in the northern colonies there were numbers of educated well-connected professional men or gentlemen of independent fortune who were capable of living up to the classical ideals of political leadership that dominated eighteenth-century culture. But there were, it seemed, never enough of these to go around. As a result, more than one established gentleman complained of the extent to which the colonial assemblies contained too many members who were not gentlemen in any sense, much less gentlemen educated in a liberal classical mode. The legislatures contained too many retailers of "Rum and Small Beer" from "poor obscure" country towns "remote from all Business"; or too many "plain, illiterate husbandmen, whose views seldom extended farther than to the regulation of highways, the destruction of wolves, wildcats and foxes, and the advancement of the other little interests of the particular counties they were chosen to represent." Even members of the councils—the colonial counterparts to the English House of Lords—were sometimes criticized by the governors for being men in "necessitous circumstances" or of "no estate in the country and much in debt." Or when they did have sufficient wealth, too often the councillors absented themselves from attendance because, as one New Jersey councillor put it, "it would too much interfere with my Interests & Business." The long and short of it was, as Governor Lewis Morris of New Jersey complained to the Board of Trade in 1745, that many wealthy individuals regarded service on the council as "a sort of tax on them to serve the publick at their owne Expense besides neglect of their business."[23]

More than anything else, it was this weakness of the colonial aristocracy—its relative lack of gentility, its openness to entry, its inability to live up to the classical image of political leadership, and its susceptibility to challenge—that accounts for the instability and competitive factiousness of colonial politics. Wherever the ruling families of a colony were entrenched—readily identifiable and beyond the resentment and rivalry of others—as in eighteenth-century Virginia and New Hampshire, then the politics were stable and factionalism was at a minimum. The strength or weakness of royal authority in any particular colony had almost nothing to do with determining this stability. In New Hampshire royal authority was extraordinarily strong, stronger than in any other colony. But this authority was only a consequence of the power exercised by a small and well-defined elite dominated by the royal governor, Benning Wentworth. By controlling the timber and naval stores trade, which was practically the sole source of great wealth in the colony, Wentworth was able for twenty-five years to manipulate the mercantile leaders of Portsmouth, virtually the only aristocracy the colony possessed, and to maintain peace within the colony. Yet in Virginia, whose politics were likewise remarkably stable, royal authority was very weak—so weak, in fact, that the royal governors virtually abandoned responsibility for ruling the colony to the forty or so aristocratic families that kept Virginia politics relatively calm for nearly a half century.

They were able to do so because they were a remarkably homogeneous and uncontested ruling group—perhaps the only colonial aristocracy whose wealth and influence approached that of the eighteenth-century English aristocracy.[24]

Elsewhere in the colonies—wherever the aristocracies or would-be aristocracies were weak and divided—politics were contentious and factious, filled with bitter clashes among the prominent individuals and families of each colony for the rewards and privileges of government. Although most colonists naturally came to believe that the intrusive presence of British royal authority and the imperial relationship in general were the source of America's political instability and factionalism, they were wrong. The problems of American politics were at bottom neither imperial nor constitutional but social; the crown was virtually irrelevant to the society's basic contentiousness. In the tiny corporate colony of Rhode Island royal authority was weaker than anywhere else; yet Rhode Island was the most faction-ridden colony of all. Only after the Revolution would some Americans come to appreciate the true nature of their social reality.

But it was not just the top of the English hierarchy that was missing or confused in America; the bottom layer—the great mass of destitute people that still burdened most European societies—was also lacking. Severe famine remained a threat to parts of Europe well into the eighteenth century, and although England itself had been free of famine since the seventeenth century, it still had plenty of poor. Nowhere in America was there anything comparable to the vile and violent slums of London—that wretched gin-soaked world immortalized by Hogarth. Although by the mid-eighteenth century the numbers of poor were increasing in the urban ports of Boston, New York, and Philadelphia, there was not, Americans realized, "the least danger of starving amongst us." Many of the American poor, especially those in an entrepôt like Philadelphia, were transients, people on their way to someplace else. Economic downturns could occasionally allow the proportion of poor in the colonies to range as high as 10 percent; but this still did not begin to compare with the poor of Hanoverian England, where as much as half the population was regularly or at least occasionally dependent on charity for subsistence. England, of course, had nothing like the nearly half million blacks held by the colonists in hereditary bondage. But it had huge proportions of marginal tenants and rural wage laborers; indeed, the bulk of its population was landless. The independent English yeoman landowner was a dream of the past in the mother country. By the eve of the Revolution three-quarters of English farmland was owned by noble and gentry landlords who leased their estates to tenants of one sort or another. Indeed, four hundred great families owned a fifth of all the land in England.[25]

By contrast, most American farmers owned their own land ("We are Lords of our own little but sufficient Estates"). The radical importance of this landownership in an English-speaking world dominated by rent-paying tenants and leaseholders cannot be exaggerated: even before the Revolution it gave Americans a sense of their egalitarian exceptionalism. The "Level" in New Jersey society that Philip Fithian thought so admirable arose "from the very great division of the lands in that Province, and consequently from the near approach to an equality of Wealth amongst the Inhabitants." Connecticut was no different, as even a spiteful Anglican victim of the Revolution, Samuel Peters, admitted. "In no part of the world," Peters wrote in his *General History of Connecticut*, "are *les petits* and *les grands* so much upon a par as here, where none of the people are destitute of the conveniences of life and the spirit of independence." Two-thirds of the white colonial population owned land, compared with only one-fifth of the English population. There were propertyless in America (maybe in some places as many as 30 percent of the adult males), but they tended to be either recent immigrants or young men awaiting their inheritance or an opportunity to move and acquire land. In no case was the overall situation of property-owning in America comparable to that of England, where more than 60 percent of the population owned no property of any kind. Freehold tenure in America was especially widespread, and freehold tenure, said William Knox bluntly, "excluded all ideas of subordination and dependence."[26]

This description of the truncated nature of American society is familiar. Both eighteenth-century observers and historians ever since have repeatedly commented on the egalitarian character of colonial society. America, it seemed, was primed for republicanism. It had no oppressive established church, no titled nobility, no great distinctions of wealth, and no generality of people sunk in indolence and poverty. A society that boasted that "almost every man is a freeholder" was presumably a society ideally suited for republicanism.[27]

Yet paradoxically this latently republican society was at the same time manifestly monarchical. American society was riddled with contradictions. It was still remarkably underdeveloped commercially compared with the mother country, it was still largely agricultural and rural, and it possessed as yet few modern alternatives to traditional personal and kinship relations to tie itself together—fewer certainly than the economically advanced society of England. Not only were the legal dependencies of white servitude and black slavery harsher and more conspicuous in the colonies than in England, but the relative backwardness of the colonists' society and economy meant that Americans had fewer opportunities than Englishmen to substitute impersonal market exchanges and a cash nexus for older personal and patriarchal connections; and thus they were more apt than Englishmen to continue to think of social relationships in familial and personal terms—as expressions of the household rather than of a market society. Colonial society was therefore a society in tension, torn between contradictory monarchical and republican tendencies. It had many exaggerated expectations of subjection and dependency but at the same time lacked sufficient personal influence and patronage power to fulfill these expectations. Consequently, the connectedness of colonial society—its capacity to bind one person to another—was exceedingly fragile and vulnerable to challenge.

8. Loosening the Bands of Society

Perhaps in time this truncated republicanized monarchical society might have matured and become more hierarchical. Already by mid-century colonial society in some areas was more stratified than it had been, and social distinctions seemed to be hardening. The rich were getting richer and the poor were growing in number. Despite pockets of instability in some areas and the spread of republican values, the ruling gentry in most colonies were more visible, interconnected, and conscious of their identity than ever before.[1]

Yet any resemblance between colonial society and that of the mother country remained superficial and partial; the hierarchies and patronage connections of American society were brittle; and little in the society had much chance to solidify. For just at the moment when some parts of American society seemed to be becoming more like England's, powerful forces were accelerating and changing everything.

These basic forces were the most important sources of the late-eighteenth-century democratic revolution. Of course, they were not unique to America; they were Western-wide. But because society in the New World was already more republican, more shallow, and more fragile, there the effects of these forces seemed magnified and overdrawn. All Europe experienced a democratic revolution in the late eighteenth century, but in America this democratic revolution was carried further than elsewhere. Extraordinary demographic and economic developments, moving as never before, reshaped the contours of the society— challenging and further eroding the older monarchical world of dependent paternal and personal relations.

Most Americans, like most Europeans, scarcely grasped the immensity of the fundamental forces at work in the Western world. They were, of course, conscious of changes and disruptions in the customs of their lives. Yet, habituated as they were to monarchical hierarchy and desirous of stability and continuity, most were not disposed to perceive, much less to understand, the structural shifts taking place in their society. In the subsequent decades, they, like the Europeans, struggled to comprehend what was happening to them, and they sought through a variety of ways to resolve the problems and anxieties created by their newly detached and independent situations. The history of America in the decades between the 1740s and the 1820s is the story of these various resolutions. The imperial crisis with Great Britain and the American Revolution itself were simply clarifying incidents in this larger story of America's democratic revolution.

The basic fact of early American history was the growth and movement of people. From the beginning of the eighteenth century, if not earlier, the colonial population had been virtually exploding; in fact, through their high birthrates and low mortality rates the North American colonists were multiplying more rapidly than any other people in the Western world. Between 1750 and 1770 they grew from one million to over two million and between 1770 and 1790 from two to four million, doubling every twenty years as they had for several generations.

Moreover, this growth was not entirely natural. During these same middle decades of the eighteenth century immigrants poured into the New World by the tens of thousands—Englishmen, Scots, and Protestant Irish from the British Isles and Germans from the Rhine Valley. Between 1764 and 1776 alone, 125,000 entered the American colonies from the home islands. From the colonial ports, particularly Philadelphia, these new migrants from the British Isles and Europe now combined with the swelling numbers of uprooted colonists to spread themselves in all directions over the eastern half of the continent.[2]

For nearly a century and a half the colonists had been confined to a several-hundred-mile-wide strip along the Atlantic coast. Now in the middle decades of the eighteenth century they began to feel pressed by the growing numbers of people. Overcultivated soil in the East was becoming depleted. Older towns, especially in New England, now seemed crowded, and greater numbers of young men were coming of age without their fathers' having land to give them. The political system was unable to absorb the increasing numbers of ambitious men. Educated, aspiring young men like William Hooper of Boston and Hugh Henry Brackenridge of Philadelphia set out for distant frontiers in North Carolina and western Pennsylvania because there was "no room" for them in their native cities. Expansionist urges among the colonists were suddenly intensified. Men dreamed of landed empires in the West, founded land companies, requested and often received grandiose grants of land from colonial and imperial authorities, and threatened the French in the Ohio Valley and Indians up and down the continent.[3]

People moved as never before—from village to village, from colony to colony, over distances of ten, a hundred, even a thousand miles. The movement was neither smooth nor orderly, nor was it directed simply into empty or sparsely settled spaces. New people poured into settled areas as others moved out, and some towns and counties long established received as many people as they sent away. Thousands upon thousands of settlers swept into western Pennsylvania and, "like the goths and Vandals of old," said William Byrd, swarmed south into the Carolinas along routes on both sides of Virginia's Blue Ridge. Along these roads strings of small towns—from York, Pennsylvania, to Camden, South Carolina—quickly developed to service the migrants and to distribute their produce to distant markets. Others, particularly dispossessed Scottish Highlanders, came to the Carolinas directly by sea.[4]

The growth of settlement was phenomenal. In Pennsylvania, twenty-nine new localities were created between 1756 and 1765—more in a single decade than in the entire previous three-quarters of a century of settlement. Between 1750 and 1775 North Carolina increased its population sixfold to emerge from insignificance and become the fourth-largest colony. "There is," wrote one commentator without exaggeration in 1767, "scarce any history, either ancient or modern, which affords an account of such a rapid and sudden increase of inhabitants in a back country, as that of North Carolina." Even tiny Georgia grew from 2,300 in 1751 to 33,000 by 1773.[5]

With the British conquest of the French in 1759 and the coming of peace in 1763 the colonists at last seemed poised to take advantage of the half billion acres of newly acquired territory in the interior between the Appalachians and the Mississippi. Immediately after General James Wolfe's victory at Quebec in 1759, speculators and settlers moved into the area around Lake Champlain and westward along the Mohawk into central New York. In the ten years between 1761 and 1771 New York's population more than doubled, from 80,000 to over 168,000. By the early 1760s hunters and explorers like Daniel Boone were beginning to open up paths westward through the Appalachians. Settlers, mostly small farmers, soon followed. Some moved southward to the valley of the Holston and the headwaters of the Cumberland and Tennessee rivers, and others spread northward into the Ohio Valley and the Kentucky basin. Some drifted down the Ohio and Mississippi rivers to join over-land migrants from the southern colonies in the new British province of West Florida, and thus completed a huge encirclement of the new west-ern territory.[6]

By the middle decades of the eighteenth century even staid New England stirred with movement. Some people circulated only from town to town, going from inland communities to the seaports or from the seaports to the interior—always in search of new opportunities and se-curity. Boston did not grow in population but many of its faces changed yearly. Beyond the eastern localities growing numbers of new towns sprang up. Between 1741 and 1780 90 percent of all new settlements in Massachusetts were founded in the counties west of Worcester. Many New England farmers gave up looking for opportunities within the es-tablished colonies of the region and set out for new and distant places, even to the very edges of the recently expanded British empire. Mas-sachusetts and Connecticut colonists not only trekked to northern New England and Nova Scotia but began moving to areas as far away as the Susquehanna in Pennsylvania and the lower Mississippi. Indeed, the largest single addition to the population of West Florida came from the settlement of four hundred families from Connecticut in 1773-74. So massive was the the migration of Connecticut farmers to the Wyoming Valley in Pennsylvania that Connecticut attempted in 1769 to extend its jurisdiction over these Pennsylvanian settlements and in 1774 to annex them as part of one of its counties; the inevitable consequence was a nasty war between the two colonies. Between 1760 and 1776 some twenty thousand people from southern New England moved up the Connecticut River into New Hampshire and what would soon become Vermont. In that same period migrants from Massachusetts streamed into Maine and founded ninety-four towns. In all, during the years between 1760 and 1776, 264 new towns were established in northern New England.[7]

More colonists needed land and suddenly in 1763 more land was available. On the frontier—in northern New England and New York, in western Pennsylvania and Virginia, and in the backcountry of the Carolinas—land remained generally cheap and accessible. But of course the more people wanted it, the more prices rose. In some desirable spots land prices skyrocketed: in the bustling, growing entrepôt of Staunton, Virginia, four town lots purchased for £10 in 1775 sold for £100 five years later. Within a decade or so these same town lots were selling for thousands of pounds. Land in the upper Shenandoah Valley in the period 1745-54 was bought and resold at anywhere from three to ten times its original price. Americans had often bought and sold land before but never on this scale.[8]

Speculative land fever seemed to infect all levels of the society. While someone like Ezra Stiles, minister at Newport, Rhode Island, and later president of Yale, speculated in small shares of land in places all over New England, Pennsylvania, and New York, more influential figures like Benjamin Franklin concocted gargantuan schemes involving millions of acres in the vast unsettled terrain of the West. Even small farmers bought and sold their land at handsome profits and, to the surprise of European visitors, prided themselves on how many plantations they had successively owned. Family farms were now thought of less as patrimonies and more as commodities. With such movement of people and such buying and selling of land, any traditional sense of community became increasingly difficult to maintain. Each move made family and social ties more tenuous, the roots more shallow. The colonists, declared one astonished British official, were moving "as their avidity and restlessness incite them. They acquire no attachment to Place: but wandering about Seems engrafted in their Nature; and it is weakness incident to it that they Should forever imagine the Lands further off, are Still better than those upon which they are already Settled."[9]

The effects of this increase and movement of people were momentous. The population outran the society's political institutions, and most of the small and exclusive colonial governments remained unresponsive to the powerful forces at work. In many of the colonies, in the middle colonies especially, representation in the legislatures did not come close to keeping up with the expansion of population. In 1730, for example, the New York assembly had one representative for 320 adult white males; by 1770 this ratio had jumped to one for 1,065. The Pennsylvania assembly was even worse: one representative to 336 white adult males in 1730 became one representative to 1,301 white adult males by 1770. On the eve of the Revolution, Pennsylvania, with a population of 250,000, had an assembly of only thirty-six members. Although such disproportionate representation was common enough to Britain (the House of Commons was a hodgepodge of inequalities and anomalies), the colonists were historically used to more direct and equal representation; and their small clublike assemblies became more and more of a grievance.[10]

The growth and movement of people strained and broke apart households, churches, and neighborhoods. Young men particularly became more autonomous and more independent of paternal and patronage relationships. Families necessarily became less involved with the larger society, and extended lines of kinship frayed and snapped. Children left their aged parents in increasing numbers to "go off among strangers," as one mother lamented. "Oh how are my children disperst over the face of the earth" became the refrain of countless American parents in the coming years. Continual migration broke apart and scattered families. Although the Preston, Campbell, and Breckenridge families had settled on Beverley Manor in the upper Shenandoah Valley only in the 1740s, within a few decades their members were spread all over southwestern Virginia and as far south as the Holston River. Each move made the next one easier; even someone as established as William Preston, who rose to become a justice of the peace, county officeholder, and member of the House of Burgesses, uprooted and replanted himself and his family three times in his lifetime, excited by the desire to sell high in one place and buy cheap in another.[11]

The increased availability of land opened up opportunities for debtors, insolvents, and others to escape their dependencies. Delinquent and insolvent tax reports of Augusta County, Virginia, show emigrants heading for various destinations, many further west into Kentucky, some to other parts of Virginia, and still others into Pennsylvania, Georgia, and Tennessee. The numbers of transients drifting from village to village, from job to job, increased dramatically. Many of these people made their way into the tiny colonial cities that were ill equipped to handle them. By 1772 in Philadelphia the percentage of poor had increased to eight times what it had been twenty years earlier, and almshouses were being constructed and filled in astonishing numbers. Everywhere older hierarchies were broken apart and traditional paternalistic ties were severed.[12]

In New England the multiplication of "idle and indigent" persons required towns to build workhouses for the poor, and in 1750 Massachusetts for the first time began regulating these "houses of industry." By 1760 the numbers of transients and wandering poor in some counties of New England had doubled or even tripled over what they had been a decade earlier. Never before had there been so many men and women living in places where they had not been born. By the end of the century even Providence, Rhode Island, with a population of only five thousand, was thought to have "a great many strangers always here."[3]

All of this movement in New England put unbearable pressure on the region's old warning-out laws. These laws had been part of the older culture of paternal dependency in which everyone was supposed to belong somewhere. If vagrants stayed in a town for a given period—three months in Connecticut and New Hampshire, one year in Massachusetts—they were then considered members of the community, which became responsible for their welfare. Warning-out was designed to absolve the community of this responsibility: men and women warned out could not claim legal inhabitancy. From mid-century the numbers of persons formally warned out in this way by various towns increased remarkably, so much so that town clerks began making lists of those warned out instead of writing separate warrants for each one. By the late 1760s Massachusetts and Connecticut began shifting responsibility for identifying transients from the communities to the individual transients themselves. In 1771 the movement of people became so much greater that Connecticut and New Hampshire could no longer maintain their short three-month period for legal residency; they extended it to one year and brought their laws into line with Massachusetts. Increasing numbers of migrants put pressure on the whole archaic system. By the 1790s New Englanders were at last willing to acknowledge the fact of population movement, and they finally abandoned the old warning-out laws. Thereafter, citizens were free to migrate from town to town, at least within their respective states, without being subjected to warnings or exclusions.[4]

In some places people moved so rapidly and in such numbers that society as people had known it was not easily re-created. Hierarchies that gradually emerged out of raw frontier areas were necessarily jerry-built and precarious. Although in 1733 William Byrd had thought that Southside Virginia was "quite out of Christendom," by 1746 the region was sufficiently filled with swarming migrants that a new county, Lunenburg, had to be carved out of it. Most of the early settlers, comprising 650 households scattered over the five thousand square miles of the county, were subsistence farmers with small landholdings; 80 percent of the households had no slaves. In such a raw society distinctions were hard to come by, and those who sought to rule had difficulty sustaining their authority. Most of the county's original twelve justices were little wealthier than the people they ruled; five of them did not own any slaves. During the first decades of the county's existence the turnover of the justices was very high: thirty-nine different men moved in and out of the twelve seats of the court. The church was no more stable. In the more settled counties of Tidewater Virginia, the justices of the court and vestrymen of the parish tended to be the same men, but in Lunenburg in the early years this was not the case: no gentlemen were distinctive enough to monopolize these positions of authority. It was not until 1759 that the county had a reputable minister who stayed for a reasonable length of time. Over a dozen years after the county's formation this minister still found large numbers of people who "had never, or seldom been at Church since they were Baptized."[5]

Although in subsequent decades Lunenburg would develop something of a social hierarchy and become reasonably civilized—by 1760, for example, claims for wolf bounties had become rare—continued immigration into the area kept this backcountry society from matching the stability of the older Tidewater counties. Thus its social distinctions remained tenuous, its politics turbulent, and its structures of authority continually susceptible to challenge. Its gentry erected no elegant brick mansions like those in the Tidewater; small frame houses painted white were the best they could do. Its leaders were quick to swear, drink, and fight and were scarcely gentlemen at all. Robert Munford, who knew the area well, drew the outrageous characters of his play *The Candidates* from personal experience. In Southside Virginia there actually existed parvenu gentlemen who promised the voters anything, magistrates who were habitually drunk, and candidates who stripped off their shirts and prepared to wrestle their way into the House of Burgesses.[6]

In some areas, even the barest elements of civilized society were hard to acquire. Orange County, North Carolina, was one of the fastest-growing areas in the colonies; yet by 1758, six years after its organization, William Few found "no schools, no churches or parson, or doctors or lawyers; no stores, grocers or taverns, nor . . . during the first two years any officer, ecclesiastical, civil or military, except a justice of the peace, a constable, and two or three itinerant preachers."[7] Conditions in the South Carolina backcountry were even worse. Thousands of the new immigrants in the 1760s, most of whom were Scotch-Irish, seemed to have no semblance of a society at all, and settlers lived in virtual isolation from one another.

They lived like "Savages," moaned Charles Woodmason, that harried and headstrong itinerant Anglican minister—a character out of a

Fielding novel if ever there was one—who has left us with an unforget-
table picture of these early Carolina settlers. Every day of his "travels"
during the late 1760s "in the Wild Woods of America" astonished
Woodmason and left him feeling harassed and victimized. There he
was: "Destitute often of the Necessaries of Life—Sometimes starved—
Often famished—Exposed to the burning Sun and scorching Sands—
Obliged to fight his Way thro' Banditti, profligates, Reprobates, and
the vilest Scum of Mankind on the one hand, and of the numerous
Sectaries pregnant in these Countries, on the other—With few Friends,
and few Assistants—and surmounting Difficulties, and braving Dangers, that ev'ry Clergyman that ever entered this Province shrunked
even at the thoughts of."[18]

He was bringing the Anglican religion to "this Wild Country,"
when it really needed all the other basic elements of civilization as well.
He had never seen people with such "abandon'd Morals and profligate
Principles—Rude—Ignorant—Void of Manners, Education or Good
Breeding." There were no institutions at all—no courts, no schools, no
churches, and very few gentlemen or even literate persons. The people
lived "like Hogs" in open cabins with "little or no Bedding, or anything
to cover them." They had multitudes of children: "There's not a Cab-
bin but has 10 or 12 Young Children in it—When the Boys are 18 and
the Girls 14 they marry—so that in many Cabbins You will see 10 or 15
Children. Children and Grand Children of one size—and the mother
looking as Young as the Daughter." But because of the lack of ministers
many did not marry and thus lived "in Concubinage—swopping their
Wives as Cattel, and living in a state of Nature, more irregularly and
unchastely than the Indians." The people seemed lazy; many lived "by
Hunting and the killing of Deer." Most of the time they lolled around,
often drunk, with no shoes or stockings and half clothed, with the women
wearing only a short shift and petticoat. ("The Indians are better
Cloathed and Lodged.") They had no shame, "for Nakedness is counted
as Nothing—as they sleep altogether in Common in one Room, and
shift and dress openly without ceremony." Woodmason could not stom-
ach their food, "all the Cookery of these People being exceedingly filthy,
and most execrable." So in his travels, he carried everything with him,
"heavy loaded like a trooper. If I did not, I should starve. . . . In many
places they have nought but a Gourd to drink out of Not a Plate Knife
or Spoon, or Glass, Cup or any thing." They lacked, in other words,
the barest accouterments of civilized living. But mainly the people lacked
religion, at least Woodmason's religion. He had trouble raising com-

municants for his services. When he did get a crowd, "out of Curiosity not Devotion," the people insulted and scoffed at him, telling him one time that "they wanted no D——d Black Gown Sons of Bitches among them." At other times they set their dogs barking during his service, or got drunk "according to Custom," or went to "firing, hooping, and hallowing like Indians." "Who but an Heart of Oak," Woodmason told himself, "could bear up Firm against such Torrents of Malice, Bigotry, and Impudence!" He bore it all, with Christian compassion and with "the Contempt and Derision befitting a Gentleman."[19]

It was mainly as a gentleman that Woodmason framed the scenes of human degradation he was witnessing. Several times he wondered what cultivated Englishmen would think of these backcountry Carolinians. "How would the Polite People of London stare." Yet this country, said Woodmason, was not a "place I would wish any Gentleman to travel, or settle." There was "no genteel or Polite Person" in the area, not even "one literate, or travel'd Person—No ingenious Mind—None of any Capacity." "How hard the Lot of any Gentleman in this Part of the World." Here was human existence in the raw—without culture.[20]

Woodmason referred time and again to a state of nature and to a comparison with the Indians. This Carolina backcountry, he could see, was a formless world starting anew. "All this must be born with at the beginning of Things" and until the country could be "reduc'd to some Form." It was not that people were too scattered for social living. Quite the contrary: although many parts of the country were "newly settled . . . the People are already together as thick as in England." These frontier people simply seemed to lack normal social relationships and the ordinary attributes of civilization. They had no benevolence, no feeling for one another. "Tis the fashion of these People to abandon all Persons when sick, instead of visiting them—So that a Stranger who had no Relatives or Connexions, is in a most Terrible Situation." Society had come apart, and nothing could bring it together. For the sociable eighteenth century, this was the ultimate horror.[21]

The South Carolina backcountry was the extreme; perhaps Woodmason exaggerated, for it did not happen like this everywhere. But everywhere in the colonies the sudden increase and movement of people in the middle decades of the eighteenth century shattered traditional monarchical relationships that were often not strong to begin with. People were freed from customary connections and made independent in new, unexpected ways. This demographic explosion, this gigantic movement of people, was the most basic and the most liberating force working on American society during the latter half of the eighteenth century, and it would remain so for at least another century after that. But it was not the only dynamic at work.

Coupled with this demographic expansion—and nearly equal a force in unsettling the society—were the spectacular changes taking place in the American economy. Exports and imports began rapidly rising in the 1740s and 1750s. Higher prices and increased demand for foodstuffs to feed the expanding populations of the Atlantic world began enticing more and more American farmers into producing for distant markets. Even Chesapeake planters, both large and small, began shifting from tobacco to grain production. Between 1760 and 1770 Virginia's exports of corn to the West Indies increased ninefold, its exports of wheat to Southern Europe, sevenfold. Its exports of flour to all destinations boomed from 15 tons to 2,591 tons. By the eve of the Revolution old Charles Carroll had seen America nearly become "the granary of Europe." No wonder Thomas Paine in 1776 was so confident of the future of American commerce: America "will always have a market," he wryly noted, "while eating is the custom of Europe."[22]

Yet while these export and import statistics provide the best measures we have of economic growth in the period, even they can scarcely convey the magnitude of what was happening. Colonial America was so economically backward, so primitive compared with Great Britain, that the effects of this sudden commercialization were exaggerated. They became both more exhilarating and more alarming. The rising demand in the Atlantic world for wheat and other foodstuffs set off chain reactions throughout the colonies. Networks of towns abruptly emerged to move the produce to the market, and hosts of new people, from wagoners to innkeepers, appeared to serve the towns. The nature of tobacco culture and its marketing had long inhibited the development of towns and marketing centers in the southern colonies; but with the shift in the upper South to grain production, strings of communities reaching deep into the hinterland now arose. Almost overnight the ports of Baltimore, Norfolk, and Alexandria grew up to distribute this swelling commerce within the Atlantic world. In the decade or so before the Revolution, Norfolk more than doubled in size to become the fifth-largest city in British North America.[23]

Almost everywhere in the colonies, but particularly in the northern and middle colonies, growing numbers of small farmers, many for the first time in their lives, were drawn into producing "surpluses" for the market. Supplying the armies that fought the French at mid-century had already helped to incite many farmers into expanded sales of provisions. But an even more important stimulus for increasing the productivity of farmers than new markets was the growing opportunities they had for consumption. The prospect of raising their standard of living and enlarging their purchase of "luxury" goods spurred farmers to work harder and produce more and more "surpluses." Higher incomes and rising expectations of ordinary people represented the beginnings of a revolution in traditional habits of consumption. Common people now had the financial ability to purchase "luxury" goods that previously had been the preserve of the gentry—from tea and tea sets to silk handkerchiefs and feather mattresses.[24]

But it was not just increased purchasing power among ordinary people that caused this consumer revolution; it was the weakness of the social hierarchy and the social emulation this encouraged. In England it was already clear that efforts by inferiors to imitate the dress and other accouterments of their superiors was a driving force behind "the birth of a consumer society." A society like England's that had, as one Englishman put it, a "gradual and easy transition from rank to rank" was bound to encourage emulative spending. If the purchase of a carriage or a Staffordshire tea set was all it took to move up a notch in the social hierarchy, then working harder in order to acquire such an item became worthwhile.[25]

How much more worthwhile was such emulative consumption in colonial America, where the distinctions of rank were even more blurred than they were in England. Already it seemed evident to observers that Americans were even more excited about emulative consumption than people in the mother country. All the "common people" in the colonies seemed "eager to make a show much above what they do in England." After all, when the ranks were squeezed together it did not take much for a person to pass upward from one to another. "In a country like this, where property is so equably divided, every one will be disposed to rival his neighbour in goodness of dress, sumptiousnes of furniture, etc." The result was to put people in "one continued Race; in which everyone is endeavoring to distance all behind him, and to overtake or pass by, all before him; every one flying from his Inferiors in Pursuit of his Superiors, who fly from him with equal Alacrity." Thus in America

every tradesman is a Merchant, every Merchant is a Gentleman, and every Gentleman one of the Noblesse. We are a Country of Gentry,

Populous generosorum: We have no such thing as a common People among us: Between Vanity and Fashion, the Species is utterly destroyed.[26]

These were the complaints of social conservatives alarmed by this conspicuous consumption and the social disorder it engendered. Clergymen and gentry spoke out against the evils of "luxury" and invoked conventional republican messages along with traditional Puritan jeremiads to extol probity and simplicity and warn of the dangers of too much wealth and riches. They knew that philosophers like Francis Hutcheson had urged high duties to be placed on imported luxuries just "so that they may never be used by the lower and more numerous orders of people, whose consumption would be far greater than those of the few who are wealthy." Common people who were tempted by refinement and extravagance, who spent too much on luxuries, were supposed to lose their incentive to work and become idle and dissolute. On the eve of the Revolution some colonists even proposed sumptuary laws in order to coerce people into living within their rank.[27]

Others, however, found in these changes in consumption and productivity the source of new ideas. Both Bernard Mandeville and later David Hume argued that, far from being an unrelieved vice, as the severe republican moralists would have it, luxury and the desires of ordinary people to acquire the goods and trappings of fashion actually stimulated manufacturing and industriousness, and helped to develop a middling group in the society standing between the aristocracy and the poor. It was precisely these developments that eventually allowed theorists like Adam Smith to perceive that, contrary to centuries of thought, labor was not based on necessity and poverty after all but was instead the principal creator of productivity and prosperity in the society; it might in fact be the sole source of wealth in the society. But these new thoughts were slow in developing, especially in the colonies. Many Americans had argued in traditional terms that poverty and the threat of starvation were the only incitements for common people to work harder. Hence the less income people had, the more frugal and more industrious they would become.[28]

Suddenly, this mid-century experience brought this traditional view into question. "Poverty," said James Otis in 1761, "is so far from being the basis of industry and frugality, that it is too often the occasion of vices directly opposite." Otis was particularly eager to distinguish himself from those rich aristocrats like Thomas Hutchinson who believed that the problems of Boston and Massachusetts were due to the fact that "the common people in this town and country live too well." As for luxury, said Otis, speaking for a new rising generation, Americans could not have too much of it. They could never be too prosperous or import too many consumer goods: "the more we have the better, if we can export enough to pay for them."[29]

Most Americans agreed that they could not have too many imports—even if they could *not* export enough to pay for them. In the years before the Revolution, colonial imports from Britain skyrocketed, going from less than a million pounds in value in 1747 to nearly four and a half million by 1772. All sorts of shopkeepers and petty mushroom traders now became involved in the importation and sale of British dry goods—that is, in the kind of trade that the richest and most prestigious of colonial merchants had long controlled. In reaction, these established merchants tried to form rudimentary chambers of commerce in order to keep such upstarts out of their ranks, but the availability of British credit and the willingness of British exporters to deal with anyone in the colonies undermined their efforts. By the 1760s a prominent London merchant house might be dealing with as many as 150 different traders in a single northern port. All this meant that traditional lines of patronage in the port cities were further weakened and the title of "merchant," theoretically still confined only to those involved in wholesale trade abroad, had lost its exclusivity.[30]

But just as important for American society as the sudden increase in exports and imports in the years after 1745 was the expansion of America's domestic or inland trade. Better roads, more reliable information about markets, and the greater number and variety of new towns all encouraged domestic manufacturing for local, regional, and intercolonial markets. By 1768 colonial manufacturers were supplying Pennsylvania with eight thousand pairs of shoes a year. In many towns 20 to 30 and even 40 percent of the male population followed a trade or craft of some sort. In 1767 the town of Haverhill, Massachusetts, with fewer than three hundred residents, had forty-four workshops and nineteen mills. By the 1760s immigrants and ex-soldiers were becoming mechanics and craftsmen in Philadelphia in such numbers as to alarm British authorities worried about American manufacturing competition with the mother country. But it was not just a case of more artisans producing for domestic and inland markets; much of the farming population itself was manufacturing and trading.[31]

We are just beginning to appreciate the degree to which Americans participated in what historians sometimes call "proto-industrialization," where rural manufacturing developed alongside commercial agricultural production. Unlike in Britain and Europe, however, American rural manufacturing was not generally the result of mercantile capitalists mobilizing impoverished cottagers and landless laborers in putting-out systems; it was more often the consequence of ongoing farm families becoming part-time manufacturers and entrepreneurs in order to better themselves. No doubt many farm families in settled areas, faced with growing population pressures on diminishing amounts of available arable land, were forced either to migrate to new western areas, as many increasingly did, or to supplement their incomes with manufacturing and trading. But many other farmers engaged in domestic industry and marketing not simply to make ends meet but also to bolster their income and raise their living standards. Even farmers who were not growing crops for export abroad were nonetheless scrambling to create goods to exchange in local markets—putting their wives and children to work spinning cloth or weaving hats, dressing deer skins and beaver pelts, making hoops and barrels, distilling rum or cider, and fabricating whatever they might sell to local stores. On the eve of the Revolution, more than one-third of the families of even the simple western Massachusetts town of Northampton had some nonfarm income. In some northern agricultural towns, people seemed to be doing everything but farming.

Although direct statistical evidence of local industry seems virtually impossible to recover, literary sources and indirect evidence suggest a significant expansion of domestic manufacturing in the countryside, particularly in homespun cloth. Royal governors in both the North and the South were surprised at the extent of household spinning and weaving in the colonies. "The planters' wives spin the cotton of this country," Lieutenant Governor Francis Fauquier reported from Virginia, not only for their own consumption but for sale in local markets. Cloth manufacturing was even more common in the middle and New England colonies. Governor Wentworth of New Hampshire estimated an annual sale of 25,000 yards of high-priced linen in his colony. During the imperial crisis and nonimportation agreements of the 1760s and 1770s some northern towns claimed yearly outputs of 20,000 or 30,000 yards of cloth; Elizabeth, New Jersey, boasted that it produced nearly 100,000 yards of linen and woolen cloth in a single year. In Philadelphia in 1775 small traders and artisans formed the "United Company for Promoting American Manufactures," employing three hundred women and children in their homes. Everywhere people sought to spin or to make something in order to increase their incomes and their capacity to buy goods. Inland commercial centers like Lancaster, Pennsylvania, sprang up to meet their expanding commercial needs and desires. In 1759 Lancaster had many retail traders, but only one person officially designated as a "merchant"; by 1770 twenty-two claimed that designation, all of them shopkeepers who had usurped the title. This was but a simple prefiguring of what in time would become the momentous shift of the basis of American prosperity from external to internal commerce.[32]

Before mid-century, inland trade in the colonies had remained limited and rudimentary compared with the century-long experience of the mother country with home markets. Now, in the middle decades of the eighteenth century, Americans suddenly began experiencing on an expanded scale what Englishmen had known for generations. A new kind of business world rapidly emerged, involving the extensive exchange of goods and services not simply with the mother country or foreign territories but within and between the colonies themselves, and no one was culturally equipped to understand or justify it. Internal trade within and between the individual colonies had, of course, gone on before, but not on this scale. This abrupt expansion of inland trade combined with the inherent weakness of America's social hierarchy to create social concerns that most Englishmen had long since learned to live with and control.

"Traffick" of one sort or another was now what every American seemed to be doing, and "subtilty and craft" in people's "dealing," it was said, had become "an accomplishment peculiar to our American colonys." It was not the traditional external commerce by those designated as "merchants" that was worrisome, but rather the extent of domestic trading among more ordinary people. Everyone seemed to have "an itch after living by their Heads rather than their Hands"; everyone wanted to be a trader buying and selling goods. Visitors and travelers were stunned by the numbers of Americans whose "whole thoughts" were "turned upon profit and gain." Sometimes it seemed "as if almost all liv'd one upon another, and that but a small Proportion was employ'd in producing any Thing from the Earth or Sea."[33]

Under these commercial circumstances borrowing among the colonists increased dramatically, as farmers and traders incurred debts in order to buy more land and livestock or to finance projects that they expected would increase their profits. This borrowing against future earnings was not the same as the informal "book debts" of the small rural communities where people knew one another, were implicated in one another's lives, and did not demand interest on their debts. Much of the new commercial borrowing involved formal, signed interest-bearing instruments of credit often between people who did not know each other well. In several Connecticut counties court actions involving such signed obligations increased from about 20 percent of all debt litigation in 1700 to 80 percent by the middle decades of the century. Because this borrowing and lending often crossed the boundaries of the local community, creditors were no longer willing to rely simply on a system of mutual notations of debts among neighbors. They now demanded that debtors, often located at some distance from them, formally write out promissory notes or take out bonds with prescribed deadlines for repayment and provisions of interest. These written contracts represented very different obligations from those of the older book accounts: they suggested a degree of mistrust and were particularly and often exclusively economic rather than being part of some ongoing social relationship based on personal familiarity. For many rural colonists these written credit obligations constituted a major intrusion of impersonal market relations into lives that hitherto had been governed by custom and communal norms.[34]

By borrowing in this way on this expanded scale, the colonists began contributing their part to the long, slow process of transforming the traditional meaning of credit and debt. Credit was often still considered less a business investment than a form of charity, a mutual aid for those temporarily distressed by the risks of life. Hence debtors who seemed to be prospering and yet refused to honor their obligations were moral delinquents who could justly be imprisoned; creditors who had been deceived had every right to squeeze out any of the debtors' concealed assets and to expect family, friends, or patrons of the debtors to bail them out.[35]

It is not surprising that the most liberal, the most entrepreneurial, and the most "modern" of the eighteenth-century colonies—Rhode Island, where nearly everyone seemed to be participating in trade—was also the colony that developed the most far-reaching terms for the relief of insolvent debtors. Rhode Island's provisions for bankruptcy were thoroughly modern and went well beyond contemporary English practice: they protected the future earnings of bankrupt debtors from being attached by creditors—in effect recognizing the new risk-taking, entrepreneurial character of debt. Yet such innovations were a long way from general acceptance.[36]

As the colonists expanded their inland trade, they necessarily increased their use of paper money, which, as one historian has noted, was "a public variant of private credit instruments."[37] By the middle decades of the century many colonists were coming to realize that paper money was not just a wartime expedient that enabled governments to pay for goods and services without suddenly raising taxes. Traders, shopkeepers, market farmers—all those involved in internal and retail trade—had discovered the value of paper currency. Without specie or paper money, as Governor William Bull of South Carolina noted in 1770, trade had to be carried on "by credit or barter," which in turn required the close and more personal patron-client relationships of a small-scale society. But in a society where increasingly "the Inhabitants [were] Strangers to each other," reliance on such personal relationships would mean that the society "could carry on no Trade." The "barter of Commodities" was "extremely troublesome and unpleasant" for people who did not know one another intimately; they were forced into "consuming near half their Time, in Bargains of the most trivial as well as material Consequence." Thus paper money opened up possibilities for increasing numbers of people to participate more independently and more impersonally in the economy. For farmers to borrow from a land bank meant that they were no longer dependent on city merchants or great moneyed men of the community for their credit. Paper money thus had a corrosive effect on traditional patronage dependencies.[38]

Paper money was attractive to entrepreneurs and retailers eager to trade and unwilling to accept the short-term credits or the deferential clientage that went with personal borrowing from established patrons and lenders. It is no wonder, therefore, that Rhode Island, where the social hierarchy was weakest and the prevalence of trading greatest, became the notorious hotbed of paper-money issues, with nine banks emitting hundreds of pounds of paper currency between 1711 and 1750. In the tiny town of Glocester, with only about 120 freemen, over one-third of them on average borrowed paper currency at each of the emissions.[39] Inland trading interests also lay behind the short-lived private Massachusetts land-bank scheme of 1740; its failure, however, suggested the still dominant position of gentry creditors and established overseas merchants, who regarded domestic trade as unproductive for the colony and too much paper currency as inflationary and destructive of their credit.

Despite parliamentary acts in 1751 and 1764 restricting the use of paper money as legal tender, the colonies continued to issue paper currency. But during the remainder of the colonial period no American attempted to argue that the demands of the internal market alone were capable of upholding the value of paper money.[40] It would take the Revolutionary War and further experience with the issuing of paper money before Americans would begin to see the significance of their domestic market and its dependence on paper currency.

Still, the development of inland trade and the resort to paper-currency emissions do suggest the various ways in which ordinary people of middling rank were becoming more independent and more free of traditional patron-client relationships. But perhaps the most vivid example of this linkage between commercial change and the loosening of paternalistic social ties can be seen in what happened to the oldest and most deeply entrenched system of small-farmer dependency in the colonial economy—that involving the international marketing of tobacco in the Chesapeake.

By the middle decades of the eighteenth century the older consignment system of marketing tobacco in the Chesapeake was being rapidly displaced by a new system that had momentous consequences for the structure of Virginia and Maryland society. From about the 1730s Scottish merchant houses, operating largely out of Glasgow, set up stores or factories all over the Chesapeake area but particularly in the developing interior. Unlike the consignment system, which had tied small planters with their small crops to the large planters with access to English merchant houses, the new Scottish marketing system was ideally suited to enhance the independence of small planters. The Scottish factors or storekeepers bought the farmers' crops outright, sold them imported goods, and extended them liberal amounts of credit. In effect they supplanted the great aristocratic planters as middlemen in the economy and society of the Chesapeake. Yet because the Scottish factors were generally only employees of their merchant firms, they had little independent standing in Chesapeake society and thus, unlike the great planters who consigned their neighbors' tobacco, never translated their economic power into political or social patronage. This change in the marketing of tobacco, together with the accompanying development of new and diverse crops, allowed small farmers, especially in the backcountry, to become more independent of personal and paternalistic ties than before. By the eve of the Revolution direct trading stores run by Scottish factors controlled probably two-thirds of the yearly tobacco crop of the region and effectively opened up participation in the market economy to many new small planters.[41]

The growing independence of small and middling Chesapeake farmers from traditional patronage connections manifested itself in a variety of ways. During the middle decades of the eighteenth century, the number of contested elections for the Virginia House of Burgesses grew markedly. This increased participation of ordinary people in electoral politics made the leading planters more anxious about their role as representatives, and in the 1750s the planters even began debating the ambiguities in the relationship between the members of the House of Burgesses and their constituents. The gentry voiced more and more concern over the mounting costs of elections and growing corruption in the soliciting of votes, especially by "those who have neither natural nor acquired parts to recommend them." There were complaints everywhere of "craft and extortion" and of social disarray. Every tobacco inspector (whose income was related to the price of tobacco) was being "made rich and above his calling" by the rising price of tobacco. Clerks of the courts were using their offices and emoluments to become "great Men." Storekeepers were able to make an estate in only seven years. And "the Smith, the Tailor, the Canoe Man, etc." were all demanding "unreasonable Prices for their Labour." By the late 1760s and early 1770s the Virginia newspapers were filled with warnings against electoral treating, bribery, and vote-seeking. The freeholders were stridently urged to "strike at the Root of this growing Evil; be influenced by Merit alone," and to avoid electing "obscure and inferior persons" to the House of Burgesses. Too many "worthy gentlemen" were being pressed by "abject competitors," and gentlemen like Robert Carter were retiring from public life rather than adjust to what Carter called the "new system of politicks" that had begun "to prevail generally." The gentry were quick to invoke those famous lines from Addison's *Cato*:

> When vice prevails and impious men bear sway
> The post of honour is a private station.[42]

In this context Robert Munford's plays *The Candidates* and *The Patriots*, written on the eve of the Revolution, less confirm the gentry planters' confidence in their superiority than betray their uneasiness with electoral developments in the colony, "when coxcombs and jockies can impose themselves upon it for men of learning." Although Munford has disinterested virtue eventually win out, his satiric comedies reveal the fears the established planters had of "men who aim at power without merit." Virginia society was by no means coming apart; but social relationships were changing, and these changes were sudden enough and on such a scale as to make many gentlemen think that the colony was on the verge of ruin.[43]

Religious developments in the Chesapeake reinforced the impression of impending ruin. The surging population and changing economic relationships unsettled traditional hierarchies and the authority of the gentry-dominated Church of England. Hundreds and thousands of Virginians, separated from customary paternal and patronage connections, found the established Anglican church unable to satisfy their emotional and moral needs and began forming new ordered evangelical communities that rejected outright the high style, the luxurious living, and the preoccupations with rank and precedence of the dominant Anglican gentry. Throughout the 1750s and 1760s the Chesapeake gentry complained in newspapers and letters of mounting defections from the Church of England, particularly among the common farmers. In these mid-century decades succeeding waves of enthusiastic New Light Presbyterians, Separate Baptists, and finally Methodists swept up new converts, mostly from among the ordinary people of the Chesapeake. Between 1769 and 1774 the number of Baptist churches in Virginia alone increased from seven to fifty-four. The gentry blamed this successful proselytizing by dissenters on the laxity and ignorance of the Anglican clergy, and the clergy in turn accused the lay vestries of Anglican gentry of not supporting them against the evangelical threat. In this atmosphere of mutual recrimination the authority of both the gentry and the established Anglican clergy was weakened.[44]

What was taking place in Virginia at mid-century was just one manifestation of a series of religious upheavals throughout all the colonies, later called the Great Awakening. Up and down the continent there were momentous religious stirrings and convulsions that ran through the middle decades of the century. They were often diverse, complicated, and local in their origins, but in general they grew out of people's attempts to adjust to the disturbing changes in their social relationships caused by demographic and commercial developments. It is not surprising, for example, that New Light religious awakenings in Connecticut centered precisely in those eastern counties most unsettled by population growth, trade, and paper-money emissions. Although the Great Awakening commonly represented an effort by people to bring some order to their disrupted lives, its implications were radical, especially since supernatural religion remained for most ordinary people, if not for enlightened gentry, the major means of explaining the world. By challenging clerical unity, shattering the communal churches, and cutting people loose from ancient religious bonds, the religious revivals became in one way or another a massive defiance of traditional authority. The individualistic logic of Protestantism was drawn out further than ever before. Revivalist clergymen urged the people to trust only in "self-examination" and their own private judgments, even though "your Neighbours growl against you, and reproach you." Some New Lights went so far as to assert the "absolute Necessity for every Person to act singly . . . as if there was not another human Creature upon Earth." The burden of people's new religious attachments now rested clearly on themselves and their individual decisions.[45] Such conditional loyalties could contribute little to the deferential faith and obedience on which monarchy ultimately rested.

9. *Enlightened Paternalism*

Throughout the eighteenth-century Anglo-American world, traditional authority was brought into question. Personal and social relations were not working properly. The social hierarchy seemed less natural, less ordained by God, and more man-made, more arbitrary. By the early 1770s, the practice of ranking entering students at Harvard and Yale by their social status had come to seem archaic and unfair and was abolished. Leaders lost some of their aura of mystery and sacredness. Subordinates and inferiors felt more independent, more free, than they had in the past. People were less willing to fulfill customary obligations. Superiors seemed more selfish and more unresponsive to those below them, and subordinates seemed more sullen and suspicious. In all the colonies, as Charles Carroll said in 1765, there seemed to be "a mean, low, dirty envy which creeps through all ranks and cannot suffer a man of superiority, of fortune, of merit, or of understanding" to go uncontested. Any mark of superiority, any pretension to aristocracy, was "sure to entail a general ill will and dislike upon the owner.'" Threats and anger were becoming more common than mutual respect and deference. Servants became more difficult to maintain, and masters complained of shortages of servants. Everywhere ordinary people were no longer willing to play their accustomed roles in the hierarchy, no longer willing to follow their callings, no longer willing to restrict their consumption of goods. They were less dependent, less willing to walk while gentlemen rode, less willing to doff their caps, less deferential, less passive, less respectful of those above them.

But this heightened questioning of authority was not simply a matter of ordinary people throwing off customary restraints and asserting themselves in new ways. It was more complicated than that. The problem really lay with authority itself, with masters and patriarchs and all those traditionally designated to govern this monarchical society. By adopting new enlightened standards of paternalism, rulers of all sorts in the Anglo-American world collaborated in weakening their own authority.

No English ruler, no English master, and certainly no superior among the American colonists—who were more English than the English themselves—ever had it easy. Liberty, insubordination, and unwillingness to truckle to any authority were what distinguished Englishmen from Frenchmen and all the other enslaved and deprived peoples of the world. The English everywhere were habitually defiant of authority, and no one at the top of any of the English-speaking world's many hierarchies ever felt as secure as he would have liked. In the colonies especially, superiors of all sorts—fathers, masters, and magistrates—were increasingly uneasy and self-conscious about the legitimacy of their position, their right to dominate.

Even in the terms of a more traditional patriarchal society, the relation between fathers and children, masters and servants, rulers and ruled, had always been described as mutual. Inferiors obviously had obligations to their superiors, but so too did superiors have a responsibility to respect the rights of their subordinates, "for," as Samuel Willard had written, "they are no more left by the Word of God to be *despotical* than the others to be *disobliged.*" English rulers could not rely on standing armies or companies of guards to frighten and compel people into obedience. "Obedience by compulsion," wrote William Livingston in 1752, "is the Obedience of Vassals, who without compulsion would disobey. The Affection of the People is the only Source of a Cheerful and rational Obedience."[2] Unlike rulers elsewhere, English superiors had to gain the natural affection and respect of their inferiors and dependents. They had to be enlightened and liberal, befitting Englishmen. Yet in the colonies, particularly by mid-century, the more those in authority sought to earn the esteem of those below them, the more fearful and resentful their subordinates became. Somehow duties and obligations hitherto taken for granted by masters and subordinates were now open to doubt. Traditional social bonds were coming apart, and authority lost confidence in its ability to hold them together.

The problem began naturally enough with the family—that model of all superior-subordinate relationships in a traditional society. Decades later, after the entire ancient structure of society in Europe and America had been transformed, John Adams knew only too well where "the source of revolution" lay: in "a systematical dissolution of the true family authority. There can never be any regular government of a nation," he told one of his sons in 1799, "without a marked subordination of mother and children to the father." But this was hindsight. In the middle of the eighteenth century few saw any political dangers in altering the nature of familial authority; indeed, many who had no desire to bring about a social upheaval were nonetheless eager to transform traditional relationships within the family. In short, they wished to republicanize the family as they were republicanizing monarchy.[3]

Certainly by 1750 ancient patriarchal absolutism no longer had the same ideological significance it had once possessed. Whatever the practice at some times and in some places might have been, few fathers, or at least few gentry fathers, now dared to justify controlling their household dependents in the arbitrary manner advocated a century earlier by Sir Robert Filmer. Married women in the colonies continued in general to have greater legal rights than their counterparts in England (though after mid-century efforts to bring colonial law more into line with English common law did at times legally restrict the rights of wives). Divorces initiated by women were a measure of women's autonomy, and they were always more common in parts of America than elsewhere in the British empire. In fact, on the eve of the Revolution the crown instructed its governors to veto all colonial efforts to liberalize the divorce laws.[4]

Patriarchy was being challenged in other ways too. Not only were sons and daughters leaving home in greater numbers, but they also claimed a greater say over their choice of marriage partners. Young people were now more apt to marry someone outside of their immediate locality, or even their religion, than they had been earlier. They may even have used premarital pregnancy as a means of compelling parental acceptance of their choices: in the last part of the eighteenth century one-quarter to one-third of all brides in some areas of America (and of England too) were pregnant before their marriage. Fathers found themselves on the defensive with their children, unable to act as arbitrarily as they had in the past. The patrimony they had to pass on had become diminished. In some parts of America, fathers could not provide land for all their sons as they had earlier, and their sons were growing up with a keener sense of both old limitations and new possibilities.[5]

Personal relationships and values within the family were transformed. Families cut some of their ties to the outside world and became much more private and insular. Servants were more difficult to acquire, and their relationship to the other members of the household became less intimate. The family core of father, mother, and children became more distinct from the household, and affection became more important than dependency in holding the family together. Lower infant-and-childhood mortality enabled parents to make a greater emotional investment in their offspring. Parents paid more attention to the individuality of each child and sentimentalized the family's inner relationships. The practice now developed of giving children affectionate nicknames, and composite family portraits including father, mother, and children became much more common. Although the family remained hierarchical, the mutual relationships of its nuclear members became more complicated. Sons were no longer seen simply as the representative of the stem line of the family, and after mid-century fathers were less apt to name a son after themselves. The individual desires of children now seemed to outweigh traditional concerns with family lineage.[6]

Parents familiar with the larger cosmopolitan and genteel culture could scarcely have avoided becoming preoccupied with the question of how best to bring up their children and with redefining their parental authority. From every quarter of the cultivated world they were besieged with advice on what it meant to be a parent. No theme was more central to the popular writing of the eighteenth century. Nearly every work of the age—whether of history, fiction, or pedagogy, from Marmontel's *Memoirs* to Goldsmith's *Vicar of Wakefield* to Chesterfield's *Letters*—dwelt on issues of familial responsibility and warned against the evils of parental tyranny and the harsh and arbitrary modes of child-rearing of an older, more savage age. Charles Rollin's *Ancient History* attacked primogeniture and other legal devices that supported an artificial patriarchal authority. Samuel Richardson's *Clarissa* criticized parents who placed family pride and wealth ahead of the desires and integrity of their children. Even Hogarth's popular series of prints *Marriage à la Mode* pointed out the dangers of parents arranging their children's marriages. Being a parent was no longer simply a biological fact; it was also a cultural responsibility. As Fénelon's *Telemachus* attested, a child's true parents were not his blood relatives but those moral preceptors like Mentor who shaped his mind and raised him to become a reasoning moral adult in a corrupt and complex world. Children were no longer merely dependents but moral beings to be cared for and educated.[7]

These changing ideas about parent-child relationships constituted what has been called a "revolution against patriarchy." The sources of this immense eighteenth-century cultural transformation necessarily ran deep—ran, indeed, all the way back to the turbulence and innovative thinking of the previous century. Although this cultural revolution was so extensive and diverse, so much a part of the general republicanization of monarchy, that the influence of no single thinker can account for it, there is no doubt that the seventeenth-century philosopher John Locke was important. More significant even than his *Two Treatises of Government* (1689-90) for the eighteenth century's assault on absolutist monarchy was his *Some Thoughts on Education* (1693). It became an authoritative starting point for the following century's ideas about education.[8]

Locke's interest in pedagogy and child-rearing flowed from his assumption, set forth in his *Essay Concerning Human Understanding*, that all knowledge was ultimately based on information received from the senses. If the mind of a child was indeed a *tabula rasa* upon which experience made impressions, then the responsibility of controlling and guiding this impressionistic experience was awesome. "Those who have Children, or the charge of their Education" during that "time most susceptible of lasting Impressions," Locke wrote, had an obligation "diligently to watch, and carefully to prevent the undue Connexion of *Ideas* in the Minds of young People." In fact, parents were largely responsible for the formation of their children's character and understanding; they, more than anything else, determined their children's fate. With the spread of such ideas—and by the mid-eighteenth century they were taken for granted by the most liberal, enlightened people—being a parent could never again be the same.[9]

Despite their power, however, the new ideas about parent-child relationships developed slowly, erratically, and confusedly, and they were largely confined to the literate and educated elements of society. This revolution against patriarchal authority was a century-long affair at least (indeed, it is still going on), and even so the new enlightened thinking about parent-child relations was never complete, never undisputed, never final. The age-old claims of blood and breeding remained persistently powerful, even among the enlightened. Indeed, throughout the century opposing monarchical and republican strains of thinking existed simultaneously in the culture, and often within the minds of individuals.

Evidence for the coexistence and struggle of the opposing strains may be found in hundreds of different places, sometimes in the most unlikely ones. Robert Munford intended his play *The Patriots*, written on the eve of the Revolution, as a satire on political behavior in Virginia, but despite his focus on politics Munford could not avoid talking about familial relationships. At the end of the play the character Melinda learns that she is the offspring of a deceased gentleman and not in fact, as she had thought, the daughter of John and Margaret Heartfree, the simple farming couple who were entrusted with her as a baby. The Heartfrees have raised Melinda as their own, and she is naturally stunned by the sudden revelation of the truth. But despite the lack of a blood relation Melinda refuses to "forget my poor old good father and mother, who have fed me, raised me, cherished and loved me so long." By the new enlightened standards of the eighteenth century the Heartfrees have the superior moral claim to parenthood, and Melinda's newly discovered gentry-uncle (her mother's brother) admits as much: the Heartfrees' "kindness . . . ," he says, "well deserves a filial attachment." Yet at the same time this Virginia aristocrat cannot but feel the overpowering connection of blood. This girl is clearly his sister's child: "These eyes tempered with sweetness, these looks of mildness declare the fountain from whence they take their origin." Munford, the Southside Virginia planter with aspirations to Tidewater gentility, could not shake off the traditional aristocratic concern with genealogy and social rank. Since Melinda was to be married to a gentleman of rank, it was important for the harmonious ending of Munford's play that she, however naturally good and kindly reared, be of gentry stock herself. Traditional opinion died hard.[10]

Indeed, it was precisely the continuing power of ancient patriarchal thought that made the revolution against it so intense and widespread. Nothing like it on such a scale had happened before in Western history. Never had so many people become so self-conscious about the problems of child-rearing and parental authority.

In his work on education, which went through numerous editions in the eighteenth century, Locke advised parents not to base their authority on fear. The ferocious brutality inflicted on children and other household dependents in the past could not produce benevolent adults. Instead, parents were now advised to work hard to cultivate the reason and affection of their children. Corporal punishment might on occasion be necessary for very young children who could not be reasoned with, but coercion could never make for effective long-lasting parental authority. "For, as Years increase," Locke told parents, "Liberty must come with them." The child gradually had to be "trusted to his own Conduct; since there cannot always be a Guard upon him, except what you have put into his own Mind by good Principles, and established Habits, which is the best and surest, and therefore most to be taken Care of." Eventually, parents had to win the respect and esteem of their children, and their other dependents, through reason, benevolence, and understanding. Parental imperiousness and severity only bred resentment and servility among the children and made them unfit for the life of independent thinking adults. The ultimate goal, as Lord Chesterfield put it, was to make one's children "equals" and "friends." Affection rather than force was to bind parents and children together. "I never saw a froward child mended by whipping," said Chesterfield."

But, of course, avoiding the whip had its own dangers. Parents, said John Witherspoon, president of the College of New Jersey (later Princeton), in a typical work of the new age, *Letters on Education* (1765), were certainly not to use "a savage and barbarous method" of training their children such as had been common "in the former age." Yet, he warned, too much "persuasion and every soft and gentle method" of education could "lead to a relaxation" of authority. "There are some families," said Witherspoon, "not contemptible either in station or character, in which the parents are literally . . . obedient to their children." All of the literature prescribed a very thin line between arbitrariness and permissiveness for parents and masters to walk in order to find "the best means of preserving authority and the way in which it ought to be daily exercised." "A middle is best," said Witherspoon."

Parents had "to establish as soon as possible, an entire and absolute authority" over their children. Yet at the same time they had to take "the utmost care" so as "not to render authority cheap, by too often interposing it." They must maintain discipline, but not by fear or force. They ought to reason with their children and all their dependents; "it is not below any man to reason in some cases with his servants." But at the same time they were never "to depart" from their "right and title to command." They were to be "always cool," but not too cool: they were not to keep their children "at too great a distance by an uniform sternness and severity of carriage." Children had to be made to obey, but that obedience was not unlimited or unequivocal; children had rights and individualities that had to be respected. Parents thus had to be caring and affectionate, but not too much so: they were not to indulge their children. "Nothing can be more weak and foolish, or more destructive of authority, than when children are noisy and in an ill humor, to give them or promise them something to appease them." It was, said Witherspoon, simply a matter of "keeping to the just middle, without verging to one or another of the extremes."[3]

When even the advisers sometimes realized that their readers might think that "all this is excessive refinement, chimerical or impossible," it is not surprising that parents became unsure of themselves.[4] The ambivalent messages of the advice manuals and the pedagogical litera- ture confused parents in the eighteenth century just as much as they do parents today. Anxiety was the burden of being an enlightened parent.

Perhaps no household more vividly illuminates the problems of pa- ternal authority in this enlightened age than that of the wealthy eighteenth-century Virginia planter Colonel Landon Carter of Sabine Hall. Carter was a well-educated leader of one of Virginia's largest and most distinguished families, an important county magistrate, and a sometime member of the House of Burgesses. Although Carter's per- sonality was anything but typical, the anxiety he experienced in main- taining his authority within his household and plantation, however uniquely depicted in his remarkable diary, only epitomized the confu- sions of authority elsewhere in the culture.

Carter shared the assumptions and values of many other eighteenth- century gentlemen in the Anglo-American world, and he was very self-conscious about the liberal dictates of the culture. Like so many others in that enlightened age, he wanted to do the right thing both for himself and for those dependent on him. Self-improvement was in fact "the whole plan of my life." In 1775, looking back at his sixty-five years, he characterized himself as a "sensible Gentleman, who has lived to an extreme age, preserving an unexceptionable character, as well in his publick capacity as in his private life." Yet somehow his "unexception- able character" was not enough to command the esteem of those be- neath him—including not only several generations of his family living within his household but also the slaves and other dependents on his plantation.[5]

His own kin were impossible. His elder son, the forty-year-old Rob- ert Wormeley Carter, was strangely disrespectful, impudent, and sulky, even though he knew "every moment that his all must come from me." His other son, John, was little better, and his grandson, Robert Wormeley's son, Landon, was "insufferable," "the most outrageous scoundrel that ever appeared in human shape." God knows he tried to be a good parent, but repeatedly his requests went unheeded, his orders unobeyed. The attitude of his children was: "can't you let us do as we will?" and this attitude was infectious, spreading to his sons' friends and all "those entertained by me." It was a good thing that "our laws prevent Parricide," or his elder son might "put his father out of the way." Throughout his life Carter had the unsettling feeling that he was not master in his own house.[16]

For his grandson's shocking "filial behavior," Carter blamed the permissiveness of the boy's "temporizing" father. It was the temper of the age: "Nothing [is] so common as to hear Parents say, 'to curb their children is to spoil their genius.' Everyone called Solomon 'barbarous' and 'a damned fool when he said spare the rod and spoil the child.' " But Carter himself was no different, toward either his own sons or his grandson. He tried reasoning with them; he threatened them with disinheritance (had not Chesterfield used his will to control his heir's behavior?); and at one point he even lashed his grandson with a whip in front of the boy's parents. But he never stood by his threats, and he repeatedly offset his displays of anger and violence by indulgence. In 1766, realizing that his grandson was "encouraged" by his parents "to insult me," he vowed to his diary to discontinue supporting the boy. "And I shall give notice." But years later he was still making the same sorts of vows and threats to his sons and grandson and never carrying them out. After he had suffered from his son "really as much abuse as could be submitted to," the "monster" had the nerve to ask him "for a pair of Pumps to go to Colo. Taylor's in and like an old fool I gave him a pair of my own." One time Carter "absolutely refused" to keep his grandson's horse, but on the very next day rescinded the refusal and "gave him to boot 2 dollars for his Pocket." Another time he even forbade the boy to come into his home "any more whilst I lived." But the next day with "tears and contrition" and "a resolution to mend," the unruly youth was welcomed back.[17]

And so it went with all Carter's dependents. He could not take the relationships with any of his subordinates for granted. He thought about them constantly, worrying about their respect or lack of respect for him and pondering ways to exact their deference and obedience. He frequently got into unbecoming wrangles with his dependents, including his slaves, and then became angry when they spoke impudently or sarcastically to him. "I will repay this treatment," he told his diary after one such incident with a slave; he called another slave "a most cursed Villain." His slaves were never beneath his contempt; he had too many doubts about his authority for that. In fact, the real question was whether he could in any degree rise above their contempt. He was continually anxious about their apparent lack of submissiveness. He tried persuading and pleading with them, and he threatened them. And sometimes in frustration he stripped and whipped them and tied them neck to heel all night. He sensed disrespect and disdain among all his dependents. After one young overseer disobeyed one of his orders, Carter actually got into a debate with him over the proper obligations a subordinate owed his superior. He even tried to imagine himself in the position of a dependent and convinced himself that he would obey even if the master were wrong. "Oh the impudence of youth!" he said of his young overseer. "A gawky boy brought up and bound to me. I rear him to life and to business. In short, I make him a useful man to society and the first instance he walks alone, he is to tell me how to step." But so it went everywhere "through this part of the world. . . . Even children just cloathing are instructing their Parents."[18]

Even as a justice of the county court, Carter sensed a lack of deference among those who should have respected him. During an exchange of insults with an attorney in court, Carter in frustration "intended to make use of my own Authority and order him to the stocks," but the rest of the court took "no notice of the behaviour." Only after he had "immediately removed home and resolved never more to go out the bench till I had satisfaction Publickly" was he able to extract a sufficient apology from the lawyer for his "ill-behaviour." "I have been a slave to everybody in the County," Carter wrote of the bitter experience, "and yet without either Severity or arbitrariness in my behaviour, nor anything but a resolution to do my duty, I am the most insulted of any man in it."[19]

He tried to act with his inferiors in what he thought was an authoritative and aristocratic manner—calm, distant, and superior—but this only made him seem ridiculous. When his children's sullen tutor acted mysteriously, Carter decided to disdain asking him about it. "I will forbear talking to him to let him see I despise him." When his son abused him in front of company for being a tyrant, "calling me Bassha for not letting everybody do as they pleased," Carter "avoided altercation" by going off to his room and pouting. The next day his son goaded him before the guests by accusing him of running off the night before with the key to the wine cellar and preventing the party from drinking. This "falsehood" was too much for Carter's pretended aloofness; "it broke through my resolution of not speaking." The whole incident ended with everyone laughing at him. Was there not some duty a son owed a parent, he asked plaintively, some deference, "of which I never receive the least shew in any one instance."[20]

The diary is filled with such pathetic complaints. Carter thought he was a good father, a kind master, a conscientious official. He was not brutal or arbitrary; he was everything the enlightened eighteenth century said a good gentleman should be—liberal and compassionate, full of "the Social Virtue of forgetting injuries." Yet somehow his enlightened compassion did not win him the honor and respect he yearned for. There must be something other "than internal goodness that goes into the Composition of esteem," he wrote with poignant bewilderment in 1775, three years before his death. "It must be a Species of love not really merited but a passion that enslaves the mind without . . . conviction; because I am sensible that in my old Age no endeavour of mine has or does Attract it."[21]

Landon Carter was no ordinary person, and his is no ordinary diary. Undoubtedly few parents and masters felt as abused and unrespected as he. But Carter's experience was not unique: it exaggerated but did not misrepresent the confusions of the society.[22] Other fathers fought with their sons, other masters quarreled with their servants, and other superiors worried about their relations with their subordinates. Already American youngsters had a reputation for being more unruly than children elsewhere. Colonial children, British observers noted, were not "overawed by their parents. There is very little subordination observed in their youth. Implicit obedience to old age is not among their qualifications." In households up and down the North American continent, family relationships were changing, and in confused, unintended ways these changes were affecting the relationships of all superiors and subordinates.[23]

All political authority in the eighteenth century was still described in paternalistic terms. These terms, however, were not those of the divine-right patriarchism made notorious by James I and Sir Robert Filmer a century earlier. To be sure, well into the eighteenth century, especially on the annual commemoration (January 30) of the execution of Charles "the Martyr" in 1649, tory high-church Anglicans and Jacobite orators and writers in England kept alive the idea that unlimited submission and nonresistance were the duty of all subjects to their rulers. But since the Glorious Revolution of 1688 and the installation of the

Hanoverian monarchy in 1714 the doctrines of indefeasible hereditary succession and absolute patriarchism steadily lost their appeal in England; in colonial America, where there were no tories to speak of (at least before the imperial crisis), such absolutist ideas scarcely existed at all.

The colonists might argue over the degrees of obedience owed by subordinates to their superiors, but that such obedience was absolute and unconditional was hardly defensible in a liberty-loving whig-dominated world. How would any supporters of the Hanoverian monarchy question the people's ultimate right of resistance and revolution? Who, shrewdly asked the Boston minister Jonathan Mayhew in 1750, could now dare to speak against the Revolution of 1688, "upon the justice of which depends (in part) his present MAJESTY's right to the throne"? For all his flirting with Jacobitism and nostalgic toryism, even Lord Bolingbroke could dismiss "the royal fatherhood of that ridiculous writer Filmer" as "a silly and slavish notion" and "one of the greatest absurdities that was ever committed to paper."[24]

Yet, absurd as Filmer's patriarchal absolutism had become, order, rank, and hierarchy were still as essential as ever, even to good whigs, and paternalism of one sort or another provided the principal image with which Englishmen described the nature of obedience to authority. Bolingbroke might ridicule Filmer, but he still believed that "the true image of a free people" remained "that of a patriarchical family, where the head and all the other members are united by one common interest, and animated by one common spirit." The idea that fathers, kings, and all other superiors in the society could be arbitrary and absolute was all but dead, "constitutionally erased out of the political creed of every *English* subject, not in or fit for *Bedlam,*" said Christopher Gadsden of South Carolina in 1769; but the new, more enlightened, liberal paternalism of the age—the kind of paternalism that had been set forth by Locke and other pedagogues—was still very much alive.[25]

Locke, of course, had not meant to identify paternal with political authority. In fact, in his *Two Treatises of Government* he had sought to destroy Filmer's patriarchism by denying that any analogy between family and government was possible. Parental authority and political authority, said Locke, were distinct and separate and had different sources: one rested on nature, the other on trust or consent. The Fifth Commandment had no political significance. It was, wrote Locke, "an Eternal Law annex'd purely to the relations of Parents and Children, and so contains nothing of the Magistrates Power in it, nor is subjected to it." Despite extensive criticism of this sort by Locke and other whig publicists, however, the familial metaphor in government persisted. It was too much in accord with the realities of a monarchical and hierarchical society to be easily displaced. English society was still a gradation of degrees and ranks held together by ties that seemed to resemble those of the family or household more than those of any other institution. The very persistence with which whig intellectuals were compelled to attack the identity between familial and political authority testified to its staying power. Indeed, Filmer was invoked most often by whig critics precisely because he had been the most absolutist and most extreme of patriarchists and hence the easiest to discredit. Whig firebrands, like Bishop Benjamin Hoadly, continued to deny, as Locke had, that the king's office was "founded upon *Paternal Authority* properly so-called." Still, even Hoadly had to admit that it had undoubtedly become "a common thing . . . to reduce, as we say, the *Duty* of *Subjects* to the Injunctions laid upon Children."[26]

In the end paternalism could remain such a compelling way of explaining authority for eighteenth-century Englishmen only because of the momentous changes taking place in family relationships and in people's attitudes toward parental authority. Once parents themselves became *limited* monarchs, then even good whigs had no trouble in equating familial and political authority. Locke eventually did destroy Filmer's patriarchal absolutism—not, as he had intended, with the *Two Treatises of Government,* but with *Some Thoughts on Education* and the new liberal ideas about the proper relation between parents and children it promoted. Parental power was not absolute after all, and children had rights as well as obligations. Parents, it seemed, had to earn the respect and trust of their children, and in some sense the children as they grew actually came to consent to their parents' rule. In just this way did the Lockean image of a trusting relationship between caring parents and respectful children come to explain the new consensual relationship between rulers and subjects in the English-speaking world. Indeed, this new enlightened paternalism became what Jonathan Mayhew in mid-century called "an easy and familiar similitude" to describe the mutual duties and rights of all superiors and inferiors in the society.[27]

This "easy and familiar similitude" meant, however, that all the ambiguity and anxiety infecting the new enlightened paternalism of the family could likewise be found in government and in all superior-subordinate relationships. Just as parents were bewildered by the mass of literature that advised them to be enlightened and liberal in the rear-

ing of their children and blamed them for any mistakes, so too were all
rulers confused by a culture that stressed the rights and liberties of subjects even more than their obligation to obey. In the English-speaking
world of the eighteenth century, paternal authority at all levels could no
longer take itself for granted.

Even the authority of the supreme father of all, God himself, was
not immune to challenge. In an enlightened age God could no longer
be absolute and arbitrary. Religion, some now said, had to rest not only
on faith and revelation but also on nature and reason. "He who would
persuade a man or prevail with him to do anything," wrote Archbishop
Tillotson, the most widely read sermonizer in America in the first half
of the eighteenth century, "must do it one of three ways, either by
entreaty or authority or argument." And for a new liberal age reasoned
argument was clearly the most preferable. It was "preposterous," said
Tillotson, "to entreat men to believe anything or to charge them to do
so" before they were "convinced . . . by sufficient arguments that it is
reasonable to do so." God, like any parent, had to earn the respect of
his children, and he had to earn it through love and affection, not fear.
God, declared Mayhew in 1765, is "a compassionate Parent." As He is
"father to all, so His government is parental, free from all unnecessary
rigor."[28]

In the thinking of many American Protestants, particularly among
those gentry most susceptible to the new ideas of parenthood, Christ
and New Testament love replaced the earlier Puritan emphasis on the
absolutism of the Old Testament's Jehovah. Deists like Jefferson and
Franklin went so far as to believe that the only thing worth keeping of
the Christian faith was the Sermon on the Mount. Many of the theo-
logical struggles of late-eighteenth-century America were cast in the same
terms as the debates over parental child-raising. Did people need coercion and the terror of eternal damnation by an absolute God to make
them righteous? Was it only fear for their future existence that could
make people bow to a sovereign God? Or could people better be brought
to humility and salvation through Christ's love and compassion?[29]

If even God was losing his absolute right to rule, the position of all
earthly rulers necessarily became less secure. In some measure all superiors in the Anglo-American world—whether parents, masters, or
magistrates—came to share the confusion and uneasiness felt by Landon
Carter in the exercise of authority. No one could be sure any longer
when discipline ran into tyranny or liberty slid into licentiousness.

Because authority was not just limited but also responsible for the behavior of those it ruled, the burden of the relationship between superiors and subordinates had shifted. If children were unruly and disobedient, if the people balked at governmental measures and rioted or rebelled, the fault more often than not now seemed to be with those in authority; for, as Witherspoon said of parents and their children, "that which begets esteem, will not fail to produce subjection." Badly behaving children—"ill words and altercations . . . between parents and children before company"—were "a sure sign that there is a defect of government at home" and that the parents were not fulfilling their responsibilities. They were not loving and caring enough. "People," said one Virginian minister, "are very apt to judge of the principles of the master, by the general behaviour of the servants." Just as children never repeatedly defied kind and reasonable parents, subjects would never rebel for light and transient causes. "All History shows," said the influential Boston preacher Samuel Cooper, "that it is no easy Matter to excite a large People into any vigorous and continued opposition to the Government they have been long habituated to respect and obey. Nothing can bring them to this, but a clear Conviction and strong Feeling of some real and important Injury. . . . This is so true, that I am persuaded it will not be easy to produce an Instance of any State agitated with long and great Commotions, without some violent and continued Pressure from the Side of Government. The Waves do not rise till the Wind blows."[30]

Against these kinds of enlightened currents traditional patriarchal authority could scarcely make any headway. By the time of the imperial crisis those who remained loyal to the paternal role of the British crown over the colonies found themselves in an impossible situation. Once Thomas Bradbury Chandler, high Anglican churchman of New Jersey, raised the question "whether *Great Britain* bears not a relation to these colonies, similar to that of parent to children," he conjured up an image that ultimately could only work against him and the cause of monarchical authority. After all, in that enlightened age parents were far more responsible than children for the harmony of the familial relationship—and even the most extreme whigs were quite willing as late as 1773 to invoke the parental analogy in defense of colonial rights. Talk as they might of the colonists' childlike "ingratitude" to the mother country and the fatherly king, the tories in the liberal atmosphere of prerevolutionary America could not turn paternalism to their advantage.

In the end Chandler was reduced to asking "whether some degree of respect is not always due from inferiors to superiors"—a pitiful question a traditional society should never have had to ask.[31]

Perhaps the most revealing and poignant example of paternalism being turned inside out during the years leading up to the Revolution was the bewildering experience of Thomas Hutchinson, a prominent colonial magistrate and royal governor of Massachusetts Bay during the crisis over the Tea Party. Although Hutchinson was learned and refined and one of the most distinguished men in all of eighteenth-century North America, by the early 1770s he had become one of its most hated. He was denounced and his effigy was burned up and down the continent. He was saddened and stunned. He felt it "grievous to be vilified & reproached by so great a party of the people," particularly to be viciously accused for failing to be what he had always prided himself on being: "father of his people." He had devoted his life to public service; even John Eliot, who did not like him, once conceded that Hutchinson "upon all occasions seemed to be influenced by public spirit more than selfish considerations." He was the most caring and affectionate of parents; indeed, "love of family and home," claims one of his biographers, was his "most notable personal characteristic." Just as he was the most loving of parents, so too did he see himself as the most benevolent of magistrates, governing not by force but by the respect and esteem of those he governed. He believed in benevolent paternalism. He especially valued his position as judge of the probate court, for it gave him "so much Pleasure to relieve the Widow & fatherless" that he said he would "rather resign my other Offices and discharge this alone without Fees or Reward." He regarded himself as a "patron" of the poor; he cared for the exiled Acadians in the 1750s as few other Massachusetts officials did; and, unlike other senior judicial officials in the colony, he never browbeat young attorneys.[32]

Hutchinson seemed to epitomize eighteenth-century enlightened values. He read Locke on toleration, supported the Baptists in Congregational Massachusetts, and struck out at "blind bigotry" of all sorts. He always tried to be fair and moderate in his opinions and courteous to opponents. He was all that an up-to-date liberal and genteel parent and ruler ought to be. "The more favor you shew the colonists in freeing them from taxes of every sort, and indulging them in such forms of constitution civil and ecclesiastical as they have been used to," he told the colony's agent in Great Britain in 1769, "the more agreeable it will be to me." He was never happy exercising authority and he was never a tory at heart. Even Jonathan Mayhew admitted that Hutchinson expressed himself just as strongly in favor of civil and religious liberty as Mayhew himself did. Hutchinson repeatedly urged the British government to treat the colonists with moderation, and he protested that Britain's closing of the port of Boston in 1774 was excessively severe. He promised "never [to] make any Encroachment upon the Rights of the People." Although he could be a spiteful paternalist, as his behavior in the tea dispute suggests, he always prided himself on his reasonableness. He felt that any resort to force created more problems than it solved. If anyone had attempted to find a "just middle," he had. He constantly sought to walk thin lines, to make delicate distinctions between power and liberty. He knew he had tried to be a good and enlightened father to his people. "I am charged with arbitrary principles," he said in 1775, "but I am so far from them as any man in the world and never wished for a greater restraint of natural liberty than is necessary to answer the end of government."[33]

But in the face of an angry whig world, which men like Hutchinson never understood, these reasoned and refined niceties conceded the case for liberty at the outset and could do nothing to bolster authority. Evidence of the arbitrariness of royal officials like Hutchinson lay in the people's very anger and turbulence: royal magistrates had simply lost the people's confidence; for when the people "see their rulers actuated by principles of benevolence and a love of justice they need little else, than this confidence, to secure their obedience." The entire obligation for obedience now seemed to rest on authority, on those who were to be obeyed. Indeed, so inherently weak, so intrinsically liberal, had traditional paternal authority become in American culture that by 1775 the Maryland preacher Jonathan Boucher came to believe that if order in America were to be defended at all, there was no alternative except to return to something resembling the archaic doctrines of Filmer's divine-right patriarchy. "The first father," said Boucher, "was the first king: and . . . it was thus that all government originated; and monarchy is its most ancient form." Since kings, magistrates, masters, and all superiors received their authority not from below but from God, the duty of all subjects and subordinates was simple: "to *be quiet and to sit still.*" That Boucher found it necessary to bypass not only Locke's *Two Treatises* but even his *Thoughts on Education* and to go all the way back to patriarchical absolutism was the ultimate symptom of the loyalists' plight.[34]

This liberalization of paternal authority spilled out to affect all economic and social relations. And precisely because American society was so economically primitive and so personally organized compared with England, the effects of this liberalization on relationships were greater in the colonies than in the mother country. The colonists had continued to think of their social and economic relations primarily in terms of the household rather than a market society and to treat them as sets of mutual rights and obligations between superiors and subordinates who were members of the same patriarchal household. Thus the colonists tried to grapple with the changes taking place in their lives almost solely in terms of their traditional personal relationships—perhaps most clearly revealed in the way in which they blended their enlightened paternalism into the new meaning they gave to contracts.

Traditionally contracts did not mean what they were coming to mean in the commercialized eighteenth century. In the past contracts had often been used in patriarchal relationships—between husbands and wives, masters and apprentices, or masters and servants—and they were not thought to be incompatible with hierarchy and inequality. These contracts were regarded as evidence that the parties to the relationship, however unequal, had mutual rights and obligations established in custom. Such patriarchal contracts did not create these rights and obligations; they merely recognized their existence. Often the contracts were informal and not written out, as befitting their entanglement in the meshwork of society. The rights and obligations of the contracts were not necessarily the result of deliberate acts of will, nor did the parties even have to consent mutually to the contracts for them to be binding. Such contacts defined relationships between people rather than specific promises of action.[35]

But increasingly in the commercialized eighteenth century contracts became much more voluntary, explicit, and consensual, much less declaratory of previously existing rights and duties and much more the consequence of conscious acts of will. Instead of defining social relationships, they now focused on individual transactions. Contracts for apprenticeship, for example, became more formal and more explicit, with obligations specified in greater detail and translated into monetary value. Contracts came to be thought of as positive bargains deliberately and freely entered into between two parties who were presumed to be equal and not entirely trustful of one another. Such formal written contracts made sense in the emerging commercial world.[36]

The new conception of contract as a consensual bargain between two equal parties was a consequence of changes in all traditional relationships between superiors and inferiors, even those between parents and children. Not only was it now thought that children tacitly assented to their parents' authority, but as children grew into adulthood they were considered to be independent equals of their parents. By the mid-eighteenth century the parent-child relationship seemed to be so conditional, so much a matter of mutual consent, as to become something akin to a voluntary contract. Had not Chesterfield in fact described the parent-child relationship evolving into "contracts" of friendship that were based on a recognition of the "reciprocal merit" of the two parties?[37]

By mid-century, positive written contracts and other impersonal legal instruments were more and more replacing the informal, customary, and personal ways people had arranged their affairs with one another. New Englanders in particular were used to thinking of patriarchal relationships in contractual terms. They had, after all, a long Puritan tradition of covenants—between the people and God, between members of congregations and their ministers, and between members of the same community. To the Puritans even marriage was more of a contractual relationship than it was to other religious groups. New England Puritans of all sorts valued "the liberty" they had "of choosing, or consenting, to their own pastor, to whom they commit care of their souls." And if their pastor did not care for their souls, they had "a natural right" to dissolve the relationship. That these New Englanders therefore would come to think of the most severe superior-subordinate relationships as only deliberate and positive bargains between two parties is perhaps not surprising. But it certainly was to the British army when thousands of New England's young men joined its war against the French in America.[38]

During the Seven Years' War in the 1750s Lord Loudoun, commander in chief of the British forces in America, was confronted with what seemed to him astonishing disobedience by the New England militia under his authority. When Loudoun attempted to get the various New England militia to serve with regular royal troops, the New England soldiers simply refused to obey. They refused on the grounds that joint service with royal troops had not been part of the contractual agreements they had made when they enlisted in the militia expeditions. And their militia officers and even their colonial civilian superiors agreed with them! In 1756 Governor Thomas Fitch of Connecticut tried to explain the situation to a bewildered and angry Loudoun. The troops, Fitch said, had to be "continued under the same Command and Employed agreeable to the Design of their Enlistments, otherwise the Contract between them and their constituents made for promoting his Majesty's service in this particular may be broken and their Rights violated.''

To Loudoun this sort of explanation was as bad as the troops' disobedience. Reared in the hierarchical military tradition of allegiance, duty, and subordination, Loudoun simply could not comprehend what the New Englanders were talking about. Bargains and contracts belonged in a counting room, not on a battlefield. But for New Englanders, contracts were part of their ordinary everyday lives. They were used to making bargains, and they treated their enlistment in the militia expeditions as just another bargain. That Britain was fighting a great war, a world war, for empire—was fighting even for the colonists' own security—was somehow lost on them. They had made agreements with their enlisting officers in which they were promised bounties and provisions in return for their services. And when their contracts were violated—as they were when they did not receive what they thought was coming to them or when Loudoun tried to merge the militia with royal regulars—they considered their agreements void, and they mutinied or deserted, sometimes heading for home in groups of dozens or even hundreds.[39]

The remarkable behavior of these militiamen reveals the peculiar nature of American social relations on the eve of the Revolution, at least in New England. The common New England soldiers lived in little awe of their officers. Indeed, the contractual relationship now often presumed an equality and a degree of suspicion between the parties. The soldiers certainly had little sense that obedience and loyalty to their superiors flowed from anything other than their voluntary contracts. Authority, even the paternal authority and majesty of the crown, commanded little natural respect. Allegiance was becoming a mere business arrangement, a coincidence of interests.

This contractual imagery mingled with and colored all paternal and all superior-subordinate relationships, including those between the crown and the colonies. Indeed, contractual imagery that emphasized the personal character of the subject's relation to state power was much more alive in America than it was in the mother country, where parliamentary sovereignty was swallowing up the ancient notions of contract and natural rights. Since the colonists were just beginning to feel the commercial revolution that was transforming English society, they were more apt to see their relationship to the state as being similar to their relationships with each other. Thus it was natural for Americans to turn their familial relationship to the crown into a contractual one, for this merely substituted one personal relationship for another; but this substitution also made it easier for them to take the awful step of rebelling against their own parents.

In the decades leading up to the Revolution scarcely a piece of American writing, whig or tory, did not invoke the parent-child image to describe the imperial relationship. The king was the "father" and Great Britain was the "mother country" and the colonists were their "children." Because the image was so powerful, so suggestive of the personal traditional world in which most colonists still lived, almost the entire imperial debate was inevitably carried on within its confines. At times the polemics between whigs and tories appeared to be little more than a quarrel over the proper method of child-rearing. Whigs argued that Britain was an unnatural parent, cruel and unfeeling in her harsh treatment of her children. "Where is maternal affection?" asked John Dickinson. In reply the tories accused the colonists of being insolent and ungrateful brats and demanded to know "whether any parent can put up with such disrespectful and abusive treatment from children, as Great Britain has lately received from her colonies." The whole imperial struggle collapsed into a family squabble.[40]

The whigs, of course, invoked the latest, most enlightened thinking about the parent-child relationship: that parents with unruly children had only themselves to blame. But for children and subordinates to disobey their fathers and masters in this still traditional world was so terrifying and unnatural that whigs inevitably resorted to the image of a contract in order to explain the imperial relationship and to justify their sense of equality and their rebelliousness. The crown had its ancient rights, its prerogatives—those vague and discretionary rights of authority that the king possessed in order to carry out his responsibility for governing the realm; but the people had their rights and liberties too, and they were just as old and just as important as the rights of the crown. Indeed, Englishmen described their history essentially as a centuries-long struggle between these conflicting rights, with the negotiating and bargaining between them resulting in the original contracts of government.

Thus the colonists, the whig polemicists said in the 1770s, were not just children whose affection for the parent state was being worn away by brutal treatment; they were also parties to contracts, deliberative agreements, legal or mercantile in character, between people and rulers in which allegiance and protection were the considerations. "Allegiance," wrote James Wilson in 1774, "is the faith and obedience, which every subject owes to his prince. This obedience is founded on the protection derived from government: for protection and allegiance are the reciprocal bonds, which connect the prince and his subjects." Not only did this contractual imagery explain the people's obedience to the prerogative powers of the king (which their consent expressed in their representative legislatures could never do), but eventually the notion of an original contract between crown and people also made sense of the colonists' developing view in 1774 that they were connected to Great Britain exclusively through the king, "Parliament" being "no party to the transaction." Their several charters (or where these were lacking "their commissions to their governors have ever been considered as equivalent securities") were now seen as "evidence of a private bargain made and executed between the King of England and our predecessors, to which the [British] nation were total strangers, and are so still, however they have in some instances strangely intermeddled." Such charters, like all contracts, were designed "to reduce to a certainty the rights and privileges we were entitled to" and "to point out and circumscribe the prerogatives of the crown." How would the sprawling British empire be held together? The king, said Alexander Hamilton in a common conclusion, would be "the great connecting principle."[41]

As feelings between the antagonists hardened, the modern contractual image tended to swallow up the traditional patriarchal idea of authority. It was as if paternalism became so liberal, so republicanized, as to surrender itself willingly to modern legal contractualism. If the empire and the colonial governments were still thought of as enlarged families, they had become remarkably artificial and voluntary ones. In the subtle, often unintended ways that the colonists prepared themselves for republicanism, some whigs now even claimed that there was no essential difference between hereditary and elective magistrates: both could be "fathers" to their people and still have their patriarchal authority rest on the consent of the people. Allegiance, which had once denoted the loyalty of an inferior to a superior, now became virtually indistinguishable from consent. Most colonists clung confusedly to the traditional patriarchal images of the king as "father" and Great Britain as the "mother country" while asserting with great vehemence that their relationship to the British crown was solely contractual, liable to be broken if the considerations were not fulfilled.[42]

All this legal talk of businesslike contracts and conditional promises left little room for natural paternal or filial feelings. Some who saw this were quick to draw out the anti-familial implications of a contractual relationship. When the arch-tory Martin Howard, Jr., of Rhode Island noted in despair that the colonies' relation to Great Britain was not really that of children to parent, as the whig Stephen Hopkins had suggested, Hopkins was quick to agree; for paternalism, even enlightened paternalism, smacked too much of hereditary dependence for good whigs to be ultimately comfortable with it as a description of the imperial relationship. "There may be a natural relation between two subjects that exists by nature," said Hopkins, "but the mother country and colony exist only by policy, and may no doubt have a political relation to each other; but can have no natural one."[43]

Others, too, in these years broke through the familial imagery and even contractual imagery to confront the ultimate logic of modern whig thinking. Government, wrote Benjamin Franklin, resembled a business company, and rulers were just "Directors" hired by the owners to carry out their wishes. "They are paid a Reasonable Consideration for their trouble." In such a relationship there "is nothing of weak and strong, Protection on the one hand, and Service on the other." These "Directors are the Servants, not the Masters" and "the Power they have is from the members & returns to them." Franklin was going further than most whigs dared go in public (even his thoughts were just marginal comments on a British pamphlet). But when even some tories like Jonathan Sewell conceded that government was "an *artificial* state of *pre-eminence* and *subordination*" that "in *fact*, and in the nature of things *must be, voluntary,*" it is not surprising that whig principles dominated the pre-revolutionary debates. Government was now being widely pictured as merely a legal man-made contrivance having little if any natural relationship to the family or to society.[44]

The conclusions were momentous and forbidding, and most colonists were reluctant to reach them. They repeatedly touched on the awesome questions their arguments were raising but never faced them directly. What would this separation of government from nature and from the natural inequalities of society ultimately mean? Would people respect rulers who were not God or their fathers or their masters, who had no visible sacredness or awesomeness, who had no inherent patriarchal authority? Was submission to be without emotion, merely a matter of utility? Were people to yield to rulers "not on account of their persons considered exclusively on the authority they are clothed with, but [only on account] of those laws which in the exercise of this authority are made by them conformably to the laws of nature and equity"? Did the injunction to obey laws and not men really mean that the dignity and natural social standing of men no longer mattered in government? Were kings really "the servants and not the proprietors of the people," as Jefferson asserted in 1774? It was true that rulers were "exalted above their brethren not for their own sakes but for the benefit of the people." But did this mean that rulers were not to be "great men," perhaps not even to be gentlemen? Were rulers really "of the same species . . . and by nature equal" with those they ruled? And do they "greatly tarnish their dignity when they attempt to treat their subjects otherwise than as their fellow-men"?[45]

These were questions implied but not followed up, suggestions thrown out in the heat of polemics, momentary and sometimes desperate efforts to bridge some of the awful chasm that had traditionally existed between superiors and subordinates, rulers and ruled. But few as yet were willing to draw out fully the significance of the incongruous belief that rulers and masters were servants and that children controlled their parents.

Even the most revolutionary could not shake off the familial imagery of the past. In 1776 in *Common Sense* Thomas Paine tried to clear the air of the "ancient prejudices" that supported hereditary monarchy and all that it implied in patriarchy and family government. Paine rejected outright the whole idea of dynastic monarchy; the king of England was a "royal brute," a "wretch . . . with the pretended title of Father of His People." "The phrase *parent* or *mother country* hath been jesuitically adopted by the king and his parasites, with a low papistical design of gaining an unfair bias on the credulous weakness of our minds." Yet only a year later Paine could find no better means to explain and justify the Revolution than to dredge up once again the familiar parent-child metaphor that he had presumably laid to rest. The colonists had simply grown up and come of age. "To know whether it be the interest of the continent to be independent," he wrote, "we need only ask this easy, simple question: Is it the interest of a man to be a boy all his life?" It was testimony to the lingering power of the old monarchical assumptions that Paine in 1777 should have still felt compelled to put the issue in these familial terms.[46]

10. Revolution

The Revolution brought to the surface the republican tendencies of American life. The "Suddenness" of the change from monarchy to republicanism was "astonishing." "Idolatry to Monarchs, and servility to Aristocratical Pride," said John Adams in the summer of 1776, "was never so totally eradicated from so many Minds in so short a Time." Probably Adams should not have been astonished, for the truncated nature of American society with its high proportion of freeholders seemed naturally made for republicanism. Yet adopting republicanism was not simply a matter of bringing American culture more into line with the society. It meant as well an opportunity to abolish what remained of monarchy and to create once and for all new, enlightened republican relationships among people.[1]

Such a change marked a real and radical revolution, a change of society, not just of government. People were to be "changed," said the South Carolina physician and historian David Ramsay, "from subjects to citizens," and "the difference is immense. Subject is derived from the latin words, *sub* and *jacio,* and means one who is under the power of another; but a citizen is an unit of a mass of free people, who, collectively, possess sovereignty. Subjects look up to a master, but citizens are so far equal, that none have hereditary rights superior to others. Each citizen of a free state contains, within himself, by nature and the constitution, as much of the common sovereignty as another."[2] Such a republican society assumed very different sorts of human relationships from that of a monarchy.

By the late 1760s and early 1770s a potentially revolutionary situation existed in many of the colonies. There was little evidence of those social conditions we often associate with revolution (and some historians have desperately sought to find): no mass poverty, no seething social discontent, no grinding oppression. For most white Americans there was greater prosperity than anywhere else in the world; in fact, the experience of that growing prosperity contributed to the unprecedented eighteenth-century sense that people here and now were capable of ordering their own reality. Consequently, there was a great deal of jealousy and touchiness everywhere, for what could be made could be unmade; the people were acutely nervous about their prosperity and the liberty that seemed to make it possible. With the erosion of much of what remained of traditional social relationships, more and more individuals had broken away from their families, communities, and patrons and were experiencing the anxiety of freedom and independence. Social changes, particularly since the 1740s, multiplied rapidly, and many Americans struggled to make sense of what was happening. These social changes were complicated, and they are easily misinterpreted. Luxury and conspicuous consumption by very ordinary people were increasing. So, too, was religious dissent of all sorts. The rich became richer, and aristocratic gentry everywhere became more conspicuous and self-conscious; and the numbers of poor in some cities and the numbers of landless in some areas increased. But social classes based on occupation or wealth did not set themselves against one another, for no classes in this modern sense yet existed. The society was becoming more unequal, but its inequalities were not the source of the instability and anxiety. Indeed, it was the pervasive equality of American society that was causing the problems—even in aristocratic South Carolina.

Perhaps the society of no colony was more unequal, more riven by discrepancies of rich and poor, more dominated by an ostentatious aristocracy than that of South Carolina. "State and magnificence, the natural attendants on great riches, are conspicuous among this people," declared a wide-eyed New England visitor in 1773. "In grandeur, splendour of buildings, decorations, equipage, numbers, commerce, shipping, and indeed in almost everything, it far surpasses all I ever saw, or ever expect to see in America." Yet, surprisingly, in the opinion of Carolinian Christopher Gadsden, society in his colony was most remarkable, not for its inequality, but for its equality, for the prevalence in it of substantial hardworking farmers and artisans—that is, of all those who "depend, almost, altogether upon their own daily labour and industry, for the maintenance of themselves and families." These honest industrious white folk were extraordinarily prosperous. Even "the poorest of them (unless some very uncommon instances indeed) but must find himself, in a very comfortable situation, especially when he compares his condition, with that of the poor of other nations," or, Gadsden might have added, with that of the black slaves in their own midst. The result, said Gadsden, was that white society in South Carolina was comparatively equal, "the distinctions . . . between the farmer and rich planter, the mechanic and the rich merchant, being abundantly more here, in imagination, than reality."

Yet because such equality and prosperity were so unusual in the Western world, they could not be taken for granted. The idea of labor, of hard work, leading to increased productivity was so novel, so radical, in the overall span of Western history that most ordinary people, most of those who labored, could scarcely believe what was happening to them. Labor had been so long thought to be the natural and inevitable consequence of necessity and poverty that most people still associated it with slavery and servitude. Therefore any possibility of oppression, any threat to the colonists' hard-earned prosperity, any hint of reducing them to the poverty of other nations, was especially frightening; for it seemed likely to slide them back into the traditional status of servants or slaves, into the older world where labor was merely a painful necessity and not a source of prosperity. "The very apprehension thereof, cannot but cause extreme uneasiness." "No wonder," said Gadsden, "that throughout *America,* we find these men extremely anxious and attentive, to the cause of liberty." These hardworking farmers and mechanics were extraordinarily free and well off and had much to lose, and "this, therefore, naturally accounts for these people, in particular, being so united and steady, everywhere," in support of their liberties against British oppression.[3]

In all the colonies in the 1760s and 1770s the circumstances were similar. The absence of a traditional European nobility and a sprawling mass of the destitute made everyone seem much more alike. At present, wrote John Adams, in 1761, "all Persons under the Degree of Gentlemen are styled Yeoman," including even laborers and those "who never owned an Inch of ground in their Lives." The lack of the customary degrees of distinction and deference was what British visitors to the colonies meant when they said that "an idea of equality . . . seems generally to prevail, and the inferior order of people pay but little external respect to those who occupy superior stations." Equality did not mean that everyone was in fact the same, but only that ordinary people were closer in wealth and property to those above them and felt freer from aristocratic patronage and control than did common people elsewhere in the Western world. And they were ready, as Edmund Burke said, to "snuff tyranny in every tainted breeze"; and as Orange County, North Carolina, stated in 1770 in a common phrase that captured the colonists' sense of the high stakes involved in their politics, they were willing "to risque our All to save our Country from Rapine and Slavery."[4]

This extraordinary touchiness, this tendency of the colonists in their political disputes to argue "with such vehemence as if all had been at Stake," flowed from the precariousness of American society, from its incomplete and relatively flattened character, and from the often "rapid ascendency" of its aristocracy, particularly in the Deep South, where families "in less than ten years have risen from the lowest rank, have acquired upward of £100,000 and have, moreover, gained this wealth in a simple and easy manner." Men who had quickly risen to the top were confident and aggressive but also vulnerable to challenge, especially sensitive over their liberty and independence, and unwilling to brook any interference with their status or their prospects.[5]

For other, more ordinary colonists the promises and uncertainties of American life were equally strong. Take, for example, the lifelong struggle of farmer and sawmill owner Moses Cooper of Glocester, Rhode Island, to rise from virtual insignificance to become the richest man in the town. In 1767–68, at the age of sixty, Cooper was finally able to hire sufficient slaves and workers to do all his manual labor; he became a gentleman and justice of the peace and appended "Esq." to his name. Certainly by this date he could respond to the rhetoric of his fellow Rhode Islanders talking about their colony as "the promised land . . . a land of milk and honey and wherein we eat bread to the full . . . a land whose stones are iron . . . and . . . other choice mines and minerals; and a land whose rivers and adjacent seas are stored with the best of fish." And Cooper might well have added, "whose forests were rich with timber," for he had made his money from lumber. Yet at the same time Cooper knew only too well the precariousness of his wealth and position and naturally feared what Britain's mercantile restrictions might mean for his lumber sales to the West Indies. What had risen so high could as readily fall: not surprisingly, he became an enthusiastic patriot leader of his tiny town of Glocester. Multiply Cooper's experience of uneasy prosperity many thousandfold and we have the stuff of a popular revolutionary movement.[6]

America was no doubt "the best poor Man's Country in the World."[7] But the general well-being and equality of the society set against the gross inequality and flagrant harshness of both white servitude and especially black slavery made many people unusually sensitive to all the various dependencies and subordinations that still lurked everywhere in their lives. Thus in 1765 at the outset of the imperial crisis John Adams's fearful and seemingly anachronistic invocation of an older feudal world of "servants and vassals" holding "their lands, by a variety of duties and services . . . in a state of servile dependence on their lords," could at once arouse the colonists' anxieties over the potentialities, however inchoate and remote, of a dependent world in their own midst. They repeatedly put into words their widespread sense that very little stood between their prosperous freedom and out-and-out oppression. Indeed, they told themselves over and over that if ever they should agree to a parliamentary tax or allow their colonial assemblies to be silenced, "nothing will remain to us but a dredful expectation of certain slavery." The tenants of one of the New York landlords may have seemed to the landlord's agent to be "silly people" by their resisting a simple extension of the services required of them out of "fear [of] drawing their Posterity into Bondage," but they knew the reality of the eighteenth-century world. They knew the lot of ordinary people elsewhere, and they knew especially the lot of white and black dependents in their own society, and thus they could readily respond to images of being driven "like draft oxen," of being "made to serve as bond servants," or of foolishly sitting "quietly in expectation of a m[aste]r's promise for the recovery of [their] liberty." The immense changes occurring everywhere in their personal and social relationships—the loosening and severing of the hierarchical ties of kinship and patronage that were carrying them into modernity—only increased their suspicions and apprehensions. For they could not know then what direction the future was taking.[8]

By the middle of the century these social changes were being expressed in politics. Americans everywhere complained of "a Scramble for Wealth and Power" by men of "worldly Spirits." Indeed, there were by the early 1760s "so many jarring and opposite Interests and Systems" that no one in authority could relax, no magistrate, no ruler, could long remain unchallenged. More and more ordinary people were participating in electoral politics, and in many of the colonies the number of contested elections for assembly seats markedly increased. This expansion of popular politics originated not because the mass of people pressed upward from below with new demands but because competing gentry, for their own parochial and tactical purposes, courted the people and bid for their support by invoking popular whig rhetoric. Opposition factions in the colonial assemblies made repeated appeals to the people as counterweights to the use of royal authority by the governors, especially as the older personal avenues of appeal over the heads of the governors to interests in England became clogged and unusable. But popular principles and popular participation in politics, once aroused, could not be easily put down; and by the eve of the Revolution, without anyone's intending or even being clearly aware of what was happening, traditional monarchical ways of governing through kin and patronage were transformed under the impact of the imperial crisis.[9] "Family-Interests," like the Livingstons and De Lanceys in New York, or the Pinckneys and Leighs of South Carolina, observed one prescient British official in 1776, "have been long in a gradual Decay; and perhaps a new arrangement of political affairs may leave them wholly extinct." Those who were used to seeing politics as essentially a squabble among gentlemen were bewildered by the "strange metamorphosis or other" that was taking place.[10]

With the weakening of family connections and the further fragmentation of colonial interests, crown officials and other conservatives made strenuous efforts to lessen popular participation in politics and to control the "democratic" part of the colonists' mixed constitutions. Some royal governors attempted to restrict the expansion of popular representation in the assemblies, to limit the meetings of the assemblies, and to veto the laws passed by the assemblies. Other officials toyed with plans for remodeling the colonial governments, for making the salaries of royal officials independent of the colonial legislatures, and for strengthening the royal councils or upper houses in the legislatures. Some even suggested introducing a titled nobility into America in order to stabilize colonial society. But most royal officials relied on whatever traditional monarchical instruments of political patronage and influence they had available to them to curb popular disorder and popular pressure—using intricate maneuvering and personal manipulation of important men in place of whig and republican appeals to the people.

After 1763 all these efforts became hopelessly entangled in the British government's attempts to reform its awkwardly structured empire and to extract revenue from the colonists. All parts of British policy came together to threaten each colonist's expanding republican expectations of liberty and independence. In the emotionally charged atmosphere of the 1760s and 1770s, all the imperial efforts at reform seemed to be an evil extension of what was destroying liberty in England itself. Through the manipulation of puppets or placemen in the House of Commons, the crown—since 1760 in the hands of a new young king, George III—was sapping the strength of popular representation in Parliament and unbalancing the English constitution. Events seemed to show that the crown, with the aid of a pliant Parliament, was trying to reach across the Atlantic to corrupt Americans in the same way.[11]

Americans steeped in the radical whig and republican ideology of opposition to the court regarded these monarchical techniques of personal influence and patronage as "corruption," as attempts by great men and their power-hungry minions to promote their private interests at the expense of the public good and to destroy the colonists' balanced constitutions and their popular liberty. This corruption had created pockets of royal influence throughout America and had made the crown itself, said John Adams, nothing but a "private interest." Such corruption had turned the colonies into a dumping ground for worthless place-seekers from Britain, "strangers *ignorant* of the interests and laws of the Colonies . . . sent over," complained William Henry Drayton of South Carolina, "to fill offices of 200£ or 300£ per annum, as their only subsistence in life." Americans were warned that they could no longer trust those "who either hold or expect to hold certain advantages by setting examples of servility to their countrymen." Men who themselves were tied to patrons simply "serve as decoys, for drawing the innocent and unwary into snares."[12] Such corruption had allowed even distinguished Americans like Thomas Hutchinson and his clan in Massachusetts to pile up offices to the exclusion of those who John Adams and James Otis felt were better men. The hatred of Hutchinson was so great that sometimes it could scarcely be contained. "Good God!" declared Josiah Quincy in 1770. "What must be the distress, the sentiments, and feelings of a people, legislated, condemned and governed, by a creature so mercenary, so dependent, and so—but I forbear: my anguish is too exquisite—my heart is too full!" The term "pensioner," Hutchinson ruefully noted, was one "which among Americans conveys a very odious Idea."[3]

By adopting the language of the radical whig opposition and by attacking the monarchical abuse of family influence and patronage, however, the American revolutionaries were not simply expressing their resentment of corrupt political practices that had denied some of them the highest offices of colonial government. They actually were tearing at the bonds holding the traditional monarchical society together. Their assault necessarily was as much social as it was political.

But this social assault was not the sort we are used to today in describing revolutions. The great social antagonists of the American Revolution were not poor vs. rich, workers vs. employers, or even democrats vs. aristocrats. They were patriots vs. courtiers—categories appropriate to the monarchical world in which the colonists had been reared. Courtiers were persons whose position or rank came artificially from above—from hereditary or personal connections that ultimately flowed from the crown or court. Courtiers, said John Adams, were those who applied themselves "to the Passions and Prejudices, the Follies and Vices of Great Men in order to obtain their Smiles, Esteem, and Patronage and consequently their favors and Preferments." Patriots, on the other hand, were those who not only loved their country but were free of dependent connections and influence; their position or rank came naturally from their talent and from below, from recognition by the people. "A real patriot," declared one American in 1776, was "the most illustrious character in human life. Is not the interest and happiness of his fellow creatures his care?"[4]

Only by understanding the hierarchical structure of monarchical society and taking the patriots' assault on courtiers seriously can we begin to appreciate the significance of the displacement of the loyalists—that is, of those who maintained their allegiance to the British crown. The loyalists may have numbered close to half a million, or 20 percent of white Americans. As many as 80,000 of them are estimated to have left the thirteen colonies during the American Revolution, over six times as many émigrés per 1,000 of population as fled France during the French Revolution.[5] Although many of these American émigrés, unlike the French émigrés, did not have to abandon their nation and could remain as much British subjects in Canada or the West Indies or Britain itself as they had been in one of the thirteen colonies, nevertheless, the emigration of the loyalists had significant effects on American society.

It was not how many loyalists who were displaced that was important; it was who they were. A disproportionate number of them were well-to-do gentry operating at the pinnacles of power and patronage—royal or proprietary officeholders, big overseas dry-goods merchants, and rich landowners. Because they commanded important chains of influence, their removal disrupted colonial society to a degree far in excess of their numbers. The emigration of members of the De Lancey, De Peyster, Walton, and Cruger families of New York, who, one historian has said, were related "by blood and marriage to more than half the aristocracy of the Hudson Valley," collapsed the connections and interests holding together large clusters of New York society.[6] Similar ramifying disruptions were felt in Pennsylvania from the departure of members of the Penns, Allens, Chews, Hamiltons, and Shippens, who formed particularly prominent, cohesive, and influential groups. Young James Allen realized only too well what the Revolution was doing. "Private friendships are broken off," he wrote in his diary, and his distinguished family and its important connections were "totally unhinged."[7]

It was the same everywhere. The removal of the loyalist heads of these chains of interest had destructive effects on the society out of all proportion to the actual numbers involved. Only forty-six Boston merchants were named in Massachusetts's banishment act of 1778, yet among these were some of the wealthiest families—the Ervings, Winslows, Clarks, and Lloyds—whose connections of kin, friends, and clients ramified throughout the society. True, the vacancies in Boston created by their removal were quickly filled by ambitious north shore merchants, including the Cabots, Lees, Jacksons, Lowells, Grays, Higginsons, and Gerrys. But the bases of the newcomers' positions were necessarily different, and the very recency of their arrival opened them to resentment and further challenge. As early as 1779 James Warren was complaining that in Boston "fellows who would have cleaned my shoes five years ago, have amassed fortunes, and are riding in chariots."[18]

Many of the loyalists' networks of kin and patronage were, of course, extensive enough to protect some of them from patriot persecution and confiscation of their property and to allow others to return quietly to the United States at the end of the war. Some departing loyalists even left members of their families in America to look after their interests. Yet neither the returning loyalists nor the patriots who took many of their places were able to re-create precisely the old prewar chains of family and patronage. Post-revolutionary society was inevitably put together on new republican terms. Social and business links formed during the war and after were thinner and more precarious, less emotional and more calculating than they had been. The lines of interest and influence created by the Revolution were looser and less personal, based less on kin and more on devotion to the patriot cause or on wealth alone. The Revolution effectively weakened or severed those loyalties of the *ancien régime* that had enabled men like William Allen or James De Lancey to form their extensive webs of personal and familial influence.

To eliminate those clusters of personal and familial influence and transform the society became the idealistic goal of the revolutionaries. Any position that came from any source but talent and the will of the people now seemed undeserved and dependent. Patrimonialism, plural officeholding, and patronage of all sorts—practices that had usually been taken for granted in a monarchical society—came under attack. It might have been possible earlier for a royal governor like Jonathan Belcher of Massachusetts to brag that "I never lost any thing I could get in an honest way." But after mid-century the piling up of offices and fees and the open exploitation of them ceased to be tolerable. "A multiplicity of public trusts" in a few persons, wrote Oxenbridge Thacher of Massachusetts in 1763, was indeed the practice "in the *infancy* of the country." It was necessary then when "gentlemen of education and ability could not be found . . . to fill up every place in government." But now "the case is very much alter'd."[19]

The prevailing revulsion against corruption and the use of patronage spilled over to affect even those who were unconnected with royal authority. Despite their stands against royal government, the self-perpetuating oligarchies of the Virginia county courts were not free from criticism. Spread of republican sentiments explains some of the anger of Virginians such as Jefferson, Patrick Henry, and Richard Henry Lee against the older clique of Tidewater planters who tended to look after one another and to restrain the entry of others into their inner circle. The scandal in 1766 involving John Robinson, speaker of the House of Burgesses and colony treasurer, who had lent to his friends paper money he was supposed to destroy, together with the easygoing way the Virginia General Court in the same year treated the murder charge against Colonel John Chiswell, smacked of corruption. Such events, one gentleman told Richard Henry Lee, fully justified Lee's "opposition to the confederacy of the great in places, family connections, and that more to be dreaded foe to public virtue, warm and private friendship."[20]

It is in this context that we can best understand the revolutionaries' appeal to independence, not just the independence of the country from Great Britain, but, more important, the independence of individuals from personal influence and "warm and private friendship." The purpose of the Virginia constitution of 1776, one Virginian recalled, was "to prevent the undue and overwhelming influence of great landholders in elections." This was to be done by disfranchising the landless "tenants and retainers" who depended "on the breath and varying will" of these great men and by ensuring that only men who owned their own land could vote.[21]

A republic presumed, as the Virginia declaration of rights put it, that men in the new republic would be "equally free and independent," and property would make them so. Property in a republic was still conceived of traditionally—in proprietary terms—not as a means of personal profit or aggrandizement but rather as a source of personal authority or independence. It was regarded not merely as a material possession but also as an attribute of a man's personality that defined him and protected him from outside pressure. A carpenter's skill, for example, was his property. Jefferson feared the rabble of the cities precisely because they were without property and were thus dependent.

All dependents without property, such as women and young men, could be denied the vote because, as a convention of Essex County,

Massachusetts, declared in 1778, they were "so situated as to have no wills of their own." Jefferson was so keen on this equation of property with citizenship that he proposed in 1776 that the new state of Virginia grant fifty acres of land to every man that did not have that many. Without having property and a will of his own—without having independence—a man could have no public spirit; and there could be no republic. For, as Jefferson put it, "dependence begets subservience and venality, suffocates the germ of virtue, and prepares fit tools for the designs of ambition."[22]

In a monarchical world of numerous patron-client relations and multiple degrees of dependency, nothing could be more radical than this attempt to make every man independent. What was an ideal in the English-speaking world now became for Americans an ideological imperative. Suddenly, in the eyes of the revolutionaries, all the fine calibrations of rank and degrees of unfreedom of the traditional monarchical society became absurd and degrading. The Revolution became a full-scale assault on dependency.

At the beginning of the eighteenth century the English radical whig and deist John Toland had divided all society into those who were free and those who were dependent. "By *Freeman*," wrote Toland, "I understand men of property, or persons that are able to live of themselves; and those who cannot subsist in this independence, I call *Servants*."[23] In such a simple division everyone who was not free was presumed to be a servant. Anyone tied to someone else, who was someone's client or dependent, was servile. The American revolutionary movement now brought to the surface this latent logic in eighteenth-century radical whig thinking.

Dependency was now equated with slavery, and slavery in the American world had a conspicuous significance. "What is a slave," asked a New Jersey writer in 1765, "but one who depends upon the will of another for the enjoyment of his life and property?" "Liberty," said Stephen Hopkins of Rhode Island, quoting Algernon Sidney, "solely consists in an independency upon the will of another; and by the name of slave we understand a man who can neither dispose of his person or goods, but enjoys all at the will of his master." It was left to John Adams in 1775 to draw the ultimate conclusion and to destroy in a single sentence the entire conception of society as a hierarchy of graded ranks and degrees. "There are," said Adams simply, "but two *sorts* of men in the world, freemen and slaves." Such a stark dichotomy collapsed all the delicate distinctions and dependencies of a monarchical society and created radical and momentous implications for Americans.[24]

Independence, declared David Ramsay in a memorable Fourth of July oration in 1778, would free Americans from that monarchical world where "favor is the source of preferment," and where "he that can best please his superiors, by the low arts of fawning and adulation, is most likely to obtain favor." The revolutionaries wanted to create a new republican world in which "all offices lie open to men of merit, of whatever rank or condition." They believed that "even the reins of state may be held by the son of the poorest men, if possessed of abilities equal to the important station." They were "no more to look up for the blessings of government to hungry courtiers, or the needy dependents of British nobility"; but they had now to educate their "own children for these exalted purposes." Like Stephen Burroughs, the author of an extraordinary memoir of these years, the revolutionaries believed they were "so far . . . republican" that they considered "a man's merit to rest entirely with himself, without any regard to family, blood, or connection."[25] We can never fully appreciate the emotional meaning these commonplace statements had for the revolutionaries until we take seriously their passionate antagonism to the prevalence of patronage and family influence in the *ancien régime*.

Of course, the revolutionary leaders did not expect poor, humble men—farmers, artisans, or tradesmen—themselves to gain high political office. Rather, they expected that the sons of such humble or ungenteel men, if they had abilities, would, as they had, acquire liberal and genteel republican attributes, perhaps by attending Harvard or the College of New Jersey at Princeton, and would thereby rise into the ranks of gentlemen and become eligible for high political office. The sparks of genius that they hoped republicanism would fan and kindle into flame belonged to men like themselves—men "drawn from obscurity" by the new opportunities of republican competition and emulation into becoming "illustrious characters, which will dazzle the world with the splendor of their names." Honor, interest, and patriotism together called them to qualify themselves and posterity "for the bench, the army, the navy, the learned professions, and all the departments of civil government." They would become what Jefferson called the "natural aristocracy"— liberally educated, enlightened gentlemen of character. For many of the revolutionary leaders this was the emotional significance of republicanism—a vindication of frustrated talent at the expense of birth and blood. For too long, they felt, merit had been denied. In a monarchical world only the arts and sciences had recognized talent as the sole criterion of leadership. Which is why even the eighteenth-century *ancien régime* called the world of the arts and sciences "the republic of letters." Who, it was asked, remembered the fathers or sons of Homer and Euclid? Such a question was a republican dagger driven into the heart of the old hereditary order. "Virtue," said Thomas Paine simply, "is not hereditary."[26]

Because the revolutionaries are so different from us, so seemingly aristocratic themselves, it is hard for us today to appreciate the anger and resentment they felt toward hereditary aristocracy. We tend to ignore or forget the degree to which family and monarchical values dominated colonial America. But the revolutionaries knew only too well what kin and patrimonial officeholding had meant in their lives. Up and down the continent colonial gentry like Charles Carroll of Maryland had voiced their fears that "all power might center in *one family*" and that offices of government "like a precious jewel will be handed down from *father* to *son*." Everywhere men expressed their anger over the exclusive and unresponsive governments that had distributed offices, land, and privileges to favorites. Real emotion lay behind their constitutional statements, like that of the New Hampshire constitution, which declared that "no office or place whatsoever in government, shall be hereditary—the abilities and integrity requisite in all, not being transmissible to posterity or relations"; or that of the 1776 Virginia declaration of rights drawn up by George Mason, which stated that

> no Man, or Set of Men are entitled to exclusive or separate Emoluments or Privileges from the Community, but in Consideration of public Services; which not being descendible, or hereditary, the Ideal of Man born a Magistrate, a Legislator, or a Judge is unnatural and absurd.[27]

More perhaps than any other revolutionary leader Mason remained preoccupied by the social implications of this republican assault on patrimonialism. A decade later in the Philadelphia Convention he warned his colleagues that they must not forget the meaning of republicanism. The new federal Constitution of 1787 seemed to suggest that the "superior classes of society" were becoming indifferent to the rights of the "lowest classes." This was foolish, he said, because "our own children will in a short time be among the general mass." Such downward mobility was inevitable in the present circumstances of America, said the younger Charles Carroll. "In a commercial nation," he said, "the glory of illustrious progenitors will not screen their needy posterity from obscurity and want." Despite these occasional premonitions, however, few of the revolutionaries realized just how devastating republicanism would be to their children and grandchildren.[28]

All of the founding fathers remained fascinated with the power of lineage and what William Livingston called "the Vanity of Birth and Titles."[29] To his dying day John Adams was haunted by the veneration for family that existed in New England. Jefferson, too, always felt the power of genealogy. He, unlike Adams, was not one to let his feelings show, but even today we can sense the emotion lying beneath the placid surface of his autobiography written in 1821 at the age of seventy-seven. There he described his efforts in 1776 in Virginia to bring down that "distinct set of families" who had used the legal devices of primogeniture and entail to form themselves "into a Patrician order, distinguished by the splendor and luxury of their establishments." The privileges of this "aristocracy of wealth," wrote Jefferson, needed to be destroyed in order "to make an opening for the aristocracy of virtue and talent," of which he considered himself a prime example.

Jefferson has often been thought to have exaggerated the power of primogeniture and entail and this "Patrician order." Not only was the docking of entails very common in Virginia, but the "Patrician order" does not appear to us all that different from its challengers. But Jefferson obviously saw a difference, and it rankled him. In the opening pages of his autobiography Jefferson tells us that the lineage of his Welsh father was lost in obscurity: he was able to find in Wales only two references to his father's family. His mother, on the other hand, was a Randolph, one of the distinguished families of the "Patrician order." The Randolphs, he said with about as much derision as he ever allowed himself, "trace their pedigree far back in England & Scotland, to which let every one ascribe the faith & merit he chooses."[30]

Benjamin Franklin likewise began his autobiography with a survey of his ancestors, concluding ruefully that he was "the youngest Son of the youngest Son for 5 Generations back"—a powerful indictment of the way primogeniture had worked to deny him through five generations. In the last year of his life, the bitterness was still there. In a codicil to his will written in June 1789 Franklin observed that most people, having received an estate from their ancestors, assumed they were obliged to pass on something to their posterity. "This obligation," he declared with emotion, "does not lie on me, who never inherited a shilling from any ancestor or relation."[31]

In their revolutionary state constitutions and laws the revolutionaries struck out at the power of family and hereditary privilege. In the decades following the Revolution all the new states abolished the legal devices of primogeniture and entail where they existed, either by statute or by writing the abolition into their constitutions. These legal devices, as the North Carolina statute of 1784 stated, had tended "only to raise the wealth and importance of particular families and individuals, giving them an unequal and undue influence in a republic, and prove in manifold instances the source of great contention and injustice." Their abolition would therefore "tend to promote that equality of property which is of the spirit and principle of a genuine republic."[32]

We have been told that such legal and constitutional changes in inheritance at the Revolution were "largely formal and symbolic," merely attempts to bring the laws of intestacy into line with what men were already doing by wills.[33] It is true that in many colonies fathers in the eighteenth century had tended to divide up their lands fairly equally among their male heirs. But, as we have seen, this partitioning of estates among more than the eldest son did not represent any modern commitment to all children sharing and sharing alike in the property. Eldest sons still had been given preference, and when land became less available fathers had resorted to more traditional patterns of inheritance in order to protect the unity of the estate.[34] The Revolution made a major change in these older patterns of inheritance, particularly in recognizing the equal rights of daughters and widows in the inheriting and possession of property.

Although some states continued the traditional practices, most new post-revolutionary inheritance laws tended to break with a patrilineal definition of kinship and to establish greater recognition of kinship ties through marriage. These new inheritance laws recognized greater equality among sons and daughters and gave greater autonomy to widows by granting them outright ownership of one-third of the estate rather than just the lifetime use that had been usual in the past. Such widows now had the right to alienate the land or to pass it on to their children of a second marriage. Most of the states also strengthened the ability of women to own and control property. In a variety of ways the new state laws not only abolished the remaining feudal forms of land tenure and enhanced the commercial nature of real estate; they also confirmed the new enlightened republican attitudes toward the family.[35]

The Revolution's assault on patriarchy inevitably affected relationships within the family, as decisions concerning women's and daughters' rights were made that conservatives later regarded as "tending to loosen the bands of society.'' Changes in the family begun earlier found new republican justifications and were accelerated—showing up even in paintings. In earlier-eighteenth-century family portraits fathers had stood dominantly above their wives and children; now they were portrayed on the same plane with them—a symbolic leveling. With the Revolution men lost some of their earlier patriarchal control over their wives and property. Although wives continued to remain dependent on their husbands, they did gain greater autonomy and some legal recognition of their rights to hold property separately, to divorce, and to make contracts and do business in the absence of their husbands. In the colonial period only New Englanders had recognized the absolute right to divorce, but after the Revolution all the states except South Carolina developed new liberal laws on divorce.[36]

Women and children no doubt remained largely dependent on their husbands and fathers, but the revolutionary attack on patriarchal monarchy made all other dependencies in the society suspect. Indeed, once the revolutionaries collapsed all the different distinctions and dependencies of a monarchical society into either freemen or slaves, white males found it increasingly impossible to accept any dependent status whatsoever. Servitude of any sort suddenly became anomalous and anachronistic. In 1784 in New York, a group believing that indentured servitude was ''contrary to . . . the idea of liberty this country has so happily established'' released a shipload of immigrant servants and arranged for public subscriptions to pay for their passage. As early as 1775 in Philadelphia the proportion of the work force that was unfree—composed of servants and slaves—had already declined to 13 percent from the 40 to 50 percent that it had been at mid-century. By 1800 less than 2 percent of the city's labor force remained unfree. Before long indentured servitude virtually disappeared.[37]

With the post-revolutionary republican culture talking of nothing but liberty, equality, and independence, even hired servants eventually became hard to come by or to control. White servants refused to call their employers ''master'' or ''mistress''; for many the term ''boss,'' derived from the Dutch word for master, became a euphemistic substitute. The servants themselves would not be called anything but ''help,'' or ''waiter,'' which was the term the character Jonathan, in Royall Tyler's 1787 play *The Contrast,* preferred in place of ''servant.''[38] ''The white servants generally stipulate that they shall sit at table with their masters and mistresses,'' declared astonished foreigners. When questioned, the servants explained that this was ''a free country,'' that they were as good as anyone, and "that it was a sin and a shame for a free-born American to be treated like a servant." Samuel Breck, a sometime senator from Pennsylvania, thought his life would be "perfectly happy" if only he had good servants. "But so easy is a livelihood obtained that fickleness, drunkenness, and not infrequently insolence, mark the character of our domestics." In one year alone Breck hired seven different cooks and five different waiters.[39]

When one English immigrant in the 1790s reported that "the worst circumstance of living" in Newark, New Jersey, was "the difficulty of getting domestic servants," then we know things were bad. Desperate would-be masters in several cities were eventually compelled to form organizations for the encouragement of faithful domestic servants. Some Northerners even concluded that the practice of keeping servants was "highly anti-republican." Consequently, in time Americans built hotels as public residences that were unlike anything existing in Europe. These hotels, combining both eating and lodging, prohibited tipping and were often occupied by permanent boarders. Many found living in these hotels cheaper than setting up a household with servants who were so hard to find. Foreigners found such hotels and boardinghouses to be peculiarly American institutions.[40]

By the early nineteenth century what remained of patriarchy was in disarray. No longer were apprentices dependents within a family; they became trainees within a business that was more and more conducted outside the household. Artisans did less "bespoke" or "order" work for patrons; instead they increasingly produced for impersonal markets. This in turn meant that the master craftsmen had to hire labor and organize the sale of the products of their shops. Masters became less patriarchs and more employers, retail merchants, or businessmen. Cash payments of wages increasingly replaced the older paternalistic relationship between masters and journeymen. These free wage earners now came and went with astonishing frequency, moving not only from job to job but from city to city. This "fluctuating" mobility of workers bewildered some employers: "while you were taking an inventory of their property," sighed one Rhode Islander, "they would sling their packs and be off."[41]

Although both masters and journeymen often tried to maintain the traditional fiction that they were bound together for the "good of the trade," increasingly they saw themselves as employers and employees with different interests. Although observers applauded the fact that apprentices, journeymen, and masters of each craft marched together in the federal procession in Philadelphia on July 4, 1788, the tensions and divergence of interests were already visible. Before long journeymen in various crafts organized themselves against their masters' organizations, banned their employers from their meetings, and declared that "the interests of the journeymen are separate and in some respects opposite of those of their employers." Between 1786 and 1816 at least twelve major strikes by various journeymen craftsmen occurred—the first major strikes by employees against employers in American history.[42]

One obvious dependency the revolutionaries did not completely abolish was that of nearly a half million Afro-American slaves, and their failure to do so, amidst all their high-blown talk of liberty, makes them seem inconsistent and hypocritical in our eyes. Yet it is important to realize that the Revolution suddenly and effectively ended the cultural climate that had allowed black slavery, as well as other forms of bondage and unfreedom, to exist throughout the colonial period without serious challenge. With the revolutionary movement, black slavery became excruciatingly conspicuous in a way that it had not been in the older monarchical society with its many calibrations and degrees of unfreedom; and Americans in 1775-76 began attacking it with a vehemence that was inconceivable earlier.

For a century or more the colonists had taken slavery more or less for granted as the most base and dependent status in a hierarchy of dependencies and a world of laborers. Rarely had they felt the need either to criticize black slavery or to defend it. Now, however, the republican attack on dependency compelled Americans to see the deviant character of slavery and to confront the institution as they never had to before. It was no accident that Americans in Philadelphia in 1775 formed the first anti-slavery society in the world. As long as most people had to work merely out of poverty and the need to provide for a living, slavery and other forms of enforced labor did not seem all that different from free labor. But the growing recognition that labor was not simply a common necessity of the poor but was in fact a source of increased wealth and prosperity for ordinary workers made slavery seem more and more anomalous. Americans now recognized that slavery in a republic of workers was an aberration, "a peculiar institution," and that if any Americans were to retain it, as southern Americans eventually did, they would have to explain and justify it in new racial and anthropological ways that their former monarchical society had never needed. The Revolution in effect set in motion ideological and social forces that doomed the institution of slavery in the North and led inexorably to the Civil War.[43]

With all men now considered to be equally free citizens, the way was prepared as well for a radical change in the conception of state power. Almost at a stroke the Revolution destroyed all the earlier talk of paternal or maternal government, filial allegiance, and mutual contractual obligations between rulers and ruled. The familial image of government now lost all its previous relevance, and the state in America emerged as something very different from what it had been.

Overnight modern conceptions of public power replaced older archaic ideas of personal monarchical government. No longer could government be seen as the king's private authority or as a bundle of prerogative rights. Rulers suddenly lost their traditional personal rights to rule, and personal allegiance as a civic bond became meaningless. The revolutionary state constitutions eliminated the crown's prerogatives outright or regranted them to the state legislatures. Popular consent now became the exclusive justification for the exercise of authority by all parts of the government—not just the houses of representatives but senates, governors, and even judges. As sovereign expressions of the popular will, these new republican governments acquired an autonomous public power that their monarchical predecessors had never possessed or even claimed. In republican America government would no longer be merely private property and private interests writ large as it had been in the colonial period. Public and private spheres that earlier had been mingled were now to be separated. Although the state legislatures, to the chagrin of many leaders, often continued to act in a traditional courtlike manner—interfering with and reversing judicial decisions, probating wills rejected by the courts, and passing private legislation affecting individuals—they now became as well sovereign embodiments of the people with a responsibility to promote a unitary public interest that was to be clearly distinguishable from the many private interests of the society.

From the outset the new republican states thus tended to view with suspicion the traditional monarchical practice of enlisting private wealth and energy for public purposes by issuing corporate privileges and licenses to private persons. In a republic no person should be allowed to exploit the public's authority for private gain. Indeed, several of the states wrote into their revolutionary constitutions declarations against any man or group of men receiving special privileges from the community. "Government," said the New Hampshire constitution, was "instituted for the common benefits, protection, and security of the whole community, and not for the private interest or emolument of any one man, family, or class of men." The North Carolina constitution stated that "perpetuities and monopolies are contrary to the genius of a State, and ought not to be allowed."

Consequently, the republican state governments sought to assert their newly enhanced public power in direct and unprecedented ways—doing for themselves what they had earlier commissioned private persons to do. They carved out exclusively public spheres of action and responsibility where none had existed before. They now drew up plans for improving everything from trade and commerce to roads and waterworks and helped to create a science of political economy for Americans. And they formed their own public organizations with paid professional staffs supported by tax money, not private labor. For many Americans the Revolution had made the "self-management of self-concerns . . . the vital part of government."[44] The city of New York, for example, working under the authority of the state legislature, set up its own public work force to clean its streets and wharves instead of relying, as in the past, on the private residents to do these tasks. By the early nineteenth century the city of New York had become a public institution financed primarily by public taxation and concerned with particularly public concerns. It acquired what it had not had before—the power of eminent domain—and the authority to make decisions without worrying about "whose property is benefited . . . or is not benefited." The power of the state to take private property was now viewed as virtually unlimited—as long as the property was taken for exclusively public purposes.[45]

Many concluded that the state legislatures could now do for the public whatever the people entrusted them to do. "A community must always remain competent to the superintendence of its concerns," wrote James Cheetham in 1802. "These general powers of superintendence must be entrusted somewhere. They can be no where more safely deposited than with the legislature. Subject to the constitution, all the rights and privileges of the citizen are entrusted with them."[46] The people under monarchy, of course, had possessed long-standing rights and privileges immune from tampering by the prerogative powers and privileges of the king. But under republicanism could such popular rights continue to be set against the government? In the new republics, where there were no more crown powers and no more prerogative rights, it was questionable whether the people's personal rights could meaningfully exist apart from the people's sovereign power—the general will—expressed in their assemblies. In other words, did it any longer make sense to speak of negative liberty where the people's positive liberty was complete and supreme? To be sure, as the Pennsylvania constitution together with other revolutionary constitutions declared, "no part of man's property can be justly taken from him, or applied to public uses, without his own consent," but this consent, in 1776 at least, meant "that of his legal representatives."[47]

Such assertions that all power to superintend and improve the society belonged to the people and was embodied in the popular state legislatures flowed naturally from republican doctrine. But well before 1800 many Americans had come to challenge the belief that such a monopoly of public power ought to be entrusted to any governmental institution whatsoever, however representative and popularly elected. Indeed, limiting popular government and protecting private property and minority rights without at the same time denying the sovereign public power of the people became the great dilemma of political leaders in the new republic; indeed, it remains the great dilemma of America's constitutional democracy.

II. *Enlightenment*

Destroying the ligaments of patronage and kinship that had held the old monarchical society together was only half the radicalism of the republican revolution. Something else would have to be put in place of these ancient social ties, or American society would simply fall apart. The first steps in constructing a new republican society were to enlighten the people and to change the nature of authority. Not only would the culture have to be republicanized, but all superior-subordinate relationships would necessarily change. If parents and masters were kind and caring, children and servants would naturally obey. If the political rulers were men of merit and talent and governed only in the public interest, they would naturally command the affection and respect of the people, and the crises of authority bedeviling American society would end. Love and gratitude would replace fear and favor as social adhesives.

The vision of the revolutionary leaders is breathtaking. As hardheaded and practical as they were, they knew that by becoming republican they were expressing nothing less than a utopian hope for a new

moral and social order led by enlightened and virtuous men. Their
soaring dreams and eventual disappointments make them the most extraordinary generation of political leaders in American history.

In many respects this revolutionary generation was very modern.
They were optimistic, forward-looking, and utterly convinced that they
had the future in their own hands. They told themselves that they had
the ability, like no people before in modern times, to shape their politics
and society as they saw fit. Can America be happy becoming independent? asked Thomas Paine. "As happy as she pleases," he answered
for all American leaders; "she hath a blank sheet to write upon." The
American revolutionary leaders had a very modern understanding of
culture. For the first time in American history they saw that their culture
was exclusively man-made. They alone were responsible for what they
thought and believed and for what would be thought and believed in
the future by those they often called the "millions unborn."

It was an awesome responsibility, and they assumed it with a sense
of excitement and anxious expectancy. They knew—it was the basic
premise of all their thinking—that people were not born to be what they
might become. Lockean sensationalism told the revolutionaries that human personalities were unformed, impressionable things that could be
molded and manipulated by controlling people's sensations. The mind,
said John Adams, could be cultivated like a garden, with barbarous
weeds eliminated and enlightened fruits raised, "the savages destroyed,
. . . the civil People increased." The revolutionaries believed with Samuel Stanhope Smith, soon to be president of Princeton, that new habitual principles, "the constant authoritative guardians of virtue," could
be created and nurtured by republican laws, and that these principles,
together with the power of the mind, could give man's "ideas and motives a new direction." By the repeated exertion of reason, by "recalling
the lost images of virtue: contemplating them, and using them as motives of action, till they overcome those of vice again and again until
after repeated struggles, and many foils they at length acquire the habitual superiority"—by such exertions it seemed possible for man to
recover his lost innocence and form a society of "habitual virtue." Virtue, said Ezra Stiles, was an art to be learned as other arts were learned.[2]

From these premises flowed the revolutionaries' preoccupation with
education—not just their interest in formal schooling but their concern
with a variety of means to create new attitudes and to remake their
culture. These comprised everything from the histories they wrote and

the advice manuals they read to the icons they created—including Jefferson's Virginia capitol, John Trumbull's paintings, and the design of the Great Seal. With the Lockean premises they had about how knowledge was acquired, everything suddenly seemed possible. The revolutionary leaders were faced with the awesome task of creating their own world.

Changing the culture meant pushing back the boundaries of darkness and barbarism and spreading light and knowledge. For the revolutionary generation America became the Enlightenment fulfilled. The settlement of America, said John Adams in 1765, was "the opening of a grand scene and design in Providence for the illumination of the ignorant, and the emancipation of the slavish part of mankind all over the earth."[3] The Revolution was simply the climax of this grand historic drama. Enlightenment was spreading everywhere in the Western world, but nowhere more promisingly than in America. It was an astonishing claim: that these obscure provinces only recently rescued from wilderness, surrounded by "savages," and perched precariously on the very edges of Christendom, should presume to be in the vanguard of the Enlightenment was enough to boggle the mind. Americans, Thomas Paine told them in 1782, had thrown off the "prejudices" of the Old World ("prejudice, that poisonous bane and pernicious pest of society," representing everything the Enlightenment hated) and had adopted new liberal, enlightened, and rational ideas. "We see with other eyes; we hear with other ears; and think with other thoughts, than those we formerly used." Ignorance was being expelled and could not return. "The mind once enlightened cannot again become dark."[4]

This pushing back of darkness and what was called Gothic barbarism occurred on many fronts. Some saw the central struggle taking place in natural science and in the increasing understanding of nature. Even the invention of a water pump for ships sent Benjamin Rush into raptures over the hope it promised "that the time will come when, comparatively speaking, 'evil there shall be none' upon the surface of the globe."[5] Others saw it occurring mostly in religion with the tempering of enthusiasm and the elimination of superstition. Still others saw it taking place mainly in politics—in driving back the forces of tyranny and in the creating of new free governments. For many Americans this political struggle became the focus of their revolution, the republican prerequisite for all other kinds of enlightenment. But for many other enlightened Americans of the eighteenth century these were just aspects of a larger struggle. For the Enlightenment represented not just the spread of science, or liberty, or republican government—important as these were—but also the spread of what came to be called civilization.

Everywhere in the Western world people were making tiny, piecemeal assaults on the ignorance and barbarism of the past. Everywhere in small, seemingly insignificant ways life was being made easier, more comfortable, more enjoyable. Decrease the pain and increase the pleasure of people: that was the Enlightenment. It seemed at times to be a mere matter of counting, of adding pleasures and subtracting pains. So William Wollaston in his *Religion of Nature Delineated* set out with mathematical exactness the way to calculate human happiness: "the man who enjoys three degrees of such pleasure as will bring upon him nine degrees of pain, when three degrees of pain are set off to balance and sink the three of pleasure, can have remaining to him only six degrees of pain; and with these therefore is his pleasure finally resolved. And so the three degrees of pain, which anyone endures to obtain nine of pleasure end in six of the latter."[6]

Such mathematical exercises were possible because the increments of happiness, the quantities of pleasure and pain, seemed small and measurable. Sometimes they were quite palpable and material— "conveniences" or "decencies" or "comforts" as they were called. Did people eat with knives and forks instead of with their hands? Did they sleep on feather mattresses instead of straw? Did they drink out of china cups instead of wooden vessels? These were signs of prosperity, of happiness, of civilization. Jefferson said that to know the real state of a society's enlightenment one "must ferret the people out of their hovels, . . . look into their kettle, eat their bread, loll on their beds under pretence of resting yourself, but in fact to find out if they are soft."[7]

But enlightenment was not simply a matter of material prosperity, of having Wedgwood dishes and finely pruned gardens. It was above all a matter of personal and social morality, of the ways in which men and women treated each other, their children, their dependents, even their animals. Such enlightened morality lay at the heart of republicanism. Americans thought themselves more civilized and humane than the British precisely because they had adopted republican governments, which, as Benjamin Rush said, were "peaceful and benevolent forms of government" requiring "mild and benevolent principles." With the Revolution they sought to express these mild and benevolent principles in a variety of reforms—most notably perhaps in their new systems of criminal punishment.

Many of the revolutionary state constitutions had promised in Beccarian fashion to end punishments that were "cruel and unusual" and to make them "less sanguinary, and in general more proportionate to the crimes." Jefferson and other leaders drew up plans for liberalizing the harsh penal codes of the colonial period, which had relied on bodily punishments of whipping, mutilation, and especially execution. Although most states did something, Pennsylvania led the way in the 1780s and 1790s in the enlightened effort, as its legislation put it, "to reclaim rather than destroy," "to correct and reform the offenders" rather than simply to mark or eliminate them. Pennsylvania abolished all bodily punishments such as "burning in the hand" and "cutting off the ears" and ended the death penalty for all crimes except murder. In their places the state proposed a scale of punishments based on fines and years of imprisonment. In the larger and less intimate worlds in which people now lived, public punishments based on shame seemed less meaningful. Instead, the criminals should be made to feel their individual guilt, by being confined in prisons apart from the excited environment of the outside world, in solitude where the "calm contemplation of mind which brings on penitence" could take place. Out of such assumptions was created the penitentiary, which turned the prison into what Philadelphia officials called "a school of reformation." By 1805 New York, New Jersey, Connecticut, Virginia, and Massachusetts had followed Pennsylvania in constructing penitentiaries based on the principle of solitary confinement. Nowhere else in the Western world, as enlightened philosophes recognized, had such reforms been carried as far as they had in America.[8]

But these penal reforms were only one manifestation of what Rush called the "gentle and forgiving spirit" that lay at the heart of the Enlightenment. The eighteenth century seemed to many to be civilized and enlightened not simply because reformers were seeking to end the barbarity of criminal punishments, but, more important, because people in general were more benevolent, conversations were more polite, manners were more gracious than they had been in the past. Everywhere there were more courtesies, amenities, civilities—all designed to add to the sum of human happiness. Not talking loudly in company, not interrupting others' conversation, not cleaning one's teeth at the table, were small matters perhaps, but in the aggregate they seemed to be what made human sociability possible. We are apt to regard the eighteenth century's preoccupation with proper social behavior—its concern for manners and decorum—as superficial and frivolous. But the enlightened of the eighteenth century knew better. "Human Felicity," wrote Franklin in his *Autobiography,* "is produc'd not so much by great Pieces of good Fortune that seldom happen, as by little Advantages that occur every Day." They realized that all those seemingly trivial improvements in social behavior were contributions to civilization and hence to enlightenment.[9]

"Civilization" was not yet a widely accepted term, but "civility" was. "Civility" was originally a legal term derived from "civil." In the first edition of his *Dictionary* in 1755, Dr. Johnson defined "civility" as "a law, act of justice, or judgment which renders a criminal process civil." But by the latter half of the eighteenth century the modern meaning of "civility," arising first in France and spreading to Great Britain, had come into use in order to express the advanced stage of enlightenment that Europe had attained. It encompassed "politeness" and "refinement" and all those new manners and decencies between people that characterized the age. Many, however—though not Dr. Johnson himself—agreed with James Boswell that another word besides "civility" was needed to designate and celebrate the kind of society the eighteenth-century Enlightenment was creating, and that word was "civilization." "Civilization," Boswell told Johnson, was better able to contrast with "barbarity" than the word "civility." Yet the origins of civilization in civility were not lost to the late eighteenth century, and politeness, good manners, and elegance remained the defining characteristics of the new society set in opposition to the rudeness and barbarism of the Gothic past.[10]

All this stress on manners, decorum, and civilization brought to a head developments that had proceeded at least since the Renaissance. For generations the enlightened people of Western society had steadily enlarged the pale of civilization and rolled back the boundaries of superstition and barbarism. Always at the center of this advance was the changing idea of a gentleman. A gentleman, Lord Chesterfield said, was "a man of good behavior, well bred, amiable, high-minded, who knows how to act in any society, in the company of any man." No word in the English language came to denote better the finest qualities of the ideal man than "gentleman," and it was the eighteenth century above all that gave it that significance. Defining a proper gentleman was a subject that fascinated the educated public, and writers from Richard Steele to Jane Austen spent their lives struggling with it.[11]

To be a gentleman now took on a moral as well as a social meaning, and in this sense gentility became republicanized. Pure monarchists might still define aristocracies exclusively by the pride of their families, the size of their estates, the lavishness of their ostentation, and the haughtiness of their bearing, but others increasingly downplayed or ridiculed these characteristics. The enlightened age emphasized new, man-made criteria of gentility—politeness, grace, taste, learning, and character. To be a gentleman was to think and act like a gentleman, nothing more. It implied being reasonable, tolerant, honest, virtuous, and candid, which meant just and unbiased as well as frank and sincere. It signified being cosmopolitan, standing on elevated ground in order to have a large view of human affairs, and being free of the prejudices, parochialism, and religious enthusiasm of the vulgar and barbaric. It meant, in short, having all those characteristics that we today sum up in the idea of a liberal arts education. Indeed, the eighteenth century created the modern idea of a liberal arts education in the English-speaking world.[12]

When John Adams asked himself what a gentleman was, he answered in just these terms of a liberal arts education: "by gentlemen," he said, "are not meant the rich or the poor, the high-born or the low-born, the industrious or the idle: but all those who have received a liberal education, an ordinary degree of erudition in liberal arts and sciences. Whether by birth they be descended from magistrates and officers of government, or from husbandmen, merchants, mechanics, or laborers; or whether they be rich or poor."[13]

America, "just emerging," as William Livingston said, "from the rude unpolished Condition of an Infant country," was primed to receive these new republican standards of gentility. The colonists were eager to create a new kind of aristocracy, based on principles that could be learned and were superior to those of birth and family, and even great wealth. They were well aware that "a thorough acquaintance with polite literature softens our manners, banishes clownish rusticity, and renders us courteous to all."[14] Such sentiments had a special appeal for the outlying provinces of the greater British world, Scotland as well as North America. Not only did both provinces exist on the edges of civilization, keenly conscious of the nearby barbarism of the Highland clans or Indian tribes, but also both societies lacked the presence of the great hereditary noble families that were at the controlling center of English life. In both North America and Scotland, unlike metropolitan England, the uppermost levels of the aristocracy tended to be dominated by minor gentry—professional men and relatively small landowners—who were anxious to have their status determined less by their ancestry or the size of their estates and more by their behavior or their learning.[15]

Historians and literary scholars have commonly characterized this cultivation of politeness, learning, and virtue the ideology of a "middle class," but this label is misleading, to say the least. To be sure, the lower gentry in the English-speaking world were becoming sufficiently separated from the great wealthy aristocratic families to permit Dr. Johnson to define a gentleman as someone "not noble," but gentlemen were not as yet equated with commoners, middling or not. The eighteenth-century North American gentry did not see themselves in quite the same way nineteenth-century gentlemen did. Thomas Jefferson and John Adams were not members of a "middle class." The eighteenth-century gentry did not describe themselves as landowners or professionals who happened to be genteel; instead they were still gentlemen who happened to be professionals or landowners. They were, in short, still aristocrats, natural aristocrats, aristocrats of virtue and talent no doubt, but aristocrats nonetheless. They were still men of leisure, graceful without foppishness, polite without arrogance, tasteful without pretension, virtuous without affectation, independently wealthy without ostentation, and natural without vulgarity. They hoped to be, in short, the kind of enlightened aristocratic gentlemen that both Edmund Burke and Jane Austen admired.

It would be difficult to exaggerate the importance of these new enlightened republican ideals of gentility for the American revolutionary leaders. They were men of high ambitions yet of relatively modest origins, and this combination made achieved rather than ascribed standards of aristocracy very appealing to them. Family and kinship had nothing to offer them, and they not only directed their anger at all hereditary and monarchical values but also were determined to establish new measures of gentility. All of them would have heartily supported William Livingston's injunctions for becoming true patriotic gentlemen:

> Let us abhor Superstition and Bigotry, which are the Parents of Sloth and Slavery. Let us make War upon Ignorance and Barbarity of Manners. Let us invite the Arts and Sciences to reside amongst us. Let us encourage every thing which tends to exalt and embellish our Characters. And in fine, let the Love of our Country be manifested by that which is the only true Manifestation of it, a patriotic Soul and a public Spirit.[16]

It is extraordinary, to say the least, to realize what a high proportion of the revolutionary leaders were first-generation gentlemen. That is to say, many were the first in their families to attend college, to acquire a liberal arts education, and to display the marks of an enlightened eighteenth-century gentleman. Samuel Adams, John Adams, Thomas Jefferson, James Otis, John Jay, James Madison, David Ramsay, Benjamin Rush, James Wilson, John Marshall—the list goes on and on, down even to the second and third ranks of revolutionary leadership— men such as William Paterson, Elbridge Gerry, Thomas McKean, Hugh Henry Brackenridge, Nathan Chipman. Those revolutionary leaders such as Benjamin Franklin, George Washington, and Nathanael Greene who did not attend college usually made up for this lack by intensive self-cultivation in liberal enlightened values.[17] The revolutionaries knew something their fathers had not known, and they were anxious to distance themselves from them socially and culturally. Sometimes, as in the case of Thomas McKean, the father's status was too lowly for the ambitious son even to acknowledge. After having been taught gentility at Francis Allison's Pennsylvania academy, McKean turned his back on his father, a failed tavernkeeper, and sought to hide his background—so clumsily, in fact, that his later political enemies quickly perceived his sensitivity over his origins and used it against him. But even when father and son shared the same social and educational advantages, as in the case of the Charles Carrolls, the son often perceived the world differently from the father. Carroll the younger, to his father's chagrin, took the wealth of the family for granted, and proclaimed grandly that great wealth did not guarantee virtue. "I am resolved to live as becomes a gentleman," said young Carroll, and that meant avoiding "every appearance of meanness" and "every appearance of prodigality and ostentation." It meant as well dedicating himself to the public good.[18]

We shall never understand the unique character of the revolutionary leaders until we appreciate the seriousness with which they took these new republican ideas of what it was to be a gentleman. No generation in American history has ever been so self-conscious about the moral and social values necessary for public leadership.

Washington's behavior, for example, is incomprehensible except in terms of these new, enlightened standards of gentility. Few were more eager to participate in the rolling back of parochialism, fanaticism, and barbarism. Washington loved Joseph Addison's play *Cato* and saw it over and over and incorporated its lines into his correspondence. The play, very much an Enlightenment tract, helped to teach him what it meant to be liberal and virtuous, what it meant to be a stoical classical hero.[19] But Washington's Enlightenment was never precisely that of, say, Jefferson or Franklin. To be sure, he was conventionally liberal on matters of religion ("being no bigot myself to any mode of worship"), and though he went to church regularly to keep up decorum, he was not an emotionally religious person. Washington never mentioned Christ in his writings, and he usually referred to God as "the great disposer of human events." On the other hand, he had no passionate dislike of the clergy or of traditionally organized Christianity as Jefferson did.[20] And although he admired learning, he was not himself a man of science as was Franklin; in fact, like many eighteenth-century gentlemen, he did not believe that "becoming a mere scholar was a desirable education for a gentleman."[21] Washington's Enlightenment was a more down-to-earth affair, concerned with social behavior and living in the everyday world of people. His Enlightenment involved civility.

One of the key documents of Washington's life is his "Rules of Civility and Decent Behaviour in Company and Conversation," a collection of 110 maxims that Washington wrote down sometime before his sixteenth birthday. The maxims were originally drawn from a seventeenth-century etiquette book and were copied out by the young autodidact. They dealt with everything from how to treat one's betters ("In speaking to men of Quality do not lean nor Look them full in the Face") to how to present one's countenance ("Do not Puff up the Cheeks, Loll not out the tongue, rub the Hands, or beard, thrust out the lips, or bite them or keep the Lips too open or too Close").[22]

All the founding fathers were aware of these conventions of civility, and all in varying degrees tried to live up to them. But no one was more serious in following them than Washington. He wanted desperately to know the proper rules of behavior for a liberal gentleman, and when he discovered those rules he stuck by them with an earnestness that awed his contemporaries. It is this purposefulness that gave his behavior such a copybook character. He was obsessed with having things in fashion and was fastidious about his appearance to the world. It was as if he were always onstage, acting a part. He was very desirous not to offend, and he exquisitely shaped his remarks to fit the person to whom he was writing—so much so that some historians have accused him of deceit.[23] "So anxious was he to appear neat and correct in his letters," recalled Benjamin Rush, that he was known to "copy a letter of 2 or [3?] sheets of paper because there were a few erasures on it."[24] His remarkable formality and stiffness in company came from his very self-conscious cultivation of what was considered proper genteel classical behavior.

Precisely because Washington had not attended college and thus had not received a liberal arts education, he became punctilious and literal-minded about observing what he had formally missed. He repeatedly expressed his "consciousness of a defective education," and he remained quiet in the presence of sharp and sparkling minds.[25] He was forever embarrassed that he had never learned any foreign languages. In the 1780s he refused invitations to visit France in part because he felt it would be humiliating for someone of his standing to have to converse through an interpreter. He said that it was his lack of a formal education that kept him from setting down on paper his recollections of the Revolution. It was widely rumored that his aides composed his best letters as commander in chief. If so, it is not surprising that he was diffident in company. Some even called it "shyness," but whatever the source, this reticence was certainly not the usual characteristic of a great man. "His modesty is astonishing, particularly to a Frenchman," noted Brissot de Warville. "He speaks of the American War as if he had *not* been its leader." This modesty only added to his gravity and severity. "Most people say and do too much," one friend recalled. "Washington . . . never fell into this common error."[26]

Franklin, like Washington, never attended college, but he certainly made up for this deficiency by becoming as much of a member of the cosmopolitan literati as he could. After his retirement from business in 1747, Franklin shed all traces of the leather-aproned mechanic he had once been, and became a gentleman philosopher and public official. He certainly felt the lack of proper social and genealogical credentials in both Philadelphia and London and did all he could to establish himself by those alternative enlightened credentials he could control. He spent his life making himself equal to "most Gentlemen from other Countries." His experiments in science, his Augustan wit, his bit of Latin, and his untiring service to the public were all part and parcel of his enlightened gentility. His mean origins made him doubly eager to stress his aristocratic values. To critics who charged him with being a rabble-rouser, he replied indignantly that he remained an independent gentleman whose offices were always obligations thrust upon him. In not one of fourteen elections, he said in 1764, "did I ever appear as a candidate. I never did, directly or indirectly, solicit any man's vote."[27] He never bragged about making money and was in fact apologetic about it. He always urged that public officials serve without salary, and he had no greater censure than to say of someone that he thought like a shopkeeper.

It is obvious that Franklin moved way beyond his father, but others sought to do the same even when their fathers were not obscure. James Otis, Jr.'s father was an important Massachusetts politician and speaker of the house of representatives. But as a self-made, uneducated Barnstable businessman the elder Otis was never able to crack the topmost levels of Massachusetts society or to get elected to the council, the bastion of such aristocracy as Massachusetts possessed. He was defeated for election to the council, it was believed, because Thomas Hutchinson thought him contemptible. The elder Otis, Hutchinson reportedly said, had wielded power in the Massachusetts legislature not by "any merit But only by Doing Little Dirty Things for Governor Shirley such as Persons of worth Refused to meddle with." If slights like these rankled the elder Otis, they enraged the son. James Otis, Jr., spent his life trying to prove that he was every bit the equal of Hutchinson, if not his superior. And he aimed to do this in the only way he could, by becoming more learned and virtuous. As a Harvard graduate, class of 1743, Otis became a member of the literary and intellectual circle of Boston. "He was," recalled John Adams, "well versed in Greek and Roman history, philosophy, oratory, poetry, and mythology. His classical studies had been unusually ardent, and his acquisitions uncommonly great." He read Pufendorf, Grotius, Barbeyrac, Burlamaqui, Vattel, Heineccius, and in civil law Domat and Justinian. No one, said Adams, was Otis's intellectual superior. His first published book was on Latin prosody and he wrote another in manuscript on Greek prosody. And he opened his library of rare books for all to consult. Otis prided himself on his enlightenment and on his sacrifices for the people. To argue the cause of the people, he would never, he said, accept a fee. It was almost as if he wanted to show Hutchinson and the world that he was not grasping and unlettered like his father.[28]

John Adams, son of a substantial but still ungenteel Braintree farmer and cordwainer, was not all that different. When Adams left Harvard and moved to Boston, he was still the wide-eyed country boy in the big city. No revolutionary leader revealed his ambitions so openly; none expressed his resentments so fully. Moving on the edges of genteel Boston society, he was awed by the wealth, sophistication, and elegance he saw. "The very rich feel their fortunes . . . their imaginations are inflated by wealth." He envied this world yet despised it at the same time. "Pomp, formalities" were abominations to him. He hated "all the great

Notions of high Family that you find in Winslows, Hutchinsons, Quincys, Salstonstals, Chandlers, Leonards, Otis's," for "tis vain and mean to esteem oneself for his Ancestors Merit."[29]

Rising from obscure country origins into the genteel world of the colonial big city was a common experience for many revolutionary leaders. Jonathan Mayhew was a member of a family that had devoted itself for several generations to missionary work among the Indians on the island of Martha's Vineyard. He was the first surviving son to attend college, and the excitement of Harvard and Cambridge convinced him that he could never again go back to Martha's Vineyard and the Indians. He decided to enter the Congregational ministry, and tried for an opening in Worcester but failed to get it. Discouraged, he was about to accept an offer from tiny Cohasset on the south shore of Massachusetts when the ministry at West Church in Boston became vacant, its occupant having upped and converted to Anglicanism. Mayhew accepted the appointment happily, for West Church was the highest-salaried Congregational post in the colony. His congregation was made up of well-to-do arriviste merchants who were as socially ambitious and anxious as their minister. Mayhew loved the life he led as pastor of West Church—the tea parties, the soirees, the high-toned conversation—and he bragged to his English correspondents of the wealth of his acquaintances and the delicacy of the tea cakes they served. He was quick to attack other Congregational ministers as "raw and unstudied in divinity," and he opposed creating another college in western Massachusetts because it would result in too many "unlettered persons" getting into the ministry. Yet at the same time Mayhew was resentful of the Boston Anglican world that scorned his origins and tempted his congregation. His liberal Congregationalism and his fiery denunciations of Anglicanism—so passionate as to bewilder even his supporters—were designed to keep his ambitious parishioners from following their previous minister into the Church of England by offering them as much respectability and formality as was possible within Congregationalism. He allowed his parishioners prosperity but at the same time condemned the luxury of the attractive Anglican world, even saying at one point that he preferred to be the poor son of a good man than the rich son of a sycophant and flatterer. In just such ways were republican values used to soothe uneasy souls.[30]

William Paterson's origins were even more obscure. He was born in Ireland of a tin-plate worker who emigrated to America when William was two years old. His father became a storekeeper in Princeton,

New Jersey, and managed to send his bright son to the college there. As with so many of the revolutionary leaders, the experience changed young Paterson's life, for at college he learned how to be a gentleman. "The true gentleman," he wrote in one of his college compositions, "is easy without affectation, grand without haughtiness, cheerful without levity, and humble without meanness." Paterson filled his notebooks with what it took to become a gentleman. He carefully catalogued the proper styles to follow in music, dance, and dress, and was quick to note the absence of grace and manners in others. A liberal arts education was more than Latin and mathematics. "Hardly anything," he wrote, "is more difficult to attain than a graceful and easy deportment." He dreamed of sometime going to London and joining in the *beau monde* of playhouses, operas, and balls. If he went, he said in 1772, he would collect anecdotes of persons eminent for station, learning, and genius. "Hardly anything is sought after more here or renders a person more agreeable in conversation."[31]

Yet all the while Paterson made fun of such pretensions. Classical values told him that too much gentility and politeness unmanned a gentleman, and while at Princeton he carried on a personal crusade against what he called "the effeminacy and dissoluteness of modern manners," including even the wearing of nightgowns by Princeton students. Like other proto-republicans, he tended to scorn what he could not fully share in. He resented the fact that college friends with better backgrounds tended to ignore his letters. He tried claiming a more significant lineage than he had, but eventually he realized that in America he did not have to be "true blue" and could actually glory in "being a Scotchman." Small wonder, then, that aspiring gentlemen could yearn for a new world where confusing fashion-mongering would disappear and only talent, liberal learning, and virtue would matter.[32]

Jefferson was probably the revolutionary leader most taken with the new enlightened and liberal prescriptions for gentility. He was the son of a wealthy but uneducated and ungenteel planter from western Virginia and the first of his father's family to go to college. From the outset he was the sensitive provincial quick to condemn the backwardness of his fellow colonials. In 1766, as a twenty-three-year-old making a grand tour up the Atlantic seaboard, he was contemptuous of the crude and barbaric behavior of the Maryland assembly he witnessed in what he sarcastically referred to as "this Metropolis" of Annapolis. The old courthouse the colonial assembly met in, "judging from it's form and appearance, was built in the year one," and its members made "as great a noise and hubbub as you will usually observe at a publick meeting of the planters in Virginia." "The mob (for such was their appearance) . . . were divided into little clubs amusing themselves in the common chit chat way." They addressed the speaker without rising, shouted out their votes chaotically, and, in short, seemed unaware of the proper or usual forms of conducting a legislature.[33]

Doing things properly and in the right manner was important to Jefferson. At the College of William and Mary and later in studying law at Williamsburg he played the violin, learned French, and acquired the tastes and refinements of the larger world. At frequent dinners with Governor Francis Fauquier and his teachers, William Small and George Wythe, Jefferson said he "heard more good sense, more rational and philosophical conversations than in all my life besides." Looking back, he called Williamsburg "the finest school of manners and morals that ever existed in America." By 1782, "without having left his own country," Jefferson had become, as Chevalier de Chastellux noted, "an American who . . . is at once a musician, a draftsman, an astronomer, a geometer, a physicist, a jurist and a statesman." He was everything an eighteenth-century republican gentleman ought to be.[34]

In time Jefferson became quite proud of his taste and his peculiar liberal brand of manners. He read widely and sought to acquire the best that was thought and said (and sipped) in the world. His excitement over the sixteenth-century Italian Andrea Palladio, whose *Four Books of Architecture* was virtually unknown in America, was the excitement of the provincial discovering the cosmopolitan and enlightened taste of the larger world. He became contemptuous and even ashamed of the "Gothic" Georgian architecture of his native Virginia; and he sought in Monticello to build a house that would do justice to those models that harked back to Roman antiquity. In everything—from gardening and wine to painting and poetry—Jefferson wanted the latest in English or European fashion.[35]

Nathanael Greene, son of a Quaker ironmonger of Rhode Island, probably summed up as well as anyone the emotions and passions of many of the revolutionary leaders. He was as ambitious as any of them, and he worked harder than most at becoming a gentleman. He especially lamented his "want of a liberal Education"—due, he said, to the "Supersticious" opposition of his Quaker family and his father's prejudice against books. So whatever he learned, he had to teach himself. But perhaps that was an advantage. It was all very well for his friend Samuel Ward, Jr., son of a distinguished Rhode Island family, "to be able to Enumerate a long train of Noble Ancestors." But that only meant that it was harder for Ward to excel his progenitors. "He that enters into Life with all the advantages of a Noble Birth, Adorned with a Liberal Education and improved by the most Pious Example, cannot be excus'd short of an improvement proportionable to the opportunity given." If one pursued virtue under such circumstances "where there is no opposition," it would be meritorious, but it would only be "the Merit of a common Man." But to pursue and practice virtue "in spite of all Opposition," that, Greene told his friend Ward, would be "the carrector of a truly great and Noble Soul."[36]

Voicing these enlightened and republican ideals was, however, one thing; implementing them was another. At the very outset of the imperial crisis in 1761, James Otis, Jr., had electrified his audience with his call for virtue. "The only principles of public conduct that are worthy of a gentleman or a man," he said, "are to sacrifice estate, ease, health, and applause, and even life, to the sacred calls of his country. These manly sentiments, in private life, make the good citizen; in public life, the patriot and the hero."[37] The Revolution became a test of the Americans' capacity for virtue.

The revolutionaries went to extraordinary lengths to fulfill classical values and to create suitable classical personae. James Warren actually wore a toga while delivering the Boston Massacre oration in 1775. And Joseph Hawley, in a supreme act of republican denial, resolved never to accept any promotion, office, or emolument under any government. John Adams yearned to have his own Ciceronian moment. Just as "Cicero's Name has been handed down thro' many Ages with Admiration and Applause," Jonathan Sewell told young Adams in 1760, "so may yours." It was true that Adams was as yet an obscure person from a little-known part of the globe, to whom the "unthinking Mob . . . dazzled with the Parade and Pomp of Nobility" as yet paid no attention. But, said Sewell, "it is not the Place where a Man lives, nor his titles of Honour in that place, which will procure him Esteem with succeeding Generations." There was a new day coming, and New England was rising. And since "a Man's Worth riseth in proportion to the Greatness of his Country, who knows but in future ages . . . , it shall be as carefully recorded among the Registers of the Leterati, that *Adams* flourished in the second Century after the Exode of its first Settlers from Great Britain, as it is now that *Cicero* was born in the Six-Hundred-&-Forty-Seventh Year after the Building of *Rome*?"[38]

But none of these revolutionaries' efforts to fulfill classical republican values came close to matching that of Samuel Adams. Adams was a Harvard-educated gentleman who literally devoted himself to the public. He was without interests or even private passions. "It would be the glory of this Age," he said, "to find Men having no ruling Passion but the Love of their Country." He had neither personal ambition nor the desire for wealth. In fact, he prided himself on being a "poor Man," and he lived in conspicuous poverty. So unconcerned was he with his personal appearance that his colleagues had to outfit him properly for his mission in 1774 to the Continental Congress. He did not even care about fame. He thought his letters were trifles and refused to keep copies of them. He despised everything that had to do with genealogy and refused to have anything to do with patronage in any form, even among his own family. He left his son to make his own way in the world, saying that no one could expect any "advantage in point of Promotion from his Connections with men." No one took republican values as seriously as Adams did. No wonder they said that "modern times have produced no character like his." He was truly "one of Plutarch's men."³⁹

Although Adams's stern display of virtue was unique, the power of classical republican imperatives among all the revolutionary leaders was impressive. Like David Humphreys, they believed the Revolution represented a recovery of antique virtue.

> What Rome, once virtuous, saw, this
>   gives us now—
> Heroes and statesmen, awful from
>   the plough.

In ancient Rome, said James Wilson, magistrates and army officers were always gentlemen farmers, always willing to step down "from the elevation of office" and reassume "with contentment and with pleasure, the peaceful labours of a rural and independent life."⁴⁰

George Washington, of course, was the perfect Cincinnatus, the Roman patriot who returned to his farm after his victories in war. Washington knew very well these classical republican values and tried to live his life by them. The greatest act of his life, the one that gave him his greatest fame, was his resignation as commander in chief of the American forces. Following the signing of the peace treaty and British recognition of American independence, Washington stunned the world when he surrendered his sword to the Congress on December 23, 1783, and retired to his farm at Mount Vernon. In order to enhance the disinterestedness of the political advice he offered in his circular letter to the states written six months earlier, he promised not to take "any share in public business hereafter." He even resigned from his local vestry in order to make his separation from the public world complete. This self-conscious and unconditional withdrawal from power and politics was a great moral action, full of significance for an enlightened and republicanized world, and the results were monumental.[41]

His retirement had a profound effect everywhere in the Western world. It was extraordinary, it was unprecedented in modern times—a victorious general surrendering his arms and returning to his farm. Cromwell, William of Orange, Marlborough—all had sought political rewards commensurate with their military achievements. Though it was widely thought that Washington could have become king or dictator, he wanted nothing of the kind. He was sincere in his desire for all the soldiers "to return to our Private Stations in the bosom of a free, peaceful and happy Country," and everyone recognized his sincerity. It filled them with awe. Washington's retirement, said the painter John Trumbull writing from London in 1784, "excites the astonishment and admiration of this part of the world. Tis a Conduct so novel, so unconceivable to People, who, far from giving up powers they possess, are willing to convulse the empire to acquire more." King George III supposedly predicted that if Washington retired from public life and returned to his farm, "he will be the greatest man in the world."[42]

Washington was not naïve. He was well aware of the effect his resignation would have. He was trying to live up to the age's image of a classical disinterested patriot who devotes his life to his country, and he knew at once that he had acquired instant fame as a modern Cincinnatus. His reputation in the 1780s as a great classical hero was international, and it was virtually unrivaled. Franklin was his only competitor, but Franklin's greatness still rested far more on his reputation as a scientist than on his long service in public affairs. Washington was a living embodiment of all that classical republican virtue the age was eagerly striving to recover.

Despite his outward modesty Washington realized he was an extraordinary man, and he was not ashamed of it. He took for granted the differences between himself and more ordinary men.[43] He had earned his reputation, his "character," as a moral hero, and he spent the rest of his life guarding and protecting it. He believed Franklin had erred by going back into public life in Pennsylvania in the 1780s. Such involvement in politics, he thought, could only endanger the international standing Franklin had achieved. In modern eyes Washington's concern for his reputation is embarrassing; it seems obsessive and egotistical. But his contemporaries understood. All gentlemen tried scrupulously to guard their reputations, which is what they meant by their honor. To have honor across space and time was to have fame, and fame, "the ruling passion of the noblest minds," was what most of the founding fathers were after, Washington above all. And he got it, sooner and in greater degree than any of his contemporaries. And naturally, having achieved what all his fellow revolutionaries still anxiously sought, he was reluctant to risk it.[44]

Many of his actions after 1783 can be understood only in terms of this deep concern for his reputation as a virtuous leader. He was constantly on guard and very sensitive to any criticism—more so than anyone else, said Jefferson. He judged all his actions by what people might think of them. He was obsessed with a concern that he not seem base, mean, avaricious, or unduly ambitious. No one, said Jefferson, worked harder than Washington in keeping "motives of interest or consanguinity, of friendship or hatred" from influencing him. He had a lifelong preoccupation with his reputation for "disinterestedness."[45]

This preoccupation explains the seemingly odd fastidiousness and caution of his behavior in the 1780s. In 1783 he welcomed the formation of the Order of the Cincinnati and agreed to be its first president. Nothing was dearer to him than this fraternity of retired revolutionary army officers, until a great popular outcry was raised against it. Washington was bewildered and shaken, and he appealed to his friends for advice. To persuade Washington to put pressure on the Order to reform itself and eliminate its hereditary character, Jefferson appealed to the one argument that Washington could not resist—that Washington's leadership of this aristocratic society would tarnish his reputation for classical virtue.[46]

In the winter of 1784–85 Washington was led into temptation once again, and it was agony. The Virginia assembly presented him with 150 shares in the James River and Potomac canal companies in recognition of his services to the state and the cause of canal-building. What should he do? He did not feel he could accept the shares. Acceptance might be "considered in the same light as a pension" and might compromise his reputation for virtue. Yet he believed passionately in what the canal companies were doing, he had long dreamed of making a fortune from such canals, and he needed the money. At the same time, he did not want to show "disrespect" to the assembly or to appear "ostentatiously disinterested" by refusing this gift.[47]

Few decisions in Washington's career caused him more distress than this one. He wrote to everyone he knew—to Jefferson, to Governor Patrick Henry, to William Grayson, to Benjamin Harrison, to George William Fairfax, to Nathanael Greene, even to Lafayette—seeking "the best information and advice" on the disposition of the shares. "How would this matter be viewed then by the eyes of the world?" he asked. Would not his reputation for virtue be harmed? Would not accepting the shares "deprive me of the principal thing which is laudable in my conduct?"[48]

The situation seems comic today, but it was not to Washington. He suffered real anguish. Once again Jefferson found the key to Washington's anxieties and told him that declining to accept the shares would only add to his reputation for disinterestedness. So Washington gave them away to the college that eventually became Washington and Lee.

Washington suffered even more anguish over the decision to attend the Philadelphia Convention in 1787. Many believed that his presence was absolutely necessary for the effectiveness of the convention, but the situation was tricky. He wrote to friends imploring them to tell him "confidentially what the public expectation is on this head, that is, whether I will or ought to be there." How would his presence be seen, how would his motives be viewed? If he attended, would he be faulted for violating his pledge to withdraw from public life? But if he did not attend, would his staying away be thought to be a "dereliction to Republicanism"? Should he squander his reputation on something that might not work?[49]

And what if the convention itself should fail? The delegates would have to return home "chagrined at their ill success and disappointment. This would be a disagreeable circumstance for any one of them to be in; but more particularly so for a person of my situation." Even Madison had second thoughts about the possibility of misusing so precious an asset as Washington's reputation. What finally convinced Washington to attend the convention was the fear that people might think he wanted the federal government to fail so that he could then manage a military takeover. So in the end he decided, as Madison put it, "to forsake the honorable retreat to which he had retired and risk the reputation he had so deservedly acquired." No action could be more virtuous. "Secure as he was in his fame," wrote Henry Knox with some awe, "he has again committed it to the mercy of events. Nothing but the critical situation of his country would have induced him to so hazardous a conduct."[50]

When the convention met, Washington was at once elected its president. His presence and leadership undoubtedly gave the convention and the proposed Constitution a prestige that they otherwise could not have had. His backing of the Constitution was essential to its eventual ratification. "Be assured," James Monroe told Jefferson, "his influence carried this government."[51] Once committed to the Constitution, he worked hard for its acceptance. He wrote letters to friends and let his enthusiasm for the new federal government be known. Once he had identified himself publicly with the new Constitution he became very anxious to have it accepted. Its ratification was a kind of ratification of himself.

After the Constitution was established, Washington still believed he could retire to the domestic tranquillity of Mount Vernon. But everyone else expected that he would become President of the new national government. Indeed, many Americans were willing to accept the strong kinglike chief executive created by the Constitution precisely because they expected Washington to be the first President. People even talked about the fact that he lacked an heir and therefore could not establish a dynasty.[52] This widespread expectation that he would be President aroused all his old anxieties about his reputation. He had promised the country that he would permanently retire from public life. How could he now assume the presidency without being "chargeable with levity and inconsistency; if not with rashness and ambition?" His protests were sincere. He had so much to lose and so little to gain. But he did not want to appear "too solicitous for reputation." He was certain, he told his friend Henry Lee, "whensoever I shall be convinced the good of my country requires my reputation to be put at risque; regard for my own fame will not come in competition with an object of so much magnitude."[53]

The more Washington weighed his decision, the more he recognized that accepting the presidency might be the only way of preserving his reputation, especially after Hamilton suggested to him that there might be "greater hazard to that fame, which must be and ought to be dear to you, in refusing your future aid to the system than in affording it." It was not easy to make decisions when a concern for one's virtue was viewed as unvirtuous. Nothing could make him abandon his retirement, Washington told Benjamin Lincoln, "unless it be a *conviction* that the partiality of my Countrymen had made my services absolutely necessary, joined to a *fear* that my refusal might induce a belief that I preferred the conservation of my own reputation and private ease, to the good of my Country.''[54]

Washington's excessive coyness, his extreme reluctance after 1783 to get involved in public affairs, and his anxiety over his reputation for virtue were all part of his strenuous effort to live up to the classical ideal of a republican leader. It shows, as nothing else so effectively can, the extent to which these enlightened values affected the actions of the revolutionary leaders.

Everywhere in America these republican values helped to shape the revolutionaries' behavior. John Dickinson's pose in 1767 as a ''Pennsylvania Farmer'' is incomprehensible except within this classical tradition. Dickinson, the wealthy Philadelphia lawyer, wanted to assure his readers of his gentlemanly disinterestedness by informing them at the outset that he was a farmer ''contented'' and ''undisturbed by worldly hopes or fears.'' Busy city lawyers were perhaps too much involved in the marketplace to make ideal republican leaders. Their constant ''Wrangling'' and their ''supporting any cause that offers'' had ''obliterated all regard to right and wrong . . . even with them Who are above pecuniary influence.'' ''Candor and integrity,'' it was said, were found ''seldom in professional Men.'' Lawyers thus were always hard pressed to justify their virtue and disinterestedness. But landed gentlemen, like the ''Pennsylvania Farmer,'' living off ''a little money at interest'' were not.[55]

Since merchants were worse off than lawyers in this respect, those with political ambitions always felt pressed to shed their mercantile activities and to ennoble themselves. John Hancock has been criticized by historians for dissipating his uncle's fortune and destroying his merchant business. But such criticism misses the point of Hancock's ambitions. Hancock wanted a public career, and the only way he felt he could have it was to become a republican aristocrat who could say ''I despise the shame of wealth.'' Henry Laurens had the same ambition, and in 1764 he began curtailing his mercantile operations. In case he himself did not make it as an aristocrat, he went to great lengths to educate his son, John, to become one. So successful was he that John Laurens, before his untimely death in 1782, emerged as everyone's ideal young republican gentleman who loved military glory and who was about as far removed from the sordid business of trade as one could get. During the Revolution, Henry Laurens, the father, became president of the Continental Congress and enough of an aristocrat himself to be able to sneer at all those merchants who were still busy making money. "How hard it is," he had the gall to say in 1779, "for a rich, or covetous man to enter heartily into the kingdom of patriotism."[56]

There was nothing unusual about these mercantile efforts at ennoblement. As Adam Smith said, "merchants are commonly ambitious of becoming country gentlemen."[57] Many American merchants in the years preceding and following the Revolution—George Clymer, William Bingham, Elbridge Gerry, George Cabot, and others—retired from business, put most of their mercantile capital into proprietary wealth, and sought to set themselves up as landed squires, often in order to pursue political office within the classical republican atmosphere.[58] But the most important merchant in the American Revolution and perhaps the richest in all North America, Robert Morris of Philadelphia, was very slow to adapt to these republican imperatives.

Morris engaged in public affairs during the Revolutionary War and became superintendent of finance in 1781 while at the same time remaining a private merchant deeply involved in the profit-making of his business. Perhaps he could never have succeeded as financier of the United States if he had not used his private trading and personal resources to aid the revolutionary cause, but he paid heavily for his mingling of private and public activities. No revolutionary leader was more severely criticized for being self-interested as Morris was. No matter that his "Exertions" in supplying and financing the Revolution were, as he said, "as disinterested and pure as ever were made by Mortal Man," the charges that he used public office for private gain kept arising to torment him, Laurens himself becoming one of his principal critics.[59]

By 1781 Morris realized that his sons ought to be better prepared for public service than he was. Like Laurens, he sent his sons abroad for the liberal education that he never had. He wanted them to read many books and to become "well grounded in the learned Languages." He hoped that when his sons returned to the "republican Governments" of America "they may probably be of some Political Consequence." Although Morris was inclined to place his older boy in "a Mercantile Character," he believed that "a liberal and well grounded Education is as necessary to this as to any other Profession, and particularly in a Country where that very Character has a tendency to lead Men into the Senate &c."[60]

Morris himself was certainly attracted by high public office, but, lacking a liberal education, he eventually became convinced that, in his own case at least, "a Mercantile Character" was not going to be acceptable for participation in an American senate. Years of harsh criticism of his self-interestedness finally drove Morris into his own attempts at ennoblement. At one moment in 1786 the vituperation was so severe that he thought he would give up his public ambitions and become exclusively a private citizen, "which suits both my inclination and affairs much better than to be in public life for which I do not find myself very well qualified."[61] But the lure of the public arena and what it represented in the aristocratic terms of civic honor were too great for him. Instead, like other merchants with political ambitions, he gradually disengaged from his mercantile business.

In the late 1780s and early 1790s he shifted all his entrepreneurial energy and much of his capital into the acquisition of speculative land—something that seemed more respectable than trade—and tried to set himself up as an aristocrat. He acquired a coat of arms, patronized artists, and hired L'Enfant to build him a huge marble palace in Philadelphia. He surrounded himself with the finest furniture, tapestry, silver, and wines and made his home the center of America's high social life. Like a good aristocrat, he maintained, recalled Samuel Breck, "a profuse, incessant and elegant hospitality" and displayed "a luxury . . . that was to be found nowhere else in America." When he became a United States senator in 1789, he was edgy and anxious to prove himself a disinterested aristocrat. When informed that the public were alarmed at the extent of "commercial influence" in the Congress, he supposed "they blame me." He seemed almost desperate to win the approval of the South Carolina nabobs Pierce Butler and Ralph Izard, who seemed to have "a particular antipathy" to him. When the Carolina senators haughtily expressed their contempt for vulgar moneymaking, Morris—to the astonishment of listeners—did "likewise": he gave himself "Compliments on his manner & Conduct in life, . . . and the little respect he paid to the common Opinions of People." Like the classical republican aristocrat he aspired to be, he was proud of "his disregard of money."[62]

But for Morris to disregard money was not only astonishing, it was fatal. We know what happened, and it is a poignant, even tragic story. All his aristocratic dreams came to nothing; the marble palace on Chestnut Street went unfinished; his dinner parties ceased; his carriages were seized; and he ended in debtors' prison. That Morris should have behaved as he did says something about the power of the classical aristocratic ideal of disinterestedness in post-revolutionary America.

12. Benevolence

At the height of the patriot frenzy in 1774–76 many of the revolutionaries wanted nothing less than a reconstruction of American society. But they had no desire to overturn one class and replace it with another. They could as yet scarcely conceive of society in these modern terms. What the whig radicals desired was to destroy all the remaining traditional ties of a monarchical society—those "secret bonds of society," as Jeremy Belknap called them: bonds of blood, family, and personal influence—and replace them with new republican adhesives.' Somehow American society would have to be tied together in new ways.

As royal authority collapsed in the colonies in 1774–75, new local authorities—committees and congresses—began putting together new popular structures of authority from the bottom up. Americans, as one Maryland official complained, were coming to believe that "they ought not to submit to any appointments but those made by themselves." Transforming the direction in which authority flowed, however, would not be easy. Whig patriots were keenly aware of the nature of the old monarchical society they were attacking. As the South Carolina General Committee told a hesitant New York Committee in March 1775, "we are not ignorant of that crowd of placemen, of contractors, of officers, and needy dependents upon the Crown, who are constantly employed to frustrate your measures."[2] Much of the activity of the revolutionary committees in 1774–76 was devoted to breaking these older personal ties of dependency on royal authority and to establishing new attachments to "the body of the people."

These whig committees and mobs took their actions very seriously. They worked out elaborate procedures and rituals for dealing with individuals who held royal commissions or whose allegiance to the revolutionary cause was in doubt. Since prominent and wealthy individuals in a monarchical society had a ramifying importance among their dependents, the patriots were always fearful, as the crowd confronting the Connecticut "River God," Israel Williams, declared, of "a man of your place and of your ability and influence." James Allen, the scion of the great Allen family of Pennsylvania, was similarly feared. In December 1776 patriot soldiers with fixed bayonets seized him and brought him before members of the council of safety, because, as Allen recounted in his diary, "Mr. Owen Biddle . . . said, that they had received accounts of the unwillingness of the Militia of Northampton County to march, that they knew my influence and property there, & were afraid of my being the cause of it."[3] But actually no person living off royal patronage was too insignificant to be challenged. In April 1775 a local committee of inspection seized a Maine lumberman under contract to provide masts to the royal navy yard in Halifax, Nova Scotia, for his "close connections with and dependence on persons employed by the Crown," an activity "contrary to the known sentiments of the people." Rarely, however, did these whig mobs hang or kill or even bring before kangaroo courts these suspected individuals. Such crown loyalists were intimidated and coerced, often by tarring and feathering and sometimes by being stuck in a smokehouse with the chimney blocked. But always the aim was to get the suspected persons to recant their former ties to the crown and to reintegrate them back into the community.[4]

Since the bond to the king was a personal and moral one, the disavowals had to be personal and moral as well. The mobs singled out suspected loyalists, subjected them to elaborate interrogations, and urged them to sign confessions of guilt and repentance. In Philadelphia, for example, thirty militiamen escorted Isaac Hunt around the city in a cart while he publicly recanted his questioning of a revolutionary committee's authority. Once the degrees of disaffection were defined and established, whether it was having drunk British tea or having denounced the Continental Congress, the mobs went to great lengths to get these individuals to swear new oaths of fidelity as "marks of friendship" to the people.[5]

The breaking of old oaths and the taking of new ones were signs of how much this new enlightened age still owed to the older medieval world of personal fealty and homage. Without such individual and personal ties, it seemed that society would necessarily fall apart. In fact, one of the principal accusations that tories made against the patriots was that their vitriolic attacks on royal officials and others, their "*electioneering,* as it is called," were "so ruinous to private attachments and good fellowship." They "set a community at variance, father against son, son against father; they dissolve in a moment the solidest friendship." Everywhere the loyalists saw what the revolutionary attack on family, heredity, and patronage, or "friendship," really meant: the patriots, tories charged, seemed to regard as important "no law, no friendship, no alliance, no ties of blood," and to be bent on dissolving all society "under the specious show of an exalted kind of virtue."[6]

These tory accusations were neither inaccurate nor misplaced. The patriots were indeed trying to destroy the ligaments of the older society and to reknit people together in new ways. All revolutionaries in the eighteenth century were fascinated with oath-taking and the need to find some republican substitute for the personal fealty and loyalty that subordinates felt toward their superiors in a monarchical society. Whig committees sought, as a character in Robert Munford's *The Patriots* declared, to make the oaths "a touchstone of public virtue, and as a trial of faith, and woe unto those who are found faithless." Late-eighteenth-century artists could not paint enough oath-taking scenes, and the American revolutionaries, like the French a few years later, could not administer enough oaths. This oath-taking was so solemn and ceremonious because the revolutionaries knew that something important was happening. They were creating new social bonds by making individuals swear a new "attachment to the body of the people" (the terms most commonly used in these mob rituals).[7]

How to attach people to one another and to the state? That was one of the central obsessions of the age. Lacking our modern appreciation of the force of nationalism, eighteenth-century thinkers had difficulty conceiving of what Bishop Butler called "the distinct cements of society" in anything other than personal terms, in terms of the individual's relationship to some other individual. Monarchy had been so powerful because its social adhesives—force, kinship, patronage, and dependencies of various sorts—had seemed so substantial. But since at least the beginning of the eighteenth century reformers had sought to republicize monarchy by replacing its social cements with other, more affective, more emotional, more natural ties. The Enlightenment came to believe that there was "a natural principle of attraction in man towards man," and that these natural affinities were by themselves capable of holding the society together.[8]

These natural affinities, the love and benevolence that men felt toward each other, were akin to traditional classical republican virtue but not identical to it. By mid-century classical virtue seemed too demanding and too severe for the civilized societies of Europe. Ancient Sparta and Rome, said Hume, were free republican states no doubt, and their citizens were virtuous and self-sacrificing. But they were also small states that were almost continually in arms. Therefore it was not surprising that their citizens were soldiers as well as farmers. "Could we convert a city into a kind of fortified camp, and infuse into each breast so martial a genius, and such a passion for public good, as to make every one willing to undergo the greatest hardships for the sake of the public; these affections might now, as in ancient times, prove alone a sufficient spur to industry, and support the community. It would then be advantageous, as in camps, to banish all arts and luxury." But Hume and many others concluded that such martial and moral spirit was "too disinterested and too difficult to support" in this modern age of sprawling commercial societies.[9]

The revolutionaries wanted a virtue that was natural. The kind of classical virtue that Montesquieu had described was unnatural; it was too forbidding, harsh, and austere. It was a "visionary principle," "the offspring of a rugged impracticability of character," and "enthusiasm" not based on reason. The antique conception of virtue was too transcending of the demands of a corrupt human nature and thus resembled the Christian conquest of self, ultimately achieved only by divine grace. It was like Chinese foot-binding; it ran against human nature. All that was needed was to allow human nature "fair play," and it would take care of itself. Man "cannot alter his nature; he can only cultivate it." Even kings were "unnatural," said Benjamin Rush, since their authority had to be "imposed by oaths, garters, guards, picture on coin &c." Without kings and other unnatural interferences, republican society could develop a new kind of virtue, could express the natural adhesives, what Rush called the natural "affections" appropriate to a modern enlightened society.[10]

Such a new, modern virtue was associated with affability and sociability, with love and benevolence, indeed with the new emphasis on politeness, which James Wilson and his friend William White defined in 1768 as *"the natural and graceful expression of the social virtues."* Politeness tamed and domesticated the older civic humanist conception of virtue. Virtue became less the harsh self-sacrifice of antiquity and more the willingness to get along with others for the sake of peace and prosperity. Virtue became identified with decency. Where the ancient classical virtue was martial and masculine, as revealed, for example, in David's painting *The Oath of the Horatii*, the new virtue was soft and feminized, and capable of being expressed by women as well as men; some, in fact, thought it was even better expressed by women.[11]

The new social virtue was much more Addisonian than it was Spartan. Indeed, the powerful appeal of Addison's play *Cato* could scarcely have rested on the austere and self-denying character of Cato himself. The hero's forbidding sternness and his inexorable suicide on behalf of liberty represented behavior not easily emulated by the prosperous and civilized audiences of the eighteenth century. More attractive was young

Juba, the Prince of Numidia and Cato's prospective son-in-law. His message was the Enlightenment's message:

> A *Roman* soul is bent on higher views:
> To civilize the rude unpolished world,
> and lay it under the restraint of laws;
> To make Man mild, and sociable to Man;
> To cultivate the wild licentious Savage
> with wisdom, discipline, and liberal arts
> Th' embellishments of life: Virtues like these,
> Make human nature shine, reform the soul
> And break our fierce barbarians into men.[12]

Promoting social affection was in fact the object of the civilizing process. "What does the idea of politeness and refinement of a people suppose? Is it not this, that they cultivate intimate friendships; that they mutually sympathize with the misfortunes of each other, and that a passionate show of affections is promoted."[13]

Although some like William Livingston stressed that "Benevolence is the Parent of Patriotism," clearly something essential in the republican tradition had changed. Classical virtue had flowed from the citizen's participation in politics; government had been the source of his civic consciousness and public-spiritedness. But modern virtue flowed from the citizen's participation in society, not in government, which the liberal-minded increasingly saw as the principal source of the evils of the world. "Society," said Thomas Paine in a brilliant summary of this common enlightened separation, "is produced by our wants and government by our wickedness; the former promotes our happiness *positively* by uniting our affections, the latter *negatively* by restraining our vices. The one encourages intercourse, the other creates distinctions." Even someone as different from Paine as James Wilson made a similar point in suggesting that government was "highly necessary" only because of man's "fallen state." Society, "particularly domestick society," said Wilson, was "better" than public life. People were wrong to consider society as merely the scaffolding of government; "in the just order of things, government is the scaffolding of society: and if society could be built and kept entire without government, the scaffolding might be thrown down, without the least inconvenience or cause of regret." It was society—the affairs of private social life—that bred politeness, sympathy, and the new domesticated virtue. Mingling in drawing rooms, clubs, and coffeehouses—partaking of the innumerable interchanges of the daily comings and goings of modern life—created affection and fellow feeling. Some now argued that even commerce, that traditional enemy of classical virtue, was in fact a source of modern virtue. "Its effects," said Benjamin Rush, were "next to religion in humanizing mankind." It formed, said James Sullivan, "a chain of confidence and friendship throughout the world."[4]

The importance of this domestication of virtue for American culture can scarcely be exaggerated. It was not nostalgic or backward-looking, but progressive. It not only helped reconcile classical republicanism with modernity and commerce; it laid the basis for all reform movements of the nineteenth century, and indeed for all subsequent modern liberal thinking. We still yearn for a world in which everyone will love one another.

No doubt this belief in the capacity of love and benevolence to hold republican societies together became for many as much of a "visionary principle" as the belief in ascetic classical virtue had been, and hard-nosed skeptics came to doubt its efficacy. But for a moment in the glow of the Revolution, Americans as cool and collected as young John Quincy Adams could imagine a new and better world emerging. In such a "vision of bliss" all violent passions will "give place to the soft control of mild and amiable sentiments, which shall unite in social harmony the innumerable varieties of the human race." Superstition would disappear, barbarism recede, and all parts of the globe be gently bound together through commerce. And then "the long expected era of human felicity which has been announced by prophetic inspiration and described in the most enraptured language of the muses, shall commence its splendid progress."[5] Men like Adams were optimistic and confident of social harmony and progress because the new modern virtue was no utopian fantasy but an enlightened conclusion of the modern science of society. Most clergymen, of course, remained satisfied with urging Christian love and charity upon their ordinary parishioners. But educated and enlightened people wanted something more: to secularize Christian love and find in human nature itself a scientific imperative for loving one's neighbor as oneself. Ultimately the Enlightenment aimed at nothing less than discovering the hidden forces in the moral world that moved and held people together, forces that could match the great eighteenth-century scientific discoveries of the hidden forces—gravity, magnetism, electricity, and energy—that operated in the physical world.

Philosophes such as John Witherspoon, president of Princeton, dreamed of a time "when men, treating moral philosophy as Newton and his successors have done natural, may arrive at greater precision."[16]

This scientific investigation of the moral and social order was not simply the work of such great minds as Shaftesbury, Bishop Butler, Francis Hutcheson, and Adam Smith. There was hardly an educated person in all of America who did not at one time or another try to describe the natural forces holding society together. By the middle of the century writers of every description—novelists, essayists, clergy-men—were excitedly exploring and promoting the natural ways people related to one another. By 1754 Esther Burr, the daughter of Jonathan Edwards and the new bride of Aaron Burr, Sr., president of the College of New Jersey, had come to realize that because of "so many just thoughts" on benevolence and compassion expressed by recent writers, "the World is agoing to have better notions about friendship than they used to." Mrs. Burr did not anticipate the half of it. "Were we not formed for Society? . . . And can that Society be carried on without a chearful and benevolent Disposition?" were questions central to the Enlightenment.[7]

"Man," it was said over and over, "is formed for social life." He had an instinct, "an irresistible urge to associate with his fellow-beings." Which is why solitary confinement as a criminal punishment was regarded by some in the eighteenth century as a terror worse than death.[18] Americans like young Nathanael Greene marveled at the way the "Spirits and minds of men" were "drawn together into communities, friendships and the various species of Society" by some "principle of attraction." This harmony "in the moral and intellectual world" was no different from the rest of the universe. "In the whole scope of Creation" there was "a certain correspondence of parts, a similitude of operations and unity of design." Liberal clergy were especially ecstatic to learn that Christian love was natural to man and in accord with the teachings of science. "Just as the regular motions and harmony of the heavenly bodies depend upon their mutual gravitation towards each other," said Jonathan Mayhew, so too did love and benevolence among people preserve "order and harmony" in the society. Love between humans was akin to gravity of the moral world, and it could be studied and perhaps even manipulated more easily than the gravity of the physical world. "Benevolence," said Samuel Cooper of Boston in 1753, "is the Cement and Support—of Families—of Churches—of States and

Kingdoms—and of the great Community of Mankind. It is the single Principle that constitutes and preserves all the Peace and Harmony, all the Beauty and Advantage of Society.''[19]

Such love, many thought, was so natural and so powerful because it rested ultimately on self-love. ''There is, in the human Breast, a social Affection which extends to our whole Species,'' John Adams told his wife in 1775 in a conventional description of the moral science at work. This affection centering on the self, said Adams, reaches outward to embrace in widening concentric circles ever larger numbers of people, to the family, the neighborhood, the town, the country, the province, the nation, eventually reaching across nations and taking in all mankind. Francis Hutcheson even thought that such love might extend into outer space. Although this love got steadily weaker as it moved outward from the self, many thought it was always tied to the self and received its strength from the self. In fact, said Samuel Cooper, self-love was ''at least as necessary to the Support and Happiness of the World as social [love].'' Benevolence was not some ''mad'' emotion by which a person ''becomes wholly devoted to the Gratification of others, without any Concern or Relish for his own private Happiness.'' Without self-love there could be no benevolence and without benevolence there could be no private happiness. Since it seemed scientifically evident that the greatest happiness for people came from their love and friendship with others, then ''the more we cultivate benevolence the more we shall promote our own happiness.'' Thus if only the natural tendencies of man were allowed to flow freely, ''unclogged by civil impediments,'' society would prosper. There would be no need any longer for compacts and charters, no need for ''municipal monitors.'' The natural feelings of love and benevolence between people could become republican substitutes for the artificial monarchical connectives of family, patronage, and dependency and the arrogance, mortification and fear that they had bred.[20]

America seemed made for such republican affection. ''In most European countries,'' Americans told themselves, ''the dependence of peasants on the rich, produces on the one side, callousness and pride, and on the other, depressing and humiliating debasement.'' But in America, where ''the feudal distinctions of tenant and lord are . . . unknown . . . the dependence of our citizens is only on each other for the supply of mutual wants,'' and this ''produces mutual confidence and good-will'' between people.''[21]

One's liberalism in this enlightened world was determined by the distance one was able to extend one's love outward. "Our Charity should be confined to no partialities, but should extend to our enemies as well as our friends, to the most remote, as well as to such as are in the vicinity." Only men who had "a benevolent temper" and reached beyond themselves and their neighborhoods were true patriots. But, of course, there were selfish persons "who live but for themselves." These tended to be those "circumscribed to the more humble walks of life," but even others more informed could act selfishly. Sometimes our self-love was "so powerful as to become partial, to blind our Eyes, and to darken our Understanding and pervert our Wills."[22] Such parochialism, bigotry, and narrowness of outlook were precisely what liberal education and refinement were designed to eliminate. Thus republicanism and cosmopolitanism were joined.

Cosmopolitanism was one of the great ideals of the Enlightenment. American military officers like Light-Horse Harry Lee were anxious to avoid being "accused of local partiality," which they conceived "improper in any officer." To be enlightened was to be, as Washington said, "a citizen of the great republic of humanity at large." English radicals believed that "every Man whatever, without any partial distinction of Nation, Distance or Complexion, must necessarily be esteemed our Neighbour and our Brother." Too intense a local attachment was a symptom of narrow-mindedness, and indeed of disease. Eighteenth-century thinkers thought there was something wrong with the Swiss, who when away from home had the reputation of breaking into tears when they heard one of their local songs. Such local feelings were common to peasants and backward peoples, but educated gentlemen were supposed to be at home anywhere in the world. The many state histories written in the aftermath of the Revolution were anything but celebrations of localism. Indeed, they were testimonies to American cosmopolitanism; they were designed to "wear away prejudices—rub off asperities and mould us into an homogeneous people."[23]

It was particularly important that artists and scientists be considered members of the "fellowship of intellect" or what was commonly called the "republic of letters." The American Revolution may have divided the British empire, said Benjamin Rush, but it "made no breach in the republic of letters." Americans showed no anger at artists and scientists, such as Benjamin West, J. S. Copley, and Count Rumford, who had left America and gone abroad. They were eager to install British scientists in the American Philosophical Society despite the war. "Science and literature are of no party nor nation," said John Adams. When

Franklin was minister to France during the Revolutionary War, he issued a document to the English explorer Captain Cook protecting him from American depredations at sea during his voyage of 1779. Franklin told all American ship commanders that they must regard all English scientists not as enemies but "as common friends of Mankind." When an American captain seized a British ship with some thirty volumes of medical lecture notes, Washington sent them back to England, saying that the United States did not make war on science. General William Howe, commander in chief of the British forces in America, in effect said the same thing when he protected David Rittenhouse's orrery in Philadelphia from damage. To be liberal-minded was to transcend such local and national boundaries.[24]

The revolutionary generation was the most cosmopolitan of any in American history. The revolutionary leaders never intended to make a national revolution in any modern sense. They were patriots, to be sure, but they were not obsessed, as were later generations, with the unique character of America or with separating America from the course of Western civilization. As yet there was no sense that loyalty to one's state or country was incompatible with such cosmopolitanism. David Ramsay claimed he was "a citizen of the world and therefore despise[d] national reflections." Yet he did not believe he was being "inconsistent" in hoping that the professions would be "administered to my country by its own sons." Joel Barlow did not think he was any less American just because he ran for election to the French National Convention in 1792–93. The truth was, said Thomas Paine in *Common Sense,* that Americans were the most cosmopolitan people in the world. They surmounted all local prejudices. They regarded everyone from different nations as their countryman and ignored neighborhoods, towns, and countries as "distinctions too limited for continental minds."[25]

To be free of local prejudices and parochial ties defined a liberally educated gentleman. One's humanity was measured by one's ability to relate to strangers, to enter into the hearts of even those who were different. And Americans prided themselves on their hospitality and their treatment of strangers. Such cosmopolitanism was a consequence of civilization. "As a man advances into the refined and complicated circumstances of civilization," said William Smith, "his mind expands and reaches out to embrace larger and larger entities, from self, family, neighborhood, to country." But even love of country was too contracted for a truly cosmopolitan person. America, by uniting the different kindred of the earth, had a duty to eradicate national prejudices and to make all humanity members of one extensive family.[26]

The institution that best embodied these ideals of sociability and cosmopolitanism was Freemasonry. It would be difficult to exaggerate the importance of Masonry for the American Revolution. It not only created national icons that are still with us; it brought people together in new ways and helped fulfill the republican dream of reorganizing social relationships. For thousands of Americans, it was a major means by which they participated directly in the Enlightenment.

Freemasonry took on its modern role in Great Britain at the beginning of the eighteenth century. The first Grand Lodge was formed in London in 1717. By mid-century, English Masonry was strong enough to provide inspiration and example to a worldwide movement. Although Masonry first appeared in the North American colonies in the 1730s, it grew slowly until mid-century, when membership suddenly picked up. By the eve of the Revolution there were dozens of lodges up and down the continent. Many of the revolutionary leaders, including Washington, Franklin, Samuel Adams, Otis, Richard Henry Lee, Madison, and Hamilton, were members of the fraternity. The Revolution disrupted the organization but revitalized the movement; in the following decades Masonry exploded in numbers, fed by hosts of new recruits from deeper levels of the society. There were twenty-one lodges in Massachusetts by 1779; in the next twenty years fifty new ones were created, reaching out to embrace even small isolated communities on the frontiers of the state. Everywhere the same expansion took place. Masonry transformed the social landscape of the early Republic.[27]

Freemasonry was a surrogate religion for an Enlightenment suspicious of traditional Christianity. It offered ritual, mystery, and congregativeness without the enthusiasm and sectarian bigotry of organized religion. But Masonry was not only an enlightened institution; it was a republican one as well. It repudiated the monarchical hierarchy of family and favoritism and created a new hierarchical order that rested on "real Worth and personal Merit" and "brotherly affection and sincerity." Masonry was an organization designed to maintain the familiarity of personal relationships in a society that was coming apart. It created an "artificial consanguinity," declared De Witt Clinton, that operated "with as much force and effect, as the natural relationship of blood." It was intended to bring people together who did not know each other as well as they had in the past. The Masonic lodges, declared Charles

Brockwell in 1750, were a means by which men who differed in everyday affairs, even in occupation, social rank, and religion, could "all meet amicably, and converse sociably together." There in the lodges "we discover no estrangement of behavior, nor alienation of affection." Masonry was looking for the lowest common denominator of unity and harmony in a society increasingly diverse and fragmented. It became "the Center of Union and the means of conciliating friendship among men that might otherwise have remained at perpetual distance." That strangers, removed from their families and neighbors, could come together in such brotherly love seemed a vindication of the enlightened hope that the force of love might indeed be made to flow outward from the self. A Mason found himself "belonging, not to one particular place only, but to places without number, and in almost every quarter of the globe; to whom, by a kind of universal language, he can make himself known—and from whom we can, if in distress, be sure to receive relief and protection." This was the enlightened cosmopolitan dream.[28]

A gentleman's cosmopolitanism rested on his ability to relate to strangers, to share in the feelings of others, including social inferiors and even animals. "He weeps with them that weep and rejoyces with them that rejoyce": that was sympathy, that was compassion. Elites earlier had scarcely ever thought about the existence of their inferiors. Now they not only thought about their inferiors, including their servants and slaves, but, like Landon Carter, they wondered and worried what their inferiors might be thinking about them! This willingness to believe that "the other" had a reality equal to one's own was a powerful force in the sentimental revolution that swept through Western culture in the latter half of the eighteenth century.[29] Gentlemen increasingly congratulated themselves on their ability to condescend, to enter imaginatively into the mind of an inferior with whom they were speaking and to assume a pose of equality. In this new republicanized world all superior-inferior relationships tended to get sentimentalized, when they were not denied altogether. Consequently it is not surprising that "friendship" became the term, the euphemism, most used to describe every conceivable personal relationship in the social hierarchy, including some of the most unequal and dependent. Even the submissiveness of the servant toward his master was occasionally sugarcoated with the term "friendship." It was as if every patron-client and dependent relationship had to be smothered in benevolence.

Many now argued that "gratitude" was "a kind of counterpart of benevolence," an enlightened republican substitute for monarchical subjection and deference. Indeed, republican theorists from Plutarch to Montesquieu had argued that gratitude was the principal source of obedience in republics and that the great vice of republics was always ingratitude. Yet there was something about the obligations of gratitude—defined as the "offspring of that gladness of heart which we feel on the reception of a favor"—that implied inequality and dependence—"dependence for friendship," John Jay derisively called it; and consequently Americans in the years following the Revolution remained uneasy over their attempts to make their republican ideas of equality compatible with gratitude and the inequality it suggested.[30]

Yet these efforts to assert the obligations of gratitude and to reconcile republicanism with hierarchy were doomed almost from the outset. For the Revolution had set loose forces in American society that few realized existed, and before long republicanism itself was struggling to survive.

iii DEMOCRACY

13. Equality

The republican revolution was the greatest utopian movement in American history. The revolutionaries aimed at nothing less than a reconstitution of American society. They hoped to destroy the bonds holding together the older monarchical society—kinship, patriarchy, and patronage—and to put in their place new social bonds of love, respect, and consent. They sought to construct a society and governments based on virtue and disinterested public leadership and to set in motion a moral movement that would eventually be felt around the globe. People "begin to know one another, and that knowledge begets a love for each other, and a desire to procure happiness for themselves, and the great family of mankind."[1]

But the ink on the Declaration of Independence was scarcely dry before many of the revolutionary leaders began expressing doubts about the possibility of realizing these high hopes. The American people seemed incapable of the degree of virtue needed for republicanism. Too many were unwilling to respect the authority of their new elected leaders and were too deeply involved in trade and moneymaking to think beyond their narrow interests or their neighborhoods and to concern themselves with the welfare of their states or their country. In many of the greatly enlarged and annually elected state legislatures a new breed of popular leader was emerging who was far less educated, less liberal, and less cosmopolitan than the revolutionary gentry had expected. These new popular leaders were exploiting the revolutionary rhetoric of liberty and equality to vault into political power and to promote the partial and local interests of their constituents at the expense of what the revolutionary gentry saw as the public good. Growing opportunities for wealth turned social mobility into a scramble. Everywhere there were laments that the "tender connection among men" that the Revolution was supposed to foster was being "reduced to nothing" by "the infinite diversities of family, tribe, and nation."[2] Expectations of raising one's standard of living—if only to buy new consumer goods—seeped deeper and deeper into the society and had profound effects on the consciousness of ordinary people. Instead of creating a new order of benevolence and selflessness, enlightened republicanism was breeding social competitiveness and individualism; and there seemed no easy way of stopping it. Since at the outset most revolutionary leaders had conceded primacy to society over government, to modern social virtue over classical public virtue, they found it difficult to resist people's absorption in their private lives and interests. The Revolution was the source of its own contradictions.

The federal Constitution of 1787 was in part a response to these popular social developments, an attempt to mitigate their effects by new institutional arrangements. The Constitution, the new federal government, and the development of independent judiciaries and judicial review were certainly meant to temper popular majoritarianism, but no constitution, no institutional arrangements, no judicial prohibitions could have restrained the popular social forces unleashed by the Revolution. They swept over even the extended and elevated structure of the new federal government and transformed the society and culture in ways that no one in 1776 could have predicted. By the early nineteenth century, America had already emerged as the most egalitarian, most materialistic, most individualistic—and most evangelical Christian—society in Western history. In many respects this new democratic society was the very opposite of the one the revolutionary leaders had envisaged.

Some now looked back nostalgically to the era of the Revolution when everything was "in the plain republican style." "Those were the patriarchal times of our country, the days of innocent pleasure, which are never to return." Others were more bitter, castigating the "democracy! savage and wild. Thou who wouldst bring down the virtuous and wise to thy level of folly and guilt! Thou child of squinting envy and self-tormenting spleen! Thou persecutor of the great and good!" But most were bewildered by what had happened.[3]

All Americans believed in the Revolution and its goals. Conservatives like James Kent had wanted as much as any radical "to dissolve the long intricate and oppressive chain of subordination" of the old monarchical society. Fisher Ames may have lost confidence in the people, but he never lost confidence in the Revolution. He remained a good republican, despite the fact that the Revolution and republicanism were the sources of all he despised. Ames had never wanted, he said, "to strip the people of all power—for then slavery would ensue." But how to prevent Americans from "sliding down into the mire of a democracy, which pollutes the morals of citizens before it swallows up their liberties''? Ames, like many American conservatives ever since, tried to draw a sharp distinction between a republic and a democracy—a republic differing "more widely from a democracy than a democracy from a despotism."[4] But since democracy was an extension of republicanism, the distinction was difficult to maintain without repudiating the Revolution itself.

Some conservatives in the 1790s and after evaded the problem by blaming the French Revolution for all that had gone wrong with America. It was not the American Revolution that had caused the popular disorder and degeneration of standards infecting America; it was the French one. The French Revolution had "done the cause of liberty an irreparable injury," said the Federalists; it was "hostile to all government, even ours, which is certainly the best." Better that the United States be "erased from existence than infected with French principles," declared a rather hysterical young Oliver Wolcott, Jr. Yet by the early nineteenth century, that seemed to many to be precisely what had happened. French Jacobinical principles, spouted by "Voltaire, Priestley and Condorcet and that bloody banditti of atheists," had poisoned the American mind and perverted the rational principles of the American Revolution. So convinced was John Quincy Adams on this point that in 1800 he translated and published in Philadelphia an essay by the German scholar Friedrich von Gentz contrasting the American and French Revolutions—promoting the pamphlet on the grounds that it rescued the American Revolution "from the disgraceful imputation of having proceeded from the same principles as the French."[5]

Thus was begun the myth that has continued into our own time—the myth that the American Revolution was sober and conservative while the French Revolution was chaotic and radical. But only if we measure radicalism by violence and bloodshed can the myth be sustained; by any other measure the American Revolution was radical—and most of the Federalists knew it. Federalists like Fisher Ames and George Cabot knew that the effort in 1804 to separate the northeastern states from the Francophiles in the rest of the country was doomed, because, as Cabot put it, the source of the evils afflicting America ultimately lay not in the southern states or in France but *"in the political theories of our country and in ourselves."*[6]

Well before 1810 many of the founding fathers and others, including most of the older leaders of the Federalist party, were wringing their hands over what the Revolution had created and most American citizens were celebrating: American democracy. "The government adopted here is a DEMOCRACY," declared the renegade Baptist Elias Smith in 1809. "It is well for us to understand this word, so much ridiculed by the international enemies of our beloved country. The word DEMOCRACY is formed of two Greek words, one signifies *the people,* and the other the *government* which is in the people. . . . My Friends, let us never be ashamed of DEMOCRACY!"[7]

Democracy became for Americans more than the broader suffrage and the competitive politics of their political system. "A most surprising revolution has taken place in the whole structure of society," declared Hugh Swinton Legaré in a Fourth of July address in Charleston, South Carolina, in 1823.[8] Democracy actually represented a new social order with new kinds of linkages holding people together. Not that in the new democratic society the monarchical influence of patronage and kinship was ever entirely lost or that the republican emphasis on affection and benevolence was ignored: no society or culture, however dynamic, could ever slough off the past that completely. Older social relationships of a monarchical and republican cast, of course, persisted into the nineteenth century and persist even today. Yet there is no doubt that the new Republic saw the development and celebration of democratic social bonds and attachments different from those of either monarchy or republicanism and the emergence of democratic political leaders different from any that had ever existed anywhere in the history of the world.

In the decades following the Revolution, American society was transformed. By every measure there was a sudden bursting forth, an explosion—not only of geographical movement but of entrepreneurial energy, of religious passion, and of pecuniary desires. Perhaps no country in the Western world has ever undergone such massive changes in such a short period of time. The Revolution resembled the breaking of a dam, releasing thousands upon thousands of pent-up pressures. There had been seepage and flows before the Revolution, but suddenly it was as if the whole traditional structure, enfeebled and brittle to begin with, broke apart, and people and their energies were set loose in an unprecedented outburst.

Nothing contributed more to this explosion of energy than did the idea of equality. Equality was in fact the most radical and most powerful ideological force let loose in the Revolution. Its appeal was far more potent than any of the revolutionaries realized. Once invoked, the idea of equality could not be stopped, and it tore through American society and culture with awesome power. It became what Herman Melville called "the great God absolute! The centre and circumference of all democracy!" The "Spirit of Equality" did not merely cull the "selectest champions from the kingly commons," but it spread "one royal mantle of humanity" over all Americans and brought "democratic dignity" to even "the arm that wields a pick or drives a spike."[9] Within decades following the Declaration of Independence, the United States became the most egalitarian nation in the history of the world, and it remains so today, regardless of its great disparities of wealth.

Equality lay at the heart of republicanism; it was, said David Ramsay, "the life and soul of Commonwealth." Republican citizenship implied equality. "Citizen" (or sometimes "cit") was a term that had been commonly used by the premodern monarchical society. It generally had meant the inhabitant of a city or town, who had been thus distinguished from a member of the landed nobility or gentry. Dr. Johnson, in fact, had defined a citizen as "a man of trade, not a gentleman." In 1762 an English comedy by Edward Ravenscroft was entitled *The Citizen Turn'd Gentleman*.[10]

By adopting the title of citizens for members of their new republics, the revolutionaries thereby threatened the distinctive status of "gentleman" and put more egalitarian pressure on their society than they meant to. After 1777 in Boston the designations of "yeoman" and "husbandman" dropped out of use, and occupational titles even among artisans were now recorded only occasionally. "Mr." increasingly came into general use among adult white males. By the 1790s the Charleston, South Carolina, city council was pressured into doing away with the titles of "Esq." and "His Honor." Already by 1793 the young conservative Joseph Dennie, who would eventually make a name for himself as founder and editor of *The Port Folio*, the best-known Federalist periodical, was chastising the revolutionaries for their encouragement of equality. "I always had a high admiration of your 'old whigs of 1775,' " he told his parents with supercilious sarcasm, "but the measure of their folly was never completely filled till they gave tarts and tailors a civic feast and taught the rabble that they were all viceroys."[11]

In embracing the idea of civic equality, however, the revolutionaries had not intended to level their society. They knew that any society, however republican and however devoted to the principles of equality, would still have to have "some Distinctions and Gradations of Rank arising from education and other accidental Circumstances," though none of these distinctions and gradations would be as great as those of a monarchical society.[12] By equality they meant most obviously equality of opportunity, inciting genius to action and opening up careers to men of talent and virtue while at the same time destroying kinship and patronage as sources of leadership. With social movement both up and down founded on individual ability and character, however, it was assumed that no distinctions would have time to harden or to be perpetuated across generations. Thus equality of opportunity would help to encourage a rough equality of condition.

Such a rough equality of condition was in fact essential for republicanism. Since antiquity theorists had assumed that a republican state required a general equality of property-holding among its citizens. Although most Americans in 1776 did not believe that everyone in a republic had to have the same amount of property, a few radicals did call for agrarian laws with "the power of lessening property when it became excessive in individuals." And all took for granted that a society could not long remain republican if only a tiny minority controlled most of the wealth and the bulk of the population remained dependent servants or landless laborers. Equality was related to independence; indeed, Jefferson's original draft for the Declaration of Independence stated that "all men are created free & independent." Men were equal in that no one of them should be dependent on the will of another, and property made this independence possible. Americans in 1776 therefore concluded that they were naturally fit for republicanism precisely because they were "a people of property; almost every man is a freeholder."[3]

Yet in the end equality meant more than even this to the revolutionaries. Indeed, if equality had meant only equality of opportunity or a rough equality of property-holding, it could never have become, as it has, the single most powerful and radical ideological force in all of American history. Equality became so potent for Americans because it came to mean that everyone was really the same as everyone else, not just at birth, not in talent or property or wealth, and not just in some transcendental religious sense of the equality of all souls. Ordinary Americans came to believe that no one in a basic down-to-earth and day-in-and-day-out manner was really better than anyone else. That was equality as no other nation has ever quite had it.

Such a view of equality was perhaps latent in republican thought. The revolutionaries' stress on the circulation of talent and on the ability of common people to elect those who had integrity and merit presumed a certain moral capacity in the populace as a whole. In the 1780s James Madison had his doubts about this moral capacity of the people stretched to the limit, but even he admitted that ordinary people had to have sufficient "virtue and intelligence to select men of virtue and wisdom" or "no theoretical checks, no form of government, can render us secure." Good republicans had to believe in the common sense of the common people. Only in monarchy were "the common people" regarded as "but little superior to the untutored herd." Ordinary people, "Cato" had written, were "the best Judges, whether things go ill or well with the Publick," for they were "the Publick." "Every ploughman knows a good government from a bad one." Ordinary people were in fact more to be trusted on some things than the aristocratic few. "Honesty and plainness go always together." Ordinary people were not deceptive or deceitful; they wore their hearts on their sleeves and were usually sincere, sincerity being defined by Archbishop John Tillotson as making "our outward actions exactly agreeable to our inward purposes and intentions." Republicanism presumed this sincerity among common people. "In republics," said David Ramsay, "mankind appear as they really are without any false colouring." Republican America would end the deceit and dissembling so characteristic of courtiers and monarchies. "Let those flatter who fear," said Jefferson in 1774; "it is not an American art."[4]

But republicanism went further. The republicanizing tendencies of eighteenth-century thinking actually challenged the age-old distinction between the aristocratic few and the common many. In our egalitarian-minded age it is difficult for us to appreciate the degree of contempt with which the aristocracy and gentry of the traditional monarchical society had regarded the lower orders: those "common wretches that crawl upon the earth," when they were noticed at all, were often regarded as little better than animals. But in the course of the eighteenth century, as we have seen, enlightened and republicanized gentry undermined this aristocratic contempt in a variety of ways. By assuming their inferiors had realities equal to their own, they in effect secularized the Christian belief in the equality of all souls before God, and in the process gave birth to what perhaps is best described as humanitarian sensibility—a powerful force that we of the twentieth century have inherited and further expanded. Often this sensibility was expressed indirectly or obliquely, but increasingly many were coming to conclude that

> Divisions into mean and great
> are bane to ev'ry virtuous state.[5]

When someone as aristocratic as William Byrd could write of the natural equality of all men, even those of different nations and races, and conclude that "the principal difference between one people and another proceeds only from the differing opportunities of improvement," then we know the force of this enlightened republicanism. So powerful were the republican tendencies in eighteenth-century Anglo-American culture that even Lord Chesterfield could say in one breath that "the herd of mankind can hardly be said to think" and yet declare in the next that "shepherds and ministers are both men; their nature and passions the same," only their "modes" of expression were "different." Chesterfield, after all, was enlightened. He counted himself among the new liberal breed of aristocrats who thought it was undignified to be proud of one's birth; he considered his servants "my equals by Nature and my inferiors only by the differences of our fortunes." Some now saw more clearly than ever before the fabricated nature of culture, and all distinctions came to seem artificial. Montesquieu said he was "human of necessity" but "French by accident."[16]

Not all Americans, of course, shared fully in these enlightened assumptions about the natural equality of mankind. Some like genteel Benjamin Prat of Boston thought that the common people were beastly, superstitious, and ignorant, and ought to remain so; education would do nothing for them except make them "conceited."[17] Others balked at including Indians or blacks within the sphere of men; and when many men thought about women in these terms, it was only to emphasize women's difference from men, not their equality. Others continued to believe that God had ordained permanent distinctions between the saved and the damned. Still others, while admitting that all men had the same senses of sight, hearing, smell, taste, and touch, argued that men of genius, the elite, might have special senses—an aesthetic sense, for example—that separated them from common people and made them more sensitive. Such a distinction justified the continued separation of gentlemen from commoners and explained the different standards of honor and shame that each group had.

Still, in the end what remains extraordinary about the views of late-eighteenth-century Americans is the extent to which most educated men shared the liberal premises of Lockean sensationalism: that all men were born equal and that only the environment working on their senses made them different. "Human nature is the same in all ages and countries," said Benjamin Rush, who as much as Jefferson came to personify the American Enlightenment, "and all the differences we perceive in its characters in respect to virtue and vice, knowledge and ignorance, may be accounted for from climate, country, degrees of civilization, forms of government, or accidental causes." Such beliefs were essential to the growing sense of sympathy for other human creatures felt by enlightened people in the eighteenth century. Once men came to believe that they could control their environment and educate the vulgar and lowly to become something other than what the traditional monarchical society had presumed they were destined to be, then they began to expand their sense of moral responsibility for the vice and ignorance they saw in others and to experience feelings of common humanity with them. The eighteenth century's feelings of equality and humanitarian concern flowed from these premises.[18]

Perhaps no one better revealed the ambivalent yet ultimately radical feelings the revolutionary leaders had about equality than did John Adams. Adams had no doubt there were great men and extraordinary characters in the world, and he hoped to be one of them. He was not ashamed to have Cicero held up as a model for him, "not ashamed to own that a Prospect of an Immortality in the Memories of all the Worthy, to [the] End of time would be a high Gratification to my Wishes." Yet at the same time he had so personally felt the arrogance and pretensions of the so-called great of Massachusetts—their "Fleers and flouts, and sneers and snubbs"—that he could not help identifying emotionally with common ordinary people—"the multitude, the million, the populace, the vulgar, the mob, the herd and the rabble, as the great always delight to call them." These "meanest and lowest of the people" were far from being mere animals; they were in fact "by the unalterable laws of God and nature, as well intitled to the benefit of the air to breathe, light to see, food to eat, and clothes to wear, as the nobles or the king." Adams believed devoutly—he had to believe—as he wrote in 1766, a decade before Jefferson's Declaration of Independence, that "all men are born equal." No revolutionary expressed more passion than Adams in denouncing aristocracy—its "certain Airs of Wisdom and Superiority," its "Scorn and Contempt and turning up of the Nose." And no revolutionary defended with more vehemence common ordinary people against that aristocracy—"against being ridden like horses, fleeced like sheep, worked like cattle, and fed and cloathed like swine and hounds."[19]

Adams was ever ready to adopt his hick-farmer persona "Humphrey Ploughjogger" in order to do battle in the press on behalf of these humble people who were "made of as good Clay" as the so-called "great ones of the World." He was not "book larnt myself, to rite so polytly, as the great gentlefolk that rite in the News-Papers, about Pollyticks," but he knew that he made better sense than they did. "The discerning few, the Choice Spirits, the better sort," as "our great knowing rich men" liked to call themselves, thought that "the talents to excel as extreamly scarce, indulged by Nature to very few, and unattainable by all the Rest." Such a view was based on "the same vanity which gave rise to that strange religious Dogma, that God elected a precious few (of which few, however, every Man who believes the doctrine is always One) to Life eternal without regard to any forseen Virtue, and reprobated all the Rest, without regard to any forseen Vice." The truth was, Adams said in 1761, the differences between men were not sharp and absolute; abilities existed on a spectrum. "We define Genius to be the innate Capacity, and then vouchsafe this flattering Title only to those few, who have been directed, by their birth, education and lucky accidents to distinguish themselves in arts and sciences or in the execution of what the World calls great Affairs." But if we apply the title of genius to all those above the median, then, said Adams, we will find that "the world swarms with them." "Planting corn, freighting Oysters, and killing Deer"—these were among "the worthy employments in which most great Geniuses are engaged." The lives of these ordinary people had "as many instances of Invention (Mr. Pope's Criterion of genius) as you will find in the works of the most celebrated Poets" or "as you will read in the lives of Caesar, or Charles or Frederick." Moreover, said Adams, this genius that the so-called great were so proud of was not innate but actually a product of circumstances. "If you pick out your great Men, from Greek or Roman, and from English history and suppose them born and bred in Eskimeaux or Caffraria, Patagonia or Lapland, no Man would Imagine that any great effects from their genius would have appeared." In the end, agreed David Ramsay, the talents for "great stations" were really the same as those for "the proper discharge of ordinary business."[20]

In egalitarian late-twentieth-century America, where nearly everyone is presumed to have a job and to make a living, we can scarcely get very excited over these eighteenth-century suggestions that ordinary people have occupations and talents that are fundamentally similar to those of the few great men of the society. But in the overall span of Western history such suggestions were novel, indeed radical, and were very much a part of the world-shaking character of the American Revolution.

Thus despite all their acceptance of differences among people—differences created through the environment operating on people's senses—most revolutionaries concluded that all men were basically alike, that they were "all partakers of the same common nature." It was this commonality that linked people together in natural affection and made it possible for them to share each other's feelings. There was something in each human being—some sort of moral sense or sympathetic instinct—that made possible natural compassion and affection and that bound everyone together in a common humanity. Even the lowliest of persons, it was assumed, had this sense of sympathy or moral feeling for others. Young divinity student and schoolmaster of Sheffield, Massachusetts, Thomas Robbins recounted in his diary the incident of a black boy of about four who asked Robbins about a cut on his thumb. The boy told him, "If I had some plaster I would give you some to put on it." Robbins was overwhelmed by the boy's sympathy. "He appears to act from the pure dictates of nature without the least cultivation. If in anyone, I think we can see nature in him." The conclusion was obvious: "Is there not then in human nature a principle of benevolence?"[21]

The revolutionaries believed in Lockean sensationalism. But they were not such out-and-out sensationalists that they counted on men and women being able by reason alone to control the environment's chaotic bombardment of their senses. Something else was needed to structure their experiences. Otherwise, human personalities, said James Wilson, quoting Hume, would become "a bundle or collection of different perceptions, which succeed each other with an inconceivable rapidity . . . in a perpetual flux and movement." A society composed only of fluctuating sensations was impossible; something had to bind people together intuitively and naturally. As Jefferson said, "the Creator would indeed have been a bungling artist, had he intended man for a social animal, without planting in him social dispositions." Americans, like others in these years, modified their stark Lockean environmentalism by positing this natural social disposition, a moral instinct, a sense of sympathy, in each human being. Such a moral gyroscope—identified with Scottish moral or commonsense thinking and resembling Kant's categories—was needed to counteract the worst and most frightening implications of Lockean sensationalism and to keep individuals level and sociable in a confused and chaotic world. If man's character were simply the consequence of the "impressions" made upon him "from an infinite variety of objects external and internal . . . ," wrote Nathaniel Chipman, "he would be the sport of blind impulses." There was a "necessity," therefore, "for a balance, as well as some arbiter of moral action."

And this balancer or arbiter was not reason, which was too unequally distributed in people, but a common moral sense—a moral intuition existing in every person's heart or conscience, however humble and however lacking in education that person may have been. This common sense, said James Wilson, "is purely the gift of heaven"; it "makes a man capable of managing his own affairs, and answerable for his conduct toward others." It made benevolence and indeed moral society possible.[22]

It was thus "natural to infer, that a disposition to do good, must, in some degree, be common to all men." From this assumption flowed not only the confidence of the revolutionaries in the natural affability of people, but the view of many that educated gentlemen had no greater sense of right and wrong than plain unlettered people. "State a moral case to a ploughman and a professor," said Jefferson, echoing Trenchard and Gordon's "Cato"; "the former will decide it as well, and often better than the latter, because he has not been led astray by artificial rules."[23]

Here was the real source of democratic equality, an equality that was far more potent than the mere Lockean belief that everyone started at birth with the same blank sheet. Jefferson and others who invoked this egalitarian moral sense, of course, had little inkling of the democratic lengths to which it would be carried. But already, even before the Revolution, there were premonitions. A gentleman's fancy education in the liberal arts did not make men free, it was suggested in 1771. "The plain, the simple and honestly well-meaning are . . . infinitely more free, than those whose self-affections are exalted by a mere formal education. Practical knowledge only is valuable."[24]

The republican revolution aggravated such anti-intellectual sentiments and rendered suspect all kinds of distinctions, whether naturally derived or not. By increasing the social scrambling and conspicuous consumption that had been obvious even before the Revolution, republican equality threatened even to destroy the notion of a social hierarchy of ranks and degrees. In a free and independent republic "the idea of equality breathes through the whole and every individual feels ambitious, to be in a situation not inferior to his neighbour." Among Americans, "the idea of inferiority, as of pursuing a mean employment or occupation . . . mortifies the feelings, and sours the minds of those who feel themselves inferior." Consequently, everyone strives to be equal with those above him, "in dress, if in nothing else." A society that had no place for these sorts of inferiorities—of occupation or of dress—was an unusual society indeed. This was drawing out republican equality faster and further than anyone had expected.[25]

For many who were captivated by such egalitarian thoughts the Revolution had only substituted one obnoxious elite for another. "There are some among *us* who call *themselves* persons of quality," declared a typical tirade from Massachusetts in the mid-1780s. But in fact such persons of quality were no different from that "set of mushroom gentry" of the colonial era who, adorned with imperial offices and connected with those "whom they condescended to admit into their circle," had attempted to assume the character of "the *better sort of people*." So absurd was this designation "the better sort" in a republic "that the very terms become thoroughly contemptible and odious in the estimation of the people."[26]

The warning was now out against all displays of superiority, whether it was attending exclusive balls and tea parties or flaunting a college degree. The formation of the Order of the Cincinnati in 1783 by retired revolutionary army officers aroused bitter opposition. Many Americans, including Samuel Adams, thought the organization represented "as rapid a Stride towards an hereditary Military Nobility as was ever made in so short a time." This sort of ferocious criticism forced the army officers to pull back and become less public in their pretensions. Indeed, by the mid-1780s aristocrats of all sorts, natural as well as artificial, were becoming increasingly cautious about claiming any superiority at all.[27]

Equality became the rallying cry for those seeking to challenge every form of authority and superiority, including the rank of gentlemen. We have usually dismissed these challenges of aristocracy as rhetorical exaggerations—bearing little relation to the presumed egalitarian reality of American society. After all, compared with Europe, America seemed to have no aristocracy to overturn. But as Louis Otto, the French minister to America, pointed out in 1786, our dismissals ignore not only the rank of gentlemen but the sense of deprivation that ordinary people now felt in relation to those gentlemen. "Although there are no nobles in America," said Otto, "there is a class of men denominated 'gentlemen,' who by reason of their wealth, their talents, their education, their families, or the offices they hold, aspire to a preeminence which the people refuse to grant them."[28]

As early as the 1780s the principal antagonists in the society were no longer patriots vs. courtiers but had become democrats vs. aristocrats. The legislative halls and the press were filled with diatribes against aristocracy, and gentlemen whose fathers were ordinary farmers suddenly found their new claims to gentility—often only a degree from Harvard, Yale, or Princeton—had become objects of bitter denunciation.

Nathaniel Chipman, son of a Connecticut blacksmith and farmer, had graduated from Yale in 1777. Like many other college graduates in these years, Chipman was intensely ambitious and full of enlightened opinions. After resigning his commission in the revolutionary army in 1778 because he lacked the income "to support the character of a gentleman" and "an officer," Chipman followed many other Connecticut migrants up the Connecticut River to Vermont, where, he felt, his college degree and his legal education might go further. "I shall indeed be *rara avis* in *terris*," he wrote to a friend in 1779, "for there is not an attorney in the state. Think . . . think what a figure I shall make, when I become the oracle of law to the state of Vermont." Although there was a good deal of self-protective humor in these revelations of ambition to a close friend, there is no doubt Chipman was serious about rising rapidly in government, eventually even into the Confederation Congress, then the highest national office in the land. All his joshing about the "many steps" he had to mount to attain "that pinnacle of happiness"—"Let's see. First, an attorney; then a selectman; a huffing justice; a deputy; an assistant; a member of Congress"—only points up his arrogant expectation that such offices naturally belonged to the likes of him.[29]

No wonder, then, that someone like Matthew Lyon regarded Chipman as a haughty "aristocrat." Lyon, like so many others in the prerevolutionary years, arrived in America from Ireland in 1764 as a fifteen-year-old indentured servant. After serving his indenture in Connecticut, Lyon married and then in 1773 migrated to Vermont. Lyon was an ambitious scrambler who seized every opportunity for personal advancement offered by the Revolution, the confiscation of loyalist lands, and the creation of an independent Vermont. Before he was done he had become a leader in the Vermont assembly and one of the richest entrepreneurs and manufacturers in Vermont, if not in all New England.

But for all his wealth, Lyon was always just an "ignorant Irish puppy" in the eyes of the educated gentry like Chipman. And naturally Lyon in turn regarded Chipman and his fellow lawyers as "professional gentlemen" and "aristocrats" who used their knowledge of the rigmarole of the common law on behalf of former loyalists, New York landlords, and other "over-grown land jobbers in preference to the poorer sort of people." However big a manufacturer and however rich he was,

Lyon was not wrong in claiming to represent the poorer sort of people, for emotionally and traditionally he remained one of them: he had not gone to Yale and he was not a gentleman. From his perspective the emerging struggle between Federalists like Chipman and Republicans like himself was indeed "a struggle . . . between the aristocrats and the democrats."[30]

The ironies of being called an "aristocrat" were not lost on Chipman and his family. "Nathaniel Chipman an aristocrat!" said his brother in amazed disbelief. "This must sound very oddly . . . to all those who have witnessed his plain, republican manners, habits, and sentiments." Yet in the levels below levels of post-revolutionary American egalitarianism, Chipman was in fact as much of an aristocrat as Vermont was to know, and Lyon, because he was wealthier than Chipman, deeply resented being made to feel his inferior.[31]

By 1791 the geographer Jedidiah Morse was already describing New England as a place "where every man thinks himself at least as good as his neighbors, and believes that all mankind have, or ought to possess equal rights." But what Morse had seen in New England was only the beginning. Others would soon discover that equality in America meant not just that a man was as good as his neighbor and possessed equal rights, but that he was "weighed by his purse, not by his mind, and according to the preponderance of that, he rises or sinks in the scale of individual opinion." That was a kind of equality no revolutionary had anticipated.[32]

14. *Interests*

In the eighteenth century democracy was not yet the article of faith that it would soon become for Americans. It was still essentially a technical term of political theory—referring to government literally by the people, which was an impossibility for any large community. But from the beginning of the revolutionary movement Americans sought to overcome this impossibility in every conceivable way; and in the process they became the first society in the modern world to bring ordinary people into the affairs of government—not just as voters but as actual rulers. This participation of common people in government became the essence of American democracy, and the Revolution made it so. Although premonitions of this democratic future appeared early in America's colonial history, only with the imperial crisis in the 1760s and 1770s did a full-scale ideological defense of the participation in government by ordinary people actually emerge.

Popular participation in politics meant something other than the mobs and rioting of the 1760s and 1770s. Mob actions by cross sections of ordinary people, artisans and laborers, were nothing new in colonial America. In all the colonies mobs had erupted almost continually in the eighteenth century, aiming at particular targets in protest against problems that the regular processes of government seemed unable to solve. Far from being symptoms of democracy, these mob protests simply demonstrated the extent to which the society was still hierarchically and paternalistically organized. Although these eighteenth-century mobs were undoubtedly anti-authoritarian and could on occasion temporarily turn "the world upside down," by their actions they always recognized "the world right side up" and usually seemed to pose no lasting threat to the political and social order; which is why they were so often tolerated by the gentry.

What alarmed the gentry of the 1760s and 1770s, however, were the growing ideologically backed claims by ordinary people to a share in the actual conduct of government. It was one thing for ordinary people to take part in a mob or to vote; for them to participate in the deliberations and decisions of government was quite another. By classical republican standards such participation would imply the participation of private "interests" in government, with the participants becoming judges of their own interests. Yet that was precisely what democracy in America came to mean.

Beginning with the Stamp Act disturbances and the formation of the Sons of Liberty in the several colonial ports in 1765, ordinary people— chiefly mechanics or artisans from many different crafts—came together to call for the boycotting of British goods. In 1772 the mechanics of Philadelphia, who comprised half the male residents of the city whose occupations are known, formed the Patriotic Society, the first organized nonreligious public pressure group in Pennsylvania's history. In New York the mechanics began convening in taverns but soon bought a meeting place for themselves and named it Mechanics Hall. Everywhere in the colonial ports artisans developed a new sense of collective identity and began speaking openly of a distinct "mechanical interest" in the society. But the artisans were not content simply to be a pressure group. They wanted to make governmental decisions for themselves, and they now called for explicit representation of their interests in government. By the 1770s artisans in the various port cities were forming slates of candidates and were being elected as artisans to various committees and congresses and other prominent offices. The traditional gentry no longer seemed capable of speaking for the interests of artisans or of any other groups of ordinary people. "If ever therefore your rights are preserved," the mechanics told each other, "it must be through the virtue and integrity of the middling sort, as farmers, tradesmen, etc. who despise venality, and best know the sweets of liberty." Artisans, they said, could trust in government only spokesmen of their own kind, only those "from whose Principles," as South Carolina craftsmen declared, they had reason "to expect the greatest assistances.'"

In 1770 artisans in Philadelphia won four of the ten elected city offices. In the wake of their success, other particular interests—religious and ethnic groups—clamored for equal recognition through representation in government. By 1774 the Philadelphia Committee of Nineteen, the principal organization of the resistance movement, invited six persons from each religious association in the city to take part in its deliberations. When in June 1774 the Philadelphia radicals proposed to add seven mechanics and six Germans to the list of nominees to the committee that would succeed the Nineteen, a significant moment in the history of American politics occurred. This marked the beginning of what would eventually become the very staple and stuff of American politics—a consciously pluralistic, ethnic, interest-group politics. By 1775 the royal governor of Georgia could only shake his head in astonishment that the revolutionary committee in control of Savannah consisted of "a Parcel of the Lowest People, chiefly carpenters, shoemakers, blacksmiths etc. with a Jew at their head.'"[2]

Such popular and pluralist representation was only the fulfillment of the localist tendencies of public life that went back to the seventeenth-century beginnings of American history. The development of what came to be called "actual representation" in government, with its corollaries of residency requirements for representatives and binding instructions from constituents, grew out of this widely held belief that in all affairs of government members of the society "should be consulted in the most particular manner that can be imagined." People increasingly felt so disconnected from one another and so self-conscious of their distinct interests that they could not trust anyone different or far removed from themselves to speak for them in government. American localist democracy grew out of this pervasive mistrust.[3]

Such popular pluralistic representation was momentous enough by itself. What made it doubly so was that these demands for interest-group representation were accompanied by a full-scale ideological defense of self-interest. As early as the 1760s groups of New York artisans were willing to say bluntly and publicly in justification of their desire for explicit representation in government that "*Self-Interest* is the grand Principle of all Human Actions" and that "it is unreasonable and vain to expect Service from a Man who must act contrary to his own Interests to perform it." Every man in the society had interests, not just noblemen and gentlemen, and therefore every man in the society had the right to hold office in government. "Every Man who honestly supports a Family by useful Employment," the New York radicals argued, "is honourable enough for any office in the State, that his abilities are equal to. And in the great essential Interests of a Nation, which are so plain that every one may understand them,—as every individual is interested, all have an equal Right to declare their Interests, and to have them regarded."[4]

The rationale for interest-group politics has never been put more explicitly than that. Nevertheless, these were as yet just marginal expressions thrown up in the confusions of the resistance movement, premonitions and anticipations of what would be more fully developed over the following decades.

Such premature demands by artisans and other plain people for participation in government were sufficiently novel and threatening, however, to provoke some responses from the gentry. However whiggish and revolutionary some gentlemen might be, they were not prepared to accept the participation in government of carpenters, butchers, and shoemakers. It was inconceivable to someone like William Henry Drayton of South Carolina that gentlemen with a liberal education who had read a little should have to consult on the difficulties of government "with men who never were in a way to study, or to advise upon any points, but rules how to cut up a beast in the market to the best advantage, to cobble an old shoe in the neatest manner, or to build a necessary house." Drayton was willing to admit that "the *profanum vulgus*" was "a species of mankind," even that mechanics were "a useful and necessary part of society," but, he said, with more courage than discretion, such men were not meant to govern. "Nature never intended that such men should be profound politicians or able statesmen. . . . Will a man in his right senses," he asked, "be directed by an illiterate person in the prosecution of a law-suit? Or, when a ship is in a storm, and near the rocks who, but a fool, would put the helm into the hand of a landsman?"[5]

It was not just their lack of ability that disqualified artisans from important governmental office. It was their deep involvement, their occupations, in work, trade, and business—their very interestedness—that made such ignoble men unsuitable for high office. They lacked the requisite liberal, disinterested, cosmopolitan outlook that presumably was possessed only by enlightened and educated persons—only by gentlemen. When artisans and other "interests" in the 1760s and 1770s defended their self-interestedness and claimed that they and their marketplace interests had a right to be personally involved in government, they were in effect demanding to be judges in their own cause; they were insisting that party or faction be made a legitimate participant in government. This was tantamount to saying that the object of government was the pursuit of private interests instead of the public good. Such ideas ran too strongly against the grain of enlightened republican thinking to be acceptable as yet. Thus in the 1760s and 1770s it was relatively easy for Drayton and other gentry to dismiss contemptuously these early defenses by artisans of interest-group politics. But such arguments did not go away.

The Revolutionary War and the reliance on American manufacturers and craftsmen that it entailed meant that artisan interests became increasingly important. But not just artisan interests: all sorts of acquisitive and commercial interests were unleashed by the Revolution, more interests than anyone had realized existed. By the 1780s a variety of self-conscious interests, many of them created by the war itself, had emerged and were clamoring for help and protection from the state governments and the weak Confederation Congress. Of course, the existence of interests in America was not new. Many of the revolutionary leaders had experienced them in their colonial assemblies. But the interests of the post-revolutionary years were different. They were more numerous, less personal and less family-oriented, and more popularly expressive of new widespread economic elements of the society than the interests of the colonial period had been. Americans virtually ceased talking about the people's "interest" in the singular; the people's "interests"—agricultural, commercial, manufacturing—were all plural now.[6]

The Revolutionary War, like the Civil War and the two world wars, had a profound effect on America's society and economy. The war effort and mobilization were enormous. The war went on for eight years (the longest war in American history until that of Vietnam); it eventually put one hundred thousand men or more under arms (perhaps as many as one in ten of the available population served); and it touched the whole of American society to a degree no previous event in American history ever had. Thomas Paine did not realize the half of it when he wrote in 1776 that "the necessities of an army create a new trade." The inexhaustible needs of three armies—the British and French as well as the American—for everything from blankets and wagons to meat and rum brought into being hosts of new manufacturing and entrepreneurial interests and made market farmers out of husbandmen who before had scarcely ever traded out of their neighborhoods.[7]

To pay for all these new war goods, at least for the American armies, the revolutionary governments issued huge sums—four hundred million to five hundred million dollars—in paper money that made its way into the hands of many people who had hitherto dealt only in a personal and bookkeeping barter economy. Under the stimulus of this wartime purchasing, speculative farmers, inland traders, and profiteers of all sorts sprang up by the thousands to circulate these goods and paper money throughout the interior areas of America. By 1778, wrote Henry Laurens, "the demand for money" was no longer "confined to the capital towns and cities within a small circle of trading merchants, but spread over a surface of 1,600 miles in length, and 300 broad." The war and rapidly rising prices were creating a society in which, as one bitter commissary agent complained, "Every Man buys in order to sell again." No event in the eighteenth century accelerated the capitalistic development of America more than did the Revolutionary War. It brought new producers and consumers into the market economy, it aroused latent acquisitive instincts everywhere, and it stimulated inland trade as never before.[8]

The paper money and the enormous amounts of debts that all these inland entrepreneurs, traders, shopkeepers, and market farmers thrived on were the consequences neither of poverty nor of anti-commercial behavior. Debt, as we of all generations in American history ought to know, was already emerging as a symptom of expansion and enterprise. Farmers, traders, and others in these revolutionary years borrowed money, just as they married earlier and had more children than ever before, because they thought the future was going to be even better than the present. Common people were eager as never before to purchase luxury goods. "Is not the Hope of one day being able to purchase and enjoy Luxuries a great Spur to Labour and Industry?" asked Benjamin Franklin in 1784—a question that flew in the face of conventional wisdom. Farmers worked harder and produced "surpluses" during the war, not, as traditional thinking would have it, out of poverty and necessity, but in order to raise their standard of living and increase, in Nathanael Greene's words, their "pleasures and diversions." And, much to the chagrin and anger of American army officers, when these consumer goods, many of them prewar imports, became less available, the farmers stopped working hard and their "surpluses" declined. Exhortations to virtue and patriotism were ignored. The farmers were not about to sell wheat or beef to the army in return for inflated paper promises to pay if they could not use that paper money immediately to buy those "pleasures and diversions" they were becoming used to.[9]

The economic troubles of the 1780s came in part from the ending of the war and the curtailing of government and military purchasing. Too many people had too many heightened expectations and were too deeply involved in the market and the consumption of luxuries to make any easy adjustments to peace. The collapse of internal markets and the drying up of paper money meant diminished incomes, overextended businesses, swollen inventories of recently imported manufactures, and debt-laden farmers and traders. The responses of people hurt by these developments were very comprehensible: they simply wanted to continue what they had done during the war. The people had enjoyed buying, selling, and consuming and desired to do more of it. And to do that they needed money, lots of it. Farmers "in a new and unimproved country," it was said, "have continual uses for money, to stock and improve their farms" or, as Madison noted, to "extend their consumption as far as credit can be obtained." And they now wanted more money than could be had by the old-fashioned means of applying "to a monied man for a loan from his private fortune." Consequently, many of these farmers pressured their governments not only to protect them from their private creditors but to print paper money or to set up loan offices that would issue paper money.[10]

These calls for paper money in the 1780s were the calls of American business. The future of America's entrepreneurial activity and prosperity lay not with the hundreds of well-to-do creditor merchants who dominated the overseas trade of the several ports along the Atlantic seaboard. Rather, it lay with the thousands upon thousands of ordinary traders, petty businessmen, and market farmers who were deep in debt and were buying and selling with each other all over America. For these people, unlike the overseas merchants who had their private bills of exchange, publicly created paper money was the only means "capable of answering all the *domestic* and *internal* purposes of a *circulating medium* in a nation" that lacked specie. The prosperity of a country, it was now argued, involved more than external commerce, more than having a surplus of exports over imports. "The *internal* commerce of the country must be promoted, by increasing its *real riches,*" which were now rightly equated with the acquisitions, improvements, and entrepreneurial activity of ordinary people. And such internal commerce, unlike foreign commerce, did not need specie; it could exist on paper money alone."

The emergence of all these business interests and their participation in the popularly elected state legislatures made the 1780s truly a critical period—perhaps, as John Fiske once said, even in the aftermath of the Civil War, the most critical moment in all the history of America.[12] For there in those few years was first clearly revealed all the latent interest-filled and enterprising power of American democracy. In the 1780s the revolutionary leaders had a glimpse of what America was soon to become—a scrambling business society dominated by the pecuniary interests of ordinary working people—and they did not like what they saw. What were release and liberation and the pursuit of happiness for the mass of ordinary Americans were for many revolutionary gentry signs of licentiousness and self-interestedness that portended the failure of the grand experiment in republicanism.

The state legislatures were greatly democratized by the Revolution—by both the increase in the number of members in each assembly and the broadening of their electorates. Men of even more humble and rural origins and less education than had sat in the colonial assemblies were now elected as representatives. In New Hampshire, for example, the colonial house of representatives in 1765 had contained only thirty-four members, almost all well-to-do gentlemen from the coastal region around Portsmouth. By 1786 the state's house of representatives numbered eighty-eight members, of whom most were ordinary farmers or men of moderate wealth and many were from the western areas of the state. Such representatives not only had a hard time passing as gentlemen but by the nature of their occupations and their lack of enlightened gentility had interests to promote.[13]

In all the states electioneering and open competition for office increased dramatically. The high levels of incumbency and stability attained by the colonial assemblies on the eve of the Revolution were now suddenly reversed, and the annual elections (an innovation for most of the state legislatures) often saw half or more of the representatives in the states turned over in any one year.[14] Under these turbulent circumstances the state legislatures could scarcely fulfill what many revolutionaries in 1776 had assumed was their republican responsibility to promote a unitary public interest distinguishable from the private and parochial interests of people. By the 1780s it was obvious to many that "a spirit of *locality*" was destroying "the aggregate interests of the community." Everywhere the gentry complained of popular legislative practices that we today have come to take for granted—parochialism, horse-trading, and pork-barreling that benefited special interest groups. Each representative, grumbled Ezra Stiles, president of Yale College, was concerned only with the particular interests of his electors. Whenever a bill is read in the legislature, "every one instantly thinks how it will affect his constituents." Instead of electing men to office "for their abilities, integrity and patriotism," the people were much more likely to vote for someone "from some mean, interested, or capricious motive." They "choose a man, because he will vote for a new town, or a new county, or in favor of a memorial; because he is noisy in blaming those who are in office, has confidence enough to suppose that he could do better, and independence enough to tell the people so, or because he possesses in a supereminent degree, the all-prevailing popular talent of coaxing and flattering."[5]

To the gentry the most alarming special-interest legislation of the 1780s was that on behalf of debtors—the printing of paper money and the enacting of stay laws and other debtor-relief measures. We have always known that the skyrocketing inflation fueled by numerous paper-money issues and the many laws passed protecting debtors were devastating to creditors, but we have not always appreciated precisely what this meant to the gentry socially and morally. Debts that were cheapened, obstructed, or not paid back not only violated the personal faith and trust that presumably lay behind the relation between creditor and debtor, but, more important, all debt-reducing devices struck directly at the kind of stable and static proprietary wealth that was the principal source of the gentry's authority and independence.[6]

We shall never understand why the inflation created by the printing of paper money aroused such extreme anxiety and such deep moral indignation among those whom George Clymer called the "honest gentry of intrinsic worth" until we appreciate better the nature of their proprietary wealth and the social identity and influence that stemmed from that wealth. Monetary inflation, they believed, threatened nothing less than "the first principles of society." Paper money, Madison told his fellow Virginian legislators, was unjust, pernicious, and unconstitutional. It was bad for commerce, it was bad for morality, and it was bad for society: it destroyed "confidence between man and man."

Therefore most gentry who stood up for credit and the honest payment of debts did not see themselves as just another interest in a pluralistic society. They were defending the only social order they could conceive of. "On one side," said Theodore Sedgwick, "are men of talents, and integrity, firmly determined to support public justice and private faith, and on the other there exists as firm a determination to institute tender laws, paper money, . . . and in short to establish iniquity by law." These rentier or proprietary gentry could not fully understand the new kind of property that was emerging—venture capital; money borrowed, not lent; property that was dynamic, fluid, and risky. As far as they were concerned, all the paper money and debtor-relief legislation of the states were simply the consequence of men using government to promote their private interests at the expense of the public good. Thus the revolutionary gentry began to appreciate for the first time what democracy in America might mean—the prevalence of private interests in government.[17]

Monarchies, of course, mingled public and private interests; indeed, they scarcely drew any distinction between public and private spheres of activity. But republics supposedly were different; they ideally embodied a distinct public interest to which people would willingly surrender some of their private pecuniary interests. Now all that seemed in doubt. Although some of the revolutionary gentry like Jefferson had hoped that ordinary farmers might be free of the interests and caprices of the marketplace, others soon came to realize that the American people were not going to be virtuous and selfless and were not going to keep their private interests out of the public arena after all. Washington, for one, quickly realized that to expect ordinary people, such "as compose the bulk of an Army," to be "influenced by any other principles than those of Interest, is to look for what never did, and I fear never will happen." Even most officers could not be expected to sacrifice their private interests and their families for the sake of their country. "The few, therefore, who act upon Principles of disinterestedness," Washington concluded, "are, comparatively speaking, no more than a drop in the Ocean."[18]

Everywhere in the war years and after, the revolutionary leaders were reluctantly forced to retreat from the republican idealism of 1775–76. Looking around at price-gouging farmers, engrossing merchants, and factious legislators, many could only conclude that private interest ruled most social relationships. It was "the only binding cement" between people. It was "the greatest tie one man can have on another." To expect most people to sacrifice their private interests for the sake of the public good was utopian. Republican citizens were apparently not all that different from the subjects of monarchies. "We may preach till we are tired of the theme, the necessity of disinterestedness in republics, without making a single proselyte," wrote an unsentimental Alexander Hamilton in 1782. All Americans, it now seemed evident, could not be like Samuel Adams. It was too bad, but that was the way it was. Human beings were like that: their "engrossing motive was self-interest."[9]

By the late 1780s many of the younger revolutionary leaders like James Madison were willing to confront the reality of interests in America with a very cold eye. Madison's *Federalist* No. 10 was only the most famous and frank acknowledgment of the degree to which private interests of various sorts had come to dominate American politics. Madison and others were now willing to allow these diverse competing interests free play in the continent-sized national republic created by the new Constitution of 1787. But Madison and the Federalists, as the supporters of the Constitution of 1787 were called, were not modern-day pluralists. They still clung to the republican ideal of an autonomous public authority that was different from the many private interests of the society. They did not expect this public authority of the new federal government to be neutralized into inactivity by the competition of these numerous diverse interests. Nor did they see public policy or the common interest of the national government emerging naturally from the give-and-take of these clashing private interests. They now knew that "the regulation of these various and interfering interests forms the principal task of modern Legislation," but they also hoped that by shifting this regulation to the national level these private local interests would not be able to dominate legislation as they had in the states and become judges in their own causes. Far, then, from the new national government being a mere integrator and harmonizer of the different special interests in the society, it would become a "disinterested and dispassionate umpire in disputes between different passions and interests in the State." And it would do so because the men holding office in the new central government would by their fewness of numbers be more apt to be disinterested gentry who were supported by proprietary wealth and not involved in the interest-mongering of the marketplace.[20]

Most of the revolutionary leaders, in other words, continued to hold out the possibility of virtuous politics. They retained the republican hope that at least a few, perhaps only those who were Washington's "drop in the Ocean," still had sufficient virtue to become disinterested umpires and promote an exclusively public sphere of activity in government.

Amid all the scrambling of private interests, perhaps only a few were capable of becoming founders and legislators who from their "commanding eminence . . . look down with contempt upon every mean or interested pursuit"; only a few were liberally educated and cosmopolitan enough to have the breadth of perspective to comprehend all the different interests of the society; and only a few were independent and unbiased enough to adjudicate among these different interests and advance the public rather than a private good.[21]

Determining who these few were was one of the crucial issues in the debate over the formation of the Constitution. Many gentry shared the certainty of Charles Nisbet, president of Dickinson College, "that men of learning, leisure and easy circumstances . . . if they are endowed with wisdom, virtue & humanity, are much fitter for every part of the business of government, than the ordinary class of people." But who were these extraordinary men? Hamilton was sure that he was one of this wise and virtuous elite, but nevertheless he lacked sufficient "easy circumstances" to remain leisured and entirely free of interested marketplace activities. As more than one friend pointed out to him, he, like many other hard-pressed gentlemen, had to live off "the hard earned profits of the law." But, explained Hamilton, this necessity did not turn lawyers into tradesmen or artisans; being a lawyer was not an occupation and was different from other profit-making activities. It may have been true, he wrote in *The Federalist* No. 35, that mechanics, merchants, and farmers were deeply involved in the marketplace and therefore had interests to promote. This was not the case, however, with members of the learned professions. "They truly form no distinct interest in society" and thus were best suited to be political leaders. They "will feel a neutrality to the rivalships between the different branches of industry" and will be most likely to be "an impartial arbiter" among the diverse interests and occupations of the society. Thus was reinforced a notion that has carried into our own time—that lawyers and other professionals are somehow free of the marketplace, are less selfish and interested and therefore better equipped for political leadership and disinterested decision-making than merchants and businessmen.[22]

The new federal Constitution was designed to ensure that governmental leadership would be entrusted as much as possible to just those kinds of disinterested gentlemen who had neither occupations nor narrow mercantile interests to promote, "men who," in Madison's words, "possess most wisdom to discern and most virtue to pursue the common good of the society." In an interest-ridden society the secret of good government was to enlarge and elevate the national government, in the manner projected by the new federal Constitution of 1787, and thus screen out the kind of interested men who had dominated the state legislatures in the 1780s—"men of factious tempers, of local prejudices, or of sinister designs"—and replace them with classically educated gentlemen "whose enlightened views and virtuous sentiments render them superior to local prejudices, and to schemes of injustice."[23]

With "the purest and noblest characters" of the society in power, Madison expected the new national government to play the same suprapolitical neutral role that the British king had been supposed to play in the empire. In fact, Madison hoped that the new federal government might restore some aspect of monarchy that had been lost in the Revolution. In monarchies, he said, the king was sufficiently neutral toward his subjects, but often he sacrificed their happiness for his avarice or ambition. In small republics the government had no selfish will of its own, but it was never sufficiently neutral toward the various interests of the society. The new extended republic, said Madison, was designed to combine the good qualities of each. The new government would be "sufficiently neutral between the different interests and factions, to control one part of the society from invading the rights of another, and at the same time sufficiently controlled itself, from setting up an interest adverse to that of the whole society." That someone as moderate and as committed to republicanism as Madison should speak even privately of the benefits of monarchy adhering in the Constitution of 1787 is a measure of how disillusioned many of the revolutionary gentry had become with the democratic consequences of the Revolution.[24]

Given this Federalist reasoning and these Federalist aims, it is not surprising that the opponents of the Constitution in 1787–88, or the Anti-Federalists, as they were called, charged that the new federal system was aristocratically designed to "raise the fortunes and respectability of the well-born few, and oppress the plebeians."[25] Because the Constitution seemed to be perpetuating the classical tradition of virtuous patrician leadership in government, the Anti-Federalists felt compelled to challenge that tradition. There was, the Anti-Federalists said repeatedly, no disinterested gentlemanly elite that could feel "sympathetically the wants of the people" and speak for their "feelings, circumstances, and interests." That elite had its own particular interests to promote. However educated and elevated such gentry might be, they were no more free of the lures and interests of the marketplace than anyone else.[26]

The consequences of such thinking were immense and indeed devastating for republican government. If gentlemen were involved in the marketplace and had interests just like everyone else, they were really no different from all those common people—artisans, shopkeepers, traders, and others—who had traditionally been denied a role in political leadership because of their overriding absorption in their private occupational interests. In short, the Anti-Federalists were saying that liberally educated gentlemen were no more capable than ordinary people of classical republican disinterestedness and virtue and that consequently there was no one in the society equipped to promote an exclusive public interest that was distinguishable from the private interests of people.

One of the crucial moments in the history of American politics—maybe the crucial moment—occurred in 1786 during several days of debate in the Pennsylvania assembly over the rechartering of the Bank of North America. The debate—the only important one we have recorded of state legislative proceedings in the 1780s—centered on the role of interest in public affairs.

The principals in this debate were William Findley, a Scotch-Irish ex-weaver from western Pennsylvania and a defender of the debtor-relief and paper-money interests in the state, and Robert Morris, the wealthiest merchant in the state, with aristocratic aspirations and a major supporter of the rechartering of the bank. Findley was precisely the sort of backcountry legislator whom gentry like Madison in the 1780s were accusing of being narrow, illiberal, and interested in the promotion of paper money and debtor-relief legislation. Now, with the issue of the rechartering of the bank, Findley had an opportunity to get back at his aristocratic accusers and he made the most of it. Morris and his genteel Philadelphia ilk had continually tried to pose as disinterested gentlemen in the classical mold, who were above crass marketplace interests and concerned only with the public good. But Findley and his western colleagues refused to let Morris and the aristocratic supporters of the bank get away with this pose. These supporters of the bank's rechartering, Findley charged, were themselves interested men; they were directors or stockholders of the bank and thus had no right to claim that they were neutral disinterested umpires only deciding what was good for the state. The advocates of the bank "feel interested in it personally, and therefore by promoting it they were acting as judges in their own cause." Their defense of the bank, said Findley, revealed "the manner in which disappointed avarice chagrins an interested mind."

There was nothing new in these charges. To accuse one's opponent of being self-interested was conventional rhetorical strategy in eighteenth-century debates. But Findley went on to pursue another line of argument that was new—startlingly new. He accepted Morris's and the other bank supporters' interestedness in the bank and found, he said, nothing unusual or improper in their efforts to obtain its rechartering; as its directors and stockholders, after all, they could hardly be expected to do otherwise, and "Any others in their situation . . . would do as they did." In sum, Morris and the other investors in the bank had every "right to advocate their own cause, on the floor of this house." But, Findley then continued, they had no right to protest when others realize "that it is their own cause they are advocating; and to give credit to their opinions, and to think of their votes accordingly." They had no right, in other words, to try to pass off their support of their personal cause as an act of disinterested virtue. The promotion of interests in politics, suggested Findley, was quite legitimate, as long as it was open and aboveboard and not disguised by specious claims of genteel disinterestedness. The promotion of private interests was in fact what American politics ought to be about.

Findley was not content merely to expose and justify the reality of interest-group politics in representative legislatures. He glimpsed some of the important implications of such interest-group politics, and in just a few remarks he challenged the entire classical tradition of disinterested public leadership and set forth a rationale for competitive democratic politics that has never been bettered. If representatives were elected to promote the particular interests and private causes of their constituents, then the idea that such representatives were simply disinterested gentlemen, squire worthies called by duty to shoulder the burdens of public service, became archaic. It may have been meaningful in the past, when such virtuous men did exist, for such a disinterested representative to make no effort on his own behalf and simply stand for election. But now, said Findley, in the democratic America of many interests where the candidate for the legislature "has a cause of his own to advocate, interest will dictate the propriety of canvassing for a seat." Such interest-group politics meant that politically ambitious men, even those with interests and causes to advocate, now could legitimately run and compete for electoral office and thus become what Madison in *Federalist* No. 10 most feared—parties who were at the same time judges in their own causes.[27]

Despite all the sarcasm and mingled emotion with which Findley in 1786 put forward this radical suggestion, he was anticipating in this one statement all of the modern democratic political developments of the succeeding generation: the increased electioneering and competitive politics, the open promotion of private interests in legislation, the emergence of parties, the extension of the actual and direct representation of particular groups in government, and the eventual weakening, if not the repudiation, of the classical republican ideal that legislators were supposed to be disinterested umpires standing above the play of private interests.

But it was not just the classical tradition of virtuous gentry leadership that Findley and other backcountry and middling Anti-Federalists contested. Without realizing the full implications of what they were doing, in the ratification debates over the Constitution they also called into question all the time-honored conceptions of society known to the revolutionary leaders. To be sure, there were a number of Anti-Federalist aristocrats like George Mason and Richard Henry Lee who had a whiggish fear of centralized power but no desire to undermine the traditional order of society. Such Anti-Federalist southern gentry could not emotionally speak for all the entrepreneurial and debtor forces of ordinary people that were emerging, particularly in the northern parts of America. But common Anti-Federalists like Melancton Smith and William Petrikin could; they shared a whiggish fear of power with aristocrats like Lee and Mason, but they also had a desire to challenge both aristocratic leadership and the social order. To these plebeian Anti-Federalists, pulling together at least two decades of intense polemics and developing reality, American society could no longer be thought of as either a hierarchy of ranks or a homogeneous republican whole. Many of them, in fact, saw a society more pluralistic, more diverse, and more fragmented with interests than even someone as hardheaded and realistic as James Madison had. Society, they said, was not a unitary entity with a single common interest but a heterogeneous mixture of "many different classes or orders of people, Merchants, Farmers, Planters, Mechanics, and Gentry or wealthy Men," all equal to one another. In such a pluralistic egalitarian society there was no possibility of a liberal enlightened elite speaking for the whole; men from one class or interest could never be acquainted with the "Situation and Wants" of those from another. "Lawyers and planters," whatever their genteel pretensions, could never be "adequate judges of tradesmen's concerns." The occupations and interests of the society were so diverse and discrete that only individuals sharing a particular occupation or interest could speak for that occupation or interest. It was foolish to tell people that they ought to overlook their local interests when local interests were all there really were. "No man when he enters into society, does it from a view to promote the good of others, but he does it for his own good." Since all individuals and groups in the society were equally self-interested, the only "fair representation" in government, wrote the "Federal Farmer," ought to be one where "every order of men in the community . . . can have a share in it." Consequently any American government ought "to allow professional men, merchants, traders, farmers, mechanics, etc. to bring a just proportion of their best informed men respectively into the legislature." Only an explicit form of representation that allowed Germans, Baptists, artisans, farmers, and so on each to send delegates of its own kind into the political arena could embody the democratic particularism of the emerging society of the early Republic.[28]

Momentous consequences eventually flowed from these Anti-Federalist arguments. In these populist Anti-Federalist calls for the most explicit form of representation possible, and not in Madison's *Federalist* No. 10, lay the real origins of American pluralism and American interest-group politics. The grass-roots Anti-Federalists concluded that, given the variety of competing interests and the fact that all people had interests, the only way for a person to be fairly and accurately represented in government was to have someone like himself with his same interests speak for him; no one else could be trusted to do so.

Ultimately, the logic of this conception of actual representation determined that no one could be represented in government unless he had the right to vote. The interests of a person were so particular, so personal, that only by exercising the ballot could he protect and promote his interests. Election in America became the sole criterion of representation. Insofar as American politics became localist and dominated by interest groups and calls for extending the suffrage, the Anti-Federalists prepared the way.

The Anti-Federalists lost the battle over the Constitution. But they did not lose the war over the kind of national government the United States would have for a good part, at least, of the next century. Their popular understanding of American society and politics in the early Republic was too accurate and too powerful to be put down—as the Federalists themselves soon came to appreciate. Even the elections for the First Congress in 1788 revealed the practical realities of American democratic life that contradicted the Federalists' classical republican dreams of establishing a government led by disinterested educated gentlemen.

Thomas Hartley of Pennsylvania, a stout Federalist, knew that the new congressmen from the state should be "men of knowledge and information, well attached to the new plan and should have characters unexceptionable as to their integrity.'' If we had such men, he told a Federalist friend in 1788, it would not matter to "what profession or interest they belong." Unfortunately, however, outside of the city of Philadelphia "there are but few men who have abilities and leisure and are fit objects for choice." There were simply not enough educated and disinterested gentlemen spread about the state; which is why Federalists in Pennsylvania, like those in several other states, urged that congressmen be elected at large instead of by districts: "you have a better chance of obtaining good men than obliging the electors to vote for separate Representatives in districts."[29] Because the Federalists in Pennsylvania soon realized that cosmopolitan and disinterested college-educated gentlemen for representatives "cannot easily be found," they began advocating representation that was as interest-ridden as that promoted by the Anti-Federalists. Northumberland County Federalists, for example, urged in October 1788 "that different men adapted to the different interests" of the state be chosen for Congress: four involved in agriculture, two in commerce, "one person remarkably attached to the principles of manufactures, and an eminent law character."[30]

But none of this interest-group participation in Pennsylvania politics had the political explosiveness of the issue of German representation. The Germans constituted about one-third of the population of Pennsylvania, but had never had numbers in government commensurate with their size in the state. Suddenly in the election of 1788 for the new federal Congress and the presidential electors, agitators raised the issue of proportional German representation in the new government and touched off a furor in Pennsylvania's politics. Both the Federalists and the Anti-Federalists scrambled to place a couple of German names on their tickets for Congress and for the presidential electors. But once aroused, German dissatisfaction "at having so small a representation" could not be appeased. Some tried to resist this ethnic pressure by pointing to its apparent logical absurdity and asked why the Germans should be singled out for attention. "If any national distinctions can possibly be made in the future laws of the empire, why are not these anxious writers equally concerned for the Scotch and the Irish? Why are they not desirous that they also should have their due proportion of federal representation?" Such "invidious distinctions" among the citizenry were ridiculous. But it soon became clear that these distinctions of ethnicity, as well as those of occupation and religion, were here to stay. The Germans, voting very much as a bloc, went

on in 1788 to elect three German congressmen from Pennsylvania—
every German candidate they could find on the Federalist and Anti-
Federalist tickets.[31]

The situation in Pennsylvania was exaggerated—because of the
particular heterogeneity of the state; but it was only an exaggeration of
what was present elsewhere in America, particularly in the North.[32]
America's democratic future of local politics, special interests, ethnic
voting, and popular electioneering was already hurdling the great heights
of the extended republic of 1788–89. Even Anti-Federalist and later Republican William Findley made it into the Second Congress. From the
outset Madison's republican remedy for republican ills did not work as
well as he and other Federalists had hoped.

For that reason Madison's remedy of an elevated and extended republic in 1787 seemed much too mild and insufficient for many Federalists in the 1790s worried about the spread of what Alexander Hamilton
called "the amazing violence & turbulence of the democratic spirit."[33]
So deeply pessimistic over the interest-ridden and unvirtuous reality of
American society were many of the Federalists of the 1790s—who clung
to the name used by the supporters of the Constitution in 1787–88—that
in filling out the new national government they went way beyond Madison's "strictly republican" remedy and sought to bring back some of
the basic characteristics and adhesives of monarchical society that many
revolutionaries had thought they had gotten rid of in 1776 once and
for all.

Despite their fears of democracy, however, the Federalists and even
their leader Hamilton were not monarchists. Although in the Philadelphia Convention Hamilton had "acknowledged himself not to think
favorably of Republican Government," he had no stake in claims of
blood and had no intention of returning to the monarchical and patriarchal politics of the *ancien régime* in which government was treated as a
source of personal and family aggrandizement. Still, he and the other
Federalists did believe that some monarchical surrogates had to be found
to strengthen government in order to keep the unvirtuous American
people from flying apart in licentious pursuits of happiness. "The mass
of men," observed John Jay, "are neither wise nor good, and virtue,
like the other resources of a country, can only be drawn to a point and
exerted by strong circumstances ably managed, or a strong government
ably administered."[34]

By the 1790s the Federalists had no confidence left in the radical
enlightened hope that governmental power was, in Hamilton's derisive

words, a mere "consequence of the bad habits which have been produced by the errors of ancient systems" and therefore not ultimately necessary for holding society together. Although many of the artisan and plebeian followers of the Republicans were quite willing, like the Federalists, to recognize the prevalence of interests, most of their leaders, and Jefferson especially, still held out hopes that virtue and the natural sociability of people were the best social adhesives. In Hamilton's view, however, these hopes were nothing but delusions. The idea that, "as human nature shall refine and ameliorate by the operation of a more enlightened plan" based on a common moral sense and the spread of affection and benevolence, government eventually "will become useless, and Society will subsist and flourish free from its shackles," was a "wild and fatal . . . scheme," even if its Republican "votaries" like Jefferson did not push such a scheme to its fullest.[35]

The Federalists thus repudiated the emerging Jeffersonian Republican view that the best government was the least government. Hamilton believed deeply in the "need" for "a common directing power" in government, and had only contempt for those who thought trade and other private interests could regulate themselves. "This is one of those wild speculative paradoxes," he said, "which have grown into credit among us, contrary to the uniform practice and sense of the most enlightened nations. . . . It must be rejected by every man acquainted with commercial history."[36]

In place of the impotent confederation of separate states that had existed in the 1780s, the Federalists aimed to build a strong, consolidated, and prosperous "fiscal-military" state in emulation of eighteenth-century England, united "for the accomplishment of great purposes" by an energetic government composed of the best men in the society. Like Madison, Hamilton recognized and accepted the prevalence of economic and commercial interests in the society, but he sought to use the national government to harness these interests for the creation of a European-like great power of a sort that Madison had never anticipated.[37] As Secretary of the Treasury, he was undoubtedly concerned with the commercial prosperity of the country—with promoting "the great interests of a great people"—but we make a mistake to see him as a capitalist promoter of America's emerging business culture.[38] He had as much contempt for the vulgarity and selfishness of that popular business culture as did Madison. Hamilton was very much the aristocratic eighteenth-century statesman—willing to allow ordinary people their profits and property, their interests and their pursuits of happiness, but wanting honor and glory for himself and for the United States.

To achieve that honor and glory Hamilton deliberately set out to "corrupt" American society, to use monarch-like governmental influence to tie existing commercial interests to the government and to create new hierarchies of interest and dependency that would substitute for the absence of virtue and the apparently weak republican adhesives existing in America. "What other chain," asked Federalist congressman Christopher Gore, would be "so binding as that involving the interests of the men of property in the prosperity of the Government"?[39] In local areas Hamilton and the Federalist leaders built up followings among Revolutionary War veterans and members of the Society of the Cincinnati. They appointed important and respectable local figures to the federal judiciary and other federal offices. They exploited the patronage of the Treasury Department and its 800 or more customs officials, revenue agents, and postmasters with particular effectiveness. The Federalists carefully managed the Bank of the United States and the national debt to connect interested individuals to the government. By 1793 or so the Federalists had formed groups of "friends of government" in most of the states. Their hierarchies of patronage and dependency ran from the federal executive through Congress down to the various localities. In the eyes of their Jeffersonian Republican opponents the Federalists seemed to be taking Americans back to the monarchy that had been repudiated in 1776.

Although Hamilton later denied, rather defensively, that he had ever made interest the weightiest motive behind his financial program, there is no doubt that he thought the debt and other financial measures would strengthen the national government "by increasing the number of ligaments between the Government and the interests of Individuals."[40] He agreed with the Scottish political economist Sir James Steuart that "self interest . . . is the main spring and the only motive which a statesman should make use of, to engage a free people to concur in the plans which he lays down for their government." Unfortunately for the Federalists, however, Hamilton attempted to tie the government largely to the holders of traditional aristocratic proprietary wealth—"who are in every society the only firm supporters of government"—and ultimately ignored the new multiplying dynamic commercial interests of those who worked for a living—commercial farmers, artisans, manufacturers, emerging entrepreneurs, and risk-taking businessmen, particularly of the mid-Atlantic states, who consequently ended up in the Republican opposition.[41]

Hamilton's dream of making the United States a great fiscal-military state dissipated in the face of America's emerging democratic society. It failed not simply because it was overwhelmed by the Jeffersonian Republicans and their waves of new entrepreneurs and venture capitalists, but, more important, because it was ultimately undone by the Federalists themselves.

Hamilton and other Federalist leaders hoped to promote a national public interest that transcended all the petty local concerns of the society. Yet by resting their government so completely on the assumption that most people were self-interested and absorbed in their private affairs, the Federalists laid virtually no civic foundations for their scheme and weakened their ability to justify their peculiar disinterested leadership against the repeated charges of their Anti-Federalist and later Republican opponents that they were as interested as everyone else in the society. The Federalists' claims of being truly disinterested and the only rightful rulers in the society thus came to depend on their remaining scrupulously uncorrupted, free of even the taint of using government to further their own private interests.

Yet many of the Federalist leaders themselves, including subcabinet officials and congressmen, were deeply involved in speculative schemes and were busy making money out of their public connections and offices. In the 1790s many congressmen, especially Federalists from the North, found, as had many army officers and other officeholders during the Revolutionary War, that their proprietary wealth did not provide sufficient earnings for them safely to ignore or neglect their private affairs; and consequently they either had to exploit their offices for profit or had to absent themselves from their responsibilities. Senator William Maclay saw at the outset what was happening in the new Congress. "I came here expecting every man to act the part of a God," he confided to his diary in August 1789. "That the most delicate Honor, the most exalted Wisdom, the refined Generosity was to govern every Act and be seen in every deed." Instead, he found only too often "rough and rude manners Glaring folly, and the basest selfishness, apparent in almost every public Transaction." At a crucial moment during the debate over the assumption of state debts, Federalist congressman Theodore Sedgwick complained that Thomas Fitzsimmons and George Clymer were absorbed in their private affairs in Philadelphia, while Jeremiah

Wadsworth of Connecticut "has thought it more for his interests to speculate than to attend his duty in Congress, and is gone home."[42]

Hamilton knew that many public officials were using their connections to get rich, but he did not want to be one of them. In 1795, at a time when he was very much in need of money and out of public office, his close friend Robert Troup pleaded with him to get involved in business, especially in speculative land schemes. Everyone else was doing it, said Troup. "Why should you object to making a little money in a way that cannot be reproachful? Is it not time for you to think of putting yourself in a state of independence?" Troup even joked to Hamilton that such moneymaking schemes might be "instrumental in making a man of fortune—I may say—a gentleman of you. For such is the present insolence of the World that hardly a man is treated like a gentleman unless his fortune enables him to live at his ease."

But Hamilton refused. "Saints," he said, might get away with such profit-making, but he knew he would be denounced by his Republican opponents as just another one of those "speculators" and "peculators." He had to refuse "because," as he sardonically put it, "there must be some public fools who sacrifice private to public interest at the certainty of ingratitude and obloquy—because my vanity whispers I ought to be one of those fools and ought to keep myself in a situation the best calculated to render service."[43] Hamilton clung as long and as hard to the classical conception of leadership as anyone in post-revolutionary America. Unfortunately for the Federalists, however, Hamilton's classical vision of aristocratic leadership required more than just himself and Washington, more than just a handful of farsighted, cosmopolitan, and great-souled gentlemen who remained virtuous and above the concerns of crass moneymaking.

To be sure, other members of the Federalist aristocracy often tried their best to live up to the classical image of being disinterested leaders standing above the marketplace of interests. Many sought to become landed gentry in the English or Virgilian manner; indeed, in the early decades of the Republic's history establishing a seat in the country became something of a mania, especially among the New England gentry. In the mid-1790s congressman and lawyer Joshua Coit of Connecticut sold his two-acre homestead in New London and purchased a nine-hundred-acre livestock farm in Montville in order to try out his "utopian . . . schemes of a Country Life." Only then, he said, could he realize his dream of "Independence," and thus real gentility, and enjoy nature and experiment, georgic style, with Lombardy poplars and new grasses suggested by the Connecticut Agricultural Society. But the livestock farm proved too expensive, and he had to sell it and eventually settle for something much smaller than even his original homestead. Similar financial pressures constrained even wealthy Christopher Gore of Massachusetts from realizing his genteel dreams. Fisher Ames thought that Gore would have to forgo retiring to his Waltham estate for a while and take up his law practice once again if he were to keep up the style of life appropriate to a gentleman of his rank. Being a gentleman, particularly a landed gentleman, demanded money. "A man may not incline to take a certain degree on the scale of genteel living," Ames told Gore, "but having once taken it he must maintain it."[44]

Other Federalists in the 1790s likewise sought to secure themselves by acquiring various sorts of proprietary wealth. Some moved into the new territory of the West with dreams of establishing landed empires for themselves on the banks of the Ohio, and others remained in the cities of the East and simply speculated in land; but all desperately sought to do what Adam Smith suggested disinterested gentry leaders must do—get money as landlords without direct exertion in the marketplace. But land in the New World was a far riskier investment than it was in Europe, and important Federalists in the 1790s, including Robert Morris, senator from Pennsylvania, Henry Knox, Secretary of War under Washington, and James Wilson, justice of the Supreme Court, ended their ventures in land speculation in bankruptcy and disgrace, and in some cases debtors' prison.[45]

These numerous bankruptcies and financial collapses in the 1790s contributed greatly to the democratization of American society. All the many failures of "those who call themselves Gentlemen," noted contemporaries, destroyed that paternalistic "confidence in men of reputed fortunes and prudence as used to exist," and opened up opportunities in business and government for new men, usually Republicans, less well educated, less liberal, less cosmopolitan, and less well-bred, men who by the traditional standards of rank were very ordinary indeed, "men, who," in the opinion of Oliver Wolcott, Secretary of the Treasury under John Adams, "possessed neither capital nor experience" and not even the inclination to be disinterested. The problem of the Federalist gentry in the 1790s was the perennial problem of American society: America's aristocracy simply did not have sufficient private means to act the public part of a classical aristocracy. Those skeptical of the appointment of James Wilson to the Supreme Court could indeed make much of "the deranged state of his Affairs,'' admitted Benjamin Rush in 1789. ''But,'' he asked, ''where will you find an American landholder free from embarrassments?'' The financial chaos of the 1780s and the states' and the Confederation's inability to pay their debts in full had ''reduced all our wealthy men to the utmost distress'' and had ''thrown a great part of their property into the hands of quartermasters—Amsterdam Jews, & London brokers.''[46] Ironically, only the South, which provided much of the Republican leadership opposed to the Federalists, was able to main¹ tain a semblance of a traditional leisured patriciate.

So much did private interests come to pervade the halls of Congress and the corridors of the various statehouses that many Americans found it harder and harder to conceive of disinterested leadership anywhere in the society. John Adams, for example, came to accept the inevitable presence of diverse interests in the society, though he believed they all could be reduced to two—''persons and property'' or ''democracy and aristocracy.'' These competing private interests might then be embodied in the two separate houses of the legislature, with the governor or executive, the only truly disinterested figure left in the state, holding the balance between the two. No wonder people accused Adams of being a crypto-monarchist: his conception of an independent disinterested executive standing above and balancing all the interests of the society was as close to a monarchy as a republic could get.

All the talk of affection and benevolence between people and nations many Federalists now dismissed as sentimental claptrap. Calls in the Senate for expressions of gratitude for France's contribution to America's independence were shouted down. ''Nothing but interest,'' it was said, ''governed all nations.'' Hamilton acknowledged that gratitude might exist between individuals, as the emotional response of a person to a benevolent and disinterested service; but nations acted only out of self-interest. The ''best lesson in moral philosophy,'' wrote Hugh Henry Brackenridge sarcastically in his comic novel *Modern Chivalry*, was ''to expect no gratitude.'' Even gratitude itself, that sublime ancient republican sentiment, actually seemed to be more and more a ''selfish rule of action'' that commands us to prefer and honor men ''not for their worth, but that they did us service.'' Interest, however disguised, now seemed to dominate all social relations.[47]

The revolutionaries' aim had been to keep private interests out of government; by the 1790s, however, many had come to accept the prevalence of interests everywhere. Even some spokesmen for the aristocratic planters of the South lost the capacity to imagine a government that did not embody private interests of one sort or another. The polemical writings of Timothy Ford of South Carolina in 1794 reveal the remarkable extent to which special interests were overwhelming the republican assumptions of 1776.

Ford spoke for the Tidewater slaveholding planters who were worried about the massive migration of small Scotch-Irish farmers into the backcountry of Carolina. After several decades of migration, these small backcountry farmers, most of whom as yet did not own slaves, were clamoring for representation in the state legislature proportionate to their numbers. The minority of eastern slaveholding planters feared they would be swamped by any such reapportionment. Ford aimed to prevent this.

Ford's argument is interesting in more ways than one. In the colonial period a conservative like Ford would have justified the unequal representation in the Carolina legislature by referring to the concept of virtual representation: that the backcountry settlers did not need additional representatives because the educated and cosmopolitan planting elite of Charleston spoke for the whole Carolina community and virtually, if not explicitly, represented everyone. But by 1794 with the weakening of patronage connections and the diversification of interests such an argument was becoming harder to make.

Instead, Ford argued that the society of South Carolina was made up of different private interests—merchants, farmers, planters, manufacturers—but that the Tidewater slaveholding planters constituted a particularly important interest. Indeed, Ford thought their interests were so "great and peculiar" that they could never be put under the legislative control of a mere numerical majority composed of people separated from the eastern planters geographically and "strangers to our interests." Interest as a motive for human behavior was in fact so strong that for the planters to place their concerns under the majoritarian power of contrary interests "would probably be fatal unto us at some time or another." Therefore out of "mere self-preservation" the planters had to stand against the simple notion of one man, one vote.[48]

Ford's argument not only anticipated John C. Calhoun's later efforts to describe concurrent majorities, but it resembled the arguments that other conservatives, frightened by the democratic power of numbers, attempted over the next two or three decades. Perhaps the best known of these are the arguments of Chancellor James Kent and his Federalist colleagues in the New York convention of 1820-21 called to revise the state constitution.

In the face of widespread enthusiasm for universal manhood suffrage, Kent and the other Federalists desperately sought to maintain a special freehold qualification for the electors of the state senate. Ten years ago, said Kent, such universal suffrage would never have been proposed, but "so rapid has been the career of our vibration" that few now could resist bowing "before the idol of universal suffrage." In their tortured polemics the Federalists tried to explain why special property qualifications for the senate's electorate were needed: that the senate had to be differently composed, that the property qualification was "a sort of moral and independent test of character, in the electorate, which we could get at in no other practicable mode," that it was the only way to protect the state against the onrushing rabble. But when confronted with Republican arguments that such a distinction in the electorate was "an odious remnant of aristocracy" perpetuating a privileged order in a republic where "there is but one estate—the people," the Federalists backed away and soon settled on the one point they thought their Jeffersonian opponents would accept—the wholesomeness of yeomen farmers and the need to protect their landed property and the "farming interest" from other opposing interests.[49]

Arguing that a specially elected senate was necessary to protect landed property or the "farming interest" was symptomatic of how much Americans were not only abandoning the eighteenth-century classical tradition of disinterested representation but also changing the meaning of property. Indeed, the entire Revolution could be summed up by the radical transformation Americans made in their understanding of property. In classical republican thought, property, landed property in particular, was not some special interest needing representation or protection. Rather, property had been considered in proprietary terms as part of a person's identity and the source of his authority. Such proprietary property was regarded not as the product of one's labor or as a material asset to be bought and sold in the market but as a means of maintaining one's gentility and independence from the caprices of the market. Landed property was the most important such guarantee of autonomy because it was the least transitory, the most permanent form, of property. Such proprietary property was designed to protect its holders from external influence or corruption, to free them from the scramble of buying and selling, and to allow them to make impartial political judgments. But by making landed property merely another "interest" among all the other market interests to be promoted or protected, Kent and the other Federalists unwittingly stripped property of its older sanctified, static meaning and turned it into a mere material possession or capital commodity. They thereby conceded the northern Republicans' more modern understanding of property at the outset—that property was changeable, based on people's labor, and "essential to our temporal happiness."[50]

If property had become just an "interest," a mere material possession, just venture capital, then, the Republicans said, everyone had an equal right to acquire it, for "the desire of acquiring property is a universal passion." Such property could no longer be an integral part of a person's identity; instead it was "only one of the incidental rights of the person who possesses it," important no doubt, but scarcely requiring specific representation in a branch of the legislature. In fact, "compared with our other essential rights," property was "insignificant and trifling." The Declaration of Independence, said the New York Republicans, had mentioned the rights of " 'life, liberty and the pursuit of happiness'—not of property." In these enterprising times there could be no distinction between real and personal property. Modern property, including land, was exclusively the product of a person's labor and entrepreneurial skills; it was commercial, dynamic, and unpredictable and could have little to do with his independence. "Independence consists more in the structure of the mind and in the qualities of the heart." Besides, the Republicans asked, how could a moral position be "guaranteed by dollars and cents?"[51]

In the end, the New York Republicans of 1820 could only gaze in amazement at the Federalists' inability to comprehend the new society they lived in. Did they not know that "the course of things in this country is for the extension and not the restriction of popular rights"? And did they not know that "our community is an association of persons—of human beings—not a partnership founded on property"? The Republicans had "supposed that the great fundamental principle that all men were equal in their rights was settled, forever settled, in this country." Hence why would the Federalists try to stand against those who advanced "with the fearless confidence of an advocate of the real and substantial rights of the people"? By 1820, if not before, there was little place left in America for old-fashioned aristocrats who talked against what Kent still had the temerity to call "the evil genius of democracy."[52]

15. *The Assault on Aristocracy*

Ultimately the weakness of the American aristocracy, at least in the North, was the source of its downfall. By the first decade of the nineteenth century attempts by aristocrats and would-be-aristocrats, especially those north of the Mason-Dixon line, to justify their political leadership had become increasingly desperate. With the weakening and disappearance of older forms of patronage, with the expansion of commerce and the fluctuating redistributions of wealth, with the spread of paper money and the widening commercial opportunities for plain and "middling" men everywhere, the gentry's position in northern society became more and more anachronistic. By the end of the eighteenth century the Federalist leaders, relatively speaking, had already lost most of the substantial economic and social power that had made aristocracies traditionally viable. By 1800 the Federalists existed essentially on borrowed time and what Abraham Bishop of Connecticut called the people's "habit of following these great men faithfully as hounds do the horn."

Bishop did his best to break this habit of "dormant acquiescence" in the people.' In fact, in the years surrounding the election of Jefferson to the presidency, Bishop launched a series of attacks on the Federalist gentry that were the most vicious and devastating of any made in the entire period of the early Republic.

Bishop, whom the Federalists called "a monstrous oddity in the world," was an unlikely critic of aristocracy.' He was the son of a respected citizen and sometime mayor of New Haven, a 1778 graduate of Yale, and a lawyer who had clerked in Philadelphia—in short, a liberally educated gentleman who had even gone on a grand tour of Europe in the 1780s. He returned to oppose the federal Constitution, hold a few petty offices in New Haven, teach school, lecture, and marry, before emerging as one of the greatest popular demagogues in American history. Whatever private demons he had within him were unleashed on the bewildered and frightened Federalist gentry of Connecticut.

In a series of speeches and pamphlets designed for audiences of ordinary people, Bishop, like other Republican polemicists in the 1790s, accused the Federalists of aiming at monarchy. They were the sort "who wish for a season when congress shall be opened with a speech from the throne to my Lords and Gentlemen . . . or they wish to hear of brilliant lives, and splendid drawing rooms." They were those who "trade under the firm of Great men and company." They yearned for a hierarchy and a distinction of ranks, which were among the "first objects" of monarchy. They had persuaded people in government to support measures, "if not by offices and bribes, yet by hopes of office, of emoluments, of honors and influence." The Federalists had used patronage and placemen in elections to engage "a host of expectants" and "sycophants and dependents," and they had built a financial structure that was "a British funding system, Americanized."[3]

All this was standard Republican rhetoric, and it was hardly what made Bishop's speeches and pamphlets remarkable. What did set them off from other Republican polemics was his acutely modern understanding of culture. Bishop realized, far more clearly than most of his contemporaries, that all that people thought and believed was a "mere human invention." No doubt, he said, Americans could look to the Far East and pity the ignorance of millions bowing to sticks and stones and adoring idols that they themselves had created; yet at the same time these Americans "seldom reflect that all our rights of conscience and opinion, that all our powers and faculties are in a state of most absolute subordination to mere human inventions."[4] Bishop thus set out, as we might say today, to "deconstruct" his culture, to bring to the surface and challenge those unspoken premises of the society that supported all those feelings of inferiority and inequality still existing everywhere despite the republican revolution. If the culture were truly man-made, as the revolutionaries had suggested, then Bishop meant to have ordinary people make it over in their own interest.

Many Americans, particularly Southerners, said Bishop, might wonder about the existence of aristocracy in Connecticut "where the distinction of rank is hardly known." But they did not know the reality of the thing. There were great men in Connecticut as elsewhere, "men whose elevated birth or talents have raised them to elevated stations and given them an immense influence over the people."

> Every country is divided into two classes of men—one which lives by the labor of the head, and the other by the labor of hands; each claims, that its services are the hardest and most important; the first professes great zeal for public good, and means nothing by it; the last does his days work, makes no professions, but brings his produce to the best markets. The first always governs the last either by deceit or force.

Deceit is the mildest way, but it requires great labor and management; force is surest.[5]

Bishop aimed to expose these great men for what they were—deluders and deceivers who were busy leading people down the garden path to monarchy. It would not be easy, he knew, to "break through the thick folds of error and imposture with which the friends of order keep the great part of mankind encompassed." The great were masters at creating feelings of inferiority and inequality among the common people. "You have been taught," he told the people, "to reverence your 'friends of order.' " That "humiliation" that ordinary people felt in the face of "wealth and power . . . has been," said Bishop, "a leading cause of all the slavery on earth."[6]

Bishop wanted the people to understand that all their feelings of inferiority and humiliation, that all that made them bow their heads and doff their caps in front of gentlemen, that indeed the whole culture that sustained rule by the gentry elite, were "delusions," "delusions" fabricated by all "the great, the wise, rich, and mighty men of the world"—"delusions" invented and maintained by all those "well fed, well dressed, chariot rolling, caucus keeping, levee revelling federalists." These were the agents of delusion, these so-called gentlemen, that "one-tenth of the society" who claimed superiority over the rest. Over and over again Bishop asked his audiences: Why should the nine-tenths of ordinary people look up "with fear and awe" to these "deceiving few"?[7]

What is most extraordinary about Bishop's attack on the Federalist aristocracy is his concession, made at the outset, that this aristocracy was indeed superior to common, ordinary people in every way—in wealth, in birth, in private character, in intellect, in education. These gentry are, he said, "the best informed men in the society." They were well versed in history, in foreign languages, in political science. They were outwardly polite, liberally educated, and cosmopolitan—everything eighteenth-century gentlemen were supposed to be. But for these very reasons, Bishop charged, these gentry were not equipped to rule the society. Precisely because they were extraordinary men, they were both dangerous and unessential for republican government. Ordinary people ought not to be ruled by men greater, wiser, and richer than they. "Through excessive indulgence we have already a number of men too great for a republic. How happens it," Bishop asked his audiences, "that these great men are so very fit to govern? Internal government is designed to control inordinate passions: great men are most proud, avaricious and tyrannical: will you then select these to curb pride, avarice and tyranny?'' What! the great cry out: "Will you leave out men of abilities and put in the base-born to govern us?'' Why not? said Bishop. Why shouldn't the people mistrust the great? "The liberties of mankind were never destroyed by any other class of men.'' Do not the "base-born'' financially support the government, and do they not thereby have a right at least to "peep through the treasury door''?[8]

The main point, said Bishop, was that these great men, these gentlemen, these "self-stiled friends of order have, in all nations, been the cause of all the convulsions and distresses, which have agitated the world.'' They fooled people with their "charming outsides, engaging manners, powerful address, and inexhaustible argument.'' They deceived them with their eloquence and skill in manipulating language. "They know well the force and power of every word; the east, west, north and south of every semi-colon; and can extract power from every dash.'' They can prove conclusively that a national debt is a blessing or a curse. They "are able to say more and argue better on the wrong side of the question than the people are on either side of it.''[9]

The subjects of the gentry's guile were "the laboring and subordinate people throughout the world. Their toil goes to support the splendor, luxury and vices of the deluders, or their blood flows to satiate lawless ambition.'' But Bishop was not content merely to list the conventional vices of great men—their lust for power and wealth. He detailed genteel tastes and behavior in a way designed to rankle. Imagine, he said, "the luxurious courtier who must have his pease and salmon before the frost has left the earth, or the ice the river, and who loathes the sight of vegetable or animal food in the season of it; who rides in a gig with half a dozen lacqueys behind him; who curses every taverner, excommunicates every cook, and hecks over the table because his eggs were not brought to him in a pre-existent state.'' Such a man "can never have any opinion of the *plebeians* who are toiling to furnish the means of his splendor.''

These gentry like to say that they are of you, Bishop told his audiences of common people, that their interests are the same as yours. Yes, *"they are indeed of you,"* he said, invoking an image that Edmund Burke had once used to praise the aristocracy, in the same way that "the oak, which shades all the small trees and draws its nourishment from the roots, [is] a part of the grove.'' "But by circumstances of fortune, birth or superior bestowments of mind, or better education they have ceased to be as you; their political condition is immensely variant from yours, they are to govern, you are to be governed. They are *well-born*, you are *base-born*!''[10]

These superior sorts speak of honor and glory, but they look only to "what they can turn to their personal advantage." These Federalists talk of energetic government and national greatness, but this was only to milk the people at every turn. They take the people's money in taxes to pay for this government at a cost of $42,000 a day. They have made the national debt "a standing dish." Washington, D.C., "begun on a system rivalling in expense and magnificence ancient Babylon, has been a sink for your money." Beware of this deluding aristocratic rhetoric about genius and glory, warned Bishop. "A nation which makes greatness its polestar can never be free." The wars that the heroic gentry exult in are paid for by the blood and treasure of ordinary people. "In war the great do not fight: they are either in the cabinet or on some distant hill, directing the carnage." Only "plain men like yourselves," on both sides, do the fighting. We are told of naval glory, but know

that privates must bleed by the thousands for the glory of admirals, commodores, and port captains; that the only glory to which the sailor or marine can arrive, is to have his name printed in the papers and against it, *"thigh badly fractured, since amputated, and likely to recover,"* and in a few months after, *"bravely fighting in the main-top, cut in two by a chain shot,"* and just under it, "we are happy to announce that though not quite successful this time, yet *the admiral and officers are in high spirits* and having put into Jamaica to refit, intend to look at them again."

"Delusion!" said Bishop, "these are thy trophies." Strong stuff, by a man way ahead of his time. Bishop even called the naming of warships "hair-strokes of delusion."[11]

This was the most outlandish assault made on aristocracy in these years, but it was scarcely the only one. Indeed, it could have had little effect if it had not been backed up by many others. Everywhere in the early Republic northern aristocrats were besieged relentlessly, mercilessly, in print and in speeches, not only by alienated gentlemen like Bishop who had gone to Yale but, more important, by countless numbers of common ordinary people who had never been to college—artisans, traders, and businessmen—and who themselves had felt the deprivations and humiliations of being common and ordinary and were bent on revenge. Such men were sick and tired of being dismissed as factious, narrow, parochial, and illiberal and were unwilling to defer any longer to anyone's political leadership but their own.

In 1797 George Warner, a sailmaker in New York, spoke for all the "tradesmen, mechanics, and the industrious classes of society" who for too long had considered "themselves of TOO LITTLE CONSEQUENCE to the body politic." In the early 1790s they organized themselves in mechanics' associations and Democratic-Republican societies, and eventually they came to make up the body and soul of the northern part of the Republican party. Everywhere in their extraordinary speeches and writings of these years, artisans, laborers, and proto-businessmen of all sorts vented their pent-up egalitarian anger at all those aristocrats who had scorned and despised them as swine and rabble—and all because they had "not snored through four years at Princeton." They urged each other to "keep up the cry against Judges, Lawyers, Generals, Colonels, and all other designing men, and the day will be our own." They demanded that people do their "utmost at election to prevent all men of talents, lawyers, rich men from being elected."[12] For a half century following the Revolution these common ordinary men stripped the northern gentry of their pretensions, charged them at every turn with being fakes and shams, and relentlessly undermined their capacity to rule. In the end they transformed what it meant to be a gentleman and a political leader in America. Here in this destruction of aristocracy, including Jefferson's "natural aristocracy," was the real American Revolution—a radical alteration in the nature of American society whose effects are still being felt today.

Most of the critics of aristocracy in these years were different from Abraham Bishop—not estranged college-educated gentry, but artisans, businessmen, and common people—and they took a different tack from that of Bishop. Most were intent on showing not the differentness of the aristocracy, not their separateness from ordinary people, as Bishop had, but rather the opposite: most sought to close the traditional and sometimes terrifying gap that had existed between common people and gentlemen; they aimed to emphasize the similarity of the two groups and thus undermine the gentry's distinctiveness and privileges. To do so they attacked the most important aspect of what it was to be a gentleman in the classical tradition: the gentry's leisure, which gave it both the time and the responsibility for public service.

Leisure, meaning not having to exert oneself for profit, had been for ages a principal source of gentry distinctiveness. It was this leisure that enabled the gentry aristocracy to stand above the competing interests of

the marketplace and at the same time obliged gentlemen to serve in government, ideally without pay. Now in the decades following the Revolution this leisure was labeled idleness and was subjected to scathing criticism—criticism that went well beyond anything experienced in England or Europe in these years. At the same time this assault on gentry idleness was coupled with a heightened appreciation of the significance and dignity of labor, which aristocrats traditionally had held in contempt. Changes in the value of labor in turn affected the traditional aristocratic meaning of property. Property became associated less with proprietary wealth and the authority of its possessor and more with the labor that produced or improved it. The claims of speculators and absentee landlords to landed property, for example, came to have little legitimacy compared with the claims of those who actually worked and improved the land; the new moral value given to labor tended to override all mere legal titles to the land.[13]

Before these developments ran their course in the second and third decades of the nineteenth century, there was nobody left, in the northern states at least, who dared publicly and proudly to claim that he did not work for a living. Not only did this celebration of work and disparagement of idleness make the South with its leisured aristocracy supported by slavery seem even more anomalous than it had been at the time of the Revolution, thus aggravating the growing sectional split in the country; but these developments had as well profound implications for the conception most Americans had of themselves as a working people.

The attacks on aristocratic idleness began early in the prerevolutionary debates. In the late 1760s the Charleston mechanics were quick to respond to William Henry Drayton's incredulous dismissal of their right to participate in the decisions of government on the grounds that, as workers, they lacked a liberal arts education. The mechanics began, as all defenders of equality did in the late eighteenth century, with an appeal to that "common sense" of which nearly everyone in the society had a portion. But Mr. Drayton, they said, seemed to lack his portion, perhaps due to "his upper works being damaged by some rough treatment of the person who conducted his birth," and of course such a deficiency of common sense "cannot be compensated by all the learning of the schools." Mr. Drayton, "in his great condescention," said the artisans in biting sarcasm, "has been pleased to allow us a place amongst human beings." But they were more than just members of the human species; they were in fact, they said, "the most useful people in a community." Which was more than they could say for "the polite

Mr. Drayton." All he ever did was inherit a fortune. Can he really "claim any merit from his possessing an estate not obtained, or obtainable, by his own industry?" If Mr. Drayton had to earn his own bread "by the labour of either his head or his hands," could he do it? Was he in fact "qualified for any one sort of business that requires knowledge or skill to conduct it?" Maybe he could earn "a scanty pittance" as a packhorseman in the Indian trade, or as a common laborer to some mechanic, or "if he behaved well," as a cartman in the city. But he could never be a carpenter, shoemaker, or butcher, though the mechanics could "not deny, that he might contrive to help himself to a slice of a dead ox, when sharp set."[4]

These were just the opening shots on behalf of common working people of what would become major barrages against aristocratic leisure in the coming years. Because we are the heirs of their democratic rise, it is difficult for us to appreciate the immense struggle these mechanics and artisans endured in establishing their self-esteem and worth in the face of the age-old scorn in which their mean occupations were held. Everywhere their claims of equality were met with genteel disbelief and "consummate and unbearing haughtiness."[5] Yet, in one of the great expressions of the democratic revolution of these years, they persevered and eventually transformed American culture. They brought aristocratic leisure into contempt and turned labor into a universal badge of honor.

It became increasingly difficult for the gentry, even those in the South, to continue to maintain the classical republican pose of being above commercial exertions and interests by their not having to work the way ordinary people did. Everyone in the society was now urged to work, and if he did not, then there was something wrong with him. Indeed, productive labor now came to be identified with republicanism and idleness with monarchy. "Monarchy delights in taking from the great body of labouring people their rank in being, by making the idle few so wealthy and powerful, as to sink mediocrity unto contempt." Monarchy had "courtiers" and "sinecures" and men receiving "princely estates" for "trifling services." Republican governments, however, had no more officers than were necessary and "gives no more than enough to secure their services."[16]

During the 1790s Jeffersonian Republicans like Matthew Lyon labeled the Federalist gentry as men brought up "in idleness, dissipation and extravagance," and associated themselves with "the industrious part of the community." They saw American society divided between those who work and those who "live on the stock of the community,

already produced, not by *their labor*, but obtained by their *art* and *cunning*, or that of their ancestors.'"[7] The struggle, said William Manning, an uneducated New England farmer writing under the name of "a Labourer," was between the many and the few, based on "a Conceived Difference of Interest Between those that Labour for a Living and those that git a Living without Bodily Labour." Those who did not have to do bodily work were "the merchant, phisition, lawyer & divine, the philosipher and school master, the Juditial & Executive Officers, & many others." These "orders of men," once they had attained their life of "ease & rest" that "at once creates a sense of superiority," wrote Manning in phonetic prose that was real and not some gentleman's satiric ploy, tended to "asotiate together and look down with two much contempt on those that labour." Although "the hole of them do not amount to one eighth part of the people," these gentry had the "spare time" and the "arts & skeems" to combine and consult with one another. They had the power to control the electorate and government "in a veriaty of ways." Some voters they flattered "by promises of favours, such as being customers to them, or helping them out of debt, or other difficultyes; or help them to a good bargain, or treet them, or trust them, or lend them money, or even give them a little money"—anything or everything if only "they will vote for such & such a man." Other voters they threatened: " 'if you don't vote for such & such a man,' or 'if you do' & cc, 'you shall pay me what you owe me,' or 'I will sew you'—'I will turne you out of my house' or 'off of my farm'—'I wont be your customer any longer' . . . All these things have bin practised & may be again." This was how the "few" exerted influence over the many.

Those who "live without Labour" (the phrase that Manning used over and over to identify the gentry) managed the government and laws, making them as "numerous, intricate and as inexplicit as possible," controlled the newspapers, making them as "costly as possible," and manipulated the banks and credit, so as to make "money scarse," especially since "the interests and incomes of the few lays chiefly in money at interest, rents, salaryes, and fees that are fixed on the nominal value of money"; that is, they lived upon proprietary wealth. In addition these "few" were "always crying up the advantages of costly collages, national academyes & grammer schools, in order to make places for men to live without work, & so strengthen their party." In fact, wrote Manning in 1798, "all the orders of men who live without Labour have got so monstrously crouded with numbers & made it fashanable to live & dress so high, that Labour & produce is scarse." Manning ended his lengthy diatribe against all gentlemen of leisure by proposing, appropriately enough, to form "a Society of Labourers to be formed as near after the order of Cincinati as the largeness of their numbers will admit of."[18]

All who lived by their labor, whatever their dissimilarities in our modern eyes, did feel as one. After all, gentlemen traditionally tended to lump together as commoners all those who worked for a living, even those who differed from each other as greatly as did Walter Brewster, a young struggling shoemaker of Canterbury, Connecticut, and Christopher Leffingwell, a well-to-do manufacturer of Norwich, Connecticut, who owned several mills and shops and was the town's largest employer. Given their common meanness as workers who had to exert themselves for a living, men like Brewster and Leffingwell naturally allied in political movements on behalf of artisans and understandably identified their "laboring interest" with "the general or common interest" of the whole state. Modern historians are often puzzled by such seemingly incongruous alliances and feelings of identity among manufacturers who differed dramatically in their wealth and scale of activity: but this puzzlement results from anticipating the future too quickly. As great as the distinction between rich capitalist employers and poor workers would eventually become, in the early decades of the Republic large-scale manufacturers like Leffingwell and small craftsmen like Brewster still shared common resentments of a genteel world that had humiliated them and held them in contempt from the beginning of time. Nor should it be surprising that Joseph Williams, a mule trader, would take up the political cause of artisans and manufacturers such as Brewster and Leffingwell. Although Williams was the richest man in Norwich (who had extorted from the town a seat in the Connecticut assembly by threatening to move his business out of the community) and as a merchant had interests that were different from those of artisans and manufacturers, he nevertheless identified with their loathing of the Federalist aristocracy of Connecticut.[19] Despite all the apparent differences between wealthy mule merchants, small shoemakers, and big manufacturers, socially and psychologically they were still the same—which has caused no end of trouble for those modern historians looking to celebrate a heroic working class but despising businessmen. Now in the aftermath of the Revolution all these workers and businessmen saw that their day was coming and joined the Jeffersonian Republicans in a democratic attack on all those gentlemen "who do not labor."[20]

So prevalent did this kind of rhetoric against gentlemen of leisure become that now even southern slaveholding aristocrats felt compelled to identify themselves with hard work and productive labor. One of the most curious anomalies in American history was the way southern aristocrats led by Jefferson and Madison assumed leadership of a Republican party that in the North was composed mostly of unaristocratic sorts—common farmers, artisans, manufacturers, and hustling entrepreneurs. The southern planters were able to link themselves with these ordinary working people in the North by stressing their common involvement in productive labor in contrast to all those northern Federalist professionals, bankers, speculators, and moneyed men who never grew or made a single thing and lived off their proprietary wealth and other men's labor.

Of course, once invoked, this celebration of productive labor could be used by others against the gentry slaveholders themselves. So professional lawyers in Virginia, struggling to gain control of the county courts from gentlemen amateurs, accused the planter aristocrats of being men raised to no "pursuit of honest industry." All this idle gentry had ever done was "learned to dress, to dance, to drink, to smoke, to swear, to game; contracted a violent passion for the very rational, elegant and humane pleasures of the turf and the cock-pit, and was long distinguished for the best horses and game-cocks in the country." Then again, lawyers found themselves open to a similar accusation: that they were unproductive parasites who lived off the cares and anxieties of others.[21]

It is not surprising, therefore, that John Adams should have concluded as early as 1790 that "the great question will forever remain, *who shall work?*" Adams himself continued to hold to the traditional distinction between the few gentry and the many commoners. Not everyone could be idle, he said; not everyone could be a gentleman. "Leisure for study must ever be the portion of a few. The number employed in government, must forever be very small." Adams was so keen on this point of gentlemen and high public officials not working that on the voyage to Europe to become minister to Great Britain he, much to the surprise of foreign observers, "scorned working at the pump, to which all the other passengers submitted in order to obviate the imminent danger of sinking, arguing that it was not befitting a person who had public status." To risk drowning rather than to lose one's honor as a gentleman speaks volumes about the power of these cultural imperatives.[22]

Others answered Adams's question "who shall work?" by concluding that, in America at least, all shall work. Gentlemen found themselves in an increasingly embarrassing position. As early as 1792,

Benjamin Rush confided to his commonplace book some of his subversive and sarcastic thoughts on the problem of gentlemanly leisure—suggesting just how constraining the traditional character of a gentleman was becoming even for members of the gentry themselves. Rush noted that John Wesley, the founder of Methodism, had forbidden "his preachers to affect to be, or even appear like gentlemen." "No wonder he gave such advice," said Rush, "when we consider how that word is abused in the world."

> A man who has been bred a gentleman cannot work, . . . and therefore he lives by borrowing without intending to pay, or upon the public or his friends. A gentleman cannot wait upon himself, and therefore his hands and his legs are often as useless to him as if they were paralytic. If a merchant be a gentleman he would sooner lose 50 customers than be seen to carry a piece of goods across the street. If a Doctor should chance to be a gentleman he would rather let a patient die than assist in giving him a glyster or in bleeding him. If a parson he loses his zeal etc. If a tradesman should happen to be a gentleman he is undone for ever, by entertaining company, by a country seat, or by wishing to secure the society and good will of gentlemen by trusting them. In a word, to be a gentleman subjects one to the necessity of resenting injuries, fighting duels and the like, and takes away all disgrace in swearing, getting drunk, running in debt, getting bastards, etc. It makes nothing infamous but giving or taking the lye, for however much gentlemen pretend to be men of their word, they are the greatest lyers in the world. They lie to their creditors, to their mistresses, to their fathers or wives, or to the public.

Rush concluded his diatribe by observing that everyone, men and women, in every society ought to work.[73]

Gentlemen had traditionally assumed that leisure, not having to work for profit, was a prerequisite of their genteel status. Now, however, such gentlemen who were "not . . . under the necessity of getting their bread by industry" were accused of living off "the labour of the honest farmers and mechanics." Their "idleness" rested on "other men's toil." Gentlemen who "do not labor, but who enjoy in luxury, the fruits of labor," had no right to "finally decide all acts and laws" as they had in the past because their "interest is at such a remove from the common interest." Even in aristocratic South Carolina the classical republican demand that government should be run by rich, leisured gentlemen who served "without fee or reward" was met with growing scorn: "enormous wealth," it was said, "is seldom the associate of pure and disinterested virtue."[24]

By the early decades of the nineteenth century working in some useful occupation was widely regarded as the new source of fame. In fact, to the chagrin of traditionalists, talented workmen and inventors of carding machines were now receiving the public applause and civic wreaths that rightly and classically belonged to government leaders.[25] The popular biographer Parson Weems helped to make the philosopher and diplomat Benjamin Franklin into a nineteenth-century hero for artisans and other laboring people. Although in the traditional sense he had not worked a day in his life since the age of forty-two and had thoroughly adopted eighteenth-century gentry values, Franklin, as a onetime printer, was no doubt the founding father most easily transformed into a workingman's symbol. But even the aristocratic George Washington was not immune to the new cultural pressures. Weems celebrated Washington, too, as someone who worked as diligently as an ordinary mechanic, and in the process Weems helped to broaden and change the older meaning of work. In a classical sense Washington had been a farmer who had exercised authority over his farm but had not actually labored on it. But for Weems exercising authority now became identified with labor and was praised as labor. Indeed, he wrote, "of all the virtues that adorned the life of this great man, there is none more worthy of our imitation than his admirable INDUSTRY." Washington "displayed the power of industry more signally" than any man in history. Rising early and working hard all day were the sources of his wealth and success. He was "on horseback by the time the sun was up," and he never let up; "of all that ever lived, Washington was the most rigidly observant of those hours of business which were necessary to the successful management of his vast concerns." "Neither himself nor any about him were allowed to eat the bread of idleness," idleness being for Weems "the worst of crimes." Weems, speaking to the rising new generation of entrepreneurs, businessmen, and others eager to get ahead, was anxious to destroy the "notion, from the land of lies," which had "taken too deep root among some, that 'labour is a low-lived thing, fit for none but poor people and slaves! and that dress and pleasure are the only accomplishments for a gentleman!'" He urged all the young men who might be reading his book, "though humble thy birth, low thy fortune, and few thy friends, still think of Washington, and HOPE."[26]

Distinctions were now so regularly drawn between "worthless idle" gentlemen and "the productive classes," between "the learned and the wealthy" and "the free laboring people . . . struggling to get a little forward in the world, and educate their children," that gentlemen who wanted a political career found it next to impossible to justify leisure in traditional genteel terms.[27] No wonder would-be aristocrats like Edward Everett pleaded with so-called workingmen's parties to believe that former gentlemen of leisure really were workingmen too. Even Demosthenes, Caesar, Bacon, Newton, Franklin, Washington, and Napoleon were all "hard workers." All value was in labor, said Everett in speech after speech and writing after writing. Man was a working being. "It is his destiny, the law of his nature to labor." "The Art of Being Happy," wrote Everett, was not leisure, as the English character "Droz" had said. On the contrary, the secret to happiness was industriousness, immersing oneself in business, even if that business involved the making of money. Consequently, the new workingmen's parties that were being formed in the 1820s, said Everett, were no artificial, temporary contrivances like other parties; they were bound to last "to the end of time," for their "first principles are laid in our nature." In America at least, these workingmen's parties necessarily had to include everyone in the society who did an honest day's work. And everyone meant gentlemen and professionals as well as artisans and common laborers. "Take the case of an eminent lawyer in full practice," said Everett. "He passes his days in his office, giving advice to clients, often about the most uninteresting and paltry details of private business, or in arguing over the same kind of business in court." He had no more leisure than a mechanic. In fact, "lawyers, doctors, and ministers, men in public station, rich capitalists, merchants," were all "very much occupied with the duties of life." There was actually no difference in this regard between "the humblest laborer, who works with his hands," and gifted geniuses like Franklin, Newton, or Shakespeare. All workers, manual laborers and gentlemen, "however various their occupations," employed both their minds and their bodies in their labor, and this united them "into one interest."

It is remarkable, to say the least, to see the audacious ease with which Everett in these speeches and writings dissolved age-old distinctions. Intellectual and bodily work, the liberal and mechanical arts, the leisured few and the laboring many, working for the public and working for profit—all these classical divisions were now casually collapsed into a single category. Consequently, argued Everett, every honest worker in the society, including a celebrated gentleman like Everett, was "entitled to the good fellowship of each and every other member of the community; . . . all are the parts of one whole, and . . . between those parts, as there is but one interest, so there should be but one feeling."[28]

Despite the heightened value placed on labor everywhere in the Western world in these years, this blurring of the ancient differences between leisured gentry and common workingmen was carried much further in America than elsewhere. And foreign visitors like Tocqueville, Michael Chevalier, and Francis Grund were surprised at what they found in the United States, at least outside of the South. The secret of America's prosperity, said Grund, was its celebration of work. Only in America had labor entirely lost its traditional association with meanness and become fully respectable. Only in America was "industry . . . an honor, and idleness a disgrace." In places such as Cincinnati, said Chevalier, it was hard to find members of "a leisure class, living without any regular profession on their inheritance or on the wealth acquired by their own enterprise in early life." Of course, there were "many persons of wealth having one hundred thousand dollars or more," but these rich, even if they had been so inclined, were prevented from living a life of leisure by a culture that prized work and attacked idleness. Everywhere in northern America, said Chevalier, there was "a constant and unrelaxing devotion to labor." In England, businessmen worked only in the morning and played at being a traditional gentleman the rest of the day. But "the American of the North and the Northwest whose character sets the tone in the United States is permanently a man of business, he is always the Englishman of the morning."[29]

Tocqueville reached the same startling conclusion. In America, he said, "everyman works for his living" and assumes "that to work is the necessary, natural, and honest condition of all men." What most astonished Tocqueville was that Americans thought not only that work itself was "honorable" but that "work specifically to gain money" was "honorable." In Europe, gentlemen had only scorn for working for profit. There the classical republican tradition of political leadership by a disinterested leisured aristocracy was still very much alive. In Europe, there were "hardly any public officials who do not claim to serve the state without interested motives. Their salary is a detail to which sometimes they give a little thought and to which they always pretend to give none." But in America, public service and profit were "visibly united." In fact, observed Chevalier, "the idea of service and salary are so inseparably connected" in Americans' thinking that in their "almanacs it is common to see the rate of pay annexed to the lists of public offices." All this had immense consequences in making people feel equal; and it was this equality, as Tocqueville pointed out, that gave Americans whatever satisfaction they had in their busy lives: it "every day confers a number of small enjoyments on every man." With everyone being alike in working for profit, no one, including servants, said Tocqueville, had to "feel degraded because they work." Who could be humiliated by working for pay when even the president of the country "works for a salary"?[30]

We have usually not given these comments on American work by foreign visitors the attention they deserve because we have not appreciated the degree to which early-nineteenth-century Americans were overturning the ancient tradition of aristocratic leisure and leadership and celebrating in its place what Emerson called "the dignity and necessity of labor to every citizen."[31]

Perhaps nothing separated early-nineteenth-century Americans more from Europeans than their attitude toward labor and their egalitarian sense that everyone must participate in it. In America, wrote Theodore Sedgwick, son of the prominent Federalist of the same name, "to live without some regular employment or industry is not reputable." Although there were individuals here and there who were idle, "there is no class that is not compelled to work." "It is true, then, in the best and strictest sense," Sedgwick concluded, "that the great body of the people of the United States are working people." With everyone claiming to work and no exclusive working class, it is not surprising that the development of a socialist movement in the United States was inhibited. In America it seemed everyone had to have an occupation, and beginning with the 1820 census every adult male was asked his occupation. All people became laborers and all activities, including public office-holding, were reduced to the making of a living—a severe leveling unprecedented in history that no other society in the modern world quite duplicated. No wonder, then, that an American, inquiring about a European visitor and being told he was a duke, could reply: "A Duke! I wonder what he does for a living?"[32]

In time new distinctions would be drawn, between "manual" and "nonmanual" labor, between "hand work" and "head work," and between "blue-collar" and "white-collar" workers. But all who made a useful contribution to society were defined similarly as workingmen. Because every free American was presumed to work at something and for pay, every free American was to that extent equal.[33]

16. Democratic Officeholding

From the outset of the Revolution the American gentry had been vulnerable to attacks on their leisured disinterestedness because for most of
them, at least in the North, their leisure was something of a fraud: they
really never had enough independent wealth and income to support
their classical image of living without working. In eighteenth-century
America it had never been easy for gentlemen to make these personal
sacrifices for the public, and it became especially difficult during the
Revolution. Gentlemen were expected to staff the officer corps of the
army and to provide for their own rations, clothing, and equipment on
salaries less than half those of British officers. Members of Congress
were no better off. Many of them, especially those of "small fortunes,"
continually complained of the burdens of office and repeatedly begged
to be relieved of these burdens in order to pursue their private interests.
Gentlemen were not used to offices that absorbed all their time and
energy and quickly concluded that the "Trade of Patriotism but ill agrees
with the profession of a practising Lawyer." Thomas Stone of Maryland
resigned from Congress in 1778 because he became "convinced that I
cannot attend Congress so constantly, as every Delegate ought to do,
without giving up the Practice of the Law." James Iredell of North
Carolina worried about how he could resign from unremunerative offices without hurting his reputation, and in 1776 he had to turn down an
appointment to the Congress because of his "cursed poverty." Periodic
retirement from the cares and commotions of the public arena for refuge
and rest at one's country seat was acceptable classical behavior. But too
often America's political leaders, especially in the North, had to retire
not to relaxation in the leisure and solitude of a rural retreat but to the
making of money in the busyness and bustle of a city law practice.[1]

Hence would-be officeholders from 1776 found themselves in the awkward position of having to urge their republican governments not only
to pay salaries but to keep raising them. In the process they gradually
undermined the two-thousand-year-old classical tradition of aristocratic
public service. In an ideal republican world, government officeholders
ought to serve without salary. Receiving profits from a public office
smacked of interestedness and tainted the officeholder's virtue. Which
is why the radical Pennsylvania constitution of 1776 abolished all "offices
of profit" in the government; there was no need for them, the consti-

tution declared, for they created "dependence and servility unbecoming freemen in the possessors and expectants, faction, contention, corruption, and disorder among the people." In place of offices of profit the Pennsylvania constitution provided "reasonable compensation" for all public servants; and if that compensation attracted too many applicants, then it had to be lessened by the legislature. For the same republican reasons Washington was anxious that he not be paid a salary as commander in chief. To the end of his life Thomas Jefferson remained committed to a classical view of officeholding—officeholding in accord with what he called "the Roman principle." "In a virtuous government," he said, ". . . public offices are, what they should be, burthens to those appointed to them, which it would be wrong to decline, though foreseen to bring with them intense labor, and great private loss." Public employment contributes "neither to advantage nor happiness. It is but honorable exile from one's family and affairs."[2]

Jefferson was never one to put his private happiness above public duty.[3] But of course he had a large plantation and several hundred slaves to support him. Other gentlemen, including most Federalists, were not so well situated. Since few would-be officeholders had Jefferson's wealth or Washington's scruples, they constantly had to press their governments to pay their officials higher salaries. If the salaries were not raised, said Gouverneur Morris in 1778, the alternative was clear: it was to elect men "who possess such Property that they can afford to sacrifice a few Thousand to the general Cause."[4]

But should anyone, even the most wealthy, have to make such sacrifices? In an unfinished essay written sometime during these years, Morris struggled to reconcile the classical tradition of disinterested public leadership with the private demands of making a living. "A Man expends his Fortune in political Pursuits," wrote Morris, expressing a common gentry complaint. Did he do this out of "personal Consideration" or out of a desire to promote the public good? If he did it to promote the public good, "was he justifiable in sacrificing to it the Subsistence of his Family? These are important Questions, but," said Morris, "there remains one more: Would not as much Good have followed from an industrious Attention to his own Affairs?" With this final question Morris went beyond the issue of salaries and cut the foundations out from under the entire classical republican tradition. An aristocracy that could pose such a question was already doomed.[5]

John Adams, cantankerous and honest as always, was also willing openly to challenge the classical republican tradition that had dictated

Washington's refusal of a salary. In several remarkable letters written in the mid-1780s to the English radical John Jebb, Adams analyzed the issue of salaries for officeholders with a thoroughness and boldness unequaled in the revolutionary era. Jebb, said Adams, seemed to agree with David Hume's view expressed in his essay on a perfect commonwealth that no representative, magistrate, or senator ought to be paid, though Hume did grant salaries to executive officials such as secretaries, councillors, and ambassadors. But Adams was not satisfied with any restrictions on salaries, and he denied that public officials' receiving pay was a violation of republican principles. The Pennsylvania constitution's abolition of offices of profit was a mistake, said Adams. It was not the "legal, honest profit" of office the Pennsylvanians ought to have worried about; it was "the perquisites, patronage, and abuse, which is the evil." If "you make it a law that no man should hold an office who had not a private income sufficient for the subsistence and prospects of himself and family," then the consequence would be that "all offices would be monopolized by the rich; the poor and the middling ranks would be excluded and an aristocratic despotism would immediately follow." Adams knew "very well that the word 'disinterested' turns the heads of the people by exciting their enthusiasm." It was central to the classical republican faith and to the views of enlightened Englishmen and French philosophes. But, said Adams, in one of the most explicit disavowals of revolutionary idealism made in the 1780s, this reliance on virtuous leaders was all wrong. "How few have they been!" Perhaps history saw only one actual disinterested character every five hundred years, but certainly it had shown us "two thousand instances every year of the semblance of disinterestedness, counterfeited for the most selfish purposes." At any rate, there was "not enough" disinterested men "in any age or any country to fill all the necessary offices, and therefore the people may depend upon it, that the hypocritical pretence of disinterestedness will be set up to deceive them, much oftener than the virtue will be practised for their good."[6]

Washington's refusal of a salary as commander in chief and his awesome and famous retirement in 1783 from public life infuriated Adams, which accounts for the passion expressed in his letters to Jebb. What did it mean, Adams asked with undisguised resentment, for an officeholder to offer to serve the people for nothing? Since serving without pay "never fails to turn the heads of the multitude," what did Washington think he was doing when he refused a salary? Did he expect the people to feel grateful to him? Gratitude, implied Adams, was no

basis for authentic republican relationships. Although gratitude had always been valued by the ancient republicans, it had lost its significance
for Adams. "The cry of gratitude," he said, "has made more men mad,
and established more despotism in the world, than all other causes put
together." The conclusion was obvious. "Every public man should be
honestly paid for his services," and then offices would be founded on
justice, not gratitude. Adams had no patience even with Washington's
retirement and renunciation of further office in December 1783. Surely,
he said, the "revolution was not undertaken to raise one great reputation to make a sublime page in history." Why were people making so
much of Washington's retirement? "Why? What is implied in this necessity? . . . Does not this idea of the necessity of his retiring, imply an
opinion of danger to the public, from his continuing in public, a jealousy
that he might become ambitious? and does it not imply something still
more humiliating, a . . . danger of setting him up for a king?" All this
could have been avoided if Washington had accepted a salary as the
other revolutionary generals had. "He should have been paid, as well
as they, and the people should have too high a sense of their own dignity
ever to suffer any man to serve them for nothing." Adams went on to
declare that "offices in general ought to yield as honest a subsistence,
and as clear an independence as professions, callings, trades, or farms,"
without spelling out the full significance of what he was saying—that
officeholders had to make a living just like everyone else.[7]

There was no doubt that paying salaries fundamentally altered the
nature of the officeholders and made them something other than virtuous leaders. Which is why French philosophes like the Abbé Mably
protested so indignantly against the articles in the revolutionary state
constitutions providing for salaries for officeholders. In 1781 James Lovell, a former Boston schoolmaster with no independent wealth, dimly
saw the implications of what was happening while serving as the Massachusetts delegate to the Confederation Congress. Why should serving
in public office not be a paid profession like any other profession such
as the ministry or teaching? asked Lovell. "Is it a Crime to serve here
as a Delegate for a Living more than to do it in the Church or in an
Academy? I thought not when I undertook it."[8] Seeing public office as
just another occupation from which one earned a living, however, was
a long way from classical republican thinking; it even suggested the
possibility of interests actually participating in government.

One of the most illuminating moments in the developing contradictions between the revolutionaries' republican idealism and their social

reality came early in the Philadelphia Convention of 1787. On June 2 Benjamin Franklin proposed that members of the executive branch "shall receive no salary, stipend, Fee or reward whatsoever for their services." This was putting the issue about as starkly as it could be put, and the response of the Convention tells us volumes about what was happening to the classical republican tradition in America.

The eighty-one-year-old Franklin felt strongly about not paying people who served in government and had written out a speech, which James Wilson delivered for him. The saving of money from the salaries was not his aim, he said. It was the evils the salaries would cause that he wished to prevent. If the government paid salaries to its executive officials, it would attract into office the wrong sorts of men, "the bold and the violent, the men of strong passions and indefatigable activity in their selfish pursuits." "By making our posts of honor places of profit," said Franklin, we would "sow the seeds of contention, faction & tumult." The old man realized that some may imagine "that this is an Utopian Idea, and that we can never find men to serve us in the Executive department, without paying them well for their services." But, he noted, the country gentry and aristocrats of England and France took up burdensome offices without pay. And had not General Washington led the Continental army "for eight years altogether without the smallest salary." These examples "shew that the pleasure of doing good & serving their Country and the respect such conduct entitles them to, are sufficient motives with some minds to give up a great portion of their time to the Public, without the mean inducement of pecuniary satisfaction." Surely America, he said, had sufficient numbers of such disinterested men.

In light of Franklin's subsequent nineteenth-century reputation as the bourgeois American, it is ironic, to say the least, for Franklin to be the founding father at the Convention most concerned with these classical sentiments of aristocratic leadership. But in fact not only was the eighteenth-century Franklin one of the most aristocratic-minded of the founding fathers, but he was also one of the wealthiest and one of those most able to serve in public office without pay.

Most of the delegates were not as well off as Franklin, and they were embarrassed by his proposal. They knew in their hearts that the old man was right, that he spoke out of a classical republican heritage of disinterested public service that went back at least to Cicero and that they still tried to pay lip service to. But they also knew that in late-eighteenth-century America serving in government without compensation was no longer possible for most gentlemen. "No debate ensued," Madison dryly noted, and Franklin's motion was postponed. "It was treated with great respect, but rather for the author of it, than from any apparent conviction of its expediency or practicability."⁹

After Franklin's proposal for the executive branch died, it was a foregone conclusion that the rest of the federal officials would receive some sort of salary. Still, there were those South Carolinian nabobs, Pierce Butler and John Rutledge, who proposed that at least members of the aristocratic Senate "should be entitled to no salary or compensation for their services." But this proposal lost, seven states to three, with one divided.¹⁰

In the end the Convention provided for compensation for all national officials but left the amounts up to the Congress. This provision itself was radical for the age: members of Parliament, after all, did not receive salaries until 1911. The First Congress, which met in the spring of 1789, easily set the compensation for the members of the other branches of the government, but it had trouble setting its own salaries. The issue had been a controversial one in the Convention, Madison having declared that for Congress to determine its own salaries was "an indecent thing, and might in time prove a dangerous one." Nevertheless, at the outset the House of Representatives agreed upon six dollars a day for both congressmen and senators. But some, including Madison and many senators, thought that senators ought to be paid more than congressmen. Otherwise, said Madison, older, able men—"the *first* characters" in the country—might prefer private retirement to public service in the Senate and thereby cause the Senate to "degenerate into an inferior and unavailing institution." Accordingly, a proposal was made to lower the salary of representatives to five dollars a day, but it was defeated by a large majority. Frederick Muhlenberg of Pennsylvania, who became Speaker of the House, told a correspondent at home that as long as the Congress continued to meet in New York City the representatives could not accept any reduction in their salary: "You have no conception," he wrote, "at what extravagant rates every thing is paid for in this place.'"¹¹

At the same time many members of the Senate were arguing that they deserved higher salaries than the members of the lower house. Senator Ralph Izard of South Carolina contended that senators needed sufficient income to maintain their dignity and character; after all, his state's delegates to the old Congress used to have £600 sterling a year, which had enabled them to "live like Gentlemen." Then Izard's colleague, Pierce Butler, who had a claim to an Irish title, rose to express his aristocratic contempt for all this wrangling about money. "A Member of the Senate," he said, "should not only have a handsome income but should spend it all. . . . It was scandalous for a member of Congress to take any of his Wages home." Better that he "give it to the poor."[12]

After months of "hard Jockeying between the Senate and the House of Representatives" over their respective pay ("it was a tryal who would hold longest out . . . a Tryal of Skill in the way of Starvation"), the Congress finally provided for six dollars a day for members of both houses. Senator William Maclay of Pennsylvania was suspicious of this clamoring for pay and for offices of profit. Indeed, he said in May 1790, "the Spirit of the last Session really was to make offices for Men, to provide for Individuals without regarding the public or Sparing Expence."[13] All these salaries for congressmen and for other federal offices, however, were never enough for many would-be gentry. New England Federalists, precarious aristocrats that they were, complained ceaselessly of "the continued disgrace of starving our public officers." Fisher Ames thought that "such a sum should be paid for service as was sufficient to command men of talents to perform it. Anything below this was parsimonious and unwise." Good men, he said, would not take up the public burden; or, as Oliver Wolcott put it, in words that by themselves repudiated the classical tradition of public service, "good abilities command high prices at market." Indeed, although the federal administration had more than enough applicants for its lower and middling offices, by the mid-1790s it was having trouble filling its highest offices. In 1795 William Smith charged in the House of Representatives that Jefferson, Hamilton, and Henry Knox had all resigned from the cabinet "chiefly for one reason, the smallness of the salary." Although this was not at all the case with Jefferson, both Knox and Hamilton had trouble maintaining a genteel standard of living on their government salaries.[14]

By the beginning of the nineteenth century the classical republican conception of government officeholding was losing much of its meaning. If each person was supposed to pursue his own private interests, and the pursuit of private interests was the real source of the public good, then it was foolish to expect men to devote their time and energy to public responsibilities without compensation. A New York report of 1800 caught the anachronism in the older republican idea of relying on private citizens serving in government without pay. On the face of it, such a reliance was "plausible, as it carries the appearance of economy and evidences a disinterested zeal for the public service.'' But in reality, this mode of governing was not successful. It evaded responsibility. ''The burthen which no one in particular is bound to sustain, is shifted from shoulder to shoulder, till at last it is left wholly unsupported: and as no compensation is to be received, no one thinks himself bound to sacrifice his own private affairs, to an object of general concern.''[15] So far then had Americans abandoned the age-old tradition that public office was the responsibility of a leisured patriciate.

It became increasingly clear that society could no longer expect men to sacrifice their time and money—their private interests—for the sake of the public. Public office could no longer be regarded merely as a burden that prominent gentlemen had an obligation to bear. No longer could it be something that gentlemen simply stood by and waited to be called to. And no longer could it be the consequence of a gentleman's previously established social wealth and authority. If anything, office in America had become the source of that wealth and authority.[16]

In the generation following the formation of the Constitution, the Anti-Federalist conception of actual or interest representation in government—the William Findley conception of representation—came to dominate the realities, if not the rhetoric, of American political life. And the intellectual world of the founding fathers, a world that went back two millennia, was rapidly undermined.

Many Americans of the early Republic, with varying degrees of reluctance or enthusiasm, came to believe that what they once thought was true was no longer true. Government officials were no longer to play the role of umpire; they were no longer to stand above the competing interests of the marketplace and make disinterested, impartial judgments about what was good for the whole society. Elected officials were to bring the partial, local interests of the society, and sometimes even their own interests, right into the workings of government. Partisanship and parties became legitimate activities in politics. And all adult white males, regardless of their property holdings or their independence, were to have the right to vote. By 1825 every state but Rhode Island, Virginia, and Louisiana had achieved universal white manhood suffrage.

With these new ideas and practices came the greater participation of more ordinary people in politics. If men were all alike, equal in their rights and in their interestedness, then there were no specially qualified gentlemen who stood apart from the whole society with a superior and disinterested perspective. All people were the same: all were ordinary and all were best represented by ordinary people. That was democracy.

Indeed, as early as the first decade of the nineteenth century it seemed to many gentlemen like Benjamin Latrobe, the noted architect and engineer, that was precisely what democracy in America had come to mean. His remarkable letter written in 1806 to the Italian patriot Philip Mazzei tells us that much of the democratic world that Tocqueville would later describe was already present. "After the adoption of the federal constitution," Latrobe explained, "the extension of the right of Suffrage in all the states to the majority of all the adult male citizens, planted a germ which has gradually evolved, and has spread actual and practical democracy and political equality over the whole union. There is no doubt whatsoever but that this state of things in our country produces the greatest sum of happiness that perhaps any nation ever enjoyed." But the cost has been high, said Latrobe. Most men have to labor, and consequently "those arts and refinements, and elegancies which require riches and leisure to their production, are not to be found among the majority of our citizens."

> The want of learning and of science in the majority is one of those things which strikes foreigners who visit us very forceably. Our representatives to all our Legislative bodies, National, as well as of the States, are elected by the majority *sui similes,* that is, *unlearned.* For instance from Philadelphia and its environs we send to congress not one man of letters. One of them indeed is a lawyer but of no eminence, another a good Mathematician, but when elected he was a Clerk in a bank. The others are plain farmers. From the next county is sent a Blacksmith, and from just over the river a Butcher. Our state legislature does not contain one individual of superior talents. The fact is, that superior talents actually excite distrust, and the experience of the world perhaps does not encourage the people to trust men of genius. . . . This government of what may be called, an unlettered majority, has put down even that ideal rank which manners had established, excepting in our great cities depending on commerce and crouded with foreigners, where the distinction between what is called the Gentlemen, and others still subsists, and produces circles of association separate from each other. . . . In Philadelphia even this distinction has almost disappeared, those who expect it having early excluded themselves from the present race of well dressed men and women. Of this state of society the solid and general advantages are

undeniable: but to a cultivated mind, to a man of letters, to a lover of the arts it presents a very unpleasant picture. The importance attached to wealth, and the freedom which opens every legal avenue to wealth to every one individually has two effects, which are unfavorable to morals: It weakens the ties that bind individuals to each other, by making all citizens rivals in the pursuit of riches; and it renders the means by which they are attained more indifferent.

The problems of governing this kind of society were overwhelming. If everyone in the society was interested and no one was disinterested, who was to assume the role of neutral umpire? Who was to reconcile and harmonize all these different clashing interests and promote the good of the whole? All the Anti-Federalists and their Republican successors could offer by way of an answer was the view, attributed to Jefferson by Latrobe, "that the public good is best promoted by the exertion of each individual seeking his own good in his own way"— with the government apparently having very little to say in the matter. Such a view marked an end to classical republicanism and the beginnings of liberal democracy.[17]

Once men decided that the public good was best promoted by allowing each individual to pursue his own good in his own way, then the relationship between the public and private spheres had to shift, as Latrobe very acutely realized. Having only ordinary people and no men of genius in government promoting an autonomous public good had little political or economic effect—since the public realm of classical politics no longer seemed to matter to the growth and prosperity of the country. "The wealth of our country, its improvements in agriculture and in mechanics, and even in some species of manufactories is rapid beyond example." And government, said Latrobe, had no hand in this rapid improvement. "We in fact do not perceive that we have a government, but on the days of election, and in the bickerings of party, which are kept up by the few who prefer the uncertainty of salaries from the public to the secure income of private industry."[18]

Despite the weakness of government and the uncertainty of public salaries in democratic America, however, competition for political office became very fierce, fiercer than in England, because, as Edward Everett observed, public office in America for some became personally and socially more important than in England. In England, said Everett, there were all sorts of areas of family and social rank for ambitious men to find scope for their talents. "In place of all these," said Everett, "we have nothing, to which the ambitious can aspire, but office. . . . Office here is family, rank, heredity, fortune, in Short, Everything, out of the range of private life. This links its possession with innate principles of our Nature; & truly incredible are the efforts Men are Willing to Make, the humiliations they will endure, to get it."[19]

This competition for office led inevitably to the emergence of politicians whose social position, private happiness, and even wealth came from holding public office and who identified their private interest with that of the public. Congressman and avid Republican Matthew Lyon, for example, saw nothing wrong with using his office to get government contracts for himself. What difference did it make, he asked on the floor of the House in 1805, if a congressman served "the public for the same reward the public gives another"? Although a member of the House of Representatives, he was also a businessman looking "for customers with whom I can make advantageous bargains to both parties. It is all the same to me whether I contract with an individual or the public."[20]

It was not easy to accept such modern democratic politics. No doubt one had to have faith in the people, said one angry and befuddled Federalist in 1816. But why did the people continue to vote for "those who seek to promote their own interest" instead of "those who seek to promote the public good"? It was discouraging. "We have advanced in the progress of avarice, and self-interest, from one step to another, till the offices of government are considered only as private property, and the election of our rulers, has become with all parties in a greater or less degree, the subject of calculation and compromise." Even former men of principle, it was said, were going over to the popular cause and adopting democratic techniques of electioneering in the scramble for political office. "Public offices are sought as a means of enriching the occupant; and their importance is graduated according to the means of corrupt influence which they afford." This classically minded Federalist could not restrain his indignation. For a man "to seek for office as means of accumulating wealth, . . . to promote his private interest, it is," he sputtered, "unpardonable."[21]

Of course, most politicians, even those openly seeking to promote their constituents' interests, were not flagrantly self-serving, but their blatant electioneering and their competitive campaigning for office made many people think they were. By 1823 *Niles' Weekly Register* already defined modern politicians as "persons who have little, if any regard for the welfare of the republic unless immediately connected with . . . their own private pursuits."[22]

These changes prepared the way for the development of modern political parties, which in the end helped to legitimate the changes the Revolution had brought about and to make democracy acceptable to Americans. The Democratic-Republican parties that emerged at the end of the second decade of the nineteenth century in some northern states, especially New York, Pennsylvania, and Kentucky, were the first modern parties in American history and perhaps in Western history. These parties were impersonal and permanent organizations of professional salaried politicians that were designed solely to recruit leaders, mobilize voters, win elections, and compete regularly and legitimately with other opposition parties. As such, they were unlike the earlier Federalist and Republican parties and indeed were unlike any party that had ever existed before.

The Federalists and the Republicans of the 1790s were not modern political parties, and their electoral competition scarcely constituted a "party system."[23] Neither the Federalists nor the Republicans accepted the legitimacy of the other, and neither was designed to be permanent. Both of them were formed by notables, who continued to decry the existence of party spirit, and both were organized essentially from the top down. The Federalists actually never thought of themselves as a party; instead they saw themselves as the natural gentry rulers of the society. The Republicans did reluctantly describe themselves as a party, but one, like the whig parties of the 1760s and 1770s, made necessary only by the need to counter monarchical tyranny; as soon as that threat from the Federalist monocrats receded, the older Republican leaders thought their party should fall away. The end of the War of 1812 and the disgrace of the Federalists, exulted Thomas Jefferson, had resulted in the "complete suppression of party."[24]

Historians have delighted in pointing out that the "Era of Good Feeling" under James Monroe's administration was filled with bitter factional contention that belied the name people gave to the era. But the title was meaningful to most people because it seemed that the earlier party competition and hateful party spirit had indeed finally disappeared. Monroe summed up traditional thinking when he remarked in 1816 that "the existence of parties is not necessary to free government."[25] However often the founding fathers in reluctant concessions to reality admitted that political parties might be necessary evils in a free society, none of them ever thought that permanent party strife was good for the harmony and stability of the Republic. Only a new generation of polit-

ical leaders—younger men born usually in obscurity during the years of
the Revolution—would be able to reach that startling conclusion.

Martin Van Buren represented just this sort of new breed of American, at ease in the chaos of the early Republic and confident of the
future. He thrived in a democratic political world that was very different
from that of the founding fathers. He believed in political parties and
in running for office. He was the first modern professional politician to
win the presidency. As the ambitious son of a tavernkeeper, he prided
himself on having risen to office "without the aid of powerful family
connexions."[26] Before his elevation to the highest office in the land, Van
Buren had no fame, no fortune, and no reputation for great achievement. He had won no battles, had written no great treatises, had made
no memorable speeches. He had no public charisma and was barely
known throughout the United States. But what this "little magician"
did do was build the best and most organized political party the country
had ever seen.

The new parties of professional politicians like Van Buren were designed for the modern democratic society. They brought together large
numbers of ordinary people in order to counter the family influence and
personal connections of Federalist gentry and older aristocratic Republicans such as De Witt Clinton of New York. Parties, like other voluntary associations of these years, combined otherwise isolated individuals
into meaningful communities. People have joined the New York Republican party, declared its leaders in 1820, not for personal benefit or
profit, "but have spontaneously and voluntarily identified their political
fortunes with ours, and thereby entitled themselves to full community
with us."[27] Parties, in fact, became a modern means by which something akin to the self-subsuming virtue of classical politics could be practiced. "Individual partialities and local attachments," declared the
leaders of the New York Democratic-Republican party in 1823, "are
secondary and quite unimportant compared . . . with the INTERESTS AND
PERMANENCY OF THE REPUBLICAN PARTY."[28]

Loyalty to the party became the sole criterion of the political worth
of a person. Family ties, personal connections, personal wealth, even
individual achievement did not matter as much as loyalty to the party
and devotion to its cause. In vain did the son of revolutionary John Jay
plead for the recognition of other characteristics besides party loyalty in
determining officeholders. No one, said Peter Jay in the New York constitutional convention of 1820, should want respectable men like himself and

other Federalists to "feel themselves aliens in their native land."
The Republican majority ought to give the Federalists some offices,
however humble, "instead of bestowing all upon men, recommended
principally as ardent political champions, or as the noisy and active
agents at our elections." But the new professional politicians like Van
Buren had only contempt for such pathetic complaints from these men
who were "Federalists from their birth." "Most of these gentlemen had
from early manhood enjoyed high and influential position in what was
called good society," Van Buren later recalled, "and the supposition
that they expected to occupy, on that account, greater consideration in
the democratic organization was not acceptable in that quarter."[29]

Despite the difficulty of defying the traditional aversion to party
spirit, Van Buren tried from the outset of his career to carve out a new
significance for parties. "Parties would always exist," he declared in
1820, "and they would always consult their interest in the selection of
candidates for public places. Their first and chief object was success."
And loyalty and discipline were the keys to success. Decades later men
recalled the iron discipline that the Albany Regency faction of the New
York Democratic-Republican party exacted from its members. No one
"was allowed to occupy a seat on the bench of whose loyalty to party
or to the acts of the regency there could be the least question." In an
enlarged, impersonal world of strangers and unknown men, connection
to the party was sometimes all that could be relied on; it was a substitute
for the friendships and personal letters of introduction of the older, more
intimate world. Nomination and appointment to office were to be made
only to loyal party members. "Give them to good and true and useful
friends who will enjoy the emolument if there is any, and who will use
the influence to our benefit, if any influence is conferred by the office,"
advised Albany Regency leader Silas Wright to a party colleague. "This
is the long and short of the rule by which to act."[30]

Such a rule created a radically new understanding of political patronage and officeholding, one that virtually repudiated all that the revolutionaries of 1776 had sought. Using offices to bind people to the
government was what monarchies did, and the revolutionaries had attacked it as "corruption." It was true that disillusionment with the
revolutionary republican experiment of having the people elect the best
and the brightest had led Hamilton and the Federalists in the 1790s to
revive some of the patronage practices of monarchy and to use federal
offices to tie influential men to the government. But Jefferson had come
into power in 1801 promising to undo all that Federalist monarchical

corruption and to restore the true republican spirit of 1776. He soon found himself, however, torn between his sincere desire to repudiate the Federalists' monarchical use of political patronage and the pressing demands of many of his fellow Republicans that he oust the Federalists and put good Republicans in their places.

No problem in Jefferson's presidency took more of his time or caused him more trouble than did that of political patronage. "Solicitations to office," he said, were the "most painful" part of being an executive magistrate. "The ordinary affairs of a nation offer little difficulty to a person of any experience; but the gift of office is the dreadful burden which oppresses him." Once the Republicans had their proportionate share of offices, Jefferson promised to "return with joy to that state of things, when the only questions concerning a candidate shall be, is he honest? Is he capable? Is he faithful to the Constitution?"[31] With Federalist officeholders replaced by Republicans, there was no further need for compromise on the issue of "corruption," and removals from office for political reasons came to an end. Under Jefferson's Republican successors, James Madison, James Monroe, and John Quincy Adams, the holders of government appointments became a more or less permanent officialdom of men growing old in their positions.

John Quincy Adams thus inherited in 1825 an administration filled with bureaucrats who were opposed to him. But, averse as he was to corruption and loyal to republican principles, Adams was unwilling to use patronage for political purposes. He retained most members of Monroe's cabinet; he even offered to keep his presidential rival, W. H. Crawford, in his cabinet. In the four years of his administration Adams dismissed only twelve of the over eight hundred civil officeholders in the federal government. When urged to dismiss more, he declared he would not. Dismissal at the pleasure of the President would be "harsh and odious—inconsistent with the principle upon which I have commenced the Administration, of removing no person from office but for cause." Adams remained committed to the ideology of the Revolution. To the astonishment of younger politicians, he said he could not remove an officer of the government "for merely preferring another candidate for the Presidency."[32]

Younger democratic politicians revealed a radically new attitude toward patronage as early as 1820 in the New York constitutional convention. During the debates the Federalists tried to out-republicanize the Republicans and use the Americans' revolutionary aversion to patronage against the Republican-dominated executive and its power to appoint officers. They argued strongly that justices of the peace, instead of being appointed by the governor, ought to be elected by the people in the localities. Rufus King, in the fashion of a good revolutionary of 1776, said that he wanted "to dissever and disconnect the magistracy from the central power at the seat of government, and to destroy this extensive means of patronage which . . . was not necessary to sustain the government." Election of local offices meant that "this great mass of patronage and power might be broken up into minute fragments, and disposed throughout the land." That the Federalists in 1820 should have been reduced to such populist and localist arguments says a great deal about the reversal of their political position since the 1790s.

The New York Republicans, who usually favored electing everyone and anyone, were obviously embarrassed by the Federalists' tactics; they after all saw themselves as the true guardians of the revolutionary spirit of 1776. Van Buren, very defensively, tried to point out that only a few thousand offices remained appointive; most were elected by the people. Besides, he said in a stunning concession to monarchical principles, retaining some patronage meant not cutting "every cord that binds together the people to the government." Republican Nathan Williams carried this argument even further. Was it not essential, he asked, "that there should be some channel through which the remotest parts of the state would feel the influence of the central administration . . . ? Could it be expected . . . that without a community of feeling, without a single tie of interest, any government would long hang together? What ligament, what cement, would there be to bind the head and the remote parts together?" "Patriotism" could not do it. It "alas! had been found, in some cases, rather weak among us." Without "influence," said Williams, "the government would be like a rope of sand." Hamilton could not have said it better. These New York Republicans were a long way from 1776 and strict republican principles, but their arguments, thrown up in the heat of debate, became part of the intellectual preparation for the Jacksonian revolution.[33]

Jacksonianism did not create democracy in America. But it legitimated it; it restrained and controlled it and reconciled Americans to it. It did so by infusing into American democracy more elements of monarchy than even the Federalists had dared to try. The Jacksonians did this, however, in the midst of the most enthusiastic democratic rhetoric that any modern country had ever experienced. Consequently, the centralizing and consolidating aspects of the Jacksonian revolution have been obscured and generally lost to us.

The administration of Andrew Jackson had a very different idea of patronage from that of the revolutionaries, one more in accord with the emerging democratic society of the nineteenth century. The Jacksonians inaugurated what came to be called the "spoils system," the systematic use of patronage to reward members of the victorious party in an intense and legitimate party competition. By ousting the losing party and appointing only party loyalists to post offices and land offices and other government positions, the party created networks of influence throughout the country and helped to hold the country together.

No wonder many thought the Jacksonians' flagrant use of patronage was a throwback to the old monarchical techniques of the eighteenth century; this is partly why Jackson's opponents called him "King Andrew" and formed the Whig party. Although the Jacksonians' justifications of patronage were sometimes similar to those of the past, its use was different—different not only from that of monarchy but from that of republicanism as well. The Jacksonian officeholders were not socially visible and respectable men. Historians and sociologists have worked hard to show that the social status of the Jacksonian officeholders was not dramatically different from that of earlier administrations.[34] But not only have these studies focused on the administrative elites of the government, ignoring the federal officeholders in the localities, but they have often applied very crude measures of social status and social background. "Occupation" is virtually no measure at all: there were lawyers and there were lawyers; an enormous social gulf, perceptible to contemporaries if not to us, separated a Harvard-educated attorney from an apprenticed lawyer who had never been to college.

Many of the Jacksonian officeholders were new sorts of democratic men. Even Amos Kendall, a member of Jackson's "kitchen cabinet" and author of Jackson's Bank veto message, was thought by some to lack "the polished conversation the graceful manner & high tone" of a real gentleman; he did "not look like a Gentleman." In fact, Jackson chose what he called "plain businessmen" for his official cabinet. "He has surrounded himself with men of narrow minds, some of them hardly gentlemen," complained the governor of Virginia.[35] Not that all Jacksonians were without wealth and power. Some were Federalist converts who found solace in the Jacksonian attack on corruption and the Jacksonian desire to restore order and virtue. Others were ambitious entrepreneurial go-getters, wealthy but unestablished and ungenteel. But many others were like the humble grocer in Frankfort, Kentucky, who became a postmaster—truly obscure men without social position in their localities; in fact, their appointment to a post office or a land office was usually the source of any social influence they might have.[36]

Regardless of the officeholders' wealth or social standing, however, what was crucial now was their loyalty to the Jacksonian cause. The sole criterion of appointment was not family, not social standing, not wealth, not ability, not character, and not reputation, but connection to the party. Nothing else was needed. "The duties of all public offices," said Jackson in his first annual message, "are, or at least admit of being made, so plain and simple that men of intelligence may readily qualify themselves for their performance. . . . In a country where offices are created solely for the benefit of the people no one man has any more intrinsic right to official station than another."[37] Anyone now could serve in any office.

But not for long. The Jacksonians used the older radical whig conception of "rotation in office" not only as a means of freeing government as much as possible from any semblance of aristocratic influence but also as a cover for the radical changes they were making in the nature of officeholding. Government office was no longer to be "a species of property" belonging to prominent gentlemen simply because of their social rank or character. Government office now belonged to the people, ordinary people, and all equally had the right and the ability to hold such office—at least for a short period of time. The result was not, of course, any sudden invasion of offices by ordinary people; college graduates and would-be gentlemen continued to dominate high public office in America. But now even they behaved as common people—a fact immediately evident to European visitors. American public officials, observed Tocqueville in June 1831, possessed little of the aristocratic distinction that Europeans expected in their government officers. "They are absolutely on the same footing as the rest of the citizens. They are dressed the same, stay at the same inn when away from home, are accessible at every moment, and shake everybody by the hand. They exercise a certain power defined by the law; beyond that they are not at all above the rest."[38]

In such an egalitarian system of rotating offices, individuals could be appointed and removed at will without damaging the integrity of government—because the nature of the offices was now to be different. Offices were to be bureaucratic in a modern sense—rationalized, depersonalized, organized by function, defined by rules and regulations, and paid set salaries.

Because many of the Jacksonian officeholders were to be faceless functionaries, presumably lacking the traditional aristocratic concern for personal honor or reputation, the government had to devise new modern safeguards against corruption. More formal structures were erected, new administrative rules were adopted, and more bookkeeping, receipts, and cross-checking were required—all designed to prevent men from exploiting their offices for personal benefit.[39] These added bureaucratic regulations and red tape in the dispensing of funds were not simply the result of the Jacksonian government's having gotten larger and assumed new responsibilities; they were the result of democracy. The new impersonal rules and the self-policing regulations were made for officeholders who were ordinary men with ordinary interests. In the Jacksonians' idea of government, "efficiency," it has been said, "lay primarily in the system (rules and regulations) rather than in men (character)." Office was defined impersonally, bureaucratically. The officeholder's creed was: "I want no discretion. I wish to be able to turn to some law or lawful regulation for every allowance I am called upon to make."[40]

The Jacksonians finally accepted the reality that most officeholders in America could no longer be leisured aristocrats serving out of a sense of honor and an obligation of rank. Instead, as experience since the Revolution had shown, officeholders in democratic America were likely to be "interested" men who could not be trusted to behave virtuously without bureaucratic checks and regulations. By today's standards Jacksonian government was minuscule, but its character was modern. It established many of the principles underlying our present democratic bureaucracy. It helped to make democracy acceptable to Americans.

17. A World Within Themselves

Beneath all these changes in interests, leisure, and officeholding were seismic shifts taking place in the structure of American society. In the half century following the Revolution what remained of the traditional social hierarchy virtually collapsed, and in thousands of different ways connections that had held people together for centuries were further strained and severed. The Revolution, complained the newly arrived Scotsman Charles Nisbet in 1787, had created "a new world . . . unfortunately composed . . . of discordant atoms, jumbled together by chance, and tossed by unconstancy in an immense vacuum." He had bumbled into a society that "greatly wants a principle of attraction and cohesion." It was not surprising that individuals were flying about, especially since their leaders were saying that it was "the moral duty of the people, at all times, to pursue their own happiness" and that each individual was his own "moral agent" with the right "to dispose of himself, and be his own master in all respects."[1]

People in the early nineteenth century sensed that everything had changed and could thus readily respond to Washington Irving's Rip Van Winkle, who woke up after several decades to find the society he had known suddenly gone. "We live in a most extraordinary age," declared young Daniel Webster in 1825. "Events so various and so important that might crowd and distinguish centuries, are, in our times, compressed within the compass of a single life." Classical Rome was now thought to be too stolid and imitative to express the restlessness and originality of this new democratic society. Ancient Greece, said Edward Everett, was a better model. Ancient Greece was tumultuous, wild, and free, said Everett, "free to licentiousness, free to madness."[2]

Everything seemed to be coming apart, and murder, suicide, theft, and mobbing became increasingly common responses to the burdens that liberty and the expectation of gain were placing on people. The drinking of hard liquor became an especially common response. By the second or third decade of the nineteenth century American consumption of distilled spirits reached an all-time high, more than five gallons per person per year—an amount nearly triple today's consumption and greater than that of any major European nation at that time. American grain farmers, particularly those in western Pennsylvania, Kentucky, and Tennessee, found it easier and more profitable to distill, ship, and sell whiskey than to try to ship and sell the perishable grain itself. Consequently, things got to the point where almost everyone or his cousin had a distillery. The number of distilleries increased rapidly after the 1780s, reaching a peak of 20,000 by 1830. In 1815 even the little town of Peacham, Vermont, had thirty distilleries. Distilling whiskey was good business because, to the astonishment of foreigners, nearly all Americans drank—men, women, children, and sometimes even babies—everywhere and anywhere, all day long. Washington, who himself had a distillery, thought as early as 1789 that distilled spirits were "the ruin of half the workmen in this Country." John Adams was mortified that his countrymen were more intemperate than any other people in the world. "The thing has arrived to such a height," declared the Greene and Delaware Moral Society in 1815, "that we are actually threatened with becoming a nation of drunkards."[3]

By 1800 Americans were already known for pushing and shoving one another in public and for their aversion to ceremony. And in the succeeding years there were frequent complaints over "the violation of decorum, the want of etiquette, the rusticity of manners in this generation." Violence was perhaps no more common than it had been earlier, but now it seemed more bizarre. During the forty-five years between 1780 and 1825 there occurred ten of the twelve multiple family murders that were reported or written about in America from the seventeenth century through 1900. It was as if all restraints were falling away. Fistfighting even broke out repeatedly in the Congress and the state legislatures.[4]

Urban rioting became more prevalent and destructive than it had been. Street, tavern, and theater rowdiness, labor strikes, racial and ethnic conflicts—all increased greatly after 1800. These eruptions of mob violence in the early Republic were uncontrolled and sometimes murderous and no longer paid tribute to paternalism and hierarchy as the mobs of the eighteenth century had done. The mobs and gangs were now composed of mostly unconnected and anonymous lowly people, full of class resentment, and thus were all the more frightening. Indeed, Republicans in New York City played upon such resentment in 1801 by telling the common people in election handbills that the Federalist mayor "hates you; from his own soul he hates you . . . ; do your duty and . . . you will get rid of a mayor who acts as if he thought a poor man had no more right than a horse."[5]

Urban societies now seemed but "a heterogeneous mass" of men with an "insatiable appetite for animal gratification" and "weak and depraved minds"; the population of the cities was now "so numerous that the citizens are not all known to each other," thus allowing "depredators [to] merge in the mass, and spoliate in secret and safety." In New York City the number of watchmen increased from 50 in 1788 to 428 by 1825, nearly double the proportionate growth in population, and still the murderous rioting continued. By the second decade of the nineteenth century some were calling for the creation of professional police forces. Social authority and the patronage power of the magistrates and gentry were no longer able to keep the peace.[6]

A new competitiveness was abroad in the land, and people seemed to be almost at war with one another. Although some were frightened by these developments, others welcomed what was described as "useful and generous strife of competition and emulation." Elkanah Watson prided himself on having done something to stimulate this competitive strife. Watson, the son of a Rhode Island artisan and representative of the new breed of middling hustlers and inventors springing up everywhere in these early years of the nineteenth century, discovered that the earlier aristocratic and enlightened techniques of stimulating agricultural reform through scientific societies of gentlemen farmers would not work in America. Because Americans were too independent for such learned paternalism, Watson in 1810 devised for Berkshire County of western Massachusetts what soon became the familiar American county fair, with exhibitions, entertainment, and prizes awarded for the best crops and biggest livestock. By such fairs Watson intended, he said, to excite that spirit of "envy" and "competition" and that desire for "personal interest" and "personal ambition" characteristic of all Americans, which in Watson's mind were, as *"practical"* sources of agricultural improvement, worth all the "studied, wiredrawn books" ever written. Watson knew, as the enlightened gentry did not, that society had to be dealt with "in its actual state of existence,—not as we could wish it." The only way of achieving public benefits "congenial to *American habits,* and the state of our *society,"* Watson concluded, was to incite emulation and individual self-interest and create "a general strife."[7]

The problem with America, complained Samuel Mitchill of New York in 1800, was that everybody wanted independence: first independence from Great Britain, then independence of the states from each other, then independence of the people from government, and "lastly, the members of society be equally independent of each other." In the western frontier areas society seemed especially weak and thin: there were "no private or publick associations for common good, every Man standing single." Indeed, could the frontier areas even "be called society where every man is for himself alone and has no regard for any person farther than he can make him subservient to his own views"? How far could American freedom be carried without ending "in the lawless and capricious liberty prevalent among savages"? Yet authority of every sort seemed unable to resist these endless challenges. By what right did authority claim obedience? was the question being asked of every institution, every organization, every individual. It was as if the Revolution had set in motion a disintegrative force that could not be stopped.[8]

All these changes and disruptions in American society were driven by the same dynamic forces at work since the middle of the eighteenth century—population growth and movement and commercial expansion. After 1800 the birthrate began to decline as people became more conscious of their ability to create prosperity for themselves and their children by limiting the size of their families. Nevertheless, the population as a whole continued to expand by leaps and bounds. Americans boasted that by 1810 the United States, numbering over seven million people, was nearly as populous as England and Wales had been in 1801 and was rapidly gaining on the former mother country.[9] The population was increasing at about 37 percent every decade, more than twice the rate of growth of any European nation. And it was a remarkably young population: in 1810, 36 percent of the white population was under the age of ten and nearly 70 percent was under the age of twenty-five.

This youthful population was moving about the country even more rapidly than it had in the past. Before the Revolution the territory of Kentucky had contained almost no white settlers. By the early 1780s, however, it had more than 20,000; by the end of the century it had grown to over 220,000 people, and people marveled at the fact that not a single adult had been born and grown up within its borders. Between 1790 and 1820 New York's population more than quadrupled and Tennessee's multiplied over ten times. In a single decade at the turn of the century Ohio grew from a virtual wilderness to become more populous than most of the colonies had been at the time of the Revolution. By 1820, only thirty-two years after the first permanent white settlers arrived, Ohio had a population of over a half million people and was already the fifth-largest state in the Union. And Ohioans were complaining that they had run out of names for their hundreds of new towns. Indeed, gazetteers in America, it was said, could not keep up with the "very frequent changes" in the dividing of territories and naming of places "which are almost daily taking place": it was a problem "peculiar to a new, progressive and extensive country." In one generation Americans occupied more territory than they had occupied during the entire 150 years of their colonial existence. "We are a rapidly—I was about to say fearfully—growing country," said John C. Calhoun in 1816. "This is our pride and danger, our weakness and our strength."[10]

It is impossible to exaggerate the significance of this westward movement of people. It was a "stupendous work of human advancement . . . of which the history of mankind certainly affords no other example." The movement was far more spectacular than the historic events revealed by the ancient ruins of the Old World. It was, Americans told themselves, "a scene, not of decay, but of teeming life, of improvement almost too rapid to seem the result of human means." By 1817 migrants could only shake their heads in amazement: "Old America," they said, "seems to be breaking up and moving westward." There was more land than people could use, and still they kept moving. The father of Joseph Smith, the founder of Mormonism, moved his family seven times in fourteen years. Others moved at least three or four times in a lifetime, selling their land to new settlers at a profit each time; "they are," it was noted, "very indifferent ploughmen" anyway. Nothing stopped them—Indians, bad weather, or poverty."

By 1820 westward-swarming Americans had created a great triangular wedge of settlement reaching to the Mississippi River. The northern side of the triangle ran from New York along the Ohio River, the southern side extended from eastern Georgia through Tennessee, and the two sides met at the tip of the wedge at St. Louis. Within this huge triangle of settlement people were distributed haphazardly and huge pockets remained virtually uninhabited. By 1820 the United States had added the territory of Louisiana and Florida, which doubled the size of the country. And the original thirteen states had become twenty-two, with over nine and a half million people. Foreigners complained that Americans were completely taken with the gigantic extent of their country and their "golden dreams of the future" and had come "to measure the importance of foreign nations by this scale."[12]

This spectacular growth and movement of people further weakened traditional forms of social organization and intensified people's feelings of equality. Such a mobile population, one Kentuckian told James Madison in 1792, "must make a very different mass from one which is composed of men born and raised on the same spot. . . . They see none about them to whom or to whose families they have been accustomed to think themselves inferior." In these new western territories, where "society is yet unborn," where "your connections and friends are absent, and at a distance," and where there was "no distinction assumed on account of rank or property," it was difficult to put together anything that resembled a traditional social hierarchy, or even a civilized community. Kentucky, like all frontier areas, travelers noted, was "different from a staid and settled society. . . . A certain loss of civility is inevitable."[13]

"The manner in which the population is spreading over this continent has no parallel in history," declared a worried observer in 1818. Americans were reversing the civilizing process, going backwards in time, losing politeness instead of, as the revolutionaries had hoped, gaining it. Usually the first settlers of any country were barbarians who gradually in time became cultivated and civilized. "The progress has been from ignorance to knowledge, from the rudeness of savage life to the refinements of polished society. But in the settlement of North America the case is reversed. The tendency is from civilization to barbarism.'' Under New World conditions "the tendency of the American character is then to degenerate, and to degenerate rapidly; and that not from any peculiar vice in the American people, but from the very nature of a spreading population. The population of the country is outgrowing its institutions.'' To some it seemed that the mind once enlightened could after all become darker.[4]

Frederick Jackson Turner was right to make so much of this western movement of people fomenting American democracy, self-sufficiency, and individualism. "The practical liberty of America is found in its great space and small population,'' said the Englishman George Flower in 1817. "Good land, dog-cheap everywhere, and for nothing, if you will go for it, gives as much elbow room to every man as he chooses to take.'' But Turner and Flower were both wrong to think that it was simply the free land and open space of the frontier that were at work. It was rather what the scale and speed of movement did to the structure of a society already weak to begin with. But equally corrosive were the republican principles the settlers carried with them. Fertile free land could never have been enough: look at the contrast with Canada, Americans said. It was "the general operation of the new political order of things on the mind and character of the country'' that explained the growth of democracy.[5]

But perhaps nothing was more important in affecting the mind and character of Americans in these years than the massive changes taking place in the economy. Often these changes have not been understood, even by expert economic historians. The changes do not seem as obvious or palpable as those that occurred later in American history. In these early decades of the nineteenth century there was little industrialization or urbanization to speak of, certainly nothing like what was going on in England in the same period. And before the 1820s there were no great technological breakthroughs, certainly nothing comparable to the railroad or the telegraph. Although by the early nineteenth century men increasingly congratulated themselves on the speed with which persons and goods were transported, in 1820 it still took weeks to travel between Boston and Washington, D.C. Consequently, most economic historians and cliometricians have been hard put to discover and agree on just what went on in these years before the Age of Jackson.

In fact, the economic data for the late eighteenth and early nineteenth centuries are so few and fragmentary and so open to misinterpretation that almost everything about America's economy in these years has been claimed. Some economic historians, often extrapolating from bits and pieces of data, have said that per capita real income was declining; others, more recently, that it was rising. Some agree that the society before 1840 got more prosperous and the per capita standard of living went up, but disagree when this happened. Others emphasize the extent to which particular groups in the society, especially craft employees, experienced decline. Still others believe that no great gains in productivity were possible before 1840 and the development of mechanization and factory machinery. But others say that factory organization and supervised divisions of labor, even without mechanization, were enough to increase productivity substantially. Most, however, seem to have a model of the English experience in the back of their minds and identify sizable economic growth and development with the expansion of manufacturing. By this measure not much economically seems to have happened in America before the 1820s. In numbers of people the United States may have been rapidly gaining on England, but its economy in the early Republic still seemed very primitive in comparison with that of the former mother country.[16]

The early Republic remained largely agricultural and rural. In 1800 nearly 75 percent of the labor force was still in farming. In fact, by 1820 the percentage of the labor force in agriculture actually increased to nearly 80 percent. In contrast, England in 1801 had only 36 percent of its workers engaged in agriculture. In America even the more urban areas of New England and the mid-Atlantic had 70 percent of their workers still on farms. The American people still lived mostly in the countryside. In 1800 there were only thirty-three towns with a population of 2,500 or more, and only six of these urban areas had populations over 10,000. Only 5 percent of Americans actually lived in cities. By 1820 the number of urban places with populations over 2,500 had increased to sixty-one, but only five of these were cities with populations over 25,000; altogether these urban places held only 7 percent of the population. England in 1821 by contrast had well over a third of its population in cities; more than 20 percent lived in cities larger than 20,000. There was London with its million and a quarter people, and there were dozens of other urban areas, twenty-eight of which had populations over 20,000.[17] At that same date the early American Republic was a very different country—still a predominantly rural agricultural society, on the surface not all that different from rural agricultural eighteenth-century colonial America.

Yet beneath that seemingly similar surface, everything had changed. America may have been still largely rural, still largely agricultural, but now it was also largely commercial, perhaps the most thoroughly commercialized nation in the world.

One measure of that commercialization was the level of literacy; for the strongest motive behind people's learning to read and write, even more than the need to understand the Scriptures, was the desire to do business—to buy and sell real estate and other goods and to make deals involving signatures and written agreements. When in the early years of the nineteenth century people in New England, including even areas along the Connecticut River in rural Vermont, attained levels of elementary literacy that were higher than any other places in the Western world (with the possible exception of parts of Scandinavia), then we know we are dealing with a population engrossed in commerce.[18]

Even at the outset of the Revolution some Americans glimpsed the significance of buying and selling among themselves, which in turn had contributed to the reform of the Articles of Confederation and the creation of a more unified country. If Americans were to be truly a nation, some said in the 1780s, they could no longer exist as thirteen separate states, living on the margin of things, sending their agricultural produce to Europe and receiving manufactured goods in return. They told themselves that they were by nature a unified empire, defined by interest and offering "a prospect of wealth and commerce which future ages alone can realize." All the massive movements of people westward, all the growing productive activity, all the endless trading, were creating a continental marketplace and a natural harmony of economic interests. Farmers could sell their produce to Americans and could buy their manufactured goods from Americans; and if the artificial political obstacles of the states could be eliminated, the whole country could be linked in trade and prosperity. "When we consider the vastness of our country, the variety of her soil and climate, the immense extent of her seacoast, and of inland navigation by the lakes and rivers," declared a Fourth of July orator in 1785, "we find a world within ourselves, sufficient to produce whatever can contribute to the necessities and even the superfluities of life."[19] Sentiments like these both prepared the way for reform of the national government in 1787 and underlay Alexander Hamilton's 1791 Report on Manufactures; in time they contributed to a radically new conception of America's economy.

America's deep involvement in overseas commerce between 1792 and 1805—largely because of the European wars—tended to mask the significance of what was happening at home. Although the Federalists and the Congress did not follow up Hamilton's Report on Manufactures, domestic manufacturing and commerce steadily grew in the decades following the Revolution. Although most Americans continued to live in the countryside, more and more were involved in proto-industrialization or rural manufacturing. By 1820 well over a quarter of the labor force in New England and the mid-Atlantic states was working in small factories, making everything from shoes to textiles. But such statistics concerning the number of factory workers are misleading; for not only was at least 30 percent of the manufacturing labor force in 1820 composed of women and children, but this factory work does not include the extraordinary amount of manufacturing taking place in rural family households. Family farms were doing more than farming; they were manufacturing as well. In 1810, for example, 90 percent of the $42 million total textile production of the nation came from family households. Only in America, said Congressman Albert Gallatin in 1799, were different occupations so blended together, "the same man being frequently a farmer and a merchant, and perhaps a manufacturer." As early as the 1790s Henry Wansey, the British visitor, observed that in both Massachusetts and New Jersey housewives in every farming household kept their families busy carding and spinning woolen and linen cloth "in the evenings and when they are not in the fields." In 1795 Brissot de Warville found "almost all" the households of Worcester, Massachusetts, "inhabited by men who are both cultivators and artisans; one is a tanner, another a shoemaker, another sells goods; but all are farmers." People, observed Tench Coxe, were selling their *"surplus* of household manufactures *out of state."* Manufactures, it was said, were "rising in all their varied form in every direction, and pursued *with an eye to profit* in almost every farm house in the United States."[20]

Everywhere in the northern states farm families were busy buying and selling with each other in ever-increasing amounts, not just "necessaries," "conveniences," and "luxuries" but capital goods as well. The bulk of the fledgling American iron and steel industry, for example, was devoted to farm implements—everything from scythes and pitchforks to axes and hoes. Home manufacturers were increasing, it was said, "because all who deal in them find their *profit* in doing so. . . . Every day brings to market some new *commodity."*[21] Gross statistics depicting the growth of this household manufacturing, even when they are available, can never fully reveal the significance of its disruptive effects on the society.

We get some sense of these effects, however, from the example of the Mann family. At the beginning of the nineteenth century Horace Mann, who would become a great educational reformer, was still a boy on his father's farm in the little town of Franklin in southeastern Massachusetts. Like so many other northern families, Mann and his mother and his brothers and sisters spent much of their spare time on handicrafts, at first just spinning and weaving for their own use. Then they began making straw braids used in ladies' hats. At first they took these braids to the local storekeeper in exchange for merchandise. But in 1804 a local hat factory began buying the braids directly from the Manns and other families in the town of Franklin and turning them into straw bonnets for sale in Providence and Boston. By 1812 the little country town of Franklin was producing 6,000 hats a year. Soon the mother and children of the Mann family were making more money from the braids than the father was from his farm. Not only did such extra disposable income in the household affect patriarchal relations between husbands and wives, but it gave these farming households the means to purchase the very sorts of luxury or consumer goods, such as straw hats, that they themselves were producing.[22]

Once it was finally realized that the desire of ordinary people to buy such consumer goods, and not their poverty or frugality as used to be thought, was the principal source of their industriousness and their productivity, then the fear of "luxury" that had bedeviled the eighteenth century died away. It no longer made any sense to say, as John Adams archaically said in 1814, that "human nature, in no form of it, ever could bear Prosperity." Prosperity was now thought to be good for people; it was their "desire of gain, beyond the supply of the mere necessities of life," that stimulated enterprise and created this prosperity.[23]

From this rapid development of internal trade arose the heightened demand almost everywhere for internal improvements—new roads, new canals, new ferries, new bridges—anything that would help increase the speed and lower the cost of the movement of goods, and, as John C. Calhoun said in 1817, in a common opinion, help "bind the republic together." All this worked to convince Americans, as the governor of Pennsylvania declared in 1811, that "foreign commerce is a good but of a secondary nature, and that happiness and prosperity must be sought for within the limits of our own country." This growing belief that domestic commerce of the United States was "incalculably more valuable" than its foreign commerce and that "the home market for productions of the earth and manufactures is of more importance than all foreign ones" represented a momentous reversal of traditional thinking. "Commerce" in the eighteenth century had usually referred exclusively to international trade. Now it was being equated with all the exchanges taking place within the country, exchanges in which both parties always gained. The Americans, said Fanny Wright in 1819, echoing a phrase heard over and over in these years, were truly forming "a world within themselves."[24]

If Americans were truly a commercial world within themselves, then they demanded as never before not only internal improvements of every sort but paper money with which to trade and deal with one another. Article I, Section 10, of the Constitution had prohibited the states from emitting bills of credit; but such a legal prohibition could scarcely have restrained the powerful entrepreneurial forces at work. People wanted, indeed needed, paper money, and despite the framers' best intentions the people simply pressed their state legislatures to charter banks that in turn issued the paper money that was desired.

Gentlemen trying to live off their proprietary wealth in 1787 had not fully comprehended the explosive entrepreneurial forces they were dealing with, and most of them certainly had not reckoned on what banks could do. Indeed, few revolutionaries understood banking at all. In 1781 the Congress had set up the Bank of North America in Philadelphia, and by 1790 there were three more banks established in New York, Boston, and Baltimore. Yet compared with England, banking in America was new and undeveloped. There was nothing yet in America that duplicated the array of different monetary notes and the dozens upon dozens of private and county banks scattered all over eighteenth-century Great Britain. When the Bank of North America was first opened in Philadelphia, it was "a novelty," said Thomas Willing, its president. Banking in America, he said, was "a pathless wilderness, ground but little known to this side of the Atlantic." English rules, arrangements, and bank bills were then unknown. "All was to us a mystery."[25]

Suddenly, as if making up for lost time, America went wild in the creation of new banks. Twenty-five banks were established between 1790 and 1800, including the Bank of the United States. Between 1801 and 1811, when the Bank of the United States was allowed to die, sixty-two more banks were established by the states. By 1816 the number of state-chartered banks had increased to 246, and by 1820 it exceeded 300. These banks, unlike the original Bank of North America or the Bank of the United States, were not just sources of credit for government, not just commercial banks, handling short-term credit for merchants, but banks for all the different economic interests of the society that wanted easy, long-term credit—mechanics and farmers as well as governments and merchants. In 1792 the Massachusetts legislature required the second state bank it created to lend at least 20 percent of its funds to citizens living outside of the city of Boston in order that the bank "shall wholly and exclusively regard the agricultural interest."[26] The state charter setting up the Farmers and Mechanics Bank of Philadelphia in 1809 stipulated that a majority of the directors be "farmers, mechanics, and manufacturers actually employed in their respective professions." New charters elsewhere had similar requirements.[27]

And these banks were to be located not merely in the large urban centers such as Philadelphia or Boston but also in such outlying areas as Westerly, Rhode Island, where a new bank established in 1800 justified itself by declaring that existing banks in the state in Providence, Newport, and Bristol were "too remote or too confined in their operations to diffuse their benefits so generally to the country as could be wished." By 1818 the state had twenty-seven banks. In 1813 the Pennsylvania legislature in a single bill authorized incorporation of twenty-five new banks. After the governor vetoed this bill, the legislature in 1814 passed over the governor's veto another bill incorporating forty-one banks. As early as 1793 John Swanwick of Philadelphia had envisioned banks sprouting up in all the provincial towns of the state. "Their number will be so far multiplied," he told the Pennsylvania legislature, "that it will be no longer a favor to obtain discounts." By the end of the second decade of the nineteenth century it seemed to one observer that nearly every village in the country had a bank; wherever there was a church, a tavern, and a blacksmith, one could usually find a bank as well. By 1818 Kentucky had forty-three new banks, two of them in towns that had fewer than one hundred inhabitants. Rhode Island, befitting its advanced commercial state, seemed to have a bank in nearly every community.[28]

These hundreds of banks now issued the paper money that the people had desired. Of course, the bank notes were not real money or specie but only promises to pay gold or silver. Yet in increasing amounts these bank notes passed as money; indeed, some Americans even grasped the fact that these banks were creating money. By 1815 over two hundred banks had deposits and note liabilities of about $90,000,000 backed by only $17,000,000 of specie. "The circulation of our country," Senator James Lloyd of Massachusetts declared in 1811, "is at present emphatically a paper circulation; very little specie passes in exchange between individuals." Some of the old revolutionaries never understood the magic of banking. Jefferson thought that the paper money issued by banks was designed "to enrich swindlers at the expense of the honest and industrious part of the nation." He could not comprehend how "legerdemain tricks upon paper can produce as solid wealth or hard labor in the earth. It is vain for common sense to urge that *nothing* can produce *nothing*." John Adams agreed: "every dollar of a bank bill that is issued beyond the quantity of gold and silver in the vaults represents nothing and is therefore a cheat upon somebody," he said in 1809. Yet such bank bills were a new source of entrepreneurial energy that enterprising Americans were eager to exploit. By 1819 Alexander Baring, the head of the great British financial family, could tell a committee of the British House of Commons that "the system of a paper currency has been carried to a greater extent in America than in any other part of the world."[29]

The public chartering of banks was just one example of the states exploiting private wealth for public purposes in an old-fashioned monarchical manner. In fact, the unwillingness of new democratically elected state legislatures to raise taxes to pay for all that governmental leaders wanted to do forced nearly all the states to fall back on the traditional mobilization of private power for public ends. As in the case of political patronage, democracy was forcing a curious reversion to older monarchical forms of governing. Instead of doing the tasks themselves, as many devout republicans had expected, the states ended up doing what the crown and all premodern governments had done—granting charters of incorporation to private associations and groups to carry out a wide variety of endeavors presumably beneficial to the public, not just in banking but also in transportation, insurance, and other enterprises. Yet because of a republican aversion to chartered monopolies, the creation of corporations did not take place without strenuous opposition and heated debate. As a consequence, these corporations were radically transformed. Within a few years most of them became very different from their monarchical predecessors: they were no longer exclusive monopolies and they were no longer public. They became private property and what Samuel Blodget in 1806 called "rivals for the common weal." And they were created in astonishing numbers unduplicated anywhere else in the world.[30]

Corporate charters had been traditional legal instruments used by governments to harness private enterprise and private wealth to carry out desirable public goals, such as founding a colony, maintaining a college, building a bridge, or running a bank. Like the appointing of wealthy individuals to be justices of the peace or other public officials, granting corporate charters was a means by which legally powerful but revenue-starved premodern governments shifted the costs of public actions to private sources. In return for the public service, such corporate grants gave to the recipients certain exclusive legal privileges, including the right to govern an area or the right to a monopoly over a particular activity. There was no sharp distinction in such corporate grants between public and private. Harvard College with its charter in the seventeenth century was no less public than one of the incorporated New England towns. These corporate privileges were not frequently granted or widely available; they were made at the initiative of the government, not private interests.

Such monopolistic grants were meaningful in a monarchical society where the recipients of these exclusive privileges were clear and visible. In the old society the holders of the corporate charters and other governmental franchises tended to be those dominant gentry in whom the hierarchical lines of patronage and influence converged. Once the Revolution severed those hierarchical lines of patronage and influence, however, these exclusive corporate charters and governmental grants became increasingly anomalous. Even in the old society of England there had been outcries against monopoly and favoritism and complaints that such corporate grants were unfairly dispersed.

These criticisms were nothing, however, compared with what happened in America. Once the old hierarchies disintegrated and the lines of influence became blurred, the new states' attempts to grant such corporate privileges to select individuals and groups immediately raised storms of protest.[31] Critics charged that such grants, even when their public purpose seemed obvious, such as those for the College of Philadelphia or the Bank of North America or the city of Philadelphia, were repugnant to the spirit of American republicanism, "which does not admit of granting peculiar privileges to any body of men." Such franchises and privileged grants may have made sense in monarchies as devices serving "to circumscribe and limit absolute power." Certainly the colonists had seen their various crown and corporate charters in just this defensive way. But now that only the people ruled, these grants of corporate privileges seemed pernicious, for "as much as the combination of citizens enjoying corporation immunities may be calculated, even at this day, to relieve from the weight of monarchical sway, to the same degree are they contrary to the equal and common liberty which ought to pervade a republic." "The unequal or partial distribution of public benefits within a state creates distinctions of interest, influence and power, which lead to the establishment of an aristocracy, the very worst species of government." "All incorporations," declared Justice John Hobart of New York, "imply a privilege given to one order of citizens which others do not enjoy, and are so far destructive of that principle of equal liberty which should subsist in every community."[32] Some like Jefferson remained deeply opposed to these corporate grants for just these reasons. To his dying day Jefferson believed that the state legislatures should grant such legal privileges only sparingly and should be able to interfere with them or take them back anytime they wished.

Given the democratic and interest-ridden nature of American society, however, it was difficult for the state legislatures to resist appeals to bestow these corporate privileges, especially since many of their members were themselves involved in the businesses they were incorporating. Legislators became in fact, as Madison had feared, judges in their own causes. In the New Jersey legislature in 1806, for example, "the peculators of both parties" cooperated in chartering dozens of turnpike associations for themselves. The "discordant names of Democrat and Federalist hath become harmoniously attuned to the pursuasive and dulcet sounds of interest." It was the same in Connecticut. The subscription list of the Hartford Bank, suggested one shrewd subscriber in 1791, had to be left open, or seem to be open—that is, if the bank hoped to be incorporated by the Connecticut legislature. There were "a number in the Legislature who would wish to become subscribers, and would, of course, advocate the bill while they supposed they could subscribe, and, on the contrary, if it was known the subscription was full, they would oppose it violently."[33] The exploitation of public office for private ends—that is, corruption—was of course not new to American politics; it had been common in the colonial governments. But the republican revolution was supposed to have created a separate public authority free from private interests.

With the representatives in the state legislatures turning over annually, it was not hard for each interest to secure its own cluster of legal privileges, with the corporate charter becoming, as James Sullivan complained in 1792, merely "an indulgence to a few men in the state, who happened to ask the legislature to grant it to them."[34] What one community or group of entrepreneurs had, another wanted, and so the corporate charters multiplied in ever-increasing numbers. There had been only about a half dozen business corporations chartered in the entire colonial period. Now such corporate grants for businesses virtually became popular entitlements. The legislatures incorporated not just banks but insurance companies and manufacturing concerns, and they licensed entrepreneurs to operate bridges, roads, and canals. The states issued 11 charters of incorporation between 1781 and 1785, 22 more between 1786 and 1790, and 114 between 1791 and 1795. Between 1800 and 1817 they granted nearly 1,800 corporate charters. Massachusetts alone had thirty times more business corporations than the half dozen or so that existed in all of Europe. New York, the fastest-growing state, issued 220 corporate charters between 1800 and 1810. It seemed clear as early as 1805, as a committee of New York City justifying multiple ferry leases put it, that "the only effectual method of accommodating the public is by the creation of rival establishments." "Thus," as one American noted in 1806, "if two baking companies are thereby permitted, where there was but one, bread may be cheaper in consequence; or if there are two banks thus instituted, and neither of them taxed, more of the people will be favoured by loans, than where there is but one bank; and a further increase will reduce even *the rate of interest.*" The thinking behind the Charles River Bridge decision of the Supreme Court in 1837 was already present a generation earlier.[35]

Eventually the pressure to dispense these corporate charters among special interests became so great that some states sought to ease the entire process by establishing general incorporation laws. Instead of requiring special acts of the legislature for each charter specifying the persons, location, and capitalization involved, the legislatures opened up the legal privileges to all who desired them. Beginning first with religious associations in the 1780s, the states, led by New York in 1811, extended the privileges of corporation to manufacturers, and later to banks and other entrepreneurial activities. With this multiplication not only was the traditional exclusivity of the corporate charters destroyed, but the public power of the state governments was dispersed. If "government, unsparingly and with an unguarded hand, shall multiply corporations, and grant privileges without limitation," then, declared a concerned Governor Levi Lincoln of Massachusetts, sooner or later "only the very shadow of sovereignty" would remain.[36]

Despite this generous bestowal of corporate charters on private interests, however, the republican belief that the government should have a distinct and autonomous sphere of public activity remained strong, especially among the new states west of the Appalachian Mountains.[37] Even in the older states many retained a republican faith in the power of majorities in the legislatures to do what they wanted with corporate charters on behalf of the public interest. "It seems difficult to conceive of a corporation established for merely private purposes," declared a North Carolina judge in 1805. "In every institution of that kind the ground of the establishment is some public good or purpose to be promoted."[38] This increasing stress on the need for a "public purpose" behind the state's activity, however, eventually forced people to distinguish between corporations such as banks and insurance companies that were now considered private because they were privately endowed and those such as towns or counties that remained public because they were tax-based.

But this distinction had its own logical consequences. If corporations such as banks and other businesses were indeed private, and not public, then it could be intelligibly argued that their charters, once granted, were actually "vested rights" of private property protected from subsequent violation or regulation by state authority.[39] No one doubted the capacity of the legislature to take private property for public purposes, but this power, it was now argued, could not be extended so far as to abridge rights expressly vested prior to the legislature's assertion of its power—at least not without some sort of compensation for such abridgments.[40] "In granting charters," declared William Robinson in the Pennsylvania assembly in 1786 in defense of the charter of the Bank of North America, "the legislature acts in a ministerial capacity"; that is, it acted as the crown had acted in mobilizing private resources for public purposes. This bestowing of charters, said Robinson, "is totally distinct from the power of making laws, and it is a novel doctrine in Pennsylvania that they can abrogate those charters so solemnly granted." There was a difference between laws and charters. Laws were general rules for the whole community; charters "bestow particular privileges upon a certain number of people. . . . Charters are a species of property. When they are obtained, they are of value. Their forfeiture belongs solely to the courts of justice."[41] It was a strained, premature argument, and it did not immediately take hold; but it pointed the way to the future. After the Constitution was adopted, some even began to argue that the corporations were actually contracts immune from state tampering by the contract clause in Article I, Section 10 of the Constitution, a position eventually endorsed by the Supreme Court in the Dartmouth College case in 1819.

Protecting private property and minority rights from the interests of the enhanced public power of the new republican governments eventually became, as Madison had foreseen, the great problem of American democratic politics. As early as the 1780s many were already contending that only the judiciary in America was impartial and free enough of private interests to solve that problem and defend people's rights and property from the tyrannical wills of interested popular majorities. The state legislatures, it was argued, should not "leave the great business of the state, and take up private business, or interfere in disputes between contending parties" as the colonial assemblies had habitually done. The evils of such legislative meddling were "heightened when the society is divided among themselves;—one party praying the assembly for one thing, and opposite party for another thing. . . . In such circumstances, the assembly ought not to interfere by any exertion of legislative power, but leave the contending parties to apply to the proper tribunals [that is, to the judiciary] for a decision of their differences."[42] These efforts to carve out an exclusive sphere of activity for the judiciary, a sphere where the adjudicating of private rights was removed from politics and legislative power, contributed to the remarkable process by which the judiciary in America suddenly emerged out of its colonial insignificance to become by 1800 the principal means by which popular legislatures were controlled and limited. The most dramatic institutional transformation in the early Republic was the rise of what was called an "independent judiciary."[43]

Judges now became the arbiters between the emerging separate spheres of public power and private rights. Law became more and more of a science removed from politics and comprehended by only an enlightened few who needed to be educated in special professional law schools. Law, Henry Chipman argued in 1806, was now "too complex to be understood by those who have not the leisure or ability to trace the intricate relations subsisting among the members of a great and busy community." Populist radicals resisted these arguments, tried to draw distinctions between *"lawyers law,* and *legislative law,"* and urged that all adjudication be purged of its *"professional mystery."* But to little avail: even after the Federalists were virtually eliminated from politics, every new effort at popular radicalization created its own conservative opposition among the Jeffersonian Republicans. The desire for an independent expert judiciary was bred by the continuing and ever renewed fears of democratic politics.[44]

Traditionally judges had been appointed to the courts because of their social and political rank, not because of their legal expertise; many were not even legally trained. They had exercised a broad, ill-defined magisterial authority befitting their social rank; they were considered members of the government and remained intimately involved in politics. Thomas Hutchinson, for example, who was no lawyer, had been chief justice of the superior court, lieutenant governor, a member of the council, and judge of probate of Suffolk County of Massachusetts all at the same time. During the 1790s both John Jay and Oliver Ellsworth performed diplomatic missions while sitting as justices of the Supreme Court; indeed, while waiting for Jefferson's return from France in 1789, Jay served simultaneously as Secretary of State and Chief Justice of the Supreme Court. Supreme Court Justice Samuel Chase saw nothing wrong with his open politicking on behalf of the Federalist cause. Congress in its Invalid Pension Act of 1792 assigned the federal courts administrative and magisterial duties that were not strictly judicial and that were actually subject to review by the Secretary of War and the Congress. Of the twenty-eight men who sat on the federal district courts in the 1790s only eight had held high judicial office in their states; but nearly all of them had been prominent political figures, having served in notable state offices and in the Continental Congress. They saw their service on the court as simply an extension of their general political activity; some of them even continued to exercise political influence and pass on Federalist patronage in their districts while sitting on the bench. Such judges were political authorities, not professional legal experts.[45]

By the early nineteenth century, however, judges began withdrawing from politics, shedding their older, broad magisterial roles, and limiting their activities to the regular courts, which became increasingly professional and less burdened by popular juries. The courts tended to avoid the most explosive and partisan political issues but at the same time attempted to designate other important issues as issues of law that were within their exclusive jurisdiction. Men began to draw lines around what was political or legislative and what was legal or judicial and to justify the distinctions by the doctrine of separation of powers.[46] As early as 1787 Alexander Hamilton had argued in the New York assembly that the state constitution prevented anyone from being deprived of his rights except "by the law of the land" or, as a recent act of the assembly had put it, "by due process of law," which, said Hamilton in an astonishing and novel twist, had "a precise technical import": these words were now "only applicable to the process and proceedings of the courts of justice; they can never be referred to an act of legislature."[47] Placing legal boundaries around issues such as property rights and contracts had the effect of isolating these issues from popular tampering, partisan debate, and the clashes of interest-group politics. Some things, including the power to define property and interpret constitutions, became matters not of political interest to be determined by legislatures but of the "fixed principles" of law to be determined only by judges. Without the protection of the courts and the intricacies of the common law, it was even argued in Pennsylvania in 1805, "rights would remain forever without remedies and wrongs without redress." Americans could no longer count on their popularly elected legislatures to solve many of the problems of their lives. "For the varying exigencies of social life, for the complicated interests of an enterprising nation, the positive acts of the legislature can provide little."[48] This was a long way from the 1776 republican confidence in popular legislative law-making and represented a severe indictment of democracy.

The result was paradoxical: as the public power of the state grew in the early Republic, so too did the private rights of individuals—with the courts mediating and balancing the claims of each. Many, including Madison in his later years, concluded that the judiciary was the only governmental institution that came close to resembling an umpire, standing above the marketplace of competing interests and rendering impartial and disinterested decisions. It seemed the only public place left in democratic America where a trace of classical aristocracy and virtue could be found. Some even thought that the very "existence" of America's elective governments depended on the judiciary—the institution most removed from the people and most immune to the pressures of private interests. "The courts of justice," concluded Tocqueville, "are the visible organs by which the legal profession is enabled to control the democracy."[49]

18. The Celebration of Commerce

In the end, no banks, no government, no institutions could have created the American economic miracle of these years. America suddenly emerged a prosperous, scrambling, enterprising society not because the Constitution was created or because a few leaders formed a national bank, but because ordinary people, hundreds of thousands of them, began working harder to make money and "get ahead." Americans seemed to be a people totally absorbed in the individual pursuit of money. "Enterprise," "improvement," and "energy" were everywhere extolled in the press. "The voice of the people and their government is loud and unanimous for commerce," said the disgruntled and bewildered Columbia professor Samuel Mitchill in 1800. "Their inclination and habits are adapted to trade and traffic. From one end of the continent to the other, the universal roar is Commerce! Commerce! at all events, Commerce!"

Mitchill's sarcastic attitude toward trade was no doubt fitting for a college professor, but not for ordinary Americans. Most of them seemed to be happily involved in buying and selling, more so than in any other country in the world. "The American," foreigners said, "is always bargaining; he always has one bargain afoot, another just finished, and two or three he's thinking of. All that he has, all that he sees, is merchandise in his eyes." English travelers were stunned to see Americans selling their landed estates in order to go into trade—the reverse of what Englishmen sought to do. There was more peddling and shopkeeping than existed anywhere else on the globe. In the 1820s Americans first used the term "businessman" to express most concisely what so many of them were doing. Americans everywhere in the country were obsessed with commerce. "It is a passion as unconquerable as any with which nature has endowed us," said young Henry Clay to the House of Representatives in 1812. "You may attempt to regulate—you cannot destroy it.'"

It was frightening and bewildering to many—that a whole society should be taken over by moneymaking and the pursuit of individual interest. Hustling entrepreneurs like Oliver Evans protested against the enlightened view of gentlemen philosophers that inventions should not be patented but be made available freely to the world of science. It was all well and good for wealthy aristocrats like Jefferson to refuse to patent and protect their inventions, but "there are few such patriots as Mr. Jefferson." The common inventor now in America was usually a poor man, and "the discovery he has made at great expense [was] the only thing perhaps which he possesses exclusively, by which he can make a comfortable living." These new kinds of enterprising inventors certainly could do good for the country, but they said they could not be expected to "do it at our own expense, without a prospect." They needed longer patent protection in order to be allowed "to enrich ourselves by our own labors, while we shall enrich our neighbors and our country." Good business sense for a new commercial world, but to enlightened philosophes like Benjamin Rush it seemed only that the "love of gold" was displacing the values of the founding fathers. The motto of the new men was:

On others inspiration flash,
Give them eternal fame—
But give me cash![2]

Gentlemen of varying tastes—ranging from Benjamin Rush to Washington Irving to Philip Freneau—shook their heads in amazement and despair and filled the air with satirical complaints or handwringing analyses of what was happening. Sensitive souls were eager to be patriotic, but many of them feared that a society so absorbed in moneymaking not only would contribute nothing to the arts and the finer things of life but would eventually fall apart in an orgy of selfishness.

By the end of the first decade of the nineteenth century, the apprehensions had increased to the point where many Americans now looked to war as a necessary regenerative act—as a means of purging Americans of their greed and their seemingly insatiable love of commerce. The War of 1812 with England became for many a way of refreshing the national character and revitalizing republicanism.[3] "War," it was said in December 1811, "will purify the political atmosphere. . . . All the public virtues will be refined and hallowed; and we shall again behold at the head of affairs citizens who may rival the immortal men of 1776." "There is," said William Crafts of Charleston, South Carolina, "a magnanimity in war, which makes even defeat glorious."[4]

The War of 1812 did not, of course, end or even lessen the Americans' involvement in commerce and their pursuit of individual self-interest. If anything, it aggravated them, by increasing home manufacturing and people's commitment to domestic markets. But the war did have the effect of clearing the air of much traditional thinking and of helping Americans come to a new and more honest appreciation of their society and its commercialism. By the end of the second decade of the nineteenth century there were far fewer despairing lamentations over the chaotic and commercial state of American society and many more realistic attempts to find new adhesives and attachments to hold people together.

It was not that the past left nothing to cement the society together. The Revolution had not dissolved all the bonds of the old monarchical society; no revolution could. People still looked after their families and kin; bank directors lent money mainly to themselves and to people they knew; and nearly everyone requested offices for relatives and friends, though now always adding that talent and merit were the prime considerations. Private patronage remained prevalent; only now there was not as much paternalism to clothe it: naked interest seemed to dominate. "The labor of my farm," said Federalist George Cabot of Massachusetts in 1801, "is performed altogether by a tenant, to whom I give specific benefits, that he may have no control over the management, and the benefits are liberal, that he may be happy, and tied to me by his interest."[5]

The national government certainly had little authority to hold things together. Jefferson had come into the presidency in his "revolution of 1800" determined to reverse the monarchizing tendencies of the Federalists; indeed, he later said his election "was as real a revolution in the principles of our government as that of 1776 was in its form." Even the symbols and ceremonies of government were simplified or eliminated, and government as a social force became increasingly weaker. By the early nineteenth century, foreign immigrants immediately noticed that "government" in America made "no sensation." "It is round about you like the air," said a startled William Sampson fresh from Ireland, "and you cannot even feel it." No people in the Western world ever dismantled its national government more completely than did the Americans of the early Republic. In time the delivery of the mail was the only way most citizens would know that such a government even existed.[6]

Yet, of course, there were continued republican appeals to the natural sociability, the sympathy, and what Joel Barlow called "the attracting force of universal love" that presumably existed in all people.[7] In the three or four decades following the Revolution newly independent American men and women came together to form hundreds and thousands of new voluntary associations expressive of a wide array of benevolent goals—mechanics' societies, humane societies, societies for the prevention of pauperism, orphans' asylums, missionary societies, marine societies, tract societies, Bible societies, temperance associations, Sabbatarian groups, peace societies, societies for the suppression of vice and immorality, societies for the relief of poor widows, societies for the promotion of industry, indeed societies for just about anything and everything that was good and humanitarian. People cut loose from traditional social relationships, it was observed as early as 1789, were "necessarily thrown at a considerable distance from each other, and into a very diffused state of society." The various voluntary associations and institutions enabled them to come together in new ways and to combine their mites for charity most effectively. By the 1820s in Massachusetts alone these associations of like-minded men and women were forming at the rate of eighty-five a year.[8]

There was nothing in the Western world quite like these hundreds of thousands of people assembling annually in their different voluntary associations and debating about everything. In other countries, said Charles Ingersoll, such "various self-created associations" gave the authorities "so much trouble and alarm" that they tried to prevent their formation. But because their own society was so dispersed and loose, Americans found these associations "not only harmless but beneficial." So prevalent did these social organizations become that eventually some people like William Channing came to fear that the social principles of these organizations were threatening that "individuality of character" that was so important to Americans and the real goal of all social action.[9]

Yet Channing and others need not have worried. For many members soon redefined their relationship to these voluntary associations. Instead of giving their time and effort to the benevolent organizations, as in the past, many persons began giving money. The societies became less mutual associations and more fiduciary ones, and philanthropic-minded people could now belong to many voluntary societies at the same time. Money had a way of multiplying people's social relationships while at the same time attenuating them.[10]

Many others came to believe that Christianity might be the best means of tying Americans together. All along, of course, varieties of Protestantism had been a major adhesive force for ordinary Americans, often the principal source of community and order in their lives. But the Revolution had disrupted American religion; it scattered congregations, destroyed church buildings, interrupted the training of ministers, and politicized people's thinking. The religious yearnings of common people, however, remained strong, stronger than any of the revolutionary leaders realized.

During the last quarter of the eighteenth century powerful currents of popular religious feeling flowed beneath the genteel and secular surface of public life, awaiting only the developing democratic revolution to break through the rationalistic and skeptical crust of the Enlightenment and sweep over and transform the landscape of the country. The consequences were far-reaching, not just for the mass of ordinary people but for many of the enlightened revolutionary leaders themselves, who were frightened and bewildered by this democratic revolution. Although some of the enlightened gentry remained immune to what was happening and like Jefferson and young John C. Calhoun in the early nine-teenth century enthusiastically predicted that the whole country was rapidly on its way to believing that Jesus was just a good man without any divinity, other liberal gentry knew better; some of them, rational and enlightened as they had been, even came to find in old-fashioned supernatural Christianity a source of salvation for both their own de-spairing souls and the shattered soul of the country. When even a once radical skeptic like Joel Barlow lamely came to insist that he had not really abandoned Christianity after all, then we know that the Enlight-enment was over.

At the time of the Revolution most of the founding fathers had not put much emotional stock in religion, even when they were regular churchgoers. As enlightened gentlemen, they abhorred "that gloomy superstition disseminated by ignorant illiberal preachers" and looked forward to the day when "the phantom of darkness will be dispelled by the rays of science, and the bright charms of rising civilization." At best, most of the revolutionary gentry only passively believed in orga-nized Christianity and, at worst, privately scorned and ridiculed it. Jef-ferson hated orthodox clergymen, and he repeatedly denounced the "priestcraft" for having converted Christianity into "an engine for en-slaving mankind, . . . into a mere contrivance to filch wealth and power to themselves." Although few of them were outright deists, most like David Ramsay described the Christian church as "the best temple of reason." Even puritanical John Adams thought that the argument for Christ's divinity was an "awful blasphemy" in this new enlightened age. When Hamilton was asked why the members of the Philadelphia Convention had not recognized God in the Constitution, he allegedly replied, speaking for many of his liberal colleagues, "We forgot."[11]

By the early decades of the nineteenth century it was no longer so easy for enlightened gentlemen to forget God. If the democratic rev-olution of the decades following the Declaration of Independence meant the rise of ordinary people, it meant as well the rise of popular evangelical Christianity; for religion was the way most common peo-ple still made meaningful the world around them. By the early 1800s these common people were asserting their evangelical Christianity in ways that gentry leaders could no longer ignore. When Aaron Burr, grandson of Jonathan Edwards, was criticized in 1801 for his neglect of religion, a close political associate reminded him of the Presbyterian vote and warned: "Had you not better go to church?" Even Hamil-ton in despair sought to wrap the mantle of popular Christianity around his Federalist cause. When Thomas Paine returned to America from Europe in 1802, he discovered that the popular world he had helped create had turned against him and his liberal "infidelity." Everywhere people noted the degree to which the freethinking world of "Hume & Voltaire & Bolingbroke" was passing away, even among the educated gentry. As the Republic became democratized, it became evangelized.[12]

Throughout the period many religious groups resisted the disintegrative effects of the Enlightenment belief in liberty of conscience and separation of church and state and urged the Republic to recognize its basis in Christianity by allowing chaplains in the Congress, proclaiming days of fasting and prayer, and by ending mail delivery on the Sabbath.[13] In 1811, in a notable blasphemy decision of Chancellor James Kent, *The People of New York* v. *Ruggles*, the connection between Christianity and republicanism was acknowledged in law. Although Kent recognized that the state had no formally established church, that its constitution guaranteed freedom of religious opinion, and that it had no statute prohibiting blasphemy, he nevertheless declared that to revile with contempt the Christian religion professed by almost the whole community, as Ruggles had done, was "to strike at the roots of moral obligation and weaken the security of the social ties." That Kent was willing to rely upon religion in this way when, like many of the founding fathers, he despised religious enthusiasm and in private called Christianity a barbaric superstition is a measure of just how much the traditional gentry had come to fear the social disorder of the early Republic.[14] Christianity, in fact, seemed to some Americans to have become the only cohesive force now holding the.nation together—"the great bond of civil society," said Federalist Leverett Saltonstall of Massachusetts, "the central attraction," said Lyman Beecher in 1815, "which must supply the deficiency of political affinity and interest."[15]

Yet the outpouring of religious feeling in the early decades of the nineteenth century—called the Second Great Awakening—actually did not bring people together as much as it helped to legitimate their separation and make morally possible their new participation in an impersonal marketplace. Even the New Divinity movement within New England Calvinism, despite its strong repudiation of selfishness, ultimately grounded Samuel Hopkins's famous concept of universal disinterested benevolence on the enlightened self-interest of people, and thus set credible moral limits to their acquisitive behavior.[16]

Others thought that religion was actually accelerating social disintegration in the new Republic by creating a "war of words and tumult of opinions" that rivaled the early days of the Reformation. In the decades following the Revolution the remains of traditional religious establishments were finally destroyed, and modern Christian denominationalism was born. Older churches—Congregationalists, Presbyterians, and Anglicans that had dominated eighteenth-century colonial society—were now suddenly supplanted by energetic evangelical churches—Baptists, Methodists, and entirely new groups unknown to the Old World, such as the Disciples of Christ. Everywhere the people were "awakened from the sleep of ages" and saw "for the first time that they were responsible beings" who might even be capable of bringing about their own salvation.[7] The American Revolution accelerated the challenges to religious authority that had begun with the First Great Awakening. Just as the people were taking over their governments, so, it was said, they should take over their churches. Christianity had to be republicanized. The people were their own theologians and had no need to rely on others to tell them what to believe. We must, declared the renegade Baptist Elias Smith in 1809, be "wholly free to examine for ourselves what is truth, without being bound to a catechism, creed, confession of faith, discipline or any rule excepting the scriptures." There had been nothing before in America on such a scale quite like the evangelical defiance and democratic ferment of this Second Great Awakening.[8]

With individuals being told that each of them was "considered as possessing in himself or herself an original right to believe and speak as their own conscience, between themselves and God, may determine," religion in America became much more personal and voluntary than it ever had been; and people were freer to join and change religious associations whenever they wished. They thus moved from one religious group to another in a continual search for signs, prophets, or millennial promises that would make sense of their disrupted lives. With no church sure of holding its communicants, competition among the sects became fierce. Each claimed to be right, called each other names, argued endlessly over points of doctrine, mobbed and stoned and destroyed each other's meeting houses. The result was a further fragmenting of Christianity. "All Christendom has been decomposed, broken in pieces" in this "fiery furnace of democracy," said a bewildered Harrison Gray Otis.[9] Not only were the traditional Old World churches fragmented but the fragments themselves shattered in what seemed at times to be an endless process of fission. There were not just Presbyterians, but Old and New School Presbyterians, Cumberland Presbyterians, Springfield Presbyterians, Reformed Presbyterians, and Associated Presbyterians; not just Baptists, but General Baptists, Regular Baptists, Free Will Baptists, Separate Baptists, Dutch River Baptists, Permanent Baptists, and Two-Seed-in-the-Spirit Baptists. Some individuals cut their ties completely with the Old World churches and gathered around a dynamic leader like Barton Stone or Thomas Campbell. Other seekers ended up forming churches out of single congregations, and still others simply listened in the fields to wandering preachers like the Methodist Lorenzo Dow.

In some areas churches as such scarcely existed, and the traditional identification between religion and society, never very strong in America to begin with, now finally dissolved. The church became for many little more than the building in which religious services were conducted, and church membership was based less on people's position in the social hierarchy and more on their evangelical fellowship. By concentrating on the saving of individual souls, the competing denominations essentially abandoned their traditional institutional and churchly responsibilities to organize the world here and now along godly lines. Consequently, the evangelical churches were less capable than they had been in the eighteenth century of encompassing the variety of social ranks within their membership. They lost their identity with the community and became more socially homogeneous; the Episcopal and Unitarian churches, for example, catered to elites, while the rapidly growing Baptists and Methodists swept up middling and lower elements of the population.[20]

Nowhere in Christendom had religion become so fragmented and so separated from society. Yet nowhere was it so vital. By the second quarter of the nineteenth century, the evangelical Protestantism of ordinary people had come to dominate American culture to an extent the founding fathers had never anticipated.

Amid this religious fragmentation, Lyman Beecher and others came to realize that making each person alone responsible for his or her salvation left nothing holding "society against depravity within and temptation without" except the force of God's law "written upon the heart" of each individual. Only the self-restraint of individuals—their moral "character"—now remained, it seemed, to hold this burgeoning, unruly society together. To be successful in America, religion had to preoccupy itself with morality.[21]

Only religion, Washington had said in his Farewell Address in 1796, was capable of supplying "that virtue or morality" that was "a necessary spring of popular government." From the beginning of America's republican experiment, the clergy had been repeatedly told that, whatever their doctrinal differences, "you are all united in inculcating the necessity of morals," and "from the success or failure of your exertions in the cause of virtue, we anticipate the freedom or slavery of our country." Faced with such awesome responsibility, religious groups and others responded to the cause of virtue with an evangelical zeal and clamor that went beyond what any revolutionary leader in 1776 could have imagined. The clergy could no longer rely on exposing the community's guilt through jeremiads; they could no longer count on reforming merely the "better part" of the society in the expectation that it would bring the rest along; and they could no longer use government to create the right "moral effect." Ordinary people themselves had to be mobilized in the cause of virtue, through the creation of both new institutions of reform and local moral societies—"disciplined moral militia," Beecher called them.[22]

Members of the moral societies, which were generally confined to rural villages, relied essentially on observation and the force of local public opinion. They united among themselves, "collecting the lovers of virtue of every name," and presented "a bold front to the growing licentiousness of the day"; and then, by erecting "a citadel, from which extended observations may be made," they exerted their "influence over the moral conduct of others," first by friendly persuasion, and then, if that did not work, by exposing the moral delinquent "to the penalties of law." The hopes were high: "Character, that dearest earthly interest of man, will thus be protected, and thousands who are now settling down into incurable habits of licentiousness, will by these means be reclaimed."[23]

The growing and sprawling cities, however, needed more than moral societies to watch over and intimidate people. They needed new and substantial institutions, such as relief societies, hospitals, free schools, prisons, and savings banks, to improve the character of the weak and vicious of the society. The proliferation in the early nineteenth century of these new institutions eventually transformed and often eclipsed the humanitarian societies that enlightened gentry had formed in the immediate post-revolutionary years in response to feelings of republican benevolence. By 1820 or so the goals and social complexion of these urban philanthropic endeavors had changed. Middling people, usually pious newcomers from rural areas, replaced the older paternalistic gentry as leaders of these charitable societies and transformed the emotional bonds tying them to the objects of their helpfulness. The patrician gentry in the 1780s and 1790s had organized charitable societies for treating the sick, aiding widowed mothers, housing orphans, feeding imprisoned debtors, or resuscitating drowning victims, out of a sense of benevolence befitting their enlightenment and their genteel social position. Their paternalistic acts of charity were disinterested acts of compassion that called for feelings of dependency and gratitude on the part of the recipients.

It was not gratitude, however, that the founders of the new reform institutions were interested in. The new middling reformers wanted to imbue people, not with deference and dependency, but with "correct moral principles"; they aimed to change the actual behavior of people. Instead of concentrating on relieving the suffering of the unfortunate, as the earlier benevolent associations had done, the new institutions tried to get at the sources of poverty, crime, and other social evils, mainly by suppressing the vices—gambling, drinking, Sabbath-breaking, profanity, horse-racing, and other profligacies—that were presumed to be the causes of those evils. The reformers sought to remove the taverns and betting houses that tempted the weak and impressionable and to create institutions, such as prisons and schools, that would instill in people a proper respect for morality. The reformers wanted to awaken the moral sense of people, and they hoped to do this by rewarding industry and good behavior and punishing laziness and bad habits.

Despite all the talk of moral persuasion, however, all the reform institutions created in these years were designed to change the conduct of people by appealing ultimately to "that which gives the keenest edge to human ingenuity,—self-interest." The savings bank introduced in New York in 1819, for example, was founded, it was said, "on principles calculated to inspire economy, produce reform, and inculcate a spirit of enterprise and industry, and self-respect, among the laboring classes of the community." People would begin "to see the progressive increase of the little capital" they had put away, and their acquisitive instincts would be aroused. Those acquisitive instincts would be stronger than their instincts for vice. They would, in fact, be the best means of binding the nation together.[24]

Of course, Americans in these years continued to rely on the traditional ligaments of kinship and patronage; and they continued to mobilize republican virtue, benevolence, and sociability to tie themselves together. But ultimately many of them came to realize that the United States would need bonds of union stronger than these and different from those possessed by any other nation. Unlike the European states, the

United States, already composed of more and more diverse peoples, could not rely on any tribal or national identity. To be an American could not be a matter of blood; it had to be a matter of common belief and behavior. And the source of that common belief and behavior was the American Revolution: it was the Revolution, and only the Revolution, that made them one people.

Therefore Americans' interpretation of their Revolution could never cease; it was integral to the very existence of the nation. Some found the meaning of the Revolution in the Constitution and the union it had created. Others discovered the meaning in the freedom and equality that the Revolution had produced. But many other Americans knew that such meanings were too formal, too legal, too abstract, to express what most actually experienced in being Americans. In concrete day-to-day terms invocations of the Constitution meant the freedom to be left alone, and in turn that freedom meant the ability to make money and pursue happiness.

It was inevitable, therefore, that many came to conclude that this unruly society could tie itself together only by bonds that were in accord with the realities of American freedom and pursuits of happiness. Nothing less than interest itself—that "most powerful impulse of the human breast"—would do as an adhesive force in this dynamic busy society.[25] Many Federalists and Republicans, like many Whigs and Democrats later, concluded that interest was about all most Americans had in common. They could not be controlled by force, or else they would have no liberty. But appeals to virtue could not contain these busy people either. Only interest could restrain them. Americans govern themselves, they said, because it was in their interest to do so. The desire to make money and get ahead helped them to develop habits of self-control. "The influence of money is wonderful, and the mind changes as the means of acquiring it are presented."[26] By the 1830s Tocqueville thought he saw what was holding this diverse, rootless, restless people together. "Interest," he concluded. "That is the secret. The private interest that breaks through at each moment, the interest that, moreover, appears openly and even proclaims itself as a social theory."[27]

Most of the Americans' defenses of interest and money as the best connecting links in society were thus not cynical or reluctant concessions to reality; they were not made obliquely or in embarrassment. Quite the contrary: these defenses were made proudly and enthusiastically, as if interest and the making of money through trade had become deserving of as much acclaim and admiration as republican virtue traditionally had been given. Interest and moneymaking after all were egalitarian and democratic. When people related to each other only through interest, there was no obligation, no gratitude required; the relationship was to that extent equal. Many had always believed, moreover, that interest was what preoccupied and moved ordinary working people, and these ordinary working people, including not just laborers and employees but master craftsmen, enterprising farmers, proto-industrialists, and businessmen, anyone and everyone who worked for profit and for a living, were "the most useful, honest part of society."[28] Indeed, some were already saying that such working people were now the only people who mattered in America.

One of the earliest and most ingenious full-scale defenses of the social benefits of business and commerce was that of Samuel Blodget, merchant, economist, and sometime architect who designed the First Bank of the United States in Philadelphia. Blodget in several pioneering essays on the American economy written during the first decade of the nineteenth century argued that commerce was the major source of cohesion in the society. Of course, from at least the beginning of the eighteenth century, many thinkers, including Montesquieu, had described commerce as beneficial to a country. It brought wealth to the society, tied different nations together, and even helped to civilize people. But by commerce most of these commentators usually had meant what Montesquieu meant: "the exportation and importation of merchandise with a view to the advantage of the state," which translated into the traditional view, as one American put it, that "only exports make a country rich."[29] Commerce was generally equated with international trade, not with mere trafficking and exchanging within the community. Such internal trading and retail dealing had traditionally possessed little of the importance and respectability of overseas commerce. But now Blodget and others identified commerce with all business activities within the community, however petty and vulgar.[30]

Indeed, Blodget celebrated economic interest itself as the best adhesive a society could have. Every people had *"social ties."* The first, said Blodget, were those of blood or kindred; the second were those of the laws; the third were those associations for the extension of the arts and sciences. The fourth, "and perhaps *the most to be depended on of all,*" were pecuniary ties. Because people were naturally so restless and quarrelsome, nothing else would work. Everywhere, he said, governments should sponsor and incorporate joint-stock companies—"minor republics"—to carry on all sorts of entrepreneurial endeavors, banks, canals, insurance companies, manufacturing and other businesses. All good republicans should do all they could to extend these stock companies throughout the country. Every town should have them, and governments and poor ordinary people alike should be able to buy small shares in them. Sometimes governments might find it necessary "to unite a bank and an insurance company together, till the town becomes sufficient to have both these in separate operations." But governments, after chartering these companies, should have nothing to do with directing them. By these means governments could "become rich with little or no dependence on taxes and yet [be] so allied, and thereby so dependent on the people as not to dare to infringe their rights in the minor republics."

Such commerce and business were the *"golden chains"* that held the society together; they created *"the best social system that ever was formed."* The principle of commerce, said Blodget, was in fact "the most sublime gift of heaven wherewith to harmonize and enlarge society. It is not only a principal stimulus to all industry; it is thence the grandparent of all the useful arts and sciences, and it is the only deity who frankly tells its votaries, 'by untouched credit and industry alone shall ye rise on my wings, to the temple of fortune and to fame.' " It was not true that only farmers and manufacturers were productive, said Blodget. Buying and selling, exchange itself, were sources of productivity in the society. In fact, Blodget went so far as to argue that merchants and traders, contrary to centuries of traditional thinking, were the only men in the society who could be fully trusted. "By the learned professions and by any other calling except that of a merchant, men may rise without that scrupulous attention to reputation and honesty, which is the basis of commercial elevation in all countries where commerce receives fair play." For too long commerce had been stigmatized "by the idle nobles and privileged orders of Europe." But America has changed all this. In a republic "alone it can flourish in full bloom."[31]

Of course, similar cultural changes were taking place throughout the Western world, but it was America, as the French theorist Comte Destutt de Tracy realized, that carried them farthest. Tracy, whose several works Jefferson translated and prepared for publication in America (though there is no indication that Jefferson ever comprehended the full import of all of Tracy's arguments), believed that the United States was "the hope and example of the world." There in the new Republic, he said, commerce had found its full identity with society. Indeed, commerce was society. "Society consists only in a continual succession of

EXCHANGES,'' and thus ''commerce and society are one and the same thing.'' Commerce for Tracy and for many Americans had shed its traditional reference to overseas merchants and external trade and had come to be equated simply with exchanges, the bulk of which took place within the country. ''All exchanges are acts of commerce, and the whole of human life is occupied by a series of exchanges and reciprocal services.'' All the agents of trade—merchants, factors, retailers, commission brokers, shopkeepers—were equally useful to society. All those innumerable petty transactions among countless insignificant individuals in which all parties gain—that was commerce, that was society. ''Commerce, that is exchange, being in truth society itself, it is the only bond among men; the source of all their moral sentiments; and the first and most powerful cause of the improvement of their mutual sensibility and reciprocal benevolence.'' And nowhere more than in republican America had commerce been allowed such full and fair play.[32]

America, at a stroke it seemed, had overturned two millennia of Western history. ''Everything relative to political economy must be original,'' declared the political economist Laommi Baldwin in 1809. ''Without recurrence to the past we have to consult futurity; we have every thing to create and little to correct; and instead of remedial institutions formed on retrospective views, we are to establish principles that shall interest posterity.''[33]

When ''exchange'' became the primary element of the economy, said Baldwin, then paper money became more important. ''The rapidity and quick succession of exchanges'' required increased quantities of money, and this paper money had democratizing effects. James Madison, like gentry creditors everywhere, may have earlier condemned paper money as destructive of ''that confidence between man & man, by which the resources of one may be commanded by another.'' But now many were extolling that same destruction of confidence between one man and another, for such confidence was simply another name for authority and dependency. In a traditional intimate society it had been possible for a gentleman with a reputation and property to deal with everyone personally. But, said the physician Erick Bollman (a former participant in the Burr conspiracy) in 1810, gentlemen could not relate to people in such a personal manner anymore. When they wished, for example, to buy a turkey from a farmer, they could not say, as they had used to, ''I own the big house at the corner of Ninth and Chestnut Street,'' and expect the farmer to tip his cap and deliver the turkey on credit. Now the farmer will say, ''What is that to me!'' Proprietary wealth, conspicuous property, personal reputation, and genteel authority did not matter as they had in the past. What the farmer wanted now was ready money, and it did not matter from whom it came: "I want a dollar," says the farmer, "or else you cannot have my turkey."[34]

All these commercial activities and exchanges had corrosive effects on what remained of the traditional patronage and hierarchical confidences between men in the society. Merchants, like the Bull brothers of Hartford in 1802, now advertised they had the "cheapest store" by setting forth "the following rules—no trust, no goods sent out, no samples given, no abatement in price first asked, no goods delivered until paid for." Paper money made these new rules possible: it destroyed personal trust, but at the same time it liberated men from older personal dependencies. All this trade and trafficking by different individuals freed men from traditional restraints and stimulated what *Niles' Weekly Register* in 1815 called "the almost universal ambition to get forward." Laborers felt freer working for money wages than they had serving apprenticeships or existing in barter relationships with superiors. Even Caesar Rodney, the attorney defending the Philadelphia cordwainers in their conspiracy trial in 1806, was willing to accept the new liberal notion that labor was a commodity bought and sold in the market. America was different from Europe, said Rodney, who was soon to become Jefferson's Attorney General. In the Old World, "statutable provisions fix and regulate the price of everything almost." But "here honesty and industry are sure to meet a due reward." It was not their newfound independence from their masters that the cordwainers objected to; they simply wanted their employers to recognize that they lived in a new country "where the poorest individual can claim the full price of his labour," and was free to withhold that labor from the market if he were not satisfied with the price.[35]

If everyone in the society was involved in moneymaking and exchanging, then to that extent they were all alike, all seeking their own individual interests and happiness. "The market house, like the grave, is a place of perfect equality," said Philip Freneau in bitter derision.[36] But he was right. All this commercial activity did promote equality, yet not, of course, equality of wealth. Quite the contrary: wealth was far more unequally distributed in the decades following the Revolution than it had been before.[37] Nonetheless, early-nineteenth-century Americans felt more equal, and for many of them that was what mattered.

After all, amid all the age-old instruments of humiliation by which superiors had kept inferiors in their place, wealth was far from being the most important and most mortifying. When the western Pennsylvanians in the state legislature declared in 1786 that "a democratic government like ours admits of no superiority," Robert Morris was stunned. "What!" he scornfully exclaimed. "Is it insisted that there is no distinction of character? Surely persons possessed of knowledge, judgment, information, integrity, and having extensive connections, are not to be classed with persons void of reputation or character." But William Findley and his western colleagues would not hear of any of these claims of superiority by Morris and his patrician crowd. They denied that Morris and his Philadelphia gentry were fundamentally different from them, denied that such would-be aristocrats were more respectable than they were; all they had was "more money than their neighbours." And more money did not justify any feelings of superiority on the one side or inferiority on the other. In America, said Findley, "no man has a greater claim of special privilege for his £100,000 than I have for my £5." That was what American equality had come to mean, and indeed still means.[38]

Only in the context of this rejection of "knowledge," "character," and "extensive connections" as the criteria of social distinction can we appreciate the celebration of what came to be called the "self-made man." This became such a familiar symbol for Americans that we have forgotten what a novel, indeed radical, notion it originally was. Of course, there had always been social mobility in Western society, sometimes and in some places more than others. Colonial America had experienced a good deal of it, and, as we have seen, many of the revolutionary leaders were the products of considerable social mobility, usually being the first in their families to go to college. But this social mobility in the past generally had been a mobility of a peculiar sort, an often sponsored mobility in which the patronized individual had acquired the attributes of the social status to which he was raised while at the same time trying to forget and disguise the lowly sources from whence he had come. The genteel sons of artisans did not usually celebrate their origins. Benjamin Franklin's *Autobiography* was unusual for doing just that. But we must remember that it was not published in Franklin's lifetime, and Franklin's countrymen made little of his obscure origins while he was alive. Indeed, in 1790 at the time of Franklin's death his principal eulogist passed over his youth as being too mean and embarrassing to dwell upon.[39] In a traditional society social mobility had not been something to be proud of, as indicated by the pejorative terms—"upstarts," "arrivistes," "parvenus"—used to disparage those participants unable to hide their rise. Although few Americans, including most Federalists, could ever easily get away with ridiculing someone else's obscure origins, many did not hesitate to raise eyebrows and jeer at those such as wealthy Republican businessmen Matthew Lyon of Vermont and John Swanwick of Pennsylvania who had not properly acculturated themselves to the rank they sought. Swanwick, for example, though one of the wealthiest men of Philadelphia, was looked down upon by the more socially established families of the city and was regarded as "our Lilliputian, [who] with his dollars, gets access where without them he would not be suffered to appear."[40]

But already in America independent mobile men were boasting not only of their humble origins but also of their lack of polish and a gentleman's education. They had made it, they said, on their own, without family influence, without patronage, and without going to Harvard or Princeton or indeed any college at all. When a South Carolina politician in 1784 was celebrated in the press for being a self-established man who "had no relations or friends, but what his money made for him," a subtle but radical revolution in thinking had taken place. During the first decade of the nineteenth century the modern image of Benjamin Franklin as the "self-made man" was first created, helped by dozens of editions of his *Autobiography* and the propaganda of ambitious artisans and businessmen. Patronage was widely condemned, and even inventors, desperate for European-like support "from opulent individuals or corporate bodies," were forced, they said, to form an association and "patronize themselves."[41] The most outrageously nouveaux riches were now getting "great pleasure in telling how they first entered Boston in Pedlars trim." For many now it was sponsored mobility and the useless ornaments of a liberal arts education that were becoming embarrassing. A man was now praised for having arrived and risen "without friends," for having been "the architect of his own fortune," or for never having been "borne on the shoulders of patronage." For many Americans the ability to make money—not whom one knew, or who one's father was, or where one went to college—now became the only proper democratic means for distinguishing one man from another. Catharine Sedgwick, author and daughter of an esteemed Federalist family, spoke for all of the old aristocracy when she said of the emerging nineteenth-century hierarchy: "wealth, you know, is the grand leveling principle."[42]

Thus our attempts to demonstrate the inequality of the society of the early Republic by measuring wealth alone misses the point of what happened.[43] It is true that by the 1820s some were already trying to put poor vs. rich in place of democrats vs. aristocrats as the major antagonists in the society.[44] Yet many could still feel equal to those of superior wealth as long as that wealth was seen as self-achieved and, more important, was not accompanied by any other pretensions to social superiority, such as those cultural attributes claimed by eighteenth-century gentlemen that money could not easily buy.

Indeed, this leveling through money put enormous pressure on the traditional distinction between ordinary people and gentlemen, between those who labored and those who did not, between those who were in trade and those who were not. For decayed aristocrats, like Hawthorne's character Hepzibah in *The House of the Seven Gables,* being forced to enter trade could be the greatest trial of their lives. Hawthorne's lengthy account of Hepzibah's agonizing decision to open a shop in Pyncheon House draws all its significance from the real pain the old lady is suffering. Her misery, wrote Hawthorne, was "the final throe of what called itself old gentility." The patrician Hepzibah, "whose religion it was that a lady's hand soils itself irremediably by doing aught for bread," is convinced that becoming the hucksteress of a cent shop has made her a plebeian; and she takes no comfort from, indeed cannot comprehend, the remarks of the young man Holgrave, who tells her that by engaging in trade she has merely joined "the united struggle of mankind. . . . These names of gentleman and lady had a meaning, in the past history of the world, and conferred privileges, desirable or otherwise, on those entitled to bear them. In the present—and still in the future condition of society—they imply, not privilege, but restriction."[45]

The distinction between gentlemen and commoners did not disappear, but it was buffeted and blurred and was eventually transformed. To visiting foreigners, it seemed that nearly every white adult male had become a gentleman. In the West, at least, "everybody that has a decent coat is a gentleman; every gentleman is as good as any other and does not conceive that he should put himself out to oblige his equal." Draymen, butchers' boys, canal workers, were all called "them gentlemen." Even men in dirty shirt sleeves were introduced as gentlemen, and blacksmiths saw nothing wrong in calling themselves gentlemen. And in their "violent intimacy" they all presumed the right to shake anyone's hand and call anyone by his first name. Federalists made fun of the vulgar for claiming to be the "people" and thus equal to gentlemen and men of education. But such satire rang hollow when no one felt embarrassed over such claims. Unlike Europe, said Joel Barlow, in America the "people" were all there were.[46]

Under such circumstances gentlemanly distinctiveness was hard to sustain. Dress became more identical for all social ranks, and fashion-mongering as a means of setting people off one from another became more frenzied. Long-existing aristocratic beliefs and practices came under increasing attack. In 1802, 1,500 mechanics and 1,200 manufacturers of Philadelphia signed a petition protesting the gentry's racing of horses in the city streets. Such an amusement, they said, "may be agreeable to a few idle landed gentlemen, who bestow more care in training their horses than in educating their children," but it was very harmful to the "mechanic and manufacturing interest."[47]

Honor, that aristocratic sense of reputation, seemed more and more difficult to understand or explain, except of course in the South. The more people talked about it, the less substantial and meaningful it appeared. "Where is *Honour*?" asked the successful printer and publisher Isaiah Thomas in 1781. "Shall we look for her in the courts of the most mighty potentates on earth, or in the stately places of the great—alas! we know too well that *self-interest* is the chief end of their politicks." To Thomas it seemed that honor in a republic could be found only among the "band of Brothers" within the Masonic craft that was increasingly composed of artisans and middling sorts like Thomas himself. Perhaps only within such Masonic societies or in other such organizations could one find the social networks that Nathaniel Chipman believed crucial for the cultivation of any sense of honor or shame. Such social networks, said Chipman, made "all the individuals of the same connection, in some measure sponsors for the actions of each." Only when enmeshed in such social webs does each person feel, "as of right, the reproach of the other's crimes, and the justice of the punishment."[48]

The proliferation of such associations in the decades following the Revolution became a testimony to the need people felt to construct artificially those social networks that earlier had been taken for granted. Simply being a gentleman, connected by that fact with other gentlemen, was no longer capable of giving individuals the sense of being involved in a select society. Outside of the South honor was attacked as monarchical and anti-republican. Honor not only fomented militarism but buttressed inequality and distorted natural relations among men.[49]

As honor came under attack, so too did dueling—as the special means by which gentlemen protected their honor. Despite growing criticism throughout the Western world, dueling continued to be practiced, especially by military officers and Southerners. Some justified dueling on the grounds that it was a civilizing agent, inhibiting gentlemen from using "illiberal language" with one another. Others saw dueling as a means of maintaining courage as a virtue amidst the spread of an effeminizing luxury. Although Aaron Burr's killing of Alexander Hamilton in 1804 in a duel did much to intensify condemnation of the practice, it was the spread of egalitarian sentiments that most effectively undermined it. When even servants began challenging others to duels, many gentlemen realized that the code of honor had lost its meaning.

Sometimes it appeared that in America's fluid society would-be gentlemen were using challenges as a means of establishing their status or their dignity. John Sevier, former governor of Tennessee, sneered at young Andrew Jackson's challenge to a duel in 1803. He condescended to notice Jackson's challenge, he said, only because the people had made Jackson a judge and thereby had promoted him to the unmerited status of a gentleman. If they had to fight, however, Sevier proposed that they fight with pistols, since he presumed, as he told Jackson, that "you know nothing about the use of any other arms," meaning, of course, fencing swords.[50]

By 1828 Noah Webster in his dictionary saw the term "gentleman" merely as a courtesy title, of general address, applied most appropriately to "men of education and good breeding, of every occupation."[51] "Of every occupation"—that was the key to the transformation. Traditionally gentlemen did not have occupations; they were not in trade or business, and they did not work for money. Even artists and members of the professions who wished to be gentlemen tried to regard their activities as something other than their source of income. When the struggling painter Samuel F. B. Morse told his parents in 1814 that he would never paint portraits and signs simply for money, that he would never make "a trade" of what was "a profession," he was drawing this traditional distinction. "If I cannot live a gentleman," he said, "I will starve a gentleman." Of course, living like a gentleman now was increasingly difficult. "Our Lawyers are mere lawyers, our physicians are mere physicians, our divines are mere divines," complained John Sylvester John Gardiner, perhaps Boston's most distinguished man of letters in the first decades of the nineteenth century. "Everything smells of the shop, and you will, in a few minutes conversation, infallibly detect a man's profession."[52]

Gentlemen like Hamilton and Burr had always been embarrassed by the fact that they had to work for money. Because neither had an independent source of funds, both periodically had been forced to interrupt their public activities to return to their New York law offices and look after their private affairs. But neither saw himself in modern terms as a lawyer who happened to be a gentleman; instead both tried to see themselves in traditional terms as gentlemen who occasionally practiced some law. For such men law was not so much a skilled professional occupation as it was a desirable attribute of a man of learning, one, as John Quincy Adams said, that was "most beneficial to man." James Kent agreed, citing Gibbon: "legal studies require only a state of place and refinement"—that is, only being a gentleman. Such gentlemen lawyers were expected to read Horace as well as Blackstone, Cicero as well as Coke, history and poetry as well as common law writs. Jefferson was a lawyer, to be sure, but he scarcely resembled a modern practitioner. He believed that the law, like all of learning, was important for a variety of reasons. "It qualifies a man to be useful to himself, to his neighbors, and to the public. It is the most certain stepping stone to preferment in the political line."[53]

But by the early decades of the nineteenth century many lawyers were forced to explain what they did in different terms. Law was no longer an aspect of being a gentleman of letters; it had become a technical and specialized profession that wholly occupied the person engaged in it. Some struggled against the changes, complaining that "you cannot be men of all work, and lawyers beside; any more than you can be in two places at the same time."[54]

In time, however, the profession was transformed. "The bar is now crowded with bustling and restless men . . . ," wrote David Dudley Field in 1844. "The quiet, decorous manners, the gravity, and the solid learning, so often conjoined in a former generation, are now rarely seen together. A new race has sprung up and supplanted the old." Lawyers were no longer as interested in classical learning. They had become workingmen like everyone else. In fact, in 1824 the Franklin Society of Philadelphia opened its first exhibition with a toast to all workingmen—doctors and lawyers as well as saddlers, coopers, bakers, and brickmakers. If lawyers were not an interest themselves, they had at least become agents for other competitive economic interests. They defended their unusual role as political representatives, however, on the same grounds that Hamilton had advanced in *The Federalist* No. 35: that they were not identified with any particular economic interest and therefore could better harmonize those interests.[55]

Those who clung to traditional standards were passed by. Richard Henry Dana, Sr., could not look at the "exalted character" of his father, Francis Dana, chief justice of the supreme court of Massachusetts for fifteen years between 1791 and 1806, "without a sense of my own littleness." Just the memory of his father's founding generation, he said in 1819, made "the present tasteless, it takes away the vigour of my hope in what is to come." He abandoned the law for a life of letters, but without independent wealth it was a struggle. His association with the learned *North American Review* was tenuous; it was "all gentlemen and no pay." It was not without ironic comment on the cultural changes that were occurring that Dana, Sr., edited *The Idle Man* in 1821–22 and assumed the title as his literary persona for the rest of his career. His son, Richard Henry Dana, Jr., felt himself even more out of place in the world in which traditional gentlemen were fast disappearing, even among the legal profession. He discovered only one gentleman among the entire practicing bar of Providence, Rhode Island—"he seemed a pearl among swine." Dana even found fault with Justice Joseph Story for arguing at dinner "like a lawyer" and talking "like a bookworm": Story "forgot that he was a gentleman dining out." Where nearly everyone claimed to be a gentleman, it was difficult to keep one's distinctiveness in mind.[56]

19. Middle-Class Order

By the second decade of the nineteenth century Americans were already referring to themselves as a society dominated by the "middling" sort. To be sure, these terms were being used in England at the same time, but their significance in America was different. In England the term "middle class" had a more literal meaning than it did in America: it described that stratum of people who lay between the aristocracy and the working class. But in America, in the North at least, already it seemed as if the so-called middle class was all there was. Middling sorts in America appropriated the principal virtues of the two extremes and drained the vitality from both the aristocracy and the working class. By absorbing the gentility of the aristocracy and the work of the working class, the middling sorts gained a powerful moral hegemony over the whole society. The aristocracy lost its monopoly of civility and politeness and the working class lost its exclusive claim to labor. Leisure became idleness, work became respectable, and nearly every adult white male became a gentleman. It happened nowhere else in the Western world quite like this.

"Patrician and plebeian orders are unknown . . . ," wrote Charles

Ingersoll in 1810, in one of the first avowed defenses of America's national character against foreign criticism. "Luxury has not yet corrupted the rich, nor is there any of that want, which classifies the poor. There is no populace. All are people. What in other countries is called the populace, a compost heap, whence germinate mobs, beggars, and tyrants, is not to be found in the towns; and there is no peasantry in the country. Were it not for the slaves of the south," wrote Ingersoll, "there would be one rank.'"

The exception is jarring, to say the least; by modern standards Ingersoll's judgment that America had become classless is absurd. We today see the distinctions of early-nineteenth-century society vividly, not only those between free and enslaved, white and black, male and female, but those between rich and poor, educated and barely literate. Yet if we are to understand the wonder, the astonishment, and judgments of observers like Ingersoll, we must see, as they did, this society of the early Republic in the context of what American society had once been and what societies elsewhere in the Western world still resembled. In that context America had experienced an unprecedented democratic revolution and had created a huge sprawling society that was more egalitarian, more middling, and more dominated by the interests of ordinary people than any that had ever existed before.

Tocqueville, too, saw almost at once what had happened. In a diary entry made only a few days after he landed in New York in 1831 he noted that in America the middle classes had attained "outward perfection," "or rather the whole society seems to have melted into a middle class." No one in America seemed to have "the elegant manners and refined courtesy of the high classes in Europe." In fact, there was "something both vulgar and disagreeably uncultivated" about American society. Yet "at the same time," said Tocqueville, no one in America was what the French would call *"ill bred."* Americans, "even to the simplest *shop* salesman," seemed to Tocqueville "to have received, or wish to appear to have received, a good education." All Americans seemed to behave the same respectable way—"grave, deliberate, reserved, and they all wear the same clothes." America, said Francis Grund, was *"mediocre par excellence.* . . . The manners of Americans, therefore, are as far removed from the elegance of courts, as they are far removed from the boorishness of the lower classes in Europe." It was as if the politeness and the vulgarity that Europeans took so much trouble to keep apart were in America somehow mingled and made one—creating, said a disgruntled James Fenimore Cooper, the "fussy pretensions" of the "genteel vulgar" who got their manners "second-hand, as the traditions of fashion, or perhaps in the pages of a novel."[2]

The blurring of the distinction between gentlemen and plain people in America corresponded to a steady vulgarization of eighteenth-century gentility. The prosperous farmers, the shopkeepers, the clerks, the manufacturers, the retail merchants, the businessmen, and others who made up the middling sort did not repudiate the genteel Enlightenment but popularized it. The new middle class extolled education, but not a classical or even a liberal arts education. They wanted education that was practical and useful, and why not? Had not the revolutionary leaders themselves told them that the people of the New World required a different kind of education from those of the Old World—"an useful American education," said Jefferson, with everyone "instructed in general, competently to the common business of life," and genius employing its talents "to the useful arts, to inventions for saving labor and increasing our comforts, to nourishing our health, to civil government, military science, &c."?[3] Many members of the revolutionary elite, including Benjamin Rush, Noah Webster, and Francis Hopkinson, had even attacked the study of the "dead languages" of Greek and Latin as time-consuming, useless, and unrepublican. Such study of Greek and Latin, Rush had said, was "improper in a peculiar manner in the United States" because it tended to confine education only to a few, when in fact republicanism required everyone to be educated. Besides, asked Webster in 1790, "what advantage does a merchant, a mechanic, a farmer, derive from an acquaintance with the Greek and Roman tongues?"[4]

Yet some of these enthusiastic republican gentlemen, when they saw the lengths to which such attacks on liberal learning could be carried, eventually backed away. Even Rush, though he retained his dislike of the heathenish classics on religious grounds, came to realize by 1810 that "a *learned* education" ought once again to "become a luxury in our country." If college tuitions were not immediately raised, he said, "the great increase in wealth among all classes of our citizens" would enable too many ordinary people, particularly plain farmers, to pay for a college education for their sons "with more ease than in former years when wealth was confined chiefly to cities and to the learned professions." It was one thing for a practical knowledge of "reading, writing, and arithmetic . . . to be as common and as cheap as air"; in a republic everyone should have these skills, and "they should be a kind of sixth or civic sense." But it was quite another thing with a liberal arts education.

"Should it become *universal*, it would be as destructive to civilization as universal barbarism." Rush had come to perceive that middlebrow adoption of liberal learning was insidiously draining and diluting its integrity without anyone's being the wiser. Better the Visigoths at the gates than this disintegration from within, or so many highbrow gentry had come to believe.[5]

These developments forced new alignments out of which the modern distinction between high and popular culture was born. In the eighteenth century cultivation in the liberal arts was thought to be a personal qualification for participation in gentlemanly society. To be a republican gentleman was to be learned and a member of the republic of letters. Such eighteenth-century genteel men of learning had no doubt of the existence of superstitious, vulgar, and barbaric customs, such as bear baiting, mummeries, witchcraft, or eating with one's hands; but they had scarcely viewed these customs as some sort of "popular culture" in competition with genteel cultivation and civilization. Yet by the early nineteenth century that was precisely what seemed to be happening. The spread of civilization, good manners, and good taste throughout the society was designed only to enlighten and elevate the public; it was not supposed to create a rival culture that diluted gentility and threatened its standards. Yet as the traditional distinction between gentlemen and nongentlemen became blurred, cultivation became popularized, breeding a middling culture that, according to high-toned Federalists, was "widely and thinly spread." Learning in America, they exclaimed, was similar to what Dr. Johnson had said about learning in Scotland: "that it is like bread in a besieged town, where everyone gets a little, but no man a full meal."[6] For some of these middling sorts, it seemed, participation in cultivated civilization had come to mean simply reading a newspaper, owning a tea service, or having a piano in the parlor.

In England, wrote James Fenimore Cooper in his *Notions of the Americans,* the aristocracy sought to distinguish itself from the upwardly mobile middling sorts by acting in eccentric and whimsical ways, thereby making it difficult for aspiring would-be gentlemen to know how to behave. But in America there was "as yet" none of this "high-bred folly." "The accession to the *coteries* are so very numerous, and are commonly made with strides so rapid," that these hordes of claimants to gentility were still likely to be "rationally polite" rather than "genteelly vulgar."

In this 1828 defense of American manners against decades of criticism by European and especially English critics, Cooper was putting as good a face on America's social situation as he thought possible; for he was by no means as sanguine about what was happening to gentility in America as his sometimes controlled arguments suggested. He admitted that an American gentleman was less polite and courteous than a European aristocrat. The American was more direct, natural, and sincere in his social relationships. He was without the European's artificiality in manners: "he will not tell you he is enchanted to see you, when, in truth, he is perfectly indifferent to the matter." But at the same time this very quality of simplicity that inhibited the "superficial courtesy" of the American gentry had the effect of "elevating the manners of the lower classes, who, considering their situations, are at all times surprisingly self-possessed and at their ease." If anything was objectionable in American social behavior, wrote Cooper, it was "the rough and hardy manner" with which ordinary Americans supported their opinions. In the end what most impressed (and frightened) Cooper about America was the degree to which "both a higher and lower order of men mingle in commerce," more so than anywhere else in the world. Commerce was what kept the society unsettled, "in a state of effervescence," and allowed the dregs to "get nearer to the surface than is desirable." Still, despite his deep uneasiness, Cooper in the 1820s remained outwardly confident that American society could eventually sort itself out and remain both republican and civilized.[7]

The struggles of individuals to rise from humble origins and achieve respectability became in time part of America's folklore. Indeed, so common did such stories become in America that, as Hawthorne later remarked, all traditional European romance in them was lost.[8] Beginning with numerous editions of Franklin's *Autobiography* in the 1790s, dozens upon dozens of accounts of youthful development—a popular American form of the European *Bildungsroman*—tumbled from American pens and presses. Most of these narratives recounted the individual's rise to respectability in conventional genteel terms. But some autobiographies were more frank and honest than others. One of the most fascinating and revealing of these is the journal, unpublished at the time, of an obscure Vermont peddler, James Guild.

Born in 1797 in Halifax, Vermont, Guild at age nine was bound out as a farm laborer for twelve years. When he finally came of age, he was not sure what he wanted to do. All he did know was that he wanted to do something other than farming. And so, like many other New England farm boys in these years, he became a peddler, wondering all the while "why I should stoop so low as to follow so mean a calling." What he really wanted, and what he eventually came to understand with compelling clarity, was to make money and to enter the promised land of gentility and respectability. His journal was in fact a parody of a traditional Puritan spiritual narrative—progressing through the familiar stages of humiliation, depression, surrender, and rebirth. Guild in the end was saved, saved not by Jesus but by money.[9]

Guild's first experiences with the larger world in Troy, New York, were mortifying: "I thought folks new everything and more to" and "I considered myself inferior to them." In fact, he was so continually humiliated by the world that he decided to give in completely to his abasement, to get a leather apron and some spoon molds, become a tinker, and thereby sink to as mean and as low a rank as possible: "so mean that no one would take notice of me" and so low that "I cared not for my looks nor reputation." If he was to be poor and insignificant, then he intended to go all the way. But such humiliation was in fact only a spiritual preparation for his conversion. In his disgrace and despondency he thought of returning home, but he worried constantly that his family and friends would despise him. In a moment of utter dejection ("O misery what shall I do?") Guild suddenly burst into tears and "boohood like a little child although I was one and twenty." "All at once" he decided he would not go back home; then and there he determined "to get into some business before they should see my face again."[10]

Guild now realized that in 1818 in democratic America life was lonely and the world "troublesome" and that "we are separated one from another to scratch our way." Experience soon taught him how to get out of scrapes by fast talking, how to size up strangers, and in particular how to trust no one. "This," he said, "learns me human nature," by which he meant: "I find people are not always what they seem to be." With this insight Guild was able to confront and deal with a capricious world. He traveled all over the East Coast, and scrambled, wrestled, and courted people. He took up the cutting of profile likenesses, the painting of miniatures, the teaching of penmanship, and for three weeks even tried "doctoring." In his travels and adventures some people deceived him, but he deceived far more; for he was always ready to use "disseption" and "to make folks think I was something I was not." He even took to calling himself "Guile." He loved to fool people, to act the vulgar clown and then reveal himself as polite and well-mannered. He was fascinated with the way "a genteel appearance" could impress people. He found "from experience if a man thinks he is something and puts himself forward he will be something." He found he could be a gentleman by acting as a gentleman. A new suit of clothes made him feel "rather large when he walked through the Streets." He polished his conversation, and when talking with people he always mentioned "some big caricter to make them think I was respected among respectable people."[11]

Yet all the while Guild knew he was not happy. He had long bouts of depression. He tried reading the Bible and praying to God, but "in vain."[12] In the end God had nothing to offer Guild emotionally. But Mammon did.

After three weeks of "solitude" and "low spirits" in Baltimore, Guild finally realized what he had been doing wrong. "I was and alwas was unhappy because I could not obtain a furtune," and he therefore concluded that he would be "one of the happiest fellows in the world If I could only be rich." If others "had began with nothin and became men of fortune," then why not he? "I said to myself money I must and will have." From that moment on, wrote Guild, "my sole object was to make money." Nothing else mattered. He cared nothing for society and for friends except "to have them treat me with politeness, and I do the same to them." He developed no deep attachments: as soon as business became dull in any community, "I was off." The pursuit of money became a means toward virtue. He developed "a strong mind" against "the weakness and folly of man." He learned self-denial. He refused to go bowling, to get drunk, or to go to places of "disipation," and he did so by concentrating on the making of money—"my whole aim" in life.[13]

Only after he had made money did he finally decide that he could go home and see his family and friends "in the caricter of an independent Gentleman, and something to foot the bill." Particularly satisfying to Guild was his visit to his old master to whom he had been bound out as a laborer only seven years earlier. At first he found it odd to see his former master bringing his horse and carriage around for him, but Guild decided finally that "it was right": he had done the same for his master in the past more times than he wanted to remember. But his middle-class world was different now from that of his boyhood. He had become, he discovered, so genteel and "so accustomed to dressing in stile and keeping Stilish company," that his former friends seemed lowly and vulgar. "The young Ladies that I used to think so very nice now look to me more like servants Girls."[14]

Still, even amidst the flood of his feelings of genteel superiority to his former friends, "who live as I used to with a tow Shirt and frock on with a beard a week old," there was a moment of regret, a pang of doubt that maybe by leaving his village home and succeeding in the larger world he had lost more than he had gained. His friends seemed so content and happy, so strongly attached to one another, with "no ambition to shine," that he could not help admiring them and wondering. But the doubt did not last, and he soon "began to feel a desire to get back again to N[ew] Y[ork] whire I could enjoy my usual occupation and visiting those families who have daughters that play so beautiful on the pianifort, and where there is constantly some new thing to attrac the eye and attention."[5]

The journal breaks off after Guild went to Europe to learn portrait painting. Perhaps the role the journal had played in Guild's life was over. He had achieved success and respectability as a member of the new middle class, and he had done it by catering to what his new middle-class customers wanted.

Indeed, by the 1820s there were dozens of itinerant painters like Guild wandering all over the countryside, advertising themselves with "Sign, Ornamental and Portrait Painting executed on the shortest notice, with neatness and despatch," and selling aspiring middling American families portraits of themselves. There existed "a decided disposition for painting in this Country," said America's first art critic, John Neal, in 1829; "you can hardly open the door of a best room anywhere, without surprising or being surprised by the picture of somebody plastered to the wall, and staring at you with both eyes and a bunch of flowers." "Wretched" as these pictures may have been, however, they did enable countless numbers of middling Americans to possess what earlier had been an exclusive luxury of the aristocracy. In just such ways did ordinary people acquire the attributes of gentility and thereby democratize the culture.[6]

At the same time as ordinary people were reaching upward and vulgarizing aristocratic and genteel culture, the gentry themselves felt increasingly compelled to reach down and embrace wider and deeper levels of the populace. Central to the republican revolution had been the desire by the revolutionary leaders to refine and improve the moral and aesthetic sensibilities of the American people. Like all educated eighteenth-century gentlemen, they had been eager to roll back Gothic barbarism and vulgar manners and extend enlightened civilization and cultivation among the general populace. Jefferson in the 1780s badgered his Virginia colleagues into erecting as the new state capitol in Richmond a magnificent copy of the Maison Carrée, a Roman temple from the first century A.D. at Nîmes, precisely because he wanted an American public building that would be a model for the people's "study and imitation" and "an object and proof of national good taste." For too long, said Jefferson, this American land had been cursed with architectural monstrosities. If Virginians put up another one of those "rude, misshapen piles" of Georgian bricks, he warned, it would simply become "a monument of our barbarism which will be loaded with execrations as long as it shall endure." He was not ashamed of his enthusiasm for the arts, he said, because its object was "to improve the taste of my countrymen, to increase their reputation, to reconcile to them the respect of the world and procure them its praise."[7]

Gentlemanly literati and artists were urged to join in this educational process—in the words of William Tudor, to "feel something of a '*missionary*' spirit" in elevating "the taste of the publick." Learned academies and critical journals were formed, not simply, as in Europe, for professional recognition and communication but also for the instruction and guidance of the people's artistic judgment. The young painter Samuel F. B. Morse wanted nothing more for his country than to have it "acquire the character of a civilized and literary nation," to let the world know "that the Americans of the present age were a civilized, refined, and literary people." The architect Benjamin Latrobe thought it the duty of every "good citizen" to promote "the education and *civilization* of the society in which he and his children are to live."[18]

Yet in their laudable efforts to reach out to the public the gentry found that their messages necessarily became popularized and coarsened. Speakers at academic commencements now saw nothing new or strange in lecturing young gentlemen on the virtues of hard work and punctuality, which were now pictured as the key to "improvement" and "respectability." Young men were told that they ought to be polite and affable only in order to gain the approval of the public. One commencement speaker even discussed the problems of too much sweat and what that could do to one's relationships in genteel company.[19]

For middle-class people busy in the making of money, clergymen issued what one of them in 1810 called "Short Sermons, Designed for the Use of Those Who Have Little Time to Read Longer Discourses." Digests and shortcuts to gentility—in particular, scores of etiquette books for anxious mobile people—became increasingly common. Etiquette books were now even written for children, as Americans realized they could no longer wait two or three generations to make a gentleman.

"Manners" became equated with sets of rules to be learned, and were now taught in schools. Some of the rules suggest how deep into the society gentility was trying to reach: people were never to sleep in any garment worn during the day, never to sit in a house with a hat on in the presence of ladies, and never to remind others of their lowly origins; it was, however, still polite to eat food off a knife as long as one's lips were not closed over the blade.[20]

These middle-class pressures worked to popularize the morality of the Revolution. Virtue, in the North at least, lost much of the rational and stoical quality befitting the classical heroes the revolutionary leaders had emulated. Temperance, for example, that self-control of the passions so valued by the ancients and one of Cicero's four cardinal virtues, became mainly identified with the elimination of popular drunkenness— "a good cause," declared the Franklin Society for the Suppression of Intemperance in 1814, in which "perseverance and assiduity seldom fail of securing the denied object."[21]

A republic, Parson Weems, the entrepreneurial biographer of Washington and a colorful spokesman for the new middle-class values, wrote in 1802, was "the best government for morals." It was a traditional statement, no doubt, but in Weems's updated early-nineteenth-century version the morals had become vulgarized. A republic meant no "sordid monopolizing *aristocracy*" to soak up money and prevent a "poor tax-ridden mother" from having enough to pay for light to mend her children's stockings. A republic was now valued for being "the cheapest of all governments, where every citizen may easily attain property sufficient to purchase books—to command leisure—and to acquire taste and knowledge." A republic was where frugality was "fashionable" and "wealth pours into every pocket." A republic was "a government where the man is looked at and not his fine coat." A republic was "the best remedy under heaven against national intemperance"; it "imparts a joy that loaths the thought of drunkenness." And finally a republic was where citizens, "seeing themselves treated with equal fairness and impartiality," knew "no pangs of jealousy and hatred: hence every countenance is bright with smiles of contentment, and every heart glows with sentiments of BROTHERLY LOVE."[22]

These middle-class pressures also worked to alter fundamentally the role and position of women in America. Since civilizations were now being ranked by the way they treated women (did not "savages" regard their women as "beasts of burden"?), enlightened men with genteel aspirations were eager to escape from those "barbarous days" when a woman was "considered and treated as the slave of an unfeeling master." That sort of traditional patriarchalism had to go. Women now had to be treated with particular delicacy and love. "A woman of virtue and prudence is a public good—a public benefactor." She had the power to make "public decency . . . a fashion—and public virtue the only example."[23]

"In the present state of society," declared Joseph Hopkinson in 1810, "woman is inseparably connected with everything that civilizes, refines, and sublimates man." Consequently, wives and mothers were now urged to use their special talents to cultivate in their husbands and children the proper moral feelings—the virtue, benevolence, and social affections—necessary to hold a sprawling and competitive republican society together. Virtue now lost what remained of its classical association with martial and masculine severity and became more and more identified with enlightened feminine sociability and affection; indeed, virtue at times seemed to mean little more than female chastity.[24]

However retarded it may appear to us, this shift in meaning gave women a new sphere of significance separate from that of men. Since they now had become the principal civilizing agents of a new and raw society—"women would effeminate even the roughness of steel and the solidity of wood"—they needed to be educated in the liberal arts even more than men. Women formed the minds of their husbands and children; it was they who were "entrusted with the care and guardianship of the rising generation." And therefore "to enlighten the sources from which society receives its earliest impressions . . . must always be regarded by the man of liberal feelings as a duty, dictated alike by gratitude and policy."[25]

Benjamin Hawkins, sometime senator from North Carolina and Indian agent, used this new understanding of the role of women to help civilize the Creeks and Cherokees. Unlike the missionaries, Hawkins did not try to teach the Indians the mysteries of religion or the intricacies of literature; instead he concentrated on the useful arts of agriculture and manufacture. When he first met the Indian chiefs and told them his plans to civilize them, he was derided and ridiculed. But he told them that "he was now done with *the men*"; he would talk with the women. He then proceeded to teach the women "the arts of carding, spinning and weaving; and to these they became soon attached, because petticoats, jackets and articles of dress could thereby be easily procured." He also taught them to exchange their surpluses of corn for material to make petticoats and other feminine items of dress. To engage in trade the women had to learn weights and measures in order to reduce all goods "to an intelligible value in money." "Progressing in these ways, the spinning and weaving of cotton increased rapidly. There were in 1805, twenty looms in the lower, and ten among the upper towns. . . . And such was the power of example prompted by interest, that some old men and boys learned to spin and seemed to take pleasure in the exercise." But among the Creeks "there was a peculiar difficulty in overcoming the aversion of the men to labour." Like European aristocrats, the Indian males were accustomed to "hunting, indolence and war," and expected others (in their case, their women) to do the degrading work of the society. The decreasing supply of game in the forests, however, made the men more dependent on the women's work and, produce; "with their pigs, maize and cotton, the females had already rendered themselves in a good degree independent of the men." Hawkins then advised "the young women to refuse favors to their sweethearts, and the married women to repel the caresses of their husbands, unless they would associate with them and assist them in their daily labours." Although this policy was not rigidly enforced, it did have some effect "in breaking the ferocity of the masculine temper, and reducing it to a milder and softer tone."

Whether Hawkins actually treated the Indians in this way is less relevant than the fact that the authors of these accounts believed that he had. These descriptions of "the business of civilizing Indians" tell us more about what white Americans of the early Republic thought were the sources of prosperity and cultivation in society than they do about the Indians.[26]

At the very moment, however, that Americans were coming to appreciate their capacity to mold and manipulate the culture of their new Republic, they were less and less sure they had that capacity under control. They knew the world had changed and changed radically since the Revolution, but had it changed in directions they had intended? By the early nineteenth century, America had become a huge bustling, boundless nation fascinated with its own expansion—"an expansion of population, of resources, of territory, of power, of information, of freedom, of everything that tends to magnify man." Early-nineteenth-century America had become the most thoroughly commercialized society in the world, where, it seemed, "everyone is a man of business; every thing is in the progress of emulation and improvement." It was a society of plain, ordinary people all busy pursuing their own private interests. All thought they had equal rights, all were in equal competition with one another, and all were "enterprising almost to a fault. What may not be expected from such a people in such a country, and doubling every twenty-five years?" "The decree has gone forth. . . . A gigantic nation has been born," and in time it will "span the mightiest dominion that ever shook the earth."[27]

But it was increasingly clear that no one was really in charge of this gigantic, enterprising, restless nation. Government was weak, the churches were divided, and social institutions were fragmented. Nevertheless, "order" somehow seemed to "grow out of chaos," and people guided themselves "without the check of any controlling power, other than that administered by the collision of their own interests balanced against each other." The promotion of self-interest did not create the predicted anarchy, for in the new commercial society it became evident that "no man can promote his own interest, without promoting that of others." The society was held together by an "interminable succession of exchanges." And every single one of these exchanges counted, such that "the minutest excess or defeat in the supply of any one article of human want, produces a proportionate effect on the exchanges of all other articles."[28]

The harmony emerging out of such chaos was awesome to behold, and speaker after speaker and writer after writer commented on it. All those isolated individuals, "each pursuing their own interests for their own sake," added up to something great and sublime. People did not have to worry about society or government anymore; they would take care of themselves. "The public happiness," said Daniel Webster, "is to be the aggregate of the happiness of individuals. Our system begins with the individual man." People did not have to feel guilty anymore about pursuing their personal happiness here and now. Even the "pursuit of gold" now had beneficial results, for "by some interesting filiation, 'there's a Divinity, that shapes our ends' . . . and free institutions may be said to have been found in following the fur trade and the fisheries."[29]

In a society of many scrambling, ordinary, and insignificant people, the power of genius and great-souled men no longer seemed to matter. "The direct action of great minds on the character of our community is," it was said, "unquestionably less at the present period, than in former days." The founding fathers, of course, had thought that eminent men and imaginative minds were in control of events and caused things to happen. But that heroic conception of society was now relegated to a more primitive stage of development. Greatness in America's colonial period may have been due almost entirely to the exertions of prominent individuals. But the American Revolution had created "something like a general will," in which the course of the society was shaped "less by the activity of particular individuals" and more by "the mass of intellectual, moral and physical powers." Indeed, no country in history ever resembled the United States "in the points of greatness, complexity, and the number of its relations." It was a country now so caught up in shifting currents, "rapid, powerful, accumulated in the mass, and uncertain in . . . direction," that it was "scarcely possible for the mind to fix upon any . . . ground of policy or just calculation" of what to do.[30] America was in the hands of "providence," people said; and this old-fashioned religious term now became identified with "progress" and with the natural principles of society created by multiplicities of busy people following their natural desires free from artificial restraints, especially those imposed by laws and government. With such a conception of the social process, educated people found it increasingly difficult to hold to the eighteenth-century conspiratorial notion that particular individuals were directly responsible for what happened.[31]

In 1791 Madison had worried that the sprawling extent of the United States would make each individual insignificant in his own eyes, a circumstance that he thought would be unfavorable to liberty. But a generation later the magnitude of the country and the smallness of each individual had become sources of strength and wonder. What would be "more striking and sublime," asked Hugh Swinton Legaré in 1823, "than the idea of an IMPERIAL REPUBLIC" spreading over an expanse of territory larger than the empire of the Caesars, "a Republic, in which men are completely insignificant," but blend "in one divine harmony" their "various habits and conflicting opinions."[32] Plain, ordinary people as individuals may no longer have been important, but together they now added up to a powerful force.

People now described society more and more as a "mass" and for the first time began using this term in reference to "almost innumerable wills" in a positive, nonpejorative sense. The individual was weak and blind, said George Bancroft in a common reckoning, but the mass of people was strong and wise.[33] From all this followed, too, a new appreciation of statistics: in 1803 the word "statisticks" first appeared in American dictionaries.[34] By itself a fact might not mean much, but collected together with others it could reveal a whole world. Of course, enlightened gentlemen like Jefferson had always spent time gathering facts, but by the early nineteenth century fact-collecting had become a national obsession. Americans collected data of all sorts—the number of tanneries, paper mills, distilleries, and so on in each state; the number of people in various villages who had lived to eighty, ninety, or a hundred; the number of leaves on a tree. No one could divine to what use all these "authentic facts" might be put; all they knew was that "the history of human science is a collection of facts," and the facts could speak for themselves.[35] "In composing a work like the present," wrote James Mease in *The Picture of Philadelphia* (1811), "the author is of opinion that the chief object ought to be the multiplication of facts, and the reflections arising out of them should be left to the reader."[36]

Everything was being left to the reader, or the listener, or the voter, or the buyer—each person—to decide. Charles Nisbet, the Scottish clergyman who became the first president of Dickinson College in Pennsylvania, thought as early as 1789 that Americans were carrying their reliance on individual judgment to ridiculous extremes. He fully expected, he said, to see soon such books as "Every Man his own Lawyer," "Every Man his own Physician," and "Every Man his own Clergyman and Confessor."[37] It was true, declared the learned journal *Medical Repository* in 1817, that there were no professional pharmacists in America as there were in Europe; in fact, in New York the situation was so bad that even several women were peddling nostrums and patent medicines on the streets. Some mistakes may result from this lack of professionalism, the *Repository* acknowledged, but these mistakes would be no more than occurred in Paris, London, or Edinburgh, "where pharmacy, as a profession, is *scientific, exclusive,* and *privileged.*" And, as in all endeavors in this "enlightened age," much more good was likely to flow from opening up pharmacy to everyone rather than keeping it secret and closed. Already new discoveries in natural philosophy and chemistry had resulted in better medical remedies, "exploding one half at least of the old pharmaceutic compounds" and justifying America's rejection of European expertise. Even American literature would have to be different and democratic: it would, in Emerson's words, "embrace the common, [and] explore and sit at the feet of the familiar, the low."[38]

The result of all these assaults on elite opinion and celebrations of common ordinary judgment was a dispersion of authority and ultimately a diffusion of truth itself to a degree the world had never before seen. With every ordinary person being told that his ideas and tastes, on everything from medicine to art and government, were as good as, if not better than, those of "connoisseurs" and "speculative men" who had college degrees, it is not surprising that truth and knowledge became elusive and difficult to pin down.[39] Knowledge and truth, it was argued, now indeed had to become more fluid and changeable, more timely and current. In a fast-moving world "many things, which we now suppose to be true or nearly so, may in a short time be found to be false, or true only under certain circumstances."[40] Americans of the early Republic experienced an epistemological crisis as severe as any in their history. Confident of their ability to determine all by themselves the truth or validity of any idea or thing presented to them, but mistrustful of anything outside of "the narrow limits of their own observation," plain, ordinary Americans were thoroughly prepared to be the prey for all the hoaxers, confidence men, and tricksters like Edgar Allan Poe and P. T. Barnum who soon popped up everywhere. They had to see everything for themselves, "for," as Herman Melville wrote of the common sailors of the *Pequod,* "nothing but their own eyes could persuade such ignorance as theirs."[41]

In vain did the Federalists and other traditionally minded gentry protest against this democratization of truth where "the unalienable right of private judgment involves the liberty of thinking as we please on every subject."[42] Most ordinary people were no longer willing to defer to the knowledge and judgments of those who had once been their superiors. Perhaps plain people did not have the college education, the extensive travel, or the intellectual power of their aristocratic neighbors, but, their spokesmen said, they had eyes and ears, and they knew what was true for them better than some "commanding genius" or "learned sage" did. Why should they trust what such gentlemen told them? "Of what avail is it to me," each of them asked, "to believe certain propositions without seeing the truth of them; but merely because my powerful neighbor believes them?"[43]

Ever since the debate over the Sedition Act of 1798, by which the Federalists had attempted to punish Republican writers and editors criticizing the rulers of the national government, the nature of truth and the ways to discover it had become public issues. While the Federalists clung to the traditional assumption that truth was constant and universal and capable of being discovered by enlightened and reasonable men, their Republican opponents argued that opinions about government and rulers were many and diverse and the truth of such opinions could not be determined simply by judges and members of juries, no matter how educated and reasonable such men might be. Thus many Republicans concluded that all political opinions, even those opinions that were "false, scandalous and malicious," ought to be allowed, as Jefferson put it, to "stand undisturbed as monuments of the safety with which error of opinion may be tolerated where reason is left free to combat it."[44]

The Federalists were dumbfounded. "Truth," they said, "has but one side and listening to error and falsehood is indeed a strange way to discover truth." Any notion of multiple and varying truths would produce "universal uncertainty, universal misery," and "set all morality afloat." People needed to know the "criterion by which we may determine with certainty, *who are right, and who are wrong.*"[45]

Yet the Republicans did have a criterion for determining who was right and who was wrong, and it was the opinion of the whole people. Their arguments in favor of freedom of speech rested on the assumption that opinions about politics, like opinions about other subjects, were no longer the monopoly of the educated and aristocratic few. Not only were all opinions equally to be tolerated but everyone and anyone in the society should be equally able to express them. Truth was actually the creation of many voices and many minds, no one of which was more important than another and each of which made its own separate and equally significant contribution to the whole. Solitary opinions of single persons may now have counted for less, but in their statistical collectivity they added up to something far more significant than ever existed before. They became what Americans obsessively labeled "public opinion."[46]

Nearly everyone in the eighteenth century had believed in the power of public opinion and had talked endlessly about it. Indeed, members of the old society were so preoccupied with their reputations and their honor precisely because of their intense concern for the judgment of others. The opinion of others, wrote Adam Smith, was a mirror by which we scrutinized the propriety of our own conduct.[47] By the word "public," like that of "society," however, eighteenth-century gentlemen had usually meant "the rational part of it" and not "the ignorant vulgar"; they often meant by the "public" men like themselves whom they knew from legislative halls and private dining rooms. When they included the larger society within the "public," they still thought of "those philosophical and patriotic citizens who cultivate their reason" as its spokesmen and representatives.[48]

The Revolution rapidly expanded this "public" and democratized its opinion. Every conceivable form of printed matter—books, pamphlets, handbills, posters, broadsides, and especially newspapers—multiplied and were now written and read by many more ordinary people than ever before in history. By 1800, wrote the Reverend Samuel

Miller in his elaborate compendium of the Enlightenment entitled *A Brief Retrospect of the Eighteenth Century,* much of the intellectual leadership of the country had fallen into "the hands of persons destitute at once of the urbanity of gentlemen, the information of scholars, and the principles of virtue." In contrast to pre-revolutionary America, the society of the early Republic had thousands upon thousands of obscure ordinary people participating in the creation of this public opinion.[49]

By the early nineteenth century this newly enlarged and democratized public opinion had become the "vital principle" underlying American government, society, and culture. It was the standard to "which all things must be brought and all subjects submitted." In every realm of endeavor—whether art, language, medicine, or politics—connoisseurs, professors, doctors, and statesmen had to give way before the power of the collective opinion of the people. Public opinion, said Federalist Theodore Sedgwick in disgust, "is of all things the most destructive of personal independence and of that weight of character which a great man ought to possess."[50] But no matter, it was the people's opinion, and it could be trusted because no one controlled it and everyone contributed to it. "The public opinion," said Samuel Williams, "will be much nearer the truth, than the reasonings and refinements of speculative and interested men." Of course, some warned that in this "age of excitement" people must not make "public opinion the standard of their faith, not the authoritative guide of their conduct."[51] But it was too late. In no country in the world did public opinion become more awesome and powerful than it did in democratic America.

Public opinion, it was said, was like vegetation, it was like sunshine: no one knew how it worked.[52] No governmental institution or even all of the political institutions together embodied it. It resembled the society, which was simply an "order" that came out of a "chaos of characters, ideas, motives, and interests." Patrons, dependencies, indeed government itself, no longer mattered in holding society together. All that was needed to tie people together was what was now called the "voluntary principle." "Afford but the single nucleus of a system of administration of justice between man and man, and under the sure operation of this principle, the floating atoms will distribute and combine themselves, as we see in the beautiful natural process of crystallization, into a far more perfect and harmonious result than if government, with its 'fostering hand,' undertake to disturb, under the plea of directing, the process."

"The choral harmony of the whole," as Emerson noted in 1834, was overwhelming to behold. "Design! It is all design. It is all beauty. It is all astonishment."[53] Yet earlier Emerson had not been so sanguine. In the 1820s he had described society as "choked with evils . . . a community composed of a thousand different interests, a thousand various societies filled with competitions in the arts, in trade, in politics, in private life."[54] He had believed in traditional fashion that the virtue of the community had depended on the virtue of individuals. But he had gradually come to realize that society was "a routine which no man made and for whose abuses no man holds himself accountable." Men now had to forget their own particularities, their private and selfish interests, and concentrate on the natural harmony of the whole. "Man is powerful only by the multitude of his affinities, or because his life is intertwined with the whole chain of organic and inorganic being."[55] Yet this new inner spiritual harmony that Emerson and others now saw amidst the outward agitation and chaos was possible precisely because the old monarchical society had come apart and set people free. "It is the age of severance, of dissociation, of freedom, of analysis, of detachment. Every man for himself. The public speaker disclaims speaking for any other; he answers only for himself. The social sentiments are weak; the sentiment of patriotism is weak; veneration is low; the natural affections feebler than they were. People grow philosophical about native land and parents and relations." The Revolution and the democracy that resulted from it had destroyed all "the ties and ligaments" of the old society.[56] It was as Tocqueville said: "Aristocracy made a chain of all the members of the community, from the peasant to the king; democracy breaks that chain and severs every link of it."[57]

This democratic society was not the society the revolutionary leaders had wanted or expected. No wonder, then, that those of them who lived on into the early decades of the nineteenth century expressed anxiety over what they had wrought. Although they tried to put as good a face as they could on what had happened, they were bewildered, uneasy, and in many cases deeply disillusioned. Indeed, a pervasive pessimism, a fear that their revolutionary experiment in republicanism was not working out as they had expected, runs through the later writings of the founding fathers. All the major revolutionary leaders died less than happy with the results of the Revolution. Even Benjamin Franklin, who died in 1790 before the full force of the democratic future had become apparent, was at the end of his life deeply angry at the way he was being treated by an ungrateful Congress.[58] Only the last of the signers of the Declaration of Independence, Charles Carroll of Carrollton, seems to have enjoyed his final years, cynically reveling in the lucrative opportunities for business that the new democratic Republic had given him.

No one had expected more from the Revolution and the American Enlightenment than Benjamin Rush. "Mr. Great Heart," Jeremy Belknap called him after the character in Bunyan's *Pilgrim's Progress* who attacked the giants and hobgoblins that stood in the way of getting to the Celestial City. Because Rush had such high hopes for the Revolution, his disillusionment was especially profound. By the early nineteenth century, his letters were filled with despair. He looked back "with deep regret" at all his public efforts on behalf of the Revolution. As "for our Constitution? I cannot meet with a man who loves it." He felt "like a stranger" in his native land. The Revolution had changed "the principles and morals" of the people and had allowed government everywhere to fall "into the hands of the young and ignorant and needy part of the community." Only by considering the people of his home state, Pennsylvania, "*deranged* upon the subject of their political and physical happiness" could he contain the anger and contempt he felt. He wanted to burn all his "dreams," and like Charles Thomson, the secretary of the Continental Congress throughout its history, Rush eventually threw all the notes and documents for his once-planned memoir of the Revolution into the fire. Americans, he felt, had no national character and little likelihood of ever acquiring one. "We are indeed," he said in 1812, "a bebanked, a bewhiskied, and a bedollared nation." America's revolutionary experiment on behalf of liberty "will certainly fail. It has already disappointed the expectations of its most sanguine and ardent friends." Like John Jay, Elias Boudinot, Noah Webster, John Randolph, and others, Rush ended by abandoning the Enlightenment and becoming a Christian enthusiast: "nothing but the gospel of Jesus Christ will effect the mighty work of making nations happy."[59]

Many others, of course, never went that far. But the numbers of old revolutionaries who lost faith in what the Revolution had done is startling: from James Warren and Samuel Adams to David Ramsay, Light-Horse Harry Lee, and Christopher Gadsden. At the end of his life, George Washington had lost all hope for democracy. Party spirit, he said in 1799, had destroyed the influence of character in politics. Members of one party or the other now could "set up a broomstick" as candidate, call it "a true son of Liberty" or a "Democrat" or "any other epithet that will suit their purpose," and the broomstick would still "command their votes in toto!" John Adams spent much of his old age bewailing the results of the Revolution, including democracy, religious revivals, and Bible societies. "Where is now, the progress of the human Mind? . . . When? Where? and How? is the present Chaos to be arranged into Order?" he asked in 1813. By the early nineteenth century, many of the founding fathers had come to share something of Alexander Hamilton's poignant conclusion that "this American world was not made for me."[60] They found it difficult to accept the democratic fact that their fate now rested on the opinions and votes of small-souled and largely unreflective ordinary people.

Even Jefferson, sanguine and optimistic as he had always been, was reduced to despair in his last years and to what seems to us today to be an embarrassing fire-eating defense of the South and states' rights.[61] He hated the new democratic world he saw emerging in America—a world of speculation, banks, paper money, and evangelical Christianity that he thought he had laid to rest. He blamed the New England Federalists for everything that was going wrong, but even in his beloved Virginia he suffered disappointment and dismay. To his astonishment he had to fight like the devil to create his state university in the face of evangelical opposition. More than any of the revolutionary leaders, he had relied on the future to take care of itself. Progress, he thought, was on the march, and science and enlightenment were everywhere pushing back the forces of ignorance, superstition, and darkness. The people in a liberal democratic society would be capable of solving every problem, if not in his lifetime, then surely in the coming years.

But Jefferson lived too long, and the future and the coming generation were not what he had expected. Jefferson was frightened by the popularity of Andrew Jackson, regarding him as a man of violent passions and unfit for the presidency. He felt overwhelmed by the new paper-money business culture sweeping through the country and never appreciated how much his democratic and egalitarian principles had contributed to its rise. Ordinary people, in whom Jefferson had placed so much confidence, more than had his friend Madison, were not becoming more enlightened after all. Superstition and bigotry, with which Jefferson identified organized religion, were reviving, released by the democratic revolution he had led. He was incapable of understanding the deep popular strength of the evangelical forces, of the real moral majorities, that were seizing control of much of American culture in these years. As late as 1822 he still believed that there was not a young man now alive who would not eventually die a Unitarian! Increasingly, however, he came to lament "the rising generation, of which I once had sanguine hopes." America, including Virginia, was not progressing, but seemed to be going backward. The people were more religious, more sectarian, and less rational than they had been at the time of the Revolution. The new generation on which he rested all his hopes did not seem to know who he was, what he had done. During the last year of his life he was pathetically reduced to listing his contributions during sixty-one years of public service in order to justify a favor from the Virginia legislature. He had lived too long and felt cast off by the democratic forces he had helped to create. "All, all dead," he wrote to an old friend in 1825, "and ourselves left alone amidst a new generation whom we know not, and who knows not us."[62]

But the disillusionment felt by Jefferson and others of the founding fathers was a strange sort of disillusionment. It was not the disillusionment that English and European liberals like Wordsworth and Constant felt over the failure of the French Revolution. That the French Revolution ended in Napoleonic despotism could to some extent have been expected; the course of the French Revolution followed the classic cyclical pattern—excessive democracy leading to dictatorship and tyranny. The failure of the French Revolution did not destroy the idea of revolution in Europe; the possibility of a successful republican revolution next time was kept alive.

In America, however, the disillusionment was different. The founding fathers were unsettled and fearful not because the American Revolution had failed but because it had succeeded, and succeeded only too well. What happened in America in the decades following the Declaration of Independence was after all only an extension of all that the revolutionary leaders had advocated. White males had taken only too seriously the belief that they were free and equal with the right to pursue their happiness. Indeed, the principles of their achievement made possible the eventual strivings of others—black slaves and women—for their own freedom, independence, and prosperity.

The very fulfillment of these revolutionary ideals—the very success of the Revolution—made it difficult for those who benefited from that success, for ordinary people and their new democratic spokesmen, to understand the apprehensions of the founding fathers. The people looked back in awe and wonder at the revolutionary generation and saw in them leaders the likes of which they knew they would never see again in America. But they also knew that they now lived in a different world, a democratic world, that required new thoughts and new behavior. We cannot rely on the views of the founding fathers anymore, Martin Van Buren told the New York convention in 1820. We have to rely on our own experience, not on what they said and thought. They had many fears, said Van Buren, fears of democracy, that American experience had not borne out.[63]

A new generation of democratic Americans was no longer interested in the revolutionaries' dream of building a classical republic of elitist virtue out of the inherited materials of the Old World. America, they said, would find its greatness not by emulating the states of classical antiquity, not by copying the fiscal-military powers of modern Europe, and not by producing a few notable geniuses and great-souled men. Instead, it would discover its greatness by creating a prosperous free society belonging to obscure people with their workaday concerns and their pecuniary pursuits of happiness—common people with their common interests in making money and getting ahead. No doubt the cost that America paid for this democracy was high—with its vulgarity, its materialism, its rootlessness, its anti-intellectualism. But there is no denying the wonder of it and the real earthly benefits it brought to the hitherto neglected and despised masses of common laboring people. The American Revolution created this democracy, and we are living with its consequences still.

Notes

Introduction

1. Hannah Arendt, *On Revolution* (New York, 1965), 49.

2. Carl Becker, *The History of Political Parties in the Province of New York* (Madison, 1968; first publ. 1909).

3. Bernard Bailyn, "Lines of Force in Recent Writings on the American Revolution," paper presented to the XIV International Congress of Historical Sciences (1975), 20.

4. For confirmation of this point, see Jack P. Greene, *Pursuits of Happiness: The Social Development of Early Modern British America and the Formation of American Culture* (Chapel Hill, N.C., 1988).

5. Bernard Bailyn, *The Ideological Origins of the American Revolution* (Cambridge, Mass., 1967), 283.

6. J. Franklin Jameson, *The American Revolution as a Social Movement* (Princeton, 1967; first published 1926), 9.

7. In fact, it is now doubtful whether any such class upheaval occurred even in the French Revolution. If the French Revolution should turn out not to be a real revolution after all, then there is obviously something wrong with our generic or sociological sense of what constitutes a revolution.

8. Bernard Bailyn, "The Central Themes of the American Revolution: An Interpretation," in Stephen G. Kurtz and James H. Hutson, eds., *Essays on the American Revolution* (Chapel Hill, 1973), 24; Jack P. Greene, "The Social Origins of the American Revolution: An Evaluation and an Interpretation," *Political Science Quarterly*, LXXXVIII (1973), 21.

1. Hierarchy

1. Blackstone, quoted in Jerrilyn Greene Marston, *King and Congress: The Transfer of Political Legitimacy, 1774-1776* (Princeton, 1987), 24; Franklin to William Strahan, 19 Dec. 1763, cited in Ralph Ketcham, *Presidents Above Party: The First American Presidency, 1789-1829* (Chapel Hill, 1984), 215.

2. Lord Adam Gordon, "Journal of an Officer Who Travelled in America and the West Indies in 1764 and 1765," in Newton D. Mereness, ed., *Travels in the American Colonies* (New York, 1916), 403; David John Jeremy, ed., *Henry Wansey and His American Journal, 1794* (Philadelphia, 1970), 123; William Eddis, *Letters from America*, ed. Aubrey Land (Cambridge, Mass., 1969), 58; Virginia Harrington, *The New York Merchant on the Eve of the Revolution* (New York, 1935), 21; Richard Beale Davis, *Intellectual Life in the Colonial South, 1585-1763* (Knoxville, 1978), III, 1428; Hugh Jones, *The Present State of Vir-*

ginia . . . , ed. Richard L. Morton (Chapel Hill, 1956), 80; "Governor William Bull's Representation of the Colony, 1770," *The Colonial South Carolina Scene: Contemporary Views, 1697–1774*, ed. H. Roy Merrens (Columbia, S.C., 1977), 268–69.

3. Montesquieu, *The Spirit of the Laws* (1748), trans. Thomas Nugent, ed. Franz Neumann (New York, 1949), Pt. I, bk. xix, ch. 27, p. 314; Arthur M. Wilson, "The Enlightenment Came First to England," in Stephen B. Baxter, ed., *England's Rise to Greatness, 1660–1763* (Berkeley, 1983), 1–28. In 1763 the Venetian ambassador in London was astounded by the shared language of English plebeians and patricians; it was so different from the great separation between popular and aristocratic culture that existed in Italy. Linda Colley, "Whose Nation? Class and National Consciousness in Britain, 1750–1830," *Past and Present*, CXIII (1986), 97.

4. John Brewer, *Party Ideology and Popular Politics at the Accession of George III* (New York, 1976), 243.

5. E. P. Thompson, *The Making of the English Working Class* (New York, 1963), 78; John Brooke, *King George III* (London, 1972), 56.

6. Derek Jarrett, *England in the Age of Hogarth* (London, 1974), 16–18, 21, 36; Voltaire, *Lettres Philosophiques* (1734) (Paris, 1964), Sixième Lettre, 47.

7. "Mr. Colden's Account of the State of the Province of New York," 6 Dec. 1765, in E. B. O'Callaghan and Berthold Fernow, eds., *Documents Relative to the Colonial History of the State of New York* (Albany, 1856–87), VII, 795; Jarrett, *England in the Age of Hogarth*, 18.

8. Harold Perkin, "The Social Causes of the British Industrial Revolution," Royal Historical Society, *Trans.*, 5th Ser., XVIII (1969), 123–43; Jarrett, *England in the Age of Hogarth*, 15, 16–23.

9. Ramsay, quoted in William Henry Drayton, *The Letters of Freeman, Etc.: Essays on the Nonimportation Movement in South Carolina*, ed. Robert M. Weir (Columbia, S.C., 1977), xxiii; Rush to Ebenezer Hazard, 22 Oct. 1768, in L. H. Butterfield, ed., *Letters of Benjamin Rush* (Princeton, 1951), I, 68; George W. Corner, ed., *The Autobiography of Benjamin Rush: His "Travels Through Life" together with his Commonplace Book for 1789–1813* (Princeton, 1948), 198.

10. Drayton, quoted in William D. Liddle, " 'A Patriot King, or None': Lord Bolingbroke and the American Renunciation of George III," *Journal of American History*, LXV (1979), 951.

11. Leonard W. Labaree, *Royal Government in America: A Study of the British Colonial System before 1783* (New Haven, 1930), 85–88; Richard L. Bushman, *King and People in Provincial Massachusetts* (Chapel Hill, 1985), 18–19; Marston, *King and Congress*, 25; Beverly McAnear, *The Income of the Colonial Governors of British North America* (New York, 1967), 69.

12. Arthur P. Scott, *Criminal Law in Colonial Virginia* (Chicago, 1930), 117–20; Douglas Greenberg, *Crime and Law Enforcement in the Colony of New York, 1691–1776* (Ithaca, 1974), 130–31.

13. A. G. Roeber, "Authority, Law, and Custom: The Rituals of Court Day in Tidewater Virginia, 1720 to 1750," *WMQ*, 3rd Ser., XXXVII (1980), 37; Greenberg, *Crime and Law*, 224; John Adams to William Tudor, 18 Dec. 1816, 29 Mar. 1817, in Charles F. Adams, ed., *Works of John Adams* (Boston, 1850–56), X, 233, 244–45.

14. John M. Murrin, "Political Development," in Jack P. Greene and J. R. Pole, eds., *Colonial British America: Essays in the New History of the Early Modern Era* (Baltimore, 1984), 408–56.

15. Jon Butler, *Awash in a Sea of Faith: Christianizing the American People* (Cambridge,

Mass., 1990), 98–128, 164–77, 197; Bruce E. Steiner, "New England Anglicanism, A Genteel Faith?" *WMQ,* 3rd Ser., XXVII (1970), 122–35; Bruce E. Steiner, "Anglican Officeholding in Pre-Revolutionary Connecticut: The Parameters of New England Community," ibid., XXXI (1974), 369–406; Patricia U. Bonomi, *Under the Cope of Heaven: Religion, Society, and Politics in Colonial America* (New York, 1986), 39–97.

16. David Hume, "The Rise and Progress of the Arts and Sciences," in Eugene F. Miller, ed., *Essays: Moral, Political, and Literary* (Indianapolis, 1985), 126; Abraham Williams, *A Sermon Preach'd at Boston . . . May 26, 1762,* in Edmund S. Morgan, ed., *Puritan Political Ideas, 1558–1794* (Indianapolis, 1965), 332; Christopher M. Jedry, *The World of John Cleaveland: Family and Community in Eighteenth-Century New England* (New York, 1979), 94. The social order was beautiful, said Jonathan Edwards, when the different members of the society "have all their appointed office, place and station, according to their several capacities and talents, and everyone keeps his place, and continues in his proper business." Norman Fiering, *Jonathan Edwards's Moral Thought and Its British Context* (Chapel Hill, 1981), 131.

17. Geoffroy Atkinson and Abraham C. Keller, *Prelude to the Enlightenment: French Literature, 1690–1740* (Seattle, 1970), 51–52, 56.

18. Edwards, quoted in Fiering, *Jonathan Edwards's Moral Thought and Its British Context,* 131; Alexander Pope, "Essay on Man," IV, ii, in Aubrey Williams, ed., *Poetry and Prose of Alexander Pope* (Boston, 1969), 148; A. Stuart Pitt, "The Sources, Significance, and Date of Franklin's 'An Arabian Tale,' " Modern Language Association, *Publications,* LVII (1942), 155–68; Adams, July 1756, in L. H. Butterfield et al., eds., *Diary and Autobiography of John Adams* (Cambridge, Mass., 1961), I, 39. On the eighteenth century's conception of order, see Arthur O. Lovejoy, *The Great Chain of Being: A Study of the History of an Idea* (Cambridge, Mass., 1936), 200–7; and Philip Greven, *The Protestant Temperament: Patterns of Child-Rearing, Religious Experience, and the Self in Early America* (New York, 1977), 194–98.

19. Richard Lucas, *Rules Relating to Success in Trade* (Boston, [1760]), 6; Williams, *Sermon,* in Morgan, ed., *Puritan Political Ideas,* 332; Donald K. Enholm, David Curtis Skaggs, and W. Jeffrey Welsh, "Origins of the Southern Mind: The Parochial Sermons of Thomas Cradock of Maryland, 1774–1870," *Quarterly Journal of Speech,* LXXIII (1987), 200–18.

20. Joseph Henry Benton, *Warning Out in New England, 1656–1817* (Boston, 1911).

21. Williams, *Sermon,* in Morgan, ed., *Puritan Political Ideas,* 333; Boston *Evening Post,* 13 Apr. 1763.

22. William Livingston et al., *The Independent Reflector,* ed. Milton M. Klein (Cambridge, Mass., 1963), 214; Browne, quoted in Carl Bridenbaugh, *Cities in Revolt: Urban Life in America, 1743–1776* (New York, 1955), 137.

23. Robert D. Mitchell, *Commercialism and Frontier: Perspectives on the Early Shenandoah Valley* (Charlottesville, 1977), 83; Melvin Yazawa, *From Colonies to Commonwealth: Familial Ideology and the Beginnings of the American Republic* (Baltimore, 1985), 60–66; Charles Moore, ed., *George Washington's Rules of Civility and Decent Behaviour in Company and Conversation* (Boston, 1926), 7–8.

24. Adams, Jan., Apr. 1761, in Butterfield et al., eds., *Diary of John Adams,* I, 198; Randolph Shipley Klein, *Portrait of an Early American Family: The Shippens of Pennsylvania Across Five Generations* (Philadelphia, 1975), 203; John Adams to William Tudor, 29 Jan. 1774, in Robert J. Taylor et al., eds., *Papers of John Adams,* (Cambridge, Mass., 1977–), II, 104; Labaree, *Royal Government,* 92–93; Purdie and Dixon's Williamsburg, *Va. Gazette,* 26 May 1774.

25. See John K. Alexander, *Render Them Submissive: Responses to Poverty in Philadelphia, 1760–1800* (Amherst, Mass., 1980), 11.

26. Mitchell Robert Breitwieser, *Cotton Mather and Benjamin Franklin: The Price of Representative Personality* (Cambridge, Eng., 1984), 241. Although women did not usually have designated occupations, and indeed, with the exception of widows, had little independent legal existence apart from their fathers or husbands, they did participate in the larger economy and often controlled the products of their own labor. See Laurel Thatcher Ulrich, "Martha Ballard and Her Girls: Women's Work in Eighteenth-Century Maine," in Stephen Innes, ed., *Work and Labor in Early America* (Chapel Hill, 1988), 70–105.

27. See Bernard Bailyn, *Voyagers to the West: A Passage in the Peopling of America on the Eve of the Revolution* (New York, 1986), 147–49; Edward M. Cook, Jr., *The Fathers of the Towns: Leadership and Community Structure in Eighteenth-Century New England* (Baltimore, 1976), 87–90.

28. Jonathan Boucher, *A View of the Causes and Consequences of the American Revolution* (London, 1797), 233.

29. Jackson Turner Main, *The Social Structure of Revolutionary America* (Princeton, 1965), 38; Carl Bridenbaugh, *The Colonial Craftsman* (Chicago, 1950), 96.

30. See Asa Briggs, "The Language of 'Class' in Early Nineteenth-Century England," in Asa Briggs and John Saville, eds., *Essays in Labour History: In Memory of G. D. H. Cole* (London, 1960), 43–73.

31. Williams, *Sermon*, in Morgan, ed., *Puritan Political Ideas*, 332. See Harold Perkin, *The Origins of Modern English Society, 1780–1880* (London, 1969), 17–62.

32. Fielding, *The History of the Adventures of Joseph Andrews*, ed. Martin C. Battestin (Middletown, Conn., 1967), II, xiii, 157.

33. Moore, ed., *Washington's Rules of Civility*, 9; [William Dover], *Useful Miscellanies: Or, Serious Reflections, Respecting Mens Duty to God, and Towards One Another* (London and Philadelphia, 1753), 31; Hunter Dickinson Farish, ed., *Journal and Letters of Philip Vickers Fithian* (Williamsburg, 1943), 161.

2. Patricians and Plebeians

1. Adams, Notes for "A Dissertation on the Canon and Feudal Law," (1765), in Taylor et al., eds., *Papers of John Adams*, I, 107; Douglass Adair, ed., "The Autobiography of the Reverend Devereaux Jarrett, 1732–1763," *WMQ*, 3rd Ser., IX (1952), 361. In the eighteenth century "the important hierarchical distinction was the one that set off the several elites from everyone else." In comparison with the great difference between the gentry and ordinary people, "differences between artisans and laborers were of no real consequence. The effect, needless to say, was to identify middling people much more closely with the bottom of society than with the top." Stuart M. Blumin, *The Emergence of the Middle Class: Social Experience in the American City, 1760–1900* (Cambridge, Eng., 1989), 33. John Adams grounded the political theory of his *Defence of the Constitutions of the United States*, written in 1787–88, on this traditional distinction: "The people, in all nations," he wrote, "are naturally divided into two sorts, the gentlemen and the simplemen, a word which is here chosen to signify the common people." *Defence*, in Charles F. Adams, ed., *Works of John Adams* (Boston, 1854), VI, 185. The best discussion of the distinction between gentlemen and ordinary people in

colonial America is in Rhys Isaac, *The Transformation of Virginia, 1740-1790* (Chapel Hill, 1982).

2. J. V. Beckett, *The Aristocracy in England, 1660-1914* (Oxford, 1986), 17-42; John Cannon, *Aristocratic Century: The Peerage of Eighteenth-Century England* (Cambridge, England, 1984).

3. Beckett, *Aristocracy in England,* 19. As John Adams wrote as late as 1788: "The distinctions which have been introduced among the gentlemen, into nobility greater or lesser, are perfectly immaterial to our present purpose; knights, barons, earls, viscounts, marquises, dukes, and even princes and kings, are still but gentlemen, and the word noble signifies no more than knowable, or conspicuous." *Defence,* in Adams, ed., *Works of John Adams,* VI, 185.

4. Speck, *Stability and Strife: England, 1714-1760* (Cambridge, Mass., 1970), 37; Steele, quoted in John Barrell, *English Literature in History, 1730-1780: An Equal, Wide Survey* (London, 1983), 37.

5. John Adams to Jonathan Sewell, Feb. 1760, in Taylor et al., eds., *Papers of John Adams,* I, 41; Peter Mathias, *The Transformation of England: Essays in the Economic and Social History of England in the Eighteenth Century* (London, 1979), 158; Washington, quoted in Richard Bridgman, "Jefferson's Farmer before Jefferson," *American Quarterly,* XIV (1962), 576; Jack P. Greene, ed., *The Diary of Colonel Landon Carter of Sabine Hall, 1752-1778* (Charlottesville, 1965), II, 795; Butterfield et al., eds., *Diary of John Adams,* II, 53; Charles Royster, *A Revolutionary People at War: The Continental Army and American Character, 1775-1783* (Chapel Hill, 1979), 317; Greene to Samuel Ward, 9 Oct. 1772, in Richard Showman et al., eds., *The Papers of General Nathanael Greene* (Chapel Hill, 1976-   ), I, 47; Butler, *Awash in a Sea of Faith,* 67-97; Morris, quoted in Gerald Stourzh, *Alexander Hamilton and the Idea of Republican Government* (Stanford, 1970), 80.

6. Jonathan Sewell to John Adams, 13 Feb. 1760, in Taylor et al., eds., *Papers of John Adams,* I, 40; John Randolph, quoted in Merrill Jensen, "The Articles of Confederation," in Library of Congress, *Fundamental Testaments of the American Revolution* (Washington, D.C., 1973), 56; Franklin, in Max Farrand, ed., *The Records of the Federal Convention of 1787* (New Haven, 1911, 1937), I, 83.

7. Hamilton to John Jay, 26 Nov. 1775, in Harold C. Syrett et al., eds., *The Papers of Alexander Hamilton* (New York, 1961-   ), I, 176; Samuel Mather, *The Fall of the Mighty Lamented* (Boston, 1738), 7; John Adams to Jonathan Sewell, Feb. 1760, in Taylor et al., eds., *Papers of John Adams,* I, 41; Samuel Kinser, ed., *The Memoirs of Philippe de Commynes,* trans. Isabelle Cazeauxe (Columbia, S.C., 1969), I, 361; John Locke, *Some Thoughts on Education* (1705), in James L. Axtell, ed., *The Educational Writings of John Locke* (Cambridge, Eng., 1968), 112-13; Jefferson's Hints to Americans Traveling in Europe (19 June 1788), in Julian P. Boyd et al., eds., *The Papers of Thomas Jefferson* (Princeton, 1954-55), XIII, 268.

8. Robert Micklus, "Dr. Alexander Hamilton's 'Modest Proposal,' " *Early American Literature,* XVI (1981), 114-15; Homai J. Shroof, *The Eighteenth-Century Novel: The Idea of the Gentleman (*New Delhi, 1978), 49; Hume, "Of Simplicity and Refinement in Writing," in Miller, ed., *Essays,* 191.

9. Adair, ed., "Autobiography of Devereaux Jarrett," *WMQ,* 3rd Ser., IX (1952), 361; Carl Bridenbaugh, ed., *Gentleman's Progress: The Itinerarium of Dr. Alexander Hamilton, 1744* (Chapel Hill, 1948), 90, 54-55; Alfred F. Young, "George Robert Twelves Hewes (1742-1840): A Boston Shoemaker and the Memory of the American Revolution," *WMQ,* 3rd Ser., XXXVIII (1981), 561-62; Courtlandt Canby, "Robert Munford's *The Patriots,* " *WMQ,* 3rd Ser., VI (1949), 500.

10. Adair, ed., "Autobiography of Devereaux Jarrett," *WMQ*, 3rd Ser., IX (1952), 361; Bartram, quoted in Carl Bridenbaugh, *Cities in Revolt: Urban Life in America, 1743–1776* (New York, 1955), 147–48.

11. James Reid, "The Religion of the Bible and Religion of K[ing] W[illiam] County Compared," in Richard Beale Davis, ed., *The Colonial Virginia Satirist: Mid-Eighteenth Century Commentaries on Politics, Religion, and Society,* American Philosophical Society, *Trans.*, New Ser., LVII, Pt. 1 (1967), 56.

12. Farish, ed., *Journal of Fithian*, 160–61; Hermann Wellenreuther, "A View of the Socio-Economic Structure of England and the British Colonies on the Eve of the American Revolution," in Erich Angermann et al., eds., *New Wine in Old Skins: A Comparative View of Some Political Structures and Values Affecting the American Revolution* (Stuttgart, 1976), 18; Josiah Quincy, *Memoirs of the Life of Josiah Quincy, Junior, of Massachusetts Bay, 1774–1775* (Boston, 1875), 88; Browne, quoted in Bridenbaugh, *Cities in Revolt*, 137; Bridenbaugh, ed., *Gentleman's Progress*, 199.

13. Jan. 1761, in Butterfield et al., eds., *Diary of Adams*, I, 198.

14. Mather, *Fall of the Mighty*, 10; Canby, "Robert Munford's *The Patriots*," *WMQ*, 3rd Ser., VI (1949), 499–500; Bridenbaugh, ed., *Gentleman's Progress*, 185–86.

15. Boucher, *View of the Causes*, 233; Reid, "Religion of the Bible," in Davis, ed., *Virginia Satirist*, American Philosophical Society, *Trans.*, New Ser., LVII, Pt. 1 (1967), 48; T. H. Breen, *Tobacco Culture: The Mentality of the Great Tidewater Planters on the Eve of the Revolution* (Princeton, 1985), 161.

16. Bridenbaugh, ed., *Gentleman's Progress*, 163, 8; Pauline Maier, *The Old Revolutionaries: Political Lives in the Age of Samuel Adams* (New York, 1980), 240; Bushman, *King and People*, 69–70; Jack P. Greene, "Society, Ideology, and Politics: An Analysis of the Political Culture of Mid-Eighteenth-Century Virginia," in Richard M. Jellison, ed., *Society, Freedom, and Conscience: The Coming of the Revolution in Virginia, Massachusetts, and New York* (New York, 1976), 18–19; Farish, ed., *Journal of Fithian*, 29; Bridenbaugh, *Colonial Craftsman*, 164; Alexander, *Render Them Submissive*, 18; I. W. Stuart, *Life of Jonathan Trumbull, Senior, Governor of Connecticut* (Boston, 1859), 118.

17. Jarrett, *England in the Age of Hogarth*, 79–80; Boston *Evening Post*, 14 Dec. 1761. See J. E. Crowley, *This Sheba, Self: The Conceptualization of Economic Life in Eighteenth-Century America* (Baltimore, 1974), 43–45; Isaac Hunt, *The Political Family: Or a Discourse, Pointing Out the Reciprocal Advantages Which Flow from an Uninterrupted Union Between Great Britain and Her American Colonies* (Philadelphia, 1775), 24–25. Despite his fresh thinking on so many topics, Bernard Mandeville still believed that it was "Folly to cure" the wants of the poor, for then they would stop working. John Barrell, *The Political Theory of Painting from Reynolds to Hazlitt* (New Haven, 1986), 48. See the important discussion of labor in Hannah Arendt, *The Human Condition* (Chicago, 1958), 79–135.

18. Mun, quoted in Crowley, *This Sheba, Self*, 44; Montesquieu, quoted in Nannerl O. Keohane, *Philosophy and the State in France: The Renaissance to the Enlightenment* (Princeton, 1980), 419; Jarrett, *England in the Age of Hogarth*, 93; Fielding, quoted in Robert W. Malcolmson, *Popular Recreations in English Society, 1700–1850* (New York, 1973), 156–57; Banks, quoted in G. E. Mingay, *The Gentry: The Rise and Fall of a Ruling Class* (London, 1976), 85.

19. *Pennsylvania Gazette* (Philadelphia), 1 Feb. 1770, in William Nelson, ed., *Documents Relating to the Colonial History of the State of New Jersey* (Paterson, N.J., 1905), XXVII, 26–29. (I owe this citation to Brendon McConville.)

20. Continental Association, 20 Oct. 1774, in Jack P. Greene, ed., *Colonies to Nation, 1763–1789* (New York, 1967), 247–50.

21. Jackson to Benjamin Franklin, 17 June 1755, in Leonard Labaree et al., eds., *The Papers of Benjamin Franklin* (New Haven, 1959–   ), VI, 77; Edward Gibbon, *The Decline and Fall of the Roman Empire* (Modern Library ed., New York, n.d.), I, ii, 48. On the luxury debate in England, see John Sekoura, *Luxury: The Concept in Western Thought, Eden to Smollett* (Baltimore, 1977).

22. Harrington, quoted in Lance Banning, *The Jeffersonian Persuasion: Evolution of a Party Ideology* (Ithaca, 1978), 28; Defoe, quoted in Speck, *Stability and Strife*, 32; Jackson to Franklin, 17 June 1755, Labaree et al., eds., *Papers of Franklin*, VI, 77; Farish, ed., *Journal of Fithian*, 161; Emory G. Evans, *Thomas Nelson of Yorktown: Revolutionary Virginian* (Williamsburg, 1975), 19–29. For an illuminating discussion of the ancient Roman aristocracy's attitudes toward work and leisure, see Paul Veyne, "The Roman Empire," in Paul Veyne, ed., *A History of Private Life: I. From Pagan Rome to Byzantium* (Cambridge, Mass., 1987), 117–59. These ideas of work and leisure, writes Veyne, "persisted from archaic Greece and India down to Benjamin Constant and Charles Maurras" (p. 123). It was the Revolution that changed these ideas for Americans.

23. One of the advantages of Thomas Jefferson's locating Monticello on the top of a mountain was that it removed from sight the production of the plantation's crops for distant markets and thus contributed to the illusion that Monticello was a self-contained and independent community. (I owe this point to information supplied by Daniel P. Jordan, executive director, and Cinder Stanton, director of research of the Thomas Jefferson Memorial Foundation.)

24. Buffon, quoted in Antonello Gerbi, *The Dispute of the New World: The History of a Polemic, 1750–1900*, trans. Jeremy Moyle (Pittsburgh, 1973), 19–20. Donald M. Scott's significant book *From Office to Profession: The New England Ministry, 1750–1850* (Philadelphia, 1978) rests on the assumption that the position of the eighteenth-century clergy was something other than that of a modern professional. And Gerard W. Gawalt is quite correct in arguing that the acceptance of lawyers as gentlemen required their having no direct tie between their work and their income. Gawalt, *The Promise of Power: The Legal Profession in Massachusetts, 1760–1840* (Westport, Conn., 1979), 16–19.

25. Locke, quoted in Harold Nicolson, *Good Behaviour: Being a Study of Certain Types of Civility* (New York, 1956), 194; Laurens to Richard Oswald, 7 July 1764, in Philip M. Hamer et al., eds., *The Papers of Henry Laurens* (Columbia, S.C., 1968–   ), IV, 338; Rachel N. Klein, "Ordering the Backcountry: The South Carolina Regulation," *WMQ*, 3rd Ser., XXXVIII (1981), 667; Edward C. Papenfuse, *In Pursuit of Profit: The Annapolis Merchants in the Era of the American Revolution, 1763–1805* (Baltimore, 1975), 141.

26. Addison, *The Spectator*, No. 549, cited in Shroff, *Eighteenth-Century Novel*, 39; *New England Magazine* (Mar. 1759), quoted in Bridgman, "Jefferson's Farmer," *American Quarterly*, XIV (1962), 568.

27. [Franklin], Silence Dogood, No. 5, 28 May 1722, in Labaree et al., eds., *Papers of Franklin*, I, 19; George C. Rogers, Jr., et al., eds., *The Papers of Henry Laurens* (Columbia, S.C., 1974–   ), V, 80n.; "Letters and Papers of John Singleton Copley and Henry Pelham, 1739–1776," Mass. Historical Society, *Coll.*, LXXI (1914), 661–66. "By the common people," wrote John Adams in his *Defence of the Constitutions*, "we mean laborers, husbandmen, mechanics, and merchants in general, who pursue their occupations and industry without any knowledge in liberal arts or sciences, or in any thing but their own trades or pursuits." Adams, ed., *Works of John Adams*, VI, 185.

28. Farish, ed., *Journal of Fithian*, 161; Harrington, *New York Merchant*, 16; Brown, *Virginia*, 35.

29. Joseph Ward to John Adams, 3 Dec. 1775, John Trumbull to John Adams, 14 Nov. 1775, in Taylor et al., eds., *Papers of John Adams*, III, 343, 300.

30. Samuel Osgood to John Adams, 30 Nov. 1775, in Taylor et al., eds., *Papers of John Adams*, III, 328; John C. Miller, *Alexander Hamilton: Portrait in Paradox* (New York, 1959), 5. For an insightful discussion of honor among the Continental army officers, see Charles Royster, *A Revolutionary People at War: The Continental Army and American Character, 1775–1783* (Chapel Hill, 1979), 88–96, 199–200, 206–10, 337–38.

31. Adams to Charles Cushing, 19 Oct. 1756, to Mercy Otis Warren, 3 Jan. 1775, in Taylor et al., eds., *Papers of John Adams*, I, 22; II, 210.

32. Montesquieu, *The Spirit of the Laws* (1748), ed. Franz Neumann (New York, 1949), Pt. I, bk. iii, ch. 7, p. 25; David Hartley, *Observations on Man, His Frame, His Duty, and His Expectations. In Two Parts* (London, 1749), II, 261, 260.

33. Boston *Evening Post*, 29 Aug. 1763.

34. John E. O'Connor, *William Paterson: Lawyer and Statesman, 1745–1806* (New Brunswick, 1979), 14. See Montesquieu, *Spirit of the Laws*, ed. Neumann, Pt. II, bk. xxviii, ch. 20, p. 117.

35. Putnam, *The Memoirs of Rufus Putnam* (Boston, 1903), 23.

36. Pierre Marambaud, *William Byrd of Westover, 1674–1744* (Charlottesville, 1971), 167.

37. Samuel Breck, *Recollections . . . with Passages from His Note Books, 1774–1862*, ed. H. E. Scudder (Philadelphia, 1877), 34–36, 91, 108–9.

3. Patriarchal Dependence

1. Montesquieu, *Spirit of the Laws*, ed. Neumann, Pt. I, bk. i, ch. 3, p. 6; Defoe, quoted in Maximillian E. Novak, ed., *English Literature in the Age of Disguise* (Berkeley, 1977), 28; Joseph Addison, Richard Steele et al., *The Spectator* (New York, 1906), No. 189, II, 79.

2. [Dover], *Useful Miscellanies*, 27; "Observations of James Glen on His General Instructions" (1753), in Leonard Woods Labaree, ed., *Royal Instructions to British Colonial Governors, 1670–1776* (New York, 1935), II, 883; Henry R. McIlwaine, ed., *Journals of the House of Burgesses of Virginia, 1752–1755, 1756–1758* (Richmond, 1909), 5; [Anon.], *Some Observations Relating to the Present Circumstances of Massachusetts-Bay* (Boston, 1750), in Andrew McFarland Davis, ed., *Colonial Currency Reprints, 1682–1751* (Boston, 1911), IV, 414, 428; Robert A. Gross, *The Minutemen and Their World* (New York, 1976), 107; Samuel Willard, *A Complete Body of Divinity in Two Hundred and Fifty Expository Lectures on the Assembly's Shorter Catechism* (Boston, 1726), 598, 600; Greven, *The Protestant Temperament*, 178–79; Liddle, "Patriot King," *Journal of American History*, LXV (1979), 955.

3. John J. Waters, "Family, Inheritance, and Migration in Colonial New England: The Evidence from Guilford, Connecticut," *WMQ*, 3rd Ser., XXXIX (1982), 71; James Lockwood, *Religion the Highest Interest of a Civil Community, and Surest Means of Its Prosperity* (New London, 1754), 33.

4. Waters, "Family, Inheritance, and Migration," *WMQ*, 3rd Ser., XXXIX (1982), 66; Robert J. Taylor, *Western Massachusetts in the Revolution* (Providence, 1954), 13–14; Kevin M. Sweeney, "River Gods in the Making: The Williamses of Western Massachusetts," in Peter Benes, ed., *The Bay and the River* (Boston, 1982), 101–16; Ronald K. Snell, " 'Ambitious of Honor and Places': The Magistracy of Hampshire County, Massachusetts, 1692–1760," in Bruce C. Daniels, ed., *Power and Status: Officeholding in Colonial*

America (Middletown, Conn., 1986), 24–25, 35; M. Eugene Sirmans, "The South Carolina Royal Council, 1720–1763," *WMQ,* XVIII (1961), 378; David Alan Williams, "The Small Virginia Farmer in Eighteenth-Century Virginia Politics," *Agricultural History,* XLIII (1969), 91–101; Leonard Woods Labaree, *Conservatism in Early American History* (New York, 1948), 17.

5. Daniel Blake Smith, *Inside the Great House: Planter Life in Eighteenth-Century Chesapeake Society* (Ithaca, 1980), 150–54, 175–230; Emory G. Evans, *Thomas Nelson of Yorktown: Revolutionary Virginian* (Williamsburg, 1975), 8–9; Allan Kulikoff, " 'Throwing the Stocking': A Gentry Marriage in Provincial Maryland," *Maryland Historical Magazine,* LXXI (1976), 517n.; Gross, *Minutemen and Their World,* 71; Fred Anderson, *A People's Army: Massachusetts Soldiers and Society in the Seven Years' War* (Chapel Hill, 1984), 42; Gary Wills, *Inventing America: Jefferson's Declaration of Independence* (New York, 1978), 36.

6. Daniel Scott Smith, " 'All in Some Degree Related to Each Other': A Demographic and Comparative Resolution of the Anomaly of New England Kinship," *American Historical Review,* XCIV (1989), 44–79; Daniel Scott Smith, "Genealogy, Geography, and Genesis of Social Structure: Household and Kinship in Early America," Conference in Anglo-American Social History, 5–7 Sept. 1985, Williamsburg, Va.

7. James A. Henretta, "Families and Farms: Mentalité in Pre-Industrial America," *WMQ,* 3rd Ser., XXXV (1978), 3–38; Jedry, *World of John Cleaveland,* 74, 77; Canby, "Robert Munford's *The Patriots,*" *WMQ,* 3rd Ser., VI (1949), 463; Smith, *Inside the Great House,* 229; Waters, "Family, Inheritance, and Migration," *WMQ,* 3rd Ser., XXXIX (1982), 76.

8. Toby L. Ditz, *Property and Kinship: Inheritance in Early Connecticut, 1750–1820* (Princeton, 1986), 57, 64, 102. See Carole Shammas, Marylynn Salmon, and Michel Dahlin, *Inheritance in America from Colonial Times to the Present* (New Brunswick, 1987).

9. C. Ray Keim, "The Influence of Primogeniture and Entail in the Development of Virginia" (Ph.D. Diss., University of Chicago, 1926), 56, 60–62, 110–14, 122, 195–96; Keim, "Primogeniture and Entail in Colonial Virginia," *WMQ,* 3rd Ser. XXV (1968), 545–86; Jedry, *World of John Cleaveland,* 80; John J. Waters, "Patrimony, Succession, and Social Stability: Guilford, Connecticut, in the Eighteenth Century," *Perspectives in American History,* X (1976), 160.

10. Ditz, *Property and Kinship,* 153–55.

11. Smith, *Inside the Great House,* 183; Margaret E. Martin, *Merchants and Trade of the Connecticut River Valley, 1750–1820* (Northampton, Mass., 1939), 15; Harrington, *New York Merchant,* 51–52; Bridenbaugh, *Colonial Craftsman,* 126–27; Arthur Cecil Bining, *Pennsylvania Iron Manufacture in the Eighteenth Century* (Harrisburg, 1979), 126.

12. Harry Roy Merrens, *Colonial North Carolina in the Eighteenth Century: A Study in Historical Geography* (Chapel Hill, 1964), 27; A. Roger Ekirch, *"Poor Carolina": Politics and Society in Colonial North Carolina, 1729–1776* (Chapel Hill, 1981), 51–85; Edward M. Cook, Jr., *The Fathers of the Towns: Leadership and Community Structure in Eighteenth-Century New England* (Baltimore, 1976), 101, and esp. ch. 4; Thomas L. Purvis, " 'High-Born, Long-Recorded Families': Social Origins of New Jersey Assemblymen, 1703 to 1776," *WMQ,* 3rd Ser., XXXVII (1980), 599; Thomas L. Purvis, *Proprietors, Patronage, and Paper Money: Legislative Politics in New Jersey, 1703–1776* (New Brunswick, 1986); Smith, "Genealogy, Geography, and the Genesis of Social Structure," Conference, 5–7 Sept. 1985, Williamsburg, Va.; Bruce C. Daniels, "Family Dynasties in Connecticut's Largest Towns, 1700–1760," *Canadian Journal of History,* VIII (1973), 99; Brown, *Virginia,* 217; John Adams, *Defence of the Constitutions of the United States* (1787), in Adams, ed., *Works,*

IV, 393; William F. Willingham, "Deference Democracy and Town Government in Windham, Connecticut, 1755 to 1786," *WMQ*, 3rd Ser., XXX (1973), 401-22.

13. Waters, "Patrimony, Succession, and Social Stability," *Perspectives in American History*, X (1976), 140; Smith, *In the Great House*, 76, 159, 160, 161, 165; Mary Beth Norton, *Liberty's Daughters: The Revolutionary Experience of American Women, 1750-1800* (Boston, 1980), 61, 63, 146.

14. Sir Robert Filmer, *Patriarcha and Other Political Works*, ed. Peter Laslett (Oxford, 1949), 96; Kathryn Preyer, "Crime, the Criminal Law, and Reform in Post-Revolutionary Virginia," *Law and History Review*, I (1983), 64; John F. Walzer, "A Period of Ambivalence: Eighteenth-Century Childhood," in Lloyd DeMauss, ed., *The History of Childhood* (New York, 1974), 365.

15. Louis Morton, *Robert Carter of Nomini Hall: A Virginia Tobacco Planter of the Eighteenth Century*, 2nd ed. (Williamsburg, 1945), 225.

16. Smith, *In the Great House*, 140-41.

17. Jedry, *World of John Cleaveland*, 73, 63-64, 73-74, 78; Alexander, *Render Them Submissive*, 12; Henretta, "Families and Farms," *WMQ*, 3rd Ser., XXXV (1978), 5-7; Waters, "Patrimony, Succession and Social Stability," *Perspectives in American History*, X (1976), 150; Waters, "Family, Inheritance, and Migration, *WMQ*, 3rd Ser., XXXIX (1982), 71; Gross, *Minutemen and Their World*, 75-76, 78; Tom Brownsword, "Moses Cooper's Tale of Wealth and Status: A Case Study of Rural Rhode Island, 1674-1808" (Honors Thesis, Brown University, 1986), 17-18; Locke, *Some Thoughts on Education*, ed. Axtell, 146; Klein, *Shippens of Pennsylvania*, 212.

18. Abbot Emerson Smith, *Colonists in Bondage: White Servitude and Convict Labor in America, 1607-1776* (Chapel Hill, 1947), 336; Marcus W. Jernegan, *Laboring and Dependent Classes in Colonial America, 1607-1783* (Chicago, 1931), 55; Eric Foner, *Tom Paine and Revolutionary America* (New York, 1976), 43.

19. Laurens, quoted in Philip Morgan, "Three Planters and Their Slaves: Perspectives on Slavery in Virginia, South Carolina, and Jamaica," in Winthrop Jordan and Sheila L. Skemp, eds., *Race and Family in the Colonial South* (Jackson, Miss., 1987), 60-61; Arthur Zilversmit, *The First Emancipation: The Abolition of Slavery in the North* (Chicago, 1967), 4; Gary Nash, *The Urban Crucible: Social Change, Political Consciousness, and the Origins of the American Revolution* (Cambridge, Mass., 1979), 107-8.

20. Thomas Jefferson, *Notes on the State of Virginia*, ed. William Peden (Chapel Hill, 1954), 162; Reid, "The Religion of the Bible," ed. Davis, *Virginia Satirist*, American Philosophical Society, *Trans.* (1967), 56.

21. Jernegan, *Laboring and Dependent Classes*, 55, 52; Richard B. Morris, *Government and Labor in Early America* (New York, 1946), 310, 345-63; Jackson Turner Main, *The Social Structure of Revolutionary America* (Princeton, 1965), 33-34; Bailyn, *Voyagers to the West*, 292; Chessman A. Herrick, *White Servitude in Pennsylvania* (Philadelphia, 1926), 271; Sharon V. Salinger, *"To Serve Well and Faithfully": Labor and Indentured Servants in Pennsylvania, 1692-1800* (Cambridge, Eng., 1987).

22. James Habersham to Laurens, 22 Feb. 1768, Laurens to Habersham, 25 Jan. 1768, to James Wright, 27 Feb. 1768, in Rogers et al., eds., *Papers of Henry Laurens*, V, 602, 565, 609; Martin, *Merchants and Trade of the Connecticut River*, 102.

23. Lawrence W. Towner, "The Indentures of Boston's Poor Apprentices: 1734-1805," Colonial Society of Massachusetts, *Publications*, XLIII (1956-63), 417-68; Robert F. Seybolt, *Apprenticeship Education in Colonial New England and New York* (New York, 1917).

24. Bridenbaugh, *Cities in Revolt*, 147; Bridenbaugh, *Colonial Craftsman*, 129.

25. Ann Kussmaul, *Servants in Husbandry in Early Modern England* (Cambridge, Eng., 1981), 3–4, 49, 38–39.

26. David Galenson, *White Servitude in Colonial America: An Economic Analysis* (Cambridge, Eng., 1981), 7–13.

27. Smith, *Colonists in Bondage*, 265, 276; Morris, *Government and Labor*, 373, 433, 437, 449, 484.

28. Eddis, *Letters from America*, ed. Land, 38; Herrick, *White Servitude in Pennsylvania*, 272–83, 213; Aleine Austin, *Matthew Lyon, "New Man" of the Democratic Revolution, 1794–1822* (University Park, Pa., 1981), 10; Galenson, *White Servitude in Colonial America*, 231n.; Ulysses Prentiss Hedrick, *A History of Agriculture in the State of New York* (New York, 1933), 78.

29. Thomas Bacon, *Sermons Addressed to Masters and Servants, and Published in the Year 1743, and Now republished by the Rev. William Meade* (Winchester, Va. [1813]), 3; Marambaud, *William Byrd*, 169.

30. Greene, ed., *Diary of Landon Carter*, II, 941; Edward M. Riley, ed., *The Journal of John Harrower* (Williamsburg, Va., 1963), 38.

31. Rowland Bertoff and John M. Murrin, "Feudalism, Communalism, and the Yeoman Freeholder: The American Revolution Considered as a Social Accident," in Stephen G. Kurtz and James H. Hutson, eds., *Essays on the American Revolution* (Chapel Hill, 1973), 270; Sung Bok Kim, *Landlord and Tenant in Colonial New York: Manorial Society, 1664–1775* (Chapel Hill, 1978), 238, 279; Patricia U. Bonomi, *A Factious People: Politics and Society in Colonial New York* (New York, 1971), 185–96; Morton, *Robert Carter*, 72–76, 80; Willard F. Bliss, "The Rise of Tenancy in Virginia," *Virginia Magazine of History and Biography*, LVIII (1950), 429; Gregory A. Siverson, *Poverty in a Land of Plenty: Tenancy in Eighteenth-Century Maryland* (Baltimore, 1977), 86, 144–49, 40–41; Jerome H. Wood, *Conestoga Crossroads: Lancaster, Pennsylvania, 1730–1790* (Harrisburg, Pa., 1979), 171–72.

32. Bliss, "Rise of Tenancy," *Virginia Magazine of History and Biography*, LVIII (1950), 435; Edward Countryman, *A People in Revolution: The American Revolution and Political Society in New York, 1760–1790* (Baltimore, 1981), 18–19; Bonomi, *A Factious People*, 192–93; Morton, *Robert Carter*, 73; Kim, *Landlord and Tenant*, 310, 328. For the conditions of American tenantry that weakened its monarchical implications, see below, ch. 7.

33. James Wilson, *Considerations on the Nature and Extent of the Legislative Authority of the British Parliament* (1774), in Robert Green McCloskey, ed., *The Works of James Wilson* (Cambridge, Mass., 1967), II, 741. See Jack P. Greene, *All Men Are Created Equal: Some Reflections on the Character of the American Revolution* (Oxford, 1976), 20, 21.

4. Patronage

1. [John Trenchard and Thomas Gordon], *Cato's Letters, or Essays on Liberty, Civil and Religious, and Other Important Subjects* (London, 1733), No. 60, II, 229; William Livingston et al., *Independent Reflector*, ed. Klein, 216.

2. Bacon, *Sermons Addressed to Masters and Servants*, 1–2.

3. See Perkin, *Origins of Modern English Society*, 49.

4. John Adams to Nathan Webb, 12 Oct. 1755, in Taylor et al., eds., *Papers of John Adams*, I, 5; John J. Waters, Jr., *The Otis Family in Provincial and Revolutionary Massachusetts* (Chapel Hill, 1968), 103; Bridenbaugh, *Colonial Craftsman*, 102; Richard J. Hooker, ed., *The Carolina Backcountry on the Eve of the Revolution: The Journal and Other Writings of Charles Woodmason, American Itinerant* (Chapel Hill, 1953), 10; Farish, ed., *Journal of Fithian*,

215; Norton, *Liberty's Daughters*, 103; Canby, "Robert Munford's *The Patriots*," *WMQ*, 3rd Ser., VI (1949), 495; Smith, *In the Great House*, 104, 136, 160, 161; Putnam, *Memoir*, 25.

5. M. J. Daunton, "Towns and Economic Growth in Eighteenth-Century England," Philip Abrams and E. A. Wrigley, eds., *Towns in Societies: Essays in Economic History and Historical Sociology* (Cambridge, Eng., 1978), 247–48; Maxine Berg, *The Age of Manufactures: Industry, Innovation and Work in Britain, 1700–1820* (London, 1985), 48; Speck, *Stability and Strife*, 66: Bridenbaugh, *Cities in Revolt*, 5.

6. Claude-Anne Lopez and Eugenia W. Herbert, *The Private Franklin: The Man and His Family* (New York, 1975), 16–17.

7. Nancy Cott, "Eighteenth-Century Family and Social Life Revealed in Divorce Records," *Journal of Social History*, X (1976–77), 22–24.

8. J. A. Leo Lemay and P. M. Zall, eds., *Benjamin Franklin's Autobiography* (New York, 1986), 54.

9. Adams to William Tudor, 4 Aug. 1774, 24 July 1774, in Taylor et al., eds., *Papers of John Adams*, II, 126, 127, 114.

10. Scott, *Criminal Law in Colonial Virginia*, 181–83; William E. Nelson, *Americanization of the Common Law: The Impact of Legal Change on Massachusetts Society, 1760–1830* (Cambridge, Mass., 1975), 39–40.

11. Bridenbaugh, ed., *Gentleman's Progress*, 146; Eddis, *Letters from America*, ed. Land, 38; *Pennsylvania Gazette* (Philadelphia), 7 Feb. 1740; Herrick, *White Servitude in Pennsylvania*, 224, 226.

12. Gordon S. Wood, "Conspiracy and the Paranoid Style: Causality and Deceit in the Eighteenth Century," *WMQ*, 3rd Ser., XXXIX (1982), 401–41.

13. Jackson Turner Main, "Government by the People: The American Revolution and the Democratization of the Legislatures," *WMQ*, 3rd Ser., XXIII (1966), 391–407; Countryman, *A People in Revolution*, 73; John J. Teunissen, "Blockheadism and the Propaganda Plays of the American Revolution," *Early American Literature*, VII (1976), 148–62.

14. Eddis, *Letters from America*, ed. Land, 22; Robert M. Weir, " 'The Harmony We Were Famous For': An Interpretation of Pre-Revolutionary South Carolina Politics," *WMQ*, 3rd Ser., XXVI (1969), 482; Victor C. Johnson, "Fair Trading and Smuggling in Philadelphia, 1754–1763," *Pennsylvania Magazine of History and Biography*, LXXXII (1959), 125–49; Bruce C. Daniels, "The 'Particular Courts' of Local Government: Town Councils in Eighteenth-Century Rhode Island," *Rhode Island History*, XLI (1982), 63.

15. Boston *Gazette*, 21 Dec. 1761; Waters, *Otis Family*, 119; Hugh F. Bell, " 'A Personal Challenge': The Otis-Hutchinson Currency Controversy, 1761–1762," *Essex Institute Historical Collections*, CVI (1970), 297–323.

16. Henry Laurens to James Habersham, 5 Sept. 1767, to George Appleby, 24 May 1768, to James Penman, 13 Oct. 1767, in Rogers, Jr. et al., eds., *Papers of Henry Laurens*, V, 297, 298, 688–89, 355; David Duncan Wallace, *The Life of Henry Laurens* . . . (New York, 1915), 137–39; Carl Ubbelohde, *The Vice-Admiralty Courts and the American Revolution* (Chapel Hill, 1960), 105–14.

17. William Smith, Jr., *The History of the Province of New York*, ed. Michael Kammen (Cambridge, Mass., 1972), II, 89, 105; Lawrence Lee, *The Lower Cape Fear in Colonial Days* (Chapel Hill, 1965), 246; Martin, *Merchants and Trade*, 159; Labaree, *Royal Government*, 163.

18. [Dover], *Useful Miscellanies*, 29; Papenfuse, *In Pursuit of Profit*, 15–29; Nash, *The Urban Crucible*, 259.

19. Adams, *Defence of the Constitutions*, in Adams, ed., *Works of John Adams*, IV, 392; George M. Curtis III, "The Goodrich Family and the Revolution in Virginia, 1774–1776," *Virginia Magazine of History and Biography*, LXXXIV (1976), 53; Thomas M. Doerflinger, *A Vigorous Spirit of Enterprise: Merchants and Economic Development in Revolutionary Philadelphia* (Chapel Hill, 1986), 38.

20. See Keith Tribe, *Land, Labour, and Economic Discourse* (London, 1978), 37, 44, 51, 56, 59, 82, 83.

21. Janet Riesman, "The Origins of American Political Economy, 1690–1781" (Ph.D. Diss., Brown University, 1983), 302–33, 146.

22. Crowley, *This Sheba, Self*, 88, 97–99, 38–39; [Smith], *Independent Reflector*, ed. Klein, 106.

23. Richard Lucas, *Rules Relating to Success in Trade* (Boston, [1760]), 10; [Anon.], *Debtor and Creditor: Or a Discourse on the Following Words, Have Patience with Me, and I will pay thee all* (Boston, 1762), 7–10; Martin, *Merchant and Trade*, 149, 153, 157; W. C. Plummer, "Consumer Credit in Colonial Philadelphia," *Pennsylvania Magazine of History and Biography*, LXVI (1942), 388–97; Peter J. Parker, "The Philadelphia Printer: A Study of an Eighteenth-Century Businessman," *Business History Review*, XL (1966), 26–37.

24. Henretta, "Families and Farms," *WMQ*, 3rd Ser., XXXV (1978), 3–32; Jedry, *World of John Cleaveland*, 64–70, 91–92; Bridgman, "Jefferson's Farmer before Jefferson," *American Quarterly*, XIV (1962), 567–77; Winifred B. Rothenberg, "The Emergence of a Capital Market in Rural Massachusetts, 1730–1838," *Journal of Economic History*, XLV (1985), 781–808.

25. Michael Merrill, "Cash Is Good to Eat: Self-Sufficiency and Exchange in the Rural Economy of the United States," *Radical History Review*, IV (1977), 42–71; Christopher Clark, "Household Economy, Market Exchange and the Rise of Capitalism in the Connecticut Valley, 1800–1860," *Journal of Social History*, XIII (1979), 169–89; Bettye Hobbs Pruitt, "Self-Sufficiency and the Agricultural Economy of Eighteenth-Century Massachusetts," *WMQ*, 3rd Ser., XLI (1984), 333–64; Christopher Clark, *The Roots of Rural Capitalism: Western Massachusetts, 1780–1860* (Ithaca, 1990).

26. Bruce H. Mann, *Neighbors and Strangers: Law and Community in Early Connecticut* (Chapel Hill, 1987).

27. Washington to Thomas Jefferson, 20 July 1770, in John C. Fitzpatrick, ed., *The Writings of George Washington* (Washington, D.C., 1931–44), III, 18.

28. George V. Taylor, "Noncapitalist Wealth and the Origins of the French Revolution," *American Historical Review*, LXII (1967), 469–96; William Doyle, *Origins of the French Revolution* (Oxford, 1980), 17–18.

29. Quincy, *Memoir*, 19.

30. Adam Smith, *An Inquiry into the Nature and Causes of the Wealth of Nations*, eds. R. H. Campbell and A. S. Skinner (Oxford, 1976), I, 265 (xi. p. 8); John Witherspoon, "Speech in Congress on Finances," in *The Works of John Witherspoon* . . . (Edinburgh, 1805), IX, 133–34.

31. Taylor, *Western Massachusetts*, 20; Robert A. East, *Business Enterprise in the American Revolutionary Era* (New York, 1938), 20–22; Aubrey C. Land, "Economic Base and Social Structure: The Northern Chesapeake in the Eighteenth Century," *Journal of Economic History*, XXV (1965), 650; Robert D. Mitchell, *Commercialism and Frontier: Perspectives on the Early Shenandoah Valley* (Charlottesville, 1977), 116, 123; Martin, *Merchants and Trade*, 159; Isaac, *Transformation of Virginia*, 133; Breen, *Tobacco Culture*, 154.

32. Thomas Hutchinson, *The History of the Colony and Province of Massachusetts-Bay*, ed. Lawrence S. Mayo (Cambridge, 1936), II, 299, 155.

33. George Athan Billias, "The Massachusetts Land Bankers of 1740," *University of Maine Bulletin*, LXI (1959), 16-31; Taylor, *Western Massachusetts*, 20-21.

34. Jacob M. Price, *France and the Chesapeake: A History of the French Tobacco Monopoly, 1674-1791, and of Its Relationship to the British and American Tobacco Trades* (Ann Arbor, 1973), I, 662.

35. Land, "Economic Base and Social Structure," *Journal of Economic History*, XXV (1965), 645, 653; Eddis, *Letters from America*, ed. Land, xvi.

36. Jay B. Hubbell and Douglass Adair, "Robert Munford's *The Candidates*," *WMQ*, 3rd Ser., V (1948), 252, 240, 241; Canby, "Robert Munford's *The Patriots*," *WMQ*, 3rd Ser., VI (1949), 457; Smith, *Inside the Great House*, 212, 255; Greene, ed., *Diary of Landon Carter*, II, 627; Charles Carroll to his son, 16 Oct. 1759, in Richard Beale Davis, *Intellectual Life in the Colonial South* (Knoxville, 1978), III, 1588; Charles S. Sydnor, *Gentleman Freeholders: Political Practices in Washington's Virginia* (Chapel Hill, 1952), 123.

37. Hendrick Hartog, "The Public Law of a County Court: Judicial Government in Eighteenth-Century Massachusetts," *American Journal of Legal History*, XX (1976), 321-23; Roeber, "Authority, Law, and Custom," *WMQ*, 3rd Ser., XXXVII (1980), 39, 46.

38. Breck, *Recollections*, 36-37; Esther Singleton, *Social New York under the Georges, 1714-1776* (Port Washington, N.Y.), I, 8-9; Linda Kealey, "Patterns of Punishment: Massachusetts in the Eighteenth Century," *American Journal of Legal History*, XXX (1986), 163-76.

39. Robert Micklus, " 'The History of the Tuesday Club': A Mock-Jeremiad of the Colonial South," *WMQ*, 3rd Ser., XL (1983), 42-61; Bushman, *King and People*, 80; Jonathan Powell, "Presbyterian Loyalists: A 'Chain of Interest' in Philadelphia," *Journal of Presbyterian History*, LVII (1979), 150-51.

40. Waters, *Otis Family*, 94; Anderson, *A People's Army*, 72; "Journal of Colonel John Winslow . . . in . . . 1755," Nova Scotia Historical Society, *Coll.*, IV (1885), 117; Samuel Osgood to John Adams, 4 Dec. 1775, in Taylor et al., eds., *Papers of John Adams*, I, 353.

41. Adams to Richard Cranch, 18 Oct. 1756, in Taylor et al., eds., *Papers of John Adams*, I, 20; James Thomas Flexner, *George Washington: The Forge of Experience (1732-1775)* (Boston, 1965), 41, 52; Waters, *Otis Family*, 91-92; Klein, *Shippens of Pennsylvania*, 143.

42. Linda Rees Heaton, " 'This Excellent Man': Littleton Waller Tazewell's Sketch of Benjamin Waller," *Virginia Magazine of History and Biography*, LXXXIX (1981), 147, 148, 149-50.

43. David Mays, *Edmund Pendleton, 1721-1803: A Biography*, 2 vols. (Cambridge, Mass., 1952), I, 11-12; Aubrey C. Land, *The Dulanys of Maryland: A Biographical Study of Daniel Dulany, the Elder (1685-1753), and Daniel Dulany, the Younger (1722-1797)* (Baltimore, 1955), 3; Hamilton to Edward Stevens, 11 Nov. 1769, in Syrett et al., eds., *Papers of Hamilton*, I, 4; Willard Sterne Randall, *Benedict Arnold: Patriot and Traitor* (New York, 1990), 34-36.

44. Lemay and Zall, eds., *Benjamin Franklin's Autobiography*, 23, 26, 45, 51, 75.

45. Paul W. Conner, *Poor Richard's Politicks: Benjamin Franklin and His New American Order* (Oxford, 1965), 152; *Poor Richard Improved* (1749), in Labaree et al., eds., *Papers of Franklin*, III, 344-45.

46. Franklin, *Proposals Relating to the Education of Youth in Pennsylvania* (1749), in La-baree et al., eds., *Papers of Franklin*, III, 400n.

47. Franklin to Hume, 19 May 1962, in Labaree et al., eds., *Papers of Franklin*, X, 84.

5. Political Authority

1. Carl Van Doren, *Benjamin Franklin* (New York, 1938), 211–12; David Freeman Hawke, *Franklin* (New York, 1976), 114–15; Lopez and Herbert, *The Private Franklin*, 53–55, 102, 111.

2. For examples of government influence, see Allan Gallay, "Jonathan Bryan's Plantation Empire: Land, Politics, and the Formation of a Ruling Class in Colonial Georgia," *WMQ*, 3rd Ser., XLV (1988), 253–79; Glenn Weaver, *Jonathan Trumbull: Connecticut's Merchant Magistrate (1710-1785)* (Hartford, 1956), 35; and the essays in Bruce C. Daniels, ed., *Power and Status: Officeholding in Colonial America* (Middletown, Conn., 1986).

3. Marston, *King and Congress*, 31; Hume, "Of the Rise and Progress of the Arts and Sciences," "Of the Independency of Parliament," *Essays*, ed. Miller, 127, 45; Rev. John Brown, *Estimate of the Manners and Principles of the Times* (1758), in E. Neville Williams, ed., *The Eighteenth-Century Constitution, 1688-1815* (Cambridge, Eng., 1960), 140.

4. William Paley, quoted in Bernard Bailyn, *The Origins of American Politics* (New York, 1968), 72–73; Bushman, *King and People*, 82.

5. Byron Fairchild, *Messrs. William Pepperell: Merchants at Piscataqua* (Ithaca, 1954), 174–75.

6. Charles G. Sellers, Jr., "Private Profits and British Colonial Policy: The Speculations of Henry McCulloh," *WMQ*, 3rd Ser., VIII (1951), 535–51.

7. Eddis, *Letters from America*, ed. Land, 16, 26; Land, *Dulanys of Maryland*, 228; William Douglass, quoted in Bushman, *King and People*, 75; Purvis, *Proprietors, Patronage, and Paper Money*, 124–27; John Murrin, "Review Essay," *History and Theory*, XI (1972), 268; William Douglass, *A Summary, Historical and Political, of the First Planting, Progressive Improvements, and Present State of the British Settlements in North America*, 2 vols. (Boston, 1749, 1751), I, 472.

8. *Constitutional Gazette* (New York), 24 Feb. 1776; 9 Feb. 1773, in Butterfield et al., eds., *Diary of John Adams*, II, 53; Gordon S. Wood, *The Creation of the American Republic, 1776-1787* (Chapel Hill, 1969), 78; Boston *Evening Post*, 5 Sept. 1763, in Taylor et al., eds., *Papers of John Adams*, I, 92.

9. Bushman, *King and People*, 97–99, 253–67.

10. Providence *Gazette*, 26 Feb. 1767.

11. [Trenchard and Gordon], *Cato's Letters*, No. 90, III, 200; Wood, *Creation of the American Republic*, 154–55; Bailyn, *Origins of American Politics*, 102.

12. Hartog, "Public Law of a County Court," *American Journal of Legal History*, XX (1976), 282–329; William E. Nelson, "The Eighteenth-Century Background of John Marshall's Constitutional Jurisprudence," *Michigan Law Review*, LXXVI (1978), 902–4.

13. Judson P. Wood and John S. Ezell, eds., *The New Democracy in America: Travels of Francisco de Miranda in the United States, 1783-1784* (Norman, Okla., 1963), 35; Robert Zemsky, *Merchants, Farmers, and River Gods: An Essay on Eighteenth-Century Politics* (Boston, 1971), 2; Douglass, *Summary, Historical and Political*, I, 507.

14. Hendrick Hartog, *Public Property and Private Power: The Corporation of the City of New York in American Law, 1730-1870* (Chapel Hill, 1983), 62–68

15. Francis Hutcheson, *A System of Moral Philosophy in Three Books* . . . (London, 1755), II, 113; Jefferson to James Monroe, 20 May 1782, in Boyd et al., eds., *Papers of Jefferson*, VI, 185–86.

16. Washington to James Wood [July 1758], in Fitzpatrick, ed., *The Writings of George Washington*, II, 251; William Pencak, *America's Burke: The Mind of Thomas Hutchinson* (Washington, D.C., 1982), 3–4.

17. Wood, *Creation of the American Republic*, 145; Williams, "Small Farmer in Virginia Politics," *Agricultural History*, XLIII (1969), 98; Klein, *Shippens of Pennsylvania*, 149; Pencak, *Mind of Thomas Hutchinson*, 4.

18. Stanley K. Johannesen, "John Dickinson and the American Revolution," *Historical Reflections*, II (1975), 34; Stephen Brobeck, "Revolutionary Change in Colonial Philadelphia: The Brief Life of the Proprietary Gentry," *WMQ*, 3rd Ser., XXXIII (1976), 423–24; Land, *Dulanys of Maryland*, 216–18; Clifford K. Shipton, "Jonathan Trumbull," *Sibley's Harvard Graduates: Biographical Sketches of Those Who Attended Harvard College* . . . (Boston, 1951), VIII, 269.

19. Taylor, *Western Massachusetts*, 24. See Smith, *Wealth of Nations*, eds. Campbell and Skinner, II, 783–85 (V.i.f. 51–54), for Smith's discussion of the incapacity of ordinary people for political office.

20. Christopher Collier, *Roger Sherman's Connecticut: Yankee Politics and the American Revolution* (Middletown, Conn., 1971), 14, 21–22; Lemay and Zall, eds., *Franklin's Autobiography* (New York, 1986), 92, 100; Louise Todd Ambler, *Benjamin Franklin: A Perspective* (Cambridge, Mass., 1975), 36.

21. Boston *Evening Post*, 26 Jan. 1767, 1 Dec. 1766.

22. Boston *Evening Post*, 1 Dec. 1766; Taylor et al., eds., *Papers of John Adams*, I, 196.

23. Jessica Kross, " 'Patronage Most Ardently Sought': The New York Council, 1665-1775," in Daniels, ed., *Power and Status*, 208; Boston *Evening Post*, 1 Dec. 1766; Bailyn, *Origins of American Politics*, 85; Wood, *Creation of the American Republic*, 145; Rind's *Virginia Gazette*, 31 Oct. 1771; J. R. Pole, "Representation and Authority in Virginia from the Revolution to Reform," *Journal of Southern History*, XXIV (1958), 23.

24. *Acts and Resolves, Public and Private, of the Province of Massachusetts Bay* . . . (Boston, 1878), III, 70; Robert E. Brown, *Middle-Class Democracy and the Revolution in Massachusetts, 1691-1780* (Ithaca, 1955), 66.

25. David S. Lovejoy, *Rhode Island Politics and the American Revolution, 1760-1776* (Providence, 1958), 16–17; Countryman, *A People in Revolution*, 33.

26. Shipton, "Jeremiah Gridley," *Sibley's Harvard Graduates*, VII, 526; Anderson, "Why Did Colonial New Englanders Make Bad Soldiers? Contractual Principles and Military Conduct during the Seven Years' War," *WMQ*, 3rd Ser., XXXVIII (1981), 438–39.

27. William M. Fowler, Jr., *The Baron of Beacon Hill: A Biography of John Hancock* (Boston, 1980), 225, 230; Charles W. Akers, *The Divine Politician: Samuel Cooper and the American Revolution in Boston* (Boston, 1982), 121, 128, 130, 141, 176, 311; John Adams to William Tudor, 1 June 1817, in Adams, ed., *Works of John Adams*, X, 260.

28. Taylor, *Western Massachusetts*, 33, 53; Snell, " 'Ambitious of Honor and Places,' " in Daniels, ed., *Power and Status*, 17–35.

29. Isaac, *Transformation of Virginia*, 65.

30. Bonomi, *A Factious People*, 170.

31. Bushman, *Kings and People*, 36–37; Gordon S. Wood, "A Note on Mobs in the

American Revolution," *WMQ,* 3rd Ser., XXIII (1966), 635–42; E. P. Thompson, "The Moral Economy of the English Crown in the Eighteenth Century," *Past and Present,* L (1971), 76–136; Peter Burke, *Popular Culture in Early Modern Europe* (New York, 1978), 175; Peter Shaw, *American Patriots and the Ritual of Revolution* (Cambridge, Mass., 1981), 197; Brewer, *Party Ideology and Popular Politics,* 190–91; Paul Gilje, *The Road to Mobocracy: Popular Disorder in New York City, 1763–1834* (Chapel Hill, 1987), 5–35; Foner, *Paine and Revolutionary America,* 50; Pauline Maier, *From Resistance to Revolution: Colonial Radicals and the Development of American Opposition to Britain, 1765–1776* (New York, 1972), 12.

32. Boston *Gazette,* 8 Aug. 1768, in Harry A. Cushing, ed., *The Writings of Samuel Adams* (New York, 1904–8), I, 237.

33. Maier, *From Resistance to Revolution,* 23.

34. Edmund S. Morgan and Helen M. Morgan, *The Stamp Act Crisis: Prologue to Revolution,* rev. ed. (New York, 1963), 166–68; Maier, *From Resistance to Revolution,* 57–58.

35. Laurens to Joseph Brown, 28 Oct. 1765, in Rogers et al., eds., *Papers of Henry Laurens,* V, 29–30.

36. Gordon S. Wood, "The Democratization of Mind in the American Revolution," Library of Congress, *Leadership in the American Revolution* (Washington, D.C., 1974), 63–89.

37. Carroll, quoted in Ronald Hoffman, *A Spirit of Dissension: Economics, Politics, and the Revolution in Maryland* (Baltimore, 1973), III; Gallay, "Jonathan Bryan's Plantation Empire," *WMQ,* 3rd Ser., XLV (1988), 278; Daniel Blake Smith, "The Study of the Family in Early America: Trends, Problems, and Prospects," *WMQ,* 3rd Ser., XXXIX (1982), 27n.; Bushman, *King and People,* 266–67; Greven, *Protestant Temperament,* 335–61.

6. The Republicanization of Monarchy

1. R. R. Palmer, *The Age of the Democratic Revolution: A Political History of Europe and America, 1760–1800,* 2 vols. (Princeton, 1959, 1964); Franco Venturi, *Utopia and Reform in the Enlightenment* (Cambridge, Eng., 1971), 90.

2. Hume, "The British Government," *Essays,* ed. Miller, 51; Linda Colley, "The Apotheosis of George III: Loyalty, Royalty and the British Nation, 1760–1820," *Past and Present,* CII (1984), 94–129.

3. Hamilton, quoted in Gerald Stourgh, *Alexander Hamilton and the Idea of Republican Government* (Stanford, 1970), 44, p. 53; Adams to Warren, 20 July 1807, Massachusetts Historical Society, *Collections,* 5th Ser., IV (1878), 353; Adams to J. H. Tiffany, 30 Apr. 1819, in Adams, ed., *Works of John Adams,* X, 378; Venturi, *Utopia and Reform in the Enlightenment,* 71, 62.

4. W. Paul Adams, "Republicanism in Political Rhetoric Before 1776," *Political Science Quarterly,* LXXXV (1970), 397–421.

5. Jefferson to Lafayette, 4 Nov. 1823, in Paul L. Ford, ed., *The Writings of Thomas Jefferson,* (New York, 1898), X, 281.

6. Hume, "Of the Rise and Progress of the Arts and Sciences," *Essays,* ed. Miller, 125; 31 July 1797, *Diary of Thomas Robbins, D.D., 1796–1854,* ed. Increase Tarbox (Boston, 1886), I, 38; Montesquieu, *Spirit of the Laws,* ed. Neumann, Pt. I, bk. vii, ch. 2, p. 97, and bk. v, ch. 9.

7. Montesquieu, *Spirit of the Laws,* ed. Neumann, Pt. I, bk. v, ch. 19; Colley,

"Apotheosis of George III," *Past and Present,* CII (1984), 94–129; [Trenchard and Gordon], *Cato's Letters,* II, 25.

8. Livingston, *Independent Reflector,* ed. Klein, 80–81; Marston, *King and Congress,* 27.

9. Venturi, *Utopia and Reform,* 63; [Trenchard and Gordon], *Cato's Letters,* II, 28; James Burgh, *Political Disquisitions: Or, an Enquiry into Public Errors, Defects, and Abuses* . . . (London, 1774–75), I, 9; II, 18; III, 173, 277, 425; Duncan Forbes, "Skeptical Whiggism, Commerce, and Liberty," *Essays on Adam Smith,* ed. Andrew S. Skinner and Thomas Wilson (Oxford, 1975), 195; Arthur Sheps, "The American Revolution and the Transformation of English Republicanism," *Historical Reflections,* II (1975), 3–28.

10. Simon Schama, *Citizens: A Chronicle of the French Revolution* (New York, 1989), 172; Paul Robinson, *Opera and Ideas: From Mozart to Strauss* (Ithaca, 1985), 8–57; John Barrell, *The Dark Side of the Landscape: The Rural Poor in English Painting, 1730–1840* (Cambridge, Eng., 1980), 7; Conyers Middleton, *The History of the Life of Marcus Tullius Cicero,* 2 vols. (London, 1741), I, ix.

11. Peter Gay, *The Enlightenment: An Interpretation: The Rise of Modern Paganism* (New York, 1966).

12. Wood, *Creation of the American Republic,* 51; Bailyn, *Ideological Origins of the American Revolution,* 25; Montesquieu, *Spirit of the Laws,* ed., Neumann, Pt. I, bk. ix, ch. 13, p. 167; Gay, *Enlightenment: Rise of Paganism,* 109; Harold T. Parker, *The Cult of Antiquity and the French Revolutionaries* (Chicago, 1937), 22–23.

13. J. G. A. Pocock, *The Machiavellian Moment: Florentine Political Thought and the Atlantic Republican Tradition* (Princeton, 1975).

14. *South Carolina Gazette,* 29 July 1749, quoted in Hennig Cohen, *The South Carolina Gazette, 1732–1775* (Columbia, S.C., 1953), 218.

15. Caroline Robbins, *The Eighteenth-Century Commonwealthman: Studies in the Transmission, Development, and Circumstance of English Liberal Thought from the Restoration of Charles II until the War with the Thirteen Colonies* (Cambridge, Mass., 1959); Isaac F. Kramnick, *Bolingbroke and His Circle: The Politics of Nostalgia in the Age of Walpole* (Cambridge, Mass., 1968).

16. Howard D. Weinbrot, *Augustus Caesar in "Augustan" England: The Decline of a Classical Norm* (Princeton, 1978), 164–65; W. Jackson Bate, *Samuel Johnson* (New York, 1975), 171–72.

17. William L. Grant, *Neo-Latin Literature and the Pastoral* (Chapel Hill, 1965), 255; Weinbrot, *Augustus Caesar in "Augustan" England,* 223, 53, 62, 64, 47–48; Hume, "Of the Parties of Great Britain," *Essays,* ed. Miller, 72.

18. Bertrand A. Goldgar, *Walpole and the Wits: The Relation of Politics to Literature, 1722–1742* (Lincoln, Neb., 1976), 135, 3, 22–23, 158–59, 26, 147–48; James William Johnson, *The Formation of English Neo-Classical Thought* (Princeton, 1967), 97–105; Reed Browning, *Political and Constitutional Ideas of the Court Whigs* (Baton Rouge, 1982), 5.

19. Alexander Pope, *An Essay on Criticism,* lines 118–21, in Aubrey Williams, ed., *Poetry and Prose of Alexander Pope* (Boston, 1969), 41.

20. McIlwaine, ed., *Journals of the House of Burgesses of Virginia, 1752–1755, 1756–1758,* 4.

21. Quentin Skinner, "The Idea of Negative Liberty: Philosophical and Historical Perspectives," in Richard Rorty et al., eds., *Philosophy in History* (Cambridge, Eng., 1984), 193–221; Michael Ignatieff, "John Millar and Individualism," in Istvan Hont and Michael Ignatieff, eds., *Wealth and Virtue: The Shaping of Political Economy in the Scottish Enlightenment* (Cambridge, Eng., 1983), 329–30.

22. David Hume, *A Treatise on Human Nature,* ed. L. A. Selby-Bigge and P. N.

Nidditch (Oxford, 1978), 587; Franklin to Colden, 11 Oct. 1750, Labaree et al., eds., *Papers of Franklin*, IV, 68.

23. Johnson, *A Dictionary of the English Language* . . . (London, 1755); Gordon S. Wood, "Interests and Disinterestedness in the Making of the Constitution," in Richard Beeman et al., eds., *Beyond Confederation: Origins of the Constitution and American National Identity* (Chapel Hill, 1987), 84.

24. Gregory H. Nobles, *Divisions Throughout the Whole: Politics and Society in Hampshire County, Massachusetts, 1740-1775* (Cambridge, Eng., 1983), 182.

25. John Brewer, *Party Ideology and Party Politics at the Accession of George III* (Cambridge, Eng., 1976), 97; Mabel H. Cable, "The Idea of a Patriot King in the Propaganda of the Opposition to Walpole, 1735-1739," *Philological Quarterly*, XVIII (1939), 119-30.

26. Jefferson, *Notes on the State of Virginia*, ed. William Peden (Chapel Hill, 1955), 165.

27. Robert R. Livingston, quoted in Bernard Friedman, "The Shaping of the Radical Consciousness in Provincial New York," *Journal of American History*, LVI (1970), 786.

28. Kenneth R. Bowling and Helen E. Veit, eds., *The Diary of William Maclay and Other Notes on Senate Debates* (Vol. IX, *Documentary History of the First Federal Congress of the United States of America, 4 March 1789-3 March 1791*) (Baltimore, 1988), 69; Adam Smith, *Wealth of Nations*, ed. Campbell and Skinner, I, 265-67 (I. xi. p. 8-10); Robert Micklus, " 'The History of the Tuesday Club': A Mock-Jeremiad of the Colonial South," *WMQ*, 3rd Ser., XL (1983), 53.

29. Jackson to Franklin, 17 June 1755, in Labaree et al., eds., *Papers of Franklin*, VI, 82; Germain, quoted in Esmond Wright, *Franklin of Philadelphia* (Cambridge, Mass., 1986), 166; Doerflinger, *A Vigorous Spirit of Enterprise: Merchants and Economic Development in Revolutionary Philadelphia* (Chapel Hill, 1986); Jessica Kross, " 'Patronage Most Ardently Sought': The New York Council, 1665-1775," in Daniels, ed., *Power and Status*, 215.

30. A. G. Roeber, *Faithful Magistrates and Republican Lawyers: Creators of Virginia Legal Culture, 1680-1810* (Chapel Hill, 1981), 107-8, 147, 156-57; William Bradford to James Madison, in William T. Hutchinson and William M. E. Rachel, eds., *The Papers of James Madison* (Chicago, 1962), I, 90-92, 95-97.

31. Greene to Samuel Ward, Apr. 1772, in Showman et al., eds. *Papers of Nathanael Greene*, I, 28; Wood, "Conspiracy and the Paranoid Style: Causality and Deceit in the Eighteenth Century," *WMQ*, 3rd Ser., XXXIX (1982), 423.

32. Gerald Stourzh, *Benjamin Franklin and American Foreign Policy* (Chicago, 1954), 17-18; Franklin, Speech on Salaries (1787), in Albert Henry Smyth, ed., *The Writings of Benjamin Franklin* (New York, 1906), IX, 591; *The Defence of Injur'd Merit Unmasked* . . . (n.p., 1771), 9.

33. Charles Turner, *A Sermon Preached Before His Excellency Thomas Hutchinson, Esq., Governor* (Boston, 1773), 11; James H. Hutson, "The Origins of 'The Paranoid Style in American Politics': Public Jealousy from the Age of Walpole to the Age of Jackson," in David D. Hall, John M. Murrin, Thad W. Tate, eds., *Saints and Revolutionaries: Essays on Early American History* (New York, 1984), 339; Laurens to John Brown, 28 Oct. 1765, in Rogers et al., eds., *Papers of Henry Laurens*, V, 30.

7. A Truncated Society

1. Jefferson to Benjamin Franklin, 3 Aug. 1777, in Boyd et al., eds., *Papers of Jefferson*, II, 26.

2. John Adams, in Adams, ed., *Works of John Adams*, IV, 68-69; Samuel Adams, quoted in Edwin G. Burrows and Michael Wallace, "The American Revolution: The Ideology and Psychology of National Liberation," *Perspectives in American History*, VI (1972), 198; Wragg, in Drayton, *Letters of Freeman*, ed. Weir, 87.

3. Eddis, *Letters from America*, ed. Land, 30; Wright, *Franklin*, 166.

4. Bushman, *King and People*, 83; Bailyn, *Ideological Origins of the American Revolution*, 303n.; McAnear, *Income of the Colonial Governors*, 70; Alonzo Thomas Dill, *Governor Tryon and His Palace* (Chapel Hill, 1955), 108.

5. Bonomi, *Under the Cope of Heaven*, 194.

6. Greene, ed., "William Knox's Explanation for the Revolution," *WMQ*, 3rd Ser., XXX (1973), 304.

7. Nicholas Cresswell, *Journal of . . .* , *1774-1777*, ed. Samuel Thornely (London, 1924), 255, 252; Doerflinger, *A Vigorous Spirit of Enterprise*, 139, 159; William T. Baxter, *The House of Hancock: Business in Boston, 1724-1775* (Cambridge, Mass., 1945), 224, 76; Richard Pares, "A London West-Indian Merchant House, 1740-1769," in Richard Pares and A. J. P. Taylor, eds., *Essays Presented to Sir Lewis Namier* (London, 1956), 107; Morton, *Robert Carter*, 207; Fiske Kimball, *Domestic Architecture of the American Colonies and of the Early Republic* (New York, 1922), 70; J. H. Plumb, *Men and Places* (London, 1966), 83.

8. Alan Gowans, *Images of American Living* (New York, 1964), 141, 142, 149; Richard Beale Davis, *Intellectual Life in the Colonial South 1585-1763* (Knoxville, 1978), III, 1148; Cresswell, *Journal*, ed. Thornely, 252; Chauncy, "A Discourse on 'the good News from a far country,' " (1766), in J. W. Thornton, ed., *The Pulpit of the American Revolution . . .* (Boston, 1860), 123.

9. Bernard Bailyn, *The Peopling of British North America: An Introduction* (New York, 1986), 82-85; Bonomi, *A Factious People*, 196-200; McAnear, *Income of the Colonial Governors*, 32.

10. Kim, *Landlord and Tenant*, 267, 261; Colden, quoted in Bonomi, *A Factious People*, 195; "A Plantation on Prince George's Creek, Cape Fear, North Carolina," *New England Historical and Genealogical Register*, LII (1898), 473; Greene, ed., "William Knox's Explanation for the Revolution," *WMQ*, 3rd Ser., XXX (1973), 299.

11. Countryman, *A People in Revolution*, 21.

12. Janet A. Riesman, "The Origins of American Political Economy, 1690-1781" (Ph.D. Diss., Brown University, 1983), 148, 152; Beckett, *The Aristocracy in England*, 339.

13. Greene, "Society, Ideology, and Politics," in Jellison, ed., *Society, Freedom, and Conscience*, 14-76; Weir, " 'The Harmony We're Famous For': An Interpretation of Pre-Revolutionary South Carolina Politics," *WMQ*, 3rd Ser., XXVI (1969), 473-501.

14. Smith, *Inside the Great House*, 146; James T. Flexner, *George Washington and the New Nation, 1783-1793* (Boston, 1969), III, 41-42; Isaac, *Transformation of Virginia*, 24-25.

15. Morton, *Robert Carter*, 224; Emory S. Evans, "The Rise and Decline of the Virginia Aristocracy in the Eighteenth Century: The Nelsons," in Darret B. Rutman, ed., *The Old Dominion: Essays for Thomas Perkins Abernathy* (Charlottesville, 1964), 73-74; Dixon Wecter, *The Saga of American Society: A Record of Social Aspiration, 1607-1937* (New York, 1937), 27; Maier, *The Old Revolutionaries*, 211-12; Carl Bridenbaugh, *Myths and Realities: Societies of the Colonial South* (New York, 1963), 27, 14; Robert L. Meriwether,

The Expansion of South Carolina, 1729-1765 (Kingsport, Tenn., 1940), 191-92; Farish, ed., *Journal of Fithian,* 101, 211, 234.

16. Greene, "Society, Ideology, and Politics," in Jellison, ed., *Society, Freedom, and Conscience,* 65-76; Breen, *Tobacco Culture,* 167-68, 111; Wood, "Rhetoric and Reality in the American Revolution," *WMQ,* 3rd Ser., XXIII (1966), 27-30; Wood, *Creation of the American Republic,* 109-14.

17. A. Roger Ekirch, *"Poor Carolina": Politics and Society in Colonial North Carolina, 1729-1776* (Chapel Hill, 1981), 81-82.

18. Bridenbaugh, ed., *Gentleman's Progress,* 13; Edward M. Cook, Jr., "Social Behavior and Changing Values in Dedham, Massachusetts, 1700 to 1775," *WMQ,* 3rd Ser., XXVII (1970), 576; John Adams, Jan. 1761, in Butterfield et al., eds., *Diary of John Adams,* I, 198, 28; Anderson, *A People's Army,* 55.

19. *Benjamin Franklin's Autobiography,* ed. Lemay and Zall, 54, 32.

20. Klein, *Portrait of an Early American Family,* 168, 292.

21. Doerflinger, *A Vigorous Spirit of Enterprise,* 20-36, 202, 46, 159-60, 140, 141, 142; Doerflinger, "Philadelphia's Merchants and the Logic of Moderation, 1760-1775," *WMQ,* 3rd Ser., XL (1983), 197; "Mr. Colden's Account of the State of the Province of New York," in O'Callaghan and Fernow, eds., *Documents Relative to the Colonial History of the State of New York,* VII, 795.

22. Robert E. Mutch, "Yeoman and Merchant in Pre-Industrial America: Eighteenth-Century Massachusetts as a Case Study," *Societas—A Review of Social History,* VII (1977), 279-302; Doerflinger, *A Vigorous Spirit of Enterprise,* 135-64, 183; Countryman, *A People in Revolution,* 113.

23. William Douglass, *A Summary, Historical and Political, of the First Planters, Progressive Improvements, and Present State of the British Settlements in North America* (Boston, 1749), I, 507; William Smith, *History of the Late Province of New York, from Its Discovery to . . . 1762,* I (New York Historical Society, *Coll.,* IV [1829]), 309; Jessica Kross, " 'Patronage Most Ardently Sought': The New York Council, 1665-1775," and Thomas L. Purvis, "A Beleaguered Elite: The New Jersey Council, 1702-1776," in Daniels, ed., *Power and Status,* 208, 251.

24. Jere Daniell, *Experiment in Republicanism: New Hampshire Politics and the American Revolution, 1741-1794* (Cambridge, Mass., 1970), 3-33; Greene, "Society, Ideology, and Politics," in Jellison, ed., *Society, Freedom, and Conscience,* 14-76.

25. Gadsden, in Drayton, *Letters of Freeman,* ed. Weir, 82; Speck, *Stability and Strife,* 34-35; G. E. Mingay, *English Landed Society in the Eighteenth Century* (London, 1963), 19-24; Wellenreuther, "A View of the Socio-Economic Structure of England and the British Colonies on the Eve of the American Revolution," in Angermann et al., eds., *New Wine in Old Skins,* 16-17.

26. Samuel Osgood to John Adams, 4 Dec. 1775, in Taylor et al., eds., *Papers of John Adams,* III, 352; Farish, ed., *Journal of Fithian,* 160; Samuel Peters, *General History of Connecticut . . .* (London, 1781), ed. Samuel Jarvis McCormick (New York, 1877), 221; Greene, "William Knox's Explanation for the Revolution," *WMQ,* 3rd Ser., XXX (1973), 299; Keith Tribe, *Land, Labour, and Economic Discourse* (London, 1978), 32-33.

27. Wood, *Creation of the American Republic,* 100.

8. Loosening the Bands of Society

1. Edward M. Cook, *The Fathers of the Towns: Leadership and Community Structure in Eighteenth-Century New England* (Baltimore, 1976), 71; James A. Henretta, "Economic Development and Social Structure in Colonial Boston," *WMQ,* 3rd Ser., XXII (1965), 75–92; Paul G. E. Clemens, *The Atlantic Economy and Colonial Maryland's Eastern Shore: From Tobacco to Grain* (Ithaca, 1980), 134.

2. Bailyn, *The Peopling of British North America,* 3–43; Bailyn, *Voyagers to the West,* 3–28, 89–125; Bernard Bailyn, "1776: A Year of Challenge—A World Transformed," *Journal of Law and Economics,* XIX (1976), 437–66.

3. Kenneth A. Lockridge, "Land, Population, and the Evolution of New England Society, 1630–1790," *Past and Present,* XXXIX (1968), 62–80; Philip J. Greven, *Four Generations: Population, Land, and Family in Colonial Andover, Massachusetts* (Ithaca, 1970); James Kirby Martin, *Men in Rebellion: Higher Governmental Leaders and the Coming of the American Revolution* (New York, 1973), 23–60; Ekirch, *"Poor Carolina,"* 27; Mitchell, *Commercialism and Frontier,* 82; Marc Egnal, *A Mighty Empire: the Origins of the American Revolution* (Ithaca, 1988).

4. Richard R. Beeman, "Social Change and Cultural Conflict in Virginia: Lunenburg County, 1746 to 1774," *WMQ,* 3rd Ser., XXXV (1978), 456; Harry Roy Merrens, *Colonial North Carolina in the Eighteenth Century: A Study in Historical Geography* (Chapel Hill, 1964), 67.

5. James T. Lemon, *The Best Poor Man's Country: A Geographical Study of Early Southeastern Pennsylvania* (Baltimore, 1972), 123; Merrens, *Colonial North Carolina,* 54; W. Stitt Robinson, *The Southern Colonial Frontier, 1607–1763* (Albuquerque, 1979), 184.

6. Bailyn, "1776: A Year of Challenge," *Journal of Law and Economics,* XIX (1976), 454–55.

7. Douglas Lamar Jones, *Village and Seaport: Migration and Society in Eighteenth-Century Massachusetts* (Hanover, N.H., 1981), 116; Bailyn, "1776: A Year of Challenge," *Journal of Law and Economics,* XIX (1976), 454.

8. Mitchell, *Commercialism and Frontier,* 84, 74, 78, 79–80, 43, 52, 83.

9. Ray Allen Billington, *Westward Expansion: A History of the American Frontier,* 2nd ed. (New York, 1960), 156.

10. Jack P. Greene, "Legislative Turnover in British America, 1696 to 1775: A Quantitative Analysis," *WMQ,* 3rd Ser., XXXVIII (1981), 461.

11. *Massachusetts in Agony . . .* (1750), in Davis, ed., *Colonial Currency Reprints, 1682–1751,* IV, 437; Smith, *Inside the Great House,* 227; Mitchell, *Commercialism and Frontier,* 52–53; Lemon, *Best Poor Man's Country,* 3, 71–97.

12. Mitchell, *Commercialism and Frontier,* 56; Nash, *The Urban Crucible,* 312–38.

13. Jones, *Village and Seaport,* 45; Louis B. Wright and Marion Tinling, eds., *Quebec to Carolina in 1785–1786: Being the Diary and Observations of Robert Hunter, Jr., a Young Merchant of London* (San Marino, Calif., 1943), 118.

14. Jones, *Village and Seaport,* 43, 47; Benton, *Warning Out in New England, 1656–1817,* 74–75, 79, 52, 114–16.

15. Richard R. Beeman, *The Evolution of the Southern Backcountry: A Case Study of Lunenburg County, Virginia, 1746–1832* (Philadelphia, 1984), 15, 27, 29, 48–49, 54.

16. Rodney M. Baine, *Robert Munford: America's First Comic Dramatist* (Athens, Ga., 1967), 160, 14; Beeman, *Evolution of the Southern Backcountry,* 88–96; Richard R. Beeman, "Robert Munford and the Political Culture of Frontier Virginia," *Journal of American Studies,* XII (1978), 182.

17. Robinson, *Southern Colonial Frontier*, 177.

18. Richard J. Hooker, ed., *The Carolina Backcountry on the Eve of the Revolution: The Journal and Other Writings of Charles Woodmason, American Itinerant* (Chapel Hill, 1953), 25.

19. Ibid., 9, 6, 38, 7, 33, 16, 39, 15, 39, 33, 32, 13, 39, 8, 13, 45, 17, 12, 30, 56, 47.

20. Ibid., 31, 61, 52, 7, 38.

21. Ibid., 31, 73, 38.

22. Carville Earle and Ronald Hoffman, "Staple Crops and Urban Development in the Eighteenth-Century South," *Perspectives in American History*, X (1976), 30; Maier, *The Old Revolutionaries*, 264; Thomas Paine, "Common Sense" (1776), in Philip S. Foner, ed., *The Complete Writings of Thomas Paine* (New York, 1945), I, 18. On the development of market farming among New England farmers, see Winifred B. Rothenberg, "The Market and Massachusetts Farmers, 1750-1855," *Journal of Economic History*, XLI (1981), 283-314; Rothenberg, "The Emergence of a Capital Market in Rural Massachusetts, 1730-1838," *Journal of Economic History*, XLV (1984), 781-808; Rothenberg, "The Emergence of Farm Labor Markets and the Transformation of the Rural Economy: Massachusetts, 1750-1855," *Journal of Economic History*, XLVIII (1988), 537-66.

23. Joseph A. Ernst and H. Roy Merrens, " 'Camden's turrets pierce the skies!': The Urban Process in the Southern Colonies During the Eighteenth Century," *WMQ*, 3rd Ser., XXX (1973), 549-74; Earle and Hoffman, "Staple Crops and Urban Development," *Perspectives in American History*, X (1976), 41.

24. Joyce Appleby, "Liberalism and the American Revolution," *New England Quarterly*, XLIX (1976), 14-15; Appleby, "Commercial Farming and the 'Agrarian Myth' in the Early Republic," *Journal of American History*, LXVIII (1982), 833-49; Carole Shammas, "The Domestic Environment in Early Modern England and America," *Journal of Social History*, XIV (1980), 3-24; Billy G. Smith, "The Material Lives of Laboring Philadelphians, 1750 to 1800," *WMQ*, 3rd Ser., XXXVIII (1981), 163-202; T. H. Breen, " 'Baubles of Britain': The American and Consumer Revolutions of the Eighteenth Century," *Past and Present*, CXIX (1988), 73-104.

25. Neil McKendrick et al., *The Birth of a Consumer Society: The Commercialization of Eighteenth-Century England* (Bloomington, 1982), 11.

26. Ebenezer Baldwin, *An Appendix, Stating the Heavy Grievances of Colonies Labour Under from the Several Acts of the British Parliament* . . . (New Haven, 1774), 51; Alexander, *Render Them Submissive*, 24-25; Charleston, S.C., *Gazette*, 1 Mar. 1773, quoted in Jack P. Greene, " 'Slavery or Independence': Some Reflections on the Relationship among Liberty, Black Bondage, and Equality in Revolutionary South Carolina," *South Carolina Historical Magazine*, LXXX (1979), 213.

27. Francis Hutcheson, *A System of Moral Philosophy in Three Books* . . . (London, 1755), II, 319; Alexander, *Render Them Submissive*, 24-25.

28. Isaac Hunt, *The Political Family: Or a Discourse, Pointing Out the Reciprocal Advantages Which Flow from an Uninterrupted Union Between Great Britain and Her American Colonies* (Philadelphia, 1775), 24-25.

29. Boston *Gazette*, 28 Dec. 1761.

30. Marc Egnal and Joseph A. Ernst, "An Economic Interpretation of the American Revolution," *WMQ*, 3rd Ser., XXIX (1972), 16.

31. James A. Henretta, "The War for Independence and American Economic Development," in Ronald Hoffman et al., eds., *The Economy of Early America: The Revolutionary Period, 1763-1790* (Charlottesville, 1988), 45-58; Blanche Evans Hazard, *The Organization of the Boot and Shoe Industry in Massachusetts before 1875* (Cambridge, Mass., 1921), 29; Victor S. Clark, *History of Manufactures in the United States, 1607-1860*

(Washington, D.C., 1916), I, 186; W. C. Plummer, "Consumer Credit in Colonial Philadelphia," *Pennsylvania Magazine of History and Biography*, LXVI (1942), 388.

32. Henretta, "War and Economic Development," and Jacob M. Price, "Reflections on the Economy of Early America," in Hoffman et al., eds., *Economy of Early America*, 60-68, 309-12; Jerome H. Wood, Jr., *Conestoga Crossroads: Lancaster, Pennsylvania, 1730-1790* (Harrisburg, Pa., 1979), 97.

33. Bridenbaugh, ed., *Gentleman's Progress*, 23, 73, 193; *A Brief Account of the Rise, Progress, and Present State of the Paper Currency of New England* . . . (1749), and *Some Observations Relating to the Present Circumstances of the Province of Massachusetts-Bay* . . . (1750), in Davis, ed., *Colonial Currency Reprints*, IV, 392-93, 419.

34. Bruce H. Mann, "Rationality, Legal Change, and Community in Connecticut, 1690-1760," *Law and Society Review*, XIV (1980), 201, 208; Bruce H. Mann, *Neighbors and Strangers: Law and Community in Early Connecticut* (Chapel Hill, 1987), 11-46, 62.

35. Rothenberg, "The Emergence of a Capital Market in Rural Massachusetts, 1730-1838," in Hoffman et al., eds., *Economy of Early America*, 137-38; Peter Coleman, *Debtors and Creditors in America: Insolvency, Imprisonment for Debt, and Bankruptcy, 1607-1900* (Madison, Wisc., 1974); William E. Nelson, *Americanization of the Common Law: The Impact of Legal Change on Massachusetts Society, 1760-1830* (Cambridge, Mass., 1975), 44-45.

36. See Sidney V. James, *Colonial Rhode Island* (New York, 1975); and Peter Coleman, *The Transformation of Rhode Island, 1790-1860* (Providence, 1963).

37. Mann, *Neighbors and Strangers*, 39.

38. "Governor William Bull's Representation of the Colony, 1770," in Harry Roy Merrens, ed., *The Colonial South Carolina Scene: Contemporary Views, 1697-1774* (Columbia, S.C., 1977), 268; [Anon.], *Elixer Magnum: The Philosophers Stone Found Out. Being a Certain Method to Extract Silver and Gold Out of the Earth in Great Plenty* (Philadelphia, 1757), 21.

39. John B. MacInnes, "Rhode Island Bills of Public Credit, 1710-1755" (Ph.D. Diss., Brown University, 1952); Tom Brownsword, "Moses Cooper's Tale of Wealth and Status: A Case Study of Rural Rhode Island, 1674-1808" (Honors Thesis, Brown University, 1986), 56; James, *Colonial Rhode Island*, 173, 178.

40. Janet Riesman, "The Origins of American Political Economy, 1690-1781" (Ph.D. Diss., Brown University, 1983).

41. Jacob M. Price, "The Rise of Glasgow in the Chesapeake Tobacco Trade, 1707-1775," *WMQ*, 3rd Ser., XI (1954), 179-99; Jacob M. Price, *France and the Chesapeake: A History of the French Tobacco Monopoly, 1674-1791, and of Its Relationship to the British and American Tobacco Traders* (Ann Arbor, 1973), I, 862.

42. Alexander White to Richard Henry Lee, 1758, quoted in J. R. Pole, "Representation and Authority in Virginia from the Revolution to Reform," *Journal of Southern History*, XXIX (1958), 23; Purdie and Dixon's *Virginia Gazette*, 25 Nov. 1773; *The Defence of Injur'd Merit Unmasked; or, the Scurrilous Piece of Philander Dissected and Exposed to Public View. By a Friend to Merit, wherever found* (n.p., 1771), 11, 8; Morton, *Robert Carter*, 52.

43. Courtlandt Canby, ed., "Robert Munford's *The Patriots*," *WMQ*, 3rd Ser., VI (1949), 450; Greene, "Society, Ideology, and Politics," in Jellison, ed., *Society, Freedom, and Conscience*, 14-76.

44. Joan Rezner Gunderson, "The Myth of the Independent Virginia Vestry," *Historical Magazine of the Protestant Episcopal Church*, XLIV (1975), 133-41; Isaac, *Transformation of Virginia*, 147-54, 161-73.

45. Richard L. Bushman, *From Puritan to Yankee: Character and the Social Order in Connecticut, 1690–1763* (New York, 1967), 107–95; Bonomi, *Under the Cope of Heaven*, 158–60.

9. Enlightened Paternalism

1. Hoffman, *A Spirit of Dissension*, 47.

2. Willard, *A Complete Body of Divinity in Two Hundred and Fifty Expository Lectures on the Assembly's Shorter Catechism*, 600.

3. Adams to Thomas B. Adams, 17 Oct. 1799, quoted in Page Smith, *John Adams* (New York, 1962), II, 1016–17.

4. Joan R. Gunderson and Gwen Victor Gampel, "Married Women's Legal Status in Eighteenth-Century New York and Virginia," *WMQ*, 3rd Ser., XXXIX (1982), 133; Daniel Blake Smith, "The Study of the Family in Early America: Trends, Problems, and Prospects," *WMQ*, 3rd Ser., XXXIX (1982), 17, 18; Norton, *Liberty's Daughters*, 230–35; Nancy Cott, "Divorce and the Changing Status of Women in Eighteenth-Century Massachusetts," *WMQ*, 3rd Ser., XXXIII (1976), 586–614; Linda K. Kerber, *Women of the Republic: Intellect and Ideology in Revolutionary America* (Chapel Hill, 1980), 157–84; Marylynn Salmon, *Women and the Law of Property in Early America* (Chapel Hill, 1986), 58–61.

5. Smith, *Inside the Great House*, 139–40; Daniel Scott Smith and Michael S. Hindus, "Premarital Pregnancy in America, 1640–1971: An Overview and Interpretation," *Journal of Interdisciplinary History*, V (1975), 537–70.

6. James A. Henretta, "Economic Development and Social Structure in Colonial Boston," *WMQ*, 3rd Ser., XXII (1965), 83; Smith, "Study of the Family in Early America," *WMQ*, 3rd Ser., XXXIX (1982), 18; Karin Calvert, "Children in American Portraiture, 1670 to 1810," *WMQ*, 3rd Ser., XXXIX (1982), 100–2; Smith, *Inside the Great House*, 41, 129, 228–29.

7. Jay Fliegelman, *Prodigals and Pilgrims: The American Revolution against Patriarchal Authority, 1750–1800* (New York, 1982), 43, 36–87; Addison and Steele, *The Spectator*, Nos. 220, 533.

8. Fliegelman, *Prodigals and Pilgrims*, 12–15.

9. James Axtell, ed., *The Educational Writings of John Locke* (Cambridge, Eng., 1968), 55; John Locke, *Essay Concerning Human Understanding*, ed. Peter H. Nidditch (Oxford, 1975), Bk II, Ch. XXXIII, Sect. 8, p. 397.

10. Canby, ed., "Robert Munford's *The Patriots*," *WMQ*, 3rd Ser., VI (1949), 499–500.

11. J. H. Plumb, "The New World of Children in Eighteenth-Century England," *Past and Present*, LXVII (1975), 64–93; Locke, *Some Thoughts on Education* (1705), in Axtell, ed., *Educational Writings of Locke*, 122–23; Edwin G. Burrows and Michael Wallace, "The American Revolution: Ideology and Psychology of National Liberation," *Perspectives in American History*, VI (1972), 239–40.

12. John Witherspoon, *Letters on Education* (1765), in Wilson Smith, ed., *Theories of Education in Early America, 1655–1819* (Indianapolis, 1973), 195.

13. Ibid., 195, 204, 194, 200, 201, 195.

14. Ibid., 194.

15. Jack P. Greene, ed., *The Diary of Colonel Landon Carter of Sabine Hall, 1752–1778* (Charlottesville, 1965), II, 13.

16. Ibid., 907, 703, 702, 941, 1004.

17. Ibid., II, 702, 765, 903, 997, 903, 997; I, 310; II, 907, 703, 903–4.

18. Ibid., II, 762, 782, 907.

19. Ibid., 726–27.

20. Ibid., 775, 1009–10, 762.

21. Ibid., 941, 923.

22. Ibid., I, 29.

23. Nicholas Cresswell, *The Journal of . . .* , *1774–1777*, ed. Samuel Thornely (London, 1924), 270; Edward M. Riley, ed., *The Journal of John Harrower* (Williamsburg, Va., 1963), 84, 103.

24. Jonathan Mayhew, *A Discourse Concerning Unlimited Submission and Nonresistance to the Higher Powers* (1750), in Bernard Bailyn, ed., *Pamphlets of the American Revolution, 1750–1776* (Cambridge, Mass., 1965), I, 242; Burrows and Wallace, "American Revolution," *Perspectives in American History*, VI (1972), 186.

25. William D. Liddle, " 'A Patriot King, or None': Lord Bolingbroke and the American Renunciation of George III," *Journal of American History*, LXV (1979), 955; Gadsden (1769), in Drayton, *Letters of Freeman*, ed. Weir, 59.

26. Locke, *Two Treatises of Government*, ed. Peter Laslett (New York, 1960), 1st, #64, p. 224; Burrows and Wallace, "American Revolution," *Perspectives in American History*, VI (1972), 183.

27. Mayhew, *Discourse Concerning Unlimited Submission*, in Bailyn, ed., *Pamphlets of the American Revolution*, I, 232.

28. Norman Fiering, "The First American Enlightenment: Tillotson, Leverett, and Philosophical Anglicanism," *New England Quarterly*, LIV (1981), 343–44, 309; Fliegelman, *Prodigals and Pilgrims*, 156.

29. Greven, *Protestant Temperament*, 265–331; Fliegelman, *Prodigals and Pilgrims*, 165.

30. Witherspoon, *Letters on Education*, in Smith, ed., *Theories of Education*, 201; Thomas Bacon, *Sermons Addressed to Master and Servants, and Published in the Year 1743 . . .* (Winchester, Va., [1813]), 16; Charles W. Akers, ed., " 'A Place for My People Israel': Samuel Cooper's Sermon of 7 April 1776," *New England Historical and Genealogical Register*, CXXXII (1978), 131–32.

31. [Thomas Bradbury Chandler], *The American Querist: Or, Some Questions Proposed Relative to the Recent Disputes between Great Britain and Her American Colonies* (New York, 1774), 5, 4; Peter Shaw, *American Patriots and the Rituals of Revolution* (Cambridge, Mass., 1981), 39.

32. Clifford K. Shipton, "Thomas Hutchinson," *Sibley's Harvard Graduates*, VIII, 203, 156; Shaw, *American Patriots*, 167.

33. Shipton, "Hutchinson," *Sibley's Harvard Graduates*, VIII, 173, 180; Bernard Bailyn, *The Ordeal of Thomas Hutchinson* (Cambridge, Mass., 1974), 74, 182, 190; Robert M. Calhoon, *The Loyalists in Revolutionary America, 1760–1781* (New York, 1973), 59.

34. David Griffith, *Passive Obedience Considered in Sermon; Preached at Williamsburg, December 31st, 1775* (Williamsburg, 1776), ed. G. MacLaren Brydon, *Historical Magazine of the Protestant Episcopal Church*, XLIV (1975), extra, 77–93; Boucher, *A View of the Causes and Consequences of the American Revolution; in Thirteen Discourses, Published in North America Between the Years 1763 and 1775 . . .* (London, 1797), 525, 535.

35. P. S. Atiyah, *The Rise and Fall of Freedom of Contract* (Oxford, 1979), 36–37, 139–93; Bruce H. Mann, *Neighbors and Strangers: Law and Community in Early Connecticut* (Chapel Hill, 1987), 25–26.

36. Mann, *Neighbors and Strangers*, 11–46.

37. Fliegelman, *Prodigals and Pilgrims*, 41.

38. Mann, *Neighbors and Strangers*, 139; Stephen Botein, "Religion and Politics in Revolutionary New England: Natural Rights Reconsidered," in Patricia U. Bonomi, ed., *Party and Political Opposition in Revolutionary America* (Tarrytown, N.Y., 1980), 23-26.

39. Fred Anderson, "Why Did Colonial New Englanders Make Bad Soldiers? Contractual Principles and Military Conduct During the Seven Years' War," *WMQ*, 3rd Ser., XXXVIII (1981), 395-417; Fred Anderson, *A People's Army: Massachusetts Soldiers and Society in the Seven Years' War* (Chapel Hill, 1984), 167-95.

40. [John Dickinson], *Letters from a Farmer in Pennsylvania* . . . (1768), in Paul L. Ford, ed., *The Writings of John Dickinson* (Philadelphia, 1895), 326; Burrows and Wallace, "American Revolution," *Perspectives in American History*, VI (1972), 217.

41. Wilson, *Considerations on the Nature and Extent of the Legislative Authority of the British Parliament* (1774), in Robert Green McCloskey, ed., *The Works of James Wilson* (Cambridge, Mass., 1967), II, 743; *Massachusetts Spy*, 23 Feb. 1775, 6 Apr. 1775; John Adams, "Novanglus," 13 Mar. 1775, in Adams, ed., *Works of John Adams*, IV, 127; Stourzh, *Alexander Hamilton and the Idea of Republican Government*, 41. On the difference between allegiance and consent, see Wilson, *Considerations*, in McCloskey, ed., *Works of Wilson*, II, 736-37: "Allegiance to the king and obedience to the parliament are founded on very different principles. The former is founded on protection: the latter, on representation. An inattention to this difference has produced, I apprehend, much uncertainty and confusion in our ideas concerning the connexion, which ought to subsist between Great Britain and the American colonies."

42. *An Essay upon Government, Adopted by the Americans, Wherein the Lawfulness of Revolutions Are Demonstrated* . . . (Philadelphia, 1775), 105; Turner, *A Sermon Preached Before His Excellency Thomas Hutchinson*, 7.

43. [Stephen Hopkins], *The Rights of the Colonies Examined* (Providence, 1765), in Bailyn, ed., *Pamphlets of the American Revolution*, I, 511, 534-35, 734; Providence *Gazette*, 2 Mar. 1765.

44. Stourzh, *Benjamin Franklin and American Foreign Policy*, 31; Boston *Evening Post*, 1 Dec. 1766.

45. Bailyn, *Ideological Origins of the American Revolution*, 309; Jefferson, *A Summary View of the Rights of British America* (Williamsburg, 1774), in Boyd et al., eds., *Papers of Jefferson*, I, 134; Samuel Cooke, *A Sermon Preached at Cambridge in the Audience of His Honor Thomas Hutchinson, Esq.* . . . (Boston, 1770), in John W. Thornton, ed., *The Pulpit of the American Revolution: Or, the Political Sermons of the Period of 1776* (Boston, 1860), 162, 163.

46. Paine, *Common Sense* (1776), "American Crisis III" (1777), in Foner, ed., *Writings of Paine*, I, 19, 79; Burrows and Wallace, "American Revolution," *Perspectives in American History*, VII (1972), 212, 215.

10. Revolution

1. John Adams to Abigail Adams, 3 July 1776, and Adams to Richard Cranch, 2 Aug. 1776, Lyman H. Butterfield et al., eds., *Adams Family Correspondence* (Cambridge, Mass., 1963), II, 28, 74.

2. David Ramsay, *A Dissertation on the Manner of Acquiring the Character and Privileges of a Citizen of the United States* (Charleston, 1789), 3. On the Revolution's creation of a new volitional allegiance of citizenship, see James H. Kettner, *The Development of American Citizenship, 1608-1870* (Chapel Hill, 1978), 173-209.

3. Josiah Quincy, *Memoir of the Life of Josiah Quincy, Junior, of Massachusetts: 1744–1775* (Boston, 1874), 88; Gadsden, in Drayton, *Letters of Freeman,* ed. Weir, 81–82. Gadsden's startling description of eighteenth-century South Carolina society as having no real distinctions was matched by Charles Pinckney's praise in the Constitutional Convention of 1787 of that "mediocrity of fortune" that existed everywhere in the United States. Such exaggerated, if not bizarre, statements are comprehensible only in the relative terms in which both men saw America, relative to the great inequalities of rich and poor they thought existed in Europe and relative especially to the great discrepancy between free white men and enslaved blacks that they knew existed in their own society. On this last point, see Edmund S. Morgan, *American Slavery-American Freedom: The Ordeal of Colonial Virginia* (New York, 1975), 376–87; and Jack P. Greene, " 'Slavery or Independence': Some Reflections on the Relationship among Liberty, Black Bondage, and Equality in Revolutionary South Carolina," *South Carolina Historical Magazine,* LXXX (1979), 193–214.

4. Adams, 3 Apr. 1761, in Butterfield et al., eds., *Diary and Autobiography,* I, 208–9; Eddis, *Letters from America,* ed. Land, 65; Burke, "Speech on Moving His Resolutions for Conciliation with the Colonies," 22 Mar. 1775, *The Works of the Right Honourable Edmund Burke,* rev. ed. (Boston, 1865–66), II, 125; Petition of the Inhabitants of Orange County, North Carolina, Oct. 1770, in William L. Saunders, ed., *The Colonial Records of North Carolina* . . . (Raleigh, N.C., 1890), VIII, 234.

5. "Mr. Colden's Account of the State of the Province of New York," 6 Dec. 1765, in O'Callaghan and Fernow, eds., *Documents of the State of New York,* VII, 797; "Journal of Josiah Quincy, Jr., 1773," ed. Mark A. DeWolfe Howe, Massachusetts Historical Society, *Proc.,* XLIX (1916), 453; Russell R. Menard, "Slavery, Economic Growth, and Revolutionary Ideology in the South Carolina Lowcountry," in Hoffman et al., eds., *Economy of Early America,* 244–74; Greene, "Slavery or Independence," *South Carolina Historical Magazine,* LXXX (1979), 201–4.

6. Tom Brownsword, "Moses Cooper's Tale of Wealth and Status: A Case Study of Rural Rhode Island, 1674–1808" (Honors Thesis, Brown University, 1986), 95, 98, 100, 104, 106; Silas Downer, *A Discourse, Delivered in Providence* . . . (1768), in Carl Bridenbaugh, *Silas Downer, Forgotten Patriot: His Life and Writings* (Providence, 1974), 100.

7. "The best poor man's country" was a common phrase to describe the colonies, applied as early as 1705 to Virginia, used by William Smith, Jr., to refer to New York, but most often invoked in reference to Pennsylvania. Robert Beverley, *The History and Present State of Virginia,* ed. Louis B. Wright (Chapel Hill, 1947), 275; Bonomi, *A Factious People,* 196; James T. Lemon, *The Best Poor Man's Country: A Geographical Study of Early Southeastern Pennsylvania* (Baltimore, 1972).

8. Adams, "Dissertation on the Canon and Feudal Law," 12 Aug. 1765, in Taylor et al., eds., *Papers of John Adams,* I, 113; Downer, *Discourse,* in Bridenbaugh, *Silas Downer,* 103; Bonomi, *A Factious People,* 203n; John MacKenzie, "Second Letter to the People," 14 Sept. 1769, in *Letters of Freeman,* ed. Weir, 24, 25; Charles Chauncey, *A Discourse on "The good News from a far Country"* (Boston, 1765), in Thornton, ed., *Pulpit of the Revolution,* 129. See Richard L. Bushman, "Massachusetts Farmers and the Revolution," in Jellison, ed., *Society, Freedom, and Conscience,* 77–124; Alan Taylor, *Liberty Men and Great Proprietors: The Revolutionary Settlement on the Maine Frontier, 1760–1820* (Chapel Hill, 1990), 13–14.

9. Richard Peters to William Smith, 28 May 1763, in *Pennsylvania Magazine of History and Biography,* X (1886), 352; Gary Nash, "The Transformation of Urban Politics, 1700–1765," *Journal of American History,* LX (1967), 605–32; J. R. Pole, *The Gift of Government:*

Political Responsibility from the English Restoration to American Independence (Athens, Ga., 1983), 117–31.

10. Edward H. Tatum, Jr., ed., *The American Journal of Ambrose Serle, Secretary to Lord Howe, 1776–1778* (San Marino, Calif., 1940), 149–50; Calhoon, *Loyalists in Revolutionary America*, 168.

11. Bailyn, *Ideological Origins of the American Revolution*, 94–159.

12. John Adams, quoted in Stephen E. Patterson, *Political Parties in Revolutionary Massachusetts* (Madison, Wisc., 1973) 9; [William Henry Drayton], *A Letter from Freeman of South Carolina, to the Deputies of North America, Assembled in the High Court of Congress at Philadelphia* (Charlestown, S.C., 1774), 9, 18; Samuel Sherwood, *A Sermon, Containing Scriptural Instructions to Civil Rulers, and All Free-born Subjects . . .* (New Haven, 1774), vii.

13. Peter Shaw, *American Patriots and the Rituals of Revolution* (Cambridge, Mass., 1981), 161, 101.

14. Adams, 9 Feb. 1772, in Butterfield et al., eds., *Diary and Autobiography*, II, 53; *Pennsylvania Magazine* (Apr. 1776), 157.

15. R. R. Palmer, *The Age of the Democratic Revolution: A Political History of Europe and America, 1760–1800: The Challenge* (Princeton, 1959), I, 188.

16. Wallace Brown, *The King's Friends: The Composition and Motives of the American Loyalist Claimants* (Providence, 1965), 94; Alexander C. Flick, *Loyalism in New York During the Revolution* (New York, 1901), 20.

17. Doerflinger, *A Vigorous Spirit of Enterprise*, 254–55; Stephen Brobeck, "Revolutionary Change in Colonial Philadelphia: The Brief Life of the Proprietary Gentry," *WMQ*, 3rd Ser., XXXIII (1976), 410–34, 432.

18. Robert A. East, *Business Enterprise in the American Revolutionary Era* (New York, 1938), 220, 232, 227.

19. Belcher, quoted in McAnear, *The Income of the Colonial Governors of British North America*, 6; Carol Berkin, *Jonathan Sewell: Odyssey of an American Loyalist* (New York, 1974), 31.

20. Joseph A. Ernst, *Money and Politics in America, 1755–1775: A Study in the Currency Act of 1764 and the Political Economy of Revolution* (Chapel Hill, 1973), 191.

21. Charles S. Sydnor, *Gentleman Freeholders: Political Practices in Washington's Virginia* (Chapel Hill, 1952), 123.

22. *The Essex Result* (1778), in Oscar and Mary F. Handlin, eds., *The Popular Sources of Political Authority* (Cambridge, Mass., 1966), 340; Jefferson, *Notes on the State of Virginia*, ed. William Peden (Chapel Hill, 1954), 165.

23. H. T. Dickinson, *Liberty and Property: Political Ideology in Eighteenth-Century Britain* (London, 1977), 89.

24. "The Constitutional Courant" (1765), in Merrill Jensen, ed., *Tracts of the American Revolution, 1763–1776* (Indianapolis, 1967), 83; Stephen Hopkins, *The Rights of the Colonies Examined* (Providence, 1765), in Bailyn, ed., *Pamphlets of the American Revolution*, I, 508; Adams, "Novanglus," 30 Jan. 1775, in Taylor et al., eds., *Papers of John Adams*, II, 242: Joyce Appleby, "Liberalism and the American Revolution," *New England Quarterly*, XLIX (1976), 23.

25. David Ramsay, *An Oration on the Advantages of American Independence* (Charleston, 1778), in Robert L. Brunhouse, ed., *David Ramsay, 1749–1815: Selections from His Writings*, American Philosophical Society, *Trans.*, LV (1965), 185, 183; *Memoirs of Stephen Burroughs* (1798, 1811) (Boston, 1988), 3.

26. Ramsay, *Advantages of American Independence*, in Brunhouse, ed., *David Ramsay: Selections from His Writings*, 184, 183; Thomas Paine, *Rights of Man: Part Second* (1792), and

Paine, *Common Sense* (1776), in Foner, ed., *Writings of Paine*, I, 368, 38. "The cottager may beget a wise son; the noble, a fool," said Samuel Adams. "The one is capable of great improvement; the other, not." Maier, *The Old Revolutionaries*, 40.

27. [Carroll], "Letters of First Citizen," 4 Feb. 1773, in Kate Mason Rowland, *The Life of Charles Carroll of Carrollton, 1737-1832* . . . (New York, 1898), I, 247, 252; Mason, First Draft of the Virginia Declaration of Rights [ca. 20-26 May 1776], in Robert A. Rutland, ed., *The Papers of George Mason* (Chapel Hill, 1970), I, 277.

28. Farrand, ed., *Records of the Federal Convention*, I, 359, 49, 56; Maier, *The Old Revolutionaries*, 174.

29. William Livingston et al., *The Independent Reflector*, ed. Klein, 359.

30. Jefferson, *Autobiography, 1743-1790*, in *Thomas Jefferson: Writings*, ed. Merrill D. Peterson (Library of America: New York, 1984), 32, 3.

31. *Benjamin Franklin's Autobiography*, ed. Lemay and Zall, 3; Codicil to the Will, 23 June 1789, in Smyth, ed., *Writings of Franklin*, X, 502.

32. Stanley N. Katz, "Republicanism and the Law of Inheritance in the American Revolutionary Era," *Michigan Law Review*, LXXVI (1977), 1-29.

33. Ibid., 13.

34. See above, ch. 3, pp. 46-47.

35. Salmon, *Women and the Law of Property in Early America* (Chapel Hill, 1986), 171; Salmon, "Republican Sentiment, Economic Change, and the Property Rights of Women in American Law," in Ronald Hoffman and Peter J. Albert, eds., *Women in the Age of the American Revolution* (Charlottesville, 1989), 448-49; Robert D. Mitchell, *Commercialism and Frontier: Perspectives on the Early Shenandoah Valley* (Charlottesville, 1977), 55.

36. Salmon, "Republican Sentiment," in Hoffman and Albert, eds., *Women in the Age of the American Revolution*, 451, 448-49; Salmon, *Women and the Law of Property*, 58-80.

37. William Miller, "The Effects of the American Revolution on Indentured Servitude," *Pennsylvania History*, VII (1940), 136; Sharon V. Salinger, "Artisans, Journeymen, and the Transformation of Labor in Late Eighteenth-Century Philadelphia," *WMQ*, 3rd Ser., XL (1983), 64-66; Steven Rosswurm, *Arms, Country, and Class: The Philadelphia Militia and "Lower Sort" during the American Revolution, 1775-1783* (New Brunswick, 1987), 16.

38. *American Museum*, XI (1792), 84; Frances Wright, *Views of Society and Manners in America*, ed. Paul R. Baker (Cambridge, Mass., 1963), 238; Richard S. Pressman, "Class Positioning and Shays' Rebellion: Resolving the Contradictions of *The Contrast*," *Early American Literature*, XXI (1986), 95.

39. David John Jeremy, ed., *Henry Wansey and His American Journal* (Philadelphia, 1970), 90; Frances Trollope, *Domestic Manners of the Americans*, ed. Donald Smalley (New York, 1960), 54; Samuel Breck, *Recollections . . . with Passages from His Note Books, 1771-1862*, ed. H. E. Scudder (Philadelphia, 1877), 299; Nancy F. Cott, *The Bonds of Womenhood: "Women's Sphere" in New England, 1780-1835* (New Haven, 1977), 28-30, 49.

40. Jeremy, ed., *Wansey and His American Journal*, 99; M. J. Heale, "From City Fathers to Social Critics: Humanitarianism and Government in New York, 1790-1860," *Journal of American History*, LXIII (1976), 26-27; Douglas T. Miller, *Jacksonian Aristocracy: Class and Democracy in New York, 1830-1860* (New York, 1967), 5-7; Arthur M. Schlesinger, *Learning How to Behave: A Historical Study of Etiquette Books* (New York, 1946), 82; Doris Elizabeth King, "The First-Class Hotel and the Age of the Common Man," *Journal of Southern History*, XXIII (1957), 173-88.

41. Sharon V. Salinger, *"To Serve Well and Faithfully": Labor and Indentured Servants in Pennsylvania, 1682-1800* (New York, 1987), 154, 156-57; Providence *Gazette*, 17 July 1824.

42. Eric Foner, *Tom Paine and Revolutionary America* (New York, 1976), 39; Sean Wilentz, *Chants Democratic: New York City and the Rise of the American Working Class, 1788-1850* (New York, 1984), 58.

43. William W. Freehling, "The Founding Fathers and Slavery," *American Historical Review*, LXXVII (1972), 81-93.

44. Hendrick Hartog, *Public Property and Private Power: The Corporation of the City of New York in American Law, 1730-1870* (Chapel Hill, 1983), 138; Harry N. Scheiber, "Public Rights and the Rule of Law in American Legal History," *California Law Review*, LXXII (1984), 217-51.

45. Hartog, *Public Property and Private Power*, 155; Harry Scheiber, "The Road to Munn: Eminent Domain and the Concept of Public Purpose in the State Courts," *Perspectives in American History*, V (1971), 363.

46. Hartog, *Public Property and Private Power*, 137.

47. J. A. C. Grant, "The 'Higher Law' Background of the Law of Eminent Domain," *Wisconsin Law Review*, VI (1930-31), 70; William Michael Treanor, "The Origins and Original Significance of the Just Compensation Clause of the Fifth Amendment," *Yale Law Journal*, XCIV (1985), 694-716.

II. Enlightenment

1. Paine, "The Forester's Letters" (1776), in Foner, ed., *Writings of Paine*, II, 82.

2. John Adams to Jonathan Sewell, Feb. 1760, in Taylor et al., eds., *Papers of John Adams*, I, 42-43; Smith to Madison, Nov. 1777-Aug. 1778, in Hutchinson and Rachel, eds., *Papers of Madison*, I, 208-9; Edmund S. Morgan, *The Gentle Puritan: A Life of Ezra Stiles, 1727-1795* (New Haven, 1962), 167.

3. Adams, "Dissertation on the Feudal and Canon Law" (1765), in Gordon S. Wood, ed., *The Rising Glory of America, 1760-1820* (New York, 1971), 29.

4. Paine, *Letter to the Abbé Raynal* (1782), in Foner, ed., *Writings of Paine*, II, 243, 244; *American Museum*, V (1789), 556.

5. Rush to John R. B. Rodgers, 25 June 1795, in Butterfield, ed., *Letters of Rush*, II, 762.

6. Wollaston, quoted in Garry Wills, *Inventing America: Jefferson's Declaration of Independence* (New York, 1978), 155.

7. Jefferson to Lafayette, 11 Apr. 1787, in Boyd et al., eds., *Papers of Jefferson*, XI, 285.

8. Louis Masur, *Rites of Execution: Capital Punishment and the Transformation of American Culture, 1776-1865* (New York, 1989), 65, 71, 80-82, 88, 87; Adam J. Hirsch, "From Pillory to Penitentiary: The Rise of Criminal Incarceration in Early Massachusetts," *Michigan Law Review*, LXXX (1982), 1179-1269; Linda Kealey, "Patterns of Punishment: Massachusetts in the Eighteenth Century," *American Journal of Legal History*, XXX (1986), 163-76; Michael Merame, "The Penitential Ideal in Late Eighteenth-Century Philadelphia," *Pennsylvania Magazine of History and Biography*, CVIII (1984), 419-50.

9. Rush to Thomas Eddy, 19 Oct. 1803, in Butterfield, et al., ed., *Letters of Rush*, II, 875; Masur, *Rites of Execution*, 68; *Benjamin Franklin's Autobiography*, ed. Lemay and Zall, 108.

10. Sheldon Rothblatt, *Tradition and Change in English Liberal Education: An Essay in History and Culture* (London, 1976), 18–19; Raymond Williams, *Keywords: A Vocabulary of Culture and Society* (New York, 1976), 57–60.

11. Henry Dwight Sedgwick, *In Praise of Gentlemen* (Boston, 1935), 130n.

12. Rothblatt, *Tradition and Change in English Liberal Education*, 23–31.

13. Adams, *Defence of the Constitutions of the United States* (1787–88), in Adams, ed., *Works of John Adams*, VI, 185.

14. William Livingston et al., *Independent Reflector*, ed. Klein, 219; Boston *Evening Post*, 2 Feb. 1767.

15. John Clive and Bernard Bailyn, "England's Cultural Provinces: Scotland and America," *WMQ*, 3rd Ser., XI (1954), 200–13; N. T. Phillipson, "Culture and Society in the 18th Century Province: The Case of Edinburgh and the Scottish Enlightenment," in Lawrence Stone, ed., *The University in Society: Europe, Scotland, and the United States from the 16th to the 20th Century* (Princeton, 1974), 425. Benjamin Rush noted as early as 1766 that "useful and pleasing" conversation was coming to characterize both Edinburgh and Philadelphia. Stephen A. Conrad, "Polite Foundation: Citizenship and Common Sense in James Wilson's Republican Theory," *Supreme Court Review—1984*, ed. Philip B. Kurland et al. (Chicago, 1985), 362.

16. Livingston et al., *Independent Reflector*, ed. Klein, 220.

17. Of the ninety-nine founding fathers studied by Richard D. Brown—that is, those who either signed the Declaration of Independence or were members of the Constitutional Convention—only eight are known to have fathers who went to college. Brown, "The Founding Fathers of 1776 and 1787: A Collective View," *WMQ*, 3rd Ser., XXXIII (1976), 465–80. Brown himself did not note the education of the founding fathers or their fathers in his study. I owe that information to Emily Widmann.

18. G. S. Rowe, *Thomas McKean: The Shaping of an American Republicanism* (Boulder, Colo., 1978), 12; Maier, *The Old Revolutionaries*, 211, 240–41, 246–47; Peter S. Onuf, ed., *Maryland and the Empire, 1773: The Antilon-First Citizen Letters* (Baltimore, 1974), 57–58.

19. Frederic M. Litto, "Addison's *Cato* in the Colonies," *WMQ*, 3rd Ser. (1966), 431–49.

20. Washington to Lafayette, 15 Aug. 1787, to Henry Knox, 20 Feb. 1784, in Fitzpatrick, ed., *Writings of Washington*, XXIX, 259; XXVII, 341. See Paul Boller, Jr., *George Washington and Religion* (Dallas, 1963), 94; Fliegelman, *Prodigals and Pilgrims*, 212.

21. Washington to Rev. Jonathan Boucher, 9 July 1771, in Fitzpatrick, ed., *Writings of Washington*, III, 50.

22. Moore, ed., *George Washington's Rules of Civility and Decent Behaviour*, 9, 5.

23. Bernard Knollenberg, as noted by Flexner, *George Washington: The Forge of Experience (1732–1775)*, I, 254.

24. Rush to John Adams, 21 Sept. 1805, in John A. Schutz and Douglass Adair, eds., *The Spur of Fame: Dialogues of John Adams and Benjamin Rush, 1805–1813* (San Marino, Calif., 1980), 37.

25. Washington to David Humphreys, 25 July 1785, in Fitzpatrick, ed., *Writings of Washington*, XXVIII, 203.

26. J. P. Brissot de Warville, *New Travels in the United States of America, 1788*, ed. Durand Echeverria (Cambridge, Mass., 1964), 344; James Thomas Flexner, *George Washington: Anguish and Farewell (1793–1799)* (Boston, 1969), IV, 488.

27. *Benjamin Franklin's Autobiography*, ed. Lemay and Zall, 57; Bernard Bailyn, *The Origins of American Politics* (New York, 1968), 143; Paul W. Conner, *Poor Richard's Politicks: Benjamin Franklin and His New American Order* (Oxford, 1965), 215, 215–17; Thomas J.

Schlereth, *The Cosmopolitan Ideal in Enlightenment Thought: Its Form and Function in the Ideas of Franklin, Hume, and Voltaire, 1694–1790* (Notre Dame, 1977).

28. John J. Waters, Jr., *The Otis Family in Provincial and Revolutionary Massachusetts* (Chapel Hill, 1968), 105; Adams to H. Niles, 14 Jan. 1818, in Adams, ed., *Works of John Adams*, X, 275; Peter Shaw, *American Patriots and the Rituals of Revolution* (Cambridge, Mass., 1981), 82, 83, 85.

29. Adams, 16 Jan. 1766, 22 June 1771, 3 Apr. 1761, in Butterfield et al., eds., *Diary and Autobiography*, I, 294; II, 38; I, 207.

30. Charles W. Akers, *Called unto Liberty: A Life of Jonathan Mayhew, 1720–1766* (Cambridge, Mass., 1964), 132, 163.

31. John E. O'Connor, *William Paterson: Lawyer and Statesman, 1745–1806* (New Brunswick, N.J., 1979), 7, 10, 26.

32. Ibid., 16, 27, 66.

33. Dumas Malone, *Jefferson the Virginian: Jefferson and His Time* (Boston, 1948), I, 8; Jefferson to John Page, 25 May 1766, in Boyd et al., eds., *Papers of Jefferson*, I, 19–20.

34. Merrill D. Peterson, *Thomas Jefferson and the New Nation: A Biography* (New York, 1970), 14, 15; Eleanor D. Berman, *Thomas Jefferson among the Arts: An Essay in Early American Esthetics* (New York, 1947), 1.

35. Jefferson came to see himself as a kind of impresario for America, introducing his countrymen to the finest and most enlightened aspects of European culture. When Americans in the 1780s realized that a statue of Washington was needed, "there could be no question raised," he wrote from Paris, "as to the Sculptor who should be employed, the reputation of Monsr. Houdon of this city being unrivalled in Europe." No American could stand up to his knowledge. When Washington timidly expressed misgivings about Houdon's doing the statue in Roman style, he quickly backed down in the face of Jefferson's frown, unwilling, as he said, "to oppose my judgment to the taste of Connoisseurs." Of course, some years later tastes had changed; for a new commemorative statue of Washington, Jefferson wanted "old Canova, of Rome," who, he said, "for thirty years, within my own knowledge, . . . had been considered by all Europe without a rival." Jefferson to Benjamin Harrison, 12 Jan. 1785, in Boyd et al., eds., *Papers of Jefferson*, VII, 600; Washington to Jefferson, 1 Aug. 1786, in Fitzpatrick, ed., *Writings of Washington*, XXVIII, 504; Jefferson to Nathaniel Macon, 22 Jan. 1816, in Andrew A. Lipscomb and Albert E. Bergh, eds., *The Writings of Thomas Jefferson* (Washington, D.C., 1903), XIV, 408.

36. Greene to Samuel Ward, 9 Oct. 1772, 26 Sept. 1771, in Showman et al., eds., *Papers of General Nathanael Greene* (Chapel Hill, 1976), I, 47, 23.

37. "Appendix" in Adams, ed., *Works of John Adams*, II, 524.

38. Jonathan Sewell to Adams, 13 Feb. 1760, in Taylor et al., eds., *Papers of John Adams*, I, 39–40; Stephen Botein, "Cicero as Role Model for Early American Lawyers: A Case Study in Classical Influence," *The Classical Journal*, LXXIII (1977–78), 313–21.

39. Maier, *The Old Revolutionaries*, 33, 47, 34.

40. David Humphreys, "A Poem on the Industry of the United States of America," in Vernon L. Parrington, ed., *The Connecticut Wits* (New York, 1954), 401; Wilson, "On the History of Property," in McCloskey, ed., *Works of Wilson*, II, 716.

41. Washington, Circular to the States, 8 June 1783, to Daniel McCarty, 22 Feb. 1784, in Fitzpatrick, ed., *Writings of Washington*, XXVI, 486; XXVII, 341; Garry Wills, *Cincinnatus: George Washington and the Enlightenment* (New York, 1984), 3–16.

42. Washington to New York Legislature, 26 June 1775, in Fitzpatrick, ed., *Writings of Washington*, II, 305; Wills, *Cincinnatus*, 13.

43. When Washington could not take those differences for granted, he cultivated them. He used his natural reticence to reinforce the image of a stern and forbidding classical hero. His aloofness was notorious, and he worked at it. When the painter Gilbert Stuart had uncharacteristic difficulty in putting Washington at ease during a sitting for a portrait, Stuart in exasperation finally pleaded, "Now sir you must let me forget that you are General Washington and that I am Stuart, the painter." Washington's reply chilled the air: "Mr. Stuart need *never* feel the need of forgetting who he is *or* who General Washington is." No wonder the portraits look stiff. In fact, when he became President and held levees, Washington was criticized for the awkwardness of his bows, which were said to be "more distant and stiff" than those of a king. James Thomas Flexner, *George Washington and the New Nation (1783-1793)* (Boston, 1969), III, 419; Barry Schwartz, *George Washington: The Making of an American Symbol* (New York, 1987), 59.

44. Washington to Lafayette, 8 Nov. 1785, in Fitzpatrick, ed., *Writings of Washington*, XXVIII, 308-9; Trevor Colbourn, ed., *Fame and the Founding Fathers: Essays by Douglass Adair* (New York, 1974), 3-26.

45. Jefferson to Madison, 9 June 1793, in Thomas A. Mason et al., eds., *Papers of Madison*, XV, 27; Jefferson to Dr. Walter Jones, 2 Jan. 1814, in Paul L. Ford, ed., *The Writings of Thomas Jefferson* (New York, 1898), IX, 448.

46. Flexner, *Washington and the New Nation*, III, 63-68.

47. Washington to Benjamin Harrison, 22 Jan. 1785, to George William Fairfax, 27 Feb. 1785, in Fitzpatrick, ed., *Writings of Washington*, XXVIII, 36, 85.

48. Washington to Harrison, 22 Jan. 1785, to William Grayson, 22 Jan. 1785, to Marquis de Lafayette, 15 Feb. 1785, to Jefferson, 25 Feb. 1785, to Fairfax, 27 Feb. 1785, to Governor Patrick Henry, 27 Feb. 1785, to Henry Knox, 28 Feb. 1785, 18 June 1785, to Nathanael Greene, 20 May 1785, ibid., 36, 37, 72, 80-81, 85, 89-91, 92-93, 167, 146.

49. Washington to Henry Knox, 8 Mar. 1787, to David Humphreys, 8 Mar. 1787, ibid., XXIX, 172.

50. Washington to Humphreys, 26 Dec. 1786, ibid., 128; Flexner, *Washington and the New Nation*, III, 108.

51. Monroe to Jefferson, 12 July 1788, in Boyd et al., eds., *Papers of Jefferson*, XIII, 352.

52. *Pennsylvania Gazette*, 5 Mar. 1788. (I owe this citation to Barry Schwartz.)

53. Washington to Henry Lee, 22 Sept. 1788, in Fitzpatrick, ed., *Writings of Washington*, XXX, 97, 98.

54. Hamilton to Washington, Sept. 1788, in Harold C. Syrett et al., eds., *The Papers of Alexander Hamilton* (New York, 1962), V, 221-22; Washington to Lincoln, 26 Oct. 1788, in Fitzpatrick, ed., *Writings of Washington*, XXX, 119.

55. Dickinson, "Letters of a Farmer in Pennsylvania" (1768), in Paul L. Ford, ed., *The Writings of John Dickinson*, I, *Political Writings, 1764-1774* (Pennsylvania Historical Society, *Memoirs*, XIV [Philadelphia, 1895]), 307; Kenneth R. Bowling and Helen E. Veit, eds., *The Diary of William Maclay and Other Notes on Senate Debates* (Vol. IX, *Documentary History of the First Federal Congress of the United States of America, 4 March 1789-3 March 1791)*, (Baltimore, 1988), 69-70.

56. W. T. Baxter, *The House of Hancock* (Cambridge, Mass., 1945), 279, 283; Laurens to Richard Oswald, 7 July 1764, in Hamer et al., eds., *Papers of Henry Laurens*, IV, 338 (see also Rachel N. Klein, "Ordering the Backcountry: The South Carolina Regulation," *WMQ*, 3rd Ser., XXXVIII [1981], 667); David Duncan Wallace, *The Life of Henry Laurens* . . . (New York, 1915), 69-70. See above, ch. 6, pp. 106-07.

57. Smith, *Wealth of Nations,* ed. Campbell and Skinner, I, 411 (III. iv. 3).

58. Tamara Platkins Thornton, *Cultivating Gentlemen: The Meaning of Country Life among the Boston Elite, 1785–1860* (New Haven, 1989), 15–56.

59. Morris to Washington, 29 May 1781, in E. James Ferguson et al., eds., *The Papers of Robert Morris, 1781–1784* (Pittsburgh, 1973–   ), I, 96; Ellis Paxson Oberholtzer, *Robert Morris, Patriot and Financier* (New York, 1903), 52–56, 70–71.

60. Morris to Matthew Ridley, 14 Oct. 1781, in Ferguson et al., eds., *Papers of Robert Morris,* III, 56–57.

61. Mathew Carey, ed., *Debates and Proceedings of the General Assembly of Pennsylvania on the Memorials Praying a Repeal or Suspension of the Law Annulling the Charter of the Bank* (Philadelphia, 1786), 81.

62. Oberholtzer, *Morris,* 285–86, 297–99, 301–3; Eleanor Young, *Forgotten Patriot: Robert Morris* (New York, 1950), 170; Barbara Ann Chernow, *Robert Morris, Land Speculator, 1790–1801* (New York, 1978); H. E. Scudder, ed., *Recollections of Samuel Breck . . .* (Philadelphia, 1877), 203; Bowling and Veit, eds., *Diary of William Maclay,* 48, 73–74, 134.

12. Benevolence

1. Belknap, quoted in W. Paul Adams, *The First American Constitutions: Republican Ideology and the Making of the State Constitutions in the Revolutionary Era* (Chapel Hill, 1980), 27.

2. Ronald Hoffman, "The 'Disaffected' in the Revolutionary South," in Alfred F. Young, ed., *The American Revolution* (DeKalb, Ill., 1976), 282–83; Bernard Mason, *The Road to Independence: The Revolutionary Movement in New York, 1773–1777* (Lexington, Ky., 1966), 46.

3. Robert M. Calhoon, *The Loyalists in Revolutionary America, 1760–1781* (New York, 1973), 278; Jonathan Powell, "Presbyterian Loyalists: A 'Chain of Interest' in Philadelphia," *Journal of Presbyterian History,* LVII (1979), 156; 25 Jan. 1777, "Diary of James Allen, Esq., of Philadelphia, Counsellor at Law, 1770–1778," *Pennsylvania Magazine of History and Biography,* IX (1885), 193–94.

4. Calhoon, *Loyalists in Revolutionary America,* 299.

5. Richard A. Ryerson, *The Revolution Is Now Begun: The Radical Committees of Philadelphia, 1765–1776* (Philadelphia, 1978), 131; Calhoon, *Loyalists in Revolutionary America,* 295–305.

6. Calhoon, *Loyalists in Revolutionary America,* 144–45, 80; Boston *Evening Post,* 13 Apr. 1767.

7. Robert Rosenblum, *Transformations in Late Eighteenth-Century Art* (Princeton, 1967, 1969), 68–69; Montesquieu, *Spirit of the Laws,* ed. Neumann, Pt. I, bk. vii, ch. 13, pp. 118–19; Cortlandt Canby, ed., "Robert Munford's *The Patriots,*" *WMQ,* 3rd Ser., VI (1949), 459.

8. Butler, "Sermons," in L. A. Selby-Bigge, ed., *British Moralists, Being Selections from Writers Principally of the Eighteenth Century* (Oxford, 1897), I, 204, 203; Norman Fiering, *Jonathan Edwards's Moral Thought and Its British Context* (Chapel Hill, 1981).

9. Hume, "Of Commerce," *Essays, Moral, Political, and Literary,* ed. Miller, 262–63.

10. *American Museum,* II (1787), 228–37; George W. Corner, ed., *The Autobiography of Benjamin Rush: His "Travels Through Life" Together with His Commonplace Book for 1789–1813* (Princeton, 1948), 199, 198.

11. Conrad, "Polite Foundation," in Kurland et al., eds., *Supreme Court Review— 1984*, 361, 363, 365.

12. Joseph Addison, *Cato: A Tragedy* (1721), act I, sc. iv, in Richard Hurd, ed., *The Works of the Right Honourable Joseph Addison* (London, 1811), I, 225.

13. *New York Magazine*, II, (1792), 406. See Lawrence Klein, "The Third Earl of Shaftesbury and the Progress of Politeness," *Eighteenth Century Studies*, XVIII (1984–85), 186–214.

14. Livingston et al., *Independent Reflector*, ed. Klein, 219; Paine, *Common Sense*, in Foner, ed., *Writings of Paine*, I, 4; Wilson, "Lectures on Law" (1790–91), in McCloskey, ed., *Works of Wilson*, I, 86–87; Rush, *Thoughts on the Mode of Education Proper in a Republic* (1786), in Hyneman and Lutz, eds., *American Political Writing*, I, 689; [James Sullivan], *The Path to Riches. An Inquiry into the Origin and Use of Money* . . . (Boston, 1792), 8.

15. *American Museum*, II (1787), 229; Adams, "Oration Pronounced July 4th 1793 . . . ," in E. B. Williston, ed., *Eloquence of the United States* (Middletown, Conn., 1827), V, 108–9.

16. *The Works of John Witherspoon* . . . (Philadelphia, 1800–1), III, 470.

17. Carol F. Karlsen and Laurie Crumpacker, eds., *The Journal of Esther Edwards Burr, 1754–1757* (New Haven, 1984), 63; Robert Micklus, " 'The History of the Tuesday Club': A Mock-Jeremiad on the Colonial South," *WMQ*, 3rd Ser., XL (1983), 60.

18. Joseph Warren (1772), in Hezekiah Niles, ed., *Principles and Acts of the American Revolution in America* (New York, 1876), 4; Tristam Burges, *Solitude and Society Contrasted* (Providence, 1797), 10, 15; Masur, *Rites of Execution*, 83.

19. Greene to Samuel Ward, Apr., 1772, in Showman et al., eds., *Papers of Nathanael Greene*, I, 27; Mayhew, *Seven Sermons upon the Following Subjects* . . . (Boston, 1749), 126; Samuel Cooper, *A Sermon Preached in Boston, New England, Before the Society for Encouraging Industry, and Employing the Poor* . . . (Boston, 1753), 13.

20. John Adams to Abigail Adams, 29 Oct. 1775, in Butterfield et. al., eds., *Adams Family Correspondence* (Cambridge, Mass., 1963), I, 318; Cooper, *Sermon Preached in Boston*, 2; John Andrews, *A Sermon on the Importance of Mutual Kindness* . . . (Philadelphia, 1790), 17; *American Museum*, II (1787), 30.

21. Jeremiah Atwater, *A Sermon Preached Before His Excellency Isaac Tichenor, Esq., Governor* . . . *on the Day of the Anniversary Election, October 14, 1802* (Middlebury, Vt., 1802), 20.

22. Zabdiel Adams, *Brotherly Love and Compassion, Described and Recommended* . . . (Worcester, 1778), 16; [Anon.], *An Oration, Pronounced Before the Society of the Social Tie, in New Haven* . . . (New Haven, 1802), 10; John Adams to Abigail Adams, 29 Oct. 1775, in Butterfield et al., eds., *Adams Family Correspondence*, I, 318.

23. Charles Royster, *Light-Horse Harry Lee and the Legacy of the American Revolution* (New York, 1981), 71; Evarts B. Greene, *The Revolutionary Generation, 1763–1790* (New York, 1943), 418; Colin Bonwick, *English Radicals and the American Revolution* (Chapel Hill, 1977), 13–14; Alan D. McKillop, "Local Attachment and Cosmopolitanism—The Eighteenth-Century Pattern," in Frederick W. Hilles and Harold Bloom, eds., *From Sensibility to Romanticism: Essays Presented to Frederick A. Pottle* (Oxford, 1965), 197; David Ramsay to John Eliot, 11 Aug. 1792, in Brunhouse, ed., *Ramsay* . . . *Selections from His Writings*, 133.

24. Lewis B. Simpson, "Federalism and the Crisis of Literary Order," *American Literature*, XXXII (1960), 256; Rush to James Beattie, 1 Aug. 1786, in Butterfield, ed., *Letters of Rush*, I, 394; Allan Guttman, "Copley, Peale, Trumbull: A Note on Loyalty," *American Quarterly*, II (1959), 178–83; Arthur L. Ford, *Joel Barlow* (New York, 1971), 59; Edward Handler, " 'Nature Itself Is All American': The Scientific Outlook of John

Adams," American Philosophical Society, *Proc.*, CXX (1976), 226; Schlereth, *The Cosmopolitan Ideal*, 30; Whitfield J. Bell, *Early American Science: Needs and Opportunities for Study* (Chapel Hill, 1955), 34.

25. Ramsay to Benjamin Rush, 8 Apr. 1777, in Brunhouse, ed., *Ramsay . . . Selections from His Writings*, 54; Ford, *Barlow*, 31; Paine, *Common Sense*, in Foner, ed., *Writings of Paine*, I, 20.

26. *New York Magazine*, I (1790), 290.

27. Catherine L. Albanese, *Sons of the Fathers: The Civil Religion of the American Revolution* (Philadelphia, 1976), 129–30; J. M. Roberts, *The Mythology of the Secret Societies* (St. Albans, Eng., 1974), 37; Conrad E. Wright, "Christian Compassion and Corporate Beneficence: The Institutionalization of Charity in New England, 1720–1810" (Ph.D. Diss., Brown University, 1980); Steven C. Bullock, "The Revolutionary Transformation of American Freemasonry, 1752–1792," *WMQ*, 3rd Ser., XLVII (1990), 347–69; and Steven C. Bullock, "The Ancient and Honorable Society: Freemasonry in America, 1730–1830" (Ph.D. Diss., Brown University, 1986).

28. Ann Lipson, *Freemasonry in Federalist Connecticut, 1789–1832* (Princeton, 1977), 40; Josiah Bartlett, *A Discourse on the Origin, Progress and Design of Free Masonry* (Boston, 1793), 15; De Witt Clinton, quoted in Steven C. Bullock, "A Pure and Sublime System: The Appeal of Post-Revolutionary Freemasonry," *Journal of the Early Republic*, IX (1989), 371; Charles Brockwell, *Brotherly Love Recommended in a Sermon Preached Before the Ancient and Honourable Society of Free and Accepted Masons in Christ-Church, Boston* (Boston, 1750), 14; John Andrews, *A Sermon on the Importance of Mutual Kindness . . .* (Philadelphia, 1790), 20.

29. Cooper, *Sermon Preached in Boston . . . 1753*, 3; Geoffroy Atkinson, *The Sentimental Revolution: French Writers of 1690–1740* (Seattle, 1966); Norman S. Fiering, "Irresistible Compassion: An Aspect of Eighteenth-Century Sympathy and Humanitarianism," *Journal of the History of Ideas*, XXXVII (1976), 199–212; John B. Radner, "The Art of Sympathy in Eighteenth-Century British Moral Thought," IX, *Studies in Eighteenth-Century Culture* (Madison, Wisc., 1979), 189–210.

30. Burges, *Solitude and Society Contrasted*, 15; Jay, quoted in Sandra F. VanBurkleo, " 'Honour, Justice and Interest': John Jay's Republican Politics and Statesmanship on the Federal Bench," *Journal of the Early Republic*, IV (1984), 260.

13. Equality

1. Robert Porter, *An Oration, to Commemorate the Independence of the United States of North America Delivered . . . Philadelphia, July 4th, 1791* (Philadelphia, 1791), 17–18.

2. De Witt Clinton (1794), quoted in Bullock, "A Pure and Sublime System: The Appeal of Post-Revolutionary Freemasonry," *Journal of the Early Republic*, IX (1989), 368.

3. Maxwell H. Bloomfield, *American Lawyers in a Changing Society, 1776–1876* (Cambridge, Mass., 1976), 37; Gouverneur Morris, in *Niles' Weekly Register*, VI (1814), 313.

4. Winfred E. A. Bernhard, *Fisher Ames: Federalist and Statesman, 1758–1808* (Chapel Hill, 1965), 344, 337; Ames, *Monthly Anthology*, II (1805), in Lewis P. Simpson, ed., *The Federalist Literary Mind: Selections from the Monthly Anthology and Boston Review, 1803–1811* (Baton Rouge, 1962), 54. For John Adams's "frantic efforts" to keep the distinction between a republic and a democracy clear, see Bailyn, *Ideological Origins of the American Revolution*, 282n.

5. Charles D. Hazen, *Contemporary American Opinion of the French Revolution* (Baltimore, 1897), 276-77, 277; Arthur Maynard Walter, *Monthly Anthology*, II (1805), in Simpson, ed., *Federalist Literary Mind*, 49; R. R. Palmer, *Age of the Democratic Revolution: The Challenge* (Princeton, 1959), I, 187-88.

6. Bernhard, *Fisher Ames*, 341.

7. Elias Smith, *The Loving Kindness of God Displayed in the Triumph of Republicanism in America* . . . (n.p., 1809), 14-15.

8. Hugh Swinton Legaré, "An Oration, Delivered on the Fourth of July 1823 . . . ," in *Writings of Hugh Swinton Legaré* (Charleston, 1846), I, 262.

9. Herman Melville, *Moby Dick* (1851), ed. Harrison Hayford and Hershel Parker (New York, 1967), ch. 26, pp. 104-5.

10. Ramsay, *An Oration on the Advantages of American Independence* (1778), in Brunhouse, ed., *Ramsay . . . Selections from His Writings*, 183; Homai J. Shroff, *The Eighteenth-Century Novel: The Idea of the Gentleman* (New Delhi, 1978), 37, 282.

11. Lawrence W. Towner, "The Indentures of Boston's Poor Apprentices: 1734-1805," Colonial Society of Massachusetts, *Publications*, XLIII (1956-63), 427; Philip S. Foner, ed., *The Democratic-Republican Societies, 1790-1800: A Documentary Sourcebook of Constitutions, Addresses, Resolutions, and Toasts* (Westport, Conn., 1976), 10; Dennie to his parents, 25 Apr. 1793, in Eugene Perry Link, *Democratic-Republican Societies, 1790-1800* (New York, 1942), 99.

12. Charles Royster, *A Revolutionary People at War: The Continental Army and American Character, 1775-1783* (Chapel Hill, 1970), 316.

13. *Pennsylvania Packet* (Philadelphia), 26 Nov. 1776; *South Carolina and American Gazette* (Charleston), 6 Nov. 1777.

14. Madison, in Jonathan Elliot, ed., *The Debates of the State Conventions on the Adoption of the Federal Constitution* . . . (Philadelphia, 1896), III, 536-37; "The Worcester Speculator" (1787), in Charles S. Hyneman and Donald S. Lutz, eds., *American Political Writings During the Founding Era*, I, 700; [Trenchard and Gordon], *Cato's Letters*, II, 35; Tillotson, quoted in Leon Guilhamet, *The Sincere Ideal: Studies on Sincerity in Eighteenth-Century English Literature* (Montreal, 1974), 16; Ramsay, *Oration on American Independence*, in Brunhouse, ed., *Ramsay . . . Selections from His Writings*, 185; Jefferson, *A Summary View of the Rights of British America* (1774), in Boyd et al., eds., *Papers of Jefferson*, I, 134.

15. *Columbian Magazine*, II (1788), quoted in Bloomfield, *American Lawyers*, 42; Norman Hampson, *The Enlightenment* (Baltimore, 1968), 154; Thomas L. Haskell, "Capitalism and the Origins of the Humanitarian Sensibility," *American Historical Review*, XC (1985), 339-61, 547-66.

16. William Byrd, "History of the Dividing Line . . . 1728," in Louis B. Wright, ed., *The Prose Works of William Byrd of Westover* (Cambridge, Mass., 1966), 221; Chesterfield to his son, 7 Feb. 1749, in *Lord Chesterfield: Letters to His Son and Others* (London, 1929), 93; Hampson, *Enlightenment*, 154, 155.

17. Richard D. Brown, *Knowledge Is Power: The Diffusion of Information in Early America, 1700-1865* (New York, 1989), 105.

18. David Freeman Hawke, *Benjamin Rush: Revolutionary Gadfly* (Indianapolis, 1971), 107; Haskell, "Capitalism and the Origins of the Humanitarian Sensibility," *American Historical Review*, XC (1985), 358.

19. Adams to Jonathan Sewell, Feb. 1760, Humphrey Ploughjogger to Philanthrop, ante 5 Jan. 1767, Earl of Clarendon to William Pym, 27 Jan. 1766, "U" to the Boston *Gazette*, 18 July 1763, in Taylor et al., eds., *Papers of John Adams*, I, 42, 179, 167-68, 71. It was his confidence in the judgment of ordinary people that accounted for Adams's

remarkable pre-revolutionary faith in popular juries. Shannon C. Stimson, *The American Revolution in the Law: Anglo-American Jurisprudence before John Marshall* (Princeton, 1990), 71-80.

20. Humphrey Ploughjogger to Philanthrop, ante 5 Jan. 1767, Humphrey Ploughjogger to the Boston *Evening Post*, 20 June 1763, Adams to Samuel Quincy, 22 Apr. 1761, in ibid., I, 179, 63, 65, 49, 50; Oscar and Lilian Handlin, *A Restless People: Americans in Rebellion, 1770-1787* (New York, 1982), 185.

21. John Andrews, *A Sermon on the Importance of Mutual Kindness* . . . (Philadelphia, 1790), 14; Increase N. Tarbox, ed., *Diary of Thomas Robbins, D.D., 1796-1854* (Boston, 1886), I, 30.

22. Wilson, "Lectures on Law" (1790-91), in McCloskey, ed., *Works of Wilson*, I, 214, 213; Jefferson to T. Law, 13 June 1814, in Lipscomb and Bergh, eds., *Writings of Jefferson*, XIV, 141-42; Nathaniel Chipman, *Principles of Government: A Treatise on Free Institutions, including the Constitution of the United States* (Burlington, Vt., 1833), 46; [John Perkins], *Theory of Agency, or an Essay on the Nature, Source and Extent of Moral Freedom* (Boston, 1771), 27. "Men are not born like blank sheets of paper, ready to receive any impression, but virtue and vice, lie latent in their nature until time brings them into action." *Massachusetts Centinel* (Boston), 19 Jan. 1785, in Wood, ed., *The Rising Glory of America*, 143.

23. *American Museum*, X (1791), 90; Jefferson to Peter Carr, 10 Aug. 1787, in Boyd et al., eds., *Papers of Jefferson*, XII, 15.

24. [Perkins], *Theory of Agency*, 19-20.

25. *American Museum*, I (1787), 462; Henry Cumings, *A Sermon Preached* . . . *May 28, 1783* (Boston, 1783), 17-18; Boston *Independent Chronicle*, 23 Mar. 1787.

26. *Independent Chronicle* (Boston), 21 July 1785.

27. Samuel Adams to Elbridge Gerry, 23 Apr. 1784, in Henry A. Cushing, ed., *Writings of Samuel Adams* (New York, 1906), IV, 301. See Wallace E. Davies, "The Society of the Cincinnati in New England in 1783-1800," *WMQ*, 3rd Ser., V (1948), 3-25. The charge of aristocracy, as William Davie of North Carolina discovered in 1803, was fatal to a political career in America. McRee, ed., *Life and Correspondence of Iredell*, II, 160. "Men of talents" had to be "kept down" in America. "Too much genius, like too much wealth destroys Equality the very soul of Democracy." James Brown to Henry Clay, 1 Sept. 1808, in James F. Hopkins, ed., *The Papers of Henry Clay: The Rising Statesman* (Lexington, Ky., 1959), I, 376.

28. Otto to Vergennes, 10 Oct. 1786, in George Bancroft, *History of the Formation of the Constitution of the United States* (New York, 1882), II, 399-400.

29. Daniel Chipman, *The Life of Hon. Nathaniel Chipman* . . . *with Selections from His Miscellaneous Papers* (Boston, 1846), 33, 29, 30, 31-32.

30. Aleine Austin, *Matthew Lyon: "New Man" of the Democratic Revolution, 1794-1822* (University Park, Pa., 1981), 46, 45.

31. Chipman, *Life of Nathaniel Chipman*, 110.

32. Jedidiah Morse, *Geography Made Easy: Being an Abridgement of the American Geography* . . . (Boston, 1791), 65; Mrs. Jarvis to Samuel F. B. Morse, in Edward Lind Morse, ed., *Samuel F. B. Morse: His Letters and Journals* (Boston, 1914), I, 100.

14. Interests

1. Ryerson, *The Revolution Is Now Begun*, 66, 31; Edward Countryman, *A People in Revolution: The American Revolution and Political Society in New York, 1760-1790* (Baltimore, 1981), 125; Staughton Lynd, *Class Conflict, Slavery, and the United States Constitution: Ten Essays* (Indianapolis, 1968), 79-108; Charles S. Olton, *Artisans for Independence: Philadelphia Mechanics and the American Revolution* (Syracuse, 1975), 55; Richard W. Walsh, *Charleston's Sons of Liberty: A Study of the Artisans, 1763-1787* (Columbia, 1959), 27.

2. Ryerson, *The Revolution Is Now Begun*, 32-33, 47, 50, 73, 75; Kenneth Coleman, *The American Revolution in Georgia, 1763-1789* (Athens, Ga., 1958), 63.

3. Essay, Philadelphia, 22 June 1774, in Wood, *Creation of the American Republic*, 183.

4. New York *Gazette*, 4 Apr. 1765, New York *Journal*, 21 Dec. 1769, quoted in Bernard Friedman, "The Shaping of the Radical Consciousness in Provincial New York," *Journal of American History*, LVI (1970), 789-90, 793-94; Olton, *Artisans for Independence*, 52.

5. Drayton, *The Letters of Freeman*, ed. Weir, 31.

6. Cathy Matson and Peter Onuf, "Toward a Republican Empire: Interest and Ideology in Revolutionary America," *American Quarterly*, XXXVII (1985), 521-27.

7. Royster, *Revolutionary People at War*, 86; Paine, "Common Sense," in Foner, ed., *Writings of Paine*, I, 31.

8. Laurens, quoted in Albert S. Bolles, *The Financial History of the United States from 1774 to 1789: Embracing the Period of the American Revolution*, 4th ed. (New York, 1896), 61-62; E. Wayne Carp, *To Starve the Army at Pleasure: Continental Army Administration and American Political Culture, 1775-1783* (Chapel Hill, 1984), 106.

9. Franklin to Benjamin Vaughn, 26 July 1784, in Smyth, ed., *The Writings of Benjamin Franklin*, IX, 243-44; Nathanael Greene to Jacob Greene, after 24 May 1778, in Showman, ed., *Papers of Nathanael Greene*, II, 404; Richard Buel, Jr., "Samson Shorn: The Impact of the Revolutionary War on Estimates of the Republic's Strength," in Ronald Hoffman and Peter J. Albert, eds., *Arms and Independence: The Military Character of the American Revolution* (Charlottesville, 1984), 157-60.

10. *Remarks on a Pamphlet, Entitled, "Considerations on the Bank of North-America"* (Philadelphia, 1785), 14; Madison to Monroe, 9 Apr. 1786, in Rutland et al., eds., *Papers of Madison*, IX, 26; [William Barton], *The True Interest of the United States, and Particularly of Pennsylvania Considered* . . . (Philadelphia, 1786), 20.

11. Ibid., 4, 25-26.

12. John Fiske, *The Critical Period of American History* (New York, 1888).

13. Jackson T. Main, "Government by the People: The American Revolution and the Democratization of the Legislatures," *WMQ*, 3rd Ser., XXIII (1966), 391-407.

14. Wood, *Creation of the American Republic*, 405; Jack P. Greene, "Legislative Turnover in British America, 1696 to 1775: A Quantitative Analysis," *WMQ*, 3rd Ser., XXXVIII (1981), 442-63.

15. Madison's Observations on Jefferson's Draft of a Constitution for Virginia (1788), in Boyd et al., eds., *Papers of Jefferson*, VI, 308-9; Stiles, "The United States Elevated to Glory and Honor" (1783), in Thornton, ed., *Pulpit of the American Revolution*, 420; *Independent Chronicle* (Boston), 19 Apr. 1787; *Connecticut Courant* (Hartford), 27 Nov., 5 Feb. 1787.

16. In fact, it was only this proprietary notion of wealth that allowed Theophilus Parsons, John Adams, and other drafters and defenders of the Massachusetts constitution of 1780 to identify property with aristocracy and hence with the senate of the

state. On this issue, see the ten illuminating articles by "The Free Republican" (possibly Benjamin Lincoln) in the *Independent Chronicle* (Boston) between 24 Nov. 1785 and 9 Feb. 1786.

17. Jerry Grundfest, *George Clymer: Philadelphia Revolutionary, 1739–1813* (New York, 1982), 177; *Providence Gazette*, 5 Aug. 1786, quoted in David P. Szatmary, *Shays' Rebellion: The Making of an Agrarian Insurrection* (Amherst, Mass., 1980), 51; Madison, Notes for Speech Opposing Paper Money (1786), in Rutland et al., eds., *Papers of Madison*, IX, 158–59; Robert J. Taylor, *Western Massachusetts in the Revolution* (Providence, 1954), 166.

18. Royster, *Revolutionary People at War*, 315; Washington to John Hancock, 24 Sept. 1776, in Fitzpatrick, ed., *Writings of Washington*, VI, 107–8.

19. Carlisle (Pa.) *Gazette*, 24 Oct. 1787, quoted in Herbert J. Storing, ed., *The Complete Anti-Federalist* (Chicago, 1981), II, 208; Washington to James Warren, 7 Oct. 1785, in Fitzpatrick, ed., *Writings of Washington*, XXVIII, 291; [Hamilton], "The Continentalist No. VI" (1782), in Syrett et al., eds., *Papers of Hamilton*, III, 103; *Pennsylvania Packet* (Philadelphia), 11 Mar. 1780; *The Federalist*, No. 10.

20. *The Federalist*, No. 10; Madison to Washington, 16 Apr. 1787, to Edmund Randolph, 8 Apr. 1787, in Rutland et al., eds., *Papers of Madison*, IX, 384, 370.

21. Stourzh, *Alexander Hamilton and the Idea of Republican Government*, 175.

22. Nisbet, quoted in Saul Cornell, "Aristocracy Assailed: The Ideology of Backcountry Anti-Federalism," *Journal of American History*, LXXVI (1990), 1162; Robert Troup to Hamilton, 31 Mar. 1795, in Syrett et al., eds., *Papers of Hamilton*, XVIII, 310; *The Federalist*, No. 35.

23. *The Federalist*, No. 57, No. 10. Madison and other Federalists were willing to allow ordinary people to pursue their partial selfish interests in the expectation that such interests would be so diverse and clashing that they would rarely be able to combine to create tyrannical majorities in the new federal government in the ways they had in the state legislatures. In an enlarged society, wrote Madison, "the people are broken into so many interests and parties, that a common sentiment is less likely to be felt, and requisite concert less likely to be formed, by a majority of the whole." This competitive situation would then allow those educated gentlemen "who possess the most attractive merit, and the most diffusive and established characters" to dominate the national government and promote the common good in a disinterested manner. Madison understood that it had worked that way in American religion; the multiplicity of religious sects in America prevented any one of them from dominating the state and permitted the enlightened reason of liberal gentlemen like Jefferson and himself to shape public policy and church-state relations and protect the rights of minorities. "In a free government," wrote Madison in *The Federalist*, No. 51, "the security for civil rights must be the same as that for religious rights. It consists in the one case in the multiplicity of interests, and in the other in the multiplicity of sects."

24. Madison, Vices of the Political System of the United States (1787), in Rutland et al., eds., *Papers of Madison*, IX, 352, 357.

25. *Providence Gazette*, 5 Jan. 1788.

26. Elliot, ed., *Debates of the State Conventions*, II, 260, 13.

27. Mathew Carey, ed., *Debates and Proceedings of the General Assembly of Pennsylvania on the Memorials Praying a Repeal or Suspension of the Law Annulling the Charter of the Bank* (Philadelphia, 1786), 19, 64, 66, 87, 128, 21, 130, 38, 15, 72–73. For a fuller discussion of the debate, see Gordon S. Wood, "Interests and Disinterestedness in the Making of the Constitution," in Richard Beeman et al., eds., *Beyond Confederation: Origins of the Constitution and American National Identity* (Chapel Hill, 1987), 69–109.

28. Philip A. Crowl, "Anti-Federalism in Maryland, 1787-88," *WMQ*, 3rd Ser., IV (1947), 464; Walsh, *Charleston's Sons of Liberty*, 132; [James Winthrop], "Letters of Agrippa," *Massachusetts Gazette*, 14 Dec. 1787, in Storing, ed., *Complete Anti-Federalist*, IV, 80; Walter Hartwell Bennett, ed., *Letters from the Federal Farmer to the Republican* (University, Ala., 1978), 10.

29. Thomas Hartley to Tench Coxe, 6 Oct., 1788, in Merrill Jensen et al., eds., *The Documentary History of the First Federal Election, 1788-1790* (Madison, Wisc., 1976-   ), I, 304.

30. Ibid., 296, 306; *Pennsylvania Gazette*, 30 July 1788, ibid., 247; Instructions of the Northumberland County Delegates, 16 Oct. 1788, ibid., 314.

31. *Federal Gazette*, 18 Nov., 1788, ibid., 347; *Pennsylvania Packet*, 25 Nov., 1788, ibid., 362, 363. As if to confirm the Anti-Federalist view that all politics were really local after all, one of the elected Federalist congressmen from Pennsylvania, Thomas Scott of Washington County in the far western part of the state, announced his resignation before he could take office. Scott did not want to give up his position as prothonotary of the county; apparently, being a federal congressman could not compare with the power of the clerk of the county court. However, the Federalists feared that if Scott did resign, the Anti-Federalist demagogue William Findley might replace him. Consequently, they worked out an agreement whereby Scott's son was appointed prothonotary and Scott took his seat as congressman. Ibid., 234, 426.

32. In Massachusetts, for example, those who wanted only "the *best* and most *competent* characters" chosen as congressmen in the election of 1788 were opposed by those who wanted an "*equal* and *real* representation" in the government of all the diverse interests of the society. Ibid., 468-72.

33. Farrand, ed., *Records of the Federal Convention*, I, 289.

34. Hamilton, in Farrand, ed., *Records of the Federal Convention*, I, 424; Jay, quoted in David Hackett Fischer, *The Revolution of American Conservatism: The Federalist Party in the Era of Jeffersonian Democracy* (New York, 1965), 7.

35. Hamilton (1794), in Morton J. Frisch, ed., *Selected Writings and Speeches of Alexander Hamilton* (Washington, D.C., 1985), 415.

36. Hamilton, "The Continentalist, No. V," (1782), in Syrett et al., eds., *Papers of Hamilton*, III, 76.

37. The emergence of England's "fiscal-military" state, in John Brewer's apt term, was the miracle of the century. England mobilized wealth and waged war as no state in history ever had; with a population only a fraction the size of France's it had built the greatest empire since the fall of Rome. Hamilton saw that the secret of England's achievement was its system of funded debt together with its banking structure and market in public securities; he aimed to build the same kind of state for the United States. John Brewer, *The Sinews of Power: War, Money and the English State, 1688-1783* (New York, 1989).

38. Hamilton, Speeches in the New York Ratifying Convention, 28, 27 June 1788, Syrett et al., eds., *Papers of Hamilton*, V, 118, 96.

39. Helen R. Pinkney, *Christopher Gore: Federalist of Massachusetts, 1758-1827* (Waltham, Mass., 1969), 37.

40. Hamilton, "The Defence of the Funding System," July 1795, in Syrett et al., eds., *Papers of Hamilton*, XIX, 40-41.

41. Sir James Steuart (1767), quoted in Stephen Copley, *Literature and the Social Order in Eighteenth-Century England* (London, 1984), 120; Hamilton to Washington, 9 Sept. 1792, in Syrett et al., eds., *Papers of Hamilton*, XII, 349; John R. Nelson, "Alexander Ham-

ilton and American Manufacturing: A Reexamination," *Journal of American History*, LXV (1979), 971-95.

42. Bowling and Veit, eds., *Diary of William Maclay*, 141; Jack N. Rakove, "The Structure of Politics at the Accession of George Washington," in Beeman et al., eds., *Beyond Confederation*, 283.

43. Troup to Hamilton, 31 Mar. 1795, Hamilton to Troup, 13 Apr. 1795, in Syrett et al., eds., *Papers of Hamilton*, XVIII, 310, 329. In his revelation in 1797 of his affair with Mrs. Reynolds, Hamilton sacrificed his reputation for private virtue, and hurt his wife deeply, rather than allow his reputation for public virtue to be tarnished. Better to be thought a private adulterer than a corrupt public official.

44. Chester McArthur Destler, *Joshua Coit: American Federalist, 1758-1798* (Middletown, Conn., 1962), 64; Fisher Ames to Christopher Gore, 5 Oct. 1802, in W. B. Allen, ed., *Works of Fisher Ames, as Published by Seth Ames* (Indianapolis, 1983), II, 1438; Thornton, *Cultivating Gentlemen*, 31.

45. On Federalist dreams of western empires, see Andrew R. L. Cayton, *The Frontier Republic: Ideology and Politics in the Ohio Country, 1780-1825* (Kent, Ohio, 1986), 12-32.

46. Wolcott, quoted in David T. Gilchrist, ed., *The Growth of the Seaport Cities, 1790-1825* (Charlottesville, 1967), 119; Ethel E. Rasmusson, "Democratic Environment—Aristocratic Aspiration," *Pennsylvania Magazine of History and Biography*, XC (1966), 155-82; Benjamin Rush to John Adams, 22 Apr. 1789, in Maeva Marcus and James R. Perry et al., eds., *The Documentary History of the Supreme Court of the United States, 1789-1800* (New York, 1985-), I, 613.

47. Fliegelman, *Prodigals and Pilgrims*, 217, 251-54; Bowling and Veit, eds., *Diary of William Maclay*, 54; Hugh Henry Brackenridge, *Modern Chivalry*, ed. Claude M. Newlin (New York, 1937), 432.

48. [Timothy Ford], "Americanus" (1794), in Hyneman and Lutz, eds., *American Political Writing*, II, 921, 924.

49. *Reports of the Proceedings and Debates of the Convention of 1821, Assembled for the Purpose of Amending the Constitution of the State of New York . . .* , ed. Nathaniel H. Carter et al. (Albany, 1821), 219-20, 216, 284, 220-21, 246, 178-79, 219, 268.

50. Ibid., 243. A few years later Kent recognized more clearly that modern property was something other than a source of dominion or independence: "the sense of property," he wrote in his *Commentaries* (1825), "is bestowed on mankind for the purpose of rousing them from sloth and stimulating them to action." Edward S. Corwin, "The Basic Doctrine of American Constitutional Law," *Michigan Law Review*, XII (1914), 262. Other jurists were reaching similar conclusions. Modern property, said Joseph Story, was not the proprietary wealth of a few "opulent and munificent citizens" that gradually spreads itself "into a thousand channels of charity and public benevolence." Rather modern property was evanescent—"continually changing like the waves of the sea"—and it belonged to everyone. It was the "general blessings, which prosperity diffuses through the whole mass of the community." It was "the source of comforts of every kind" and the promoter of "private happiness; and every man, from the humblest possessing property, to the highest in the State, contributes his proportion to the general mass of comfort," even those who possess "but a single dollar." Merrill Peterson, ed., *Democracy, Liberty, and Property: The State Constitutional Conventions of the 1820's* (Indianapolis, 1966), 79-82. On the new democratic understanding of property as the product of labor, see Alan Taylor, *Liberty Men and Great Proprietors: The Revolutionary Settlement on the Maine Frontier, 1760-1820* (Chapel Hill, 1990), 25, 28.

51. *Report of the Debates of the New York Convention of 1821*, ed. Carter et al., 243, 235, 178, 235, 274.

52. Ibid., 179, 243, 314, 319.

15. The Assault on Aristocracy

1. Abraham Bishop, *Connecticut Republicanism: An Oration on the Extent and Power of Political Delusion* . . . (Albany, 1801), 34, 35.

2. [David Daggart], *Three Letters to Abraham Bishop* . . . (Hartford, 1800), 3.

3. Bishop, *Connecticut Republicanism*, 28, 31, 32, 46, 47; Bishop, *Proofs of Conspiracy, against Christianity, and the Government of the United States* . . . (Hartford, 1802), 29; Bishop, *Oration Delivered in Wallingford, on the 11th of March 1801, before the Republicans of the State of Connecticut* . . . (New Haven, 1801), 59.

4. Bishop, *Oration in Wallingford*, 30.

5. Bishop, *Connecticut Republicanism*, v, 30–31; Bishop, *Proofs of Conspiracy*, 19–20.

6. Bishop, *Oration in Wallingford*, 18, 28–29; Bishop, *Proofs of Conspiracy*, 26.

7. Bishop, *Connecticut Republicanism*, 8, 5, 40; Bishop, *Oration in Wallingford*, 38.

8. Bishop, *Connecticut Republicanism*, 32, 41, 40; Bishop, *Proofs of Conspiracy*, 27.

9. Bishop, *Oration in Wallingford*, v; Bishop, *Connecticut Republicanism*, 8, 35, 32.

10. Bishop, *Connecticut Republicanism*, 8, 61–62, 34. Burke's celebration of the great aristocratic families as "the great Oaks that shade a country and perpetuate [their] benefits from Generation to Generation" came in his famous 1772 letter to the Duke of Richmond. Quoted in Isaac Kramnick, *The Rage of Edmund Burke: Portrait of an Ambivalent Conservative* (New York, 1977), 4–5.

11. Bishop, *Oration in Wallingford*, v, 76; Bishop, *Connecticut Republicanism*, 62, 15–16, 18, 19, 21.

12. George Warner, *Means for the Preservation of Political Liberty: An Oration Delivered in the New Dutch Church, on the Fourth of July, 1797* . . . (New York, 1797), 13–14; Alfred Young, "The Mechanics and the Jeffersonians: New York, 1789–1801," *Labor History*, V (1964), 274; Donald H. Stewart, *The Opposition Press of the Federalist Period* (Albany, 1969), 389; Richard E. Ellis, *Jeffersonian Crisis: Courts and Politics in the Young Republic* (New York, 1971), 173.

13. Taylor, *Liberty Men and Great Proprietors*, 24–29.

14. Drayton, *Letters of Freeman*, ed. Weir, iii–12, 113.

15. Harold B. Rock, *Artisans of the New Republic: The Tradesmen of New York City in the Age of Jefferson* (New York, 1979), 50, see esp. 5–7, 53–57.

16. Bishop, *Oration in Wallingford*, 54.

17. Austin, *Matthew Lyon*, 74, 67; Stewart, *Opposition Press*, 390.

18. Samuel Eliot Morison, ed., "William Manning's 'The Key of Libberty'," *WMQ*, 3rd Ser., XIII (1956), 202–54.

19. James P. Walsh, " 'Mechanics and Citizens': The Connecticut Artisan Protest of 1792," *WMQ*, 3rd Ser., LXII (1985), 66–89.

20. Stuart M. Blumin, *The Emergence of the Middle Class: Social Experience in the American City, 1760–1900* (Cambridge, Eng., 1989), 33–34. As Blumin suggests, much of our confusion over what was happening socially in the late eighteenth century comes from our inability to appreciate the extent to which the gentry were set off from all common people who worked for a living, middling as well as poor.

21. A. G. Roeber, *Faithful Magistrates and Republican Lawyers: Creators of Virginia Legal*

Culture, 1680-1810 (Chapel Hill, 1981), 247, 251; Ruth Bogin, *Abraham Clark and the Quest for Equality in the Revolutionary Era, 1774-1794* (East Brunswick, N.J., 1982), 32; Austin, *Matthew Lyon,* 64.

22. [John Adams], *Discourses on Davila: A Series of Papers on Political History* (1790) (New York, 1973), 91; Antonio Pace, ed., *Luigi Castiglioni's Viaggio: Travels in the United States of North America, 1785-1787* (Syracuse, 1983), 335.

23. Corner, ed., *The Autobiography of Benjamin Rush,* 225.

24. Bogin, *Abraham Clark,* 32; Bishop, *Proofs of Conspiracy,* 20; Jerome J. Nadelhaft, " 'The Snarls of Invidious Animals': The Democratization of Revolutionary South Carolina," in Ronald Hoffman and Peter J. Albert, eds., *Sovereign States in an Age of Uncertainty* (Charlottesville, 1981), 77.

25. *Port Folio,* 3rd Ser., 4 (1810), 571-72.

26. Mason L. Weems, *The Life of Washington* (1809), ed. Marcus Cunliffe (Cambridge, Mass., 1962), 203-14.

27. [Samuel Blodget], *Economica: A Statistical Manual for the United States of America* (Washington, D.C., 1806), 4; Nowal Neil Luxon, *Niles' Weekly Register: News Magazine of the Nineteenth Century* (Baton Rouge, 1947), 37-38.

28. Everett, "Lecture on the Workingmen's Party" (1830), "Advantage of Knowledge to Workingmen" (1831), *Orations and Speeches on Various Occasions,* 2nd ed. (Boston, 1850), 285, 287, 320, 292, 294, 303; *North American Review,* XXVII (1828), 115.

29. Francis J. Grund, *The Americans, in Their Moral, Social, and Political Relations* (Boston, 1837), 157; Michael Chevalier, *Society, Manners, and Politics in the United States: Letters on North America* (1836), ed. John William Ward (Gloucester, Mass., 1967), 201-2.

30. Alexis de Tocqueville, *Democracy in America* (1835), ed. J. P. Mayer (New York, 1969), I, 373; II, 550-51; Chevalier, *Society, Manners, and Politics in the United States,* ed. Ward, 284.

31. Emerson, "The American Scholar," in Brooks Atkinson, ed., *The Complete Essays and Other Writings of Ralph Waldo Emerson* (New York, 1940), 55.

32. Sedgwick, quoted in Marvin Meyers, *The Jacksonian Persuasion: Politics and Belief* (Stanford, 1957), 174-75; James Fenimore Cooper, *Notions of the Americans Picked Up by a Travelling Bachelor* (1828) (New York, 1963), I, 161n.

33. Stuart M. Blumin, "The Hypothesis of Middle-Class Formation in Nineteenth-Century America: A Critique and Some Proposals," *American Historical Review,* XC (1985), 316-17.

16. Democratic Officeholding

1. Jack N. Rakove, *The Beginnings of National Politics: An Interpretative History of the Continental Congress* (New York, 1979), 216-39, 230, 235, 237; George A. Billias, *Elbridge Gerry: Founding Father and Republican Statesman* (New York, 1976), 138-39; McRee, ed., *Life and Correspondence of James Iredell,* II, 55, 56; Chipman, *Life of Nathaniel Chipman,* 29, 33. In America, noted Jefferson in 1782, "offices of every kind, and given by every power, have been daily and hourly declined and resigned from the declaration of independence to this moment." Jefferson to James Monroe, 20 May 1782, in Boyd et al., eds., *Papers of Jefferson,* VI, 185-86.

2. Jefferson to Richard Henry Lee, 17 June 1779, in Paul L. Ford, ed., *The Writings of Thomas Jefferson* (New York, 1893), II, 192; Jefferson to William Duane, 1 Oct. 1812, in Lipscomb and Bergh, eds., *Writings of Jefferson,* XIII, 186; Jefferson to Francis Willis,

13 Apr. 1790, in Ford, ed., *Writings of Jefferson*, V, 157. In fact, said Jefferson, the very "drudgery" of office and the bare "subsistence" provided for officeholders in a republic were "a wise & necessary precaution against the degeneracy of the public servants." Such aristocratic views naturally increased Jefferson's popularity among Republican plebeians who resented paying taxes to pay for what seemed to be the high salaries of their public officials. Some of these Republican plebeians in New Jersey even regarded the difference between what a militiaman got for travel—ten cents a day—and what a congressman got for travel—thirty cents a mile—as "an aristocratical distinction." Jefferson to De Meunier, 29 Apr. 1795, in Paul L. Ford, ed., *The Works of Thomas Jefferson: Federal Edition* (New York, 1904), VIII, 174; Leonard D. White, *The Federalists: A Study in Administrative History* (New York, 1948), 292–93.

3. At a moment of despair and withdrawal following his troubled term as governor of Virginia, Jefferson did complain that the burdens of public service had become too heavy even for him. Leisured gentlemen like himself, he admitted, had an obligation to the state to serve their "tour of political duty." But the public had no right to their "whole existence." "If we are made in some degree for others," he said, "yet in a greater are we made for ourselves." Jefferson to Monroe, 20 May 1782, in Boyd et al., eds., *Papers of Jefferson*, VI, 185–86.

4. Morris, quoted in Rakove, *Beginnings of National Politics*, 237.

5. Morris, "Political Enquiries," in Willi Paul Adams, ed., " 'The Spirit of Commerce, Requires that Property be Sacred': Gouverneur Morris and the American Revolution," *Amerikastudien/American Studies*, XXI (1976), 329.

6. Adams to John Jebb, 21 Aug. 1785, in Adams, ed., *Works of John Adams*, IX, 533–35.

7. Adams to Jebb, 10, 25 Sept. 1785, ibid., 538–42, 543–44.

8. Lovell, quoted in Rakove, *Beginnings of National Politics*, 227.

9. Farrand, ed., *Records of the Federal Convention*, I, 78, 81–85. In his will Franklin stated that it had "long been a fixed opinion of mine, that in a democratical state there ought to be no offices of profit." When he had been elected president of Pennsylvania he had, he said, devoted "the appointed salary to some public uses." Codicil to Franklin's will, 23 June 1789, Smyth, ed., *Writings of Franklin*, X, 501.

10. Farrand, ed., *Records of the Federal Convention*, I, 211, 219. Connecticut, Delaware, and South Carolina voted to deny salaries to senators; Massachusetts was divided.

11. Farrand, *Records of the Federal Convention*, I, 216; Madison, Salaries for Congress, 16 July 1789, Madison to Wilson Cary, 18 July 1789, in Rutland et al., eds., *Papers of Madison*, XII, 293, 295.

12. Bowling and Veit, eds., *Diary of Maclay*, 134. Butler, by his manner and his flaunting of his Anglo-Irish aristocratic connections, probably did more to discredit classical republican sentiments than a multitude of artisan-businessmen: he made himself obnoxious to his fellow senators, said William Maclay, by "ever and anon declaring how clear of local Views [and] how candid and dispassionate he was." Ibid., 73.

13. Ibid., 134, 149, 259.

14. White, *Federalists*, 292, 301, 271. By 1797, public office for a classically minded figure like Hamilton had lost some of its former attractiveness. "The pecuniary emolument is so inconsiderable as to amount to a sacrifice to any man who can employ his time with advantage in any liberal profession. The opportunity of doing good, from the jealousy of power and the spirit of faction, is too small in any station to warrant a long continuance of private sacrifices." Hamilton to William Hamilton, 2 May 1797, in Syrett et al., eds., *Papers of Hamilton*, XXI, 78.

15. Hartog, *Public Property and Private Power*, 133.

16. It was hard to sustain the pretense that office was a burden that prominent gentry were obliged to bear when the hesitancy of men like John Jay to accept a position in the new federal government was attributed to his "waiting to see which Salary is best, that of Lord Chief Justice or Secretary of State." Samuel A. Otis to John Langdon, [16–22] Sept. 1789, in Marcus and Perry et al., eds., *Documentary History of the Supreme Court*, I, 661. Part 2 of this volume is full of the awkward letters of men who desired appointment to the Supreme Court but were culturally inhibited from expressing their desires too boldly. See especially the shuffling delicacy of John Lowell. Lowell to Elbridge Gerry, 20 July 1789, ibid., 637–38.

17. Benjamin Latrobe to Philip Mazzei, 19 Dec. 1806, in Margherita Marchione et al., eds., *Philip Mazzei: Selected Writings and Correspondence* (Prato, Italy, 1983), 439. See Chipman, *Principles of Government*, 62–63: In the absence of an impartial arbiter, Chipman suggested an "amicable compromise" among the competing interests; but of course "in matters that depend on a mutual compromise, every man is, under the best regulated government, of right allowed to be the judge of his own interest, and an actor in his cause."

18. Latrobe to Mazzei, 19 Dec. 1806, in Marchione et al., eds., *Mazzei: Selected Writings and Correspondence*, 439.

19. Everett, quoted in Shaw Livermore, *The Twilight of Federalism: The Disintegration of the Federalist Party, 1815–1830* (Princeton, 1962), 266–67; Leonard D. White, *The Jeffersonians: A Study in Administrative History, 1801–1829* (New York, 1951), 364–68.

20. Austin, *Matthew Lyon*, 134.

21. *As You Were! A Word of Advice to Straight-Haired Folks: Address to the Freemen of Connecticut* (New Haven, [1816]), 14, 3.

22. Niles, quoted in M. J. Heale, *The Making of Modern Politics, 1750–1850* (London, 1977), 130.

23. Ronald P. Formisano has been making this point for years. Formisano, "Deferential-Participant Politics: The Early Republic's Political Culture, 1789–1840," *American Political Science Review*, LXVIII (1974), 473–87; and his *The Transformation of Political Culture: Massachusetts Parties, 1790s–1840s* (New York, 1983).

24. Jefferson to Lafayette, 14 May 1817, in Ford, ed., *Writings of Jefferson*, X, 83.

25. Monroe, quoted in Hofstadter, *The Idea of a Party System: The Rise of Legitimate Opposition in the United States, 1780–1840* (Berkeley, 1969), 196.

26. Martin Van Buren, *Autobiography*, ed. John C. Fitzpatrick, *Annual Report of the American Historical Association for the Year 1918* (Washington, D.C., 1920), I, 7.

27. Albany *Argus*, Feb. 29, 1820.

28. Albany *Argus*, Aug. 26, 1823, quoted in Michael Wallace, "Changing Concepts of Party in the United States: New York, 1815–1828," *American Historical Review*, LXXIV (1968–69), 461.

29. Jay, in *Reports and Debates of the New York Convention of 1821*, ed. Carter et al., 345; Van Buren, *Autobiography*, 105.

30. *Reports and Debates of the New York Convention of 1821*, ed. Carter et al., 262; Robert V. Remini, "The Albany Regency," *New York History*, XXXIX (1958), 344, 345.

31. Jefferson to James Sullivan, 3 Mar. 1808, Lipscomb and Bergh, eds., *Writings of Jefferson*, XII, 3; Jefferson to Elias Shipman and others, 12 July 1801, in Ford, ed., *Works of Jefferson: Federal Edition*, IX, 274.

32. White, *Jeffersonians*, 380; Carl Russell Fish, *The Civil Service and the Patronage* (New York, 1905), 72.

33. *Reports and Debates of the New York Convention of 1821*, ed. Carter et al., 386, 387, 321, 385–86.

34. Sidney H. Aronson, *Status and Kinship in the Higher Civil Service* (Cambridge, Mass., 1964).

35. Lynn Marshall, "The Strange Still Birth of the Whig Party," *American Historical Review*, LXXII (1967), 452n.; Harry L. Watson, *Liberty and Power: The Politics of Jacksonian America* (New York, 1990), 99, 101.

36. Marshall, "Strange Still Birth of the Whig Party," *American Historical Review*, LXXII (1967), 452.

37. Jackson, First Annual Message, 8 Dec. 1829, in James D. Richardson, ed., *A Compilation of the Messages and Papers of the Presidents, 1789–1897* (Washington, D.C., 1900), II, 449.

38. James T. Schleifer, *The Making of Tocqueville's Democracy in America* (Chapel Hill, 1980), 143.

39. Matthew A. Crenson, *The Federal Machine: Beginnings of Bureaucracy in Jacksonian America* (Baltimore, 1975).

40. Marshall, "Strange Still Birth of the Whig Party," *American Historical Review*, LXXII (1967), 456, 457–58.

17. A World Within Themselves

1. Charles Nisbet (1787), quoted in Samuel Miller, *Memoir of the Rev. Charles Nisbet, D. D., Late President of Dickinson College, Carlisle* (New York, 1840), 167; William Findley, *Observations on "The Two Sons of Oil" Containing a Vindication of the American Constitution . . .* (Pittsburgh, 1812), 291; Alexander McLeod (1802), quoted in Steven Watts, *The Republic Reborn: War and the Making of Liberal America, 1790–1820* (Baltimore, 1987), 113.

2. Webster, "Address of Bunker Hill" (1825), in *Writings and Speeches of Daniel Webster: National Edition* (Boston, 1903), I, 238–39; Edward Everett, "An Oration Pronounced at Cambridge . . . 1824," in Joseph L. Blau, ed. *American Philosophic Addresses, 1700–1900* (New York, 1946), 77.

3. W. J. Rorabaugh, *The Alcoholic Republic: An American Tradition* (1979), 3–21, 87; Ian R. Tyrell, *Sobering Up: From Temperance to Prohibition in Antebellum America, 1800–1860* (Westport, Conn., 1979), 3–32; Randolph A. Roth, *The Democratic Dilemma: Religion, Reform, and the Social Order in the Connecticut River Valley of Vermont, 1791–1850* (Cambridge, Eng., 1987), 48; Elizabeth Cometti, ed., *Seeing America and Its Great Men: The Journals and Letters of Count Francesco dal Verme, 1783–1784* (Charlottesville, 1969), 15.

4. Esther B. Aresty, *The Best Behavior: The Course of Good Manners—From Antiquity to the Present as Seen through Courtesy and Etiquette Books* (New York, 1970), 189–90, 229; *North American Review*, I (1815), 20; Neil K. Fitzgerald, "Towards an American Abraham: Multiple Parricide and the Rejection of Revelation in the Early National Period . . ." (M. A. Thesis, Brown University, 1971), 8–9, using Thomas M. McDade, comp., *The Annals of Murder: A Bibliography of Books and Pamphlets on American Murders from Colonial Times to 1900* (Norman, Okla., 1961); David Hackett Fischer, *The Revolution of American Conservatism: The Federalist Party in the Era of Jeffersonian Democracy* (New York, 1965), 187.

5. Paul A. Gilje, *The Road to Mobocracy: Popular Disorder in New York City, 1763–1834* (Chapel Hill, 1987), 123–288; Howard B. Rock, *Artisans of the New Republic: The Tradesmen of New York City in the Age of Jefferson* (New York, 1979), 59.

6. Gilje, *Road to Mobocracy*, 268, 274, 279.

7. Charles Stewart Daveis, *An Address Delivered on the Commemoration at Fryeburg, May 19, 1825* (Portland, Me., 1825), in Joseph L. Blau, ed., *Social Theories of Jacksonian Democracy: Representative Writings of the Period 1825-1850* (New York, 1954), 49; Elkanah Watson, *History of the Rise, Progress, and Existing State of Modern Agricultural Societies on the Berkshire System, from 1807 to the Establishment of the Board of Agriculture in the State of New York, January 10, 1820* (Albany, 1820), 114, 142, 160, 177-78, 168n., 169, 182.

8. Samuel Latham Mitchill, *An Address to the Citizens of New York . . .* (New York, 1800), 7-8; Grundfest, *George Clymer*, 141; Lucius Versus Bierce, *Travels in the Southland, 1822-1823: The Journal of Lucius Versus Bierce*, ed. George W. Knepper (Columbus, Ohio, 1966), 103.

9. *Niles' Weekly Register*, I (1811-12), 10.

10. Joan Wells Coward, *Kentucky in the New Republic: The Process of Constitution Making* (Lexington, Ky., 1979), 3; R. Carlyle Buley, *The Old Northwest: Pioneer Period, 1815-1840* (Bloomington, Ind., 1950), 125; Andrew R. L. Cayton, *The Frontier Republic: Ideology and Politics in the Ohio Country, 1780-1825* (Kent, Ohio, 1986), 112; Calhoun, quoted in William A. Schaper, *Sectionalism and Representation in South Carolina* (New York, 1968; first publ. 1901), 139.

11. Everett, "Speech at Nashville" (1829), *Orations and Speeches*, I, 191, 192; Cayton, *Frontier Republic*, 116; Henry Wansey, *The Journal of an Excursion to the United States of North America in the Summer of 1794* (New York, 1969), 183; Malcolm J. Rohrbough, *The Trans-Appalachian Frontier: People, Societies, and Institutions, 1775-1850* (New York, 1978), 36-37, 96-97.

12. C. F. Volney, *A View of the Soil and Climate of the United States of America*, trans. C. B. Brown (Philadelphia, 1804), 3.

13. Patricia S. Watlington, *The Partisan Spirit, Kentucky Politics, 1779-1792* (New York, 1972), 46; Morris Birkbeck, *Letters from Illinois* (London, 1818), 14; Rohrbough, *Trans-Appalachian Frontier*, 55; William C. Preston, *Reminiscences*, quoted in Charles L. Sanford, ed., *Quest for America, 1810-1824* (New York, 1964), 26.

14. *The Panoplist and Missionary Herald*, XIV (1818), 212-13.

15. Flower, quoted in Alice Felt Tyler, *Freedom's Ferment: Phases of American Social History from the Colonial Period to the Outbreak of the Civil War* (Minneapolis, 1944), 18; Everett, "Speech at Yellow Springs, Ohio" (1829), *Orations and Speeches*, I, 209, 210; Stephen Hahn and Jonathan Prude, eds., *The Countryside in the Age of Capitalist Transformation: Essays in the Social History of Rural America* (Chapel Hill, 1985), intro., 4.

16. For the most important works, see George Rogers Taylor, "American Economic Growth before 1840: An Exploratory Essay," *Journal of Economic History*, XXIV (1964), 427-44; Donald R. Adams, Jr., "Wage Rates in the Early National Period: Philadelphia, 1785-1830," *Journal of Economic History*, XXVIII (1968), 404-17; Paul A. David, "The Growth of Real Product in the United States before 1840: New Evidence, Controlled Conjectures," *Journal of Economic History*, XXVII (1967), 151-97; Douglass C. North, *The Economic Growth of the United States, 1790-1860* (Englewood Cliffs, N. J., 1961); Kenneth L. Sokoloff, "Productivity Growth in Manufacturing during Early Industrialization: Evidence from the American Northeast, 1820-1860," in Stanley L. Engerman and Robert E. Gallman, eds., *Long-Term Factors in American Economic Growth* (Chicago, 1986), 679-736; Sokoloff, "Inventive Activity in Early Industrial America: Evidence from Patent Records, 1790-1846," *Journal of Economic History*, XLVIII (1988), 813-50, and the articles by Winifred B. Rothenberg cited above in note 22, ch. 8.

17. Adna Ferrin Weber, *The Growth of Cities in the Nineteenth Century: A Study in Statistics*

(New York, 1969), 40–47; Philip Abrams and E. A. Wrigley, eds., *Towns in Society: Essays in Economic History and Historical Sociology* (Cambridge, Eng., 1978), 247–48.

18. William J. Gilmore, "Elementary Literacy on the Eve of the Industrial Revolution: Trends in Rural New England, *1760–1830*," American Antiquarian Society, *Proc.*, XCII (1982), 87–177; Gilmore, *Reading Becomes a Necessity of Life: Material and Cultural Life in Rural New England, 1780–1835* (Knoxville, 1989).

19. Matson and Onuf, "Toward a Republican Empire," *American Quarterly*, XXXVII (1985), 496–531.

20. Claudia Goldin and Kenneth Sokoloff, "Women, Children, and Industrialization in the Early Republic: Evidence from the Manufacturing Censuses," *Journal of Economic History*, XLII (1982), 745–46; Thomas C. Cochran, *Frontiers of Change: Early Industrialism in America* (New York, 1981), 57; Gallatin, quoted in Joyce Appleby, *Capitalism and a New Social Order: The Republican Vision of the 1790s* (New York, 1984), 43; Wansey, *Journal of an Excursion* (New York, 1969; first publ., 1796), 47, 101; James A. Henretta, "The War for Independence and American Economic Development," in Hoffman et al., eds., *Economy in Early America*, 81, 80; *Niles' Weekly Register*, III (1812–13), 328. Perhaps nothing is more revealing of what was happening than the pathetic letter written in 1808 by the little border town of St. Albans, Vermont, to President Jefferson protesting his April 19, 1808, proclamation that the town was in a state of insurrection for violating the Embargo. The town inhabitants told the President that they could not understand how stopping their trade with Canada could possibly help the United States if it hurt the people of St. Albans. "Exchanging their surplus production for many of the conveniences, and even necessaries, of life," they said, was what the townsmen did; it was the source of their daily existence. *American Register*, III (1808), 450–52.

21. Stanley Lebergott, "Labor Force and Employment, *1800–1960*," in *Output, Employment, and Productivity in the United States after 1800*, XXX, *Studies in Income and Wealth*, National Bureau of Economic Research (New York, 1966), 128; *Niles' Weekly Register*, III (1812–13), 328.

22. Jonathan Messerli, *Horace Mann: A Biography* (New York, 1972), 16; Thomas Dublin, "Women and Outwork in a Nineteenth-Century New England Town: Fitzwilliam, New Hampshire, 1830–1850," in Hahn and Prude, eds., *Countryside in the Age of Capitalist Transformation*, 51–69.

23. Adams to Jefferson, 16 July 1814, in Lester J. Cappon, ed., *The Adams-Jefferson Letters: The Complete Correspondence between Thomas Jefferson and Abigail and John Adams* (Chapel Hill, 1959), II, 436. Others, even some of the most radical spokesmen for ordinary people, had no better understanding of economic developments. Abraham Bishop, for example, continued to believe that the amount of wealth was fixed and all that it did was circulate about. Taking out mortgages and borrowing money were the consequence of extravagance, he said; they could not add to the amount of wealth. "A state of commerce neither stimulated nor restrained is the natural state for a republic." Statements like these reveal how difficult it was for people in this dynamic period to grasp exactly what was happening to the economy: everything was so unprecedented, and conventional wisdom died hard. Bishop, *Connecticut Republicanism*, 12; Bishop, *Oration in Wallingford*, 21.

24. Calhoun, quoted in Oscar and Lilian Handlin, *Liberty in Expansion, 1760–1850* (New York, 1989), 197; *Niles' Weekly Register*, I (1811–12), 282, 3; Mathew Carey (1822), quoted in Nathan Miller, *The Enterprise of a Free People: Aspects of Economic Development in New York State during the Canal Period, 1792–1838* (Ithaca, 1962), 42; Frances Wright, *Views of Society and Manners in America*, ed. Paul R. Baker (Cambridge, Mass., 1963), 208.

"There is no word in the English language that more deceives a people than the word *commerce*," wrote Hezekiah Niles in his *Weekly Register* in 1814. People everywhere "associate with it an idea of great ships, passing to all countries—whereas the rich commerce of every community is its *internal*; a communication of one part with other parts of the same. . . . In the United States (were we at peace) our *foreign* trade would hardly exceed a *fortieth* or *fiftieth* part of the whole *commerce* of the people. These assertions," said Niles, "may surprise many, but they are founded on what I esteem indisputable data." *Niles' Weekly Register,* VI (1814), 395.

25. Bray Hammond, *Banks and Politics in America from the Revolution to the Civil Wa* (Princeton, 1957), 66.

26. Pauline Maier, "The Debate over Incorporations: Massachusetts in the Early Republic," paper delivered at Bicentennial Conference of the Massachusetts Historical Society, 18–19 May 1990, 32; J. Van Fenstermaker, *The Development of American Commercial Banking: 1782–1837* (Kent, Ohio, 1965), 4–14.

27. Hammond, *Banks and Politics,* 145, 165.

28. Hammond, *Banks and Politics,* 147, Philadelphia *General Advertiser,* 16 Feb. 1793; Richard Gabriel Stone, *Hezekiah Niles as an Economist* (Baltimore, 1833), 94–95; Fenstermaker, *American Commercial Banking,* 8.

29. Hammond, *Banks and Politics,* 188, 196, 189; Jefferson to Col. Charles Yancey, 6 Jan. 1816, in Ford, ed., *Works of Jefferson: Federal Edition,* XI, 494.

30. [Samuel Blodget], *Economica: A Statistical Manual for the United States of America* (Washington, 1806), 17.

31. When in the Philadelphia Convention James Madison proposed that the federal government be given the explicit power to grant charters of incorporation, the framers decided to finesse the issue by saying nothing in the Constitution about incorporations out of fear of arousing popular opposition to "mercantile monopolies." Frank Bourgin, *The Great Challenge: The Myth of Laissez-Faire in the Early Republic* (New York, 1989), 44.

32. Hartog, *Public Property and Private Power,* 90.

33. Walter R. Fee, *The Transition from Aristocracy to Democracy in New Jersey, 1789–1829* (Somerville, N.J., 1933), 146; Joseph S. Davis, *Essays in the Earlier History of American Corporations,* IV, *Eighteenth Century Business Corporations in the United States* (Cambridge, Mass., 1917), 321; P. H. Woodward, *One Hundred Years of the Hartford Bank . . .* (Hartford, 1892), 50.

34. [Sullivan], *Path to Riches,* 37–38, 10, 43.

35. Cochran, *Frontiers of Change,* 21; Hartog, *Public Property and Private Power,* 153; [Blodget], *Economica,* 17.

36. Oscar and Mary Handlin, *Commonwealth: A Study of the Role of Government in the American Economy: Massachusetts, 1774–1861* (Cambridge, Mass., 1947, 1969), 106–33; Ronald E. Seavoy, *The Origins of the American Business Corporation, 1784–1855: Broadening the Concept of Public Service During Industrialization* (Westport, Conn., 1982); Lincoln, quoted in Maier, "The Debate over Incorporations," 18.

37. Sandra F. VanBurkleo, " 'The Paws of Banks': The Origins and Significance of Kentucky's Decision to Tax Federal Bankers, 1818–1820," *Journal of the Early Republic,* IX (1989), 480–87; Sandra F. VanBurkleo, " 'That Our Pure Republican Principles Might Not Wither': Kentucky's Relief Crisis and the Pursuit of Moral Justice, 1818–1826" (Ph. D. Diss., University of Minnesota, 1088), ch. 6.

38. R. Kent Newmeyer, *Supreme Court Justice Joseph Story: Statesman of the Old Republic* (Chapel Hill, 1985), 132; Harry N. Scheiber, "Public Rights and the Rule of Law in American Legal History," *California Law Review,* LXXII (1984), 217–51.

39. "The proposition, that a power to do, includes virtually, a power to undo, as applied to a legislative body," wrote Hamilton, "is generally but not universally true. All *vested rights* form an exception to the rule." Hamilton, "The Examination," 23 Feb. 1802, in Syrett et al., eds., *Papers of Hamilton*, XXV, 533. Edward S. Corwin called the protection of vested rights "the basic doctrine of American constitutional law." Corwin, "The Basic Doctrine of American Constitutional Law," *Michigan Law Review*, XII (1914), 247–76.

40. In 1776 most of the revolutionary state constitutions did not provide for just compensation for the public taking of private property; but, following the adoption of the Fifth Amendment to the federal Constitution in 1791, this provision was explicitly added in nearly all the constitutions of states subsequently admitted to the Union. In the following years, where such a specific reference to just compensation remained absent from the constitutions of the original states, judicial interpretation often inserted it. J. A. C. Grant, "The 'Higher Law' Background of the Law of Eminent Domain," *Wisconsin Law Review*, VI (1930–31), 70.

41. Carey, ed., *Debates of the General Assembly of Pennsylvania*, 11–12; Davis, *Essays in the History of American Corporations*, 313.

42. *Pennsylvania Packet* (Philadelphia), 2 Sept. 1786.

43. "It is the regular administration of the laws by an independent judiciary," declared a Federalist in the New York constitutional convention of 1820–21 in a common reckoning, "that renders property secure against private acts of violence." *Reports of the Debates of the New York Convention of 1821*, ed. Carter et al., 242.

44. [Henry Chipman], *An Oration on the Study and Profession of the Law* (Middlebury, Vt., 1806), 7; Richard E. Ellis, *The Jeffersonian Crisis: Courts and Politics in the Young Republic* (New York, 1971), 163, 176, 177.

45. Sandra F. VanBurkleo, " 'Honour, Justice, and Interest': John Jay's Republican Politics and Statesmanship on the Federal Bench," *Journal of the Early Republic*, IV (1984), 263–64, 269; Russell Wheeler, "Extrajudicial Activities of the Early Supreme Court," *Supreme Court Review* (1973), 123–58.

46. George L. Haskins and Herbert A. Johnson, *Foundations of Power: John Marshall, 1801–15*, in Oliver Wendell Holmes Devise, *History of the Supreme Court of the United States*, II (New York, 1981), 189, 193–95, 203–04, 246, 297, 336, 354, 395–96, 400, 421; George L. Haskins, "Law versus Politics in the Early Years of the Marshall Court," *University of Pennsylvania Law Review*, CXXX (1981), 1–27; Jennifer Nedelsky, "Confining Democratic Politics: Anti-Federalists, Federalists, and the Constitution," *Harvard Law Review*, XCVI (1982–83), 351–60; Morton J. Horwitz, *The Transformation of American Law, 1780–1860* (Cambridge, Mass., 1977), 257; Newmeyer, *Jospeh Story*, 38, 54. The controversy that arose over the constitutionality of the Congress's assigning of administrative duties to the courts in its 1792 Invalid Pension Act was a consequence of this emerging distinction between political and legal matters. Some of the justices, on the grounds that they would violate the separation of powers, objected to becoming pension commissioners and making such magisterial decisions. J. M. Sosin, *The Aristocracy of the Long Robe: The Origins of Judicial Review in America* (Westport, Conn., 1989), 285–87.

47. Hamilton, Remarks in New York Assembly, 6 Feb. 1787, in Syrett et al., eds., *Papers of Hamilton*, IV, 35. The view expressed by Hamilton did not of course immediately take hold. The attorney general of North Carolina, for example, argued in 1794 that the clauses of the state constitution referring to due process and the law of the land were not limitations on the legislature; they were "declarations the people thought

proper to make of their rights, not against a power they supposed their own representatives might usurp, but against oppression and usurpation in general . . . , by a pretended prerogative against or without the authority of law.'' Thus the phrase that no one could be deprived of his property except by the law of the land meant simply ''a law for the people of North Carolina, made or adopted by themselves by the intervention of their own legislature.'' Edward S. Corwin, ''The Doctrine of Due Process of Law before the Civil War,'' *Harvard Law Review*, XXIV (1911), 371-72. Blackstone had written that one of the absolute rights of individuals was ''the right of property: which consists in the free use, enjoyment and disposal of all his acquisitions, without any control or diminution, *save only by the laws of the land*''—which of course for Blackstone included those laws enacted by Parliament. Corwin, ''Basic Doctrine of American Constitutional Law,'' *Michigan Law Review*, XII (1914), 254.

48. Alexander J. Dallas, quoted in Ellis, *Jeffersonian Crisis*, 179; Michael Les Benedict, ''Laissez-Faire and Liberty: A Re-evaluation of the Meaning and Origins of Laissez-Faire Constitutionalism,'' *Law and History Review*, III (1985), 323-26.

49. Harry N. Scheiber, ''The Road to *Munn*: Eminent Domain and the Concept of Public Purpose in the State Courts,'' *Perspectives in American History*, V (1971), 366; George Dargo, *Law in the New Republic: Private Law and the Public Estate* (New York, 1983), 40; Madison to Jefferson, 27 June 1823, in Gaillard Hunt, ed., *Writings of Madison* (New York, 1900-10), IX, 140; Tocqueville, *Democracy in America*, ed. Phillips Bradley (New York, 1956), I, 278.

18. The Celebration of Commerce

1. Samuel L. Mitchill, *An Address to the Citizens of New York* . . . (New York, 1800), 23; Chevalier, *Society, Manners, and Politics in the United States*, 283; J.A. Leo Lemay, ''Poe's 'The Business Man': Its Contexts and Satire of Franklin's *Autobiography*,'' *Poe Studies* XV (1982), 30; Clay, Speech in the House of Representatives, 22 Jan. 1812, in Hopkins, ed., *Papers of Clay*, I, 626.

2. *Niles' Weekly Register*, V (1813-14), 1-16; Corner, ed., *Autobiography of Benjamin Rush*, 338; Harriet Silvester Tapley, *Salem Imprints, 1768-1825: A History of the First Fifty Years of Printing in Salem, Massachusetts* (Salem, 1927), 106.

3. Steven Watts, *The Republican Reborn: War and the Making of Liberal America, 1790-1820* (Baltimore, 1987), 63-107.

4. *Niles' Weekly Register*, I (1811-12), 252; William Crafts, *Oration on the Influence of Moral Causes, on National Character* . . . (Cambridge, Mass., 1817), 40.

5. Cabot, quoted in Fischer, *Revolution of American Conservatism*, 3.

6. Jefferson to Spencer Roane, 6 Sept. 1819, in Ford, ed., *Writings of Jefferson*, X, 140; Bloomfield, *American Lawyers*, 37.

7. Ford, *Joel Barlow*, 89.

8. *American Museum*, V (1789), 555; Richard D. Brown, ''The Emergence of Urban Society in Rural Massachusetts, 1760-1820,'' *Journal of American History*, LXI (1974), 29-51; Brown, ''The Emergence of Voluntary Associations in Massachusetts, 1760-1830,'' *Journal of Voluntary Action Research*, II (1973), 64-73.

9. Ingersoll, ''Influence of America on the Mind'' (1823), in Blau, ed., *American Philosophic Addresses*, 36; William E. Channing, ''Remarks on Associations'' (1829), in *Works of William E. Channing* (Boston, 1877), 139-40.

10. On the changing nature of these benevolent societies, see Conrad E. Wright. "Christian Compassion and Corporate Beneficence: The Institutionalization of Charity in New England, 1720-1810" (Ph.D. Diss., Brown University, 1980).

11. Nicholas Collins, "An Essay on those inquiries in Natural Philosophy which at present are most beneficial to the United States of America," *American Philosophical Society, Trans.*, II (1793), vii; George H. Knoles, "The Religious Ideas of Thomas Jefferson," *Mississippi Valley Historical Review*, XXX (1943-44), 194; Henry May, *The Enlightenment in America* (New York, 1976), 72-73; Butler, *Awash in a Sea of Faith*, 195-96, 214-15; Trevor Colbourn, ed., *Fame and the Founding Fathers: Essays by Douglass Adair* (New York, 1974), 147n.

12. M[arinus] Willet to Aaron Burr, 8 Mar. 1801, in Mary-Jo Kline et al., eds., *Political Correspondence and Public Papers of Aaron Burr* (Princeton, 1983), I, 522; Colbourn, ed., *Fame and the Founding Fathers*, 149-59; May, *Enlightenment in America*, 326-34.

13. In 1806 St. George Tucker of Virginia, although a lifelong deist, became frightened enough by the social chaos that infidelity supposedly had caused that he was willing to support state subsidies for Christian teachers regardless of sect. May, *Enlightenment in America*, 331.

14. John T. Horton, *James Kent: A Study in Conservatism, 1763-1847* (New York), 190. Joseph Story in his *Commentaries* (1833) also discovered that Christianity was part of the common law. Franklin Hamlin Littell, *From State Church to Pluralism: A Protestant Interpretation of Religion in American History* (New York, 1962), 48.

15. Salstonstall, in *Journal of Debates and Proceedings in the Convention of Delegates, Chosen to Revise the Constitution of Massachusetts, Begun and Holden at Boston, November 15, 1820, and Continued by Adjournment to January 9, 1821* (Boston, 1853), 207; Beecher, *On the Importance of Assisting Young Men of Piety and Talents in Obtaining an Education for the Gospel Ministry* (New York, [1815]), 16.

16. William Breitenbach, "Unregenerate Doings: Selflessness and Selfishness in New Divinity Theology," *American Quarterly*, XXXIV (1982), 479-502.

17. Joseph Smith, *The Pearl of Great Price* (Salt Lake City, 1974), 47; John Rogers, *The Biography of Elder Barton Warren Stone . . .* (Cincinnati, 1847), 45.

18. Elias Smith, *The Loving Kindness of God Displayed in the Triumph of Republicanism in America . . .* (n.p., 1809), 27. See in general Nathan O. Hatch, *The Democratization of American Christianity* (New Haven, 1989), for the popular effects on religion of the Second Great Awakening.

19. Abel M. Sargent, *The Destruction of the Beast in the Downfall of Sectarianism . . .* (n.p., [1806]), 15; Otis, quoted in Josiah Quincy, *The History of Harvard University* (Cambridge, Mass., 1840), II, 663.

20. Donald M. Scott, *From Office to Profession: The New England Ministry, 1750-1850* (Philadelphia, 1978), 34, 47-48.

21. Lyman Beecher, "The Necessity of Revivals of Religion to the Perpetuity of Our Civil and Religious Institutions," *The Spirit of the Pilgrims* (1831), 467-71.

22. Washington, "Farewell Address" (1796), in W. B. Allen, ed., *George Washington: A Collection* (Indianapolis, 1988), 521; Rush, "To the Ministers of All Denominations," 21 June 1788, in Butterfield, ed., *Letters of Rush*, I, 461-62; Beecher, *A Reformation of Morals Practicable and Indispensable: A Sermon Delivered at New Haven on the Evening of October 27, 1812* (Andover, Mass., 1814), 18.

23. "Formation and Constitution of the Columbia Moral Society," *Columbia Magazine*, I (1814-15), 179-85.

24. Josiah Quincy, quoted in Frederic Cople Jaher, *The Urban Establishment: Upper*

Strata in Boston, New York, Charleston, Chicago, and Los Angeles (Urbana, Ill., 1982), 41; M. J. Heale, "Humanitarianism in the Early Republic: The Moral Reformers of New York, 1776–1825," *Journal of American Studies*, II (1968), 161–75.

25. Ford, "Americanus," in Hyneman and Lutz, eds., *American Political Writing*, II, 924.

26. Jeremiah Atwater, *A Sermon Preached before His Excellency Isaac Tichenor, Esq., Governor . . . on the Day of the Anniversary Election, October 14, 1802* (Middlebury, Vt., 1802), 18–19; *Niles' Weekly Register*, III (1812–13), 328.

27. Tocqueville, quoted in Wood, "Interests and Disinterestedness," in Beeman et al., eds., *Beyond the Confederation*, 103.

28. Christopher Manwaring, *Republicanism and Aristocracy Contrasted . . . Exhibited in an Oration, Delivered at New London, July 4th, 1804* (Norwich, Conn., 1804), 9.

29. Montesquieu, *Spirit of the Laws*, ed. Neumann, Pt. I, bk. xx, ch. 13, p. 323; [Anon.], *The Commercial Conduct of the United States of America Considered, and the True Interest thereof, Attempted to Be Shewn by a Citizen of New York* (New York, 1786), 4.

30. "Perhaps the most controversial subject of political economy," said De Witt Clinton in 1814, "is whether the home or foreign commerce is most productive of national wealth." De Witt Clinton, *A Discourse Delivered before the New-York Historical Society, at Their Anniversary Meeting, 6th December 1811* (New York, 1814), 37.

31. [Blodget], *Economica*, 12, 9, 102; [Samuel Blodget], *Thoughts on the Increasing Wealth and National Economy of the United States of America* (Washington. D. C., 1801).

32. [Antoine Louis Claude Destutt de Tracy], *A Treatise on Political Economy . . .* (Georgetown, 1817), xvi, xix; [Destutt de Tracy], *A Commentary and Review of Montesquieu's Spirit of the Laws . . .* (Philadelphia, 1811), 232; Emmet Kennedy, "A Philosophe in the Age of Revolution: Destutt de Tracy and the Origins of Ideology," American Philosophical Society, *Memoir*, CXXIX (Philadelphia, 1978), 212; Joyce Appleby, "What Is Still American in the Political Philosophy of Thomas Jefferson?" *WMQ*, 3rd Ser., XXXIX (1982), 287–309.

33. Laommi Baldwin, *Thoughts on the Study of Political Economy, as Connected with the Population, Industry and Paper Currency of the United States* (Cambridge, Mass., 1809), 67.

34. Baldwin, *Thoughts on Political Economy*, 45; Madison. Notes for a Speech Opposing Paper Money, ca. 1 Nov. 1786, in Rutland et al., eds, *Papers of Madison*, IX, 158–59; [Erick Bollman], *Paragraphs on Banks* (Philadelphia, 1810), 24.

35. Margaret E. Martin, *Merchants and Trade of the Connecticut River Valley, 1750–1820* (Northampton, Mass., 1939), 148; *Niles' Weekly Register*, IX (1815), 238; Rodney, in John R. Commons et al., eds., *A Documentary History of American Industrial Society: Labor Conspiracy Cases* (Cleveland, 1910), III, 170.

36. Freneau, quoted in Watts, *Republic Reborn*, 81.

37. See James T. Lemon and Gary Nash, "The Distribution of Wealth in Eighteenth-Century America: A Century of Change in Chester County, Pennsylvania, 1693–1802," *Journal of Social History*, II (1968), 1–24; Allen Kulikoff, "The Progress of Inequality in Revolutionary Boston," *WMQ*, 3rd Ser., XXVIII (1971), 375–412; Lee Soltow, "Economic Inequality in the United States in the Period from 1790 to 1860," *Journal of Economic History*, XXXI (1971), 822–39; Jackson Turner Main, "Trends in Wealth Concentration before 1860," *Journal of Economic History*, XXXI (1971), 445–57.

38. Carey, ed., *Debates of the General Assembly of Pennsylvania*, 38, 21, 130.

39. William Smith, *Eulogium on Benjamin Franklin, LL.D. . . . Delivered March 1, 1791, . . . before the American Philosophical Society . . .* (Philadelphia, 1792).

40. Roland M. Baumann, "John Swanwick: Spokesman for 'Merchant-Republicanism' in Philadelphia, 1790–1798," *Pennsylvania Magazine of History and Biography*, XCVII (1973), 141.

41. *Gazette of the State of South Carolina* (Charleston), 13 May 1784; [Anon.], *Remarks on the Rights of Inventors, and the Influence of their Studies in Promoting the Enjoyments of Life, and Public Prosperity* (Boston, 1807), 15.

42. William L. Hedges, "Washington Irving: Nonsense, the Fat of the Land and the Dream of Indolence," in Matthew J. Bruccoli, ed., *The Chief Glory of Every People* (Carbondale, Ill., 1973), 156; Messerli, *Horace Mann*, 90; Stanley Elkins and Eric McKitrick, "A New Meaning for Turner's Frontier: Democracy in the Old Northwest," *Political Science Quarterly*, LXIX (1954), 334; De Witt Clinton, "Oration before the New York Alpha of the Phi Beta Kappa Society, at Schenectady, July 22, 1823," in Williston, ed., *Eloquence of the United States*, V, 516–17; Sedgwick, quoted in Stow Persons, *The Decline of American Gentility* (New York, 1973), 50.

43. Edward Pessen, "The Egalitarian Myth and American Social Reality: Wealth, Mobility, and Equality in the 'Era of the Common Man,'" *American Historical Review*, LXXVI (1971), 989–1034. For an acute criticism of Pessen's formulations, see Jaher, *Urban Establishment*, 68–71.

44. *Observations on Public Principles and Characters; with Reference to Recent Events* (n.p., 1820), 29–31.

45. Hawthorne, *The House of the Seven Gables* (Boston, 1883), ch. ii, 55–64.

46. Chevalier, *Society, Manners, and Politics in the United States*, 212; Frances Trollope, *Domestic Manners of the Americans*, ed. Donald Smalley (New York, 1960), 99–100; Jane L. Mesick, *The English Traveler in America, 1785–1835* (New York, 1920), 307, 308; Grund, *Americans, in Their Moral, Social, and Political Relations*, 25; Port Folio, (1804), 214; Joel Barlow, *Advice to the Privileged Orders in the Several States of Europe Resulting from the Necessity and Propriety of a General Revolution in the Principles of Government* (1792) (Ithaca, N.Y., 1956), 18. In 1802 the buyer of a church pew in a New England meeting house called himself a "gentleman," but the seller labeled him a "blacksmith." Jonathan Prude, *The Coming of Industrial Order: Town and Factory Life in Rural Massachusetts, 1810–1860* (Cambridge, Eng., 1983), 32.

47. Peter Goldberger, "The Trial of Journeymen Shoemakers and the Collapse of Philadelphia's Artisan Community" (Honors Thesis, Brown University, 1982), 16.

48. Isaiah Thomas, *An Oration Delivered in . . . Lancaster . . . Massachusetts . . . 1779 . . .* (Worcester, Mass., 1781), quoted in Steven C. Bullock, "The Revolutionary Transformation of American Freemasonry, 1752–1792," *WMQ*, 3rd Ser., XLVII (1990), 368; Steven C. Bullock, "The Ancient and Honorable Society: Freemasonry in America, 1730–1830" (Ph. D. Diss., Brown University, 1986), 124; Nathaniel Chipman, *Sketches of the Principles of Government* (Rutland, Vt., 1793), 55.

49. Tunis Wortman, *Oration on the Influence of Social Institution upon Human Morals and Happiness . . .* (New York, 1796); Lyman Beecher, *The Remedy for Duelling . . .* (Sag Harbor, N. Y., 1807); Evarts B. Greene, "The Code of Honor in Colonial and Revolutionary Massachusetts," Colonial Society of Massachusetts., *Trans.*, XXVI (1924–26), 368–87; Kenneth S. Greenberg, *Masters and Statesmen: The Political Culture of American Slavery* (Baltimore, 1985), 23–41.

50. David Ramsay to Benjamin Rush, 29 July 1774, in Brunhouse, ed., *David Ramsay . . . Selections from His Writings*, 51; *American Museum*, XI (1792), 218–19; Robert C. McLean, *George Tucker: Moral Philosopher and Man of Letters* (Chapel Hill, 1961), 214–15; *Reports of the Debates of the New York Convention of 1821*, Carter et al., eds., 208; Thomas

P. Abernethy, *From Frontier to Plantation in Tennessee: A Study in Frontier Democracy* (Chapel Hill, 1932), 177–78.

51. Noah Webster, *An American Dictionary of the English Language* . . . (New York, 1828), I.

52. Morse, ed., *Samuel F. B. Morse: His Letters and Journals*, I, 164; Gardner (1806), in Simpson ed., *Federalist Literary Mind*, 81.

53. Robert A. Ferguson, *Law and Letters in American Culture* (Cambridge, Mass., 1984), 12; Kent, "An Introductory Lecture to a Course of Law Lectures" (1794), in Hyneman and Lutz, eds., *American Political Writings*, II, 945; Jefferson to Thomas Mann Randolph, Jr., 30 May 1790, in Boyd et al., eds., *Papers of Jefferson*, XVI, 449.

54. Ferguson, *Law and Letters*, 27.

55. Ferguson, *Law and Letters*, 201; Gerald W. Gewalt, *The Promise of Power: The Emergence of the Legal Profession in Massachusetts, 1760–1840* (Westport, Conn., 1979), 39–69; Bruce Sinclair, *Philadelphia's Philosopher Mechanics: A History of the Franklin Institute, 1824–1865* (Baltimore, 1974), 40–41.

56. Ferguson, *Law and Letters*, 244, 246.

19. Middle-Class Order

1. [Charles Jared Ingersoll], *Inchiquin, the Jesuit's Letters* . . . (1810), in Wood, ed., *Rising Glory of America*, 387.

2. George Wilson Pierson, *Tocqueville in America*, abridged by Dudley C. Lunt (New York, 1959), 44; Grund, *Americans, in Their Moral, Social, and Political Relations*, 14–15; Cooper, quoted in Edwin H. Cady, *The Gentleman in America: A Literary Study in American Culture* (Syracuse, 1949), 121.

3. Jefferson to John Banister, Jr., 15 Oct. 1785, in Boyd et al., eds., *Papers of Jefferson*, VIII, 636; Jefferson to Joseph C. Cabell, 28 Nov. 1820, in Ford, ed., *Writings of Jefferson*, X, 166. See Lawrence A. Cremin, *American Education: The National Experience, 1783–1876* (New York, 1980), II, 249–334.

4. Meyer Reinhold, *Classica Americana: The Greek and Roman Heritage in the United States* (Detroit, 1984), 129, 124.

5. Rush to James Hamilton, 27 June 1810, in Butterfield, ed., *Letters of Rush*, II, 1053. Others too thought that the number of those attending colleges and academies in the United States ought to be limited, "since but few men can, or ever ought to live by their learning." David Barnes, *A Discourse on Education* (Boston 1803), 11.

6. Joseph Stevens Buckminster (1809), in Simpson, ed., *Federalist Literary Mind*, 100.

7. Cooper, *Notions of the Americans*, I, 153–54, 155, 172, 176, 164, 165.

8. Hawthorne, *The House of the Seven Gables*, ch. xii, 211.

9. "From Tunbridge, Vermont, to London, England—The Journal of James Guild, Peddler, Tinker, Schoolmaster, Portrait Painter, from 1818 to 1824," ed. Arthur Wallace Peach, Vermont Historical Society, *Proc.*, V (1937), 250.

10. Ibid., 256, 258, 260.

11. Ibid., 276, 262, 298, 261, 300, 279, 288, 304.

12. Ibid., 278.

13. Ibid., 300, 301, 305.

14. Ibid., 306, 307, 308.

15. Ibid., 308.

16. David Jaffe, "One of the Primitive Sort: Portrait Makers of the Rural North, 1760–1860," in Hahn and Prude, eds., *Countryside in the Age of Capitalistic Transformation*, III, 110.

17. Jefferson to Madison, 20 Sept. 1785, in Boyd et al., eds., *Papers of Jefferson*, VIII, 535; Jefferson, *Notes on the State of Virginia*, ed. Peden, 153.

18. William Tudor, *North American Review*, II (1815–16), 161; Oliver W. Larkin, *Samuel F. B. Morse and American Democratic Art* (Boston, 1954), 16; Latrobe to Hugh Henry Brackenridge, 18 May 1803, in John C. Van Horne and Lee W. Formwalt, eds., *The Correspondence and Miscellaneous Papers of Benjamin Henry Latrobe* (New Haven, 1984), I, 300.

19. *Port Folio* (1810), 499.

20. *Youth's Guide to Happiness, Consisting of Poems, Essays and Sermons, Particularly Calculated for the Pious Instruction of the Rising Generation* ([New York], 1810); Schlesinger, *Learning How to Behave*, 22.

21. *Franklin Society for the Suppression of Intemperance* (Broadside: Greenfield, Mass., 23 Feb. 1814).

22. Mason L. Weems, *The True Patriot: Or an Oration on the Beauties and Beatitudes of a Republic* . . . (Philadelphia, 1802), 37.

23. Destutt de Tracy, *Commentary and Review of Montesquieu's Spirit of the Laws*, 72; Joseph Hopkinson, "Annual Discourse, Delivered before the Pennsylvania Academy of the Fine Arts" (1819), in Wood, ed., *Rising Glory of America*, 333.

24. Hopkinson, "Annual Discourse," in Wood, ed., *Rising Glory of America*, 333; Ruth H. Bloch, "The Gendered Meanings of Virtue in Revolutionary America," *Signs: Journal of Women in Culture and Society*, XIII, No. 1 (1987), 37–58.

25. *Literary Magazine*, V (1806); Charles G. Ferris, *An Oration, Delivered before the Tammany Society . . . on the Fourth of July, 1816* (New York, 1816), 10; *Niles' Weekly Register*, I (1811–12), 61.

26. Samuel L. Mitchill, "The Progress of the Human Mind from Rudeness to Refinement . . . ," *American Monthly Magazine*, III (1818), 358–63.

27. [Ingersoll], *Inchiquin, the Jesuit's Letters*, in Wood, ed., *Rising Glory of America*, 385, 388; Elkanah Watson, *History of the Rise, Progress, and Existing Condition of the Western Canals in the State of New York* . . . (Albany, 1820), 91; Charles Sprague, "Oration, 4 July 1825," in Willison, ed., *Eloquence in the United States*, V, 339.

28. Wright, *Views of Society and Manners*, ed. Baker, 174; Edward Everett, "Accumulation, Property, Capital, Credit" (13 Sept. 1838), in *Orations and Speeches*, II, 291.

29. [Bollman], *Paragraphs on Banks*, 8; Webster, "The Boston Mechanics' Institution" (1828), in *Writings and Speeches of Daniel Webster: National Edition* (Boston, 1903), II, 40; Daveis, "Address," in Blau, ed., *Social Theories of Jacksonian Democracy*, 40.

30. Theron Metcalf, *An Address to the Phi Beta Kappa Society of Brown University, Delivered 5th September, 1832* (Boston, 1833), 4; *North American Review*, III (1816), 345–47.

31. Jacob Viner, *The Role of Providence in the Social Order: An Essay in Intellectual History* (Philadelphia, 1972), 111; Gordon S. Wood, "Conspiracy and the Paranoid Style: Causality and Deceit in the Eighteenth Century," *WMQ*, 3rd Ser., XXXIX (1982), 440–41.

32. Gordon S. Wood, "The Democratization of Mind in the American Revolution," in Robert H. Horwitz, ed., *The Moral Foundations of the American Republic* (Charlottesville, 1977), 125–26; Legaré, "Oration on Fourth of July 1823," in *Writings*, I, 268–69.

33. Everett, "An Oration Pronounced at Cambridge before the Society of Phi Beta

Kappa'' (1824), in Blau, ed., *American Philosophical Addresses*, 75; Bancroft, "The Office of the People in Art, Government, and Religion," ibid., 107.

34. Patricia Cline Cohen, *A Calculating People: The Spread of Numeracy in Early America* (Chicago, 1982), 151, 154.

35. Everett, *Orations and Speeches*, I, 272.

36. Cohen, *Calculating People*, 154.

37. James H. Smylie, "Charles Nisbet: Second Thoughts on a Revolutionary Generation," *Pennsylvania Magazine of History and Biography*, XCVIII (1974), 201.

38. *Medical Repository*, XVIII (1817), 269-70; Emerson, "American Scholar," in Atkinson, ed., *Complete Essays and Other Writings*, 61.

39. Hopkinson, "Annual Discourse," in Wood, ed., *Rising Glory of America*, 328; Samuel Wileiams, *The Natural and Civil History of Vermont* (Burlington, Vt., 1808), II, 394.

40. John H. Wilkins, *Elements of Astronomy . . .* , 2nd ed. (Boston, 1823), vi, quoted in William J. Gilmore. " 'The Annihilation of Time and Space': The Transformation of Event and Awareness in American Consciousness, c. 1780-1850," paper delivered at Conference on Printing and Society in Early America, American Antiquarian Society, 24-25 Oct. 1980, 50.

41. George Tucker (1827), quoted in Gordon S. Wood, "Evangelical America and Early Mormonism," *New York History*, LXI (1980), 369; Neil Harris, *Humbug: The Art of P. T. Barnum* (Boston, 1973), 61-89; Melville, *Moby Dick*, ed. Hayford and Parker, ch. 124, p. 425.

42. David Tappan, *A Discourse Delivered in the Chapel of Harvard College, June 19, 1798* (Boston, 1798), 4-5.

43. Edward Everett, *An Oration Delivered at Concord, April the Nineteenth 1825* (Boston, 1825), 49; Bishop, *Oration in Wallingford*, iii, iv.

44. [George Hay], *An Essay on the Liberty of the Press . . .* (Philadelphia, 1799), 40; Jefferson, Inaugural Address, 4 Mar. 1801, in Adrienne Koch and William Peden, eds., *The Life and Selected Writings of Thomas Jefferson* (New York, 1944), 322; Wood, "Democratization of Mind," in Horwitz, ed., *Moral Foundations*, 123-28.

45. Judge Addison (Pa.), quoted in John C. Miller, *The Federalist Era, 1789-1801* (New York, 1960), 232; Isaac Chapman Bates, *An Oration, Pronounced at Northampton, July 4, 1805* (Northampton, Mass., 1805), 6-7, 15.

46. Wood, "Democratization of Mind," in Horwitz, ed., *Moral Foundations*, 124-25.

47. Adam Smith, *The Theory of Moral Sentiments* (1759), ed. D. D. Raphael and A. L. Macfie (Oxford, 1976), 112.

48. Madison to Rush, 7 Mar. 1790, in Charles Hobson et al., eds., *Papers of Madison*, XIII, 93.

49. Samuel Miller, *A Brief Retrospect of the Eighteenth Century . . .* (New York, 1803), II, 254-55.

50. Tunis Wortman, *A Treatise Concerning Political Enquiry, and the Liberty of the Press* (New York, 1800), 180; Daveis, "Address," in Blau, ed., *Social Theories of Jacksonian Democracy*, 45; Richard E. Welch, Jr., *Theodore Sedgwick, Federalist: A Political Portrait* (Middletown, Conn., 1965), 211.

51. Williams, *History of Vermont*, II, 394; Metcalf, *Address to Phi Beta Kappa*, 4, 21-22.

52. Daveis, "Address," in Blau, ed., *Social Theories of Jacksonian Democracy*, 49-50.

53. Emerson, "Science" (1834), *The Early Lectures: 1833-1836*, ed. Stephen E. Whicher and Robert E. Spiller (Cambridge, Mass., 1964), I, 49.

54. Emerson, *The Journals and Miscellaneous Notebooks*, ed. William H. Gilman and Alfred R. Ferguson (Cambridge, Mass., 1963), 103-4.

55. Emerson, "Human Culture," "The Philosophy of History," *The Early Lectures: 1836–1838*, ed. Stephen E. Whicher et al. (Cambridge, Mass., 1964), II, 218, 17.

56. Emerson, "Historical Notes of Life and Letters in New England," *Lectures and Biographical Sketches*, in *The Complete Works* (Boston, 1883), X, 326.

57. Marvin Zetterbaum, *Tocqueville and the Problem of Democracy* (Stanford, 1967), 59.

58. Franklin to Charles Thomson, 29 Dec. 1788, in Smyth, ed., *Writings of Benjamin Franklin*, IX, 691–97.

59. Rush to John Adams, 19 Feb., 29 June, 14 Aug. 1805, 2 Apr. 1807, 13 June 1808, 2 Oct. 1810, 27 June 1812, in John A. Schutz and Douglass Adair, eds., *The Spur of Fame: Dialogues of John Adams and Benjamin Rush, 1805–1813* (San Marino, Calif., 1980), 22, 28, 31, 32, 79, 108, 109, 169, 227; Rush to Granville Sharp, 8 Oct. 1801, in John A. Woods. "The Correspondence of Benjamin Rush and Granville Sharpe, 1773–1809," *Journal of American Studies*, I (1967), 35. Following the defeat of the Federalists in 1800, even Alexander Hamilton underwent a deep religious conversion. Douglass Adair, "Was Alexander Hamilton a Christian Statesman?" *Fame and the Founding Fathers: Essays by Douglass Adair*, ed. Trevor Colbourn (Chapel Hill, 1974), 154–56; May, *Enlightenment in America*, 329.

60. Washington to Jonathan Trumbull, 21 July 1799, in Fitzpatrick, ed., *Writings of Washington*, XXXVII, 312–13; May, *Enlightenment in America*, 335; Adams to Jefferson, 15 July 1813, in Cappon, ed., *Adams-Jefferson Letters*, II, 358; Hamilton to Gouverneur Morris, 29 Feb. 1802, in Syrett et al., eds., *Papers of Hamilton*, XXV, 544.

61. Robert E. Shalhope, "Thomas Jefferson's Republicanism and Antebellum Southern Thought," *Journal of Southern History*, XLII (1976), 529–56.

62. Jefferson to Dr. Thomas Humphreys, 8 Feb. 1817, to Francis Adrian Van De Kemp, 11 Jan. 1825, in Ford, ed., *Writings of Jefferson*, X, 77, 337.

63. *Reports of the Debates of the New York Convention of 1821*, ed. Carter et al., 261.

Index

Adams, John, 3, 74, 266; background of, 196, 197; on balanced government, 267; on banking, 318; on Cicero, 204; on common people, 27, 374n; cosmopolitanism of, 221; on courtiers, 175-6; disillusionment of, 366-7; on education, 190; on enlightenment, 191; on equality, 171, 237; on fame, 40, 59-60; on family authority, 48, 147, 182; on freedom and servitude, 172, 179; on friendship, 58; on gentlemen, 31, 118, 195, 374n, 375n; on government salaries, 288-9; as "Humphrey Ploughjogger," 237-8; on intemperance, 306; on interest, 175, 267; on Mass. government, 16-17, 410-11n; on moneylending, 69; on Otis, 200; on patronage, 64, 80, 88; prosperity feared by, 315; on republicanism, 95, 407n; on social affection, 220; on social rank, 21; on religion, 330; resentments of, 200-1, 289-90; on Revolution, 169; on Washington, 40, 288-9; on work, 281

Adams, John Quincy, 218, 231, 301, 346

Adams, Samuel: background of, 197; disinterestedness of, 253; disillusionment of, 366; on English example, 110; as Freemason, 223; on heredity, 400n; on mobs, 90; on Order of the Cincinnati, 241; and republicanism, 205

Addison, Joseph, 38, 103; and *Cato*, 143, 197-8, 216-17; on commerce, 37; on patriarchy, 43; and politeness, 216

African-Americans, 90, 236

Albany Regency, 300

Alexandria, Va., 134

allegiance, 11, 15, 40; and consent, 166, 397n

Allen, James, 84, 176, 213-14

Allen, William, 73, 76, 177

Allen family, 176

Allison, Francis, 197

America: compared to England, 16-17, 110, 112-17, 296-7; compared to

Europe, 306; population of, 6; *see also* society, colonial; society, U.S.; United States

American Revolution, *see* Revolution, American

Ames, Fisher, 230, 231, 266, 293

Amory family, 119

Anglican church, *see* Church of England

Annapolis, Md., 37

Anti-Federalists, 255, 258-9, 294, 296, 412n

antiquity, classical, 100-1, 284-8, 369

apprenticeship, 23, 51, 52, 162, 185-6; *see also* servitude

Arendt, Hannah, 3, 376n

aristocracy, 8, 320, 363; and American Revolution, 276; attacks on, 240-1, 242, 243, 255, 305, 409n; in Conn., 272-3; in England, 15, 25-6, 122; and government salaries, 291, 416n; and judiciary, 325; introduction into colonies, 174; nature of, 25, 27, 150, 273, 293; passions of, 27, 28, 39-40, 273-4; and proprietary wealth, 68, 410-11n; revolutionaries' idea of, 195, 196, 237, 262-3, 291, 375n; in South, 71, 115-17, 281; weakness of, 30, 113, 121, 266, 271; *see also* gentlemen

Arnold, Benedict, 75

Articles of Confederation, 313

artisans, 22, 23, 317, 341; and Freemasons, 344; and government, 85, 244-7; and interests, 85, 107; and labor, 37, 277; and mobs, 244; and patrons, 63-4; as Republicans, 276; status of, 23, 38, 185-6, 280, 341, 344, 426n; weakness of, in South, 115

assemblies, colonial, 174

Association, Continental, 35

associations, voluntary, 328-9

Athens, ancient, 100

Augustus Caesar, 102-3

Austen, Jane, 68, 194, 196